THE HEALTH SERVICES
SINCE THE WAR

VOLUME I

THE HEALTH SERVICES SINCE THE WAR

Volume I

PROBLEMS OF HEALTH CARE THE NATIONAL HEALTH SERVICE BEFORE 1957

BY

CHARLES WEBSTER

LONDON

HER MAJESTY'S STATIONERY OFFICE

© *Crown copyright* 1988
First published 1988

ISBN 0 11 630942 3

HMSO publications are available from:

HMSO Publications Centre
(Mail and telephone orders only)
PO Box 276, London, SW8 5DT
Telephone orders 01-622 3316
General enquiries 01-211 5656
(queuing system in operation for both numbers)

HMSO Bookshops
49 High Holborn, London, WC1V 6HB   01-211 5656 (Counter service only)
258 Broad Street, Birmingham, B1 2HE   021-643 3740
Southey House, 33 Wine Street, Bristol, BS1 2BQ   (0272) 264306
9-21 Princess Street, Manchester, M60 8AS   061-834 7201
80 Chichester Street, Belfast, BT1 4JY   (0232) 238451
71 Lothian Road, Edinburgh, EH3 9AZ   031-228 4181

HMSO's Accredited Agents
(see Yellow Pages)

And through good booksellers

Printed in the United Kingdom for Her Majesty's Stationery Office

Dd 239479 C15 2/88 G443 10170

CONTENTS

CHAPTER VI: CONSERVATIVES AND CONSENSUS

CHAPTER VII: THE ADVISORY SERVICES

CHAPTER VIII: THE HOSPITAL SERVICE

CHAPTER IX: PRIMARY AND PREVENTIVE SERVICES

CONCLUSIONS

NOTES

ABBREVIATIONS

INDEX

TABLES

MAPS

The health of the people is really the foundation upon which all their happiness and all their powers as a State depend.

Disraeli (1877)

The unanimous opinion of the meeting, made clear in the expressions of both men and women, appeared to be that the Health Service, according to their experience of it, was not only a success but a blessing. For the first time, it was said, men felt secure so far as the medical care of their families is concerned, and women felt freedom in this regard in respect of their children which they had never before experienced. I was quite touched, and hoped inwardly that we should be able to see to it that everyone had in fact a fair deal.

A K Bowman (1949)

PREFACE

This volume fulfils a commission given in 1980 to write, with respect to the National Health Service, 'a fairly compact volume concentrating on the central issues from the immediate post-war period into the early fifties'. Presentation of a balanced account of post-war developments necessitated a review of antecedent events. Consequently three short chapters deal with problems of health care and planning before the end of World War II. No obvious date suggested itself as the terminal point for this first part of what was originally conceived as a study of the NHS up to and including the reorganisation of 1974. Generally 1956 has been adopted as the terminus for the current exercise. Where possible the topics under review have been discussed up to the most appropriate natural break. Consistent with the above remit, this volume makes no pretence at being a total history of medicine and health care in mid-century Britain. It is specifically concerned with policy issues relating to the National Health Service. No apology is offered for this bias. Many of the issues upon which this study concentrates have acquired permanent interest.

After a long period of relative neglect, the early history of the NHS is now attracting much attention. I have benefited greatly from the work of Abel-Smith, Eckstein, Stevens, and Titmuss, and the recent books by Honigsbaum, Klein and Pater. While there are inevitable points of overlap between my work and theirs, I am satisfied that a fresh approach, exploiting many hitherto inaccessible records, has been justified. The collective volume on the Scottish health services edited by McLachlan, studies on hospital regionalisation by Fox, and on the London hospital system by Rivett unfortunately appeared after my work was complete.

A few points relating to presentation should be mentioned. Typographical errors, etc, are silently corrected in quotations. Frequently, longer quotations are slightly abbreviated where there is no risk of altering the sense. First names or initials of individuals or full titles of books are given on first mention, or again thereafter where strictly necessary. The index will aid location of these key references. Because statistical information is derived from a variety of sources there is an absence of complete consistency between the figures relating to particular points of detail.

I owe a great debt of gratitude to the many friends and colleagues who have assisted me in the course of this project. Among retired officials I am indebted to Dame Enid Russell-Smith, Dr J E Pater, and especially Sir George Godber. The latter's prompt and detailed attention to my tiresome queries is greatly appreciated. I am indebted to Dame Enid for permission to quote from letters written to her brother. The late Sir Douglas Haddow kindly commented on sections of the draft relating to Scotland. I would like to thank Lady Macleod and Lord Tranmire for allowing me to interview them. I am obliged to very many other former officials and medical colleagues who have advised me on points of specific detail.

I am particularly grateful to the departmental record staff of the DHSS, the Department of Education and Science, OPCS, the Treasury, and the Cabinet Office for their prompt attention to my requests for files. I have also been assisted in many ways by my immediate colleagues in the Historical Section of the Cabinet Office.

Given fairly strenuous academic commitments in Oxford, the completion of this study would not have been possible without the support of colleagues in the Wellcome Unit for the History of Medicine. The project has impinged on the work of most members of the Unit. Of assistants directly involved, the work of Dr Geoffrey Bowles is especially reflected in sections (ii) and (iii) of chapter IX, while the work of David Cantor is relevant to the sections relating to the blood transfusion service and the public health laboratory service. Geoffrey Bowles' great reliability and aptitude were indispensable at the start of this work. Dr P Gouk and especially Dr Jonathan Barry are Wellcome Unit research assistants who have helped with background work on newspapers and period- icals. Jonathan Barry's keen participation was of major value in keeping up the pace of work. In the final preparatory phase, which has involved a great deal of work according to a tight timetable, I am especially indebted to Ann Cheales and Elizabeth Peretz, and to Vivian Peto for preparation of the index. The whole project has depended on direct advice on the text and support in the manage- ment of the Wellcome Unit from Margaret Pelling, the Deputy Director. Finally I would like to thank my family for their tolerance and kindness during a particularly busy time.

CHAPTER I

Incessant Construction

Quite fortuitously, establishment of the National Health Service in 1948 came exactly one hundred years after the first Public Health Act, and about two hundred years after the inception of the voluntary hospital movement. The National Health Service was designed to bring order to an inheritance of health care institutions representing the accretion of more than a century of 'incessant construction'.[1] But this piecemeal, cumulative process was inevitably deficient in system and rational planning. By the inter-war period it was evident that the impact of progressive developments was lessened by a variety of deficiencies. Urgently required modernisation and improvement was held back by such limitations as anachronism, administrative complexity, duplication, parochialism, inertia and stagnation variously evident in crucial sectors of the services. Expansion in scientific and technical knowledge outpaced improvements in services. Rising aspirations among the public also exposed the inadequacy of existing medical services. It was realised that the 'masses, quite naturally and rightly, will not tolerate much longer a position in which they become, when overtaken by serious illness or injury, the objects of charitable help and treatment. Flag days do not fit into the picture of a comprehensive National Health Service'.[2]

Radical improvement of the health services came high in popular expectations for post-war reconstruction. From the outbreak of World War II the proposal for a comprehensive National Health Service was greeted with spontaneous acclaim. In terms reminiscent of Disraeli, Willink described the new scheme as the 'very root of national vigour and national enterprise . . . the biggest single advance ever made in this country in the sphere of public health'.[3] The new sense that health was being elevated into a universal right was gratifying to the Ministers responsible for the National Health Service legislation. Bevan detected a 'new freedom from anxiety in sickness'. He was touched by an 'almost unplumbable well of gratitude' expressed particularly by old people.[4] Woodburn noted the 'quiet but general satisfaction on the part of the general public that the hospital and specialist service is now more freely available to all, irrespective of social position'. He was also gratified by the possibility in Scotland of 'bringing the most highly skilled resources to the help of the individual patient, especially in the smaller towns and villages, in a way that they have never and could not have been brought before'.[5]

From the outset there was a sense of the special importance of the British National Health Service, identified by admirers and critics alike as the first experiment in socialised medicine to be undertaken by a major western industrialised nation. Bevan thus argued that they should 'keep it intact for its own value; I also hope that we keep it intact to demonstrate to those in other countries, who are watching with a great deal of interest, that it is something which can be done and is worth doing'.[6] Quite irrespective of its positive qualities or shortcomings, the National Health Service has become sanctified at home as the inalienable foundation of the welfare state, whereas abroad it is known as a characteristic British institution.

Although widely portrayed as a revolutionary departure, the National Health Service as a mechanism was in most respects evolutionary or even traditional. For instance, although originally conceived as a unified structure, the service was effectively split into three distinct component parts coinciding with the three nuclei around which health care institutions had aggregated in the course of the previous century, the most antique part being the voluntary hospitals. Health services provided at public cost were also of venerable origin, having their source in the mechanisms evolved for poor relief in the sixteenth century. However, it was only in the nineteenth century that public health services developed on an extensive scale. Finally, state-administered compulsory national health insurance was established in 1911 as a replacement for a variety of earlier contributory medical schemes.[7] What was the condition of these three major elements of the health service as they approached the challenge of World War II?

(i) VOLUNTARY HOSPITALS

The senior voluntary hospitals were old and prestigious. The oldest went back to the middle ages. But the majority of leading voluntary hospitals, including the teaching hospitals, originated in the second part of the eighteenth century. These hospitals were the most expansive manifestations of medical philanthropy, which had spawned a tumultuous variety of other institutions, ranging from substantial dispensaries to minor food charities. The pattern of development roughly followed the process of urbanisation, although hospital provision in rapidly expanding industrial centres lagged well behind population expansion.[8] Nevertheless, the voluntary hospital system showed considerable resilience. Between 1911 and 1938, in England and Wales the number of institutions increased from 783 to 1,255, while the beds provided per thousand population increased from 1.20 to 2.12. In 1938 the voluntary hospital sector was providing one in every three beds for the physically ill, at least half of all beds for acute cases, and the great majority of beds for the most specialised and difficult treatments.[9] As noted below voluntary hospitals were also playing some part in hospital services of the kind delegated to local authorities. On an annual budget of only £16m in 1938, voluntary hospitals were still occupying a crucial place in health care.[10]

Voluntary hospitals were an extraordinary collection of heterogeneous institutions, ranging from teaching hospitals with an average of over 500 beds in 1938, to minute cottage hospitals, the great expansion of which in the present century forced down the bed average for all general voluntary hospitals to 68.[11] Small size, together with haphazard distribution and the demands of modern therapy, resulted in major problems of expansion, relocation and modernisation, which the majority were quite unable to meet.

Problems of survival were particularly serious in London, where in 1938 half the teaching beds and one-third of special hospital beds in England and Wales were located.[12] Beds for acute cases were generally concentrated in inner city areas, whereas population was increasingly migrating to the suburbs.

Voluntary hospitals were faced with a major dilemma. In order to maintain local esteem and attract revenue they were committed to modernisation, but the latter tended to exacerbate their financial problems because modernisation was becoming increasingly more costly owing to the pace of technical advance and related staffing requirements. The response was uneven. Hospitals frequently indulged in extravagant expenditure on modern equipment as a public relations exercise, but were unable to make efficient use of this equipment because of the shortage of trained staff. Thus modern operating theatres, X-ray equipment, and radium therapy were often applied to doubtful effect.

Enforced economies were undertaken at the expense of desirable developments in staffing. Salaries and wages were increasingly recognised as being unrealistically low. Growth of the public hospital sector only emphasised the adverse position of the staff of voluntary hospitals. By 1938 the low pay of nursing staff was having serious effects on recruitment and morale. Voluntary hospitals were fortunate in employing the majority of their medical staff on an honorary basis. However the demands of modern care necessitated building up a sizeable corps of full-time junior medical staff, while there was growing doubt whether general practitioners, who formed the backbone of the medical staff of smaller provincial voluntary hospitals, were capable of keeping up with the demands of a modern service. During the 1930s there emerged a call for a more uniform and perhaps salaried consultant service for voluntary hospitals.

In their increasingly desperate struggle for survival voluntary hospitals resorted to a variety of new means for raising money. The economic relations of voluntary hospitals with the local community changed decisively. For instance in England and Wales in 1891 provincial hospitals were deriving 88% of their revenue from voluntary gifts and investments. They thus conformed to the classic model for a charitable institution. However, by 1921 this element had sunk to 55%, and by 1938 to 33%. Between 1891 and 1938 payments from patients jumped from 11% to 59%.[13] In Scotland fees from patients also grew in importance, but in 1937 this source was only accounting for 25% of voluntary hospital income.[14] Traditionally in Scotland fees and subscriptions were not important, but even here these sources were providing 48% of current income by 1937.

By degrees voluntary hospitals opted to admit private patients (usually building separate private blocks for this purpose), to exact charges from classes of patients hitherto treated gratis, to receive payment for services from local authorities and finally to rely on regular weekly payments, whether from workmen's schemes operated through factories, Hospital Saturday Funds, or the Hospital Savings Association.[15] One estimate suggested that half the insured population were protecting themselves and their dependants against the risk of the costs of hospital treatment through the savings movement.[16] Such contributions, although made voluntarily, conferred rights on contributors and their dependants to out-patient treatment, and they also helped with access to in-patient treatment. For lower-wage earners these schemes offered a minor form of medical insurance, involving not only more obvious forms of hospital benefit, but also ophthalmic and dental treatment, and even nursing home facilities. The middle classes responded by establishing parallel schemes such as the British Provident Association. Although the development of contributory schemes temporarily salvaged the finances of voluntary hospitals, they also created extra strains on resources by increasing the demand for services.

Despite all of their problems, voluntary hospitals never lost their prestigious status or fell in public esteem. Other arms of voluntary activity also continued to play a major role, especially in smaller towns and rural areas. Increasingly, voluntary organisations operated in partnership with local authorities in such fields as maternity and child welfare, district nursing, midwifery, tuberculosis after-care, or mental and physical handicap.[17] But the financial and administrative burden gradually passed to local authorities, and their full-time employees were of growing importance in mounting these services.

(ii) PUBLIC HEALTH SERVICES

The largest segment of the publicly funded hospital and institutional services grew up almost accidentally as an appendage to the workhouse system established under the Poor Law Amendment Act of 1834.[18] Even before this date parishes had provided outdoor medical relief, while larger districts had become involved in the development of accommodation for both mentally and physically sick patients.[19] Inevitably the inmates of the burgeoning workhouse system required medical treatment. Boards of Guardians also continued with their traditional responsibility for outdoor medical relief. Temporarily it looked as if Guardians would assume major sanitary responsibilities, but in the later nineteenth century this trend was reversed. Guardians nevertheless retained important responsibilities with respect to the poor. They were under no obligation to provide extensive medical services, although by the inter-war period a minority of these authorities had established hospitals providing an almost full range of services, from maternity care to emergency services and even radiotherapy, as well as catering for the heterogeneous masses of the chronic sick. At the height of this development Poor Law authorities were providing more than 90,000 beds in England and Wales, and 5,600 in Scotland, in their infirmaries and sick wards. In England and Wales they were employing about 5,000 doctors, one-fifth of whom worked entirely in institutions, numbers which had declined slightly by 1929.[20] Under the Local Government Act of 1929 about half of these beds were appropriated by Public Health Committees of local authorities to form the nucleus of their general hospitals. A smaller number were adapted into mental deficiency institutions.[21] The same trend occurred in Scotland, although to a lesser extent, under its Local Government Act of 1929, the only major conversion of a poorhouse undertaken before 1939 being the establishment of the three General Hospitals in Edinburgh.[22]

After 1929 Public Assistance Committees were responsible for a large residuum, mainly of elderly people, for whom institutional care was necessary. The arbitrariness of the division of responsibility between Health and Public Assistance Committees is disclosed by the evidence that of the 149,000 residents in Poor Law institutions in England and Wales in 1939, nearly 60,000 were classified as 'sick'.[23]

In the above reorganisation the responsibilities of Boards of Guardians were transferred to Public Health and Public Assistance

Committees of county councils and county borough councils. Local authorities had been steadily expanding their public health functions since the mid-nineteenth century. Their involvement began with sanitation and housing. By World War II they had assembled a formidable array of specialist health services, largely overshadowing their work in the more conventional environmental health field.[24] The absorption of Poor Law institutions noted above represented a major increment in this process. Even before 1929, either singly or on a joint board basis, local authorities were responsible for an elaborate system of institutions for mental and mental deficiency patients, as well as infectious diseases hospitals and tuberculosis sanatoria.

Before 1930 only three authorities had exercised their powers under the 1875 Public Health Act to establish general hospitals.[25] The position was transformed during the 1930s. By 1938 local authorities were providing 72,500 general hospital beds in England and Wales, and 5,400 in Scotland.[26] Local authorities were consequently emerging as major hospital administrations. Indeed the LCC, with 75,000 beds (including 35,000 mental), was arguably the largest hospital authority in the world, rivalling in size the entire voluntary sector of England and Wales. In principle, recipients of local authority hospital care were required to pay for this service on a means tested basis, but the scale seems to have been applied leniently, while some authorities were in effect providing free hospital treatment to their ratepayers. Overall it was thought that local authorities were not recovering from patients more than 10% of the total cost of their hospitals.[27]

Alongside development of their hospital services, local authorities also ran multifarious clinics for groups exposed to special risk. For instance, fears of racial deterioration in the wake of the Boer War resulted in the establishment of a medical service for children of school age. Medical inspection and supplementary feeding were introduced before World War I. In 1921 Local Education Authorities were given a duty to secure for elementary children 'such adequate and suitable arrangements as may be sanctioned by the Ministry of Health for attending to the health and physical condition, and to provide for medical inspection' of school children.[28] By 1938 the School Medical Service was engaged in diverse activities, ranging from special schools, school meals and milk, physical education, to inspection and treatment of minor ailments. Notwithstanding its positive qualities the School Medical Service was insufficiently equipped to make more than a minor indentation on many of the most serious problems with which it was engaged.[29]

The prevailing fear gradually switched from overpopulation to depopulation, with special concern over the declining birth rate, and excess infant and maternal mortality. In response to this anxiety, voluntary agencies established numerous infant welfare clinics. Then, under the Maternity and Child Welfare Act (1918), local authorities were given a statutory responsibility for services for mothers and infants. During the inter-war period local authorities created large numbers of antenatal and child welfare clinics. These varied in character from sessions held in village halls, where routine examination of expectant mothers and infants was conducted, to purpose-built 'health centres' where a much fuller consultative service was available and where ambitious educational programmes were introduced.[30] Authorities varied greatly in the degree to which they provided free or subsidised milk and health foods for mothers and infants. Postnatal care was relatively neglected. By 1938 only 28 postnatal clinics had been established.[31] The use of public maternity and child welfare clinics for dispensing birth control advice, although not prohibited, was only permissible in cases of the most dire medical need. Because of their enormous diversity maternity and child welfare services were variable in their utility. These services also illustrate the great extent of regional variation. Antenatal 'attendance' is admittedly an imperfect index, but this reached 73% in London in 1935, whereas levels elsewhere were much lower. The average for county boroughs in England was 63%, and 17% for counties, whereas in Scotland and Wales the levels were 35% and 36% respectively.[32]

Responsibility of local authorities to provide a fully co-ordinated midwifery service dates from the Midwives Act (1936) and the Maternity Services (Scotland) Act (1937).[33] The Scottish arrangements were the more comprehensive. Despite this element of rationalisation, maternity services retained a bewildering complexity. For instance it was pointed out that in London an expectant mother was faced with a choice of nine different routes to confinement.[34] By 1938 local health and welfare authorities were providing in their own hospitals about 6,500 maternity beds in England and Wales and 1,000 beds in Scotland.[35] By this date about 35% of notified births took place in hospital. Levels of provision varied enormously from one area to another.

Although gradually declining in its virulence, tuberculosis was the single most important cause of death among adults in Britain before World War II.[36] Alarm over tuberculosis was signified in 1911, when this condition was the only one for which dependants of insured workers could claim treatment under National Health Insurance. Tuberculosis treatment was rationalised by the Public Health (Tuberculosis) Act of 1921, under which this service became the responsibility of local authorities. The most elaborate scheme was developed in Wales, where the service was conducted by the

King Edward VII Welsh National Memorial Association, which established the Sully Sanatorium near Cardiff, one of Britain's most modern hospitals. But this case of regional planning was a mixed blessing, because 'the very excellence of the Memorial Association scheme on the diagnosis and treatment side seems to have been an excuse for neglect on the prevention side'.[37] By 1938 local authorities were providing about 16,000 beds in the tuberculosis hospitals and sanatoria in England, 2,000 in Wales, and 4,700 in Scotland, in addition to their clinic and after-care services, undertaken in association with voluntary agencies.[38] Selection for treatment often involved a crisis for tuberculosis sufferers and their families because of the doubtful efficacy of surgical treatment and because the stigma of this disease resulted in difficulties in maintaining employment.

The inter-war period also exposed inadequacy of arrangements for the detection and treatment of cancer. Although voluntary effort had resulted in the establishment of 22 radium centres, the majority of cancer sufferers were deprived of the opportunity for early diagnosis and treatment. The Cancer Act of 1939 laid the foundations for a mechanism of diagnosis under the control of county councils and county borough councils, and for co-ordination of diagnosis and treatment at a regional level. Despite the inadequacies and hazards of existing treatment at that time, the cancer scheme is of permanent interest as an early model for regional planning of health and hospital services, although this innovation came too close to World War II to be put into practice.[39]

Most of the services provided by local authorities were 50% exchequer-aided. Between 1900 and 1938 the gross cost of local authority administered health services expanded from £3m to c £50m. The scope of these services had expanded to such a degree that this system was already occasionally called a 'National Health Service' in policy discussions. Where permissive powers were applied to the utmost degree, when rate revenue was buoyant, and where the local Medical Officer of Health was sympathetic with modern developments, the standard of service bore comparison with later counterparts under the National Health Service. In local cases capital investment in new hospitals and clinics easily outstripped the performance of the National Health Service. However, sparkling and expensive initiatives such as the Sully Sanatorium (1934), the Finsbury Health Centre (1938), or the Impington Village College (1938), were not representative of the whole. There was a great contrast between better developed services in more prosperous areas like greater London, and conditions in smaller authorities or the depressed regions. The areas of greatest need were least able to sustain effective health and social services.[40] In such places permissive powers were least used and their Medical Officers of Health tended to be least responsive to advanced developments taking place elsewhere. The worst public services were fairly censured as the 'last word in a despairing effort to dodge obligations'.[41] The quality of local authority health services was thus wildly uneven. The services themselves, including hospitals, were frequently stigmatised for being unnecessarily bureaucratic and inhumane. This reputation does much to explain the antagonism towards local authorities by representatives of the medical profession in the course of the National Health Service negotiations.

Superimposed on difficulties peculiar to deprived areas, the general policy of retrenchment during the inter-war period placed serious constraints on the development of new services and on the expansion of existing ones. Thus, despite their complexities, such services as the School Medical Service and the Maternity and Child Welfare Service remained relatively modest operations, the two together involving cost to public funds of about £3m in 1929, the same cost as the tuberculosis service at that stage. This expenditure can be compared with the beet sugar subsidy, which stood at £5m in 1933/34.[42] Paradoxically many of the services that had been delayed during peacetime were taken up more actively during World War II, when for instance the first systematic effort was made to supplement the diets of mothers, infants and school children.

(iii) MENTAL HEALTH SERVICES

Although services for the mentally ill and mentally handicapped were the responsibility of local authorities, they had evolved separately and tended to be administered independently, involving the largely autonomous Boards of Control at the centre, operating from London and Edinburgh, with statutory local authority committees at the periphery.[43]

The County Asylums Act of 1808 constituted a significant precedent because it was the first occasion in legislation in which public funds were made available in all administrative areas for providing hospital accommodation. In practice, county asylums were not developed into a comprehensive system until after the 1845 Lunatic Asylums Act. County asylums filled up with 'pauper lunatics' whose fees were paid by their local Guardians. This provision was modernised with the Lunacy Act of 1890 which placed on local authorities an obligation to maintain institutions for the mentally ill.[44] In 1938 local authorities were providing for 131,000 patients in mental hospitals in England and Wales, and 13,000 patients in District Asylums in Scotland.[45] By contrast with

9

the position in England many Scottish local authorities discharged their responsibilities towards mental patients through contracts with the seven voluntary Royal Mental Asylums.

With hindsight, the major limitations of the mental and mental deficiency system relate to the predominantly custodial and legal approach towards these problems, which resulted in a system administered in isolation from other health and social services. Under the jealous eye of the Board of Control the system ossified and it failed to adapt substantially to limited proposals for integration contained in the Mental Treatment Act of 1930. Modern mental hospitals were firmly set in the mould of the Victorian asylums in which they were housed. Only two new mental hospitals were built in the inter-war period; the Bethlem Hospital was rebuilt for the fourth time in its long history, and a completely new hospital was built at Runwell, Essex. The latter, although containing 1,000 beds, as dictated by norms of that time, humanised conditions to some extent by dividing the hospital into small units. With the longer life of mental patients and failure to mobilise the forces of rehabilitation, mental hospitals were becoming increasingly overcrowded and they were also seriously understaffed. The same problems affected mental deficiency hospitals to an even more severe extent.

The eugenist-inspired drive to segregate the mentally deficient resulted in the Mental Deficiency Act (1913), with a parallel Act for Scotland. By 1938 46,000 institutional places were provided in England and Wales, and 3,900 in Scotland.[46] Following from the alarmist note of the Wood Report (1929), specialists in this field regarded this task as only partly accomplished. It was felt that a further 78,000 mental defectives in the population should be segregated into institutions, while strong moves were made to introduce voluntary sterilisation among the estimated 164,000 mental defectives remaining at large.[47]

(iv) NATIONAL HEALTH INSURANCE

The celebrated Lloyd George National Insurance Act of 1911 is traditionally regarded as an important step towards the National Health Service. Indeed, in the popular imagination of the older generation, 1911 was frequently identified as the beginning of the National Health Service. As far as workers were concerned this scheme was the most important direct intervention of the state in health care prior to 1948, by virtue of its introducing a compulsory system of contributory health insurance for a major section of the manual workforce. The '10d for 4d' scheme survived with remarkably little modification until 1948, and its spirit lives on into the

National Health Service to a much greater degree than was intended by the architects of the new system.

The National Health Insurance income limit was extended, partly because of inflation, from £160 to £250 in 1920, and to £420 in 1942. The number of workers covered by this scheme increased from 11.5m (27.4% of the population) at the outset to 20.3m (43% of the population) in 1938.[48] In addition to receipt of weekly cash sickness benefit, members were eligible for 'adequate medical attendance and treatment' without payment, from their chosen 'panel' doctor.[49] Despite their initial deep reservations concerning the Lloyd George scheme, and continuing unhappiness about capitation levels, the great majority of general practitioners joined the panel system. By 1938 90% of active general practitioners were playing some part in the scheme. During the Depression the panel did much to stabilise their incomes and protect them against decline in proceeds from private practice.

As far as recipients were concerned, the major disadvantage of National Health Insurance was limitation of treatment, except in the case of tuberculosis, to care within the 'competence of an ordinary practitioner', which in effect ruled out hospital and specialist treatment.[50] The quality of treatment was often criticised for retaining too many affinities with the old club practice, 'lightning diagnosis and a bottle of physic'.[51] Also, because the system was administered through some 7,000 Approved Societies there was considerable diversity in additional benefits offered. More fortunate workers generally received half the cost of dental and ophthalmic treatment, whereas the less fortunate were deprived of such additional benefits. The worst defect of this system related to absence of coverage for dependants. The latter were reliant on the patchy services provided by public agencies. Otherwise family resources were strained to pay a doctor's bills or to subscribe to some voluntary contributory scheme in order to obtain the services of the local doctor, some public dispensary, or an out-patient department of a hospital. Because of the inadequacy of cash benefits offered to sick workers, their family budgets came under the greatest strain at the time of their sickness.

General practitioners had been reluctant participants in the National Health Insurance scheme. Although their fears concerning interference from the state or Approved Societies proved to be unjustified, general practitioners were increasingly disgruntled by consistent refusal of the authorities to agree to favourable adjustment of the National Health Insurance capitation fee. Increasing overcrowding in the profession offered the very real prospect that National Health Insurance list sizes, already only averaging about 1,000, would further diminish. General practitioners anticipated the erosion of their base income, and they were not confident about the future of their private practice earnings. They looked forward to a bleak future, dependent on scraps of fees derived from a multiplicity of sources. They also feared that modern clinic services developed by voluntary hospitals and local authorities were rapidly turning their predominantly single-handed practices into an archaic backwater of medical care.[52]

(v) THE BALANCE SHEET

Looking back on more than a century of incessant construction expert opinion was impressed by the scope and complexity of the British health services. The 1944 White Paper opened with a declaration that 'The record of this country in its health and medical services is a good one'. The planning process abounded with tributes to the high level of development of the nation's health services. Creation of a comprehensive health service thus seemed logical, attainable and indeed an almost inevitable next step.

The sense of forward motion in the health services is suggested by evidence from various directions. The extensive scale of health legislation and innovation is evident from the above survey. Health expenditure seems to have benefited from the known growth in social service and public expenditure.[53] The cost of public health services in England and Wales (excluding environmental services) increased from £5.6m in 1900/01, to £38.7m in 1927/28, reaching about £51m in 1938/39.[54] Between 1911 and 1938 expenditure of voluntary hospitals increased from £3m to £17m.[55] These increases look more modest when seen as a proportion of GNP. For Britain as a whole, expenditure on public health services, excluding environmental services, seems to have been 1.2% GNP in 1938/39, representing only a minor increase on earlier decades.[56] Consistent with this finding Gough suggests that health and welfare spending was constant at 1.8% GNP in 1931 and 1937.[57]

Various estimates of total expenditure on health services are included in Table I. These calculations suggest a fairly close agreement that between £140m and £150m was being absorbed by the major components of the health services just before World War II.

Taking the above details into account, and also correcting for rising costs, it is necessary to qualify superficial impressions concerning expansion of the health services during the inter-war period. It is arguable that the predominant feature was diversification within a framework of constant expenditure, rather than substantial expansion of the system as a whole.

Perhaps the other primary feature of the inter-war situation was unevenness of provision, especially with respect to hospital services

TABLE I

Contemporary Estimates of the Gross Cost of the Pre-War Health Services in Britain

Service				£ million
	(A)	(B)	(C)	(D)
Local Authority Hospital Services	22	14.5	16.5	23.4
Poor Law Hospital Services	7	8	8	
Mental & Mental Deficiency Hospitals	12	13	14.5	12.3
Other Local Authority Services	2	12	13.0	4.6
NHI Doctors' Fees	10	11	8	8.4
NHI Medicines	4	3	5	2.4
Voluntary Hospitals	18	15.5	17	[15]
Fees to Doctors and Dentists	45	47	38	[40]
Self-medication	20	25	20	[20]
Total	140	149	140	126.1

Source (A) L. T. Hilliard and L. C. J. McNae, 'If the Medical Services are Free', *Medicine Today and Tomorrow*, March 1941, pp 11–15.

(B) *PEP Report,* pp 388–92.

(C) Medical Planning Research, 'Interim General Report', *The Lancet,* 1942, ii, p 609.

(D) *WP,* pp 80–4.

Notes (1) The differences in these estimates are largely accounted for
(a) by the slightly different dates from which the data originated;
(b) by inclusion of different entities in each category.

(2) (A), (B) and (C) relate to Scotland, England and Wales; and (D) to England and Wales. In (D) notional estimates from official sources have been included for the private sector.

Adding certain miscellaneous items the *Lancet* estimate (excluding cash payments) was £160m, which is reasonably consistent with the PEP estimate of £149m for a slightly earlier date, and which amounts to 3.0% GNP for expenditure on health from all sources.

and more innovatory features of health care. As noted above, prosperous urban areas witnessed a transformation of their local authority health services. Deprived areas and smaller rural authorities fell steadily behind in this process of modernisation. Large tracts of Britain, especially in the north and west, were lumbered with obsolete services and backward-looking attitudes in health administration. Non-working women were a further particular victim of discrimination since they were excluded from National Health Insurance benefit, and because of the poor development of obstetric and gynaecological services. In their case care was provided in inverse proportion to need.

Diversity in the quality and quantity of services undermines the value of aggregate data. This conclusion also emerges with respect to data concerning the state of health of the generations born before World War II.

On the basis of aggregate statistics MacNalty had some justification for claiming that 'the standard of public health at the outbreak of war had reached a high level of excellence unprecedented in history'.[58] On the positive side, infant mortality was slowly declining; maternal mortality, after reaching a peak in the mid-thirties, was in decline; life expectancy for males and females was increasing; most of the major infectious diseases were in retreat.[59] MacNalty was also no doubt justified in claiming that 'some part of the improvement must be due to the health services', although he frankly admitted that quantifying this contribution was impossible. It is likely that the major part of the increase in average life expectancy after the first months of life was attributable to improved diet and rising standards of living among certain segments of the population. A further helpful factor was the autonomous remission of some of the major infectious diseases such as tuberculosis, diphtheria, measles, whooping cough and scarlet fever.[60].

On the negative side, Britain's performance in the health field was steadily declining by comparison with other English-speaking countries and Scandinavia. Lack of co-ordinated services for cancer, orthopaedics, gynaecology, etc, underlined the failure of the hospital service to adapt to growing problems of ill health. Within Britain health standards precisely mirrored diversities within the health services. Levels of mortality and morbidity, to the degree that reliable data are available for the latter, were noticeably worse in Scotland, Wales and Northern Ireland than in England. Within each of these areas health standards were noticeably worse in inner city slums or depressed districts, and among certain occupational groups such as miners and their families. The masking of these striking class differentials of health in the aggregate data was compellingly revealed by Titmuss, who pointed out the large-scale needless wastage of human life still taking place among less privileged classes.[61] These findings underlined the great scope for improvement in the provision of health and social services. They also brought into question the suitability of services as then constituted to provide a quality of health care appropriate to an advanced western civilisation in the later twentieth century. There was a growing distaste for services marred by the taint of charity, less eligibility, minimum standards, or heavy-handed bureaucracy. Diffusion of news about superior standards elsewhere and mounting confidence in the capabilities of modern medicine resulted in a general rise in expectations. During the late thirties the new philosophy of social medicine, positive health, and optimum standards, spread to a wide public.

It was no longer acceptable to measure the success of health care in terms of protection against major infectious diseases. The propaganda of the new, stylish, Peckham Health Centre reinforced the view that health was more than freedom from disease. This health centre swept into prominence as the medical institution for the future. The first and only comprehensive survey of the health services to be undertaken in twentieth-century Britain concluded, with conscious reference to the Peckham model, that the new health services must aim at 'creating and maintaining good physique, energy, happiness or resistance to disease', rather than merely work of a 'salvage nature . . . patching up ill-health'.[62] With this utopian goal in mind existing health services looked distinctly inappropriate to meet the challenge of the future.

CHAPTER II

Visions of Utopia

The idea of establishing a unified comprehensive health service was sometimes dismissed as an unrealisable, utopian objective. This was certainly the response to schemes evolved in the context of post-war reconstruction in 1918. When the reconstruction exercise was repeated during World War II, and the health scheme was again introduced, Churchill warned his colleagues against deceiving the people with 'false hopes and airy visions of Utopia and Eldorado'.[1]

Paradoxically, the very high level of development of health services in Britain stood in the way of any radical reconstruction. Deeply entrenched professional interest groups, or institutions shrouded in venerable traditions, presented formidable obstacles to anything other than incremental change. Movement towards a comprehensive National Health Service involving a strong element of innovation was thus hesitant and indecisive. It was only during World War II that the ascendancy was gained by forces favouring complete overhaul of the health services.

It is arbitrary to identify a starting point for initiation of planning for the National Health Service. The Labour Government in 1945 clearly built on the experience of the Wartime Coalition Government. Conventionally the wartime crisis and the Emergency Medical Service are regarded as crucial to the generation of a climate of opinion favourable to ambitious schemes for social reconstruction. The wartime commitment to planning and the ferment of ideas associated with the wartime experience admittedly constituted an important catalytic influence. Yet, as noted above, the inter-war crisis also played its part in exposing the instability and inappropriateness of the ramshackle edifice of medical services.

Retrenchment delayed reaction to the increasingly serious problems apparent in most arms of the services. Once recovery began it was realised in both official and outside circles that major reorganisation was a necessary condition for survival. In some respects piecemeal reforms had made the position worse. For instance, dismantling the Poor Law medical services in 1929 and the consequent strengthening of the public health sector helped to precipitate a crisis within the rival spheres of National Health Insurance and the voluntary hospitals. The action of 1929 itself represented a partial and belated response to an assault on the Poor Law begun much earlier in the century. Poor Law reformers were by 1910 enunciating principles that were taken up with more chance of success during World War II, in their attack on 'overlapping, confusion and waste', and in their appeal to principles of 'efficiency and economy' in the social services.[2] Wartime solutions to social problems were thus not entirely new inventions. They fell into a pattern determined by a complex sequence of pre-war events, in the course of which political and economic pressures for substantial change had built up to the point when they could no longer be contained.

The idea of arresting the process of fragmentation and division of responsibility in the field of health care by unifying health services had already commended itself to the 1869 Sanitary Commission, which declared that 'All powers requisite for the health of town and country should in every place be possessed by one responsible local authority . . . so that no area shall be without such an authority, or have more than one'.[3] Notwithstanding this recommendation, publicly provided services in a county area became divided between Boards of Guardians, county councils, district councils, and insurance committees, as well as being distributed between a variety of statutory committees of any one local authority. At the centre public health agencies were superintended and largely kept apart by the different arms of the labyrinthine Local Government Board, while the new National Health Insurance system was administered entirely separately under two National Insurance Commissions. Thus, by 1918, events had led in exactly the opposite direction to that recommended by the sanitary commissioners.

(i) SEARCHING FOR SYSTEM: 1900–1940

The scheme of Sir John Simon for a separate Ministry of Health presiding over unified local medical services was frustrated, but his *English Sanitary Institutions* (1890 and 1897) persisted in its influence as powerful propaganda for this cause. The first major opportunity to achieve a degree of unification occurred with the Royal Commission on the Poor Laws (1904–1909) where the assertive minority group headed by Beatrice Webb pressed for integration of public health and poor law health services into a 'Public Medical Service' or 'State Medical Service'.[4]

The Minority Report of the Poor Law Commission provided renewed incentive to comprehensive health planning. The model laid down in this report gained widespread acceptance and it gradually came to dominate official thinking. To the degree that significant steps towards a National Health Service were taken between 1904 and 1946, the Minority Report was the effective blueprint.

Of the two rival public agencies providing extensive health services, the Minority Report reversed the recommendation of the sanitary commissioners and declared firmly against the Boards of Guardians. Services determined by proof of destitution and regulated by destitution agencies were thought inappropriate to health care. Equally firmly the Minority Report held up the local authority health services as the model for the future. Despite the apparent profligacy of providing comprehensive health services on an indiscriminate basis, the Minority Report argued that prevention of health problems at source would result in economies in expensive treatment or institutional facilities, while it would also more effectively protect the population at large from the spread of disease. The primary responsibilities of the state medical service should accordingly embrace 'searching out disease, securing the earliest possible diagnosis, taking hold of the incipient case, removing injurious conditions, applying specialised treatment, enforcing healthy surroundings and personal hygiene, and aiming always at preventing either recurrence or spread of disease—in contrast to the mere "relief" of the individual'.[5] For this purpose the Minority Report suggested the expansion of public health committees of county boroughs and county councils, where sufficient in size, to provide a unified medical service undertaken by a staff of full-time, salaried medical officers, including 'clinicians . . . sanitarians, institution superintendents as well as domiciliary practitioners'.[6] Many of the services would not in the event have been universal because patients were to be subject to a means test, an arrangement designed to allay the fears of medical practitioners about the erosion of their established mode of private practice among the better off.

Introduction in 1911 of unemployment and sickness insurance made major groups of workers less dependent on poor relief during times of difficulty. Advocates of a unified health service found this system objectionable on account of its entirely separate administration, its ties with the complex and uneven machinery of Approved Societies, and because of disapproval of a 'publicly subsidised system of letting the poor choose their own doctors'.[7] It was realised that once the National Health Insurance system was firmly established, it would be difficult to dismantle. Continuing pressures for the separate administration of family practitioner services, and the persistence of administrative characteristics of the panel system bear witness to the tenacity of the arrangements introduced in 1911.

Formation of the Ministry of Health in 1919 at least drew the National Health Insurance Commission into the department taking over the health and poor law functions of the dismantled Local Government Board. In the context of elaborate plans for post-war reconstruction and for the radical overhaul of machinery of government, an expectation was aroused that the new Ministry of Health would fulfil the chief aspirations of previous generations of public health reformers. Indeed both Sir Robert Morant, the first Permanent Secretary to the Ministry, and Lord Dawson, Chairman of the newly formed Consultative Council on Medical and Allied Services, cherished ambitious plans for the development of a comprehensive and unified health service.[8] Building on Dawson's own wartime experiences of medical planning, the interim report of the Consultative Council approached this problem from the point of view of the most efficient and rational use of resources. Morant worked towards the same objective, but with a more realistic understanding of limitations imposed by the existing pattern of administration. After the premature death of Morant in March 1920, and the replacement of Christopher Addison, the first Minister of Health, in April 1921, the Consultative Council lapsed, proposals for Poor Law reform were further postponed, and the Ministry of Health fell into a cautious and routine mode of operation consistent with the growing pessimism of the times.[9] Failure of the Consultative Council might have been compensated for by the establishment in 1930 of an informal Medical Advisory Committee, under the Chief Medical Officer, but it was later noted that this Committee 'functioned spasmodically and ineffectively during the next ten years'.[10] Dawson's plans for a universal system of health centres, elaborate co-ordination of medical effort, and his guiding principle that the 'best means of maintaining health and curing disease should be made available to all citizens' were consigned to the world of medical utopias.[11]

The scheme prepared by Dawson was designed to draw private medical practitioners into participation with the state medical service. Otherwise, he feared, new services would be introduced on an ad hoc basis by local authorities until the position of the independent medical practitioner became completely untenable.

The prediction of 'a state medical service by instalments, almost by stealth', albeit a depressing prospect to Dawson, proved an accurate prognosis for the direction of events during the inter-war period.[12] From the Maternity and Child Welfare Act in 1918 to the Cancer Act of 1939 a long succession of measures added to the health responsibilities of local authorities. There was also a slow drift towards increasing the authority of county councils and county borough councils at the expense of district councils, the most important step in this direction being the transfer in 1929 of health responsibilities from 635 Poor Law Unions to 145 local health authorities. But the haphazard system of local government stood firmly in the way of complete consolidation of services in the larger local authority units. Awkward divisions of responsibilities persisted between the LCC and metropolitan boroughs, and between county councils and larger district councils. Small sizes of many local authority units resulted in functions being inadequately performed, or delegated to largely unsatisfactory ad hoc joint boards, which sprang up for provision of tuberculosis sanatoria, infectious diseases hospitals or mental and mental deficiency institutions.[13]

The cumbersome machinery of local government cranked out services of uneven distribution and quality. The inefficiency of this system was underlined by cases of unnecessary duplication, such as the tuberculosis sanatoria of Nottingham County Borough and Nottinghamshire County Council that were situated a short distance apart in Sherwood Forest.

The worst disjunction within the system was between the municipal and voluntary hospital sectors. From the time of the Cave Committee (1921) pressure built up for closer co-ordination between the two systems. However it was almost as an afterthought that section 13 was added to the 1929 Local Government Act (and section 27 to the Scottish Local Government Act), requiring local authorities to consult with voluntary hospitals in planning an extension of their hospital services. In the event it was only in isolated instances such as Liverpool, Manchester or Oxford that extensive co-operation took place. On the whole, local authorities expanded their hospital services without reference to their voluntary neighbours, or even in a spirit of competition or emulation.

If they were guided by any longer-term objectives at this time it is likely that department officials subscribed to the aims of Morant, whose great imagination cast a long shadow over the department he had created. Morant wanted:

> to disentangle the health services from the rest of the Poor Law and to transfer them to the new Local Health Authority, which he hoped would be the County and the County Borough. In this his mind reverted to the plan of the 1902 Education Bill. He contemplated the County and County Borough as the Health Authority administering not only the health services at present under the Poor Law, but also practically all other health services, including infectious diseases, lunacy, tuberculosis, maternity and child welfare.[14]

The most radical side of Morant's proposals involved bringing voluntary hospitals directly under local authority control, partly because he believed that voluntary hospitals were 'doomed', but also because of the 'immense loss of efficiency' under the current fragmented system of hospital administration. Morant had also

considered the desirability of establishing separate health authorities, but he abandoned this idea because this was likely to
lay 'too much stress on treatment to the neglect of preventive
medicine'.

Memoranda reflecting the plans of Morant also provided a
vehicle whereby the spirit of Simon and the Webbs was resusci-
tated. These earlier ideas again became relevant when a new
impetus towards comprehensive planning arose after further expansion of health services came under consideration during recovery
from the worst effects of the Depression.

Sir Kingsley Wood, Minister of Health from June 1935 until
May 1938, possessed experience of health administration extending
back to 1911 when he had advised the industrial insurance companies
on national health insurance. The Medical Advisory Committee,
newly reconstituted in 1936, discussed a wide variety of proposals
for expansion of services, extending from birth control to cancer.[15]

In December 1936 Sir Arthur MacNalty, the Chief Medical
Officer from 1935 to 1940, was asked to prepare proposals for the
provision of specialist and other diagnostic services, either for the
population as a whole or at least for the insured population in the
first instance. MacNalty's memorandum concluded that recent
developments had rendered local authority services a more appropriate basis for a comprehensive scheme than the National Health
Insurance system, which was judged inappropriate for further
development. Least disruption would be incurred by transfer of
medical benefit to local authorities, despite the likely resistance to
such a change from Approved Societies, the Insurance Committees,
and the profession.[16]

The above thinking was consistent with Morant's philosophy.
MacNalty noted the support of medical colleagues in the department, and it was later stated that development of public health
services was the agreed policy of the Ministry of Health. This
policy was sufficiently firm for a positive scheme to be worked out
in 1936 to transfer National Insurance medical benefit to local
authorities.[17]

The next trace of steps towards a unified health service is evident
from four office conferences held between February and June 1938
to discuss 'Development of the Health Services'. This renewed
effort was prompted by the prediction that this issue was likely to
appear in election programmes in the near future. Also the Minister
was speculating that in light of the new cancer scheme 'further
developments of the health services were not excluded'. A group
of about eight senior officials went over the disadvantages of
National Health Insurance medical benefit and they considered

plans for extending benefits to dependants of insured workers under a scheme administered by local authorities.[18]

The above discussions were interrupted by news of the serious financial difficulties of voluntary hospitals, including the London teaching hospitals.[19] The scale of this problem placed it beyond the means of the King's Fund, which was already distributing about £300,000 pa to London hospitals. All the solutions discussed relied on raising substantial sums from public sources. In particular it was hoped that the LCC would use voluntary hospitals on an agency basis, and perhaps also provide other subsidies. However, an LCC delegation, led by Herbert Morrison, was unresponsive to appeals for support.[20] No progress had been made when the introduction of the wartime Emergency Hospital Service provided voluntary hospitals with an unexpected injection of exchequer revenue. The largescale anticipated wartime need for access to beds in the voluntary sector, the substantial scale of the required exchequer subsidy, and the dilemma over a post-war hospital settlement resulted in active discussion of the possibility that a voluntary system 'approaching demise' might best be rescued by nationalisation and direct administration of a national hospital service, and perhaps all health services, by the Ministry of Health. This avowedly radical proposal received a cool reception from some officials, one of whom informed the Permanent Secretary that a 'national scheme is legislatively impracticable and administratively not worthwhile'.[21]

It was rapidly conceded that despite the appeal of 'a centrally directed organisation of all health services from Whitehall . . . from the point of view of preventive and curative medicine and of national efficiency' the friends of such a scheme were too few to merit its further consideration.[22] In any case, throughout 1940 officials were primarily concerned with short-term questions of the wartime emergency, rather than with abstract schemes for a distant and unpredictable future.

It was said at the time that Hitler and the Ministry between them had accomplished in a few months what might have taken the British Hospitals Association twenty years to bring about.[23] It might have been added that the Spanish Civil War also contributed to this development, because the devastation wreaked by Fascist air forces brought home the fearful risk of aerial bombardment.[24] It was initially estimated that 290,000 hospital beds would be required for civilian air-raid casualties. The Emergency Hospital Service created as a temporary expedient marked a secular shift towards a nationally planned and rationalised hospital service. As the 1944 White Paper acknowledged, this wartime experiment had translated 'a collection of individual hospitals into something of a related hospital system'. On points both of structure and detail the Emergency Hospital Service left a permanent mark on the post-war hospital system. The long-term impact of this wartime commitment was not universally appreciated at the time.[25]

Whereas the British Hospitals Association proposed fifteen hospital regions for England and Wales, the emergency scheme adopted twelve regions. Both plans divided Scotland into five regions.[26] In most of the cases the headquarters of the Regional Hospital Officers coincided with a teaching hospital centre. The intractable problem of organisation within London was solved by dividing greater London into ten sectors radiating out from teaching hospitals in the centre.[27] Although to a lesser extent than military service, the emergency hospital scheme introduced medical staff to public work on a salaried basis. Mutual distrust was broken down as hospital staff from the two sectors became used to working together. A leading hospital surveyor was impressed by 'the extent to which whole-time service is already in being. We are watching a transformation in some fields that amazes by its rapidity'.[28] The wartime emergency also necessitated attention to the long-running problem of low pay and staff shortage within the nursing profession. In 1941 the Government imposed a uniform pay structure for nurses as a condition for its grants to voluntary hospitals. The Rushcliffe Committee was then set up to look more closely into the problem of pay and conditions for nurses. The opportunity was also taken to establish a separate roll for assistant nurses.[29]

The shortage and maldistribution of beds was solved by an expansion programme, involving the addition of some 44,000 beds in England and Wales and 16,000 beds in Scotland. In Scotland the Department of Health itself built and directly administered seven new general hospitals, supplying an additional 7,000 beds.[30] When Gleneagles Hotel was not required for emergency hospital facilities it was diverted to a much publicised experiment in social medicine, involving rehabilitation of workers from the Clyde Basin.[31] In Scotland it was concluded that emergency hospitals had 'effectively drained off the waiting lists; then they started a service to supplement GPs'.[32]

Existing hospitals were subjected to an extensive programme of 'upgrading', to increase their efficiency and to provide modern facilities. Because of the wartime emergency, a regionally organised Blood Transfusion Service and a national Emergency Public Health Laboratory Service were established.[33] Hospital transport was also organised on a level unknown previously.

The above changes involved extensive state investment in the hospital services. Generous exchequer payments to voluntary hospitals in respect of beds set aside for emergency use entailed   a subsidy which soon became indispensable. The services themselves, initially intended for casualties became available on an increasingly liberal scale to civilians. As early as 1942 the Scottish Department of Health accepted the use of emergency beds in voluntary hospitals for almost all persons on waiting lists, with the exception of chronic cases.[34]

Given the improvement in standards effected by the emergency scheme, it was realised that the Government would be unavoidably committed to maintaining these standards after the war.[35] It was concluded that the effect of the Emergency Hospital Service on hospital and specialist services 'assumes almost the proportions of a revolution'.[36]

(ii) SCHEMING FOR RECONSTRUCTION

The urgency of official discussions on post-war policy greatly intensified during 1941, particularly because of the Government commitment to evolve detailed proposals for post-war social reconstruction, but also partly because of the still unsolved problem of the fate of voluntary hospitals after the run-down of the Emergency Hospital Service, and finally because outside parties were publishing and even putting into operation their own long-term plans.[37] The health departments needed to move quickly to prevent this latter process getting out of hand.

Rival and incompatible planning proposals were emanating from influential sources.

First, among the major political parties, the Labour Party was committed to a particularly radical reorganisation of the health services.[38] Since 1934 Labour had been pledged to establish a comprehensive service provided free to all, the employment of all staff on a full-time salaried basis, administration under a reformed multi-purpose regional government, and the provision of a comprehensive system of publicly provided health centres. More detailed proposals, worked out by Labour's Public Health Reconstruction Committee formed in July 1941, closely approximated to official thinking at that time. This similarity is simply explained, because both the Labour Party and the Ministry of Health were anticipating that the future health service would be developed by extending local authority health services and reforming local government. Plans for a state medical service along these lines became known to a wider audience through a variety of popular expositions.[39] The Permanent Secretary was advised that they must prepare for a full 'state and rate medical service', involving 'equality of treatment and benefit', because these principles were supported by 'considerable weight of vocal political opinion'.[40]

The Labour movement made a direct representation to the Government on 6 February 1941 when the two Health Ministers received a TUC deputation to discuss union views on social security. The paper circulated by this deputation strongly attacked voluntary hospitals, National Health Insurance and the Approved Societies. Among the demands of this delegation was 'A comprehensive national medical service covering everything that medical science can command for prevention and cure of sickness'.[41]

Secondly, the BMA became committed to health planning in the light of increasing pessimism about the future of general practice. The territory of general practice had suffered incursions from both public health services and hospital contributory schemes. Extension of the National Health Insurance system to serve a wider population and to provide additional services now seemed the best basis for protection of the interests and professional reputation of general practitioners. The BMA standpoint was expounded in *A General Medical Service for the Nation* (1938), a revised version of a report originally issued in 1930. This document risked being overtaken by events. Its obsolete character was indeed accepted by the BMA Secretary.[42] For instance, it advocated extension of National Health Insurance benefits to dependants, but failed to take up the almost universal demand to raise the income limit above £250. However, in one respect the document lived on, because its first basic principle ('That the system of medical service should be directed to the achievement of positive health and the prevention of disease no less than to the relief of sickness') was enshrined in the report of the Medical Planning Commission and in the Beveridge Report, and it was echoed in many subsequent planning documents.[43]

In order to update its image and seize the initiative, in August 1940 the BMA convened a Medical Planning Commission comprising more than seventy representatives drawn from the major professional organisations. This body was asked to examine the likely long-term impact of the war on the nation's medical services.[44]

The *Draft Interim Report* of the Medical Planning Commission issued in June 1942 was a disjointed document, but it attracted widespread interest because it was less monolithic than the 1938 report.[45] Its liberal tone suggested greater receptivity to change within the medical profession than was previously evident. More directly than the report of 1938 the Medical Planning Commission formulated the requirement to 'render available to every individual all necessary medical services, both general and specialist, and both domiciliary and institutional'.[46] Indeed from the MPC report it seemed as if general practitioners were looking forward to joining

25

into teams working from health centres. It was less noted in official circles that the report was given a poor reception at the BMA Annual Representative Meeting in September 1942. The Medical Planning Commission and its report were not further pursued. Opinion within the BMA reverted to positions stated in its previous policy documents.

Thirdly, as they sank deeper into financial trouble, voluntary hospitals increasingly recognised the necessity of co-ordination. Since the beginning of the century the King Edward Hospital Fund for London had striven for greater efficiency in the use of the resources of London voluntary hospitals. In 1937 a Commission established by the British Hospitals Association advocated grouping of voluntary hospitals under regional councils.[47] This policy was given added strength by the Nuffield Provincial Hospitals Trust, established in 1939 with the primary aim of 'co-ordination on a regional basis of hospital . . . services'. The Nuffield Hospitals Trust immediately set about forming regional and divisional councils, representing both voluntary and local authority hospitals with a view to consolidating these institutions into a permanently viable National Hospital Service.[48] Lord Nuffield's initiative evoked from Walter Elliot, Minister of Health from May 1938 to May 1940, an expression of general encouragement on the grounds that the Trust would further the intention of the 1929 Local Government Act to promote co-operation between the municipal and voluntary sectors of the hospital system.[49] Advisers sympathetic to the voluntary hospitals sought a public undertaking from the Minister that 'he proposes to adopt regionalisation and to take the initial steps for its universal application'.[50]

Fourthly, an avalanche of plans for the post-war reconstruction of medicine were prepared by specialist and lay groups, as well as keen individuals, the whole effort contributing to a sense of dissatisfaction with the past and of inevitable progression. At the summit of the profession, the Royal College of Physicians established committees to prepare reports on key issues in the modernisation of health care and medical education. More informally, from his important post at the London School of Hygiene, Wilson Jameson in 1939 initiated weekly discussions on the future of medicine and the health services. These discussions involved experts who later occupied important positions in medical administration, research and education.[51]

Expressing the more radical and iconoclastic mood taking root within the medical profession was Medical Planning Research, a group of scientifically-minded younger medical practitioners, 200 of whom contributed drafts to its rapidly prepared, but substantial

'Interim General Report', an impressive and informative piece of analysis, even if somewhat out of touch with political realities.[52]

Medical Planning Research was indebted to Political and Economic Planning, whose influential *Report on the British Health Services* appeared in 1937. Building on its extensive work on the health and social services, PEP advised that 'Medical and allied services should be financially and administratively divorced from social insurance and the Poor Law, and unified into one national system providing its services for the whole population on the basis of common citizenship'. Along with 'all the other public health activities', those services should be 'supported from the general public funds'.[53]

At the popular end of the spectrum of opinion *Picture Post* was probably echoing a widespread mood in calling for a comprehensive health service as part of its 'Plan for Britain'.[54] It has been noted that this special issue of *Picture Post* unleashed more letters from the public than any other issue in the magazine's history.[55] A British Institute of Public Opinion Survey undertaken at this time indicates that 85% of those questioned supported a state-organised medical service, while 55% were favourable to placing all hospitals and doctors under state control.[56] The Nuffield College Social Reconstruction Survey undertaken for the Beveridge Committee discovered a universal demand for radical alteration of the panel system. Their investigators detected general sympathy for establishment of a unified state medical service. Typically, in Devon it was discovered that 'the most obvious reform which has been advocated throughout the whole course of our inquiries is that medical service should become a state matter. The desire for this among insured persons and among the younger and more progressive doctors in the county appears to be fairly widespread'.[57] This conclusion was tested by Beveridge's committee in a visit to Lancashire, when it was concluded that in the light of apparent loss of public confidence in general practitioner services 'one meets in many quarters an expressed preference for the resolution of the whole question by means of a whole-time state medical service'.[58]

A Ministry of Information survey summed up the public mood on the health services:

There are a number of points on which feeling is very strong and in some cases unanimous:

i. In the future, the best possible medical, surgical and hospital treatment should be available to everyone, and 'without the stigma of charity'.

ii. The panel as run at present is strongly and widely disliked, primarily because of the discrimination which doctors are thought to show between panel and private patients; and secondly, because no provision is made for dependants.

iii. There is growing feeling in favour of regular periodic medical examination.

iv. There should be much more prevention of disease . . .

v. A majority appear to favour the national ownership and control of hospitals.[59]

In the light of such mounting evidence it is not surprising that the Permanent Secretary advised that 'public opinion will not . . . be satisfied with less than a scheme under which hospital treatment . . . is available to anyone who needs it'.[60] Consequently, the first steps of the Coalition Government towards a National Health Service were taken against a background of overwhelming public pressure for a change in this direction.

Although the competing interests within the health care world also realised that it would be impossible to return to the pre-war system, their spirit of wartime solidarity was insufficient to overcome sectarian pressures. The wartime emergency appeared like a once-and-for-all opportunity for the various interest groups to consolidate their position within a peacetime settlement.

(iii) A NATIONAL HOSPITAL SERVICE: 1941

In view of the radically different perceptions of the planning process, it is difficult to discern a strong common core within the mass of competing programmes for the future of the health service. *The Times* noted that 'the need for improvement is universally conceded, as also the need for planning in one form or another', but otherwise there was little sign of consensus.[61] It is also evident that the health departments were finding it difficult to exercise effective leadership.

Instead of planning in isolation, as had been the case in 1936, the health departments were by 1941 holding the ring between competing interests, recognising that prospects of a long-term solution might be irrevocably sacrificed if one side was allowed to take premature initiatives. A particular problem arose over the headlong rush of the Nuffield Trustees towards regionalisation, a trend viewed with deepening suspicion, especially by larger local health authorities such as the LCC, as a threat to their interests and independence. Consequently, policy discussions in 1941 became directed towards the hospital problem. Indeed, it was assumed that the hospital service would be reformed in advance of any attempt to modify the panel system.[62]

Important changes of personnel introduced at both the ministerial and official level placed responsibility for post-war planning in entirely new hands. In 1940 Malcolm MacDonald became the eleventh Minister of Health since the department was founded in 1919. MacDonald's own appointment lasted only from May 1940 to February 1941, but his brief spell in office was important, because of both staff changes and increasing commitment to hospital policy. MacDonald was replaced by A E Brown whose appointment lasted until November 1943. Ernest Brown was already experienced in health affairs by virtue of his previous appointment as Secretary of State for Scotland (May 1940–February 1941). Thomas Johnston, Brown's successor at the Scottish Office, remained in the post until the end of the Coalition Government.

In 1940 MacDonald replaced both his Permanent Secretary and his Chief Medical Officer. Sir George Chrystal, an outsider with predominantly Ministry of Pensions experience, was replaced as Permanent Secretary by Sir John Maude, whose whole career had been spent in the National Health Insurance Commission and at the Ministry of Health. Maude remained in the post until the 1945 Labour Government. MacNalty was replaced by Sir Wilson Jameson, who was persuaded to become Chief Medical Officer on the understanding from MacDonald that major changes in the health services would be implemented.[63] Jameson played a major role in the complex health negotiations, under both the Coalition and Labour Governments.

At the Scottish Office, W R Fraser, who was appointed as Secretary of the Department of Health in 1939, continued until his retirement in 1943, when he was replaced by Sir George Henderson, who retired in 1953. Henderson had ascended the scale in the Scottish Department of Health in very much the same manner as Maude in London. J M Mackintosh left his post as Chief Medical Officer in 1940 to succeed Jameson at the London School of Hygiene, being replaced by Sir Andrew Davidson, who retired in 1954.

The above changes created useful stability within the health departments between 1941 and 1945. During this period there was only one senior ministerial change (Willink for Brown in November 1943) and one replacement among the four senior officials, and even this preserved continuity.

Both personal and political characteristics affected ministers' responses to the challenge of post-war reconstruction. Differences were evident within parties, as well as between them. For instance, action on post-war reconstruction in education was slower under the President of the Board of Education, Herwald Ramsbotham, than under his younger Conservative successor, R A Butler, who held office from July 1941. As a parallel example, the National Labour Minister, MacDonald, was less lethargic than Brown, his National Liberal colleague in Scotland.

On some occasions Party differences were evident. In January 1941, for example, the Labour Scottish Parliamentary Under-Secretary of State wanted the department to prepare for a comprehensive and free health service, but Brown agreed with his officials that it was 'premature' to consider post-war problems.[64] Upon Brown's transfer to the Ministry of Health, Thomas Johnston, his Labour successor, was more positively committed to post-war planning. Given Brown's background he and Johnston should have been ideally suited companions, but they failed to work together, with the result that the English and Scottish plans for the health services drifted awkwardly apart. Notwithstanding their own inclinations, neither Johnston nor Brown could resist the momentum of events on the hospital front.

As noted above, under both Kingsley Wood and Walter Elliot the Ministry of Health had, before the war, recognised the inevitability of radical change within the hospital sector. The wartime emergency reinforced this conclusion. However, before 1941 Ministers had not committed themselves collectively to going beyond the vague prescription about co-operation contained in the 1929 Local Government Acts. Before the establishment of a firm Cabinet mechanism for handling proposals for long-term civil planning, MacDonald seems unilaterally to have entered into stronger commitments on hospital policy than were merited by the state of Government thinking. Apparently without obtaining sanction from his Cabinet colleagues MacDonald instructed officials to assume that a radical reorganisation of the hospital service would take place after the cessation of hostilities. The new arrangements would involve acceptance by the Government of an obligation to provide adequate hospital facilities for the whole population.[65] Responding to continuing pressures from the Nuffield Trustees, MacDonald gave firm support for two principles, first, the co-existence and co-operation of local authorities and voluntary hospitals; secondly, the need to plan with respect to regional units larger than existing local government areas.[66]

The Times viewed the above formula as the preferred means to retain 'the best features of the old voluntary system . . . side by side with public health and other public medical services'.[67] The Permanent Secretary interpreted MacDonald's letter as committing the Minister, 'and to some extent the Government, on three points—a measure of regionalisation, a local government system, and co-operation between municipal and voluntary hospitals'.[68] Commitment on 'a local government system' had not in fact been contained in MacDonald's letter, although this view was influential in the thinking of his department.

Departmental discussions revealed substantial worries concerning pursuit of all three of these objectives.[69] Officials were far from certain that maintenance of the voluntary hospital system was possible or desirable. It was felt that enhancing the role of the state sector would inevitably hasten the decline of voluntary hospitals. The value of some form of regional organisation was admitted, but it was doubted whether this mechanism should extend further than advisory planning functions. While it was agreed that local authorities should assume statutory responsibility for the provision of services, it was realised that authorities would need to combine together before they could provide comprehensive hospital services. Finally, it was predicted that all administrative reforms currently under consideration were likely to provoke fierce opposition.

In view of these awkward dilemmas it is not surprising that the progress of departmental discussions and informal consultations was slow and sporadic. Although little advance was recorded by the autumn of 1941, a formal ministerial statement on policy was unavoidable in the light of forceful initiatives from the Nuffield Trustees, and increasingly inflammatory responses from local authorities. By the end of 1941 three Regional Councils, one Regional Advisory Council, and eight Divisional Councils had been established.[70] In a widely publicised outburst directed against the voluntary hospital planners, Charles Latham, Leader of the LCC, asserted that 'Fifth-Columnists against democracy are preparing to steal the people's municipal hospitals'.[71]

With a view to defusing the situation, Brown prepared a statement agreed by the Secretary of State for Scotland (Johnston), the Chancellor of the Exchequer (Wood), and the Minister without Portfolio (Greenwood), which was duly read in the House of Commons.[72] For the first time Brown publicly stated the Government's positive objective 'as soon as may be after the war to ensure that by means of a comprehensive hospital service appropriate treatment shall be readily available to every person in need of it'. It was emphasised that the service was not to be free. The Government intended to maintain 'the principle that patients should make reasonable payment, either through contributory schemes or otherwise'. Brown talked vaguely about 'co-operation' or 'partnership' between voluntary and municipal hospitals and, without using the term 'region', about the need to design the service on the basis of areas substantially larger than existing local authorities. Representing a substantial concession to local authority pressure, it was stated that major local authorities would have the duty to secure the provision of the new hospital service. Furthermore it was announced that, with the support of the Nuffield Provincial Hospitals Trust, surveys of hospital resources would be undertaken with a view to establishing guidance on future planning. By this device the energies of Nuffield planners were channelled into surveying rather than regional organisation. In the event, the teams of surveyors not only gave the health departments their first precise insight into the state of the nation's acute and chronic hospitals, but they also provided an avenue for local intelligence and commentary during the formulation of plans for a comprehensive health service.

The press release associated with Brown's official statement stressed that the above policies were carrying to a logical conclusion principles about co-operation laid down in the 1929 Local Government Acts.[73] Brown's low-key approach was unsuccessful in allaying disquiet in ministerial circles about the risk of premature commitments on national hospital policy. Apart from Brown's discussions among immediate colleagues concerning the text of his announcement, relatively little opportunity had been available for wider consent to an initiative on national hospital policy. At its first meeting, the Cabinet Committee on Reconstruction Problems asked Brown and Johnston to report on National Health Insurance, hospital organisation and nutrition policy.[74] Brown mentioned that initiative on hospitals was being left to the Nuffield organisation, which he was actively assisting. The momentum of the Reconstruction Committee rapidly ran down, with the result that hospital policy was not again subjected to scrutiny until the committee was reconstituted in 1943.

There were few other opportunities for Ministers to raise the hospital issue. However, at the Lord President's Committee Attlee asked for clarification of Brown's statement.[75] Brown was invited to produce a memorandum for fuller discussion.[76] Brown's paper gave Ministers their first opportunity to discuss hospital policy. Building on hints contained in his press release, and in some detail, Brown presented his scheme as the culmination of developments since 1909 which had progressively increased the responsibilities of county councils and county borough councils for hospital services. The regional principle was already implicit in the Cancer Act; a precedent for financial arrangements between local authorities and voluntary hospitals was located in the 1875 Public Health Act; while the Emergency Hospital Scheme had proved that co-operation could apply on a general scale.

In discussion Brown stressed that the voluntary hospitals would be partners, yet also be subordinated to local authorities. Brown's approach was generally supported, but Bevin insisted that the new service must not leave workers in the position of depending on 'charity or favour'.[77] Interventions in subsequent debates by Labour members reproached Brown for being over-conciliatory to the voluntary hospital interest.[78] It was thus already clear that bipartisanship would be difficult to obtain on this key problem in post-war reconstruction.

The Scottish Department of Health was faced by even stronger pressure for consolidation of the voluntary sector position than was evident in England and Wales. In Scotland a stream of inter-war official reports on hospitals and health services had emphatically insisted on the supremacy and independence of voluntary hospitals. Armed with the last and most formidable of these reports, the Cathcart Report, the Scottish branch of the British Hospitals Association formulated a scheme for dividing Scotland into five health regions. In 1941 they submitted a plan for full co-ordination to the three local authority associations. Negotiations between the various agencies were promoted by the newly formed Nuffield Advisory Committee on Regionalisation of Hospital Services in Scotland.[79]

The momentum of this operation was already strong when Thomas Johnston, the new Secretary of State, convened a Council on Post-War Problems under his chairmanship. This committee considered all aspects of post-war reconstruction.[80] At first it was anticipated that the Reconstruction Committee in London would provide a lead on policy and timing. In the absence of such an initiative Johnston began discussions with interested parties, assisted by his Office Committee on Post-War Hospital Policy formed in April 1941.[81] As in earlier discussions in London, this committee appreciated the advantages of a unified state-administered hospital service, but it was felt that this alternative was politically impracticable. Johnston was nevertheless determined that his department's direct hold over hospital services developed in the context of the Emergency Hospital Service would not readily be relinquished. He identified his department with Brown's statement, but it was added 'that certain important differences in the Emergency Hospital Service and in methods of financing voluntary hospitals in Scotland are being given special consideration'.

Johnston then held meetings with the hospital interests, in the course of which he repeated the main principles outlined in the ministerial statement. He was firm that local authorities would become legally responsible for the administration of health services, but assurances were given that the position of voluntary hospitals would be protected. Johnston made no commitment about the fate of the State Emergency Hospitals, but his statements suggested continuing firm involvement by the Department of Health in hospital administration.[82] Although disappointed by the prospect of statutory local authority responsibility for the future hospital service, voluntary hospital representatives acquiesced in Johnston's proposal to establish a committee to investigate means of realising the goals described in Brown's ministerial statement. The remit of this committee was to 'consider and make recommendations within a policy aimed at the post-war development of a comprehensive and co-ordinated hospital service in Scotland on a regional basis'. This committee was also asked to consider the fate of Government-provided hospitals under the Emergency Hospitals Service, arrangements for securing co-operation between voluntary and municipal hospitals, and financial arrangements between the various parts of this service.[83] This committee was chaired by Sir Hector Hetherington, Principal of Glasgow University, who had previous experience in organising hospital co-ordination in Liverpool. Hetherington had also been Chairman of the Royal Commission reviewing workmen's compensation since 1938, on which account he was in line to chair the wartime Committee on Social Insurance, until Beveridge was interposed in order to secure the support of Bevin for this committee.[84] Because of this intervention the energetic mind of Beveridge became applied to questions having vital bearing on post-war health services.

(iv) BEVERIDGE AND THE GENERAL PRACTITIONER SERVICE: 1942

Thinking about the National Hospital Service was still at a preliminary stage when the equally intransigent problem of National Health Insurance forced itself to the head of the agenda. This occurred because the panel system was the aspect of the health services impinging most on the general problem of social security, and because the latter had emerged as the focal point of Government action on post-war social reconstruction. As far as the health departments were concerned immediate pressures over social security were resolved by increasing the National Health Insurance income limit to £420 and by appointing an Inter-departmental Committee on Social Insurance and Allied Services under Sir William Beveridge 'to undertake, with special reference to the inter-relation of the schemes, a survey of the existing national schemes of social insurance and allied services, including workmen's compensation, and to make recommendations'.[85] Beveridge's appointment was announced by Greenwood on 10 June 1941.[86]

Beveridge's energetic mind swept over the whole system of social security, including most aspects of health care.[87] His committee received evidence from a wide variety of lay and professional organisations involved in health planning. Beveridge was therefore ahead of the health departments in sounding out opinion on health policy. Furthermore, his range of intelligence sources was broader, and he was in advance of the health departments in his appreciation of the wider social and economic context of social security policy. The Inter-departmental Committee was so evidently outpaced by its chairman that its inquiries rapidly took on the character of a personal mission. In order to avoid any sign of premature Government commitment it was arranged that the report would appear under Beveridge's own name. Beveridge thundered ahead, circulating a draft in July 1942. After minor alterations of the draft his report was completed in October. Following some vacillation on the part of the Government the famous document was published in December 1942.

At the outset of his deliberations Beveridge stated that a first premise, or 'Assumption A' of his comprehensive social security scheme was a 'national health service for prevention and comprehensive treatment available to all members of the community'.[88] It was anticipated that the Social Security Fund itself would only bear part of the cost of the new service, the larger part being provided from public revenue. This principle was ultimately translated into 'Assumption B' of the final Beveridge Report, which thereby became the first official source signifying that the Government was considering undertaking a full reconstruction of the health services, rather than merely sponsoring rationalisation of the hospital service.[89] Beveridge also became the main publicist for the idea of a National Health Service by virtue of the remarkable demand for the original report, official and unofficial summaries, as well as popular expositions, including those by Beveridge himself. 'Disease' was identified by him as one of the 'Five Giants' standing in the way of reconstruction. This particular obstacle would be felled by a health service ensuring 'that the best that science can do is available for the treatment of every citizen at home and in institutions, irrespective of his personal means'.[90]

On the question of a comprehensive health service Beveridge was voicing aspirations of the public at large. Thus, regardless of Government dilatoriness Assumption B emerged as a commitment that would be very difficult for any administration not to honour.

Beveridge gave the Ministry of Health early warning of his intentions.[91] One of his problems was deciding whether a health service should be free at the point of use, like police protection or the use of roads, or whether it should be charged on consumption as in the case of public transport. He concluded 'It seems clear that, if at all possible, a medical service without any charge on consumption at any point for any person is the right solution. If there is any prospect whatever of a charge, the patient may delay applying. If the line is taken that health of the individual is a national and not an individual interest, medical service should be provided as freely as the services of a policeman or soldier'. The only objection occurring to Beveridge against a free service was the possibility of frivolous use, but because access to the service was determined by a doctor, it was felt that this abuse would be reduced to the level at which it could be tolerated. On questions of detail, Beveridge was persuaded that the panel system should give way to 'community service', the doctor being employed on the same basis as a civil servant or university teacher. He was uncertain whether the voluntary element could be preserved in the hospital system. The precise pattern of hospital administration was left an open question.

The final report was rather different in its perspective since its primary emphasis was on the contributory insurance principle, at least with respect to domiciliary services, leaving open the degree to which the insurance contribution would also cover hospital costs. The Insurance Fund was thus expected to make a substantial grant towards the medical service. Beveridge also liked the idea that this Fund, as the representative of the consumer, should have a major voice in the administration of the health service. The final report was less firm on the necessity for a free service. In sections omitted from the Brief Report Beveridge considered the possibility of a 10s 'hotel expenses' charge for hospital patients, and also charges for 'subsidiary services', as well as for dental and optical appliances.[92] He was clearly impressed by the degree to which workers had subscribed to the Hospital Savings Association and he favoured inducements for them to continue these contributions in order to ensure survival of voluntary hospitals.

The Ministry of Health was shaken by the 'Utopian' character of Beveridge's initial proposals.[93] The certainty of opposition from the profession weighed heavily against unifying health services under local authorities, which was the most practicable way of realising the Beveridge scheme. Notwithstanding such formidable difficulties inherent in the available options, the Ministry of Health was now forced to declare its hand and produce 'some sort of scheme for a general medical service, if only for the reason that in its absence Beveridge, who is thirsting to do the job himself, will probably induce Greenwood to invite him to make a report on the subject'.[94] With some difficulty Beveridge was dissuaded from pursuing his ideas on the detailed organisation of the new health service.[95] In return the health departments now took on an active planning role. In March 1942 Jameson instructed his officials 'about the Beveridge committee and plans for a salaried medical service'.[96] Beveridge thus provided the final catalyst, stimulating Maude to translate earlier departmental thinking into a positive set of proposals. The guidelines adopted at this critical moment of decision involved:

First, taking the 'revolutionary' step of transition from an 85% or 90% scheme of the kind wanted by the BMA to a service for the whole population, in line with the comprehensive scope of the Beveridge social security scheme and other publicly funded social services. This arrangement avoided the invidiousness of evolving criteria for exclusion.[97]

Secondly, bearing in mind the known and asserted defects of the part-time panel system, the widespread incursion of salaried service through expansion of the local authority and military sectors, and the strong support of Jameson and others for non-competitive practice in health centres provided and equipped at public expense, full-time salaried service seemed the only tenable basis for employing general practitioners in the new service.[98]

Thirdly, it was felt that administration of general practitioner services would be less objectionable to the profession if remuneration and conditions of service were determined by a strong 'Central Medical Board' appointed by the Ministry, but containing representatives of the profession.

Pessimism about the reaction of the profession was compensated for by the sense that the Beveridge scheme for general expansion of the services presented a propitious moment for making a decisive break with arrangements that had persisted since 1911.

In adopting the more adventurous course of discarding the panel system and opting for a radical alternative, officials were heartened by signs within the medical press that the profession was becoming more receptive to innovation. Particular significance was attached to the Medical Planning Commission, and to the utterances of such leaders of the profession as Sir Farquhar Buzzard and John Ryle, Regius Professors at Oxford and Cambridge respectively.[99] It was confidently asserted that both Henry L Souttar (Chairman of the Medical Planning Commission) and Charles Hill (identified as the chief MPC draftsman) believed that the proposals 'would inevitably lead eventually to a whole-time salaried service'.[100]

Although officials noted some significant differences between their own plans and the Medical Planning Commission Report, these obstacles were not felt to be insuperable.[101] The new scheme looked sufficiently hopeful to merit production of a fully costed version, which estimated £35m for a salaried general practitioner service for England and Wales.[102]

A mature proposal prepared for Ministers was completed by Maude in November 1942. Consistent with principles adopted earlier in the year the general practitioner service was to be planned on a whole-time salaried basis, with groups of six to twelve doctors working from health centres serving populations of between ten and twenty thousand. Health centres would be administered in local authority units of not less than 200,000 population, this size being determined by the minimum required for a comprehensive public medical service.[103]

It was realised that the profession would need substantial guarantees concerning protection of its traditional freedoms 'To convert at a stroke one of the oldest and most honourable professions into a public service amenable to all the discipline which public service involves is an operation quite without precedent'. Consequently besides appointing a Central Medical Board as 'honest broker' between the professions and local authorities, it was proposed (a) to strengthen the central Medical Advisory Committee, (b) possibly to appoint local advisory committees, and (c) even to permit co-option of medical representatives on to local authority statutory committees. Although the BMA was known to be strongly in favour of part-time service and capitation payment, it was not proposed to depart from the principle of full-time salaried service 'The general principle applicable to public service, civil and military, that exceptional competence or zeal should find its reward in the shape of promotion in the service must, in our view, apply to the present case'.

Maude's proposals received a cool reception from the Treasury, partly because of indecision about the Beveridge Report, but also because of caution about making such a radical transition away from the settled system of National Health Insurance.[104] In Scotland the Department of Health approved of Maude's paper, which was judged to be in line with their own thinking. The main Scottish concern related to adverse reactions to the Medical Planning Commission Report evident at the BMA Annual Representative Meeting.[105] It was pointed out that group practice in health centres was accepted only in a severely amended form; a 100% service was approved by only a small majority; whole-time salaried service was rejected; and finally the BMA conference had firmly supported insurance schemes, or direct payment of fees. It was concluded: 'in effect the medical profession is hesitating'.[106]

A further manifestation of the gulf between BMA elders and the health departments issued from the BMA Presidential Address, which was sceptical about the Medical Planning Commission and openly hostile to the Ministry of Health. The BMA was warned: 'The bond between the Ministry of Health and the various health services administered by the local public health authorities is growing, communal services are increasing, and we may awake one day soon to find ourselves members of a co-ordinated state health service'. The President presented a depressing prospect of the profession being coerced into 'regimented units of a system of bureaucratic control', which he declared was repugnant to his colleagues and contrary to the British tradition of medical practice.[107] The problem for the planners was to determine whether the trend of opinion was represented by the Buzzards or by the Beckwith Whitehouses of the profession.

(v) GOVERNMENT COMMITMENT: 1943

Further steps towards a National Health Service were dependent on Government commitment to Assumption B of the Beveridge Report. This issue was inseparable from broader questions of policy and priorities for post-war reconstruction. Appearance of the Beveridge Report necessitated much closer attention within the Government to reconstruction than had occurred up to that time. The Committee on Reconstruction Problems established under Greenwood (Minister without Portfolio, earlier Minister of Health in the 1929 Labour Government) in February 1941 met on only four occasions before its chairman was removed from office in February 1942. This committee was no more effective under Sir William Jowitt, the Paymaster General, having only met fourteen times by December 1942, when it was restructured and strengthened in the light of the Beveridge Report. The new Committee on Reconstruction Priorities was chaired from November 1942 to November 1943 by the Lord President, Sir John Anderson, whose varied civil service experience had involved work with Morant on the transition from the Local Government Board to the Ministry of Health. The major political influence on this committee was divided between Anderson and Wood (Chancellor of the Exchequer and former Minister of Health), and on Labour's side, Bevin (Minister of Labour) and Morrison (Home Secretary).

The first task of the Reconstruction Priorities Committee was to advise the War Cabinet on the line to be adopted in the debate on the Beveridge Report. Health policy proved to be uncontentious. The advice of the Official Committee looking into the Beveridge Report was accepted in turn by the Reconstruction Priorities Committee and by the War Cabinet without discussion or dissent. It was accepted that 'the time has come when steps should be taken to set up a comprehensive health service covering all forms of preventive and curative treatment'.[108] The War Cabinet agreed that the Government spokesmen would announce acceptance of the principle of a comprehensive service, although pointing out that it would be many years before the full range of services could be provided, and also giving assurances that this would not exclude the continuation of voluntary hospitals or private practice.[109]

In the debate on the Beveridge Report Anderson duly confirmed the Government's commitment to 'ensure, through a publicly organised and regulated service, that every man and woman and child who wants it can obtain—easily and readily—the whole range of medical advice and attention, through the general practitioner, the consultant, the hospital and every related branch of professional care and up-to-date method'. Anderson gave solemn assurances that there would be no obligation on the side of patient or doctor, and that the scheme was no threat to voluntary hospitals or professional interests. Although the service would utilise local government machinery, it was stressed that its execution would involve full consultation and co-operation with voluntary agencies.[110]

In amplification of Anderson's statement, Wood confirmed that responsibility for the service would lie with the Minister of Health, while Morrison underlined its free and universal character.[111] The health service was mentioned briefly in Churchill's first broadcast on peacetime reconstruction, where he promised a four-year plan involving five or six large measures of reform.[112]

The above pronouncements were not a complete expression of the Government's position. Churchill was opposed to committing a future peacetime government to policies on reconstruction determined by a wartime coalition, whereas Labour wanted to press on without delay with plans for reconstruction.[113] Such issues severely strained the consensus within the Government. Doubts on the right are apparent from the remarks of Churchill and others cited above about the hazards of utopianism. Such critics infused the debate with what they regarded as realistic pessimism, seeking to avoid binding successors to commitments entered into by the War Coalition. On the left, the Parliamentary Labour Party was in revolt against its Cabinet members on the grounds of what were seen as their excessive concessions to their coalition partners. With such criticisms in mind senior Labour members of the Government grew restive about lack of progress towards post-war social reconstruction. They were disturbed by interpretations of Churchill's speech suggesting that legislation would be delayed until the state of the peacetime economy was determined. As indicated below, arguments boiled over into active strife between the coalition partners between July and October 1943, one of the outcomes being reconstitution of the Reconstruction Priorities Committee.[114]

Notwithstanding continuing doubts and disagreements within the Government the official pronouncement of February 1943 jolted health planning on to a new plane of realism. As noted above, the health departments had previously been inhibited from commitment to a definite scheme because of the prospect of unavoidable conflict with one or other of the major vested interests in the health field. However, as the war progressed, movement towards a permanent settlement became unavoidable owing to a variety of new factors, the major ones being (a) the imminent run-down of the Emergency Hospital Service, (b) the Government pledge to comprehensive social security reform, (c) the emergence of new specialised health services instigated by other government departments such as Labour and Education, (d) the need to integrate newly established laboratory and blood transfusion services with other health services, and (e) the need to remove uncertainty about prospects for the large corps of demobilised doctors. As noted above, confidence within the health departments was strengthened by compelling evidence of public demand for a state medical service, and by some, albeit uncertain, evidence of receptivity to change within the medical profession.[115] Because their views had been maturing for some time, the health departments were well placed to formulate their proposals without delay. Indeed, in advance of Anderson's announcement, in January 1943 the Ministry of Health prepared its first drafts of a Bill, anticipating that legislation would be introduced during the following session.[116]

The general lines of thinking at this stage are best indicated by reproducing the statement of objectives for the new service:

(1) Public provision to be made for a comprehensive health service for all who wish to take advantage of it.

(2) No compulsion to take advantage of it; freedom to resort to private medical advice and private institutional arrangements, if anyone prefers to do so.

(3) No compulsion of the profession to take part in it; freedom to continue private practice outside the new service, if any doctor wishes.

(4) The new public service to cover the whole field of medical treatment and advice (hospital, clinic and personal practitioner) and to include specialist and consultant services; and also the provision of prescribed drugs and appliances; but to exclude, for the present, treatment under the Mental Treatment Act.

(5) The service (with nursing, midwifery, health visiting and other ancillary services) to be directed to 'positive health' and the prevention of sickness and disability, as much as to treatment and cure.

(6) The service to absorb or replace existing services of local authorities in respect of hospital and institutional treatment (under public health or Poor Law powers), tuberculosis, infectious diseases, maternity and child welfare and midwifery, cancer, venereal diseases, parts of the school medical services, domiciliary medical treatment under the Poor Law, district nursing and

health visiting, and all existing medical services under National Health Insurance.

(7) The service to be universally available, without distinction of income or means. To be a free service, subject to 'social security' or other insurance contribution (though possibly with some exception in respect of 'hotel' costs for in-patient hospital maintenance). (For the moment it is left an open question.)

(8) The main organisation of the service to be decentralised and based on the local government principle. Responsibility to be put on major designated authorities (covering combined areas, where necessary, of county and county borough councils), with statutory representation of interests other than 'local authority' in the strict sense.

(9) Professional interests of the service to be centred in a new Central Medical Board, with machinery to maintain the quality and safeguard the well-being of doctors engaged in the service. Provision for interests of existing practitioners, etc, in the transition to the new service.

(10) Principles of 'free choice' of doctor and 'family relationship' of doctor and patient to be retained as much as possible in the new service; minimum interference with existing personal relationship of doctor and patient.

(11) Voluntary hospitals to play an essential part in the service, where willing to do so; to retain their full identity and status; to comply with the arrangements and conditions of the service while they take part in it, and to receive financial contribution from public funds in respect of their part in the service.

(12) Better provision for regulating consultant practice; and for relating hospital and specialist services, university and medical teaching interests and the work of the general practitioner.

(13) The whole new service to be the subject of exchequer support.[117]

Objectives (1) to (5) and (10) bear a generic resemblance to the 'General Principles' announced by the BMA in 1938. Mental health was omitted from (4) out of fidelity to the views of the Board of Control. The Beveridge proposals for health charges in addition to a social security contribution were left undecided. The proposed organisation of the services, (8) to (13), followed the lines of the ministerial statement of October 1941, except that the local authority role was emphasised at the expense of regionalisation. Consistent with departmental thinking a Central Medical Board was proposed to protect the interests of the profession.

A brief paper submitted by the Health Ministers to the Committee on Reconstruction Priorities amplified the above objectives.[118] Here the local authority bias was further stressed. It was, for instance, 'inevitable that the service form part of local government'; 'the comprehensive service must be one and indivisible in each area of the country'; 'the alternative course of removing the existing health services from the local authorities would go far to discredit and destroy local government'; 'it follows that the new services should be treated as local government services'.[119] The Ministry of Health favoured realisation of its objectives by adoption of multi-purpose elected regional authorities of the kind proposed for Tyneside in 1937. However, given absence of agreement on local government reform, the health departments opted for the less desirable alternative of local authority joint boards.[120] The paper contained two significant differences in emphasis from the October 1941 statement. First, arrangements for co-ordination of health services on a larger regional level were now relegated to a minor consideration.[121] Secondly, reference to charges was less firm than in either the 1941 statement or indeed in the Beveridge Report.[122]

Proposed changes within the hospital service were mainly evolutionary and they involved little administrative innovation. By contrast the reform of National Health Insurance medical benefit seemed to entail a 'much bigger undertaking than rationalisation of the hospital system of the country'. Consequently the Reconstruction Priorities Committee was provided with an elaborate justification of the new model for the general medical services based on a system of health centres and whole-time salaried service.

The above relatively adventurous scheme was accepted by the Reconstruction Priorities Committee as the appropriate vehicle for realising Assumption B of the Beveridge Report.[123] It is, however, noticeable that processing through the War Cabinet machinery resulted in a public statement from Anderson much closer in spirit to Brown's more orthodox pronouncement of 1941. This change in perspective demonstrates the underlying tension between utopian and pragmatic considerations respecting the character of the future health service.

CHAPTER III

Infinite Regress

Initially the architects of the new health service anticipated that their timetable might be geared to the forthcoming education legislation. This synchronisation was desirable to obtain full integration between comprehensive health services for school children and for the rest of the population.

The above expectation was undermined by Anderson's promise that the form of the new service would be worked out in consultation with the parties involved.[1] This process was regarded differently by the various participants. For instance, the Ministry of Health wanted preliminary 'advice and assistance', whereas the profession demanded a full, negotiated agreement. Consequently the timetable for the National Health Service was slowed down, not only by elements in the coalition wary about incurring ambitious commitments to social reconstruction, but also by the arduous task of reconciling powerful groups holding incompatible positions. By the end of 1943 the health and education legislative timetables were irrevocably disengaged.[2]

The health White Paper was eventually published in February 1944. Although possessing special importance by virtue of containing the first full declaration of the Government's intentions concerning a comprehensive health service, it carried insufficient authority to stem the tide of criticism. Because the White Paper was neither a declaration of firm policy, nor a presentation of alternatives for adjudication by interested parties, it occasioned further debilitating negotiations rather than a swift transition to legislation. By the beginning of 1945 it was evident that the National Health Service was an unlikely candidate for wartime legislation. Eventually the Coalition and Caretaker Governments faded away without even an official statement concerning the outcome of nearly eighteen months of negotiations on the White Paper.

(i) THE BROWN PLAN AND ITS RECEPTION: JANUARY–JULY 1943

The health departments initially hoped that outside parties would be won over by the boldness and rationality of their new scheme. Brown urged the BMA to participate in 'the greatest single step forward in public health in the history of this country'.[3] In a major speech at Watford, Brown claimed that his reform would 'eventually contribute more to human welfare and human happiness, and to the strength of the British nation, than any of the historic social advances of the present century'.[4] Notwithstanding this superficial optimism there was already doubt in official circles concerning the likely reception of their scheme. The official committee making recommendations on the Beveridge Report concluded with respect to a comprehensive health service that 'the change is a radical one involving the whole status of a powerful and historic profession, and it is difficult to predict with confidence how medical and lay opinion would react to this proposal'.[5]

The health departments intended to adopt a tight schedule involving confidential discussions with the major interested parties in the late spring of 1943, with a view to issuing a White Paper in June. This would allow for the Bill drafted early in 1943 to be introduced during the parliamentary session 1943/44.[6] When discussions ran into difficulties it was agreed to delay publication of the White Paper first until the autumn, and then eventually until the new year. Even this timetable proved difficult to meet.

It was thought that confidentiality of discussions would permit the departments substantially to modify their scheme and issue a White Paper commanding a broad degree of agreement. However, secrecy allowed for the circulation of distorted rumours about the Government's intentions, with the result that anxiety and animosity was whipped up, especially within the profession. *The Times* warned the Government to settle the fears of the profession, which in particular 'must be allowed to play an important part locally and centrally, in order to secure a high standard of professional integrity'.[7] It was urged that 'in that planning process the medical profession can be trusted to take a share worthy of its tradition of disinterested social service'.[8]

The serious newspapers were inundated by letters from doctors concerned that their fundamental liberties were under threat. These fears were exacerbated by increasingly impassioned letters and speeches from the BMA leadership. In terms reminiscent of the Beckwith Whitehouse address, the BMA secretary alerted the public to the danger of 'transformation' of their doctors into local government officials.[9] Officials were particularly stung by a speech made by Charles Hill, the deputy secretary of the BMA, on 16 May 1943, in which he amplified leaks already appearing in the press into a full and unsympathetic review of the Government's proposals. This speech was received with 'unusual acclamation' from the packed 'mass meeting' of the Metropolitan Counties Branch of the BMA, and the alarm generated spread through the profession like a forest fire.[10]

The confidential memorandum, in later literature often called the 'Brown Plan', was a short document of only twelve paragraphs, presenting the ideas of draft legislation and PR(43)3 in a brief and relatively non-contentious form.[11] Notwithstanding the formal secrecy of this document, its contents could easily be surmised from Government statements or deliberate leaks. Although local government organisation of the new service was presented as an historically inevitable and constitutionally inescapable feature of the scheme, the Central Medical Board was offered as a counterbalance sufficient to protect the interests of the profession.[12] The proposal to adopt health centres as the basis for general practice was presented as official endorsement of the views of the Medical Planning Commission. Although nothing explicit was mentioned about restriction to full-time salaried service, suspicions were aroused by the intention to allow the 'individual doctor to choose whether to apply for enrolment in the service or to practise privately outside it'.[13]

Supposedly confidential discussions took place between early March and the end of July 1943. The London meetings involved Scottish representatives, but separate, parallel discussions were held in Scotland. Although there were differences in detail between the two sets of negotiations they proceeded along similar lines. In both London and Edinburgh separate meetings were held with representatives of voluntary hospitals, local government, and the medical profession.

Despite their reservations concerning the Government plan, discussions with the voluntary hospital representatives were relatively uncomplicated.[14] The voluntary lobby argued that granting statutory powers to local authorities undermined any conception of partnership. Introduction of regionalisation was seen as a means to restore the position of voluntary hospitals. Voluntary hospital representatives were divided over the extent of their demands. Their general aim was ensuring effective insulation from local authority control. Stronger voices wanted an independent Central Hospitals Board or Council which would oversee policy and make exchequer grants to both voluntary and municipal hospitals. Contributions to voluntary hospitals from local authorities would then be confined to fixed payments for services rendered. Voluntary interests would be further protected by their strong representation on regional authorities, and also on local hospital committees. The latter were to be established as statutory sub-committees of Local Health Authorities. Ideally the voluntary hospitals wanted representation on the authorities themselves.

The above demands gained support from the Hetherington Committee.[15] This committee favoured regional organisation, involving equal partnership between local authorities and voluntary hospitals.[16] The committee gave no support to Johnston's proposal for continuing with direct state management of hospitals after the war.[17]

The English voluntary hospitals were embarrassed by the Scottish conclusion that voluntary contribution schemes should be replaced by compulsory insurance arrangements, so that assessment and recovery of charges from patients could be terminated.[18] Scottish consideration of a separate insurance scheme for hospital care rapidly gave way to the simpler alternative involving extension of the Beveridge social security scheme to cover the whole cost of hospital treatment, which was very much against the policy of the English branch of the British Hospitals Association.

Local authority representatives initially welcomed the new proposals.[19] Their primary reservations related to amalgamation for the purposes of establishing sufficiently large areas to exercise a full range of health functions, and they were also divided among themselves about delegation of responsibilities between the different levels of local government. But they were united in their resistance to the incursion of non-elected representatives into their committees. There was most resistance to co-option of medical representatives on to Local Health Authorities, but more acceptance of co-option to sub-committees, providing that elected members were in a majority. Gradually the local authorities became more suspicious. Representatives from Edinburgh and Glasgow accused the Department of Health of permitting 'undue domination of medical interests', arguing that unification was being sacrificed and that two parallel health services were being established. It was generally felt that proposals for central funding of voluntary hospitals were decisively removing these institutions beyond the reach of public accountability, a trend seen as a 'fatal blot on the scheme'.[20] By this stage Maude realised that the local authorities were being alienated by mounting concessions to voluntary hospital and general practitioner interests.[21]

As feared by the health departments the medical profession was the group most difficult to handle. The BMA harboured deep-seated fears of state control. The organisation was defeated in 1911 over National Health Insurance, and during the inter-war period it suffered repeated setbacks in its battles with the Ministry of Health over levels of capitation payments. Then in 1941 the Government had adversely affected private earnings by extending the threshold of National Health Insurance from £250 to £420. Yet the BMA was slowly increasing in internal cohesion and growing more adept at resistance. By 1943 it was in a position to lead the whole profession into confrontation with the Government, not only to defend what it saw as fundamental matters of principle, but also using the occasion to right a succession of past wrongs.

An initial meeting with the Minister's Medical Advisory Committee exposed basic lack of sympathy with major tenets of official thinking.[22] This impression was dramatically amplified in meetings held in London and Edinburgh, particularly by the large 'Representative Committee' of thirty-five members, drawn from very much the same organisations which had served on the Medical Planning Commission, but more conspicuously dominated by leading medical politicians of the BMA.[23] From the outset this committee squabbled with the health departments over procedure, the status of the meetings, confidentiality, and even minute taking. The Ministry of Health was pleased when the Representative Committee delegated its work to a Negotiating Committee comprising eight members.[24]

The profession opposed the official plan both in principle and in detail. Arguing from various angles they were particularly insistent against employment by local authorities. Anderson repeated the conclusion recently expressed by him in *The Times* that the majority of the profession objected to 'translation of a free profession into a branch of local government service'. Guy Dain, chairman of the BMA Council, agreed that 'the professions were united in the view that they would not accept employment by Local Authorities as known at present'.[25] In Scotland Cameron argued that the 'new service should not be an administrator's paradise, or even a paradise for the Medical Officer of Health. It was the glory of the profession that they were masters in their own house'.[26] Maude warned the Minister that a 'fundamental difficulty with the medical profession would be to induce them to accept service under a local authority'.[27] Objection to local government service was partly related to what were perceived as the inadequacies of local authorities as they were currently organised. From the Medical Advisory Committee, Rock Carling criticised such areas as Lancashire 'with its seventeen County Boroughs, their local jealousies, excess of local patriotism and blighting parochial limitations'.[28]

Opposition to local government organisation was also related to its associations with full-time salaried service, which it was thought would be inevitably associated with stultifying bureaucracy. All the negotiating groups stood firm on the right of all medical practitioners in public service to retain professional independence and on the right to practise privately. Anderson warned that salaried service would lead to 'stereotyped mediocrity'. In Webb-Johnson's view the health departments had 'struck at the root of the freedom of a great profession'.[29] He described protection of

private practice as the 'central issue' in their disagreement with
the official plan.[30] Maude appreciated that 'the opposition to a
universal and compulsory system of salaries will be bitter and
sustained'.[31] Because health centres were central to the official
argument in favour of full-time salaried service, the professional
team turned against this seemingly uncontroversial innovation.

A further implication of the defence of private practice was
resistance to establishing a service for the whole population. The
profession favoured adopting an income limit, above which a
voluntary contribution scheme would be developed to support
continuing access to private practice for the middle classes.[32]

Sir Arthur Robinson, the experienced former Permanent Secretary in the Ministry of Health, concluded that the profession
would not accept more than extended National Health Insurance
benefit, and this view was indeed expressed in the course of the
negotiations, but it was not dominant.[33] At one stage the BMA
made a move to refer the problem to a Royal Commission, but
this was resisted by the Health Ministers as a delaying tactic.[34] As
in the case of the voluntary hospitals, the profession favoured
options most remote from local government.[35] A general plan was
emerging among the negotiators involving hiving off the National
Health Service to a separate Board or Commission within the
Ministry of Health, in order that a high degree of autonomy
should be achieved, as in the case of the Assistance Board within the
Ministry of Labour. Running parallel with the Central Hospitals
Council, and possibly amalgamated with the Central Medical
Board, would be a professional advisory body (a 'Medical Services
Council' or 'Medical Advisory Committee') having statutory
responsibilities regarding general practitioner services and a great
deal of independence from Ministers. The profession also expected
to occupy a strong position on regional and local health authorities,
which themselves would preferably be separate from local government. The profession favoured introducing the new health service
by stages over a long period. No advantage was seen in rushing
forward with a unified health scheme.[36]

The above proposals were totally at variance with the outlook
of the health departments. The case in favour of full-time salaried
service in health centres was strongly argued at the meetings by
both Ministers, Maude, Jameson and Henderson. Johnston
attacked ad hoc health authorities as a 'system of continental
dictatorships', inconsistent with the principles of representative
government.[37] It seemed out of the question for publicly financed
service to be controlled by non-elected bodies of professionals.
Maude described one BMA proposal for health centres to be
provided, equipped and staffed with ancillary workers by local

authorities, but containing a medical staff contracted to the Central Medical Board, as an 'unworkable dyarchy'.[38]

(ii) RECONSTRUCTION COMMITTEE AND WAR CABINET: JULY 1943–FEBRUARY 1944

Notwithstanding their objections to counterproposals emanating from the profession, officials faced the inevitability of compromise. Some comfort was derived from occasional hints that the official plan might be acceptable, providing that the profession was given sufficient voice in its administration. The official side was faced with an unenviable dilemma. If they stood by the PR(43)3 recommendations there would be a re-enactment of the 1912 confrontation with the BMA. Goodwill of the profession could be bought, but only at the cost of sacrificing long-standing policy goals of the departments, thereby surrendering to professional vested interests and alienating local authorities and their political allies.[39]

A White Paper containing revised proposals was prepared by July 1943 with the aim of publication in September. It was first necessary to obtain sanction of the Reconstruction Priorities Committee and the War Cabinet.[40] This stage exposed disagreement between the coalition partners, occasioning further delay in the departmental timetable.

In February the two Ministers issued a joint memorandum. In July Johnston offered separate commentary from the Scottish point of view on the proposals made by Brown.[41] Speed and decisiveness were not assisted by Brown's long and rambling memorandum which, in surveying the confidential discussions, exposed all the ramifications of disagreement, without producing convincing solutions. This document strikingly testifies to the loss of self-confidence within the Ministry of Health. Already, after brief initial discussions, their plan for a unified health service was falling to pieces, while substitute proposals were sufficiently indecisive to invite further destructive criticism at the hands of the politicians.

It was still proposed to use local authorities as the backbone of organisation. Some 42 health authorities in England and Wales (16–18 in Scotland) were envisaged. They would be constituted by amalgamation of existing major authorities into joint health authorities.[42] Partly in order to preserve the Welsh National Memorial Association, it was proposed to make Wales into a single health authority. Out of conformity with educational provision and as a concession to local interests, elaborate provision for delegation to districts was provided for. In order to conciliate medical interests in England and Wales it was accepted that voluntary hospital and medical representatives would be co-opted to both health authorities and their district committees, but without voting rights.[43] However,

Johnston argued that such an arrangement was fundamentally unsound because it would undermine the position of democratically elected authorities.[44]

The voluntary hospitals were promised their Central Hospitals Council, representation on local committees, and economic independence from local authorities.[45] Regional organisation was mentioned only in Johnston's memorandum and then only in response to an interim statement from the Hetherington Committee. Brown's memorandum reluctantly opted for operation of two separate and entirely different organisations for the general practitioner services. Alongside full-time salaried practice in health authority provided health centres, it was proposed to allow other practitioners to continue with a modified panel service organised by updated National Health Insurance administration. In order to improve the panel system it was intended to control the distribution of doctors centrally, abolish sale and purchase of practices, introduce superannuation, impose a basic salary element in remuneration, tighten up regulations concerning employment of assistants, reform arrangements for certification, and improve co-ordination between general practice and other health services.[46] Restriction on the right to practise privately was now reduced to the extent of limiting obligatory full-time service to new entrants for their first five or seven years.[47]

Johnston proposed a simpler organisation for general practice in Scotland, involving the whole general practitioner service being administered by the Department of Health, which would itself undertake responsibility for providing health centres.[48] The whole somewhat untidy package was presented to the Reconstruction Priorities Committee, which handled this business with little sense of urgency at meetings spaced at about monthly intervals between July 1943 and January 1944, followed by a rapid burst of activity on 10 and 11 January 1944 during which uneasy agreement was reached on the text of the White Paper.

The slow pace of progress on post-war reconstruction provoked growing frustration within Labour ranks. Even the *Economist* began writing about the failure, or refusal of the Government to give a lead on post-war domestic policy.[49]

The Labour position was strengthened by the appearance on the Reconstruction Priorities Committee of Attlee in his capacity as Lord President, an office to which he was appointed upon the death of Kingsley Wood. Anderson was at the same time made Chancellor of the Exchequer, in which capacity he continued to chair the Committee for a brief time, until another Cabinet reshuffle in November 1943 introduced Woolton as Minister of

Reconstruction, and chairman of a strengthened 'Reconstruction Committee'.[50] In the latter ministerial changes the National Liberal, Ernest Brown, was displaced by the Conservative, Henry U Willink, as Minister of Health. It was no doubt hoped that a new Minister would stand a better chance of regaining the confidence of the profession than the architect of the doomed 'Brown Plan'. Indeed, Willink, as a lawyer rather than career politician, might have struck a chord of sympathy with the sister profession, although it was also felt that his lack of political experience would prove disadvantageous.[51]

Aiming to restore his Government's image in the reconstruction field, Churchill delivered a major speech on their peacetime programme, using the slogan 'Food, work and homes for all'. No doubt reflecting pessimism concerning health policy discussions he made no direct reference to this major facet of the reconstruction process.[52]

Disagreements within the Government were as wide as those outside. Kingsley Wood, in line with his long-standing loyalty to the Approved Societies favoured extending the panel system. At the other extreme Bevin saw the advantages of a centrally controlled state medical service.[53]

Largely owing to the persistence of Morrison the largest debate within the Reconstruction Committee related to the relatively minor issue of the respective merits of joint boards and individual local authorities.[54] Taking the side of the Association of Municipal Corporations, Morrison argued against joint boards on grounds of their past unsatisfactory record and because of predicted adverse effects on local government. Morrison even preferred a state-run health service to any joint board mechanism. Brown admitted that joint authorities were a reluctant necessity for the sake of viable units of hospital administration, but he urged that negative effects on local democracy would be counteracted by extensive delegation to districts.[55] As a concession to Morrison it was suggested that the White Paper should set out alternatives without stating Government commitment. Agreement was also given to Bevin's proposal that joint health authorities would only be a temporary expedient pending local government reorganisation. Brown was asked to work out a plan for a service based on individual county boroughs and county councils, except in special instances.[56] Brown was most disinclined to sacrifice his new style health authorities, but he argued that maintenance of the current system of local administration was preferable to a halfway house arrangement involving weak joint health authorities competing with strong county councils and county borough councils.[57]

Increasing divergence between the Scottish and English plans was not welcomed. It was thought that divergences would be exploited by critics of the National Health Service.[58] Scotland was more inclined to adopt centralisation because of enthusiasm within the Department of Health for co-ordination and administration of the Emergency Hospital Service. Flying in the face of the Hetherington Committee, Johnston was reticent about relinquishing state control of the new emergency hospitals.[59] He was quick to propose central administration of general practitioner services and health centres. Such alternatives were thought to be more viable in Scotland because of its relatively small population.[60]

Having proposed to remove general practice from local authority control, Johnston was unwilling to coerce medium-sized towns into amalgamating with neighbouring county authorities for the purpose of providing clinic services, a point which Willink recognised would be exploited by larger district councils in England facing transfer of their services to major authorities. It was eventually agreed that the White Paper would allow for different arrangements in the two countries on grounds of their particular local circumstances.

The strongest general concern within the committee related to the Health Ministers' retreat from their declared policy concerning full-time salaried service and health centres.[61] In his first intervention Attlee pointed out the incompatibility between their proposals for 'grouped and non-competitive practice in publicly provided health centres, with the current proposal for the old system of panel doctors receiving capitation fees'. Commitment to health centres was reaffirmed by the Health Ministers, but they urged a gradualist approach. The meeting agreed that the White Paper would make it clear that 'they regarded the development of such centres as one of the main objectives of their policy'. The draft White Paper was still not positive enough about health centres to satisfy Ministers. Anderson, Bevin and Morrison pressed for much stronger commitment on this point. Adopting a line quite opposed to that of his predecessor as Chancellor of the Exchequer, and perhaps betraying his own civil service sympathies, Anderson called for the Government to 'go out boldly for the health centre scheme, and the health departments would find that they had the support of all the more progressive doctors'.[62]

The most evident sign of a Party split during the committee's discussions occurred over direct payments by patients.[63] Growing public antipathy to contributory schemes was represented by Bevin, who argued that hospital treatment should be fully covered by the national insurance scheme. Brown warned that ending the voluntary contributory schemes would remove a source of income upon which voluntary hospitals depended. Such a move would, in his view, alienate the voluntary interest, and constitute a retreat from the earlier Government pledge concerning partnership. Brown was not supported by Johnston, who invoked the Hetherington Committee in support of the conclusion adopted by Bevin.[64] The Reconstruction Committee opted for deduction from disability payments rather than hospital charges, a view sustained at their final discussions of the White Paper, despite the opposition of Willink, who believed that voluntary hospitals would be 'dealt a mortal blow' by this decision. Johnston was unrepentant. As far as voluntary hospitals in Scotland were concerned, fees were an 'anachronism'.[65]

On 10 January 1944 Woolton was commissioned by the Reconstruction Committee to revise the White Paper and then circulate the text for final approval on 26 January. He was specifically asked to improve the firmness of tone. At their last collective discussion of the text, Labour members of the committee pressed successfully for further modifications to render the proposals for general practitioner services less offensive to Labour Party opinion.[66] Labour Ministers were dissatisfied with the final production which they pronounced still too indefinite in tone and over-conciliatory with respect to unacceptable aspects of professional practice. Attlee even objected to any sentiment contemplating the continued existence of voluntary hospitals as more than a short-term expedient.[67]

Countervailing pressures for modification of the White Paper emerged from the opposite direction. At the instigation of Beaverbrook, Churchill tried to re-open discussions on private medical practice, the status of voluntary hospitals, and the terms of employment of consultants. In response Attlee reminded Churchill that Labour members of the Reconstruction Committee had accepted so much that was unpalatable in the White Paper that they risked censure within their own Party. He warned that any resumption of discussions would force Labour Ministers to renew their demands for full-time salaried service and for other policies 'far more repugnant to Conservative feeling'.[68] Woolton, sensing danger, warned his Conservative colleagues that the White Paper was indeed very difficult for Labour to swallow.[69] Although one further Cabinet discussion was held, Churchill allowed his mind to be settled. The Cabinet agreed to publish the White Paper without further emendation on 17 February 1944.[70]

As indicated above, the health departments originally hoped to issue a White Paper in June 1943, and indeed the first draft of the English and Welsh side of the document was ready for circulation in August 1943.[71] The Scottish commentary and additions were submitted at the end of November. The two departments argued over many points of detail. For instance, the Scottish expert on

National Health Insurance argued that the White Paper was unduly critical of the system of medical benefit. On the other side the author of the White Paper felt that the Scottish document was 'too long and repeats ours. Utterly wrecks our Paper'.[72]

Redrafting involved radical restructuring and rewriting. The tone of the final version was noticeably less positive and more reserved than the original drafts. The latter for instance announced that the aim of the new service would be 'for the first time, to ensure, through a nation-wide organisation for health, that every benefit of up-to-date medical science and skill—the whole range of modern preventive and curative medicine—may be equally and universally available to the men and the women and the children of this country, no matter who they are and what they are or where they are', sentiments that were systematically toned down in the equivalent paragraph of the White Paper.[73] In drafting, the most serious difficulties were presented by the sections outlining the role of the new joint health authorities and related local medical services committees, and also by the sections on general practitioner services, especially the parts on group practices, health centres, private practice and the sale of practices.

The White Paper, *A National Health Service* (Cmd. 6502) and its popular exposition, *A National Health Service: The White Paper Proposals in Brief*, provided the first detailed public statement of the Government's intentions concerning a comprehensive health service.[74] These two documents were slimmer than the Beveridge equivalents published just over a year earlier. Although the original drafts were presented as a sequel to the Beveridge Report, this connection was gradually obscured with redrafting until in the final text reference to Beveridge was minimal, mainly comprising a passing reference in the account of antecedent discussions (p 74). Direct mention of Beveridge in the opening paragraphs of both documents was expunged at the late proof stage upon request of the Cabinet.[75]

No doubt to underline historical continuity and allay fears concerning the innovatory character of the new scheme, both the text and appendices gave prominence to accounts of the historical development of the British health services. The comprehensive health service was presented as a timely and logical culmination of an accelerating trend towards state participation in health care.[76]

'Free' and 'comprehensive' were the keynotes of the new service, yet both were subject to significant reservations. It was recognised that the service would not supersede well-entrenched special services such as the industrial or school medical services controlled by other government departments. It was acknowledged that the mental health service was included only as an afterthought, while doubts were expressed concerning the feasibility of introducing in the short term dental or ophthalmic services for non-priority classes. Although the service was to be free at point of delivery, following the precedent of the Beveridge Report, the way was left clear for direct or indirect charges for appliances and for hospital treatment.[77]

On the administration of the service the White Paper maintained the 'principle of local responsibility, coupled with enough central direction to obtain a coherent and consistent national service'.[78] The primary vehicles for central direction would be the Central Health Services Council and its sub-committees, together with the Central Medical Board.[79] At the local level only perfunctory reference was made to the possibility of adopting regional organisation in England and Wales. By preference, as 'the most convenient— and indeed, in the Government's view, the only course possible at the present time' it was proposed to combine county councils and county boroughs into an unspecified number of joint authorities (called Area Health Authorities in earlier drafts). These new authorities would plan the service as a whole, but they would only assume direct control over local authority hospital services. Clinic services would remain the direct responsibility of county councils and county boroughs, which would also superintend the new health centres.[80]

The White Paper guaranteed the full independence and autonomy of voluntary hospitals under the new scheme. Their role in joint planning would be assured, and arrangements were outlined precluding local authorities from gaining financial control over voluntary hospitals.[81]

General practice provided the most troublesome moments in the drafting of the White Paper.[82] It was now acknowledged that 'universal change' to a full-time salaried state or local authority service was impracticable. Although it was intended to give such 'grouped' practice in health centres 'full trial on a large scale', arrangements would also be available for 'separate' participation in the new service along the lines of the National Health Insurance scheme, but with allowance for payment by salary in particular circumstances.[83] New entrants would be required to practise on a full-time salaried basis, first as assistants, and then for a number of years to be determined by the Central Medical Board.[84]

In Scotland the new service was explicitly designed on tripartite lines.[85] Clinic services were to remain with existing local authorities. General practitioner services and health centres would be administered directly by the Department of Health. In line with the recommendations of the Hetherington Committee and its antecedents it was proposed to organise hospitals on a regional basis.

With the exception of the Highlands region the other four regions would be based on the catchment areas of medical schools. These Regional Hospital Advisory Councils would contain equal representation from local authorities and the voluntary sector. However the Regional Councils were to be consultative and advisory only. Joint Hospital Boards composed entirely of local authority representatives would own and administer all publicly provided hospitals, and in consultation with voluntary hospitals prepare plans for the hospital service in their areas for submission to the Secretary of State and the Regional Councils.[86]

A brief financial appendix to the White Paper estimated the cost to public funds of the new service as £148m per annum, compared with a total of £170m for health and rehabilitation services contained in the Beveridge Report.[87] Insufficient detail was presented to explain the difference between these two estimates.

(iii) RECEPTION OF THE 1944 WHITE PAPER
Slow gestation assured the White Paper of eager anticipation and a keen reception. Its authors tried to rekindle a spirit of idealism and bi-partisanship. The White Paper was represented as the equivalent to the Beveridge Report, a veritable Magna Carta for positive health. Also like the Beveridge Report, 'it had the advantage of being the product not of several pens but of one—that of (Sir) John Hawton—and its style and presentation were widely praised'.[88] The immediate reception was positive. *The Times* congratulated the coalition partners on subordinating Party interest in favour of an agreed plan. The White Paper marked a 'fresh stage in the course of domestic reconstruction', a statement of objectives that 'could scarcely be bettered and cannot be seriously open to question'.[89] Privately, the great Lord Dawson conceded that the White Paper was 'a remarkable piece of work—well written and lucid—containing the principles on which a great new service could be built'. Even the BMA official statement contained a hint of warmth, 'Our immediate reaction is one of cautious welcome'.[90]

Departmental confidence in the White Paper was less robust than was suggested by outward appearances. As indicated above, informal consultations and ministerial deliberations taking place during the previous year necessitated substantial departures from the preferred plan. First Brown, and then Willink emphasised the provisional character of their proposals. Officials thus witnessed the progressive collapse of their original scheme for a fully unified health service. It was difficult to prevent fragmentation into all the existing components. The resultant compromises embodied in the White Paper involved pressing forward with evolutionary adjustments to the existing system to the maximum extent permitted by prudence.

Greatest unhappiness related to the abandonment of unity in organisation. In light of Johnston's acceptance of a tripartite structure, Brown was advised that 'our best course would be to follow suit and at great sacrifice of system and order, placate the interested parties by putting the hospital and clinic services on a county and county borough basis . . . and centralising the general practitioner service'. However, such a tripartite construction made a 'travesty of our original conception of a single unified service'. Such an arrangement was only defensible in Parliament if presented as a temporary expedient.[91] It was also realised that such compromises were likely to increase pressure for further regress, as was experienced in the case of health centres. Maude admitted that a 'dual system' was a painful alternative; 'anything further would mean the abandonment of the co-operation and health centre idea and a continuation of the panel with such minor improvements as could be grafted on to that system'.[92] A colleague thought that such compromise would involve 'more row and difficulty than a firm adherence to our original conceptions about general practice'.[93]

In some respects it was felt that concessions were being taken too far. For instance, the Press Officer warned that dropping the title 'National Health Service' from the White Paper would be taken as a fundamental departure from the concept of a comprehensive service prevalent in Government statements since the Beveridge Report.[94]

The White Paper disappointed advocates of firm policy. One of the most active hospital surveyors contended that 'it is at once too timid and too conciliatory. Too timid in failing to indicate frankly the size and comprehensiveness of the new health authorities, and in stating baldly and boldly the urgent need for big areas. Too conciliatory in encouraging a perpetuation of isolation of Voluntary Hospitals from the County and Municipal'.[95] Another advocate of hospital regionalisation pointed out that voluntary hospitals had already changed out of all recognition. The logic of their situation pointed to complete reliance on exchequer funding. In this context Buzzard called for unified hospital administration under the joint authorities proposed by the White Paper, envisaging that the traditions of voluntary hospitals would be protected by maximum delegation to the hospital unit.[96]

Regardless of self-doubt and reservations among advisers or within the health departments, external reactions to the White Paper in lay circles were consistently favourable. *The Times, Manchester Guardian, Economist* and *Spectator* gave continuing editorial support for the Government's line, and these journals were not impressed by the mounting tide of BMA opposition. *The Lancet* broke ranks with the *BMJ* and accepted the White Paper as a satisfactory compromise.[97] The TUC and Labour Party were content with the White Paper as an interim solution. However, a Gallup Poll indicated that only 55% of those questioned were satisfied with the Government's proposals, whereas 32% were opposed, perhaps indicating that the adverse publicity emanating from the profession was reducing public confidence in official handling of the new health service.[98] Among the popular newspapers the *Daily Express* was conspicuous for its sniping against the Government's plan.

In the parliamentary debates on the White Paper the Commons gave a reasonably positive, but by no means unanimous response.[99] Influential Labour voices warned that they would be pushed no further in the direction of compromise.[100] The weightiest reservations emanated from the Lords' spokesmen for voluntary hospitals, and from the medical peers, Dawson, Horder and Moran. On hospitals pleas were made for regionalisation, representation of voluntary hospitals on health authorities, and on behalf of contributory schemes. On administration the Lords distrusted both the Central Medical Board and joint authorities, while they urged strengthening of the Central Health Services Council to protect the profession's authority against the state. Moran and Horder appealed for an independent central authority to run the health service. Full-time salaried service and health centres fell under suspicion from Dawson, the originator of the health centre idea. Dawson's change of heart illustrates how deep-seated were anxieties concerning the threat of state regimentation to the traditional freedoms of the profession. Much capital was made of the Ministry of Health's cavalier attitude to its pre-existing advisory and consultative machinery.[101] The public response by Ministers to the above criticisms and to the growing onslaught from the BMA was relatively muted. Indeed Lord Cherwell sought assurance that the health departments were mounting a concerted defence of their position. Willink's public self-justification was made in two short addresses designed to allay Conservative fears of 'a bureaucratic and regimented service denying to the medical profession and the voluntary hospitals the freedom they need to develop in their own way'. By underlining the provisional character of the White Paper Willink hoped to deflect the BMA from making 'preposterous accusations' and to channel energies towards acceptable compromises.[102]

By the time the White Paper was published opposition within the medical profession to the Government's plans had been boiling up for nearly a year. Government steps to counter objections had been inhibited by the supposedly confidential nature of initial discussions.

A particularly vigorous and effective part in mobilising the profession against the Government plan was played by Charles Hill, the BMA assistant secretary, known to a wider public as the 'Radio Doctor'. As noted above, Hill had breached confidence when, before the strategically sensitive Metropolitan Counties Branch of the BMA, he launched an inflammatory attack on the Brown Plan in the spring of 1943.[103] In September the Annual Representative Meeting adopted 14 principles which demonstrated that the membership was unprepared to go much beyond the modest scheme for extension of the National Health Insurance system envisaged by the BMA in 1938.[104]

Consistent with the above indications it is not surprising that the *BMJ* gave the White Paper a hostile reception. The carefully presented edifice of evolutionary change embodied in the White Paper was denounced as a 'brilliantly camouflaged' exercise in deception. The new service was portrayed as a further move in the unremitting process toward state control of the medical profession.[105] Hill repeated his attack on the scheme in a further address to the Metropolitan Counties Branch on 5 March 1944.[106] Hill's standing was now greatly increased by his recent appointment as secretary of the BMA, following the sudden illness and death of Anderson.

The larger Representative Committee of the profession addressed 44 questions to the Minister seeking further elucidation of the White Paper, which were discussed by officials with Hill and Dain on 4 and 12 April 1944.[107]

The first definitive statement of opposition of the BMA to the White Paper was contained in a report of the Council prepared for the Annual Representative Body.[108] Because of preparations for the Normandy invasion this meeting was postponed from July until December.[109]

The BMA consequently took almost a year to determine its negotiating position. Notwithstanding this lengthy preparation, the Council and Representative Body essentially confirmed positions taken by negotiators at the first confidential discussions of the Brown Plan in the spring of 1943. The posture of the BMA was basically static and uncompromising.

Ideally the BMA leadership wanted abandonment of the entire scheme to which the Government was committed, delay until a new Government was elected after the war, examination of the health services by a Royal Commission, and eventually introduction of new services by stages.

With respect to the White Paper proposals the BMA sought relaxation of control by central administration, possibly involving hiving off the National Health Service to an autonomous Board, strengthening the Central Health Services Council, and abolishing the Central Medical Board. The last had been evolved in response to professional antipathy to employment by local authorities, but the profession decided that this medicine was worse than the disease, since it opened the way to central bureaucratic control over the distribution of doctors.

Because joint authorities signified continuing local authority dominance in local health administration, this aspect of the White Paper was vigorously contested. The BMA favoured creation of an additional regional tier of administration, with arrangements for substantial professional representation at the regional, joint authority, and individual local authority levels. Doctors would retain the position of independent contractors, with rights to undertake private practice, and with the opportunity to benefit materially by limitation of the service to 90% of the population. Health centres would be reduced to limited trials superintended by the CHSC.

Reflecting confidence in its position the BMA authorised the British Institute for Public Opinion to undertake an opinion survey among its membership. This exercise elicited a 48% response, involving 25,000 replies.[110] Similar success was encountered with a parallel poll conducted among medical students. Although this survey generally supported the BMA line, it was scarcely a gesture of unrestrained approval. Despite being inundated with propaganda against the White Paper, it emerged that the rank and file was well in arrears of the leadership in its militancy. Granted, only 39% were generally in favour of the White Paper compared with 53% against, but service doctors, salaried doctors and students showed a majority in favour. Against the line adopted by the leadership a substantial majority favoured a 100% free and comprehensive service, health centres, salaried service in health centres, abolition of sale and purchase of practices, and Central Medical Board control over distribution of doctors. The leadership's only consolation derived from vigorous opposition to joint authorities, or to local authority contracts for health centre doctors. This unmilitant response from the membership little assisted the health departments because it failed to temper the hurricane unleashed by the leadership of the profession.

Departmental communications with the voluntary hospital and local authority lobbies were not delayed by the requirement to consult a mass membership. These organisations reacted to the White Paper relatively quickly. They were primarily concerned with the general organisation of the hospital service, the dominant sector of the health service in which the two parties were direct competitors.

The White Paper was seen by the voluntary hospitals as a threat to their status and independence. In May 1944 a nation-wide campaign was launched to publicise the case of the voluntary sector. Both the British Hospitals Association and the King's Fund came forward with counterproposals, which were broadly in harmony, and which echoed views expressed by their representatives and by medical peers in the recent Lords' debate.[111] Pre-war schemes for regionalisation provided the obvious common ancestry for their thinking.

These proposals constituted the voluntary hospitals' criteria for the restoration of 'partnership' with the state sector. They wanted formation of an independent Central Hospitals Board similar in status to the Central Health Services Council for the purposes of general policy and central administration. A second innovation was introduction of a tier of Regional Hospital Councils which would become the 'keypoint' in the system, with overall responsibility for planning and consultant services. At the county level they proposed establishment of Local Hospital Councils to deal with local planning. Joint authorities in England and Wales, or joint hospital boards in Scotland, would then become redundant for purposes of planning and ownership of hospitals, except in special cases. At all three levels the voluntary hospitals demanded parity with local authorities over representation. The independence of the voluntary sector would be further strengthened by superseding local authority payment for services by exchequer grants paid on a three or five-year basis.

The two associations representing local authorities were not entirely in accord, the counties standing to benefit and the county boroughs to suffer by the establishment of joint authorities. Acute hospital services for county areas tended to be located in the large towns.[112] Joint authorities would thus give counties an interest in the administration of these key elements in the new health service. Nevertheless, in preliminary negotiation, neither the County Councils Association, the LCC, nor the Association of Municipal Corporations favoured the joint authority arrangement, largely because of a disinclination to disrupt their painfully constructed and prestigious public health departments. The joint authority arrangement involved a fragmentation of responsibility between joint and unitary authorities, with the inevitable weakening of the latter due to loss of control of the hospital service. The AMC warned that progressive county boroughs would be held back by their backward rural neighbours under the joint arrangements. The local authorities realised that most of the attractions of the Brown Plan were lost. They were no longer going to preside over a unified service. Indeed the new scheme was not even a vehicle for their ascendancy over voluntary hospitals in the sphere of hospital development. It seemed to local authorities that their services were being forcibly split up whereas voluntary hospitals were granted privileged autonomy. Local authorities resented what they saw as the protected status of voluntary hospitals under the new scheme. They wanted elimination of exchequer grants to voluntary hospitals and warned that the latter's representation on joint authorities and their committees was unacceptable. It was recognised by each of the two rival hospital sectors that in the agency dispensing public funds resided power over the system as a whole.

(iv) RECASTING GOVERNMENT PROPOSALS: 1944

In the absence of a Government plan for local government reform the Ministry of Health evolved its own scheme for geographical units appropriate for the new health service. It was proposed to establish between 35 and 40 joint authorities to take over public hospital services and assume planning responsibility for health services as a whole. These new authorities were the linchpins of the whole system. They effectively combined planning and executive functions in units capable of providing an almost comprehensive service. Although existing county councils and county boroughs would be left in charge of clinics and health centres, and voluntary hospitals guaranteed continuing independence, it was thought that the planning powers of joint authorities would secure ordered development of the system. Although the Ministry sympathised with the arguments against precepting and it knew all about the weakness and unpopularity of the multiplicity of joint boards spawned in the health field, officials were confident that larger and more powerful joint authorities would prove superior to limited joint boards, and that they would improve on the performance of existing major authorities. One of the great benefits of the new arrangement was its opportunity to erase such 'stupidities' as Rutland, Canterbury and other small authorities incapable of mounting extensive hospital services.[113]

Joint authorities were in keeping with the trend of the times towards establishing ad hoc authorities with responsibilities extending over counties or even larger areas for administering such services as water, gas, electricity or major roads. The White Paper was silent about the number and character of joint authority areas. Local authorities feared that the Government would accept the 12 regions wanted by the voluntary hospital lobby. Not until June 1944 was it officially stated that the Ministry favoured much smaller joint authority units. Even then no specific proposals were made in order to avoid frictions that would inevitably accompany plans for amalgamation. It was envisaged that joint authorities with populations of 500,000 or more would command a sufficient range of services to avoid the need for a regional tier in planning or administration. The advantage of joint authorities against regions was a consistent theme of office memoranda.[114]

As noted above, joint authorities were given a hostile reception from Morrison in the Reconstruction Committee. Unhappily for the Ministry of Health the virtues of joint authorities were also opaque to the parties involved in negotiation. It was indeed a cruel irony that it should have been this prided innovation, and linchpin to the whole system that provoked disparate elements into an almost unique display of united opposition. Apart from marginal appeal to the shires, joint authorities were anathema to all others. To county boroughs they threatened dilution of their influence, in all likelihood a dangerous prelude to stripping away other major responsibilities. To voluntary hospitals these joint authorities symbolised the growing imperialism of local authorities. To the profession these bodies were a warning of growing strength of the state machine and mounting pressures for full-time salaried employment. Antipathy to joint authorities by the above uneasy partnership resulted in renewed appreciation of the advantages of regionalism. If hospital planning were delegated to weak, distant, regional committees, local authorities might be left with executive control of their existing services. The voluntary lobby aspired to strong regional authorities which they might dominate and thus achieve ascendancy in the hospital partnership. The profession saw regional authorities as bodies of experts with a capacity to withstand interference from the state. 'Not only County Boroughs, but the voluntary hospitals, the Nuffield Trust, the minor authorities, and probably even the doctors, will like it' was the verdict of officials concerning regional councils.[115]

Yet official thinking was only slowly reconciled to sacrificing its joint authorities. As an additional tier regional councils were criticised because they introduced further complexity into a system that had already sacrificed the appealing simplicity of earlier plans. If adopted as an alternative to joint authorities, regions introduced what officials regarded as a fatal divorce between planning and execution. In either of its forms regionalism was dismissed as 'very poor second best . . . we ought to go all out for the joint authority principle as long as we possibly can', if need be offering minor compromises to render the joint authority scheme more palatable.[116]

The possibility of introducing small, expert, regional advisory bodies was broached informally to a local authority representative in September 1944, as part of a package in which local authorities were asked (a) to agree to 40% voluntary hospital and professional membership on Local Health Service Councils which would supersede joint authorities and take over their general planning function, and (b) to accept 50% voluntary hospital membership on new planning bodies called Local Hospital Councils, which would operate in tandem with Local Health Service Councils. With joint authorities replaced by planning councils the path was clear to leave statutory responsibility for hospital services with existing major local authorities. The Minister would set up joint authorities to take over hospitals 'not universally as in the White Paper, but only where he was satisfied that it would be impracticable to obtain an efficient service'.[117]

The Minister himself expressed interest in a regional tier to the voluntary hospital representatives, as part of an arrangement in which they were asked to accept a minority role on Local Hospital Councils. The Minister was less yielding on other points, flatly opposing an executive Central Hospitals Board, or Docker's demand that all payments to voluntary hospitals should come directly from the exchequer.[118]

In explaining these proposals to Moran it was confirmed that the region was 'fundamental to our new ideas'. Regional bodies were also to control consultant appointments.[119] By Christmas 1944, although the Minister's position was still formally undecided, officials were satisfied that the old joint authority scheme was defunct and should not be revived.[120]

In Scotland the Secretary of State faced fewer pressures to modify the White Paper scheme than his colleague in England. Many of the features of the Scottish scheme were justified on relatively non-controversial geographical grounds. Also Johnston had avoided conflict by accepting separate organisation for the three major components of the health service. Finally the authority of the Hetherington Committee and the logic of Scottish geography persuaded him to accept at the White Paper stage a regional tier of planning.[121]

The Department of Health faced the same pressure as in England for strengthening the independent central councils, particularly by including a majority of elected professional representatives and by guaranteeing independence to initiate investigations and publish reports. The Scottish profession preferred a single Central Health Services Council with functional sub-committees. None of these proposals unduly disconcerted the Department of Health.

For the purpose of hospital development regions were welcome to the Scottish voluntary hospitals and the profession. In line with the Hetherington Committee they sought to strengthen the region at the expense of joint authorities by making regions responsible for initiating planning in their areas. This proposal was accepted by local authorities and by the department.

The above adjustment marginally weakened the position of joint hospital boards which the department hoped to retain in Scotland because of the small size of most local authorities. However, the Scottish BHA, despite being guaranteed 50% membership of regional councils, remained suspicious about the powers of local authorities. They stayed convinced that the Secretary of State's proposals were placing voluntary hospitals in a position of dependence rather than partnership. In their turn the larger local authorities were unenthusiastic about joint hospital boards, although by December 1944 they had not collectively insisted on reverting to administration of the hospital service by existing local authorities. Johnston was willing to accede to such a request if it were made.

On general practitioner services the Scottish BMA adopted a similar position to its English counterpart. Apart from insisting on the continuation of private practice the other primary concern was playing down the health centre experiment. Perhaps the most surprising concession in Johnston's mind was willingness to introduce the new health service in stages, a possibility more easy with his compartmentalised scheme than with the English version, which retained at least an element of unified structure.[122]

No doubt the Secretary of State was responding to a much publicised letter from Captain E C Cobb MP and other Conservative MPs proposing introduction of the health service in two stages, the first being re-organisation of the hospital services and extension of the panel to 90% of the population.[123] Webb-Johnson, commenting favourably on this scheme, reminded Willink of the profession's reason for resisting a 100% service 'The danger of making insurance for general practitioner service universal in its application is that this may undermine the freedom of the profession and eventually steer us towards a whole-time salaried service'. In Webb-Johnson's view the move to a service for the whole population was a 'revolutionary proposal' inconsistent with promises made by Churchill that controversial measures would not be advocated by his Coalition Government.[124]

After its deliberations over the White Paper at the beginning of February 1944 the Reconstruction Committee met on more than fifty occasions without considering the health service. This problem was not introduced again until October, when the Health Ministers provided brief interim reports of their negotiations. This was in fact the last occasion when the Reconstruction Committee was invited to comment on the scheme as a whole.[125] Its further brief deliberations in March 1945 related to a single minor issue. This last round of ministerial discussions under the Coalition Government was not particularly consequential. The Health Ministers were sympathetic to strengthening the central professional council, but their colleagues stood by their earlier objections. The committee was more accommodating to the new thinking on local organisation, providing that local authorities were kept in a majority position on Local Health Service and Hospitals Councils.

The Labour side of the Reconstruction Committee was becoming increasingly restless concerning rumours that additional compromises were being offered to the profession. Further departures from the White Paper scheme were likely to test to breaking point the delicate bipartisanship maintained within the committee.

(v) NEGOTIATING BY COMMITTEE: JANUARY–MAY 1945

The process of compromise was not completely over. Indeed, as far as elements within the profession were concerned, it had scarcely begun. Commencement of formal negotiations was delayed until after the Representative Meeting in December 1944. Only then was the Negotiating Committee of the profession formally constituted, comprising 31 members, 16 of whom came from the BMA, and 6 from Scotland.[126] The effective voice of this body was a small sub-committee comprising H Guy Dain (Chairman, and Chairman of the BMA Council), Sir Alfred Webb-Johnson (Vice-Chairman, President, Royal College of Surgeons), Lord Moran (President, Royal College of Physicians), Eardley Holland (President, Royal College of Obstetricians and Gynaecologists), Professor R M F Picken (President, Society of Medical Officers of Health), S Wand (Chairman, BMA General Practice Committee), R W Cockshut (BMA), A Talbot Rogers (BMA), and E A Gregg (BMA). Perhaps as a sign of the expected permanence of their vocation, the Negotiating Committee soon adopted its own headed notepaper. Although united in many of their criticisms of the White Paper, sectional tensions occasionally surfaced. For instance, Moran was at pains to emphasise the independence and rank of the Royal College of Physicians against the imperialism of the BMA.[127]

Although the most intensive discussions were held with the representatives of the profession, separate talks with the voluntary hospitals and local authority associations continued, and consultations were extended to such groups as dentists, nurses, and the TUC. In London some forty meetings were held between the new year and the end of May 1945. Scottish negotiations were almost exclusively limited to the local authorities. The English negotiations were broken off on 24 May, owing to the collapse of the Coalition Government, an outcome which suited the BMA because fresh soundings needed to be taken at the Annual Representative Meeting scheduled for the end of July 1945.

The most notable step in the negotiations was submission of interim proposals by Willink. These were distilled into a report produced by the Negotiating Committee, for distribution to the BMA membership in April and for consideration by a Special Representative Meeting at the beginning of May 1945.

The main feature of negotiations was continuing resistance by the profession to departing from its declared lines of policy. For instance, ever since the thirties the BMA had insisted that the comprehensive service should include all civilian health services and that the Ministry of Health should be concerned with no other function. This view was confirmed in the opening resolution of the Special Representative Meeting.[128] The only notable concession made at this point was acceptance that the service should be available to the whole population, rather than to only 90% as previously stipulated. This concession was matched by ample reciprocation on the other side, since Willink completely abandoned the idea of full-time salaried service with the consequence that all general practitioners would be allowed to practise privately in addition to their public work.[129]

The central advisory machinery captured disproportionate attention. The Minister offered to take account of the views of the profession in appointing central advisory committees, but the profession continued to press for direct election of their representatives and finally for a professional veto over membership as a whole.[130] It was eventually agreed to include 19 medical representatives on a Central Health Service Council of 37, a level resented by local authorities who argued for a majority of elected representatives at all levels in administration.[131] Having gained this majority representation, the profession pressed for CHSC control over the membership and terms of reference of subordinate committees such as the standing advisory committees proposed for hospitals, and for medical services.[132] Right to initiate as well as to give advice on request was demanded by the profession.[133] The Minister was sympathetic to this and also agreed to increase ex officio membership on the CHSC although, as instructed by the Reconstruction Committee, he opposed election of CHSC members, as well as the unrestricted right to publish reports.[134]

Reacting to earlier criticisms, the Minister reduced the powers of the Central Medical Board. It was now proposed to scrap the requirement for full-time service from new entrants. Instead of controlling the distribution of all doctors seeking a practice it was agreed to limit action of the Board to closing areas judged to be over-doctored. Since contracts were to be placed with local committees rather than the Board, Hill proposed that the Board might be scrapped completely, a view confirmed at the Representative Meeting.[135]

The division of responsibility between regional and local administration absorbed the greatest energies of the negotiators. The most vociferous advocate of the region was Moran. His pleas for enhancement of the authority of the region permeated the meetings. His view that the region was 'the most important instrument in securing a good service, and the essential protection of the profession against local authority control' was inadequately understood by the BMA according to Moran.[136] He remained dissatisfied because (a) insufficient guarantees were given concerning the rights of the region to initiate planning and exercise final sanction over local plans before they were forwarded to the Minister, and (b) the regions were given insufficient control over the execution of the agreed plan. Moran wanted regions to exercise an advisory role, and perhaps even to operate sanctions in the disbursement of exchequer grants to local authorities.[137] These extensions of power for the region were regarded as fundamental in the resolutions adopted by the Special Representative Meeting.[138] The clear tenor of these changes was in the direction of establishing the regional council of experts in a position of sovereignty over area councils with their elected majorities. The Minister accepted that regional councils should be dominated by experts. He had in mind a membership of 15, including only 4 local authority representatives, but he objected to extension of advisory functions beyond planning, consultant selection, and surveys.[139] Willink argued that it was intolerable to prevent democratically constituted area authorities from submitting their plans to the Minister.[140]

The mature proposals of the Minister involved establishing at the area level Local Health Service Councils (also called Planning Councils) comprising 31 members, 60% of whom would be elected, while the rest would contain a 'sizeable' medical element.[141] As a concession, giving the 'last word to the region', plans were to be submitted simultaneously to the region and the Minister, an arrangement which was criticised because it fell short of the 'subordinate' role for local councils demanded by the profession.[142] The profession also wanted stronger medical representation on the local councils. The position of elected representatives was further weakened by the Minister's proposal to delegate the hospital side of planning to a Hospital Group containing equal local authority and voluntary hospital membership.[143] The BMA demanded a similar committee for planning the general practitioner service, an idea which officials recognised would annoy local authorities who, 'rightly, regard this as stripping them of practically all their public responsibility in planning'.[144]

In order to avoid direct financial relations between local authorities and voluntary hospitals it was proposed to establish a 'clearing house' at planning authority level to distribute local authority payments for services rendered. Even without the final concessions demanded by the profession the influence of local authorities on local councils was being drastically eaten away. Given their strong position at the regional and area level the profession could have afforded to be lenient over administration at the local authority level. Even here however the profession wanted co-option on to statutory public health committees in line with the arrangement in education, but this innovation was resisted by the AMC and the LCC.[145] An alternative proposal involved establishment of non-statutory local medical advisory committees of the kind already in existence in some local authority areas.[146]

In response to pressure for perpetuation of the existing mechanism of employment of general practitioners, the Minister fell back on Local Practitioner Committees, which would be direct replacements for existing National Health Insurance Committees.[147] Officials acknowledged that this aspect of the service was the 'merest shadow' of the White Paper proposals.[148]

In line with his other concessions on points involving departure from existing arrangements for general practice, the Minister conceded that health centres would only be introduced as a 'centrally controlled experiment'.[149] The profession was nevertheless sensitive about this vestigial scheme.[150] They wanted local authorities cut out of health centre contracts, a tempting proposal, but officials warned the Minister that this might jeopardise any chance of general health centre development in the longer term.[151] The profession was also resistant to payment of part salaries to health centre doctors. Because salaries 'should be ruled out as opposed to the principles of the profession', capitation payment and competition should be permissible even in health centres.[152]

The medical profession in Scotland left action to their delegates on the Negotiating Committee. They had not commented separately on the White Paper proposals before the lapse of the Coalition and Caretaker Governments. The Secretary of State accepted elaboration of the central advisory machinery. He was inclined to maintain the Central Medical Board, anticipating that this would be wanted by the profession. In response to the rebellion of the Scottish BHA against its leadership Johnston agreed to strengthen the planning powers of the five Regional Hospital Advisory Councils. However, Johnston was unable to satisfy the BHA demand for an equal say in the local administration of the new hospital service. In response to the wishes of the profession Johnston agreed to elevating Local Medical Service Committees from an advisory position into administrative bodies for general practitioner services. Given the general erosion of powers of the proposed joint boards the larger local authorities predictably questioned the desirability of continuing with these joint authorities. By April 1945 it was evident that Johnston was at risk of alienating the last of his erstwhile allies, by driving local authorities into alliance with the BHA and profession in opposition to his scheme.[153]

(vi) BREAKDOWN OF THE COALITION

With the collapse of German resistance strains within the Government became increasingly apparent. The Reconstruction Committee was a particularly tender spot. In the few meetings held in 1945 sharp disagreements surfaced over unification of electricity supplies, nationalisation of the iron and steel industry, and over sale and purchase of medical practices.

Traditionally doctors had purchased and resold their practices. Their value was an important asset for retirement, and compensation for substantial debts incurred as new entrants. Proposals for salaried service would have swept away sale and purchase, with appropriate compensation being offered to current incumbents. This arrangement would have been particularly attractive to the sizeable batch of new entrants soon to emerge from the forces. Subsequent reversion to NHI norms meant that the sale and purchase tradition was not necessarily threatened, except in the case of doctors transferring to health centres. This issue was raised in negotiations with the profession, but it assumed little prominence. Dain wanted sale and purchase to continue in health centres, but he preferred total abolition to any dual system.[154] Officials agreed that a dual system was unworkable.

This problem was taken to the Reconstruction Committee, ostensibly because uncertainty was impairing the value of practices, but privately Woolton informed the Prime Minister that BMA acceptance of Government proposals was conditional on a statement promising continuation of sale of practices.[155] Willink wanted to oblige 'in view of the many problems which would complicate the introduction of the new medical service, the question of the disposal of practices should be deferred until some experience had been gained of the results' and then the matter should be considered by a committee of inquiry. Johnston disagreed and pressed for immediate action. He could see no reason for delay. The Government would be accused of evasion and the health centre experiment jeopardised.[156]

Discussion within the committee exposed strong differences of opinion. Woolton was asked to discuss the problem further with the Health Ministers, and he secured acceptance of Willink's proposals.[157] Privately Woolton conceded that it had been difficult to dissuade Labour colleagues from insisting on immediate suspension of sale of practices.[158]

The above controversy may explain why Willink refrained from reporting to the Reconstruction Committee on other aspects of his negotiations on the health service. In the year since the debate on the 1944 White Paper negotiations had been conducted in private. The Minister had tentatively offered many concessions, but he had not committed the Government to a new scheme. The Cabinet, Parliament and the public were not briefed on developments. Of course rumours abounded, especially after a detailed report was circulated to the medical profession in March 1945. The popular press was astir with allegations about 'surrender' to the doctors.[159]

With increasing urgency *The Times* called on the Minister to declare his position.[160] Complaints were made in the House of Commons about the Minister's silence, answered in a brief non-committal speech merely admitting that the shape of new proposals was beginning to emerge, but that an alternative scheme had not yet crystallised.[161] Outside Parliament Labour MPs were making inflammatory speeches declaring that the White Paper was an 'ugly confidence trick' to disguise a conspiracy by the Tories in league with the old guard of the medical profession.[162] The Labour Party Annual Conference also rang with accusations of betrayal.[163]

Uncertainty and suspicion penetrated the Reconstruction Committee. Bevin asked Willink for information on the negotiations. Willink furnished Bevin with outlines of the scheme shown to the medical profession, claiming that no essential departure from the White Paper was involved. A declaration in the draft that he wanted the modified proposals 'settled in a coalition Bill and not left till after the election' was deleted from Willink's reply.[164]

Capitulation of Germany on 9 May raised the question of the continuation of the coalition. There was support on both sides for extension, but the Labour Party National Executive Committee would not agree to continuing beyond October.[165] In response Churchill resigned on 23 May and was appointed Prime Minister of a Caretaker Government holding office until the election on 5 July.

In the new administration Willink remained as Minister of Health, Woolton as Minister of Reconstruction, and Anderson as

Chancellor of the Exchequer. The Earl of Rosebery replaced Johnston as Secretary of State for Scotland.

Much greater progress had been made in formulating legislation than was publicly known or officially acknowledged. An outline sketch of a Bill was prepared early in January 1945. Forty pages of 'First Notes' were circulated on 20 January. Instructions to Parliamentary Counsel were sent on 15 February. The first printed draft of the 'Health Service Bill' is dated 6 April 1945.[166] On 8 May the Minister promised local authorities that he would present a Bill at an early date.[167] On 18 May Woolton reacted to the public anxiety about the intentions of the Government by asking Willink to be ready to bring his Bill before the Reconstruction Committee at an early date.[168] Immediately after formation of the Caretaker administration, Willink announced that he was in favour of the Government making a clear statement of its intentions before the election.[169]

Willink duly prepared a report of 'Progress with the Proposals for a National Health Service', which was circulated as a confidential proof at the beginning of June. This report related only to England and Wales. It was felt that the Scottish proposals were still consistent with the scheme outlined in the 1944 White Paper. Even for England and Wales Willink claimed that the fundamental objectives of the White Paper were maintained. The changes affected 'only ways and means and not ends'. These modifications were to the benefit of the service since they strengthened individual freedom, eliminated 'any possible excess of standardisation', and encouraged variety and individuality throughout the service.

A statement of the kind prepared by Willink was demanded by *The Times* in order to give credence to the Conservative election manifesto claim that they were ready to introduce a comprehensive health service. *The Times* wondered in the light of Willink's record whether the plan would be ready. Preparations to meet the post-war situation were already in arrears. *The Times* demanded answers to controversial issues without delay.[170]

Having shed his coalition partners the way was now clear for Willink to make the last few adjustments to his scheme with a view to finally appeasing the profession. The National Health Service could then be presented as a decisive contribution of Conservatism to post-war social reconstruction.

Woolton circulated a brief Cabinet paper recommending publication of the report prepared by Willink. The latter's draft covering note warned that 'distortions would now hold the field unanswered . . . if the discussions were left to fizzle out in an official silence, with no statement of any Government intentions'.[171] Willink recognised a precious opportunity for the Government to realise the basic objectives of the White Paper with the assurance of unanimous support from the major interests involved. In order to conciliate the profession his memorandum proposed concessions on a few issues upon which general practitioners were most sensitive. There was to be no restriction on distribution, and for health centre doctors no contract with local authorities, and payment by capitation. These points were relevant to only a handful of doctors, but they were assuming major symbolic importance. Outside the general practitioner service the memorandum froze to positions taken throughout the recent negotiations.[172] The Minister continued to evade (a) elected membership on the central advisory machinery (para 15), (b) unrestricted right of the central advisory committees to publish reports (para 15), (c) placing regions as intermediaries between the Minister and area in planning (para 18), (d) extending powers of regions into the financial arena (para 21), and (e) deriving all payments to voluntary hospitals directly from the exchequer (para 25).

On the controversial question of the scale of the health centre experiment, the report was ambiguous, acknowledging that this development would be centrally 'controlled', but also promising a 'substantial scale' (paras 34, 38, 40).

Willink's report was discussed at a meeting of six Ministers, who were also considering the section on health for the election manifesto.[173] Willink's recommendation of immediate publication of a full report on Government intentions for the health service was not accepted. Whereas Willink dwelled on the positive aspects of his proposals, his colleagues believed that the new scheme would contain ample election capital for Labour. The Ministers feared that the public were likely to regard Willink's concessions as substantial retraction from the White Paper proposals, offered to placate professional pressure groups. There was doubt whether election candidates would be able to justify the new plan. It was agreed that candidates should give assurances that the 1944 White Paper would be suitably modified. The question of further action was referred to a full meeting of the Cabinet.

Having failed to secure publication of his full report, Willink now fell back on a proposal for a general public announcement on the scope of the new service together with a short published statement. The Cabinet was provided with a full list of modifications to the 1944 White Paper.[174] This more prudent course was accepted by the Cabinet and a draft statement was prepared for circulation on 20 June.[175] Willink was yet again disappointed. It was decided that his statement should await the concerted attack on the Conservative record on health policy which it was anticipated would be mounted during the election campaign. Because this threat never materialised the Conservatives left a discreet veil over their intended contribution to post-war reconstruction in the field of health.

CHAPTER IV

Labour Ascendant

In the 1945 General Election Labour emerged triumphant to secure the only substantial electoral mandate in its history. Socialist doctors reflected the air of anticipation on the left, declaring that 'a new world is in the making and everywhere the democratic forces are gaining in the struggle against reaction'.[1] The new Cabinet, facing the formidable challenge of implementing their socialist programme, was headed by those stalwarts of the Reconstruction Committee, Attlee, Bevin and Morrison. In the selection of his Cabinet, it was generally agreed that Attlee's most unexpected, audacious and 'unconventional stroke' was the appointment of Aneurin Bevan as Minister of Health.[2]

Among officials there were rumours of the choice of either Ellen Wilkinson or Edith Summerskill.[3] Whatever alternatives were rumoured, Attlee's draft Cabinet list suggests no wavering with respect to Bevan.[4] At the age of 47 Bevan was the youngest member of the Cabinet, and one of the minority never before to have held ministerial office.

Attlee's move was undoubtedly shrewd. A leader of backbench revolt was removed and submitted to Cabinet discipline. Furthermore, the Ministry of Health was an obvious political graveyard, as the experience of Brown and Willink testified. This appointment was thus an utmost test of the capacity of Bevan to perform 'good service'.[5] The prediction that the status of Bevan's office would be reduced by transfer of its housing function to the Ministry of Town and Country Planning did not materialise in 1945, although this change was no doubt under consideration and it was effected in 1950.[6]

The press regarded Bevan as the right type to restore firmness in health service negotiations. Similar thoughts were aroused among officials. The departing Willink was praised for his niceness and sincerity, but it was felt that he lacked the fighting qualities needed in the health field. Bevan was identified as a formidable fighter. Doubts concerning his 'weight and judgement' were soon dispelled. He seemed to possess 'great drive, an able and clear mind and a capacity to listen'. Officials were also impressed by his sincerity. He 'really cared about the way in which the people lived'.[7]

The former Secretary of State for Scotland, the energetic and successful Thomas Johnston, was not interested in resuming this appointment, preferring to cultivate Scottish interests in a non-political capacity. The post fell on Joseph Westwood, previously a member of the Cathcart Committee and former Parliamentary Under-Secretary of State to Brown and Johnston. Westwood, an ex-miner of 61, was in decline and he was arguably the least able member of the Cabinet. Attlee was presumably content to have a less assertive Secretary of State than Johnston, but Westwood carried this characteristic to the point of ineptitude. Westwood was retired somewhat unceremoniously by Attlee in October 1947 and he died in 1948.[8]

Westwood was succeeded by Arthur Woodburn, whose career had been spent in adult education before entering Parliament during the war. From 1941 he served as Parliamentary Private Secretary to Johnston. Attlee gave him a junior appointment in the Ministry of Supply and Aircraft Production in 1945 before his promotion to the Scottish Office in October 1947. More adequate to the task than Westwood, Woodburn remained in office until the 1950 General Election, when he was replaced by the more assertive McNeil.[9] By this stage it was necessary to pay heed to patriotic sentiment. It was complained that the 'two epigoni of Mr Johnston [Westwood and Woodburn] caused great dissatisfaction even among moderate Scots'.[10]

At the junior level in the Ministry of Health Alderman Charles Key was appointed Parliamentary Secretary. Key was a Poplar celebrity, with special knowledge of housing and London local government. In February 1947 he was appointed Minister of Works, in which capacity he came into the public eye in the Stanley affair. Key was succeeded briefly by L J Edwards, and then by Arthur Blenkinsop, who remained in his post until the end of the Labour Government, and continued thereafter to be active in health affairs in the House of Commons.

The Joint Parliamentary Under-Secretary of State for Scotland with primary responsibility for health was George Buchanan, followed by Thomas Fraser in 1948. In practice Westwood delegated to Buchanan the major share of the work in preparing for the Scottish NHS legislation, as well as many of the delicate and prolonged negotiations with the profession before the Appointed Day in July 1948.

With the retirement of Sir John Maude as Permanent Secretary, the link of the Ministry with Morant was broken. Maude was only the third Permanent Secretary in the department's history, whereas Bevan was the fourteenth Minister. Maude's successor was selected from outside the department. Sir William Scott Douglas had served at the Treasury and Ministry of Supply during the war. Previously he had been Secretary of the Scottish Department of Health. He remained in office until 1951. During this time Sir George Henderson remained his counterpart in Scotland. Jameson in London and Davidson in Edinburgh also provided continuity as Chief Medical Officers during this period. Of the two Deputy Secretaries in London, Sir John Wrigley also stayed until 1951, but Sir Arthur Rucker was succeeded by J M K Hawton in 1947. This change was significant because it replaced an official who had reservations about the new scheme by a much younger colleague who was greatly trusted by Bevan, and who possessed intimate knowledge of the plans for a comprehensive service from their inception.

Although 1945 provided Labour with its first opportunity for an extended term of office, the Party and the movement were by no means fresh to the idea of a comprehensive health service.[11] As noted above, the early Labour Party was bound by a pledge to dissolve the Poor Law. Under the guidance of the Webbs this principle was associated with plans for a comprehensive health service administered centrally by a functional Ministry of Health and at the periphery by committees of elected local authorities. In the course of the partial fulfilment of these objectives after World War I, Addison and Dawson were aware of their proximity to Labour thinking. The first Minister of Health went over to the Labour Party shortly after his removal from office.

The commitment of the Labour Party to a modern comprehensive health service took place in the 1930s. Official policy changed remarkably little between 1934 and 1945, except for conciliatory gestures towards the 1944 White Paper when wartime legislation looked likely. The real strength of the Labour position lay in its increasing ascendancy in local government. Development of public health and hospital services became a major objective of the LCC and Labour-controlled metropolitan boroughs. By the outbreak of World War II it was noted that the LCC had become the 'largest hospital authority' and 'also the largest public health authority in the world'.[12] Opinions differed about its qualitative supremacy, but the LCC had demonstrated the capacity of a major local authority to build up a complex health service and to undertake a radical reorganisation of hospital services within the space of ten years. The LCC constituted a crucible for experiment, a state within the medical state, and it was strategically well placed to influence the Ministry of Health during the evolution of its thinking on a comprehensive health service.

As previously indicated, the Ministry of Health prepared contingency plans for a comprehensive health service with the above Labour initiatives in mind. During the war Labour became directly involved in preparations for a National Health Service by virtue of the position of Thomas Johnston as Secretary of State for

Scotland, a strong presence on the Reconstruction Committees, involvement of the LCC and other local authorities in the negotiation process, and finally through pressure exerted by union and Labour organisations for full realisation of Beveridge's Assumption B. Officials even drew close to the relatively left-wing Socialist Medical Association because this was one of the few professional organisations to sympathise with their own thinking on the future of the health service.[13] Rumours concerning retractions of the Caretaker Government reconsecrated the Labour movement to its health and social security objectives. Bearing in mind the extent of its commitments in the health field, the health content of the 1945 Labour election manifesto, *Let Us Face the Future*, was brief and inconsequential, ironically reading rather like a precis of the Conservative manifesto, except for its explicit advocacy of 'health centres where the people may get the best that modern science can offer'. During what turned out to be an unexpectedly low-key election, disagreements on health policy remained below the surface. Neither party was forced to reveal its colours.[14]

Bevan had played conspicuously little part in agitation on health matters. He was, of course, intimately familiar with the health problems of the mining areas at the height of the Depression, and also with the characteristic Medical Aid Societies of the Welsh coalfields. This firsthand experience occasionally showed in his ministerial speeches. The chorus of complaints about prevarication over the Beveridge Report was joined by Bevan. On just two occasions he made what may appear with hindsight to be providential interventions. First, he interrupted Brown's announcement on hospital policy to declare that 'subvention by public funds and flag days is becoming increasingly repugnant to the conscience of the public', calling for a hospital scheme more 'in accord with civilised notions of organised society'.[15] Secondly, he interrupted Anderson's statement on social security precisely at the point where the question of a comprehensive health service was raised.[16] Brown and Anderson were two Ministers for whom Bevan felt particular disregard.

The remoteness of Bevan from the Labour health experts is suggested by a briefing letter from the Propaganda Secretary of the Socialist Medical Association in which she provided him with elementary information about the association and its literature. It was no doubt hoped that Bevan would be guided by the nine SMA members in the House of Commons.[17] Although Bevan received numerous communications from the SMA, apart from some initial confidential exchanges his relations with this group were not particularly close.

(i) FRESH BEARINGS

Although the negotiations conducted under Willink had been debilitating and to some degree destructive, they had been of material value in exploring the territory of the proposed health service in minute detail. Consequently, although uncertain about major policy options, by the time of Labour's return officials were furnished with legislation in an advanced stage of preparation. It was thus possible to move forward with speed.

Bevan's first major speech struck a cautious note. He predicted that his proposals would be announced within the year. However, soon afterwards he promised to present a Bill early in the new year.[18]

The precise direction of Labour thinking was not easy to predict. Willink's final concessions to the profession, although minor in extent, had shattered the fragile consensus over the White Paper. The 1945 Labour Conference sanctioned a fresh appraisal of the White Paper proposals, and the first ministerial statements suggested that material departures from Willink's scheme were in prospect.[19] The promise of 'unorthodox' intentions contained in Bevan's first major speech gave the same impression.

The new Minister was faced with a treacherous political equation requiring an estimate of the degree to which long standing policy commitments of his Party needed to be tempered in order to secure smooth progress to early legislation. The solution adopted indeed resulted in early legislation, but this task was accomplished in the face of an unanticipated volume of opposition emanating success-ively from officials, Ministers, and from the three major interest groups involved in the health service.

Bevan's mind was quickly made up concerning his preferred scheme. The main lines of his proposals were worked out in August 1945, and they were communicated to the Socialist Medical Association and other select witnesses in September.

Given the great variety of alternatives already considered it was virtually impossible to come up with entirely new proposals. In the main Bevan was dealing in fresh permutations of already known options. But his package was sufficiently radical to cause a stir, and his plan for the hospital service constituted a major surprise. On the other hand, some of Bevan's proposals left intact certain of the much lamented compromises wrung out of Willink by the profession.[20]

With respect to the central machinery, Bevan upheld Willink's agreement to publish annual reports of the Central Health Services Council, except where contrary to the public interest. He also accepted the long standing agreement to consult the profession on appointment of members to the CHSC, but like Willink he resisted the unrestricted right of the profession to nominate members. Whereas Willink agreed to specify in his Bill the range of Standing Advisory Committees to be adopted, Bevan intended to leave the choice to the Minister.

The department had fought hard to unify all health services under a single planning authority, but its schemes had been slowly whittled away until the residual plan for area planning bodies was unattractive to all parties. Bevan followed this trend to its logical conclusion, adopting Johnston's precedent in Scotland by splitting the new health service into its three traditional component parts, and pushing responsibility for co-ordination to the ministerial level. At first Bevan considered transferring all local authority services to the regional and district administration devised for hospitals. But ultimately he fell back on the arrangement of previous schemes in which planning and administration of clinic services were the responsibility of county and county borough councils, with delegation of maternity and child welfare services to authorities responsible for the school health service. By contrast with Willink's scheme, it was proposed to transfer maternity and child welfare services from metropolitan borough councils to the LCC. Health centres were allocated to county and county borough councils. Bevan removed restrictions on this development, but he followed Willink by placing health centre doctors' contracts with local committees supplanting Insurance Committees, now called Executive Committees, rather than with local authorities. The degree of change within the general practitioner services depended on the Government's capacity to develop a system of health centres. Otherwise the proposed administration of general practitioner services retained the essential features of the panel system, but with certain minor differences:

(a) it was proposed to institute part-salary plus capitation payment, the precise arrangement depending on whether the doctor worked in a health centre or not;

(b) the 1944 White Paper machinery for controlling the distribution of new entrants would be reintroduced;

(c) following earlier prevarication on this issue, the sale and purchase of practices would be prohibited.

Earlier indecision about inclusion of a full dental and ophthalmic service in the new health service was ended by Bevan. In the short term, the general dental and eye services would be available under the Executive Committees apart from the hospital-based ophthalmic service which it was hoped to expand, and the services to priority groups which would continue as local authority responsibilities. The eventual aim was to locate all dental services in health centres, staffed by full-time salaried dentists. Pending the development of a full consultant ophthalmic service the temporary Supplementary Ophthalmic Service would be left with opticians. In response to mounting pressure from the profession and the TUC, Bevan wanted to reverse the agreement between Bevin and Brown reached in 1943, and transfer responsibility for the industrial health services to local authorities.[21]

The most unexpected feature of Bevan's scheme related to hospitals and consultant services, which constituted by far the largest component of the new service. Ever since the 1941 ministerial statement, plans for the post-war hospital service had been based on the idea of partnership between the municipal and voluntary sectors. At the outset it looked as if the expansion of municipal hospitals would continue until voluntary hospitals lost their identity. By the time of Willink's scheme the position of the voluntary hospitals was strengthened to the degree that their long-term future seemed assured.

Bevan gave up the attempt to reconcile the two rival hospital systems, deciding instead to merge all hospitals as the 'direct responsibility of the Minister and financed wholly from the exchequer'.[22] The recently adopted regional advisory machinery could be readily modified to take on a more general administrative function as the agent of the Minister. Indeed a change in this direction had been urged on Willink by the profession. It was envisaged that some 16 to 20 regions would exercise general direction over a large number of Hospital Management Committees which would administer local hospital groups. After more than momentary hesitation about challenging the independence of voluntary teaching hospitals it was decided that they also should be taken over, but accorded a special status, each under its own Board of Governors which would act as the direct agent of the Minister.

Although slow to gain acceptance in official circles, hospital regionalisation of one kind or another had been a dominant theme for nearly ten years. In left-wing thinking the idea of regional administration was increasingly associated with a call for public ownership of all hospitals. The Socialist Medical Association had long favoured 'regional elected authorities administering a national plan and employing whole-time salaried officers in health centres and large hospitals'.[23] The SMA envisaged that all voluntary hospitals would eventually be absorbed into this system. Immediate public take-over of voluntary hospitals was the declared policy of the 1945 Labour Party Conference. The maverick Medical Practitioners' Union was author of a widely-known memorandum advocating state control of all hospitals and their administration under hospital sub-committees of Area Health Committees.[24] Sir Frederick Menzies regarded the LCC as an ideal prototype hospital and health region. Already in 1941 he described regionalisation as the order of the day, the 'New Order' or 'New Deal', already adopted for wartime purposes and destined to be generally applied in peacetime.[25] At an early stage both English and Scottish officials had considered hospital nationalisation as one of the alternatives for post-war reconstruction, but this dangerous idea had been rapidly discarded on account of likely antagonism from both voluntary hospitals and local authorities, because the Ministry of Health was not perceived as a sufficiently strong entity to mount such an operation, and because there seemed no particular reason to intervene in what seemed like an irreversible evolution towards municipalisation.

From his fresh vantage point Bevan realised that imperfections in the current system of local government fundamentally undermined schemes for municipalising health services. In the case of the hospital service nationalisation offered an opportunity to evolve a more rational geographical framework, and a chance to create a system of administration that would be more palatable to the profession and the voluntary lobby. Bevan held out the attractions of 'worker control' to the profession and to health workers as one of the positive merits of hospital nationalisation and indeed of nationalisation in general.[26] Where Bevan was noticeably less radical than socialist pressure groups was in applying his rational framework only to the hospital sector. He thereby sacrificed an opportunity to unify health administration, which had been one of the major themes of early plans for a comprehensive health service. By following the tripartite organisation already adopted in Scottish plans, Bevan calculated that local authorities and general practitioners would be to some extent conciliated by the prospect of maintenance of the status quo in their sectors.

Bevan's scheme was attractive to Buchanan in Scotland because it produced greater uniformity between the two schemes, and also because hospital nationalisation fitted in with aspirations of the Department of Health to extend its influence in the hospital sector. Bevan's proposal was greeted by Buchanan as a means to 'get rid once and for all of any purely historical impediments'.[27] However, the proposal to exclude teaching hospitals from the regional boards was unacceptable to Buchanan and it had never been seriously contemplated in Scotland, where teaching hospitals performed the general hospital function for their areas. There was less certainty about the status of Regional Hospital Boards proposed for Scotland. Advantages could be seen in establishing small Boards, but in the interests of democracy it was likely that the Boards would be large. The Department of Health favoured Boards acting as agents of the Secretary of State, but it was appreciated that in practice they would need to enjoy a maximum degree of independence. Arriving at a solution to this problem proved to be one of the most troublesome aspects of the early National Health Service.[28]

(ii) INTERNAL DISSENSION: OCTOBER 1945–MARCH 1946

While most aspects of Bevan's scheme were accepted within the Government without difficulty, agreement to nationalisation of hospitals was only secured after much dispute. The dissension provoked by this issue stirred up within the Cabinet ill-ease about the National Health Service as a whole; it soured relations between Bevan and some of his senior colleagues, and contributed to their hostility towards Bevan's management of the early service.

Bevan's first problem was overcoming scepticism within his department concerning nationalisation of hospitals. Bevan quickly came round to the nationalisation idea in his discussions with J M K Hawton. The first document to reveal these new thoughts suggests some 25 to 30 'Divisional Councils' covering areas with populations of at least 500,000. These Divisions would be 'the Minister's local agent, the owner of the hospitals, and the employer of all their staff'. At the local level, 'District Management Committees of the Divisional Council would act as the governing body of all the hospitals in the District'. In view of the comprehensiveness of this arrangement it was argued that local authority services might be assimilated into this regional structure.[29]

Notwithstanding this bold initiative, memoranda prepared for Bevan by his senior officials argued forcefully against departure from the hospital scheme handed down by the previous administration.[30] It was appreciated that greater public accountability of voluntary hospitals might be required, but there seemed to be no justification for taking these hospitals into public ownership. Political considerations were not regarded as sufficient grounds to merit a course which would be violently opposed by voluntary hospitals. It was also pointed out that Bevan's solution was subversive to local government. Douglas advised Bevan that it was 'a pity to discard a plan which gives us much, if not all, of what we want, which is practically ready, and which would have a very large measure of agreement in its passage'.[31] Bevan was warned that he was embarking on a dangerous adventure which was likely to undermine any possibility of early legislation and destroy all hope of regaining consensus.

Disregarding such pessimistic prognostications Bevan presented preliminary thoughts on hospital nationalisation to the Cabinet. He now reverted to the ten regions then favoured by the voluntary hospital planners. Although 'regional boards' and 'District Committees' were primarily advocated for the purposes of hospital administration, he left open the possibility that he would propose inclusion of local authority services, 'in order to ensure a unified health service' (para 14(8)). At this stage he excluded the larger voluntary teaching hospitals, an idea strongly criticised in a counter-memorandum by Buchanan.[32] The latter argued that the political benefits gained from leaving the major teaching hospitals with their freedom would be more than offset by disadvantages to the system as a whole. In discussion Bevan acknowledged that it was not his intention to exclude the teaching hospitals altogether, but that 'special provision should be made for them within the scheme', a point of view that was not evident from the comments about 'exemption' in his memorandum.

In the short initial Cabinet discussion tentative support was forthcoming from some of Bevan's colleagues.[33] Morrison was silent at this meeting, but soon afterwards he circulated a memorandum sharply critical of Bevan's plan, and the latter replied before the discussion was taken up again.[34] Morrison mainly relied on the argument that nationalisation of hospitals deprived local government of one of its major functions, at a time when local government was already weakened by transfer of other services to ad hoc authorities. In Morrison's view it was necessary to halt the erosion of local democracy, not only as a matter of principle, but also because of the importance of local government to the Labour movement. Morrison was doubtful whether the new structure would function as Bevan claimed. If under firm ministerial direction, the Boards would lack vitality; if given greater authority they would be insufficiently accountable over their policy and expenditure.

Bevan took advantage of the admission by Morrison that nationalised services were inherently more efficient than local government agencies. He also capitalised on Morrison's difficulty in coming up with a suitable alternative. Morrison had somewhat incongruously ended up by defending joint boards, precisely the arrangement attacked by him during the Coalition Government. Bevan reasserted that nationalisation was the alternative offering fewest disadvantages. Local government in his view possessed sufficient functions and new opportunities to retain its vitality. It was unsound to leave local government with a service largely financed by the exchequer. His scheme represented a correct 'rationalisation of local government services to ensure a sensible distribution both of function and cost as between local authorities and the state'. As on the previous occasion Bevan received relatively passive support, Addison being the sole Minister to express agreement in both discussions. Attlee therefore signified approval of Bevan's plan in principle, but he allowed for further discussion when the scheme was submitted in its detailed form.[35]

A summary of the whole scheme was submitted for consideration by the Cabinet before Christmas.[36] It is not necessary to describe this document in detail because the proposals have already been outlined in the previous section. For the first time what turned out to be the permanent classification of services was introduced— Part I Central Administration, Part II Hospital and Specialist, Part III Local Authority, and Part IV Family Practitioner.

The administrative bodies for Part II hospital services were now called Regional Hospital Boards and Local Hospital Management Committees. It was considered that about twenty regions would be established; each was to be related to a teaching hospital in one of the eleven existent teaching centres. Teaching hospitals were to be publicly controlled, but accorded 'special provision' under their Board of Governors (para 12). Local clinics, domiciliary and welfare services, and even the ambulance service were detached from the hospital service in order to appease advocates of local government, and included as local authority services under Part III. Local authorities were also given a stake in Part IV services by virtue of providing health centres, which it was envisaged would house both local authority and Local Executive Committee services, and also serve as outposts for consultants. Health centres would be 'developed as fast and as widely as possible' (para 32). It was proposed to control the distribution of doctors by a new Central Committee, replacing the Central Medical Board which had been abandoned by Willink. Industrial health services, which had made a brief appearance as a putative local authority responsibility, were now dropped from consideration.

Relatively minor differences were proposed for Scotland. The ambulance service was to be administered by the Regional Hospital Boards. Because of the small size of local authorities Executive Committees administering family practitioner services would be formed by amalgamation of a number of districts. The Department of Health intended to keep control of the development of health centres in line with the proposal in the 1944 White Paper, despite the intention to develop health centres on a more extensive scale. The Scottish document was silent about administration of teaching hospitals.

Bevan's memorandum ended with a summary of the service from the point of view of the consumer. After a transitional period it was intended to provide everybody with 'a personal or family doctor, of their own choice, working in a publicly provided and equipped health centre, and undertaking the whole care of the patient in his home or at the centre' (para 54).

Opening the Cabinet discussion Bevan explained that his complex arrangements for employing general practitioners would
achieve an even distribution of doctors, eliminate the worst features
of the capitation system and 'lead eventually to a full-time salaried
service'.[37] Once again the discussion was diffuse and inconsequential. Addison and Buchanan were supportive. Greenwood was
pessimistic about the chances of early legislation. The burden of
criticism was now concentrated on financial arrangements. Morrison, Chuter Ede and Dalton were concerned that transfer of the
cost of the hospital service to the exchequer would not be offset
by a compensating reduction in the block grant to local authorities.
There was approval for Attlee's suggestion that, notwithstanding
these difficulties, Bevan should prepare a summary of his Bill.

Heads of a Bill were presented without delay. Bevan urged speed
because of uncertainty and confusion concerning the Government's
intentions. He sought authorisation for preparing a Bill and beginning confidential negotiations with interested parties.[38] His Cabinet
colleagues sought clarification on various points. They wanted an
assurance that the opportunity given to doctors to undertake private
practice would not undermine the quality of general practice.
Suggestions were made about improving recruitment and in-service
training of general practitioners. There was concern that local
authorities and trade unions might not be sufficiently represented
on what were now called 'Hospital Management Committees'.
Bevan confirmed that industrial health services would be left out
of his scheme.

The major concern was again finance. Behind the scenes Dalton
had concluded that 'the financial basis is quite unacceptable as it
stands'. He would not accept handing out large sums of exchequer
money to delegated bodies, and he realised that it would not be
possible to reduce exchequer grants to local authorities to the
required degree. Dalton agreed that either the Minister or local
authorities be made rigidly accountable for the service.[39] At the
Cabinet meeting Dalton signified these difficulties, but they were
not pressed to the point of holding up progress on the National
Health Service Bill.

The opportunity to deflect Bevan from his chosen path was now
past. Bevan soon reappeared with a report on his negotiations and
with the draft Bill.[40] Both he and Westwood were confident that
criticism could be contained. No significant changes in his Bill
were called for. Government supporters had opposed the concession
allowing private practice and private beds in a state service. They
were also suspicious about leaving remuneration to be settled by
regulation, but Bevan had explained to them that these arrangements were unavoidable. The Secretary of State reported that he

was working out a closer association between teaching hospitals and Regional Boards than was intended in England. Only two significant obstacles were introduced in this final stretch. Dalton asked for an assurance that local authorities would be warned of reductions in their exchequer grant. Secondly, Morrison and Greenwood raised difficulties about scheduling the NHS legislation in the current parliamentary session.[41] It was agreed that neither problem need impede the progress of Bevan's Bill, which was duly introduced to Parliament on 20 March 1946.

(iii) EXTERNAL DISCUSSIONS: OCTOBER 1945–MARCH 1946

Bevan's predecessor had tried to evolve a health service by negotiation. After three years of this process Bevan decided that the scheme accepted by the Government would not be open to negotiation. But he was willing to consult as widely as necessary to ensure the most effective realisation of his policy. Although called 'consultation' this new round of discussions was both as protracted and as acrimonious as the earlier negotiations. This process of attrition was also effective in wrenching further concessions out of a reluctant Minister.

In his early relations with the medical profession Bevan combined affability with inscrutability over his policies. He flirted with the élite of the Negotiating Committee at the Café Royal.[42] He made witty speeches at meetings of medical specialists. He visited the Council of the BMA. But he refused to be drawn into revealing his plan.

Bevan's intentions were not hidden for long. Early in November the left-wing popular press boldly announced 'Voluntary Hospitals to Go', 'Great Hospital Move', 'Hospital Nationalisation', and provided a rough sketch of the new hospital service.[43] Churchill immediately questioned Attlee in the House of Commons about this leak. Attlee was unforthcoming. His annoyance at the indiscretion of his colleagues was duly communicated to them.[44] In a lesser scoop the *Daily Mirror* described the whole scheme on 7 January 1946, but the additional information involved few surprises. Indeed, the proposals as a whole were regarded as a great concession to doctors. Because of these leaks the public was informed about the general nature of Bevan's proposals before they were finally accepted by the Government, and before they were released on a confidential basis to the organisations involved in negotiations. For this latter purpose Bevan produced a memorandum that was a slightly revised version of the outline of the service discussed at the Cabinet meeting on 20 December 1945.[45] Perhaps the most significant change was deletion of reference to the intention to develop health centres as fast and as widely as possible. Bevan's confidential hand-out was probably first given to a deputation from the TUC on 8 January 1946, at a meeting which initiated an intensive round of discussions which lasted until the publication of the National Health Service Bill. Having begun with the representatives of organised labour, the Minister's second meeting introduced him to the Negotiating Committee of the profession. Thereafter Bevan worked steadily through organisations in approximate order of their importance and relevance, beginning with the local authorities and the organisations representing voluntary hospitals, passing to bodies acting for major professional groups, and ending for the sake of prudence or completeness with minor groups such as medical auxiliaries and chiropodists, and with cognoscenti from alternative medicine, such as herbalists and homoeopaths. In his Second Reading speech Bevan pointed out that he had personally attended twenty conferences, and that his officials had held thirteen more. Either Westwood or Buchanan were present at the first meetings with major bodies convened by Bevan. Thereafter Westwood's officials conducted parallel discussions with representative organisations in Scotland.

Bevan's exchanges with groups associated with the Labour movement were affable. The TUC was disappointed that industrial health services were excluded from the National Health Service, but trade unionists were pleased with Bevan's assurance that unions would be represented on Regional Hospital Boards.[46] Among the local authority associations the least receptive was the County Councils Association, but following the lead of the LCC the local authority associations came into line with Bevan's scheme, on the understanding that they would be given strong representation on Regional Hospital Boards, Executive Committees, and on the central advisory machinery. Local authorities in Scotland were insistent that teaching hospitals should not be accorded 'quasi-independent' status.[47] The Socialist Medical Association was unhappy about Bevan's departure from some of Labour's favoured policies. Besides meeting Bevan its leaders kept up a lively correspondence with him, especially defending full-time salaried service in health centres, the inclusion of teaching hospitals in the regional hospital organisation, and criticising the intended segmentation of the service on the ground that co-ordination would be jeopardised.[48]

Not surprisingly the new scheme elicited the fiercest initial hostility from the voluntary hospital lobby. During negotiations preceding the 1945 election, the tide had flowed strongly in the interest of voluntary hospitals. Nationalisation looked like total reversal. Leaders of the British Hospitals Association took violent exception to 'extinction of entity, confiscation, elimination of

personal interest and a most autocratic method of appointing . . .
management'.[49] Bevan retorted that ownership was a 'fundamental
principle' of the Government upon which there could be no
retreat.[50] The two sides seemed set on a collision course. Yet the
impact was less destructive than the BHA predicted because a
sizeable element within the voluntary sector recognised positive
aspects of the Government's scheme. Substantial concessions
reduced opposition among medical staff of voluntary hospitals.
Part-time contracts would facilitate continuation of private work;
private beds were to be retained in state hospitals; guaranteed
salaries and superannuation provided protection against the vagaries of private income; hospital medical staff were promised freedom
from centralised bureaucracy together with a substantial voice
in administration at all levels; teaching hospitals were awarded
independence and special status. An added incentive of an
attractive system of merit awards, controlled by the profession
itself, was later introduced as an extra lure for better-off consultants. Given the inevitability that voluntary hospitals would in
future rely almost entirely on public funding for survival and
development, their medical staffs were easily converted to the view
that the new system introduced substantial tangible advantages to
offset any losses consequential on transfer of voluntary institutions
to state ownership. The collective mind was prepared for such a
change because leading planners among the consultants such as
Buzzard and Cohen had been pointing towards this direction of
events for some time.[51]

Reflecting this drift in opinion, representatives of the King's
Fund and the Nuffield Provincial Hospitals Trust were far less
recalcitrant than their brethren in the British Hospitals Association.
Bevan's scheme was generally accepted subject to adequate safeguards being introduced to preserve the status of teaching hospitals
and protect hospital endowment funds.[52]

Consistent with previous experience consultations with the profession were delicate and turbulent. Besides consideration of the
National Health Service scheme as a whole it was necessary to
take immediate action on certain important practical problems
touching on the income and security of doctors. The Government
needed to clarify its position concerning the sale and purchase of
practices, and in order to obtain the goodwill of doctors it was
essential to settle, once and for all, the grievances over levels of
remuneration that had been accumulating since 1911.

Willink's announcement of 3 May 1945 that sale and purchase
would not be abolished in the short term was inconsistent with
Labour thinking. A scheme in which doctors worked in publicly
provided health centres and where the Minister appointed doctors

to vacant practices rendered the sale of practices obsolete. Uncertainty over the Labour Government's policy was already undermining the value of existing practices. In order to forestall damaging consequences within the profession this minor issue was pushed to the head of Bevan's agenda. He proposed to announce the abolition of sale and purchase, with the payment of compensation at retirement or death of general practitioners, sufficient to offset the loss in the goodwill value of their practices.[53] Buchanan was unfavourable to compensation, preferring substitution of improved superannuation terms.[54] The Secretary of State was not associated with the paper on this subject presented to the Cabinet, and no Scottish representative was in attendance at the Cabinet discussion. Notwithstanding critical remarks from Morrison on procedural points, Bevan's suggestion was accepted and a draft public statement agreed. Dalton understood that £40m in compensation would be involved.[55]

Before the publication of the NHS Bill the reincarnated Negotiating Committee was more concerned with the terms of compensation than with any other issue. Once the Government's resolve was accepted, the committee set about securing advantageous terms for its clientele. Gradually the committee was weaned from its original demand for immediate compensation, but its argument for an assessment based on a standard superior to 1939 practice values was accepted. Initially the committee demanded £71.6m compensation, a figure considerably higher than originally given to the Cabinet by Dalton. In response Government representatives offered £60m, which by degrees was raised to £66m. This figure was agreed by the Negotiating Committee on the eve of publication of the NHS Bill.[56]

For the purpose of estimating compensation the BMA representative had based his calculations on the assumption that the average practice value was £4,000 and that the average net income of a general practitioner was £1,600 in 1939. Estimates of pre-war levels of remuneration of general practitioners were also relevant to the determination of appropriate income for practitioners working under the new scheme. This issue was referred to a special committee chaired by the veteran Sir Will Spens, Master of Corpus Christi College, Cambridge, since 1927, and known primarily for his committee work in the field of education. Although the Spens Report on remuneration of general practitioners was not published until 9 May 1946, the committee undertook most of its work before the Labour Government was elected. Consequently Labour became tied by findings evolved in the ethos of the Willink era.

As early as 1943 establishing accord over remuneration was regarded as a necessary precondition to gaining professional confidence in the new health service. Brown had promised to investigate capitation 'from the ground up'. The profession was persuaded to collaborate in such an inquiry only when it was made clear that new scales of payment would not presuppose full-time salaried service.[57] Brown's statement aroused the expectation that the new settlement would clear up all past injustices. The committee began work in February 1945. Spens was persuaded by the BMA that under the new scheme, although private practice would not be forbidden, its yield would be so little that the income from 'publicly organised service . . . will be in the future the only source of professional income'. In this context it was claimed by the BMA that the mean net income of general practitioners was less than £1,300, which was regarded as unjust and inadequate. The BMA was looking for an average net income of at least £2,000 for the new service, with differentials determined by list sizes rather than by salary scales.[58] Although the BMA knew 'precious little of this Government's intentions', Spens was warned that 'we are opposed to the solution by this external discretionary judgement of a man's work'.[59]

The Spens Committee was fair to the profession. Its four expert lay members were balanced by four representatives from the BMA. Since the major part of the statistical evidence and oral testimony also came from the profession it is not surprising that the findings of this committee flowed strongly in the BMA direction. The profession also scored on the remit of the committee, which authorised not only estimation of incomes required to protect past standards, but also reference to the 'social and economic status of general medical practice and its power to attract a suitable type of recruit to the profession'.[60] This broader remit opened the committee to propaganda from the profession to the effect that a radical improvement in career prospects was required in order to stave off complete collapse of professional standards.

The committee was also impressed by the strength of resistance within the BMA to any mode of payment other than capitation. While not prescribing the capitation system for the future the committee worked on the assumption that the current system of remuneration would continue because 'capitation affords a method of differentiation which is acceptable to the majority of the profession'.[61] While not explicitly obstructing a salaried service, the Spens Committee placed a formidable obstacle in the path of this alternative.

In order to adjudicate between the Ministry and the BMA concerning doctors' income, the committee was advised by Professor A Bradford Hill, the medical statistician, who conducted an investigation into pre-war earnings of a sample of 5,000 doctors.[62] The findings of Hill were more favourable to the BMA than to the health departments. On the basis of this sample the 35–65 age group was found to earn a gross income of £1,819 in 1939, which upon correction for 38% expenses gave a net income of £1,128.[63] The official side concentrated on its evidence that doctors' income from the National Health Insurance source alone mounted to an average of £1,572 in 1939, and it was argued that 25% expenses was a more realistic level. More than averages, Spens was impressed by the apparent great extent of low earnings among doctors, which he regarded as a major potential disincentive to recruitment. Spens believed that this problem could be solved by creating a prospect of high earnings for the most successful general practitioners. The formula included in the Report involved paying half the 40–50 cohort a net income of £1,300, one quarter £1,600 and one tenth £2,000, with prospects of £2,500 or more for the few highest earners. The draft proposals of Spens were slightly more generous, suggesting that 15% should earn above £1,900. At the other end of the scale Spens proposed to protect new entrants with not less than £500, which the BMA was anxious should not become translated into a basic salary.[64]

It was thought that the above proposals could be implemented by increasing the capitation fee from 10s 6d to 15s 6d, which figure was disputed by officials, who initially suggested that a capitation fee of 13s 6d would be sufficient.[65] The department estimated that the Spens package would cost £4.5m plus whatever betterment was required to take account of adjustment of professional incomes since the outbreak of war.[66]

The Spens Report attracts virtually no attention in accounts of the National Health Service negotiations. Nevertheless it is important because of its relevance in pushing the Government off course over salaried employment for general practitioners. It was even more significant in indicating the new superiority of the BMA in negotiations over levels of remuneration. It was finally a reminder that the National Health Service would face a series of incremental increases in the cost of its wages bill, which the Government would be impotent to restrain.

Neither the Negotiating Committee nor the BMA wanted negotiations to be limited to points of detail such as sale of practices or income levels. Following the precedent set by Brown and Willink they expected Bevan to work out his legislation in dialogue with them. The negotiators therefore leapt into action immediately leaks concerning Bevan's intentions appeared in the press.[67] The Minister responded that he would let them comment on his Bill, but he would not permit a 'long series of protracted negotiations'.[68]

Left somewhat in the cold the BMA responded with a grandiose gesture, announcing seven points of its basic philosophy upon which there could be no compromise. Most of the 'freedoms' defended by the BMA were not under attack or were intangible. Of the more meaningful points the Minister was warned of the strength of opposition to salaried service and to any direction of labour.[69] The Government's scheme was explained to the Negotiating Committee on 10 January 1946.[70] Only one informal discussion of the proposals was held before the publication of the Bill. In addition to the above points some traditional tenets were repeated: the Ministry of Health should give up services not directly connected with health and take over health functions of other Government departments. Doctors also demanded a 'predominant' voice in administration. Reflecting the deep-rooted fear of local authorities, assurances were sought that the latter would not dominate hospital administration, and it was urged that health centres should be transferred from local health authorities to the new regional authorities.[71]

(iv) THE NATIONAL HEALTH SERVICE ACT, 1946

As noted above, the National Health Service Bill, eventually published on 20 March 1946 (eighteen months overdue according to *The Times*), had experienced a long gestation period.[72] A complete printed Bill, dated 6 April 1945, was ready before the breakup of the wartime Coalition Government. A revised printed version is dated 2 August 1945. The first full draft of the 1946 Bill is dated 18 January 1946. Consequently, the 1946 Bill was more a product of metamorphosis than spontaneous generation. Much from the 51 clauses of April 1945 was salvaged in the 57 clauses of March 1946.[73] It is instructive to examine the major points of similarity and difference between the 1945 and 1946 versions of the Bill.

Part I in the 1945 version is considerably longer than its equivalent of 1946, because it outlines the complete central and local structure of administration. The complicated arrangements for balancing the participation of all the different agencies at the periphery in the preparation and submission of plans for the entire service find no equivalent in the 1946 Bill. The 12 clauses of Part I of the August 1945 draft are compressed to two clauses in March 1946. In both the 1945 and 1946 versions clause 1 defines the duty of the Minister to promote a comprehensive health service. The Labour version added its famous provision determining that all services would be free of charge except where express provision for a charge was made in the Bill. The second clause of 1946 described the central advisory machinery, but in rather different terms to the 1945 equivalent.

Part II in 1945 and 1946 described Hospital and Specialist Services. But the contents were strikingly different as a result of transition from a form of service provided by local health authorities drawing on facilities of voluntary agencies, to one in which the Minister took on the whole of this responsibility. Consequently the major complication of Part II in 1945 was the set of clauses (14–22) describing arrangements for contracting with voluntary hospitals, whereas in 1946 the major complication was the set of clauses (6–10) dealing with transfer of voluntary and local authority hospitals to the Minister. The 1945 version (clause 13) had permitted local authorities to provide accommodation requiring payment from patients. The 1946 Bill persisted with this provision, now proposing two classes of beds requiring payment, the lesser Amenity beds (clause 4), and the Private Patient Accommodation (clause 5).[74] A generous concession added in 1946 (clause 3(3)) provided for reimbursing patients and their escorts for travelling expenses to hospital. The ambulance service in both 1945 (clause 11) and 1946 (clause 27) was consigned to local authorities with the effect that in the 1946 Bill ambulances were not administered by their major user.

The innovations of 1946 greatly simplified the structure of hospital administration, which was now essentially reduced to only four clauses (11–14). The new Regional Hospital Boards, Hospital Management Committees, and Boards of Governors were enjoined to administer the service consistent with the directives of the Minister and relevant regulations, but the general emphasis was on devolution and autonomy. The elaborate arrangements for evolving hospital plans which had formed such a dominant element in earlier discussion documents and draft Bills were now completely abandoned. The tail end of Part II of the 1946 Bill made provision for incorporation of unincorporated medical and dental schools of London University (clause 15), provision of powers for the Minister and Hospital Boards to undertake research (clause 16, added 1 March), and for two ancillary services to be provided by the Minister, the bacteriological and blood transfusion services (clauses 15 and 16), which in the 1945 drafts had been included under miscellaneous services to be provided by the Minister in association with local authorities (clauses 44 and 45).

In the 11 February 1946 draft an important structural change was introduced, reversing the order of Parts III and IV, which dealt respectively with general medical and local authority services in 1945. Before the 1946 drafts the bulk of local authority services had been covered in Part II under hospitals, leaving only residual clinic services to be listed in Part IV, following the more substantial general medical services in Part III. Promotion of local authority services to Part III in 1946 created a logical order, beginning with nationalised hospital services, continuing with municipalised services around the nucleus of health centres, and ending with Part IV private contractor arrangements. In the new order adopted on 11 February, Part III, which at the earliest stage had comprised an unheaded list of local authority services, was entitled 'Health Services Provided by Local Health Authorities'. Notwithstanding this reordering, the list of services and contents of relevant clauses remained remarkably constant from the first printed draft of 1945 to Bill (94) of March 1946, especially with respect to Maternity and Child Welfare, Midwifery, Home Nursing, Vaccination and Immunisation, Prevention, Care and After Care, and Home Helps (clauses 32, 37, 38, 39, 40–43 in 1945; clauses 22, 23, 25, 26, 28–29 on 11 February 1946, etc). The innovations of 18 January 1946 included insertion of detailed specifications for submission of plans for services (perhaps a residue of the more elaborate planning arrangements of older drafts), a new health visiting service, and the ambulance service. In the 18 January 1946 draft the trivial health centre clause of the 1945 version (clause 33) was strengthened (clause 18) but left under general medical services; then in the 11 February draft this clause was moved to a strategically more important position at the head of local authority services (clause 18), in which position it remained on 19 March when it had become clause 21.

Apart from relegation to Part IV, the clauses dealing with general medical and dental services, pharmaceutical services and ophthalmic services underwent relatively little transmutation in the process of revision. The most obvious superficial difference, introduced at a late stage in the 1 March 1946 draft, removed the subheadings for the dental, pharmaceutical and ophthalmic services, instead lumping these under a single heading.

The Central Medical Board of the April 1945 draft was already dropped in the August 1945 draft, leaving 'Local Medical Services Committees' as the local administrative authority for these services. These bodies were rechristened 'Executive Councils' in the Labour drafts (19 March, clause 31). The essential modifications to the 1945 Bill were introduced at an early stage in drafting the Labour legislation, and not much modification occurred during subsequent drafts. The most important changes to the general medical service as embodied in the 19 March Bill comprised: insertion of elaborate arrangements for regulating succession to practices, involving establishment of a Medical Practices Committee (clause 34); prohibition of sale and purchase (clause 35), and payment of £66m compensation (clause 36). Arrangements for the other private contractor services were largely carried over from the 1945 drafts. However there were some significant changes of procedure and emphasis. In 1946 the dental service was to be directed by Executive

Councils rather than by the Central Dental Board of 1945. In 1945 local health authorities were left to organise an eye service partly involving contracting with local opticians. In 1946 Executive Councils were given responsibility for this service, and it was emphasised that this was a 'Temporary Eye Service' persisting only until it was supplanted by a hospital clinic eye service.

In drafts up to 1 March 1946 mental illness was covered by a clause included in Part II. In redrafting this clause was eliminated, and a separate Part V was created containing three clauses dealing with special provisions relating to mental and mental deficiency services.

The Second Reading debate on the National Health Service Bill in the House of Commons was relatively uneventful. Its one moment of distinction was the opening speech by Bevan, who was at his most eloquent and persuasive, or 'restrained and conciliatory' according to The Times.[75] Particularly dismal moments were the stumbling reply to Bevan by Richard Law[76] and especially an ill-considered winding-up speech by Arthur Greenwood.[77] On behalf of the Liberals, Clement Davies expressed pride in the part played by Welshmen in introducing both NHI and NHS legislation. He also pointed out that Law's father had led opposition to national health insurance on very much the same grounds as his son's opposition to the NHS Bill.[78] Notwithstanding their disagreements over means, speakers from all parties and all regions were united in their call for radical improvement of existing services.

Bevan urged that his formula was the only practicable way to 'universalise' or 'generalise the best health advice and treatment'. The profession was tempted by the guarantee of security, generous remuneration and compensation, the opportunity to continue with private practice, and more active participation in administration and policy than ever known before. The reality of such industrial democracy for doctors was offered as the antidote to irrational fears concerning civil service control. Bevan's major concession to the profession involved acceptance that the time was not ripe for introduction of full-time salaried service. Accordingly, apart from a basic salary element to assist young doctors it was proposed to adopt the profession's preference of rewarding zeal through capitation payments.

In line with the structure of the Bill, Bevan defended his tripartite organisation as a rational solution that would not impede co-operation across boundaries. The three major 'instruments' of this system were hospitals, general practitioner teams, and health centres, the last being an innovation 'to which we attach very great importance indeed'. With respect to local administration it was promised that the NHS would be an 'elastic, resilient service, subject to local influence as well as to central control'.

Despite his general exhortatory tone, Bevan warned that he would not be deflected from his course by 'sectional' or 'vested interests'. From the vantage point of his decisive electoral mandate he declared that Parliament must cease its vacillations and remember that 'the House of Commons is supreme, and the House of Commons must assert its supremacy'.[79]

The debate followed predictable lines. Conservatives complained most about the nationalisation of voluntary hospitals, which was regarded as a gratuitous assault on charitable institutions. Willink made capital out of Labour Ministers' statements in favour of voluntary hospitals during their previous incarnation in the Coalition Government.[80] Conservatives were also suspicious of Labour's intention to relegate the issue of doctors' salaries to regulations, which they exposed as a subterfuge for introducing a full-time salaried service. On the Labour side, Bevan came under criticism for not committing himself to full-time salaried service and for permitting pay beds in state hospitals.

Critics from the two sides converged in arguing against the erosion of local government involvement in the field of health. Notwithstanding his earlier conversion to regionalisation, Willink now argued that regionalisation was appropriate to mechanical and impersonal services such as electricity, but not to personal services. The Bill contained a particularly pernicious form of regionalisation because it established 'a non-elective body subject to the directions of the Minister'.[81] The most effective critique of non-elected regional authority and defence of the smaller elected authority came from Bevan's colleague, Fred Messer, an experienced Labour public health expert from Tottenham. Messer's intervention provoked irritated interruptions from Bevan. In response Messer quoted Labour Party documents and *Tribune* against Bevan. Messer wanted the Bill to be modified to 'make it democratic, make it comprehensive, and make it unified',[82] most of which was applauded by Conservative apologists for the county councils.[83] Notwithstanding the Government's supporters' timorousness about adventuring into the terra incognita of non-elected, ad hoc regional authorities for personal services, the Conservative amendment against the Bill moved by Willink was defeated by 359 to 172 votes.[84]

Despite vigorous campaigning by the BMA and the British Hospitals Association against the Bill, the Government offered no material concessions during the remaining parliamentary stages. During the Standing Committee, Committee and Report stages in the House of Commons most of the amendments emanated from the Government and they were of a technical nature. Considering the hysteria worked up outside Parliament the Conservative contribution was dutiful rather than spirited. Amendments from the Opposition were introduced to strengthen the central advisory machinery, reverse hospital nationalisation or at least increase the independence of individual Hospital Management Committees, complicate procedures for introducing health centres, transfer functions from the LCC and county councils to metropolitan and other boroughs, reduce opportunities for including a salary element in the payment of general practitioners, and eliminate arrangements for control over the distribution of doctors. The National Liberals tried to prevent the Bill coming into operation before January 1950. The only amendment to achieve success, and then only temporarily, involved substituting the High Court for the Minister in appeals against decisions of the disciplinary Tribunal introduced in connection with Part IV services. The Government were narrowly defeated at the Committee stage, but this decision was reversed at the Report stages. It was pointed out that the Tribunal was introduced as an additional protection for the profession, the Minister alone having possessed disciplinary powers under National Health Insurance.[85]

The Opposition took an unusual initiative by attempting to enforce rejection of the Bill at the Third Reading. In very much the same terms as the Second Reading amendment the new amendment invoked 'mutilation of local government', 'dangerous increase in ministerial power and patronage', 'appropriation of trust funds and benefactions', and loss of freedom and independence of the profession as its reasons for rejection of the original Bill, all of which was summed up by Key as 'five inexcusable inexactitudes'. Elimination of the Opposition amendment was carried by 261 to 113 votes.[86]

The House of Lords stepped prematurely on to the stage when Moran introduced a motion, 'while regretting any measures which might impair the general practitioners' service, welcomes proposals for the better co-ordination of the hospital services of the country'. General practitioners were an adventitious consideration, but Moran sympathised with their objections to salaried service, providing that any alternative adopted contained incentives for efficiency. Moran believed that the hospital problem was the key to the National Health Service and he was satisfied that Bevan's Bill offered the most palatable solution. Ministerial control was acceptable as a condition for injection of exchequer revenues on which voluntary hospitals were to be dependent; voluntary institutions would be immune from the 'menace' of local authority control; and teaching hospitals, 'the very essence of the voluntary hospital system' would be preserved. For the system as a whole Bevan's plan at last embodied the principle of regionalisation in its definitive form. Providing that Regional Hospital Boards were comprised of experts rather than representatives and if Hospital Management Committees were granted sufficient autonomy, Moran was satisfied with the Government's proposals.[87] Lords Donoughmore and Inman, representing voluntary hospitals of London, supported Moran's line. Horder maintained a rearguard action, damning the Bill as a fundamental assault on the liberties of the profession, but his presentation of a solid wall of opposition from the Royal Colleges was undermined by the freshly expressed qualified support of his own Royal College of Physicians for the Government's proposals.[88]

Moran's timely intervention was of material assistance to the Government in steering the NHS Bill through the House of Commons, and it was subversive to Opposition attempts to invoke unanimous support from the profession. The April debate also provided a useful rehearsal for the much later formal deliberations of the House of Lords on the NHS Bill. The Second Reading debate exposed no changes of heart. Aware of the much greater strength of the Opposition in the House of Lords, Jowitt gave assurances that the Minister would not exercise heavy-handed control, that regulations approved by Parliament would entail further protection for the profession, and that there would be effective delegation to Hospital Management Committees. Following publication of the Spens Report on the remuneration of general practitioners, a similar review was promised for consultants.

Presenting the Opposition case Lord Munster repeated the main points of criticism made earlier in the House of Commons. Moran, Horder and the voluntary hospital speakers repeated their lines. They were still in discord. Bevan received the blessing of Lord Beveridge who saw this Bill as the appropriate antidote for the giant of disease. For the first time there would be a 'true Ministry of Health, a national authority with the duty and with the power of attacking disease as a national enemy'.[89]

Consideration of the NHS Bill in the House of Lords occasioned re-enactment of recent Commons debates over amendments, and with similar results. For instance the Government resisted elevation of Hospital Management Committees to the status of Boards of Governors, compulsory delegation from county councils to non-county boroughs, or substitution of the High Court for the Minister in disciplinary appeals. In general the Government tried to bend with the wind, offering minor concessions, with the hope of avoiding major defeats. This strategy was largely successful, although in some cases confusion emerged over the handling of promised concessions. The Lords stage therefore produced a small crop of amendments and clarifications inspired from Opposition circles. Thus Lord Llewellin and his associates were rather more successful than their counterparts in the House of Commons.

In response to a battery of amendments concerning protection of the endowments of voluntary hospitals the Government offered two small concessions, one securing respect for the objects of transferred endowments and the other removing the disincentive to making gifts to hospitals between the passage of the Act and the Appointed Day.[90] Although at the Commons Committee stage Bevan had resisted enhancement of the formal status of Hospital Management Committees he had promised that their responsibilities would be protected by regulation. In the Lords Committee stage Lord Luke and others complained that the responsibilities of HMCs were not defined clearly enough in the Bill. Following a sympathetic response from Jowitt, a more explicit statement concerning the degree of control and management exercised by HMCs was introduced at the Report stage by the Government.[91] Although not regarding it as necessary, the Government also agreed to an amendment allowing HMCs to sue and be sued in their own name, even when acting as agents of RHBs.[92] Moran was unsuccessful in persuading the Government to accept amendments making statutory provision for House Committees and Medical Staff Committees although he was promised that this outcome would be encouraged where practicable.[93]

Addington withdrew an amendment concerning delegation of local authority clinic functions from county councils to non-county boroughs on the understanding that the Government would give 'willing and friendly consideration' to introducing discretionary arrangements to this effect. However this concession met with rooted objections from officials. Addington was left to reintroduce his amendment at the Report stage, where it was withdrawn.[94] Lord Balfour of Burleigh was more successful with his amendment to attain delegation from the LCC to metropolitan boroughs. This proposal had been debated and defeated at the Committee and Report stages in the House of Commons. However, exploiting the division in London local government, and urging fidelity to the agreement reached between Willink and the rival parties, Balfour achieved a majority for his amendment.[95]

Llewellin introduced an amendment determining that regulations relating to terms and conditions of medical practice would be published at least three months before the Appointed Day. Although Jowitt expressed sympathy at the Committee stage, no concession was offered on the grounds that late emendations might be required. However, assurances were forthcoming that as much notice as possible would be given with regulations.[96] Llewellin achieved more with an amendment on the controversial issue of payment by salary. The Government had already resisted an attempt at the Commons Committee stage to establish payment by capitation except under exceptional circumstances. Llewellin reintroduced this amendment at the Lords Committee stage. Despite the Government argument that a salary element was fundamental to its thinking about the general practitioner service, and notwithstanding its contention that determination of salary structure by regulation was consistent with National Health Insurance precedent, Llewellin's amendment was carried with both Conservative and Liberal support. At the Third Reading Llewellin conceded that he would be satisfied if a guarantee was provided that the salary element would not be more than 25% of total NHS income.[97]

Some minor concessions concerning the general practitioner service were more willingly offered. It was agreed to take account of the views of relatives and partners in determining succession to practices; penalties connected with the sale of good-will were slightly modified; and it was agreed that general practitioners could be represented by counsel at the disciplinary Tribunal.

There was much discussion concerning introduction of a new clause specifically guaranteeing a service for the deaf, but it was unclear whether such a provision should be included under Part II or Part IV of the Act. Despite the sympathetic backing of Addison, Bevan refused to accept a new clause, asking the deaf to be content with his assurances that the comprehensive service would take care of their needs.[98]

A final minority issue related to denominational hospitals. Bevan had already given an assurance on this subject at the Commons Committee stage. A new clause ensuring the preservation of denominational hospitals was proposed by the Earl of Iddesleigh. This was withdrawn on the understanding that an equivalent clause would be introduced by the Government, which was done at the Report stage. But the new clause left Iddesleigh dissatisfied because it gave no guarantee that the denominational character of hospital staffs would be protected. However, Bevan was unwilling to offer further concessions to the denominational interest.[99]

Of the 82 Lords' amendments considered by the House of Commons about 12 were Opposition-inspired. Of the latter, 10 were accepted without demur. The two most substantial Opposition amendments, relating to delegation from the LCC to metropolitan boroughs and payment of general practitioners by capitation, were defeated by 296 to 134, and 303 to 128 votes respectively. The slight difference in these margins may have reflected disquiet in Labour circles over the arrangements for local authority services in London.[100] The House of Lords did not insist on either of their rejected amendments. The Bill received the Royal Assent on 6 November 1946.[101]

The smooth passage of the NHS Bill through the House of Lords testifies to the consistency with which the Government held to its firm but conciliatory line on its controversial health service legislation. The Government had patiently steered the NHS Bill through 32 days of Commons' and 10 days of Lords' deliberations. Bevan almost merited election to the rank of statesman. The consistency of his performance was spoiled by an ill-considered quip made at the Committee stage. Responding to taunts about his Second Reading comment that the medical profession was not ripe for salaried service, he retorted that 'there is all the difference in the world between plucking fruit when it is ripe and plucking it when it is green'. For a leadership of the BMA desperate for tangible evidence that Bevan was lacking in good faith, this remark was the key to rejuvenating their campaign against the new Act.[102]

(v) THE NATIONAL HEALTH SERVICE (SCOTLAND) ACT, 1947

As one of the great nurseries of modern medicine Scotland jealously guarded its medical traditions. Scotland's health service legislation in general paralleled that applied south of the border, but was more than a mirror image of the English version. The requirement to produce a separate National Health Service Act for Scotland was never in doubt.

Separate legislation was advantageous in that it permitted adaptation to the characteristic administrative and geographical conditions of Scotland. This separation also enabled the Secretary of State to take up certain options that could equally well have been introduced in England and Wales. But the two Bills were so similar in general composition that critics could castigate the Secretary of State's Bill as a faint echo of its English counterpart. In order to avoid confusion, parliamentary discussion of the Scottish Bill was deferred until the English Bill had completed its passage through the House of Lords.[103] Instructions for 'translation' of the English Bill into the Scottish form were given to the parliamentary draftsman in March 1946. A first print was available in May 1946. The Legislation Committee gave permission for the Bill to go forward, and it was laid before the House of Commons at the end of the session, and again in its final form on 26 November 1946.[104] It then took some six months to complete the legislative process, leaving only just over a year before the eventually adopted

Appointed Day, and creating difficulties in synchronising the delicate negotiations with the medical and dental professions in the two countries.

The major differences between the English and Scottish Bills were relatively few, and they have already been mentioned in the above account of the evolution of policy. First, it was planned to deal with the contentious issue of hospital endowments by temporarily vesting them in the new Boards of Management, while evolving a reallocation scheme through a Hospital Endowments Commission (modelled upon the School Endowments Commission of 1928 upon which Westwood had served) to be appointed for a five-year term by the Secretary of State (clause 7). Secondly, it was intended to place all hospitals under Boards of Management and within a unified regional hospital framework (clause 11), an arrangement which itself ruled out the English method for dealing differently with the endowments of teaching and non-teaching hospitals. Thirdly, responsibility for the development of health centres was located with the Secretary of State, with powers of delegation to local authorities (clause 15). Fourthly, the ambulance service was to become the responsibility of the Secretary of State rather than local authorities, with the result that ambulances would be provided under the hospital service (clause 16).

The above points by no means exhaust the differences between the two Bills. A multiplicity of minor differences included: absence of ex officio members on the Scottish Health Services Council; a closer and more explicitly defined relationship between Regional Hospital Boards and Boards of Management; greater university representation on bodies concerned with hospital administration and appointments; arrangements for compulsory amalgamation of local authority areas for the purpose of establishing local health authorities or Executive Councils; appointment committees for medical and dental specialists to include nominees of a national panel of specialists; and the ability of Executive Councils to provide houses for doctors and dentists, in line with the existing Highlands and Islands Medical Service.

The Second Reading debate on the Scottish Bill opened with a laborious and pedantic exposition of differences between the two health schemes by Westwood. It was promised that the special virtues of the Highlands and Islands Medical Service would be protected and extended to the nation as a whole. Identification of the new service with the older pioneer scheme was particularly useful to the Government because the latter involved payment of grants to general practitioners which it was claimed provided a respectable precedent for introduction of universal basic salaries.

For the Opposition, J S C Reid proposed an amendment taking exception to the Bill on grounds of over-centralisation of power in the hands of the Secretary of State, unjustifiable diversion of endowments, interference with the doctor-patient relationship, and inconsistency with the Scottish traditions of medical education and research. Reid was less pedestrian than Westwood and his statement of the Opposition case was superior to the performance of Law at the equivalent stage in the English proceedings. Among the Opposition speakers Elliot and Galbraith were particularly competent. In addition to their use of standard objections against both Bills the Opposition concentrated on lack of even-handedness respecting the status and endowments of the teaching hospitals in England and Scotland. They also alleged that the Secretary of State was aspiring to even greater centralised control of the service than his English counterpart. Following Buchanan's reply to objections, framed somewhat autobiographically, the Government carried the division by 273 to 123.[105]

The Standing Committee stage lasted from 28 January to 20 March 1947. Because of concern about the timetable, in late February Buchanan persuaded the committee to increase its meetings from twice to three times a week, much to the irritation of the Opposition.[106] Neither this stage nor the day into which the Committee, Report, and Third Reading were compressed resulted in difficulties for the Government.[107] Numerous minor Government amendments were taken. At the Standing Committee and afterwards both sides criticised the wording concerning the boundary between benefits to mothers and children available free and those for which charges could be levied. Labour speakers were reminded of the indignity of means-tested benefits pre-war.[108] The more sustained Opposition amendments designed to protect the number of private beds, modify penalties relating to sale of practices, and remove powers of the Secretary of State to provide services where these would otherwise have been inadequate, were comfortably defeated.

Introducing the Third Reading, Westwood's speech folded up prematurely owing to a misjudgement. Gallacher dismissively called Westwood 'Wee Joe'. Buchanan was congratulated by Elliot for his handling of the Bill at the Standing Committee stage. In a spirited critique of the Bill Conservatives dwelt on the good qualities of the voluntary system and the achievements of Scottish medicine. The Communist Gallacher reminded them that the Scottish people enjoyed the poorest health of any nation in Western Europe. Macpherson gave as his grounds for opposing the Bill destruction of local initiative, absence of co-ordination between the three branches of the organisation, and insufficiency of personnel to mount an effective service. In summing up Galbraith stated the more conventional objections to the Bill, 'centralisation of control, the unnecessary interference with the freedom and independence of the medical profession and of medical institutions, and the incursion of officialdom into the field of medical education'. Buchanan replied to critics and extolled the merits of the scheme, securing a majority of 143 against 54.[109]

In a quiet Second Reading debate in the House of Lords the Bill was explained and defended in concluding remarks by Lord Morrison.[110] The Committee, Report and Third Reading stages took place on 12 May 1947. In amicable exchanges between a small group of peers a number of minor amendments were introduced, all of which were duly accepted by the House of Commons. Following pressure from Lord Elgin and Kincardine concerning clauses 7 and 8 it was agreed to limit reallocations by the Hospital Endowments Commission to hospital uses, and to extend the life of the Commission from five to seven years.[111] With respect to clause 11 it was agreed in response to the Earl of Rosebery that Regional Hospital Boards should not limit their consultations to universities in framing schemes for Boards of Management.[112]

The Earl of Selkirk and the Marquess of Linlithgow eventually succeeded in devising a form of words acceptable to the Government giving more flexible arrangements for the composition of committees responsible for consultant appointments. The effect of this change was to ensure under clause 14 appropriate university representation on teaching appointment committees.[113] With respect to clause 15, the Government introduced an amendment making it explicit that school health services would be among the facilities available at health centres.[114] Having resisted efforts by the Duke of Montrose to obtain specific mention of services for the deaf in earlier clauses of the Bill, the Government acquiesced to an insignificant change in clause 17 which included research into hearing aids among the research functions permissible under this legislation.[115]

Tension was at its greatest in discussion of the Government's intentions with respect to salaried service of general practitioners. Somewhat reluctantly the peers allowed this issue to be decided in discussions between the Government and the profession, and the outcome to be reflected in regulations. No division was forced and the only accepted amendment to clause 34 stemmed from Lord Saltoun, the effect of which was to make it explicit that patients could change, as well as choose, their family doctor.[116] A minor amendment in clause 43 emanating from the Earl of Selkirk was accepted to ensure that in disciplinary tribunal hearings the accused would be given a written statement of the charge and complaint.[117]

The only other House of Lords amendment was introduced by the Government to clarify arbitration procedures concerning the transfer of hospitals to the Secretary of State.

The Third Reading debate in the House of Lords was a fittingly mild affair with the participants in the previous discussions coming together in harmony to applaud the new service, with Morrison serving as their choragus.[118] Thus, emerging consensus among the politicians was at least evident in the last scene of the legislative process. But this reckoning takes no account of reactions within the medical profession. When the hard task of gaining the confidence of the medical profession began in earnest in the autumn of 1947 Westwood was replaced by the more formidable Woodburn.

(vi) INEVITABLE CONFLICT

When devising means for translating the National Health Service legislation into practice the Government was entering a house haunted with ghosts from 1911. The acrimonious controversy leading up to the Appointed Day was punctuated with reference from both sides to parallels with the 1911 National Health Insurance legislation. From the Government's point of view the Lloyd George experience showed the necessity for standing firm in the name of democracy and on the authority of Parliament against irresponsible elements within the BMA. From the perspective of the BMA the humiliation of 1911 had given the Government the sense that it could ignore the traditions of a liberal profession. To the elderly BMA leadership events before 1914 were not such distant memories. Guy Dain, their Chairman, had served on the BMA Council since 1921. Most of the prominent negotiators had qualified before 1918. The whole tenor of the BMA campaign was conditioned by the fear that history was likely to repeat itself. The credibility of the BMA Council rested on its policy of vigilance, which retrospectively looks like overreaction, but on this occasion they were determined to prevent the lapse of their membership into the defeatism and complacency that had proved their downfall in earlier times. The Government view that its legislation embodied ample and special concessions to the profession was consequently not shared by the BMA leadership.

The primary difficulty for the Government was persuading a BMA which was deeply disenchanted with the NHS legislation to collaborate amicably in framing regulations and setting up the machinery for administration of the new health service. A further major complication was presented by the long-running dispute between the doctors, dentists and the Government over levels of remuneration. Discord over NHI capitation and interpretation of the Spens Report permeated discussions between the Government

and the profession concerning the new service, and the remuneration issue contributed to souring relations between the two
sides. A final complication worth noting was created by the late
completion date of the Scottish legislation, which caused difficulties
in synchronising discussions concerning the two divisions of the
health service.

Naturally the Government hoped that the medical profession
would bow to the will of Parliament and participate constructively
in setting up the new service. The leadership of the BMA regarded
matters differently. In their view, since the Government had
been unwise enough to undertake legislation at variance with the
traditions of the profession, it should make belated concessions not
only in framing regulations, but also through introducing amending
legislation. The gulf between the partners in the great new experiment in health care was formidable.

With characteristic pugnacity Dain pronounced that 'a conflict
is inevitable'.[119] Yet at the outset the omens were not entirely
inauspicious. Henry Souttar, President of the BMA, expressed
confidence that the profession would accept the Government's
scheme. Charles Hill, the influential secretary of the BMA, advised
the Government to make concessions over part-salary and control
of distribution of general practitioners, in which case the profession
would accept the abolition of sale and purchase of practices despite
its reservations concerning legal difficulties likely to be faced under
certain partnership arrangements.[120] These three issues were raised
at Bevan's first meeting with the profession to discuss the NHS
Bill, but no concessions were offered because it was held that
controls over distribution and the basic salary had already been
reduced to a minimum necessary for consistency with the principles
upon which the new service was based. It was explained that the
basic salary was essential to protect the position of young entrants,
while the ability to close over-doctored areas was necessary to
guarantee correction of imbalance in the distribution of doctors.
Amendment of the complex clauses concerning abolition of sale
and purchase was promised, but only if the courts exposed ambiguities in the Act. Harsh penalties for offenders were defended as
necessary consequences of the generous compensation offered for
the abolition of the sale of goodwill.

Subsequent meetings between Bevan and the Negotiating Committee of the profession exposed the extent of their disagreement
and also the limitations of compromise from the Government side.
Bevan was for instance unaccommodating on certain issues upon
which pressure was being exerted in Parliament for amending the
NHS Bill. Thus Bevan opposed emendation of the structure of

hospital administration, and introduction of right of appeal to the courts for general practitioners facing disciplinary charges.

Bevan resisted amendments to the legislation, but he was not entirely intransigent. He pointed out that his acceptance of private beds in state hospitals had run into opposition from Labour colleagues. He was willing to extend this scheme to admit a proportion of beds upon which there was no ceiling to private fees, but he refused to provide grants for private patients equivalent to the cost of NHS treatment. He was also not prepared to guarantee that private clinics would not be taken over by purchase, but he offered to tolerate profit-making nursing homes and also to affirm that take-over would be an unlikely event. He offered to give consultants more protection under complaints procedures, and to give greater autonomy to Hospital Management Committees. Unit house committees and medical committees were given Bevan's blessing, but he argued that it was impracticable to force their establishment in all situations. He agreed to take note of the recommendations of hospital medical committees in making appointments to Hospital Management Committees, but refused to accept direct nominations.[121] Concerning Part III services Bevan agreed to consult the Central Health Services Council on health centre development. He also accepted that local authority plans should be submitted to Regional Hospital Boards for comment. He was not willing to coerce local health committees to co-opt representatives from the medical profession, but he agreed to encourage this practice.

With respect to succession to general practice under Part III of the Bill, Bevan promised that the role of Executive Councils and Local Medical Committees would be strengthened to ensure that in the normal course of events selection would be made at the local level rather than by the Medical Practices Committee.

Any credit gained by Bevan with the profession as a result of the above concessions was wiped out by his apparent evasiveness concerning implementation of the Spens findings, which implied increasing capitation from 10s 6d to 15s. The official side offered an increase of NHI capitation to 12s 6d, on condition that the profession entered into discussions concerning application of the Spens recommendations to the National Health Service. The profession responded by refusing to discuss any remuneration issues relating to the NHS until the Government conceded full application of Spens principles to the NHI situation. Faced with impasse Bevan threatened to impose a capitation of 12s 6d on an interim basis.[122]

The above events were taken as a sign of the Government's ill-will towards the profession, thus contributing to the inflamed tone of the Annual Representatives Meeting held in July 1946, where Dain unleashed rhetoric that was to become a commonplace during the next two years. Bevan was denounced as a 'dictator'; doctors were warned that they would fall under the control of civil servants and that they would be themselves reduced to civil servant status. The Government's proposals seemed inexcusable on grounds of efficiency, in which case the BMA leadership was persuaded that they were the product of doctrinaire socialism. The NHS was being used as a vehicle for subjecting their profession to the policy of nationalisation being applied elsewhere in the economy. The Annual Representative Meeting agreed to hold a plebiscite to determine whether the profession would co-operate in framing regulations for the new service.[123] In the run-up to this vote Dain delivered one of his most vitriolic speeches, repeatedly castigating Bevan as the 'Medical Service Dictator' intent on making doctors into salaried civil servants. Both Dain and Hill referred ominously to striking. Hill declared that doctors could not be forced into a choice between 'Bevan or Belsen'.[124] Unfortunate publicity for the Government, coming at the worst time, and confirming the fears of the BMA leadership, was provided by the 'Willesden affair' in which the local authority attempted to force its medical staff into unions.[125]

Bearing in mind the strength of the campaign for a negative vote, and the self-denial of Bevan over defending his position in public controversy, the plebiscite result was not completely disastrous for the Government. On an 81% poll, 46% voted in favour of discussions on the regulations, whereas 54% voted against. However it was ominous that 11,400 out of 17,800 general practitioner principals were against discussions, despite the known risks of a boycott.[126]

Bevan met this rebuff with stoic resignation, issuing a brief conciliatory statement calling for 'wiser counsels'. The Times was critical of both parties. The reckless and emotional BMA leadership had not been sufficiently countered by persuasive argument by Bevan, with the result that his concessions were overlooked and his policies had become too readily 'interpreted as the first sinister steps in a socialist conspiracy to rob doctors of their freedom'.[127]

Having assisted the Government in the House of Lords over its NHS legislation, Moran now worked behind the scenes for an accommodation between the BMA and the Ministry of Health. After overcoming objections from his physician colleagues Moran obtained support from the Presidents of the other two Royal Colleges for a joint letter to Bevan appealing for clarification on points standing in the way of further negotiations with the profession. In response Bevan repeated that he had rejected full-time salaried service and that remuneration would be based substantially on capitation. Although expressing a preference for a universal salary element, he now agreed to negotiate on this point. On the appeals Tribunal, Bevan reiterated his view that the new system gave enhanced protection for doctors. With respect to the direction of labour he argued that a Medical Practices Committee comprising seven out of nine members who were medical practitioners appointed after consultation with the medical profession was likely to be sensitive to the local situation, where in any case the initiative for appointments would normally lie.[128] In view of the likelihood that the Royal Colleges would enter into separate negotiations with the Minister on regulations, the BMA Council agreed to recommend a Special Representative Meeting to follow suit, providing that it was understood that a further plebiscite would be held to pronounce on the results, advice which the Meeting accepted by an overwhelming majority.[129] After brief formalities the Negotiating Committee was back in action, the negotiating parties splitting into six groups to investigate proposed regulations in microscopic detail.[130]

Between March and November 1947, the best part of a year, the experts were locked in confidential discussions. The most intractable problems were faced by the General Practice sub-committee. After seven meetings this sub-committee ground to a halt at the beginning of October 1947. The meetings were largely concerned with technical issues, although the differences of opinion evident in May 1946 were still very much apparent.[131] In late October the Negotiating Committee withdrew to prepare its case in the light of the previous discussions. On 7 November the committee issued a comprehensive document which was already printed for distribution to the profession when the two sides met for their last meeting to consider the extent of their remaining disagreements. This meeting demonstrated that virtually no progress towards a settlement had been made. The two sides were ossified in the stances assumed in May 1946. Gone were the niceties exchanged at the earlier stage in negotiations. Bevan and Woodburn defended their entrenched positions competently and with aggression. Bevan accused Dain of betraying the conditions upon which the negotiations were mounted by preparing a printed statement in advance of completion of the exercise. The accusation of dictatorship was now turned on Dain, whose 'pronunciamento' was taken as a demand for a new Act in defiance of the will of Parliament. The whole ground of the previous negotiations was covered, but with little will toward compromise. An example of one of the longer discussions was the one and a half hours spent on the function of the Medical Practices Committee, in which both sides repeated their positions, with no further concessions emerging from Bevan.[132]

Shortly after the above meeting the 'Case' of the Negotiating Committee was published, together with a formal reply and a special message to the individual doctor from Bevan.[133] The Negotiating Committee was uncompromising in its insistence on unrestricted movement of doctors, maintenance of sale and purchase of practices, and payment by capitation, as well as on its other more minor demands for strengthening the position of consultants and general practitioners. Bevan's response conceded virtually nothing beyond what had been offered to the Negotiating Committee in May 1946 and made public during parliamentary debates on the NHS Bill. The only significant modification introduced at this stage was acceptance that from 1949 onwards Executive Councils would be allowed to elect their own chairmen. Bevan's document argued for support from the profession on the basis of compromises already made. He believed that the scheme was now consistent with the seven principles announced by the profession in December 1945. The Minister reserved only those powers essential for his accountability to Parliament. The Act 'will be found to represent a degree of decentralisation and a degree of professional administration which is probably unequalled in any other field in which a Minister remains completely answerable to the nation for its good or ill administration'.

In the judgement of the BMA Council Bevan had failed to respond to their legitimate requests. His proposals were in conflict 'with traditions and standards of a great profession'. This view was strongly supported by a Special Representative Meeting which agreed to take a majority adverse vote including 13,000 general practitioners as sufficient for rejection of the Minister's proposals.[134] In the few weeks before the plebiscite the BMA campaign reached its crescendo. Members of the Royal Colleges came under pressure not to break ranks with the BMA leadership, conciliatory gestures being denounced as apostasy. The Government's proposals were assailed in the columns of the *BMJ* by numerous letters from anxious doctors, apocalyptic captions calling for resistance against dictatorship in the name of liberty, fierce editorials, and reports of angry speeches by Dain and his henchmen. Most of the stories concerning Bevan's lack of civility towards the negotiators derive from this period. The profession increasingly fell under the spell of the BMA ghazis, losing sight of the more impartial stance taken at this time by *The Lancet* and *The Times*.[135]. Both of these journals felt that Bevan had needlessly sacrificed the advantage of his position by resisting concessions on minor points to which the profession attached great importance. The trickle of concessions offered were thought to be no substitute for a properly negotiated agreement. Illustrative of minor points of sacrifice which contributed little towards improving the general situation was the offer made by Bevan to *The Lancet* early in 1948 that he would appoint an impartial committee of lawyers to examine interpretation of the controversial clauses concerning partnership agreements. This concession made in response to an isolated query was a more tangible gesture towards the doctor's position than anything conceded in the protracted negotiations of 1947.[136]

After exhibiting a degree of self-control quite alien to his temperament for more than two years Bevan's patience was at last exhausted. The aggressive instinct apparent at his meeting with the profession in December 1947 was given full vent in the new year. A speech on his own ground in Pontypridd attacked the slogans and distortions of the BMA leadership. The profession was entreated to submit to the will of Parliament.[137]

The sharp deterioration in relations with the profession and Bevan's sense that there would be a heavy vote against participation in the NHS necessitated consultation with the Cabinet, where agreement was given to the above-mentioned announcement regarding examination of the adequacy of safeguards for partners under existing partnership agreements. Bevan was satisfied that no further concessions were called for and that none should be given before the Appointed Day. The Cabinet agreed that participation of doctors in the scheme would only be secured if the Government mounted an effective publicity campaign, which it was agreed to initiate by the unusual device of a motion in the House of Commons welcoming the new service.[138] The agreed terms for this motion noted that the Appointed Day for the National Health Service was fixed for 5 July. The House of Commons was invited to welcome 'the coming into force on that date of this measure which offers to all sections of the community comprehensive medical care and treatment and lays for the first time a sound foundation for the health of the people; and is satisfied that the conditions under which all the professions concerned are invited to participate are generous and fully in accord with their traditional freedom and dignity'.[139]

Bevan warmed up for the debate on the above motion by attacking the BMA's conduct of its plebiscite, warning well in advance that he was not willing to accept the validity of a negative vote.[140] The speech introducing the Government motion on 9 February is remembered by Bevan's biographer as 'one of the most coruscating he had ever delivered'. The BMA leadership was called 'raucous voiced', 'politically poisoned', and it was accused of 'organised sabotage' and of 'squalid political conspiracy'. But the major part comprised a spirited but straightforward defence of the Government's position concerning abolition of sale and purchase, basic salary, partnership agreements, and the appeals procedure. The Government's record of concession was defended, while the blame for inflexibility was aimed back at the Negotiating Committee. Leading the Opposition assault Butler scored points against the formidable Minister, but his approach was more conciliatory than other Opposition contributions. The Government carried the vote by 337 against 178.[141] While Bevan's speech was heartening to Government supporters as a public vindication of their record, elsewhere it was viewed as a further set-back to a negotiated settlement.

The BMA plebiscite confirmed a hardening of attitude among doctors. On an 82% poll, only 4,735 approved of the Act in its current form, whereas 40,814 disapproved. Of consultants, general practitioners, assistants, and whole-time hospital doctors 25,340 were against accepting the scheme in its current form, while 4,084 were in favour. A similar majority supported abiding by the Representative Meeting's decision concerning boycotting the service.[142] The above results were greeted with ecstatic jubilation at a long Special Representative Meeting on 17 March.[143]

Breakdown of negotiations concerning broader issues disrupted the long-running negotiations over implementation of the Spens Report on general practitioners' remuneration. After narrowly avoiding withdrawal of contracts by doctors, discussions had resumed in October 1946 when the Government conceded that Spens principles should be applied to NHI capitation. Quite quickly the official side increased its offer of an interim increase in capitation from 12s 6d to 15s 6d, which satisfied the profession and cleared the way for consideration of levels of remuneration under the NHS.[144] Argument on suitable capitation levels for the new service was held up pending conclusions of the General Practice Negotiating sub-committee concerning such issues as the percentage of the population for whom coverage should be provided. The doctors hoped for a capitation of 20s; the Treasury favoured 17s. Just before the sensitive meeting in December 1947, Cripps gave his agreement to 18s, the figure favoured by the health departments, and regarded by Bevan as his final non-negotiable offer.[145]

The 18s capitation fee and the method proposed for applying Spens principles to general practitioners' remuneration were explained to the Negotiating Committee and to the wider profession in the memorandum circulated by Bevan in December 1947. These proposals were also explained to Spens and accepted by him as a fair implementation of his Report, although he was not satisfied that sufficient weight was given for increase in practice expenses.[146]

The doctors' representatives made the same point, and they also argued that 20% betterment was inadequate. However at this stage their primary objection related to the proposed £300 basic salary component rather than to the level of remuneration. By way of demonstrating the principled root of this grievance the BMA policy document declared that their argument with the Government was not about money.[147]

The increasing tendency of the dental profession to echo the militancy of the BMA introduced a further irritating complication for the Government. Dentists experienced inhibitions about the scheme similar to those of their brethren in general practice. The future service was designed to employ dentists on a full-time salaried basis working in health centres. When it emerged that health centres were an uncertain future projection, dentists became more concerned with securing an advantageous position with respect to the interim service arrangements derived from the existing NHI dental benefit model. As in the case of general practitioners, dentists wanted substantial improvement of existing NHI rates before agreeing to participate in the Spens review of dentists' incomes. Warding off incipient dental strikes, the Government's offer of an interim increase and the promise to backdate any Spens agreement provided respite and drew the dental organisations into the exhaustive deliberations of the Spens Committee, the report of which was not published until May 1948. In the meantime the relatively smooth negotiations about framing regulations for the new service were interrupted when a meeting of the Dental Consultative Committee with the Minister exposed fundamental differences concerning the new service. Led by the BDA the dentists wanted abandonment of the scale of fees method of payment and substitution of a grant-in-aid mechanism, and they objected to continuation of prior approval, except for extractions and dentures for the under-21s. Neither of these proposals was acceptable to Bevan.[148] Shortly afterwards the BDA Council recommended its members to boycott the new service until the Government accepted revised terms of service.[149]

The BMA plebiscite result of March 1948 illustrated how little progress had been made since the previous plebiscite of December 1946. If anything relations between the BMA and the Minister had hardened; hostilities were being conducted on more fronts; and the urgency for settlement was the greater in view of the imminence of the Appointed Day. The various arms of the press differed in apportionment of the blame, although there was unity in prognostication of disaster. But the threatened storm faded and suddenly there was light.

As in the winter of 1946 Lord Moran was the agent of mediation. He engineered a resolution of the comitia of the Royal College of Physicians calling for an amendment Act to preclude whole-time salaried service and thus attract willing co-operation from all branches of the profession.[150] The resolution was forwarded to Bevan first informally, and then formally. On the latter occasion the other two Royal Colleges also wrote advocating a similar solution.[151] The Government response was a short statement delivered by Bevan in the House of Commons and repeated by Addison in the House of Lords on 7 April 1948.[152] The soothing tone of Bevan was suggestive of major compromise. In reality the new concessions offered were of relatively limited importance. It was agreed that the assurances given concerning salaried service should now be backed up by legislation. Such legislation had previously been resisted on the grounds that it would become the thin end of the wedge to more extensive revising legislation. But the already announced decision, now repeated, that legislation would be introduced if necessary on partnership agreements, rendered legislation on other outstanding items easier to accept.[153]

The most sensitive issue touched upon in the above statement concerned treatment of basic salary in the draft regulations. It was now proposed to abandon universal imposition of basic salary in favour of its application to new entrants for three years, and to other practitioners on request.

Bevan was warmly congratulated in both Houses, by Moran among others. Moran also wrote separately to express his delight.[154] Bevan thanked Moran for contributing 'the most helpful thing said by any doctor in the whole of this business'.[155] The new spirit of reconciliation ushered in a brief flurry of final conclusive negotiations, beginning with a conference between the Health Ministers and six representatives of the BMA (Dain, Horder, Hill, A L Abel, J A Brown and E A Gregg) on 12 April to review their differences.[156] Despite the civil tone of their exchanges Bevan argued his case vehemently and was clearly reluctant to go beyond concessions already announced. The summary of official replies to BMA queries was received calmly by the leaders of the profession, in which atmosphere three further meetings were held to reach a final decision concerning amending legislation and remuneration.[157]

The official side pressed the advantages of a short Bill to give immediate effect to the most basic demands of the profession. It was hoped to limit the Bill to two or three areas, first, the already promised prohibition of full-time salaried service, secondly, the minor provision allowing Executive Councils to elect their own chairmen, and thirdly the clarification of provision on sale and

purchase with respect to partnership agreements if such a recommendation was made by the legal committee.

Undeterred by the threat of delay, the profession wanted the
Amendment Act extended to cover a further nine points. The
latter included a variety of long-standing demands concerning
limitation of the powers of the Medical Practices Committee, and
right of appeal to the courts, both points upon which the Government was unwilling to make concessions. The Ministry of Health
was however willing to accept a provision for co-option of medical
representatives on local authority health committees, but this idea
was abandoned in view of opposition from Scotland. The profession
made a strong bid to obtain upward revision of the £66m compensation for abolition of sale of practices, but this demand for
amendment was dropped in the light of counter-arguments that
the £66m was over-generous.

Bevan agreed to extend the legislation to include more elaborate
arrangements for selecting the medical member of the disciplinary
Tribunal, and also permit a levy upon relevant practitioners to
support local medical, pharmaceutical and dental committees, in
line with the arrangement existing under National Health
Insurance. It was agreed to take care of other worries of the
profession in the course of framing regulations, or by discussion
at the appropriate moment.

The discussions in May 1948 were as much preoccupied with
remuneration as with the amending legislation. Thus two years
after publication of the Spens Report on general practitioners'
remuneration, agreement was at last reached on salary terms for
entry into the new service.

Reluctantly Bevan accepted the profession's suggestion for a
further limitation on the payment of the £300 basic salary. It was
agreed that the basic salary should be paid only in cases of proven
need as determined by Executive Councils in consultation with
Local Medical Committees. Bevan insisted on retaining a last
vestige of authority by introducing right of appeal to the Minister
for rejected applicants.

The profession was divided over arrangements for paying general
practitioners for attendance in maternity cases. Responding to
pressure from the Royal College of Obstetricians and Gynaecologists and other improvers, the health departments wanted to restrict
payments to more highly trained general practitioners included on
special local obstetric lists. It was impossible to prohibit other
doctors from undertaking this work, but it was not proposed to
reward them with the maternity fee. Much to the consternation of
the Treasury the maternity fee was forced up from the existing

level of 3gn to 7gn, and it was agreed to pay 5gn to practitioners excluded from the obstetric list.[158]

The profession made a case for increase of the capitation fee from 18s to 20s, primarily on the ground that the 20% betterment offered by the Government was inadequate. Evidence was adduced by the BMA in favour of 30% betterment. Backed by strong Treasury resistance the Ministers opposed further increase in capitation. The profession grudgingly acceded although Hill warned that 'we accept the translation of Spens with the exception of the issue of the 20%' betterment.[159] For the moment level of remuneration was not invoked as an obstacle to acceptance of the new service.

A separate Spens Committee spent a year investigating the remuneration of consultants and specialists. The report of this committee was published in May 1948 and its acceptance by the Government was announced on 3 June 1948. Because of the lateness of submission of this Spens Report it was necessary to place hospital medical staffs on temporary contracts pending negotiations with the profession to devise a scheme for implementation of the Spens recommendations. The appearance of this report was helpful in finally consolidating support for the NHS from hospital medical staffs. The immediate problem for consultants and specialists related less to the Government than to their own professional organisations because it was far from obvious what body would negotiate on their behalf.[160]

From the outset it was understood that the results of the above negotiations would be put to a further plebiscite of the BMA membership. On this occasion the BMA agreed to refrain from adverse publicity. Before the plebiscite the BMA Council dropped its objections to abolition of sale of practices and also to the Medical Practices Committee. However the Government's concessions were still insufficient to gain the full confidence of the BMA Council. The membership was advised that the 'freedoms of the profession are not sufficiently safeguarded'. Returns from the plebiscite showed that in the less tense atmosphere opinion was drifting away from the militant line evident two months earlier. On a 77% poll, a majority of 25,842 against 14,620 disapproved of the NHS Act in its amended form. Among consultants, general practitioners, assistants and whole-time hospital staff, 12,799 were in favour of entering the service whereas 13,891 were against. However the latter group contained only 8,493 general practitioners out of the 13,000 regarded as necessary for a boycott of the service.[161] More than 8,000 general practitioners had relinquished their opposition between the heady days of February and the eve of the service in May. Alfred Cox, who had been secretary of the BMA in 1911, warned the BMA leadership that it was facing 'humiliating retreat'. Unless they recommended ungrudging acceptance of the result of the plebiscite and gave wholehearted support for the new service their organisation risked being irrevocably weakened.[162]

Advice from the spirit of 1911 was followed, albeit not without mutual recriminations at a further long special meeting of the Representative Body on 28 May 1949, where newly submitted terms of the amending legislation were accepted and objection to entering the service was dropped.[163] Horder and his fellow Adullamites scrambled away to found the Fellowship for Freedom in Medicine which attracted some 3,000 followers to prosecute a campaign against the NHS.[164]

'Strength and unity in order to mould the service' was the new mandate given to the BMA leadership by the Representative Meeting. With just one month to spare before the Appointed Day, with one major exception, all major arms of the profession were united in acquiescing to the new service.

The Government's residual difficulties lay with the dental profession. Only reluctantly had the latter been drawn to participate in the Spens Committee's investigation into dental incomes, which proved to be the most exacting of the Spens series, with the result that the report was not published until 10 May 1948.[165] On the basis of an estimated working week at the chairside, the report recommended for dentists an average salary of £1,600 per annum, plus allowances for betterment and expenses. The profession had pressed for £2,000 per annum at 1939 values. The Treasury regarded £1,600 as excessive. But such criteria as shortage of dentists were invoked to excuse generosity. Cripps reluctantly agreed that the Government had no choice but to proceed on the basis of Spens.[166]

The leadership of the BDA was still wedded to payment by grant-in-aid, unsympathetic to the NHI itemised fee procedure which was used for calculating salaries in the Spens Report, and positively opposed to the proposal for full-time salaried service in health centres. Bevan's meeting with the Consultative Committee of the profession on 7 June was unproductive. The Minister flatly refused to accept payment by grant-in-aid, to restrict prior approval any further, to include adolescents in the class eligible for priority treatment, or to extend to dentists the exclusion of full-time salaried service promised to general practitioners and consultants under the amending legislation. On just three other, trivial points it was promised to extend to dentists already agreed provisions of the Amendment Bill. Only one significant concession was offered. It was agreed that the prior approval mechanism operated by the Dental Estimates Board would possibly be relaxed.[167]

Representatives of the profession promised to consult their membership. Without much hope of success Bevan circulated to dentists a summary of his concessions.[168] Reflecting opinion expressed at regional meetings, an Extraordinary Meeting of the BDA on 20 June 1948 endorsed a recommendation that the membership should boycott the new service. The leadership of the two smaller dental associations were undecided and divided, with the result that they offered no firm counsel to their members. Consequently as the Appointed Day approached the dentists were isolated in their opposition to the National Health Service, and even their fugitive army was in disarray.

(vii) THE APPOINTED DAY

Intransigence from major sections of the medical and dental profession added to the already substantial difficulties of bringing into being the administrative bodies required for the National Health Service in the short interval of time between the passage of the two Bills and the Appointed Day. At first it was hoped to introduce the new service in January 1948. Throughout the parliamentary proceedings relating to the two Bills the Appointed Day was given as 1 April 1948. Meeting this deadline was a strain for the health departments, but the date was not changed to 5 July 1948 at their behest, but rather at the suggestion of the Approved Societies, when it was pointed out that 1 April was a peak period for handling sickness forms. The Approved Societies persuaded the Minister of National Insurance to defer the starting date to a low point of sickness. Bevan considered upstaging his colleagues by introducing the National Health Service ahead of other parts of the new social security scheme, but Ministers agreed that a single date should be adopted for the introduction of the whole package of reforms. The new date was announced by Attlee on 9 June 1947.[169]

The magnitude of the operation undertaken by the health departments was greatly increased by the Labour Government's decision to nationalise hospitals. Previously within official circles nationalisation was an almost disregarded option. There was little appetite or sense of capacity to take on such a colossal commitment. Before World War II the health departments exercised little influence in the hospital sphere. Even with respect to local authority hospitals the central departments played a relatively remote role. Firmer central department participation was envisaged in schemes evolved during the war, but the official preference placed the centre of gravity for administration of the new health service on local authorities, with only limited accretion of power to the centre being envisaged. This slight shift was occasioned less by positive aspiration of the Ministry than by pressure from the voluntary hospitals and the medical profession for creation of a buffer against the threat of municipalisation.

Bevan's bold scheme for hospital nationalisation permitted greater unification of the hospital system, but it involved launching the health departments on an experiment in administration for which they were ill-prepared. The administrative model adopted for the hospital service reverted to a regional scheme revolving around teaching centres of the kind favoured in voluntary hospital circles. Rather by accident this pattern coincided with other nationalised undertakings such as coal, electricity, gas, or transport, although the hospital service was unique in following the departmental rather than public corporation model. The hospital service was also dissimilar to other regionally organised services in the degree to which it was intended to decentralise the administration, largely to preserve a sense of local responsibility in a large organisation and so to some degree to overcome the anomaly that the hospital service, alone of personal services, lay outside the local authority framework.

Amalgamation of all hospitals into a single system also produced an organisation rivalling the largest national corporations in size.[170] The scale of the National Health Service as an organisation is indicated by illustrative data cited in Table I. The National Health Service, of which the hospital service was by far the largest component, with about 500,000 employees or contractors, was the third largest non-military organisation in Britain, only exceeded by the British Transport Commission and the National Coal Board, with 900,000 and 800,000 employees respectively.

The agenda of work for the health departments involved forming a large number of administrative bodies, and laying down regulations for their guidance.[171] At the centre it was necessary to undertake consultations and establish the Central Health Services Council (or Scottish Health Services Council), and devise appropriate subsidiary Standing Advisory Committees.

For Part II services it was first necessary to determine boundaries of hospital regions, and then form Regional Hospital Boards after undertaking appropriate consultation. In England and Wales designation of teaching hospitals and appointment of Boards of Governors for each were needed. Once the Boards were in operation, they were required to draw up schemes for hospital groups and appoint Hospital Management Committees. One of the most complex operations involved transfer of all hospitals and their endowments to the state.

Part III services involved relatively little action since the Acts largely perpetuated existing local health administration. However,

TABLE I

The National Health Service: Institutions & Workforce

	England & Wales	Scotland	Britain
Part II			
Voluntary hospitals	1,143	191	1,334
Municipal hospitals	1,545	226	1,771
Total	2,688	417	3,105
Voluntary hospital beds	90,000	27,000	117,000
Municipal hospital beds	390,000	37,000	427,000
Total beds	480,000	64,000	544,000
(including Mental & MD beds)	190,000	7,000	197,000
Total hospital staff	315,000	47,000	362,000
(including: medical and dental	15,500	1,500	17,000
: nursing & midwifery	128,000	19,500	147,500
: administrative & clerical	22,500	3,000	25,500
: others)	149,000	23,000	172,000
Part III			
Medical and dental staff	3,000	370	3,370
Other staff	20,000	3,000	23,000
Part IV			
General practitioners	17,600	2,000	19,600
Dentists	9,000	1,100	10,100
Pharmacists	14,000	2,800	16,800
Eye service	6,200	1,000	7,200

Note on sources: the above estimates relate to the eve of the NHS, a variety of sources being used. In view of wide divergence in the data, selection has been made with a view to taking the best available estimates on each point.

Staff numbers have been reduced to whole-time equivalents.

it was still necessary to initiate and monitor preparation of schemes for carrying out obligations imposed by the Acts.

By the time that positive action was required most of the proposals for radical overhaul of Part IV services had been abandoned. Every new concession brought the Executive Council services nearer to the National Health Insurance model they were designed to replace. Ultimately Part IV services from an administrative point of view involved relatively minor adjustments of the National Health Insurance structure, the primary changes being occasioned by the intention to make the services available on an unrestrictive basis rather than just to the insured population. The only structural innovation was insertion of the controversial central regulatory Medical Practices Committee. Otherwise the Dental Estimates Board, disciplinary Tribunal, Executive Councils, Local Medical, Pharmaceutical and Dental Committees were all lineal descendants of identifiable NHI ancestors. Nevertheless drawing up and negotiating professional agreement to elaborate regulations relating to Part IV services was itself a major exercise, even assuming willing participation of the profession.

Preparations for the huge Part II services were not handicapped by lack of co-operation from the major agencies involved.[172] After a month spent in consultations the Statutory Rule and Order defining Regional Board areas was made on 18 December 1946. There followed the laborious process of selecting RHB chairmen and board members which was completed by June 1947. The chairmen met the Minister for the first time on 23 July 1947, following which Bevan addressed a mass meeting of RHB members.[173] Most of the key staff of RHBs were appointed between August and October 1947, but they were not in office until the end of the year. With the regional apparatus in place the RHBs prepared schemes for grouping of hospitals, being guided by the philosophy of RHB (48)1 'The Planning of Specialist Services' of January 1948. By the spring of 1948 370 Hospital Management Committees had been formed. Between March and May 1948 first the provincial and then the London teaching hospitals were defined. Consequently the Appointed Day arrived before the new management bodies had taken effective control of their groups. Consultants and specialists were issued with temporary NHS contracts, partly because of delay in working out the Spens settlement, and partly because of the need to undertake a review of consultant services before adopting settled staffing complements. The whole of the hospital edifice depended on decisions made about disposition of the consultant grade. The winding up of accounts of the institutions of the old regime and transfer of assets to the new service was not completed until the end of March 1949.

Local health authorities were given their timetable for preparation for schemes relating to services under their control in February 1947. Some 1,200 schemes were submitted by the end of 1947. The work of scrutiny and revision was largely completed before 5 July 1948.

Executive Councils for Part IV services were established between May and November 1947. These bodies shadowed the insurance committees, the staff of which prepared for transfer to the Executive Councils on 5 July. Active preparations by the ECs for establishing the new service were relatively limited before March 1948. After this date the elaborate machinery of local professional committees was established, and arrangements made to accept practitioners. Regulations relating to general medical services, pharmaceutical, dental and eye services, were approved between March and June 1948. Because of objections to the Medical Practices Committee by the profession names for this body were not submitted in January 1948 as requested, but they were sent in after the thaw had begun in late May. By the end of May 26% of English and about 36% of Scottish and Welsh general practitioners had joined the service. By 5 July the lists of general medical practitioners kept by Executive Councils were virtually fully subscribed. By the Appointed Day about half of the dentists had joined the EC list, indicating that the BDA-backed boycott was only imperfectly observed. Negotiations with chemists concerning their terms of remuneration were not completed until 18 June 1948 in England and Wales, and 1 July in Scotland. These arrangements secured the entry of chemists into the new service. Following an agreement reached in 1947 Executive Councils established Ophthalmic Services Committees which enrolled opticians to operate the Supplementary Ophthalmic Service. Removal of the threat of their exclusion from the service ensured the willing co-operation of dispensing opticians.

Discussions concerning publicity for the National Health Service began in October 1946. After a great deal of discussion a final plan was agreed in December 1947.[174] This subject was not given particularly high priority and the arrangements for publicity were unspectacular, but it was appreciated that the public needed basic information about the new service in order to induce them to enrol in good time. It was thought that special efforts would be required to encourage the middle classes and their general practitioners to forsake private practice and enter the scheme. Finally it was necessary to establish local machinery for dealing with individual queries.

In the course of discussions there occurred some curtailment of the publicity arrangements. Realisation that publicity might become fundamental to preventing collapse of public confidence in the new service only emerged in the early months of 1948, when relations between Bevan and the medical profession reached their lowest ebb. As noted above the Cabinet decided that BMA domination of the media should be ended. Bevan's speech in the House of Commons on 9 February 1948 opened the Government's publicity campaign with explosive albeit destructive impact.

Under the chairmanship of Morrison, Ministers met to consider publicity for the Appointed Day.[175] Morrison realised that the new social security scheme deserved publicity as a notable achievement in post-war reconstruction, but he was obsessed by fears that national resources might be insufficient to meet the cost of potentially expensive new services. For him publicity was primarily a vehicle for inspiring workers to greater productivity in order to generate the tax revenue to sustain the burden of social security. At this meeting Bevan adopted an entirely different approach, insisting that the National Health Service required entirely separate publicity from the rest of the social security scheme. Otherwise the public would believe that the new service, like National Health Insurance, was paid for entirely through national insurance contributions. Separate publicity was also needed to gain the confidence of middle-class patients and thereby exert pressure on doctors to participate in the service. It was agreed that the primary vehicle for informing the public about the new service should be a house-to-house leaflet, preparations for which should be kept secret in order to prevent forestalling action from the BMA.

The idea of a leaflet distributed to 13 million homes featured in the original publicity plans of the health departments. This method of communication with the public was becoming favoured by the Government. It was used to distribute the highway code and a leaflet on fuel economy, while it was also agreed to circulate information about the new social security scheme on the same basis. A thirty-two page illustrated booklet was issued by the Ministry of National Insurance.[176] The Treasury suggested that the NHS could be covered by an additional paragraph in this booklet, a suggestion which was immediately rejected by the Ministry of Health. It was not until the summer of 1947 and after overcoming objections from HMSO and the GPO that a separate NHS leaflet was accepted.[177]

The Ministry of Health next ran into trouble over its ideas concerning production details. Bevan insisted on high quality. It was reported that he 'attaches very great importance to this leaflet', which he regarded as 'the most powerful instrument in the armoury of publicity' for the NHS.[178] The Minister consulted Philip Zec of the *Daily Mirror* for advice on layout and he wanted art paper instead of the telephone directory paper that was offered. A compromise was reached whereby slightly better paper was used, but the leaflet was cut from six pages to four pages.

The final proof of 'The New National Health Service' leaflet was agreed at the end of January 1948. The leaflet was delivered by HMSO to the GPO in February, but after two 'leaks' the stock was recalled. In the meantime a rival leaflet was being distributed to patients from the opponents of the NHS warning them that 'doctors expect to be obliged to disclose personal medical details of their patients to officials of the Ministry of Health'. Bevan and his officials were dismayed by this 'scandalous travesty' and they appealed to the Labour press for counter-publicity.[179] Distribution of the official leaflet was eventually timed to begin on 26 April, partly with a view to counteracting a polemical speech made by Dain.[180] Copies of the leaflet were delivered to virtually all households in Britain by 10 May, a separate Welsh language version being distributed in Wales.

The New National Health Service contained a brief and uncontroversial summary of the services to be made available under the new scheme. Its most controversial element was the advice given to patients to 'Act at once' to choose their doctor by completing forms available at local post offices and other places. In addition local health authorities, as the most reliable and experienced of the existing agencies, were asked to co-operate in publicising the new service locally. These authorities were asked to produce 'authoritative' guides, containing not only information about Part III services, but also details about hospital and family practitioner services in order to combat the idea that three separate health services were being established. Local health authorities were slow to respond to this request. The booklets produced differed greatly in character and quality. Only a few authorities (eg Kent CC) issued a comprehensive guide to services. Some medical officers of health sponsored articles in local newspapers. Local arrangements were made to handle personal enquiries. On the whole, the National Health Service was ushered in without a display of local propaganda on its behalf.[181] The main newspaper coverage comprised advertisements in national and local newspapers and in the *Radio Times* aimed at reinforcing the house-to-house leaflet. Similar information was given by the BBC on its 'Can I Help You' programme. A 'Friday Forum' discussion underlined the tensions surrounding the new service, on account of a heated exchange between Stephen Taylor, the Labour MP and medical journalist, and Dr R W Cockshut of the BMA.[182]

Films were more important for the publicity campaign than radio. Plans for a 4-reel film were jettisoned at Treasury request. A shorter documentary film entitled 'A Doctor in the House' was produced, its title being abandoned in favour of 'Here's Health'. The latter was not regarded as a success and it was shelved, but a ten-minute cartoon 'Your Very Good Health', in the 'Charley' series of Halas and Batchelor was both memorable and successful as propaganda directed toward the middle classes. This group was also the main target of a widely shown trailer entitled 'Doctor's Dilemma'.[183] A useful forum for the above films was a large exhibition 'Health of the People' mounted at the Government exhibition centre on Oxford Street. This exhibition marked both the centenary of the 1848 Public Health Act and the inception of the new service.[184]

The above effort scarcely merits the accusation made in the *British Medical Journal* that the Government, aided and abetted by their masters, the trade unions, had mounted a 'huge publicity campaign' of films, posters and pamphlets, aimed at exposing the medical profession to intolerable pressure. Although this indignation melted away after the rapprochement between the Government and the profession reached at the end of May 1948, publicity concerning the health service emanating from the two sides was not entirely in accord. Officials criticised a BMA leaflet for encouraging patients to remain on doctors' private lists.[185] The more glamorous BMA leaflet *The New Health Service and You* issued just after the inception of the new service rather upstaged its official competitor.

As the Appointed Day approached expressions of public reconciliation emanated from the former combatants. On behalf of the BMA Council Dain promised that the 'profession will do its utmost to make the new service a resounding success'.[186] Bevan responded that he would give the profession 'all the facilities, resources, apparatus and help I can' to enable the two partners to embark on 'quite the most ambitious adventure in the care of national health that any country has seen'.[187]

The National Health Service was formally launched by a broadcast given by Attlee on Sunday 4 July at 9.15 pm. Preparations for this speech involved extensive inter-ministerial deliberations. Attlee was given conflicting advice concerning the tone of his broadcast. Whereas Morrison advised being as 'objective and non-controversial as possible', Bevan argued that it was absurd to give credit to their political enemies with respect to the genesis of the National Health Service.[188] Bevan's invitation to partisanship was resisted, but the text was modified at his request to emphasise that the National Health Service was unconnected with insurance payments, and that it would be universally available and of equal standard for all social classes.[189]

On 5 July *The Times* carried a large Government advertisement placed by the Central Office of Information and headed 'This Day Makes History'. *The Times* editorial comment applauded the new social security scheme, and the whole press was supportive. But differences of perspective were still apparent even among official pronouncements. Morrison used the above advertisement as a vehicle for calling for 'more and more production'. Bevan stole the limelight of the day primarily because of a speech in which he undermined Attlee's conciliatory tone, ending up by calling the Conservatives 'lower than vermin', which earned him a stiff rebuke from the Prime Minister.[190]

Within the department it was proclaimed that 'Today is the Appointed Day and our great new scheme is thrust upon an astonished world'.[191] After weeks of frenzied preparation, last-minute deals, and changes of plan, the Appointed Day was unexpectedly uneventful. The following days were also quiet, showing that fears about major lapses in preparation were unfounded.[192] The case of the doctor who sent a telegram to the Minister on 5 July rather than follow the custom of applying to the local hospital for admission of a patient was an exception. Such an outcome dispelled the myth of overweening power of the Minister.[193] In general the start of the NHS was pleasing to Bevan, and he pleased others. Addressing the chairmen of Executive Councils on 28 July Bevan gave a 'rousing and inspiring address with that touch of leadership which so few public men can master and he then spent an hour answering quick fire questions and giving the right answers by some means of telepathy'. Such magnificence enabled this reporter to forgive him his weaknesses.[194]

The official verdict on the Appointed Day was disarmingly modest:

The Service is new, but July 5th, 1948 did not introduce at once new facilities previously unavailable. The public had had access to all the services in some degree before, but they had secured them in many ways, through a medley of local and central government and voluntary agencies. The National Health Service did not provide on July 5th some elaborate new thing but rather sought to ensure that all necessary services should thenceforth be available without financial obstacles and that there should be the means to develop whatever is lacking in the service in future. The great immediate advance was not that all things were at once available, but that there was now a way to secure them in the future. The main problem of July 5th, 1948 was to ensure that the change-over from the old to the new entailed no disturbance of the quality or availability of any necessary health service. It would be vain to hope that fundamental changes such as had to be made could take place without confusion, but such confusion as occurred was for the most part in offices rather than in hospital wards, doctors' surgeries or any of the other places where the patient is served.[195]

Although the service was not perfected in all of its parts, the major structures were in place and the most severe obstacles had been overcome. Within a short span after the Appointed Day the great majority of general practitioners had been shepherded into the service and the show of resistance by dentists was collapsing. The Government's somewhat skeletal publicity campaign was successful in prompting the public to join the new service. By 10 July in England and Wales 16 million names had been entered on Executive Council lists in addition to the 19.5 million already in place through National Health Insurance arrangements.

(viii) THE NATIONAL HEALTH SERVICE (AMENDMENT) ACT, 1949

Although concessions won from the Government through confrontation were insignificant, their embodiment in amending legislation was of great symbolic importance to the BMA. An Amending Act would vindicate in the eyes of the profession the hard line taken by its negotiators from the outset, and it was presented as a belated token of reparation by a penitent Government. The Government resisted amending legislation out of fear that, once conceded, its scope was likely to be widened until the basic framework was undermined. However, once it became apparent that concessions to the profession could be kept in check, amending legislation was accepted as a necessary and convenient mechanism for tidying up the recent health service legislation.

The 1949 NHS (Amendment) Act was not an unqualified success as an exercise in harmony. Undeterred by past failures, and again largely without success, the BMA pursued many of its perennial objectives.[196] Unsuccessful demands included permitting HMCs and BGs to appoint their own chairmen; allowing private patients in hospitals a grant-in-aid towards the cost of treatment; giving medical staff committees in hospitals statutory recognition; providing statutory protection against arbitrary termination of contract for specialists; arranging for private patients of general practitioners to obtain drugs and appliances at public expense; augmentation of the £66m compensation allowed for abolition of sale and purchase of practices; further limitation of the powers of the Medical Practices Committee with respect to distribution; and replacement of the Minister by the Medical Practices Committee in appeals against Executive Council decisions on basic salary.

The department showed some sympathy for the BMA suggestion that the old NHI disciplinary procedure should be revived to deal with patients calling doctors out on trivialities, but this idea was firmly resisted by Bevan.[197] BMA support for exclusion of aliens from NHS benefits, although initially resisted, contributed to the pressure for action on this front. The only real concession to the new round of BMA demands was agreement to permit ECs to remove from their lists practitioners who were no longer practising.

The Government responded to BMA demands for right to arbitration over remuneration and conditions of employment, but the negotiators were indignant when they discovered that the new legislation would deny them automatic access to arbitration.

Officials argued that the proposed practice was consistent with established norms elsewhere in the civil service. The BMA objected to being treated like civil servants. They claimed that a fundamental pledge had been dishonoured and the atmosphere 'poisoned'.[198] The arbitration issue was part of a broader complaint by the BMA that the Government had broken its promise to take the profession fully into its confidence in framing the amending legislation. The Permanent Secretary responded that promised discussions had been held, but the profession had never been invited to participate in framing the legislation itself.[199]

Instructions to Parliamentary Counsel for the amending Bill were issued on 27 June, shortly after the final accord with the profession. The Bill steadily expanded from the six clauses originally intended to the twenty-three of the form presented to the House of Commons on 11 May 1949.[200] Morrison expressed his annoyance at Bevan's department's inability to predict the length of its Bill.[201] There was no separate Scottish Bill on this occasion, the necessary applications to Scotland being contained in the relevant clauses.

Expansion of the Bill was primarily a consequence of the work of the committee established under Mr G O Slade, KC to consider revision of sections 35 and 36 of the 1946 Act relating to the effect on partnership agreements of the abolition of the sale and purchase of practices. This committee had been established on 20 April 1948 with the expectation that its report would determine the response of partnerships at the Appointed Day. The delay of this report until after the Appointed Day resulted in additional complications in the amending Bill. The relatively small issue of partnership agreements took up Part I and clauses 1–9 of the Bill. Part II comprised miscellaneous provisions, many of which enshrined concessions made to the profession in the May accord. Clause 10 determined that section 33 of the 1946 NHS Act could not be employed to establish by regulation a full-time salaried general practitioner service. Clause 12 extended this provision to specialists. Clause 14 permitted greater flexibility in selecting the professional member for the disciplinary Tribunal established under section 42 of the 1946 NHS Act. Enabling ECs to appoint their own chairmen from 31 March 1949 and local professional committees to levy charges on their members were covered in schedules of the Bill. Clause 12 extended application of the Conciliation Act (1896) and the Industrial Courts Act (1918) to cover contractors paid by fees and also cases where remuneration and conditions of service were determined by statutory regulation. Automatic and binding arbitration was not provided for these groups. The Government kept to its line that arbitration required the consent of both parties and the Minister, with the Minister also preserving overriding authority over implementation. The remaining clauses (15–23) were mainly of a minor and technical nature, designed to correct anomalies exposed since the Appointed Day.

The one significant concession promised at the Standing Committee of this Bill involved agreement to insert a new clause prohibiting the introduction by regulation of full-time salaried service for dentists, except in health centres. This clause was duly added at the Report stage.[202]

The more important changes in the Bill were introduced at the Report stage and in the House of Lords. Following pressure from the CHSC a new clause was introduced at the Report stage relaxing the Government's long-standing objection to doctors using health centre facilities for their private paitents. The new clause was tempered with the proviso that higher charges would be made to the doctors, while the arrangement was made subject to ministerial agreement.[203] Also at the Report stage Elliot and his colleagues pressed for health service charges to be introduced for non-residents. While the Minister was sceptical about the practicality of such a scheme he agreed to introduce an amendment giving effect to this proposal.[204] Bevan was by no means new to this idea. Perhaps influenced by reference to this concession in one of Sir Waldron Smithers' outbursts against the NHS, in April 1949 Morrison began nettling Bevan about the information leaflet concerning the NHS handed to foreigners upon their arrival in Britain.[205] But the opportunity to exploit this issue more fully was not offered until the autumn, when it was introduced in the somewhat unlikely context of promoting co-operation between the Brussels Powers in the social service field.[206] Bevan argued that because NHS benefits were freely accessible to foreign visitors to Britain, other Brussels Powers ought to concede similar rights to the British. The Cabinet was deflected into discussion of abuse of the NHS by foreign visitors, no doubt recalling newspaper stories currently circulating concerning foreign seamen landing in droves in Liverpool to collect false teeth which subsequently turned up for sale in bazaars in Baghdad. An official check in fact revealed that only ten foreign seamen had used the dental service in the first year of the NHS.[207] Bevan argued that the cost of such services provided for foreign visitors would not exceed £200,000 pa, but the Cabinet felt sufficiently sensitive about adverse publicity connected with this issue to insist that legislation should be introduced to give the Ministers power to restrict access to NHS facilities for foreign visitors, and in appropriate cases to permit levying of charges.[208] A new clause allowing a charge for visitors was introduced in the House of Lords, where it was accepted without demur, and it prompted no adverse repercussions in the House of Commons.[209]

Much greater significance attaches to another new clause introduced in the House of Lords, which allowed charges for prescriptions to be introduced by regulation. This proposal was accepted in the House of Lords with virtually no debate. It was, however, unsuccessfully resisted by a group of Labour MPs in the House of Commons. This provision, rather than the ones for which the Act was designed, is the section for which the 1949 Act is remembered. Its consideration therefore more correctly belongs to the discussion of the crisis of expenditure into which the National Health Service was plunged from the moment of its inception.

CHAPTER V

Crisis of Expenditure

(i) THE GATHERING CRISIS: JULY 1948–JULY 1949

The National Health Service had barely begun before it was overtaken by the crisis over expenditure. This problem was to some extent anticipated. During the initial Cabinet exchanges on hospital nationalisation it was predicted that expenditure on Regional Hospital Boards would be difficult to restrain. It was also doubted whether increased exchequer liability to the health service could be offset by proportionate reductions in exchequer grants to local authorities. Although these problems were recognized as a major disadvantage of the new scheme, they were not regarded as insuperable obstacles to its acceptance, and suggestions about strengthening controls over Regional Hospital Boards were not pursued. Cost was not invoked as a major problem during parliamentary debates on the National Health Service Bill.

The estimated net cost of the National Health Service was given as £130m in the Beveridge Report, £108m in the 1944 White Paper, £122m in Cabinet papers in December 1945, and as £134m in the Financial Memoranda appended to the National Health Service Bills.[1] Independent calculations suggested that the burden of a comprehensive health service would be somewhat higher. The PEP report of 1937 gave £161m as the combined cost of current health services. In 1941 two Socialist Medical Association members estimated the cost of a reorganised service as £140m. Perhaps the most scientific estimate, from Medical Planning Research, assumed that a comprehensive service would cost £230m. In 1944 an Oxford doctor prompted heart searching among officials when he questioned the adequacy of Appendix 'E' to the 1944 White Paper and estimated that the new service would cost at least £200m at the outset and considerably more as it became genuinely comprehensive.[2] Official estimates tended to the low side, expecting that services could be kept within bounds, and perhaps not taking sufficient note of warning signs that limitations which were successfully imposed during the inter-war period would no longer be apposite in the system that they were creating. This lapse of judgement may look puzzling with hindsight, but there was no rush to correct these misapprehensions until well after the Appointed Day.

The estimates laid before Parliament in February 1948 for the first nine months of the service included a gross figure of £198.4m and a net figure of £149.7m. The net total for England and Wales was £132.4m (£175.5m pa), reached after the submitted estimate was cut by £22.3m at the Chancellor's request.[3] During the latter part of 1948 it was becoming increasingly clear that expenditure was running well ahead of the estimates and that it would be necessary for the 1949/50 estimates to be substantially higher than originally anticipated. Besides the Treasury becoming alerted to this problem, it seems that Morrison, ever vigilant on matters concerning Bevan, was urging Attlee to initiate some kind of inquiry into the workings of the National Health Service, with a view to permitting the Cabinet to decide future policy, rather than allowing matters to be decided on financial grounds between the Treasury and the health departments.[4] No inquiry as such was conducted at this time and the suggestion was again to fail when it was repeated by Morrison in October 1949, but it eventually succeeded in April 1950 when the NHS Cabinet Committee was set up. But Morrison's incursion was probably not without its effects. Perhaps sensing gathering anxiety and criticism, Bevan seized the initiative and submitted a Progress Report on the NHS to the Cabinet. This report was unsolicited and it occupied no obvious place in the Cabinet discussions of the time. Cripps was annoyed that inflated estimates for 1948/49, presented without prior consultation with the Treasury, were baptised as 'progress'.[5]

In his document Bevan touched relatively lightly on expenditure, which was now announced as £225m gross for the part year 1948/49 (£300m pa gross) and estimated as £272m net and £330m gross for 1949/50. He admitted that this 'cost remains unquestionably big', but it was excused as the reasonable cost of social innovation. It was thus formally confirmed that there would be need for a substantial Supplementary Estimate for 1948/49, and a radical increase in the health service budget for 1949/50.[6]

Both Bevan and Woodburn fixed upon similar grounds for their difficulties over expenditure; first, high level of demand, representing a backlog inherited from earlier times; secondly, difficulty in providing precise estimates for an entirely new organisation; thirdly, the effects of operation of the Whitley or any alternative pay machinery. The Ministers were quietly confident about ironing out these difficulties. It was felt that demand would naturally subside, that the new hospital system would quickly fall into a settled state, and that salaries could be adjusted to ensure proper rewards without permitting abuse.

It was intended to hold a full Cabinet review of NHS expenditure in January 1949. But behind-the-scenes manoeuvring associated

with growing Treasury alarm resulted in this subject being deferred eventually until the end of May. Thus virtually a year elapsed before the Cabinet reviewed the service and its increasingly acute expenditure crisis. However the Cabinet received a foretaste of this problem when the two Health Ministers were called to explain their requirement for Supplementary Estimates of £52.8m and £5.6m for 1948/49.[7]

Within the Treasury there were always dormant fears because of the difficulty in drawing up a balance sheet for expenditure of pre-NHS health services. There was thus no effective yardstick for evaluating the performance of the new service. Initially little concern was expressed over the lack of a mechanism for controlling hospital establishments, but this attitude quickly changed when it was realised that hospital costs were leading the escalation of NHS expenditure. From November 1948 onwards the Treasury engaged in an unremitting struggle with the Ministry of Health over control of hospital staff numbers. From the outset all demands for tighter control of hospital spending ran up against the fundamental tenet of Bevan's policy that both RHBs and HMCs should exercise maximum autonomy within the constraints of their annual budgets. The Treasury came to deplore this arrangement as a licence to regard budgets as a floor, rather than as a ceiling to expenditure. The initial freedom of action granted to individual hospital authorities in fixing their budgets introduced strong pressure at the periphery for expansion, primarily inhibited by practical barriers such as market forces serving, for instance, to limit opportunities for recruitment of staff. But nevertheless staff numbers steadily expanded, and when the Whitley Councils ground into operation major salary increases rapidly appeared on the horizon. Consequently the NHS was hit simultaneously by increases both in staff numbers and pay levels, the inevitable result being unforeseen escalation in staff costs in the hospital sector. This was merely one, although the greatest of the indications for the Treasury that NHS expenditure was out of control. It was predicted that when the old regime accustomed to rate financing passed away, the new philosophy of 'easy money' would take root, and become 'infinitely demoralising'. These gloomy predictions seemed to be confirmed by the 1949/50 provisional estimate submitted by the Ministry of Health in November 1948, which indented for £280m, compared with the £132.5m for the part-year 1948/49. Even when the 1948/49 figure was scaled up to an annual rate the increase was £108m. It was clear that costs were expanding very unevenly: 24% in the case of non-teaching hospitals but 90% for teaching hospitals; 300% for local authority services; only 8% for the general medical service; 39% for chemists; 320% for dentists; and 460% for opticians. The Scottish estimate revealed a precisely similar pattern. This situation was regarded as 'very frightening' in Treasury circles, and likely to result in an outcry potentially damaging to the service.[8] The revelation in the Progress Reports that the gap between 1948/49 and 1949/50 levels of spending was likely to be less owing to the 1948/49 estimates being exceeded gave little comfort within the Treasury. Cripps fully shared the alarm over the financial aspects of Bevan's Progress Report. Action on the tentative 1949/50 estimates was frozen while urgent discussions with Bevan were held.

In the run-up to the Budget, Cripps relied on persuasion with the Ministers concerned rather than taking the matter to the Cabinet as he was invited to do by Attlee. In the interval between two meetings with Bevan, Cripps wrote to the two Ministers demanding drastic cuts of £100m and £12.5m in the net NHS estimates for 1949/50, a reduction virtually cancelling out the increase above the original 1948/49 estimates claimed in the provisional estimates for 1949/50.[9]

In reply Bevan delicately sidestepped Cripps' letter, referring only to their conversation, in response to which he offered an extended and elaborate seventeen-page justification of his expenditure plans. With respect to each arm of the service it was argued that expenditure was being pegged down to the minimum and that unavoidable increases represented only minor increments above anticipated outcomes for 1948/49. However cuts amounting to £27.75m were offered in services, the main element of which was a drastic reduction in hospital capital expenditure. Of the minor cuts offered by Bevan the most curious involved withdrawing the $2\frac{1}{2}$d container cost payment to chemists, in anticipation that in future the patient would 'bring—or buy—his own bottles or containers for the medicine'.[10] Fortunately for Bevan, because of higher than anticipated yields from Appropriations in Aid, the estimate could be reduced from £280m to £234m, which he regarded as the maximum concession necessary.[11] Firmly precluding the introduction of charges he declared 'I must say at once that I am entirely opposed to any idea of obtaining additional appropriations in aid by requiring payments from the beneficiaries under the service'. Bevan defended this conclusion at length, pointing out that the yield from charges would be insignificant compared with the extent of administrative inconvenience. Furthermore, charges would involve a premature and fundamental reversal of policy, raising the spectre of the means test and harking back to the discredited Poor Law. He invited Cripps to rejoice that the service was in great demand, a sign of the success and popular appeal of the NHS. In order to maintain this standard he believed that it was to increase expenditure still further, rather than 'taking the attract-iveness out of the service' and reducing it to an austerity level. Without further commitment of resources the service would become 'so niggardly and unattractive that it will be considered by many to be a cheat'. Coming at the outset of the long argument over the imposition of charges in the NHS, this letter provides a useful reminder of Bevan's depth of feeling on this issue, and an indication of his grounds for attaching great symbolic importance to the principle of a service free from direct charges.

Cripps answered promptly with some fifty words, thanking Bevan for his efforts, but reminding him that the £100m savings target remained only half met.[12] Treasury officials took up this problem in earnest, no inhibitions being felt about charges, 'In principle, I think a charge is right. I have never been able to see why people should get dentures and spectacles for nothing any more than houses, food and clothing'.[13] However, in one major respect there was agreement with Bevan: the demands of the health service on exchequer resources would continue to expand unless there was a change of policy. Of the more obvious policy options, imposition of charges was strongly preferred to increasing the National Insurance employee's contribution by 1s per week.[14] Convinced of the seriousness of the crisis of NHS expenditure, Cripps wanted Bevan to explore the whole range of possibilities for reducing exchequer liability. Cripps confided to Attlee that the 'finances of the service are giving me very serious concern', not only in the short term, 'but even more from the point of view of the long-term implications if the facilities which it provides are expanded and developed, as we all hope may be possible'.[15] Cripps met Bevan armed with a variety of plans for economies and charges to offset increased costs, including: the 1s increase in the National Insurance contribution, dental and ophthalmic charges, ending the supplementary ophthalmic service, with Bevan's own container charge of $2\frac{1}{2}$d being translated into a prescription charge of 6d, later revised to 1s, in symmetry with the putative 1s National Insurance increase.[16]

Bevan was by no means insensitive to the dangers of the situation. He called together members of the management side of the Whitley Councils, who were also leading figures on the Hospital Boards, and delivered them a strong lecture on incomes policy. He also reminded them of the international economic situation and Marshall Aid. On this occasion his commitment to labour discipline permitted sympathy with the American point of view: 'The American Nation was entitled to ask us whether we were spending American money to raise the standard of living beyond that obtaining in America'. He also invoked the recent White

Paper on *Personal Incomes, Costs and Prices*, which had warned that 'there is no justification for any general increase of individual money incomes', even when intended to restore past relativities.[17]

Under Cripps' incomes policy increases were permissible in very limited cases, for instance where industries were experiencing labour shortages. His White Paper extolled productivity, but left it unclear whether this would merit wage increases in the short term. This policy was backed by the TUC, and until 1951 it was moderately successful in holding off pay claims in the industrial sector where in the space of two-and-a-half years wage rates increased by only 5%. Bevan urged the Whitley Councils to preach restraint and self-sacrifice, only permitting increases in exceptional cases of severe labour shortage.[18] But Bevan's rhetoric was a feeble instrument to stem the tide of pay increases already streaming through the negotiating machinery, where the pace had already been set by a 30% award to nurses. Already it was clear that in terms of annual rates, the hospital salaries bill for 1949/50 would be 22% higher than for 1948/49. Such steep increases for large groups of workers appeared to be subversive of the Government's incomes policy. No account was taken of the low base point of the remuneration of nurses and allied workers.

Cripps drove home the message of the White Paper in speeches in the House of Commons on 6 July and 27 September 1949.[19] From September 1949 onwards the Ministry of Health was asked by the Treasury to apply restraint in its Whitley negotiations. However, as a joint memorandum by Bevan and Woodburn pleaded, their ability to interfere with the Whitley negotiations was extremely limited, unless completely arbitrary action was taken. Cabinet discussion in November 1949 produced no insight into a means of breaking the wage spiral.[20] A further six months then elapsed before a further unsuccessful attempt was made to achieve wage restraint in the health sector.

The climax of Cripps' pre-Budget effort to stabilise health expenditure was marked by a plea for the departments never again to exceed their estimates. Cripps declared that he was 'as anxious as yourselves that the NHS shall be an unqualified success and that the policy which has inspired its creation has my warmest support', but this development could not go beyond what the nation's resources could sustain. He therefore appealed for the utmost economy in NHS administration.[21]

Woodburn replied with a matter-of-fact account of steps being taken to control hospital expenditure. Bevan was more aggressive, blaming the 1948/49 Supplementary Estimate on cuts in the original estimate imposed by the Treasury, and baldly stating that a

Supplementary Estimate for 1949/50 was an inevitable consequence of salary awards.[22]

In preparing the 1949/50 Budget the Treasury committee was concerned with the general rise of public expenditure. Health was one of three main sectors where 1948/49 estimates had been exceeded to a major degree. The others were defence and food subsidies, where Supplementary Estimates of £61m and £52 had been incurred. The Chancellor was warned that the point had been reached when extension of the social services was being financed by taxes levied on the lower social groups, thereby reducing the income available for personal use. The Chancellor was urged to consider carefully before committing the state to further encroachment on individual incomes. This message was introduced into the Budget speech, but it was toned down in successive drafts. In the final version health expenditure was mentioned only obliquely. Cripps restated his obligation to increase expenditure on the social services, but warned that the limit of what could be achieved through taxation had been reached. He announced a thorough review of social service expenditure and emphasised that Supplementary Estimates would in future only be permitted in special cases, for instance where changes of policy were made. His broadcast on the Budget devoted even less attention to economy in the social services, instead concentrating on the positive benefits to health and happiness brought about by 'the great new free Health Service' and other social services.[23]

The Treasury was by no means confident that the Chancellor would be able to honour his Budget pledge to avoid future Supplementary Estimates in the social services. Of the not inconsiderable £53.5m and £3.2m net savings extracted from Bevan and Woodburn respectively, about half was to be derived from extra receipts in the form of lump sum payments from local authorities with respect to their pension liabilities. Only £27.75m and £2.2m represented a squeeze on the service, the greatest element here being reduction of remuneration to dentists. The pension fund payments had invaluable cosmetic effects, but they were unrepeatable windfalls.[24]

Notwithstanding exhortations by Cripps, NHS expenditure was continuing to rise. By the spring of 1949 it was clear that a Supplementary Estimate of at least £50m for 1949/50 was looming. Ministers were urged to face the 'heroic decision that experience shows that it was premature for us to think that we could put on the taxpayer the whole cost of the health services of the country without any charge to the recipients'.[25] But there was no expectation that the Government was yet ready to reverse its policy on a free service, although a pessimistic review of the two Progress

Reports undertaken for Morrison also tentatively raised the possibility of charges as one of the methods of holding down health expenditure.[26]

The cause of the pessimists was not assisted by the report of the Select Committee on Estimates which seized the initiative to investigate the new health services, but which failed to uncover any compelling grounds for major criticism. All obvious cases of wasteful expenditure were already being subjected to control. It was concluded that 'all branches of the Health Service are making great efforts to work the new machinery efficiently'.[27] The slightly perfunctory and unenergetic activities of the Select Committee left Morrison and his allies without significant new ammunition.

When the Health Ministers finally submitted their updated Progress Reports at the Cabinet meeting on 23 May 1949, Bevan presented the Cabinet with the stark choice between cuts in services or a Supplementary Estimate. In Bevan's view the former meant withholding services 'which the community has proved it urgently needs—dental treatment and spectacles must be refused, beds must be closed, staff dismissed, and waiting lists already appallingly long must grow even longer'. The Secretary of State's argument followed similar lines. Both Ministers drew attention to Treasury-imposed cuts as one reason for their difficulties, and neither risked a firm forecast of expenditure for the current financial year, although in discussion the figures of £52m and £5m were offered as tentative predictions for their Supplementary Estimates.[28]

The most striking feature of Bevan's contribution was his explicit opposition to charges for services, especially for hospital treatment. He argued that charges would reduce the prestige of the service and involve introduction of expensive and complex administrative machinery to handle exemptions from charges. Woodburn also opposed charges and favoured higher National Insurance contributions to raise additional revenue.

Cripps was embarrassed by the prospect of supplementing the 1949/50 health estimates, especially in the light of his Budget speech which had declared that future Supplementary Estimates would only be considered in special circumstances. He sanctioned assurances that vital hospital services would not be cut, providing stringent measures were taken to keep within the approved estimates. For the longer term, Cripps urged much tighter mechanisms of financial control within the hospital service. It was agreed by the Cabinet that a decision on the Supplementary Estimates should be delayed pending action on financial control and economies within the service, to be devised by the Treasury and health departments. Although charges for services were undoubtedly in the collective mind no reference to this option was recorded in the minute.

Morrison was therefore not successful in stirring his colleagues into adopting radical measures to control NHS expenditure. He also failed to persuade Griffiths to criticise the NHS from the Ministry of National Insurance perspective. The brief prepared for Morrison in connection with the Cabinet meeting argued strongly for charges, both as the most desirable option to raise additional revenue, and as the means to suppress demand.[29]

Treasury officials were overcome by a sense of helplessness. Because of the complexity of hospital financing it was virtually impossible to impose short-term economies without sacrificing services. As the summer of 1949 passed by without more than tentative action being agreed, there seemed no escape from further substantial Supplementary Estimates. In the absence of tangible measures to control hospital recurrent expenditure, officials concentrated increasingly on the easier alternative of charges to patients. Charges were liked by the Treasury because they represented a way both of raising revenue and because of their psychological effect. Charges were seen as an 'education of the public who use the service' and they also proved that a ceiling existed to the public money available for the health service.[30]

As early as July 1949 a major Supplementary Estimate for 1949/50 had become an inevitability. Mounting expenditure on the health service was accepted with resignation at the Economic Policy Committee, and by the Cabinet in the autumn of 1949, when provisional estimates of £356m for 1950/51 and £387m for 1951/52 were crystallising out.[31]

(ii) THE PRESCRIPTION CHARGE

Bevan's momentary capitulation on the prescription charge occurred in the context of Cripps' drive to reduce domestic consumption by £280m as a means of combating inflation. Among the demands for reductions, the most painful for Bevan related to housing rather than health. Reversing the preference displayed in earlier Treasury discussions, Cripps now opted for a 1s increase in the National Insurance contribution, calculated to yield £40m, rather than direct health charges. But Bevan was strongly opposed to either 'any increase in the National Insurance contribution or any general introduction of charges for medical service', such as 'a direct charge for in-patients in hospitals, or a charge for part of the cost of dentures, spectacles and other appliances'. All such proposals were condemned as 'drastic modifications of the basic principles of the Health Service'. No particular reasons were given for assimilating National Insurance into his general objection to health charges. He doubtless knew that increase in the National Insurance contribution was not favoured, even among the critics of the National Health Service.

Bevan gave his customary lecture on general belt-tightening within the service. He promised substantial saving from measures being adopted to reduce the cost of the pharmaceutical services. In place of direct charges to hospital in-patients Bevan asked for further reductions in their National Insurance benefit. This possibility was explored, but quickly abandoned. Somewhat surprisingly Bevan accepted the suggestion, made in the Treasury memorandum, for a 1s prescription charge, with an estimated annual saving of £10m. At this stage the prescription charge was not viewed like other charges as fundamental infringement of the principle of a free service. Bevan argued that free dental and ophthalmic services were more important because they were benefits unavailable to the poor before the NHS and therefore greatly valued and widely needed aspects of the service. But he frankly admitted that the pharmaceutical service was subject to abuse. The bottle of medicine was in his view generally a routine item, the value of which was often questionable, as Bevan was apt to remind his audiences. As noted above, he himself had set in motion the prescription charge by accepting that patients should pay the container charge. He viewed an enforced charge as a useful deterrent to unnecessary resort to medication.[32]

It is quite possible that the prescription charge was also offered as a minor palliative in the hope of disarming his critics, and in preparation for a stout defence against the proposed cut of £35m in the council housing building programme proposed later in the agenda. However, having let Bevan off lightly on the health service, the Committee was unrelenting on housing cuts.

There is no record of Bevan's opposition to the prescription charge when the Economic Policy Committee's recommendations for economies were placed before the Cabinet. Indeed the Prime Minister's memorandum stated that Bevan was positively in favour of a flat rate prescription charge as a contribution 'to the efficiency of this scheme'. But others pointed out that this charge would be a special injustice to old people who had contributed for years to the National Health Insurance scheme, and who were now to be denied benefits in old age. It was argued that this would create pressures for increases in the old age pension. The Cabinet agreed to exempt old age pensioners from the prescription charge, seemingly without Bevan's objection.[33] Having jettisoned the major National Insurance charge proposed in connection with the health budget, he now made a last-ditch but unsuccessful attempt to reverse the Economic Policy Committee's recommendation and the Cabinet decision on housing cuts, hinting at resignation, while also unleashing his celebrated remarks concerning inflated defence spending. Attlee with equally characteristic terseness replied that it 'really does not advance matters to talk about gorged and swollen defence estimates any more than it does to talk of grossly extravagant Health Services'.[34]

The drafting of Attlee's announcements to Parliament and the public concerning the package of cuts proved troublesome. All sides wanted their point of view expressed. On health charges Attlee stressed that the prescription charge was introduced as a deterrent against extravagance, rather than as an economy.[35] The resultant saving of £10m pa was presented as an incidental bonus. In drafts of the broadcast the reference to exemptions for old age pensioners underwent a variety of mutations. In the end it was explained that all pensioners would receive relief, not simply those in need as indicated in some of the drafts. Morrison unsuccessfully pressed Attlee to declare that because of the need to reduce public expenditure the public should be ready to pay for services which in principle should be free.[36]

Prescription charges were welcomed as a realistic gesture by *The Times*, but only as a half-measure pointing the way to charges for dentures and spectacles. Indeed, failure to introduce such charges was regarded as 'astonishing'. Charges as a whole were criticised as an inadequate response. *The Times* called for a complete reconstruction of dental and eye services to establish a system of cheap and efficient clinics providing basic ophthalmic and dental services.[37] The prescription charge was regarded by the press as a substantial retraction from the principle of a free service. Bevan meanwhile defended the prescription charge both to the Parliamentary Labour Party and other audiences, employing his graphic remark: 'I shudder to think of the ceaseless cascade of medicine which is pouring down British throats at the present time'.[38] At this time Bevan insisted that charges were a specific short-term deterrent, to be withdrawn as soon as practicable, whereas after his resignation he claimed that it was never his intention to allow the prescription charge to be introduced.[39]

From the point of view of Bevan's critics the health services, although representing the most rapidly expanding point of Government spending, had escaped virtually unscathed from an important round of public spending cuts.[40] Skilful evasion by Bevan led Morrison to revive his notion of a Cabinet inquiry into the health service. Bevan wanted a similar intervention over defence expenditure. Attlee allowed the two combatants to cancel one another out. Neither health nor armaments were to be scrutinised, but neither Morrison nor Bevan lost sight of his target.[41]

The prescription charge issue was by no means settled. Rather than welcoming amelioration of the charges Bevan reacted sharply against exemptions, and against proposals to involve the health departments in evolving machinery for reclaiming charges. Before the Lord President's Committee he argued vigorously against concessions on the grounds that they reduced the return from the levy, because they inspired further demands for concessions, and because they undermined the deterrent aspect of the charge. Perhaps the most potent objection stemmed from the medico-political situation. All complications of the system would need co-operation from both chemists and doctors. Given the strained relations between these professions and the Government, Bevan was not confident in securing their co-operation and he was in no mood to seek it.[42]

Concessions to certain groups were unavoidable. For instance, the claim of the war-disabled could not be resisted. Sensing the danger of infinite regress, extension of exemption beyond old age and war pensioners was vigorously opposed by the Treasury. But the damage was already done. The effect of exclusion of old age pensioners reduced the anticipated yield from £10m to £6m. Once the erosion of his simple formula was conceded, Bevan reverted to his more natural mood, reducing the burden to those patients requiring more complicated treatment, by opting to charge on the basis of the script rather than on each item on the script. This technical readjustment further reduced the yield from the prescription charge.[43] Delay ensued while the mechanism for collecting the charges was agreed between the departments involved. Bevan pressed for universal charges, all exempted classes being required to reclaim their fees from the National Assistance Board. This was the easier option for the health departments, but much the more unattractive for the patient.[44] Only in mid-November 1949 did the Ministry of Health accept the inevitability of an exemption scheme.

Parliamentary sanction for prescription charges was obtained by the insertion of a new clause into the NHS Amendment Bill during its later stages. In view of lack of agreement on matters of detail, it was decided to seek 'wildest and wooliest powers' for the Minister.[45] The clause introduced at the Lords Committee stage sought Regulations for 'making and recovery of such charges in respect of such pharmaceutical services, as may be prescribed, and the Regulations may provide for the remission or repayment of the charges in the case of such persons as may be prescribed'.[46] At Bevan's insistence, the Government spokesman defended this clause as a temporary expedient, expectations for longer-term economies in the drug bill being vested in the newly established Cohen Committee. The Lords agreed to this proposal without a division. In the House of Commons this was the only Lords amendment to spark off a division. Even here, the amendment was carried by 138 to 9 votes.[47] As section 16 of the new Act, the provision for a prescription charge immediately became the object of acute controversy.

In normal circumstances, taking powers to levy prescription charges would naturally lead to imposition of these charges. But Bevan's reluctance to implement his new powers was soon evident. When the Parliamentary stages of the 1949 Bill were completed, Bevan drew Cripps' attention to the practical difficulties of imposing charges, 'Surely we must review again among ourselves whether these exemptions make the game worth the candle'. Woodburn was also unenthusiastic about the charges and he reminded the Chancellor of his reservations concerning the measure.[48]

Cripps was determined not to sacrifice this single specific economy, relying on the Lord President's Committee to prevent backsliding. In Bevan's absence owing to a cold, Sir William Douglas passed on a message advising the Committee to delay action, partly because there would be an inevitable delay, also because of the reduced yield, and finally because the time was not propitious for negotiation with the medical profession. It was reported that the Secretary of State for Scotland now accepted the charge, providing it was levied on a script basis. Notwithstanding a variety of reservations concerning the scheme, the Committee agreed to introduce the prescription charge. By this time exemptions extended to 'the class entitled to cheap tobacco' (ie $4\frac{1}{4}$m pensioners), the $\frac{3}{4}$m receiving National Assistance, and $\frac{3}{4}$m war service disability pensioners.[49] This decision met with a hostile reception from Bevan, who produced a battery of arguments why the measure should not be introduced. His most telling point concerned the political damage likely to be done in the run up to the General Election. By way of conciliation he held out the prospect of extensive savings as a result of a major review of the service that he had just initiated. Given this prospect Bevan urged that it was politically insensitive to press ahead with an unpopular measure yielding trivial savings.[50] He added that introduction of charges would necessitate consultation with the BMA, the secretary of which was standing as Conservative candidate for Luton, so ensuring that the Government's action would be subjected to 'grotesque misrepresentation by the Opposition'. Attlee promptly agreed that any action should be deferred until after the election.[51] Looking back over these events Bevan admitted that he could be accused of 'bad tactics' over the prescription charge, but he defended his manoeuvres to circumvent this charge, claiming that he knew from the outset that it would never be imposed because it was impracticable.[52]

The Treasury was dismayed at the failure of its campaign for economy in the National Health Service. Receding expectations from the prescription charge exacerbated anxieties concerning likely future trends in expenditure. In preparation for the 1950/51 estimates Treasury officials prepared a list of drastic charges and economies relating to the Ministry of Health vote.[53] Only three were adopted by Cripps, abandonment of the supplementary ophthalmic service, termination of merit awards, and lowering of council house standards.[54] Bevan pointed out that abolition of the supplementary eye service and merit awards, although desirable objectives, would present him with serious practical difficulties. Reacting to mounting pressure for reductions in the scope of the health service, he called on the Chancellor either to preserve the scheme in its entirety, or to 'substitute a revised, interim and austerity scheme', a course which he regarded as infinitely preferable to 'whittling away' at his service. Woodburn was more optimistic about being able to amend distinction awards, but he was unwilling to consider cutting back the ophthalmic or dental service before the election.[55] In the light of predicted increases in health expenditure Bridges found Bevan's response 'pretty frightening'.[56]

The crisis over NHS expenditure had now been developing for over a year. But the election had arrived with very little tangible progress towards a solution. Action on charges had effectively been blocked. Apart from a mild circular designed to tighten up hospital budgeting, virtually nothing had been done to hold down hospital expenditure. The only substantial success emanated from correcting obvious defects in the system of estimating payments to dentists. With growing concern over the advance of social service spending, and because the health services were leading this advance, with the hospital services representing the cutting edge of the trend, it was inevitable that economy in the National Health Service would be at the head of the social service agenda of the next Government.

(iii) CRIPPS' LAST CAMPAIGN: FEBRUARY–APRIL 1950

By contrast with the 1945 manifesto, the 1950 Labour election manifesto made only passing and general reference to the National Health Service. On the other hand, the Conservative manifesto, as well as containing a pledge to maintain and improve the health service, specified action in four areas, administrative efficiency, balance in the dental service, strengthening the position of the family doctor, and improving appointments to hospital boards of management. Iain Macleod is credited with this contribution to the manifesto.[57]

The General Election of 23 February 1950 returned Labour with an overall majority of only six seats, and with 315 seats compared with 298 for the Conservatives and their allies.[58] Attlee left the upper echelons of his Cabinet virtually unchanged, although one important promotion affected health. The adequate but uncharismatic Arthur Woodburn was swept aside somewhat unceremoniously to make way for Hector McNeil at the Scottish Office. McNeil was fifteen years the younger, indeed the youngest appointee to have held this office. He had been promoted rapidly, in 1946 replacing Noel-Baker as Minister of State at the Foreign Office when the latter was transferred to the Air Ministry. McNeil wanted to succeed Westwood as Secretary of State for Scotland, but Bevin refused to release him. Both Bevin and Gaitskell were impressed by McNeil. Ultimately McNeil was mentioned as a possible successor to Bevin.[59] In view of these associations it is not surprising that Bevan and McNeil were at odds both on domestic issues and foreign affairs.

Bevan's biographer attaches little weight to speculations that Bevan was thirsting for promotion. Nevertheless there was widespread feeling that Bevan wanted to move and that he favoured transfer to the Colonial Office, the post granted to James Griffiths. Gaitskell, who hoped to be appointed Minister of Health, was convinced that it was a mistake from the point of view of finance to leave Bevan in this post.[60] Within the department it was doubted whether Bevan had enough commitment to overhauling and pruning the service to merit his retention.[61] It was variously rumoured that either Bevin or Morrison persuaded Attlee that Bevan should be left at his department to clear up the mess critics claimed that he had created.[62]

There was one further complication. Attlee returned to the proposal for transferring housing from the Ministry of Health to Town and Country Planning. Dalton was chosen to head the new housing and planning department, but as a condition of acceptance he wanted Bevan replaced by Griffiths at the Ministry of Health. At first Attlee refused to move Bevan, leaving Dalton with the small department of Town and Country Planning, although retaining his Cabinet rank. Dalton's enhancement was only delayed for a year, until Bevan's removal from the Ministry of Health became an imperative rather than desirable objective.[63]

During its second short term the Labour Government took more decisive action to curb health expenditure. A slender majority and greatly strengthened opposition opened the Government to sharper attack on the always controversial health issue. Bevan's critics within the Cabinet were running out of patience with him, while his patience with them was also virtually exhausted. The Treasury line was strengthened by the arrival of Gaitskell. Finally, many of the excuses for high and unpredictable expenditure acceptable at the outset of the service were now inapplicable.

The storm broke immediately over the new Government with the arrival of a fresh round of Supplementary Estimates. In January 1950 it was anticipated that Supplementary Estimates of about £90m for the year 1949/50 would be required.[64] In the event Supplementary Estimates amounting to £89m were published on March 1950. The Opposition now took advantage of a particularly prominent target and faced the Government with a motion introduced into the Committee of Supply on the Civil Supplementary Estimates, deprecating the failure of the Chancellor to carry out his declared intention of requiring civil departments to keep within the limits of their original estimates. The National Health Service was inevitably at the centre of this storm. In preparation for the defence Bevan was requested to prepare a memorandum setting out arrangements for future control of expenditure.[65] This document was essentially a descriptive survey of the workings of the service. It offered little prospect of immediate economies. Bevan was quite unrepentant on the crucial issue of hospital expenditure, where he urged the Cabinet to recognise that 'the plain fact is that the cost of the hospital service not only will, but ought to, increase . . . . The position cannot be evaded that a nationally owned and administered hospital service will always involve a very considerable and expanding Exchequer outlay'.[66] Hospital charges were firmly ruled out as a device for reducing this burden on the exchequer.[67] On the cost of prescriptions, Bevan again offered only limited hopes of savings, and he was insistent that if charges were introduced, prescription charges should not be introduced in isolation. This did not imply sympathy for across-the-board charges. When it came to the point of considering dental and ophthalmic charges he argued that introduction of these charges was premature because it would constitute a 'basic alteration of the whole principle of the health service on the evidence of these early, and unreliable, experiences of its working'.[68] Bevan's paper warned against panic measures in response to unforeseeable hazards which had affected the new service. He was satisfied that the ongoing process of tightening up financial control, together with natural fall in demand, would resolve the expenditure problem without necessitating either cuts or charges.

In the Cabinet meeting Bevan urged his colleagues to accept Supplementary Estimates as an inevitable consequence of a new and expanding service.[69] Rather than committing themselves to panic measures he appealed for them to await the judgement of experts, particularly Sir Cyril Jones, whom he had appointed to undertake an independent examination of the financial administration of the service. And this was merely the cornerstone of a range of inquiries to be conducted by the department or its advisory committees, as well as by independent research bodies. Bevan repeated his opposition to charges, either for hospital treatment, or for the supply of drugs or appliances.

In reply Cripps pointed out that such large Supplementary Estimates laid the Government open to the charge that public expenditure was out of control. The least he could do in defending the Supplementary Estimates was to promise that the estimates for 1950/51 would be strictly observed, and that effective means of controlling hospital expenditure were being evolved. Following discussion there was general agreement that the service should keep within its estimates and that unexpected expenditure in one field should be compensated for by savings in another. Some Ministers felt that this degree of financial control would obviate the need for a system of charges. Bevan was clearly satisfied with an arrangement that effectively shelved charges in return for acceptance of the 1950/51 estimates as a fixed ceiling for NHS expenditure. It was also minuted that the Cabinet agreed to defer discussion of health services finances until a later date.[70] This latter minute was received with consternation by Bevan, who complained to Attlee that he deserved 'a little peace to get on with my proper work without this continual nibbling'.[71] At the first opportunity Bevan questioned the accuracy of the minute, but this attempt at decisive consolidation of his gains proved counterproductive. Cripps affirmed that he was still thinking of imposing charges as a means of keeping under the agreed ceiling. While asserting that it had not been necessary to mention charges in his statement to the House of Commons on 14 March, Cripps successfully sought his colleagues' agreement to reconsidering health charges before the Budget. Bevan was thus faced not only with a resumption of deliberations on NHS expenditure, but also with a Cabinet commitment to reopen the question of charges.

In fact the debate on Supplementary Estimates passed off without incident. Crookshank predictably accused the Government of failing to honour its pledges to economise, singling out the health service as 'a very big hole through which the money has been pouring'—an image explicitly derived from Bevan's celebrated remark concerning cascades of medicine.[72] Cripps likewise concentrated on the health service, reminding the House of Commons that he had always accepted the need for additional expenditure, for instance to provide improved conditions for nurses and hospital staffs.[73]

Crookshank's aggressive line failed to set the tone for the debate. Conservatives were not baying for cuts and charges. In particular Hill and Macleod, two newly arrived health experts, were decidedly conciliatory in their approach. Charles Hill, in his maiden speech, limited himself to constructive suggestions concerning the relation between Regional Hospital Boards and Hospital Management Committees.[74] A more substantial contribution was made by Iain Macleod, also in a maiden speech where, apart from condemning overpayment of dentists, he was generally supportive of the social services.[75] Bevan found himself in the unusual position of having nothing to attack and being able to concur with Hill. Rises in hospital expenditure were excused by Bevan as a universal feature of health care in advanced industrialised societies.[76]

By contrast with relative calm in Parliament, an almost apocalyptic tone was creeping into the briefs prepared by officials for certain of the senior Cabinet Ministers, while there were also signs of agitation concerning delay in handling the expenditure crisis. Morrison was told that Bevan was 'heading the Government straight for another 1931 financial crisis in the very near future, and unless the Government can show that it knows how to adopt a pace of development of the Health Service which the national economy can bear, something will have to go before long'. Bevin demanded information about discussions between the health departments and the Treasury over the costs of the health service.[77] Within the Cabinet Office it was the firm view that delays in grappling with this problem were primarily the responsibility of the Treasury and Chancellor of the Exchequer, the latter having failed to implement decisions reached at the Cabinet a year previously.[78] Other Ministers were therefore not justified in claiming that the Minister of Health had failed to bring this matter before his colleagues. The Secretary of the Cabinet informed the Treasury that he was making these facts clear to the Prime Minister in order to forestall recriminations. It was recommended that Cripps should now seize the initiative and bring the matter to the Cabinet before Easter.[79] The ailing Cripps was at this stage joined by Hugh Gaitskell, who was transferred from Fuel and Power after the 1950 election to join the Treasury as Minister of State for Economic Affairs. Prior to this date Bevan and Gaitskell had enjoyed minor social contacts. Bevan was among the leading politicians to congratulate Gaitskell on his promotion. By contrast with both Attlee and Cripps, Gaitskell appreciated Bevan's qualities as a politician without being linked to him by bonds of sentiment forged by common pre-war experiences.[80]

Gaitskell immediately joined the party favouring imposition of a ceiling on NHS spending set below the 1950/51 estimates in order to force the health departments into making cuts or accepting imposition of charges. Looking back on the previous inconclusive attempts to achieve this objective, Gaitskell blamed 'policy compromise' resulting from Bevan's threat of resignation and the unwillingness of the Cabinet to abandon the principle of a free service. Gaitskell believed that 'cuts would have done us a lot of good'.[81] Morrison was informed that the Chancellor was now 'thoroughly alive to the need for imposing a ceiling', but the Minister of Health was as far as ever from being willing to accept any kind of financial control. In Morrison's view the Chancellor's ceiling of £392m for 1950/51 was too generous by some £42m.[82]

Attlee was told by the Cabinet Secretary that strong political and personal feelings generated over NHS expenditure had precluded consultation between officials of the departments involved. Even the Secretary of State for Scotland had produced his more constructive paper for the forthcoming Cabinet meeting without consultation with the Treasury or Ministry of Health. The Cabinet Secretary noted that the Chancellor wanted the Cabinet to approve the principle of charges. To the basic question facing the Cabinet, 'is it politically possible for a Government to abandon the principle of a free and universal health service?' the Cabinet Secretary replied unequivocally that charges were necessary. Already a precedent was set; the IS charge had received legal sanction. Charges would provide insurance against the 'fatal' risk of exceeding the estimates for 1950/51. Finally an expanding service must offer counterbalancing savings.[83]

Cabinet exchanges in March 1950 had produced agreement on introduction of a ceiling for health expenditure, but the Cabinet had not arrived at an unambiguous definition of this ceiling, and it had not agreed on sanctions to be applied in case the ceiling was not observed.

In preparing the Budget, the Treasury committee conveyed the message that the 'economy is overloaded' and that strong countermeasures were required.[84] Of the main alternatives, there seemed to be no room for major saving on defence or food subsidies. An increase in the National Insurance contribution was thought undesirable. By a process of elimination the committee reached the conclusion that the National Health Service offered the only avenue for substantial economies, which might be achieved by temporarily eliminating parts of the service, or introducing a substantial package of charges.

As generally recounted, the next step involved dramatic intervention by Harold Wilson to preclude Bevan's resignation and achieve a workable compromise. On the basis of Wilson's own testimony it is suggested that Bevan, perhaps sensing that pressures for health service economies and charges were becoming uncontainable, openly threatened resignation. Wilson staved off this crisis, by persuading Cripps yet again to defer charges, while obtaining Bevan's agreement to accept a Cabinet Committee to monitor control of NHS expenditure. With this compromise 'charges, including the prescription charges, had been stopped, and Bevan lived to threaten to resign another day'.[85]

Records relating to the three Cabinet meetings held in the first week of April suggest that the compromise described by Wilson was only slowly worked out and that Bevan was once again assisted by wavering among his colleagues concerning health charges.

Because rival papers circulated by the Health Ministers and himself suggested that it would be difficult to reach a compromise, Cripps wrote to Attlee indicating that Bevan's resignation was a real possibility. In Cripps' view their discussion on the health service would lead to a 'very strong clash of opinion and may in certain events lead to the (real) resignation of the M of H'.[86] Cripps suspected that overspending would become apparent within a couple of months. Accordingly he wanted to be forearmed with means of preventing over-spending rather than waiting until limits were exceeded and then attempting belated action to effect controls. £350m was mentioned as the right level of spending for the NHS, but in practice this target was unrealistic for 1950/51. His compromise involved abandoning 'this cutting down but only providing that some certain means of preventing supplementaries were devised'. Cripps agreed with McNeil's contention that the extent of charges needed to keep NHS expenditure within its agreed limit could not now be predicted, but Cripps refused to accept this as an argument for inaction. It was necessary to agree 'to the powers being taken now but the actual charges not being imposed until such time as it becomes clear that the rate of expenditure is exceeding that allowed for in the estimates'. The final decision on the implementation of charges should then be taken before the end of the session if it seemed that the £392m ceiling of the current estimate was being exceeded. In return for this compromise Cripps wanted a 'high-level body' established to decide on charges and their order of priority. It was envisaged that charges would be introduced from time to time in order to keep expenditure within the agreed limit. It is clear from his note that Cripps wanted charges to compensate for expansion of the service, but he was not explicit in committing himself to a £350m ceiling as a target for the next few years.

Attlee supported Cripps, 'Clearly we must take a firm stand on this expenditure'.[87] Any ambiguity concerning the ceiling to be imposed on health expenditure was cleared up in the Cabinet memorandum circulated by Cripps, proposing the tougher alternative, which was defended by Cripps at the first of three Cabinet meetings held to discuss NHS expenditure. It was suggested that expenditure should be kept within the £392m limit for 1950/51 and thereafter reduced to £350m, for which purpose a package of charges would be worked out with the Ministers involved, and then introduced. Cripps was vehemently supported by Morrison, who pointed out that Bevan's memorandum failed to offer guarantees that the original estimate would not be exceeded. He believed that the Government had been over-ambitious in introducing its comprehensive health service, with the result that priority classes were suffering reduction in the quality of their services.[88]

Bevan only circulated a short memorandum, repeating his objection to charges in principle and pointing out that the charges under consideration would yield nothing like the revenue needed to reduce the health service budget by the 10% requested by the Chancellor. In discussion he appealed to his colleagues to stand by their previous decision not to impose charges. In the new parliamentary situation he believed that a charges Bill might not be accepted by the House of Commons. Finally such action would have deeper symbolic importance as 'a shock to their supporters in this country and a grave disappointment to Socialist opinion throughout the world'.[89]

McNeil, the new Secretary of State for Scotland, departed from the line adopted by his predecessor and broke ranks with Bevan. His long memorandum bypassed the question of principle and considered practical means to yield a 10% reduction in NHS expenditure. The only major concession sought was delaying charges until 1951/52. He agreed with Bevan that it would be a mistake to overestimate possible yields from hospital charges, pointing out that real savings were only possible by decisive measures such as abandoning the dental service for those over 21. He was in favour of delaying decision on such drastic retrenchment for a few months, while it was discovered whether more routine economies were achieving significant savings.[90]

The second Cabinet meeting reviewed in detail the various openings for economy within the service, the most notable concession being Bevan's suggestion that a Cabinet Committee should be appointed under the chairmanship of the Prime Minister to review monthly reports from the health departments on progress with economies.[91] Despite identification of about ten areas in which distinct economies were being made, 'some Ministers', probably led by Morrison, argued that these economies added up to very little and that they offered no prospect of achieving the Chancellor's £350m target. In their view, both charges and cuts in services were needed. Some Ministers then spoke for hospital charges; the majority were against, but they were favourable to some charges in the ophthalmic and dental field, primarily to contain abuses. They were generally unsympathetic to the prescription charge, particularly because it would seem that benefits were now charged for which had been available free to insured workers since 1911. National Insurance contributors would perceive themselves as being charged twice for their general medical service benefit.

Following the failure to reach a conclusion at the Cabinet meetings on 3 and 4 April, Attlee called a special meeting of Ministers representing the two sides on the evening of 4 April which eventually agreed a compromise draft Budget statement prepared by Cripps.[92] Even then disagreements again surfaced and further concessions were made at the Cabinet meeting on 5 April.

Cripps now defended his last-ditch position, insisting on the £392m limit for 1950/51 and requesting to announce in his Budget powers to impose charges should this limit be exceeded. The ceiling met no objection, but Cripps faced such strong opposition to the announcement of powers to impose charges that Attlee found it impossible to conclude that the Cabinet was in favour of 'the general application of the principle of Charges throughout this Service'. The prospects of reducing the health budget for future years to £350m had now quite evaporated. In Attlee's summing up for the purpose of the Budget statement the Chancellor was requested to specify that the Health Ministers had the necessary powers to maintain their expenditure within the specified ceiling, but that an amending Bill would be introduced should these prove to be insufficient.[93]

In his abandoned draft Budget statement Cripps was pledged to take whatever steps were necessary 'whether by reduction of services, by contribution to their expenditure, or by any other necessary means, so as to keep the charge on the Exchequer down'.[94] In the agreed revision of this statement, direct reference to prescription charges was added, the clear implication being that the power to impose these charges would be used should other economies in the general medical service not come to fruition. Despite all the energetic opposition of Bevan and inhibitions of the Cabinet, prescription charges were by no means a dead issue. Regardless of lack of specificity concerning economies Cripps was firmly committed to his £392m ceiling. There was 'no excuse for exceeding the estimates in the coming 12 months'. It was not possible 'to permit any overall increase in the expenditure on the Health Service. Any expansion in one part of the Service must in future be met by economies or, if necessary, by contraction in others'.[95]

(iv) BEVAN INTRANSIGENT: MAY 1950–JANUARY 1951

The above events contained certain elements of compromise. Cripps conceded a high ceiling for NHS expenditure, while Bevan fell under the suzerainty of a Cabinet Committee. But the central issue of charges remained unresolved. Any increase beyond the £392m 1950/51 estimate would open the way to charges, and there was a strong view that charges should be introduced in any case in order to peg down NHS expenditure to the £350m regarded as the proper level by the Chancellor of the Exchequer.

The hard-won ceiling was punctured almost before it was imposed. The labyrinthine pay negotiation machinery of the NHS was rolling inexorably forward. By April 1950 it was clear that imminent Whitley awards would raise 1950/51 expenditure above the newly agreed limit. The Ministry of Health asked for confirmation of Bevan's advice that the Chancellor had excluded Whitley awards from the ceiling. This construction was strongly denied by the Treasury where it was observed that this precedent would rapidly turn the ceiling into a floor. Cripps was turned to for confirmation, 'What I said was that I could not expect that there would be included in the estimates awards as to which no forecast could have been made—ie entirely unpredicted. They should nevertheless try to keep within the ceiling by savings'.[96] Within the Treasury it was believed that Bevan's line was 'clean contrary both to what the Cabinet had decided' and to the agreed text of the Chancellor's Budget speech.[97] It was hoped to hold up Whitley negotiations until the issue of principle was considered by the Cabinet Committee, but reluctantly Cripps agreed, first to allow negotiations concerning senior nurses to go ahead without waiting for the committee, and then to exclude Whitley awards altogether from the ceiling.[98]

Once it was decided to establish a Cabinet Committee to watch over the National Health Service, the terms of reference and composition of this Committee were agreed with little dissent. The terms of reference agreed at the first meeting on 22 April had been circulating in draft for ten days. The committee's remit comprised:

1. To fix limits for the total cost of the NHS in the financial year 1951/52 and succeeding years.
2. To keep under review the course of expenditure on this Service, on the basis of monthly statements by the Health Departments, and if the cost seems likely to exceed the limits set for the current year, to devise appropriate remedies.
3. Generally to assist the Health Ministers in securing due economy in the administration of this service.[99]

The Cabinet Secretary proposed a committee of seven, which Attlee slightly, but significantly amended by adding the Lord

President, Morrison.[100] Attlee also wanted to know whether Cripps himself wished to join the committee in place of the Minister of State for Economic Affairs, but Cripps deferred to his keen adjutant Gaitskell. Morrison at first demurred until he was satisfied that the committee's powers were sufficiently substantial and that the committee would be fully involved in expenditure matters raised between the Treasury and health departments. Morrison complained bitterly that this committee would not have been needed if problems of expenditure had been brought before the relevant committees at an earlier stage.

As finally constituted, the Cabinet Committee on the National Health Service comprised: the Prime Minister (Attlee), Lord President (Morrison; from 9 March 1951, Addison); Lord Privy Seal (Addison; from 9 March 1951, Bevin; from 26 April 1951, Stokes), Minister of Health (Bevan; from 17 January 1951, Marquand), Secretary of State for Scotland (McNeil), Minister of State for Economic Affairs (Gaitskell, continuing from 19 October 1950 as Chancellor of the Exchequer), Minister of National Insurance (Summerskill), Minister of Pensions (Marquand; from 17 January 1951, Isaacs).[101]

The new committee began work with the melancholy realisation that NHS expenditure was already running at least £10m beyond its limit for 1950/51, the excess resulting primarily from lost revenue occasioned by non-imposition of the prescription charge, Whitley awards, and rising costs of hospital supplies.[102] This excess dwarfed the health departments' catalogue of actual and prospective savings, mainly achieved by tightening up on payments to practitioners and cutting back in the ophthalmic and dental fields, which were anticipated to yield about £2m. Among these reductions the only substantial economy offered on the hospital side involved abolition of travelling expenses for hospital patients, which would save less than £½m. The Secretary of State concluded hopefully that their accounts represented a 'literal increase', but a 'comparative saving'.[103] The Prime Minister was advised that the health departments' proposals for economies in the family practitioner services could be taken further, but that these could never make a significant contribution to economy because the real problems lay in the hospital area, which threatened a 'flood' of expenditure. It was argued that additional resources were being swallowed up by extravagant staffing rather than by improvements to patient care. There was thus an urgent need for the health departments to create effective means of controlling hospital expenditure without 'creating a vast administrative machinery to play cat and mouse with the voluntary bodies'. It was hoped that the report by Sir Cyril Jones would settle predicaments concerning hospital expenditure.[104]

At the first meeting of the Cabinet Committee Bevan elaborated on the health departments' action to 'secure a grip on expenditure', expressing confidence in closer monitoring of expenditure by means of monthly returns, standardisation of accountancy procedures, control of new developments, and introduction of norms for establishments. This battery of measures was greeted with pessimism and the Health Ministers were pressed to place finance operations in the hands of civil servants accountable to the central department, thus resurrecting a proposal first made in 1946, and reacted to favourably at that time by Bevan, but now resisted by both Health Ministers. Neither was confident that this change would improve matters. Consequently they were chary about tampering with the much cherished autonomy of local health administration. However the committee wanted to return to this proposal again.[105]

The initial meeting seems not to have raised particularly controversial issues, but Bevan felt humiliated by the very existence of the committee. Even this meeting had demonstrated propensities to interfere with policies central to the philosophy of Bevan's service. Already Gaitskell was identified as the most dangerous intruder, 'the pedantic spokesman of the Treasury's most arid doctrines'. Jennie Lee recalled that Bevan came home from this meeting 'white with passion'.[106] Gaitskell's diary made no reference to this event. It was not until the summer that he remarked on Bevan's impetuous behaviour.[107]

Bevan also felt isolated on the committee. Woodburn had generally gone along with him, but McNeil had moved away from the principle of a comprehensive and free health service. McNeil aligned himself with Morrison, offering at the right time to reintroduce his earlier proposals for cuts and charges.[108]

Despite Bevan's officials' request to slow down the pace of meetings, Attlee called the next meeting for 23 May.[109] The meeting itself was desultory. Ministers skirmished lightly on widely scattered topics without coming to positive conclusions on anything. Once again the most tangible hints about cuts occurred in the family practitioner arena. Gaitskell warned that Supplementary Estimates might be accepted for wage increases, but not for routine hazards such as epidemics.[110] Morrison was restive. He blamed Attlee for allowing the initiative to slip away and threatened to resign from the committee if Attlee was not more decisive in his leadership.[111]

The morale of the critics was restored by a stern memorandum from Gaitskell reminding the committee that it was set to renege on a firm Government commitment by sliding into a yet further Supplementary Estimate for the health services. He put forward proposals for a more rigorous assault on the hospital expenditure problem, invoking hotel charges and curtailment of services as one of the three main courses of prospective action.[112] Gaitskell's memorandum came into headlong conflict with a clutch of memoranda from Bevan, who, clearly on the offensive, bypassed the question of economies, and instead pressed the case for greater resources to develop services. Pointing to the difficulties in mounting major capital projects under the current budgetary system, he proposed that hospital authorities should raise capital by loan, which was regarded by the critics as much the more expensive alternative and a dangerous precedent for other services. To underline the parlous state of hospital service, and possibly as an antidote to claims about extravagance, Bevan pointed to the severe congestion of facilities 'gross overcrowding, as in mental hospitals particularly; early discharge, as in maternity cases; long waiting lists, which tend to grow rather than fall in spite of increased numbers of patients treated; and congested out-patient departments or long waits for appointments'. As the analogue to hospital development, Bevan urged the introduction of health centres as the base for efficient and modern family practitioner services. On points of detail, Bevan requested additional funds to expand the supply of hearing aids, and he told the Committee that the recovery of spectacle lenses was not a practicable proposition.[113] McNeil gave Bevan no support. His own memoranda pointed out that Bevan's modernisation proposals would drive up the cost of the family practitioner services. Neither was he in favour of loans for hospital building, instead preferring simpler changes to facilitate longer-term planning.[114]

Bevan had held his critics at bay since the late autumn of 1948. His star had reached its apogee. Now it was on the wane. Events were turning decisively against him.

At the next committee meeting on 28 June 1950, Bevan needed to explain why it was still not possible to provide reliable figures for monthly hospital expenditure.[115] He was also uncomfortable about the recently produced Jones report, which he now played down on the grounds that it had little short-term relevance. On expenditure, unrepentantly he offered no guarantee that the estimates would not be exceeded, 'The hospitals, and the other health services, were living organisms and it was difficult to keep within conventional financial limits'. This uncompromising challenge to financial orthodoxy was the cue for McNeil's lament that he was 'driven to the view' that estimates could be observed by cutting back the dental service and suspending the ophthalmic service. Despite having been briefed by Gaitskell just before the meeting, Attlee now demonstrated some sympathy with Bevan, by opposing 'drastic pruning of individual services' and favouring the case for summation of minor savings.[116] Bevan offered the controversial alternative of restrictions on prescribing of proprietary medicines rather than the 1s prescription charge as a vehicle for major economy in the general medical service.

This digression was unsuccessful. Discussion returned to the cost of the hospital service. A freeze on hospital establishments was urged. Bevan objected, but Gaitskell pressed on, forcing Bevan to defend steps already taken to control hospital staffs. Once again Bevan refused to undermine the authority of local hospital administrations by introducing an extension of central control. Although not minuted it is probable that at this meeting Gaitskell raised his hospital charges option, this being the likely cause of Gaitskell's report that Bevan 'provoked by something I had said, slammed his papers down and started to walk out of the room. The PM, however, summoned him back and smoothed him down . . . It is a very wearing affair—always having to nag one's colleagues, and especially when they are as slippery and difficult as the Minister of Health'.[117]

Bevan was now gripped by the spectre of the collapse of his health service; he had fallen into a climactic struggle between socialism and its enemies, 'He pictured several of his Cabinet colleagues, now assisted by this glorified civil servant, banded together, contentedly it seemed, to undermine the greatest Socialist achievement of the Labour Government. He noted not the will and courage but the other aspects of Gaitskellism, the parched political imagination, the pedantic insistence on lesser truths in the presence of great ones'.[118]

Thus, at the very first meeting of the Cabinet Committee to tackle points of substance, Bevan sensed that he was entering a major political confrontation, a struggle for survival between himself and Gaitskell. His immediate instinct was to broaden the front of opposition and withdraw from the regular Thursday dinners held by Cripps for Ministers involved with the Treasury. Bevan remarked that it was known that he would resign rather than accept health charges, but Gaitskell had gone on pressing this solution. Gaitskell's 'unjustifiable needling' on this question was invoked to explain his outburst of resentment at the Cabinet Committee.[119]

Compared with the heat of June the temperature subsided during the summer. Memoranda submitted by Bevan to the July committee meeting were relatively uncontroversial, and the Jones Report generated a degree of superficial harmony.

Bevan reported progress on limiting the prescription of proprietary medicines and on cutting back travelling expenses to out-patients, and he delivered the first quarterly report on expenditure, which showed that spending was not running ahead of the estimate.[120] It was beginning to look as if administrative economies in the hospital field would eliminate the need for charges or cuts. Subject to minor reservations the Jones Report was welcomed by Bevan as a 'useful assessment by an independent observer'. On the tightening up of hospital administration, the central issue of the Jones Report and the one upon which the committee most looked for guidance, Bevan was favourable to reduction in the authority of the RHBs and increasing contact between his department and HMCs. Thus RHBs would 'drop back into an advisory position; they were a necessity in getting the service going, but they become less necessary as it gets under full weigh'. It was 'inherently impossible to ensure a proper implementation of national policy at the periphery when that policy is mediated through fourteen separate regional bodies, all naturally watchful of their prestige and their independence'. In fact Bevan offered to go further than Jones by denying Boards a voice in the appointment of consultants and in planning capital works. He was, however, unwilling to follow Jones on the removal of doctors from management bodies. Bevan reminded colleagues that this participation had been a condition of their entry into the service. Their removal from management bodies would be bitterly resisted. Any gains would be outweighed by losses of goodwill and co-operation. Bevan was thus willing to follow Jones part of the way, but he was unwilling to extend central control to the point of undermining the devolutionist philosophy of the NHS.[121]

The Treasury saw the Jones Report as confirmation of their long-held view that there existed 'lack of financial control over the hospital service'. It was agreed that the primary aim should be tightening the links between the Ministry of Health and HMCs. Treasury thinking generally coincided with the Ministry of Health memorandum, but it was still felt that key officers should either enjoy 'protected status' or become civil servants.[122]

Morrison was advised that Jones had produced 'a most useful and important report', substantially supporting Morrison's criticism of the health services. The Cabinet Office also saw Jones as an ally, 'It shows quite clearly that the present form of hospital administration allows waste and fails to put first things first'. Bevan's new spirit of flexibility was recognised but he was still not sufficiently aware of the intrinsic defects of the system and was using 'philosophy' as an escape from a reality in which 'waste, misdirection of energies and inefficiency have to be accepted as the price for the degree of freedom which should be accorded to an HMC'.[123]

The Jones Report, like Dr Chasuble's sermon on The Manna in the Wilderness, was adaptable for all occasions and everyone's tastes. The July meeting of the Cabinet Committee was primarily concerned with the Jones recommendations. Attlee urged rapid implementation of hospital 'reorganisation' under which 'regional hospital boards should be purely advisory in character' before the current system became too entrenched. However, McNeil was resistant to applying such a radical modification in Scotland, where he believed there was a more positive role for RHBs. Opinion was divided over the status of key officers of health authorities; arguments were rehearsed in favour of protected status and the civil service alternative. The Health Ministers wanted to wait until the new organisation was functioning to see whether such a change was advisable, but the rest of the committee preferred immediate action.[124] In the course of discussions Bevan made an unfortunate slip about the number of HMCs which he gave as 2,000. After the meeting he wrote apologetically to Gaitskell, admitting that there were only about 380.[125]

Signs that the committee was reaching conclusions destined to have a major impact proved to be illusory. As the summer passed the Cabinet Office became increasingly agitated about the failure of the Ministry of Health to produce heads of legislation for a Bill to dissolve Regional Hospital Boards. Attlee still wanted legislation early in the session and an announcement in the King's Speech at the opening of Parliament. Although the Ministry produced the requested outline of legislation in September, this was accompanied by a memorandum arguing forcefully against this change, and suggesting that such disruption would undermine attempts at economies in the hospital service. The associated idea of altering the status of officers was asserted to be 'contrary to the whole spirit of administration by responsible voluntary bodies on which the hospital service depends'.[126] McNeil's parallel memorandum was also totally antagonistic to reorganisation. McNeil even co-opted Jones for support, persuading Jones to admit that 'changes in the Scottish organisation are unnecessary and uncalled for'.[127] The Health Ministers were assisted by reports showing that hospital expenditure was still under control.[128] But little comfort could be gained from this new-found financial probity, because the Prime Minister was being advised that the recent decision of the Government to instigate a 'large increase in our preparations on defence' would necessitate all civil expenditures being 'pruned to the greatest practicable extent', including abandonment of desirable services. Attlee was urged to reopen the question of charges as a means of guaranteeing against future increases in health service costs during the armaments drive.[129]

The October committee meeting was again a low-key event. In Gaitskell's absence Douglas Jay attended on behalf of Cripps, whose resignation on health grounds was then imminent. Bevan tried to instil an air of calm by invoking favourable trends on most expenditure fronts. The committee was by no means content to abandon the scheme for hospital reorganisation, but the issue was not pressed to a conclusion unfavourable to the Health Ministers.[130]

Slackening of pressure on Bevan proved to be only temporary. Already in the late autumn notes were being exchanged between the Treasury and Cabinet Office concerning the level of NHS expenditure to be fixed for 1951/52—regarded by them as a 'hot potato'. It was thought that the Lord President would be the best agent to raise this delicate issue before the committee.[131] There was also an urge to reintroduce the idea of staffing limits, something 'irreconcilable with the present powers of HMCs and BGs. It is no use giving orders to the chauffeur if the steering column is not connected to the front wheels'.[132] Of the specific hospital questions under review, consultants' remuneration had been under increasing discussion since the summer. There was feeling in the press, among medical researchers, and even within the profession against merit awards and the artificially advantageous position of part-time consultants. Moran defended merit awards before the House of Lords.[133]

Newly appointed as Chancellor of the Exchequer, Gaitskell circulated a strongly worded memorandum to the November committee meeting urging that the remuneration of both whole-time and part-time consultants should be brought down. Gaitskell believed that inflated incomes of consultants had resulted in an 'interminable succession of claims' from aggrieved professional groups. It was argued that consultants enjoyed the best of both worlds, security of their state salaries and pensions, but also levels of remuneration hitherto only available to the elite of the private sector. In order to restore balance Gaitskell proposed that new entrants to the consultant grade should be paid on a lower salary scale.[134] Gaitskell's intervention provoked a strong riposte from Bevan, but a more sympathetic response from McNeil. Bevan denied all Gaitskell's basic assertions and argued that there was no basis for altering the structure of rewards to consultants, except with respect to incidental points such as income-tax allowances.[135]

The Prime Minister was presented with arguments for scrapping the Spens consultants agreement, which it was believed constituted a barrier to effective rationalisation of their salaries. It was thought that at the committee, Morrison and Addison would 'recommend a root and branch attack on merit awards', based on their fidelity to the MRC position. It was noted that Bevan 'does not seem to be prepared to go far enough in altering the present system', and that in this respect he seemed at variance with the Jones Report.[136]

The committee meeting on 21 November 1950 was destined to be the last one attended by Bevan, whose sense of grievance and humiliation was now heightened by witnessing his most formidable critic from the younger generation securing the succession to Cripps.[137] Gaitskell now faced him with enhanced authority, as well as being armed with a strongly critical memorandum. However Bevan and McNeil were not in an entirely weak position. Their reports on expenditure were still favourable. Their departments were still marginally within their estimates. Minor proposals were announced to ensure final consolidation of their economies. Bevan proposed controls on entry to training and tighter regulation of remuneration for part-time consultants, but he was strongly against 'root and branch' attacks on the Spens system.[138] The Committee was not satisfied that Bevan was bringing part-time consultants under sufficient control. They called on the Health Ministers to reconsider consultants' pay and to discuss ways of reducing the remuneration of this group. The more serious immediate danger of a major rise in general practitioners' incomes was scarcely noticed by the committee.

Throwing caution to the wind, and defying his critics, Bevan mused that it would be unwise to permit a surplus in the health budget, and he even suggested that spare resources should be directed into the tuberculosis or mental deficiency services.

This meeting was more controversial than the final minutes suggest. Bevan questioned the accuracy of the minute relating to consultants' pay and eventually agreed to the generalised instruction noted above rather than to a more specific recommendation about the pay of new entrants.[139] The contested minute had in fact been introduced to pacify Bevan. His intervention had unwittingly restored a minute more to the taste of the Treasury because it opened the way for wider action on consultants' pay. Other members of the committee were distressed because Bevan's speculations about profitable use of surpluses had been minuted without recording the 'shock' response to this remark emanating from Gaitskell, Morrison and others.[140] But it also seems that this group had refrained from arguing in detail against Bevan, thus, according to the secretary to the committee, spurring Bevan on to making the point twice or even three times. Attlee made no attempt to inhibit Bevan or to draw out a response.[141] Treasury and Cabinet Office officials were unhappy about the outcome of the contest. Bevan had indeed left open the question of consultants' pay, but he had fought off reconsideration of merit awards. The committee had still not come to terms with its first and prime responsibility of determining the ceiling on health expenditure for 1951/52, a problem intimately connected with the imposition of charges and introduction of cuts in services.[142]

After the November meeting of the Cabinet NHS Committee pressures built up for Bevan's transfer to the Ministry of Labour, an option refused by him only shortly before. It is quite likely that experiences of the November meeting convinced Bevan that his powers of resistance were waning and that the enhanced influence of Gaitskell on this committee would soon drive him into an untenable position. Remaining at the Ministry of Health was likely to involve frustrations and policy decisions intolerable to Bevan.[143] Consequently when, according to Foot, Attlee offered to protect the social services from further cuts, Bevan accepted the transfer, not as promotion but perhaps as the only option presented to him for remaining with the Cabinet.[144] Attlee may have thought that Bevan would lapse from his increasingly entrenched position concerning health charges when saddled with responsibility for labour discipline. However experience at the Ministry of Labour failed to diminish Bevan's uncompromising stand on health charges and it was uncongenial because it plunged him into conflict with organised labour.[145]

(v) BEVAN'S RESIGNATION: FEBRUARY–APRIL 1951

Attlee used Bevan's departure as the occasion to reintroduce his long-awaited scheme to dismember the Ministry of Health. At its establishment in 1919 this large department had absorbed most of the work of that Victorian gothic folly, the Local Government Board. The close attachment of housing to health was itself a hangover from Victorian sanitarianism. The strength of the Ministry of Health had been progressively enhanced since its inception, particularly by such measures as the Local Government Act (1929) and the National Health Service Act (1946). The Cabinet status of the Ministry had lapsed only during the wartime emergency. Under Bevan this department had reached the zenith of its influence and it had become the most rapidly expanding sector of public spending. Faced with the new policies of retrenchment Bevan found himself resisting major cuts on both the housing and health fronts.

Changes introduced since 1945 had made this department vulnerable to being fractured into its component parts without the appearance of irrationality or arbitrariness. Creation of the National Health Service itself distanced health from local government services, so weakening the traditional close association between health and housing, and paving the way for transfer of the latter to the newly formed Ministry of Town and Country

Planning. Officials speculated that political motives were also relevant. 'It is more likely the result of Dalton's ambition to get back into large departments, and sudden fear, possibly by PM possibly by Bevan that reamalgamation [Health and Town and Country Planning] would result in a Ministry which was too powerful'.[146] One major consequence, not lost on critics of the National Health Service, was that the new Ministry of Health would become a second-class department, headed by a Minister without Cabinet rank. Thus rationalisation reduced the Ministry of Health into an entity easier to control by senior Ministers.

Gaitskell favoured Robens as a replacement for Bevan, but it proved more convenient to recruit his second choice, Hilary Marquand from the Ministry of Pensions.[147] The latter office provided broad familiarity with the problems of health of various groups of the disabled and the growing mass of the elderly. The Ministry of Pensions ran its own hospitals, manufactured a wide range of surgical appliances and employed on a contract basis both consultants and many other classes of health worker. Any gaps in Marquand's education would have been filled by experience on the Cabinet Committee on the National Health Service.

Marquand had made a spirited intervention in discussions about the introduction of the 1s prescription charge. He made the case for exemption for the war disabled, partly on the ground of long standing obligation, partly to relieve pressure for an increased disability pension.[148] Marquand later reminded Bevan of the administrative tangles resulting from failure to consult the Ministry of Pensions over prescription charges, and he also offered his department's assistance over hospital organisation.[149] Marquand described the economical operation of Ministry of Pensions' hospitals to the Cabinet Committee on the NHS, but his brief memorandum sank without trace in its contorted deliberations.[150] At Bevan's last attendance of the Cabinet Committee Marquand had made a further small contribution. Experience of his department was invoked in support of the chorus of complaints that part-time consultants were overpaid.[151]

In dispensing his advice Marquand told the Cabinet Secretary that he was 'keenly interested in the development of the NHS', in response to which Bridges favoured bringing Marquand more closely into high-level discussions concerning the health services. Thus in the course of 1950 Marquand had gradually emerged as a natural successor to Bevan.[152]

The contrast between Marquand and his predecessor was immediately noted: Bevan's faults were on a very big scale, the new person appeared to be 'a man of peace', helpful perhaps with the profession, but it seemed likely that the Treasury would 'make mincemeat' of him. Whereas Bevan had been faulted for being too inflexible about changes in the NHS it seemed as if the new Minister was struggling 'to save some at least of his Health Service, at which his colleagues are picking like vultures round a corpse'. Marquand's obituary notice confessed that he was 'dull' and 'no orator'.[153]

Marquand was faced with an immediate test. At the very moment of his appointment the health departments were framing estimates of £423m for 1951/52, on an understanding, strongly disputed by the Treasury, that the £393m ceiling applied only to 1950/51. The Treasury was adamant that expenditure must be held at the level of the estimates for 1950/51, which meant that a package of charges and/or cuts was inevitable.[154]

In practice initial Treasury preparations for the 1951 Budget displayed mild confidence over NHS expenditure, anticipating stabilisation at about £400m. However charges and economies assumed new importance, partly because of the need to offset what were seen as unavoidable increases in the hospital sector, also to pay for an increase in the old age pension, but especially because of the increasing demands of rearmament. Gaitskell aimed to keep social service expenditure constant so that the whole increase in taxation could be deflected into defence expenditure, the latter being estimated to increase from £824m to £1250m in 1951/52. Within social service expenditure the National Health Service was the only candidate capable of yielding sizeable economies. The immediate goal adopted was pegging 1951/52 expenditure at the 1950/51 level, which immediately raised the likelihood of the introduction of charges.[155]

The Treasury was faced with a dilemma over the size of NHS Estimates to be published in the *Vote on Account* on 21 February 1951. In the light of his commitment to stabilising the NHS estimates Gaitskell favoured publishing £393m rather than £423m, although this had the disadvantage of being a 'phoney estimate', likely to arouse fears that cuts in the ophthalmic and dental services were being instituted. It was therefore suggested from Treasury and Ministry of Health sources that the true figure of £423m should be published, but that the Budget speech would then describe the package of cuts and charges designed to stabilise expenditure at £393m, thus allowing the departments to derive political advantage from their efforts at economy.[156] Gaitskell objected 'I do not like this: there will be a major row at once if the health estimates show this increase. We shall then find it more difficult to get the economies through because it would be said to look as though we were giving way to opposition clamour. I cannot see the objection to leaving the Hospital Finance at last year's level and the others at the department estimates level. This, I fancy, would give us a total fairly close to last year'.[157]

This conclusion was communicated to Marquand and McNeil.[158] Marquand immediately demonstrated that he was not an entirely pliable instrument by disputing what he saw as Gaitskell's attempt to tie him to an arbitrarily determined cut in expenditure. He had promised to seek cuts and to put forward proposals, but the yield was yet to be decided. He therefore refused to agree to Gaitskell's proposal. Marquand showed every sign of picking up Bevan's defensive style, pointing out that cuts in the health service would appear to be paying for armaments. Furthermore, cuts in the hospital service would result in strong opposition throughout the constituencies. He reminded Gaitskell that the NHS was 'the most popular of all our new institutions'.[159] By contrast McNeil agreed to publishing an estimate around £400m, but he supported Marquand in resisting cuts in the hospital service.[160] A last-minute meeting with the Health Ministers resulted in their agreement to Gaitskell's line, although a minor concession was made, increasing the *Vote on Account* estimate to £398m. This figure was formally agreed at the first meeting of the Cabinet NHS Committee to be attended by Marquand in his capacity as Minister of Health and it was the only item of business at that meeting.[161]

Marquand and McNeil quickly presented the Cabinet Committee with their preferences concerning cuts. Marquand rejected suspension of the dental and ophthalmic services, and he thought that the committee would continue to be unsympathetic to hospital charges. In his view the hospital service was underfinanced and there was no room for more than their current efficiency drive. He rejected the most lucrative package (suspension of the dental and supplementary ophthalmic services, plus the prescription charge), instead opting for the prescription charge, together with dental and ophthalmic charges (the latter conceded reluctantly), which would yield only £11m in the first year, but £32m per annum subsequently. His department would need to find more than £10m in the first year by other savings.[162] McNeil was less inhibited than Marquand about hospital charges, but his order of priorities was similar. He was 'reluctantly driven to the conclusion that we must resurrect' the 1s prescription charge but this should be imposed with exemptions as previously agreed. Despite the political shock involved, he maintained that the greatest saving should come from restriction of the dental service to priority classes.[163]

Despite their constructive and conciliatory approach, the Health Ministers' proposals were not viewed kindly within the Treasury. They were judged misguided in adopting the 'fiction' of £398m as their target, rather than the £393m wanted by the Chancellor.

There was no confidence in the Ministers' assessment of the hospital situation. The Treasury felt that there was room for both economies and charges, but these would need more time for preparation than was then available. In the short term it was recommended that the Chancellor should be 'quite flat-footed' on other economies, the dental and ophthalmic services should be suspended, and the prescription charge introduced without exemptions.[164] Gaitskell communicated a demand for further savings, criticising the Ministers for not clearing their schemes with the Treasury. He set them a £40m target for savings. It was explained that these savings were needed to support a rise in benefits to old age pensioners, and because of increasing defence obligations.[165]

The Health Ministers were naturally disappointed that their response was held to be insufficient, but at a meeting with Gaitskell on 28 February 1951, they were persuaded to accept £393m as the target for cuts, on the understanding that the National Insurance Fund would bear part of the cost. It was intended that this charge would be met by increasing employees' contributions. Gaitskell wanted this measure to be first considered by the NHS Committee rather than by the full Cabinet. Undoubtedly, Bevan's objections to increasing the National Insurance contribution were still fresh in memory.[166]

Having prepared the health departments for a major package of economies, Gaitskell tested the reactions of his senior Cabinet colleagues. On 6 March he met Attlee, Bevin and Morrison to announce the introduction of 'a new principle into the Health Service viz the levying of charges', which Gaitskell presented as the alternative preferable to suspending services, or limiting them to priority classes. He reported the agreement of the Health Ministers to the £393m target, which would be reached by means of implementation of the package of charges proposed by Marquand, plus a cut in hospital expenditure of £10m (England and Wales) and £0.25m (Scotland) with a total yield of £38m in a full year. Gaitskell complained that his suggestions were 'greeted with no enthusiasm at all'; his proposals for health savings were not opposed, but his colleagues failed to sanction an increase in the National Insurance contribution.[167]

In working out the technicalities of the package of cuts, at a meeting on 8 March McNeil needed persuading not to exempt old age pensioners from the 1s prescription charge. Otherwise there was little disagreement. It was proposed to charge half the cost of dentures, £1 on a pair of glasses, and 1s for each prescription, giving a total of £34.3m for a full year. A number of minor economies, including charges for hearing aids, amounting in all to £5.1m, were agreed for reserve purposes.[168] The proposals to introduce charges and a cut in hospital expenditure to make up for the lower yield of these charges in the first year, was then presented to the Cabinet NHS Committee.[169] This might have been a difficult moment for the Chancellor, particularly in view of the recent loss of Morrison from this committee. However, by virtue of Gaitskell's thorough preparations, the weighty and controversial issues facing the Cabinet Committee were handled almost as a formality. £393m was taken as the ceiling for 1951/52 expenditure and the agreed package of cuts was accepted without emendation. The only recorded discussion concerned the 1s prescription charge, where there occurred a virtual re-enactment of the discussions held in the autumn of 1949 between Bevan and his colleagues.[170]

Marquand was faced with fewer pressures for exemptions, with the result that he successfully included old age pensioners in the scope of the charges, with only the war disabled and National Assistance Board relief recipients being excluded from payment. Old age pensioners failed to escape because it was argued that their pension increase would cover their increased liabilities, but this decision also probably denoted a slackening of pressure on behalf of the elderly owing to a more economy-minded atmosphere prevailing within the committee.

The next hurdle in Gaitskell's campaign occurred on 15 March when he presented the decisions of the NHS Committee and other social service proposals to an ad hoc meeting attended by Attlee, the Health Ministers, the Minister of Labour (Bevan), Secretary of State for Colonies (Griffiths), and Minister of Local Government (Dalton). At this delicate meeting Gaitskell conveyed the 'unpalatable' message concerning NHS charges and cuts. It was predicted that no agreement would be reached and that the matter would be referred to the Cabinet meeting on 22 March, the short time interval being designed to inhibit leakage.[171]

The meeting on 15 March proved to be even more turbulent and awesome than anticipated. Bevan stepped out of the shadows, for the last time to exercise his fascination over health affairs. His limited instincts for compromise had been further eroded by Morrison's promotion to the Foreign Office. This change was precipitated by the illness of Bevin, who now arrived in the Cabinet NHS Committee in his capacity of Lord Privy Seal, a post which he occupied for a few weeks before his death on 15 April 1951.[172]

On 15 March Gaitskell's carefully elaborated edifice was subjected to the blast of Bevan's disapproval. As on previous occasions the strength of Bevan's conviction shook the resolve of his colleagues. Although Gaitskell had prudently solicited the support of Addison,

Attlee's particular confidant, at the meeting itself the Prime Minister was variously reported as 'extremely weak', 'wobbling', or disinclined to intervene. Bevin surprised Gaitskell by positively supporting Bevan and pleading for a more lenient policy towards the NHS. Griffiths, whose inclusion in discussions was merited by his former experience with National Health Insurance, expressed unhappiness about the proposed prescription charge. Although the Cabinet veterans were hesitant to drive towards a system infiltrated with charges, Gaitskell felt that he enjoyed majority support. At this point both Bevan and Gaitskell elevated this issue into a matter of confidence. They were set on their final collision course. Adding to the crisis McNeil decided after the meeting to support Gaitskell by resigning if necessary.[173]

The meeting of 15 March was adjourned without agreement being reached, and it was not reconvened. Consequently the wider Cabinet was drawn into the unresolved conflict. In the few days before the Cabinet meeting scheduled for 22 March, Gaitskell turned to his senior colleagues for greater support. He met Attlee, Morrison and Bevin on 20 March. Bevin proposed a compromise under which the ceiling for health expenditure would be raised from £393m to £400m, with the understanding that Gaitskell would express the firm intention of the Government to adhere to this figure for two or three years in order to soften the burden of defence expenditure. Having granted this concession, Gaitskell emphasised that 'under no circumstances can I as Chancellor of the Exchequer accept an expenditure from the Exchequer of more than £400m for NHS either in original or revised estimates or in supplementary estimates'. Gaitskell agreed to abandon the prescription charge on this condition, providing dental and ophthalmic charges were increased.[174] This proposal was approved by Attlee, but in line with his own and Bevan's previous statements on the prescription charge, he urged presentation underlining 'means of eliminating waste from the services and not solely as a method of raising revenue'. Such an interpretation was scarcely compatible with Gaitskell's conception of charges.[175]

The sensitive Cabinet meeting was held on 22 March. This and subsequent Cabinet meetings held until after Bevan's resignation were chaired by Morrison because of Attlee's removal to hospital on 21 March. Having ascertained that he was assured of support from his colleagues, Gaitskell pointed out that savings on the health service were reluctantly imposed but were the only means at his disposal to compensate for the cost of urgently needed pension increases. It was stressed that his original intention was to hold health expenditure down to £393m, but the Lord Privy Seal's compromise had raised this to £400m, an arrangement permitting abandonment of the shilling prescription charge. Gaitskell's review of recent events was significantly in error in claiming that the NHS Committee had sanctioned £393m as the level of expenditure for 1951/52 to be included in the *Vote on Account*. As indicated above, the agreed figure was £398m, and initially the Health Ministers adopted this as their target for expenditure cuts. Gaitskell realised that his concession would seem more generous if the additional £5m was kept 'up my sleeve'. Bevin's 'compromise' resulted in adoption of a ceiling only £2m higher than the level originally sanctioned by the NHS Committee, before the health departments were beaten down a further £5m by Gaitskell.[176]

Both Bevin and Morrison (the latter partly reporting Attlee's views), emphasised that dental and ophthalmic charges were tolerable on the grounds that the public accepted that abuses existed in these services. Neither Attlee nor Bevin wanted to depart from the principle of a free service, but Morrison was happy to accept charges because they had been a feature of socialist health policy in earlier days.

Bevan saw no point in making charges because it seemed that health expenditure had been brought under control. Any increases now reflected the rising cost of living. It was absurd to 'depart from Labour Party principles for the sake of a paltry increase in revenue'. Bevan asserted that backing for such charges over the last three years was not 'financial in character'—a clear implication that charges were being advocated on doctrinaire grounds. He then shifted ground to blame defence expenditure for the charges, claiming that the large sums allotted to defence would not be spent wisely. Consequently any cuts in public expenditure should be aimed in that direction. He also reminded the Government of its promise to protect the social services in the period of rising defence expenditure. Finally he pointed to the political disadvantages stemming from a decision to abandon the conception of a free National Health Service.[177]

Apparently Bevan once again threatened to resign and leave the meeting. His battle with Gaitskell over charges was enlivened by a skirmish with Shinwell, who took exception to Bevan's remarks on defence expenditure. Shinwell supported the proposed health charges, as did Dalton, Alexander, Addison and Isaacs. Marquand and Summerskill were persuaded, both expressing satisfaction that the prescription charge was dropped, while McNeil conceded that the charges were needed.[178]

Griffiths and Ede were unenthusiastic supporters of the compromise. Griffiths' contribution was especially critical. He predicted that imposing a ceiling on health spending would render further charges inevitable. He also suspected that old age pensioners would feel cheated by having their pension benefit levels eroded by health charges. Griffiths also objected to encroachment on the principle of a free service.[179] Wilson likewise invoked this principle as the ground for his objection. Like Bevan, he opted for defence rather than health cuts, and privately he too felt that health charges were being pursued as a 'mission or an obsession' by Gaitskell rather than on grounds of merit.[180] Notwithstanding the above objections the Cabinet agreed to impose 'for the time being' a £400m limit on health expenditure, and to set in motion charges for dentures and spectacles to take effect on 12 April. It also approved the rise in old age but not war pensions.

In the interval between the above meeting and settlement of the Budget speech, there could have been further moves to accommodate Bevan and other dissenters. The Health Ministers were certainly not averse to Bevan pleading their cause. They were the beneficiaries of his actions. Morrison gave satisfaction to neither party by his diffidence.[181]

Perhaps inadvertently, in the heat of the moment, when stung by an audience of heckling dockers in Bermondsey, Bevan let it be known that 'I will never be a member of a government which makes charges on the National Health Service for the patient'. The day afterwards, on 4 April, this speech was widely reported, but only the *News Chronicle* noticed the resignation threat.[182] Indeed, Bevan's remark was not generally noted until 11 April when it was carried by the *Daily Mirror, Daily Worker,* and *Daily Telegraph.* Even the press was inclined to discount rumours of Bevan's impending resignation. But there was no complacency or delayed reaction at the front line. News of Bevan's ultimatum was immediately transferred through Wilson to Dalton and thence to Gaitskell. Dalton's conversations with Bevan and Gaitskell figure in the relevant biographies.[183] Despite the evident dangers of political damage to the Government neither side was in a mood for compromise.

Continuing deadlock was confirmed when on 9 April the Cabinet met to discuss the Budget statement.[184] Gaitskell asked his colleagues to stand by their decision to limit health expenditure to £400m, a goal only attainable by imposition of charges. Bevan immediately widened the argument to consider the prospective £13m savings from charges in the light of a Budget of over £4,000m and defence estimates of £1,250m. He cited the President of the Board of Trade (Wilson) and Under-Secretary at the Ministry of Supply (Freeman) in support of his contention that savings could be made from the defence budget, which he regarded as an alternative preferable to 'a serious breach of Socialist principles'. The Cabinet was reminded that imposition of charges would entail his resignation. Gaitskell argued that his Budget had rightly balanced the various competing sectors of expenditure, and he resisted Bevan's suggestion that the £13m saving might be arrived at by drawing on the Budget surplus, or taking more from the National Insurance Fund. Even if more resources were available, Gaitskell was not satisfied that they should be directed into the health service. Ministers were divided over the likely adverse political repercussions stemming from adoption of Gaitskell's line. His supporters argued that it would be no more difficult to obtain support for the new charges than it had been in 1949 when the prescription charge was sanctioned. Bevan, Wilson and Ede (Home Secretary, and since March 1951 Leader of the House of Commons) were less confident about being able to secure the passage of this legislation without Conservative support, and 'several Ministers' hinted that resignations from the Government would precipitate an acute political crisis. Of the fifteen Ministers attending this meeting, it is likely that Bevin, Ede, Griffiths and Tomlinson supported Bevan and Wilson, or at least were reticent to push the issue to the resignation point.

In view of this impasse, it was agreed to postpone discussions until the evening, allowing Morrison to consult with Attlee at St Mary's Hospital. Attlee's views were communicated by Morrison to the reconvened meeting.[185]

Whatever his vacillation in the past, Attlee now unequivocally stood behind his Chancellor of the Exchequer, and he appealed to his colleagues to place loyalty to the Government before their departmental interests. None of their budgets should be treated as sacrosanct. His greatest concern related to the adverse electoral consequences of a Government split, 'after such a debacle, the Conservatives might remain in office for a long period'—according to Morrison's notes Attlee had predicted ten years—a gloomy prognostication, but in the event falling short by three years. The meeting seemed to be fully appraised of the gravity of its deliberations. It was recorded that 'the Labour Party had given an example to the world of stable and progressive Government in a difficult period of transition after the end of the war and in the dangerous period of international tension which had followed it; and it would be a tragedy if at this juncture the inspiration of its leadership in world affairs were cast away'. While appreciating these arguments Bevan and Wilson urged that questions of principle were at stake. Neither felt able to share in the collective decision to introduce charges. Accordingly, they would be forced to resign. Bevan retorted that the initiators of proposals for health charges would bear the heavy responsibility of adverse political consequences.

Last-minute proposals for compromise were then considered. Possibilities included postponing the introduction of charges for six months; adoption of £400m as the ceiling, but not making a commitment on measures to be taken to secure this objective (an idea stemming from Tomlinson); introducing economies in NHS administration; imposing the prescription charge, but abandoning charges for dental and ophthalmic services.

Gaitskell and his supporters explained that all of these alternatives had been considered by the Cabinet Committee and that none of them had been found acceptable. In the face of a refusal to concede Bevan was more explicit than ever before that his reservations about health charges were connected with wider disagreements concerning the pace and volume of the rearmament programmes of the Western powers.

Although not mentioned in the record Gaitskell offered his own resignation rather than reverse the decision of 22 March. According to Gaitskell he was given 'very strong support' by Addison, Dalton and Shinwell, while Ede and Griffiths, although unconvinced, felt bound by the earlier Cabinet decision. Only Bevan, Wilson and Tomlinson recorded their dissent from the Cabinet's reaffirmation of its decision reached on 22 March.[186]

However, this decision had taken two long meetings, and matters were not finally resolved until moments before Gaitskell presented his Budget on the afternoon of 10 April. Bevan and Wilson visited Attlee at 10.30 am on that date to represent their position and they felt that the Prime Minister's response was sympathetic.[187] In the meantime Bevin had tried to mediate between Bevan and Gaitskell. Morrison on two occasions directly and again through the medium of Gordon Walker pressed Gaitskell to accept the formula proposed by Tomlinson. The same proposal was made by Attlee when Gaitskell arrived at 11.00 am.[188] Gaitskell remained intransigent and offered his resignation, whereupon Attlee decided that he would keep his Chancellor and sacrifice the rebels.[189] Even then the pressure for compromise was not finally dissipated. In considering means to make the economies more palatable, Gaitskell offered to drop his proposal to introduce charges on the date of the Budget, in order to avoid criticism over retrospection.[190] This concession was not at first adopted, but there was a last-minute change of mind. At the request of Morrison Gaitskell amended his Budget statement only moments before he entered the chamber to deliver his speech.[191]

Gaitskell's hearers could not have realised the dominance assumed by that minor recommendation for health charges. The announcement of 'a modest charge in respect of some dental and optical services' was accompanied by expressions of regret, and it constituted a miniscule element in the Budget speech, evoking virtually no immediate reaction in the House and very little comment in the subsequent Budget debate.[192] But this impression of calm was illusory. Bevan, Wilson with Freeman again visited Attlee on the evening of 10 April, when they were persuaded by him to delay their decision about resignation until after the meeting of the Parliamentary Labour Party on 11 April. Bevan's unexpect-edly conciliatory stance at this meeting generated a flood of press comment predicting that he would not after all resign.[193] But this did not signify compliance with the Cabinet decision. At the Cabinet meeting on 12 April Bevan and Wilson announced that they would not support a Bill for the introduction of charges which it was now proposed to introduce on 17 April.[194] It was reported that the Legislation Committee sanctioned publication of the Bill 'in great fear of Bevan', and not confident of victory.[195] Even at this late moment various compromises were floated and Bevan was besieged with advice on his impending resignation.[196] Attlee, obviously out of touch with events, wrote to Bevan as if differences were being settled in the interests of Party unity.[197]

When, at the last Cabinet meeting Bevan was ever to attend, it was announced that the Second Reading of the health charges Bill would be taken on 24 April, he declared that this would not secure his vote in favour and that he would resign if the Bill was carried at the Third Reading.[198] This discussion led Shinwell to propose a further concession, in response to which Gaitskell agreed that the charges might be established on a temporary basis. The Ministers were sent away to work out an appropriate form of words, but Bevan, although at first seeming to favour this course, ultimately found that he could not collaborate in this exercise.[199] Morrison and Gaitskell, together with the Home Secretary and Chief Whip, visited Attlee to report on this new impasse.[200] Attlee wrote immedi-ately to remind Bevan of his responsibilities to the Government, in response to which Bevan tendered his resignation.[201] As in his last contributions at Cabinet meetings Bevan linked this 'beginning of the destruction' of the social services with a 'physically unattain-able' burden of rearmament. In his view Labour was sacrificing that 'moral leadership of the world' built up by the post-war Government. Attlee pointed out that Bevan had widened his area of disagreement with the Government, thus ruling out further attempts to accommodate him. Bevan himself was made the obstacle to dropping the health charges.[202] Harold Wilson resigned on 23 April, and John Freeman on the following day.[203]

Liberated from the Cabinet, Bevan railed at the Government with tempestuous fury, first in the House of Commons[204] and then at a Parliamentary Labour Party meeting.[205] Wilson's more restrained resignation speech made a more favourable impact.[206] The resignations were not successful in generating a major Labour revolt, but they were instrumental in consolidating Bevan's sympathisers into a more coherent faction.[207] Bevan's formal connection with the Government and the National Health Service was now finally severed.

(vi) IMPOSING ECONOMIES: APRIL–OCTOBER 1951

The storm raised by Bevan over health charges cast a deep shadow over the Health Ministers Marquand and McNeil. Changes of posture within the Cabinet associated with the Bevan upheaval greatly added to their discomfiture over the introduction of health charges. Upon Marquand's assumption of office departmental officials began preparations for imposing health charges. As mentioned above, the Cabinet Committee agreed to introduce the package of health charges at its meeting on 14 March. Of these, the prescription charge required Regulations, while the dental and ophthalmic charges needed fresh legislation. It was intended to introduce a Bill immediately after the Budget and forestall attempts to evade charges by making the Regulations retroactive. Somewhat optimistically, it was anticipated that the meeting of Ministers on 15 March would clear the way for drafting the Bill. It was hoped to introduce a simple Bill the day after the Budget and obtain passage through all stages in two days. Charges would thus come into operation at least by 16 April, and possibly as early as 13 April.[208]

Important changes of plan took place in the run-up to the presentation of the Bill. First, because of easing of the NHS ceiling to £400m, it was possible to leave the prescription charge in abeyance, a concession wanted by Marquand on account of his principle that the sick should not be charged, and designed to remove the greatest cause of objection among Labour MPs.[209] Secondly, Gaitskell's last-minute concession removed the element of retroactivity, and it also undermined the elaborate preparations made by the health departments to put charges into operation without delay. Thirdly, immediately after the Budget, Ministers pressed for limiting charges to the minimum number of items. They agreed that charges would be specified in the Bill, and that power to vary them would be subject to the Affirmative Resolution procedure. These concessions involved sacrificing anticipated charges for sight-testing, dental inspection, and minor flat-rate charges for dispensing, ophthalmic or conservative dental treatment.[210] Fourthly, against the wishes of the Treasury and McNeil, but consistent with his view that payments should be restricted to the fit, Marquand succeeded in exempting hospital in-patients

from charges. Fifthly, in discussions associated with Bevan's resignation, the Cabinet agreed that Government spokesmen would
describe health charges as a strictly temporary expedient.[211] Sixthly,
in order to satisfy Government supporters, the Cabinet agreed to
amending the Bill to prevent charges being increased without fresh
legislation.[212] Finally, the Cabinet agreed to limit charges to a
period of two years, after which fresh legislation would be required.
Under pressure from his officials Marquand pushed forward the
terminal date from 1953 to 1954.[213]

Of slight comfort to the Bill's sponsors, proposals to exempt old
age pensioners from these charges were resisted. The above delays
and concessions were nevertheless inconvenient and unwelcome to
the departments concerned. The Ministry of Health was thrown
into confusion by the instability of Cabinet attitudes. All previous
instructions on dental and ophthalmic services were cancelled; then
the cancellation was reversed; and ultimately out of the ruins of
the original Bill it was necessary to produce a new Bill within a
few days.[214]

In order to avoid 'another fiasco of withdrawal of instructions',
the Permanent Secretary favoured introduction of the charges after
the passing of the Bill, rather than with its introduction, despite
the loss of revenue consequent on this further delay, and notwithstanding the stampede for free benefits in the interim.[215] Erosion
of the anticipated yield from the charges from £12.7m to £9m was
a primary irritation to the Treasury, while the Cabinet Secretary
warned Morrison that the £13m was 'quietly draining away'.[216]

The first print of the Bill dated 22 March 1951 was considered
by the Legislation Committee on 10 April. This Bill in its revised
form was eventually presented to the House of Commons on
17 April 1951 and was given its Second Reading on 24 April.[217] As
in the case of the 1949 Act, it was not necessary to introduce a
separate Scottish Bill.

The Bill comprised only five clauses. It was intentionally uncomplicated. The main substance was contained in Clause 1 and the
relevant schedule, which outlined charges for dentures representing
about half their cost, and ophthalmic charges of 10s for each lens
plus the actual cost of the spectacle frames. The charges applied
to Part IV (family practitioner) services, and to out-patients in
Part II (hospital) services. There was thus continuing provision
for free dental and ophthalmic treatment to priority classes (infants,
children of school age, and pregnant and nursing mothers).
Another unavoidable concession was made to war pensioners.
Otherwise all those unable to pay the charge were referred to the
National Assistance Board. The National Assistance Act (1948) was
amended to enable payments to be made for medical purposes.

Marquand felt vulnerable to criticism on the appropriateness and adequacy of National Assistance. The Cabinet was unhappy about dealing with hardship cases through National Assistance.[218] This issue continued to cause difficulties. The National Assistance Board remonstrated with Scottish officials because McNeil had given Parliament an unduly optimistic impression of income levels eligible for relief from charges, whereas Foot made his complaints concerning delay in evolving NAB scales relating to this relief.[219]

As a 'little sugar for the pill' the Bill was amended to permit tuberculosis patients to be treated at public cost in Swiss sanatoria. This proposal emanated from Scotland, but the scheme itself was applied also, somewhat less successfully, to England and Wales.[220]

In his Second Reading speech Marquand argued that urgently needed hospital development could only be accommodated by making cuts elsewhere. By a process of elimination 'appliances' had been settled on for economies. Use of charges to inhibit demand in the dental sector was also defended as a means of restoring the service to priority groups, and the support of the Dental Standing Advisory Committee was quoted on this issue. He denied the claim of critics that charges had resulted in provision under the NHS of a service inferior to that given under National Health Insurance.

Marquand was frequently interrupted by Labour members. His Bill was greeted with little enthusiasm on the Labour side. Representative of Labour critics, William Griffiths attacked the measure as a 'thoroughly miserable Bill' not rendered more acceptable by the attempt to gild the pill through the introduction of a clause permitting tuberculosis patients to be treated abroad.

On behalf of the Conservative Opposition Sir Hugh Lucas-Tooth announced qualified support for the Bill. The connection between increased defence commitments and social service economies was freely admitted from the Opposition side. For the Liberals Grimond spoke of 'overriding present need to defend this country'. Macleod urged that 'there can be no social security unless there be national security first'. Lucas-Tooth and others pointed out that the only threat to the Bill came from deserters, or 'bandits', on the Government side. The primary Opposition criticism, voiced at length by Macleod, Powell and Elliot, lay in the use of the National Assistance Board to deal with cases of hardship. Powell attacked the 'transformation of this social service into another by the application of charges linked with a means test'.

Clause 3 concerning tuberculosis treatment was calculated to win, and predictably received, a sympathetic response from all sides. Elaboration on this clause figured prominently in McNeil's brief winding-up speech. On the health charges he admitted that this step would not have been undertaken without 'overriding economic necessities' imposed by the defence programme.[221]

At the Committee stage the Government faced a handful of destructive amendments from its own side, mainly aiming to reduce the impact of the charges. All such amendments were resisted and they gave no real difficulty to the Government.[222]

The Government also resisted amendments to end the charges in 1952 or 1953, but Marquand agreed to introduce a new clause at the Report stage bringing charges to an end in April 1954.[223] Perhaps the greatest difficulty was caused by the definition of the group constituting hospital 'in-patients' eligible for free treatment. Embarrassment over this point was taken by Scottish officials as confirmation of their view that all hospital patients should be included in the charges, and that even mental patients should be forced to claim relief through the National Assistance Board.[224]

On the Conservative side Iain Macleod was active at the Committee stage of the 1951 NHS Amendment Bill, being particularly associated with two substantial proposals, the first and more radical seeking to place responsibility for recovering charges with Regional Hospital Boards and Executive Councils rather than with the independent contractors.[225] This alternative was vigorously resisted by the Government. The second involved restricting alterations of charges made by Order in Council to reductions, so limiting the Government's capacity to revise scales upwards without fresh legislation. Similar amendments emanated from Messer and from Stross on the Labour side. The Government conceded this amendment subject to minor changes in wording.[226]

The climax of opposition to the Bill was a surprise intervention from Bevan in which he visibly discomfited Marquand. He then departed to leave his lieutenants to attack the front bench 'who appeared as grinding the faces of the poor with all the malice of the Tories but without their excuse of believing in it'. The demonstration ended with only three votes being cast against the measure.[227]

The remaining stages of the Bill were taken in the House of Commons on 7 May and the House of Lords on 9 May. The measure was introduced and greeted with some euphoria in the House of Lords, provoking a gesture of discord from Bevan's friend Lord Faringdon and from Lord Strabolgi. Lord Haden-Guest's last words in the House of Lords proceedings claimed support on the grounds that 'in helping to back up National Defence, we are performing a service to the National Health Service'. Royal Assent was given on 10 May.[228] At this point the Labour Government reached the end of its slow and faltering journey towards the introduction of health charges. Marquand's more conciliatory attitude towards charges did something to ease relations between the Ministry of Health and the Treasury.

On the Treasury side regrets were expressed concerning their own negative approach to the National Health Service, but this had been 'practically . . . forced on us by the old regime'. Under the new dispensation it was possible to work in a more harmonious relationship with 'our friends and colleagues' at the Ministry of Health.[229] Within the Ministry itself the question of economies moved sharply up the agenda immediately Bevan was replaced by Marquand, 'In view of the changes announced today we had better review our various suggestions for economies in the Health Service'.[230] Ministry of Health officials even signalled to the Treasury that they were willing to engage in talks concerning a 'completely different kind of system for the Health Service'.[231]

However the new concord was not complete, largely because in the Treasury view imposition of health charges was merely a first step towards introduction of tighter financial control within the health service. One official described their current achievements as a 'drunken stagger from expedient to expedient'.[232] In the freer atmosphere after the imposition of charges it was hoped that the Cabinet Committee on the National Health Service would move decisively towards action on many unfinished items of business connected with the efficiency of the National Health Service. Marquand found himself retracing Bevan's steps in resisting schemes finding favour with the committee. He reiterated Bevan's view that the abolition of Regional Hospital Boards should be delayed until after the period of retrenchment; he ruled out any general attack on the Spens pay arrangements for consultants; he objected to changing the status of RHB officers; and finally he wanted to keep open discussions on financing capital works on a loan basis.[233] In all of these respects Marquand was adopting positions that had led his predecessor into conflict with both the Treasury and with Morrison.

At two meetings in May 1951 the Cabinet Committee held desultory discussions concerning Regional Hospital Boards, consultant salaries, the status of officers, and the difficulties of restraining prescription of expensive proprietary drugs, but no decisions were reached.[234] A few new papers were prepared for the committee, mainly comprising lists of unfinished business, but it was clear to officials that the momentum had been lost.[235] The major conflict over charges had been resolved; health service expenditure was stabilised; most other issues required long-term deliberation by the departments concerned. The Cabinet Committee was not well placed to make a constructive contribution. The Ministry was increasingly preoccupied with the mounting conflict over doctors' pay, a problem beyond the capacities of the Cabinet Committee. Attlee was unwilling to terminate the committee, but he was not confident that it could make a further useful contribution until after the summer recess.

The National Health Service Committee was never reconvened. Having decided against a May poll, Attlee opted for 25 October as the date for the General Election. By virtue of internal dissension and adverse external publicity the National Health Service had ceased to be an indisputable electoral asset to Labour. The Labour Government was defeated. Some comfort was taken from the small scale of the losses, which was seen as justification for optimism about the future. This expectation turned out to be erroneous. None of the committee was ever to hold office again. When the next Labour Government was returned after an intermission of thirteen years, it was headed by Harold Wilson, Bevan's principal ally in the battle over NHS expenditure.

CHAPTER VI

Conservatives and Consensus

Neither of the election manifestos of 1951 contained much reference to health and both manifestos showed signs of being hastily compiled revisions of their 1950 counterparts. The Conservative manifesto virtually eliminated the 1950 section on health, whereas the Labour manifesto slightly expanded its comment to boast that the British National Health Service was the 'admiration of the post-war world'.[1]

The Conservative Party came into office with 321 seats against 295 for Labour and 13 for other parties. Churchill announced his senior Government appointments on 28 October. Eden was designated Foreign Secretary and Leader of the House, while Butler became Chancellor of the Exchequer. In the second batch of Cabinet appointments announced on 30 October, H F C Crookshank replaced Eden as Leader of the House in addition to being appointed as Minister of Health. Health thus returned to the Cabinet, albeit accidentally on account of Crookshank's other responsibilities. James Stuart assumed responsibility for Scottish health affairs as Secretary of State for Scotland.[2]

The Conservative Party possessed no obvious choice for the Health Ministry. Willink, the former coalition Minister, left Parliament to become Master of Magdalene College Cambridge in 1948. Walter Elliot, an even earlier Minister of Health, had effectively reached the end of his political career. Richard Law had not proved his effectiveness. Of the younger generation Selwyn Lloyd and Sir Hugh Lucas-Tooth had been active in the Select Committee on Estimates deliberations on the health service, and they spoke on health matters in Parliament, but both were given posts elsewhere in Churchill's administration. At this period health was not particularly high in Conservative political estimations. Furthermore, the attractiveness of this assignment was diminished by the recent reduction in the responsibilities of the Ministry, together with persistent controversies and an aura of financial irresponsibility hanging over the National Health Service. There was thus no scramble to occupy Bevan's former seat. Events fully justified the dangerous character of the health assignment.

Crookshank has been described as a 'somewhat withdrawn bachelor, fastidious . . . and a strict observer of protocol, he was little known in the country or even in his own Party. He had held a number of ministerial jobs, without particular distinction, becoming a senior figure in the Party in Opposition, largely through his first-class debating ability'.[3] Crookshank was an old associate of Harold Macmillan, but he was never particularly close to Churchill.[4] As a former Financial Secretary to the Treasury he was thought to be in line for a senior economic appointment. Health was perhaps below his expectations and he took the first opportunity to stand down from this post. It is likely that Crookshank's association with health was never regarded as more than a temporary expedient. His appointment introduced into a potentially troublesome area an experienced politician and specialist on economic affairs. These skills were particularly valuable when the Government was running into renewed trouble with the doctors, and when there was fresh risk of health expenditure breaching its bounds.

Crookshank made an initially favourable impression with officials, who were heartened by his Cabinet rank and sound professional experience. They found him 'pleasant . . . acute; intelligent and penetrating mind'. But this enthusiasm rapidly waned as it became clear that Crookshank was suspicious of the National Health Service because of its Labour associations.[5] 'Cold-blooded' was the epithet most readily called to mind by him. His public and office appearances were described variously as 'adequate and dull', 'woolly and uninspired', or 'woefully inadequate'. Crookshank's cold and dull professionalism was not calculated to inspire commitment and enthusiasm among his civil servants. Neither was he a particularly keen attender at his office in the Ministry of Health.[6] This reticence created an impression of 'lack of leadership and preoccupation with other matters'.[7]

In many respects, the obvious choice for the Scottish office was Walter Elliot, who had served both as Secretary of State and as Minister of Health in pre-war Governments. He had been one of the most active opposition speakers on health affairs. However, age and other factors militated against his appointment.[8] J S C Reid, another active health speaker, had become a Lord of Appeal in 1948.

James Stuart, the Secretary of State for Scotland, had served as Chief Whip (1941–48). Stuart was an influential and well-liked figure within the Cabinet. Churchill was known to have much warmer regard for him than for Crookshank. Stuart is widely credited with having encouraged Churchill to appoint Macleod as Crookshank's successor in 1952.[9]

The experienced Thomas D Galbraith was selected as the senior Scottish Parliamentary Under-Secretary with responsibility for housing, health and local government. Notwithstanding Galbraith's skill in parliamentary debate, he was subjected to rough handling when representing his department in the debate on health charges.[10]

The Parliamentary Secretary to the Ministry of Health throughout Churchill's administration was Miss M P Hornsby-Smith, MP for Chislehurst. Officials felt that she had been conscripted to boost to two the token force of women in the Government. Notwithstanding their reservations about Miss Hornsby-Smith, they breathed a sigh of relief that 'the Radio Doctor' had gone to the Ministry of Food rather than the Ministry of Health as a Parliamentary Secretary. Miss Hornsby-Smith they found nervous and inexperienced, and for them perhaps too much of a Party politician.[11] It seems at one point in his diary that Crookshank was referring to Hornsby-Smith as his 'Minister of Health'.[12]

Between 1950 and 1952 important changes took place at the senior level among officials in the Ministry of Health. First, on 31 May 1950, having reached the age of 65, Sir Wilson Jameson retired as Chief Medical Officer. Jameson had occupied this office during the ten stormiest years in his department's history. His calm judgement and 'unruffled courtesy' earned him credit on all sides.[13] He was succeeded by Dr John A Charles, one of two Deputy Chief Medical Officers, and formerly Medical Officer of Health for Newcastle-on-Tyne. Charles, a much lesser figure than Jameson, occupied this post until 1960. He was increasingly overshadowed by Dr George E Godber, his energetic and visionary Deputy CMO and successor as Chief Medical Officer.

The reorganisation of his department in the spring of 1951 was taken as the opportunity for retirement by the Permanent Secretary, Sir William Scott Douglas. The latter was absolved from blame by the BMA secretary with respect to the stormy proceedings between the Labour Government and the profession.[14] Douglas was succeeded by J M K Hawton, Deputy Secretary since 1947 and unrivalled expert on the National Health Service. Hawton occupied this office for the rest of the decade. He did not enjoy his predecessor's easy terms with the profession. The scars of bitter controversy left a deep imprint on his sensitive personality. Hawton's Deputy Secretary from 1951 until 1956 was I F Armer, formerly a Chairman of the Welsh Board of Health, who was knighted in 1954. Upon Armer's retirement in 1956 he was succeeded by Dame Enid Russell-Smith, who remained in office until her retirement in 1963. She was the first woman to hold this post in the history of the department. The above changes illustrate the manner in which the Ministry of Health in the late 50s was dominated by internal appointees.

At the Scottish Department of Health Sir George Henderson retired in 1953 after ten years as Secretary. His long tenure was followed by the more normal modern pattern of regular succession: Harold Ross Smith (October 1953–March 1956), John Anderson (March 1956–August 1959), and the experienced planner of the Scottish NHS, Thomas Douglas Haddow (August 1959–1962). Sir Andrew Davidson retired as Chief Medical Officer to the Department of Health in 1954. His replacement was Dr H K Cowan, former Medical Officer of Health for Essex County Council who like his predecessor, occupied this post for a long spell, ending with his retirement in 1964.

(i) THE CROOKSHANK INTERMISSION: OCTOBER 1951–MAY 1952

The new team was not encumbered with specific commitments to health policy deriving from its recent election manifesto. However the more ample 1950 manifesto was more than a faint memory. As a consequence of their controversies with the previous Government the spectre of waste and inefficiency in the NHS was uppermost in the collective mind of the new administration. The way seemed open for the application of new resolve to the many problems that had defeated the defunct Labour Cabinet Committee on the NHS. There seemed to be a fresh opportunity to build on the experience gathered during the troubled formative years of the new health service, without interference from the personal and political disagreements previously standing in the way of firm action. Yet the Conservatives were by no means unified in their approach to the social services. Indeed Crookshank was poles apart from the ascending One Nation Tories who had flooded into the House of Commons in 1950. Even the Cabinet was by no means united in its attitude towards the social services. The impetus for a decisive break with policies adopted by Labour was therefore not irrepressible.

The strain of Crookshank's office was possibly underestimated. It was perhaps thought that a freeze on NHS expenditure would reduce his problems and facilitate a caretaker role. Churchill asked Crookshank to let him know if he 'felt the burden of two offices too much'.[15] In the event Crookshank's brief spell at the Ministry of Health was anything but tranquil. Hospital expenditure continued its inexorable rise. The dispute over remuneration of the medical profession reached a new peak. The substantial award given to general practitioners was seen as a humiliating defeat for Crookshank's department. Pressure for a comparable increase to consultants and related professional groups looked like giving a sharp twist to the inflationary spiral. A stream of other pay demands in the health sector was grinding through the Whitley machinery. In a desperate bid to hold down expenditure the new Minister was faced with bringing in legislation to introduce fresh charges only a few months after similar legislation had been passed by the Labour Government. The new Government was also committed to sponsoring a Bill to establish a General Dental Council so that the dental profession would be placed on a more secure formal footing.

Seemingly irresistible pressures for increased expenditure on the National Health Service put an end to any Tory expectation of a substantial cut in the cost of the service. The primary goal became avoiding the political embarrassment occasioned by exceeding the £400m ceiling set by the previous Government.

From the Conservative perspective the challenge of economy and efficiency within the health service had been only half grasped by their predecessors. Crookshank in particular was free from inhibitions which had hitherto prevented firm action on economy. Yet such instincts were not readily translatable into action. When examined in detail the seemingly endless opportunities for economy evaporated, until the imposition of fresh cuts and charges became almost as difficult for the Conservatives as it had been for Labour. Even when areas for saving were identified Crookshank found that his colleagues lacked the political will to commit themselves to unpopular measures.

Notes composed shortly after his appointment show that Crook-shank was especially concerned with economy. Citing a recent Conservative policy document he accepted that sacrifices were inevitable. He called for review and alteration of charges in order to establish proper priorities. Echoing Churchill he queried the high level of expenditure on the social services.[16] After only a few days in office, Butler wrote to Crookshank, as he had written to other Ministers, pointing to the consequences of mounting defence commitments. It was 'imperative that we should make a big reduction in civil expenditure'. His colleagues were called on to be 'zealous' in the saving of material and human resources, calling for sacrifices where possible in the public services.[17] Butler was concentrating on health and education in his drive to save £100m on civil expenditure.[18]

During November 1951 officials in the Treasury and health departments exchanged ideas on 'batting orders' for fresh cuts and charges. They were unanimous in preferring to work out a solution among themselves and between the Ministers concerned rather than by reviving the Cabinet Committee on the health service.[19] Major opportunities for savings explored by them included intro-duction of charges for prescriptions, dental and ophthalmic service charges, restriction of medicines available under the NHS, hospital maintenance charges, extending the pay-bed sector, and abolition of the dental and ophthalmic service.

In the Chancellor's view the prescription charge was 'in the bag'. Initially Treasury opinion favoured higher dental and ophthalmic charges rather than 'hacking about with the service', but abolition became the favoured option when it emerged that the Ministry was positively in favour of eliminating dental and ophthalmic services because of the possibility of obtaining a high saving of £35m by this relatively simple means.[20] Such expedients were regarded as only limited contributions to the problem of NHS economy. The Treasury recognised that a permanent solution necessitated control of hospital expenditure. In this area long-term hopes were pinned on application of rigorous standardisation. In the meantime it was proposed to introduce a freeze on establishments.

The list of economies given by Crookshank to his officials included introduction of the prescription charge, a 1gn per week hospital maintenance charge, graduated charges for hospital appliances, abolition of the dental service except for priority classes, as well as a general exhortation to economy within the hospital service. At this stage he was also still seriously considering the abolition of Regional Hospital Boards. The major reservation of officials related to hospital charges, where it was pointed out that unavoidable exemptions would substantially reduce the yield.[21] Officials were also unenthusiastic about the Minister's proposals to introduce charges for aliens using the services.[22]

Stuart favoured a 10s 6d hospital charge, abolition or a 50% charge for the dental service, a 2s 6d ambulance charge, and a scale of charges for 'non-essential' proprietary drugs.[23]

Although officials within the Ministry of Health were exploring sixteen different avenues for charges or cuts, they concluded that many of these alternatives would be unproductive or positively damaging. Especially strong defences were mounted of the Supplementary Ophthalmic Service and the General Dental Service. The Board of Control however took no exception to charges being levied on mental and mental deficiency patients for their hospital care.[24]

Provisional NHS estimates of £431m for 1952/53 showing an increase of £32m on the projected outcome for 1951/52 suggested that more than £30m should be adopted as the target for cuts.[25] Following the Minister's instructions economies amounting to £37m or £42m were itemised, the main savings comprising prescription charges, hospital maintenance charges with reduction or exemption for children and for infectious diseases, a £1 dental charge reduced to 5s for priority classes, and suspension of the Supplementary Ophthalmic Service. In addition it was proposed to raise small sums on charges for hospital appliances, increased amenity bed charges, and charges for the use of day nurseries.[26]

Although the above package was presented to the Economic Policy Committee,[27] the Treasury believed that the necessary economies would not be attained without cuts in services. The Chancellor now proposed to 'preserve the main branches of the service' and sacrifice the General Dental and Supplementary Ophthalmic Services. Butler discussed with Crookshank means for holding his 1952/53 estimate down to the 1951/52 level, following which Crookshank secured his officials' agreement to suspending the dental and ophthalmic services in order to avoid introduction of charges for hospital maintenance.[28]

The Economic Policy Committee vacillated about NHS economies. All proposals for cuts and charges, even the prescription charges, were found objectionable according to some telling criterion. The committee eventually opted for the prescription charge without exemptions, and for abolition of the dental and eye services.[29]

The above half-hearted decision by no means settled the issue. Both at the Economic Policy Committee meetings and in private, Cherwell in particular was critical of the line agreed by the Treasury and health departments. His point of view was important because of his closeness to Churchill.[30] Cherwell argued vehemently that cuts should fall on the hospital service, where he believed the major source of waste was located, and where 'fancy' services were giving poor value. He resented cuts aimed at primary services, believing that it would be difficult to justify such cuts against the accusation that the 'poor man's social services' were being axed. Cherwell also argued that it would be politically disadvantageous to announce charges in advance of the Budget.

Butler and Crookshank called their officials together to discuss concessions to Cherwell's view. Notwithstanding Crookshank's stand as a 'committed abolitionist' on both departmental and political grounds, it was decided to revert to dental charges, but without reintroducing hospital maintenance charges. The shortfall was to be made up by adding 2d to the National Insurance stamp, an attractive solution for the health departments, but very much a last resort, which had been considered in connection with the 1951 Budget, but not implemented.[31]

The Cabinet agreed without difficulty on the 1s prescription charge, and on some other insignificant charges. The proposal to abolish the non-priority dental and ophthalmic services was now formally abandoned. The hospital service was discussed, but hospital maintenance charges were not reintroduced. The health departments and the Treasury were left to work out a means of yielding a saving of £7.5m on the dental services, with a preference for a flat rate charge for treatment. It was agreed that any shortfall would be taken up by an increased employees' contribution to National Insurance. The target for savings on the NHS was reduced from £38m to £25m.[32]

There now took place a recapitulation of previous discussions concerning the undesirability of increasing the National Insurance charge, which was estimated to be disadvantageous to industry and a fundamentally unsound way of raising revenue for the health service on account of its regressive character. Butler was quickly persuaded to abandon this economy.[33]

Although spared overt political confrontation, Conservative attempts to introduce health charges ran into most of the difficulties experienced by Labour.

The prescription charge was at first accepted without demur, but it was difficult to resist claims for exemption. In addition to unavoidable exemptions for the war disabled, the Minister of Education made a strong bid for exemption of school children from the prescription and dental charges in view of the obligation placed on education authorities to provide free treatment under the 1944 Education Act. The Economic Policy Committee agreed to free school children from dental charges but refused their exemption from the prescription charge on grounds of loss of revenue.[34] Ministers were sharply divided over the machinery to be adopted for handling exemptions. Lord de la Warr, the Postmaster General, put up stiff opposition before conceding that exemptions would be claimed through post offices.

By the time Butler announced the new health charges on 29 January 1952, the original substantial package of economies had been radically whittled down. There was to be no abolition of services, no hospital maintenance charges, while plans for extensive charges for hospital appliances had been narrowed down to small charges for a few items. The prescription charge was to be introduced more or less as envisaged when it was announced in 1949, while a new flat rate charge for dental treatment was being added to the payment for dentures imposed in 1951.

In opposing the new economies Labour put up a show of unanimity. Speeches by Bevan, Blenkinsop, Gaitskell, Griffiths, and Wilson, as well as by Clement Davies the Liberal leader, attacked the charges. The Government cleared its hurdle comfortably with a majority of 31.[35]

Except for the *Daily Mirror* and the *Daily Worker* the press gave a favourable reception to the new charges, which were treated as a minor gesture to economy but a step in a direction firmly advocated by the press for some time. The Bill to introduce additional charges was published on 31 January 1952.

The above reception gives little insight into the extent of the adverse reaction prompted by this Bill among Government supporters. Because of the unexpected measure of opposition among Conservative MPs, the Second Reading was delayed until after the Budget.[36] Then, by virtue of delaying tactics by the Opposition, it was necessary to impose a guillotine on the Bill, before it eventually received Royal Assent on 22 May. There was no separate Scottish Bill. The charges, originally scheduled to coincide with the publication of the Bill, and then for 1 April, were eventually delayed until 1 June. It was estimated that the delay would sacrifice £4m out of the anticipated £20m savings. The hope of salvaging the situation by prior introduction of the prescription charge was disappointed because of a defect discovered in the 1949 legislation.[37]

The first snag over implementing the Cabinet's decision occurred when Crookshank, without previous warning to the Treasury, persuaded his colleagues to delay introduction of the charges until after the Royal Assent. This option was no doubt favoured by the health departments in the light of their previous unsuccessful attempt to introduce the 1951 charges ahead of completion of the legislative process. The Treasury was dismayed by the prospect of loss of revenue (calculated at £500,000) occasioned by evasion of charges in the inevitable scramble for free treatment before the Bill became law.[38] The above losses were augmented by the decision to postpone the Second Reading of the Bill until after the Budget. This timing was urged by Cherwell, notwithstanding granting notice long enough in advance to permit a rush for free treatment before the impending charges.[39]

In view of the revenue lost by postponement in the timing of the new levies the Treasury was strongly opposed to further reductions in its slender package of charges. However demands for further concessions emanated from the constituencies, as well as from the Conservative Research Department and the Conservative Health and Social Services Committee. Officials were taken aback by the 'hostile attitude of the Conservative Backbenchers to the charges generally'.[40] The adverse reception to health charges was reported by Robert Boothby, 'backbencher after backbencher got up, really understanding the subject and expressing consternation at the harm being done to the Health Service'. It looked to him as if the Bill would have to be withdrawn and modified to meet Tory objections.[41]

Demands reaching Ministers included exemption of adolescents from the dental charge; elimination of the charge for dental examinations; special arrangements to ease prescription charges for the chronic sick; exemption of appliances from the charges, especially hearing aids and batteries; and easing of National Assistance Board scales for those seeking repayment.[42]

In the face of this unanticipated hostility Ministers were driven to abandon, first the dental charge to adolescents, and then the charge for preliminary dental examinations. They agonised over whether to give way on hearing aids and batteries, finally deciding to retain the charge for the latter, but not for hearing aids, which was the cheapest way of granting this concession.[43] Butler wanted the charges introduced a month earlier to provide some compensation for the £½m cost of the above concessions, but this point was ultimately not insisted upon.[44] It was hoped that the three concessions agreed on 20 March and announced during the Second Reading debate on 27 March would stem the tide of Conservative criticism.[45] Crookshank was dismayed by the above display of 'reluctance to face facts' on the part of his ministerial colleagues as well as backbenchers.[46]

In addition to the above reluctantly granted concessions, in response to a request of James Stuart, who was warned of the likely harmful effects of charges on Scottish dental schools, it was agreed that Ministers would be granted the right to waive charges in the case of patients volunteering for treatment in dental schools.[47]

Negotiations with the professional associations concerning the imposition of charges were stormy but they revealed no insoluble problems. None of the professional associations was enthusiastic about charges. The British Dental Association in particular found the manner of their imposition 'most damaging to the dental health of the nation', a conclusion not denied by the officials concerned.[48] The officials were particularly unenthusiastic about imposing charges for conservative dentistry and they were comforted to find that Macleod shared their view that such charges should be scrapped.[49]

In his Second Reading speech Crookshank emphasised that he was acting on precedents established by the Labour administration.[50] The Government was merely bringing to life measures agreed by Labour. As much as possible the new proposals were supported by quotations from Labour Ministers, including Bevan. Crookshank admitted that the £1 charge for dental treatment was 'rather rough and ready', but this charge would damp down demand, and so revive the priority dental services. Announcement of an amendment largely freeing adolescents from dental charges was presented as an earnest of the Government's commitment to the priority classes. It was also pointed out that by exempting clinical examinations from charges, regular visits to the dentist would not be discouraged. With regard to the prescription charge, Crookshank pointed out that Bevan's ceaseless cascade of medicine had now become a Niagara Falls. The deterrent use of this charge was thus more necessary in 1952 than when Attlee had first announced it in 1949. It was impossible for Crookshank to avoid reference to the substantial Danckwerts award, inconveniently announced only two days before, but he assured the House of Commons that the burden of backpayments would not be counted against the £400m health budget ceiling for 1952/53. The new charges were defended as a reluctant necessity towards meeting the obligation to stabilise health expenditure. The Bill was portrayed as a minor yet constructive contribution towards improving the National Health Service, rather than as a sign of major retrenchment.

Crookshank ended by reminding members of his Party's contribution to the establishment of the National Health Service, the continuation of which would be in jeopardy unless the Government protected the foundations of the economy.

The following debate was particularly notable for the aggressive contribution made by Macleod.[51] The sense of occasion was enhanced by an unanticipated chance for him to follow and make a spirited reply against Bevan. The latter's own speech exploited the Government's difficulties over Danckwerts, but it was a lacklustre performance, it is claimed, owing to ill-health and deference to Party considerations.[52] Macleod made the most of divisions and discomfiture within the Labour Party concerning health charges. He baited the Labour right about surrendering to Bevan. The Bill obtained a majority of 25 on its Second Reading.

Macleod's intervention did much to disguise Conservative inhibitions about the Bill. Nevertheless Crookshank felt that the Second Reading had gone 'very badly. I had a miserable and hateful day'.[53] Crookshank's difficulties were not over. The opposition united and used this Bill as the occasion for the first major assault on the new Government. By 1 April 91 amendments had been tabled on a Bill comprising only six short clauses. The 1951 Bill had been disposed of in 22 hours. In the course of three days (3, 8, 9 April) of the Committee stage of the 1952 Bill, about 22 hours were absorbed on five lines of the first clause. By introducing its first guillotine, the Government avoided further delay over the NHS Bill, but at the cost of a major procedural wrangle over the application of the guillotine and over suspension of operation of Standing Order No 41, as a means to bypass the Business Committee established for the purpose of dealing with procedural issues.[54]

Amendments flowed almost exclusively from the Labour side, yet there was Conservative concern over some points of substance. Macleod pressed Crookshank to remove the inconsistency between the 1951 and 1952 legislation with respect to arrangements for modification of charges. Macleod pointed out that the Conservatives were vulnerable on this point because their amendments had been responsible for the 1951 arrangements. Crookshank declined to accept this advice, and Macleod agreed not to press his amendments.[55] Although few Conservative amendments were tabled, it was clear to observers that among Conservative backbenchers there was no diminution in antipathy to the Bill.[56]

The Opposition amendment stampede was led by Marquand. Seriousness of purpose on the Labour side was indicated by willingness to push amendments to a division. On the first day of the Committee stage an amendment to end the new charge on 1 April 1954, in consistency with the 1951 Act, was defeated by 275 to 262.[57] An amendment to remove the power to levy charges on hospital out-patients was defeated by 281 to 269.[58] This latter amendment set the tone for the majority of the others, which sought to reduce charges or to exclude a wide variety of patients from the proposed charges. A particularly determined attempt was made to remove the charge from all dental treatment costing less than £1.[59]

Exemptions were vigorously resisted on the grounds that concession over one case was likely to set a precedent for all. In the Bill exemptions were limited to four clearly defined groups, National Assistance beneficiaries, war disability pensioners, limited exemption with respect to supply of appliances by out-patient departments for children under 16 or in full time attendance at school, and venereal disease patients for reasons of international obligation. The only concession to Labour involved an amendment to exempt patients from charges for repair or replacement of defective appliances. Although Bevan was not particularly active in speaking on the amendments, it was clear to observers that he was still deeply concerned with the National Health Service, and determined as ever to resist charges.[60] Bevan had wanted the Labour spokesman to give assurances that Labour would restore the cuts, but the Parliamentary Committee had at first refused. Attlee equivocated. Bevan then reminded Attlee that they had granted an amendment in the 1951 legislation limiting the cuts to the three years of rearmament. Because these charges would lapse in 1954 Bevan pressed Labour to give an undertaking that it would end the new charges at this date. On second thoughts Labour decided to declare in favour of ending all health charges on 1 April 1954, and Marquand gave a pledge to this effect on 1 May on the basis of a unanimous decision of the Parliamentary Labour Party.[61] An editorial in *The Times* denounced this statement as an act of irresponsibility.[62] Sensing the opportunity to embarrass the Opposition at the final stages of the Bill, Macleod (now Minister of Health) wrote to Woolton suggesting that Lord Jowitt should be pressed to dissociate the Labour peers from Marquand's statement.[63]

Progress of the Bill through the House of Lords in May 1952 produced no notable changes, but it was characterised by strong pressure on behalf of the chronic sick and terminally ill.[64] Amendments were rejected, but Macleod offered sufficient minor concessions to be implemented by Regulations that criticism was contained. Woolton's lack of competence in handling these debates seriously worried both the new Minister and officials. Lord Salisbury in particular was applauded for having compensated for the deficiencies of Woolton.[65]

Crookshank stepped into another minefield by introducing the long-delayed Dentists Bill into the legislative programme for 1951/52. This Bill was required for implementation of recommendations of the Teviot Committee. It was required for two primary reasons, first to establish a central body, eventually known as the 'General Dental Council', to control registration and standards within the profession; secondly, to define conditions for the use of ancillaries to supplement the work of qualified dentists. The first objective was technically complex but relatively unproblematical, the second was highly controversial.

A draft Bill produced at the beginning of 1947 had been circulated to relevant bodies for comment. The original draft contained no special provision for hygienists, reliance being placed on section 1(3)(c) of the 1921 Act. Consultations proceeded slowly and difficulty was experienced in finding parliamentary time for the Bill. Work resumed in 1949, and a revised Bill was completed in 1950. The revised Bill empowered the Privy Council to make an order establishing a register of ancillary workers who would be entitled to engage in dental work specified in the order. It was envisaged that the new Dental Board would control the education and qualifications of such ancillary dental workers. The Bill was put down for the 1950/51 session, but lengthy consultations about dental ancillaries delayed its revision, with the result that in March 1951 it was dropped from the programme. Redrafting continued over the summer. The Bill was ready for presentation just after Crookshank took office. It was timetabled for introduction in the House of Lords in February 1952. In the intervening period it became clear that the BDA was campaigning among peers and MPs in order to delete the clauses relating to dental ancillaries.

From the Government point of view these clauses were vitally important because dental ancillaries were seen as the most hopeful means to restore the declining services for priority groups, and generally to introduce much-needed efficiency and economy into the dental service. A recent mission to New Zealand had inspired new confidence in the potentialities of a dental nurses scheme.[66]

Initially Woolton had made a good impression when being briefed on the Dentists Bill, but both he and to a lesser extent Onslow proved over-conciliatory to their critics in the House of Lords.[67] At the Second Reading Woolton omitted the part of his speech referring to the importance attached to the dental ancillary clauses by the Government. He also inclined to accept a greater degree of control over ancillaries than the Government wanted. Onslow inadvertently agreed to ancillaries being limited to the extraction of deciduous teeth. The Government came under pressure from a group headed by Webb-Johnson, and containing Teviot himself, either to drop the clauses relating to ancillaries, or to limit ancillaries to work on children under the personal supervision of registered dentists. Although the Government withstood these pressures, the Bill was abandoned after its First Reading in the House of Commons in March 1952. Further progress was interrupted by the death of King George VI. It was then decided not to reintroduce the Bill in the next session.[68]

Ironically Crookshank had been overtaken by events. The shortage of dentists in the priority services, which provided one of the main grounds for extending the use of dental ancillaries, was alleviated by the reduction in demand in the general dental service occasioned by the 1951 and 1952 legislation. Consequently the profession could argue that the decline of the priority dental service was a temporary phenomenon which had been corrected without recourse to 'dilution' of the kind proposed by the Government.

Crookshank's final and most embarrassing difficulty related to the remuneration of the medical profession. He inherited his predecessor's agreement with the BMA to seek resolution of their long-standing argument with the Government concerning 'betterment' by reference to an independent adjudicator. On 15 August 1951 the Labour Cabinet accepted arbitration, thereby narrowly averting the mass resignation of general practitioners announced for 27 September. The Conservative Government was also constrained by an agreement reached late in September 1951 on the selection of an adjudicator and his terms of reference, as well as on a working party which would deal with technical matters. The long process of obstruction of BMA salary demands, followed by preparation for arbitration, effectively removed this important issue from the agenda of high-level discussions on NHS finances.

In December 1951 Harold Danckwerts, a Judge of the High Court of Justice, was invited to act as adjudicator. The two parties prepared their cases, each confident in the impregnability of their incompatible positions. The health departments were in a difficult position, being constrained to a hard line by the Treasury, but deflected from pursuing this course by Crookshank. Officials were impressed by the contrast between Crookshank's tenacity with respect to health charges and his lack of firmness towards doctors' salaries.[69] Yet this single arbitration award stood to wipe out savings achieved by the charges imposed under three hard-won pieces of legislation. Because of the coincidence of events it seemed as if damaging dental charges were being imposed in order that money should be 'poured into the laps of the doctors'.[70] Crookshank had indeed inherited a vague election pledge to assist doctors, which he felt would be prejudiced if the health departments scored too well in the Danckwerts arbitration.

The main recommendation of Danckwerts related to the appropriate adjustment of general practitioners' remuneration to take account of changes in the value of money since 1939. The Government had adopted a betterment of 20% in 1948 and it was argued that no upward revision was required, although it was conceded that a change in the method of distribution was desirable. The Danckwerts award, announced on 24 March 1952, involved total acceptance of the BMA case, allowing that betterment in 1948 should have been 85%, adjusted to 100% for the year 1950/51.[71] The total liability of this award was £9.7m for 1950/51. Including payment of arrears it was calculated that the total cost in the year 1952/53 would be £40m, for which a supplementary vote would be required. The Cabinet frankly accepted that the Danckwerts award represented 'total rejection' of their case. It was feared that repercussions in other parts of the wage sector would cause acute embarrassment. Any credit derived by Crookshank from economies obtained under the 1952 Act was more than wiped out by the £40m liability stemming from the Danckwerts award.[72]

It was predicted that the departments would now face 'really serious trouble' from the Government. The Chancellor admitted to the Permanent Secretary that the award 'had knocked all his plans endways and would gravely upset the TUC just as he had succeeded in getting them to acquiesce in a plan of wage restraint'.[73] Churchill was equally indignant, 'Can anything be done about this and are we bound hand and foot to pay the £40m? I sympathise greatly with you on this heavy blow and would gladly help if there was any way out'.[74] Simultaneously Churchill had been consulting Moran about the introduction of further charges to counteract rising NHS costs. Moran suggested a hotel charge for hospital patients and introduction of a scale of charges for medicines deemed inessential. He also favoured increasing general practitioner involvement in hospital work in order to cut back on hospital staff costs.[75] At the same time in the House of Lords Moran warned that consultants would demand parity with general practitioners, again invoking hotel charges as a means to compensate for the cost, all of which was listened to by Crookshank, 'head buried in his hands'.[76]

A Treasury memorandum prepared for the Cabinet described the Danckwerts award as a 'heavy blow' for the Government. Particular concern was expressed about an inevitable chain reaction which would be set up in the National Health Service, universities, civil service, and other public sector areas. Although it was recognised that there was no escape from Danckwerts, possible containment measures included decisively repudiating association between the cost of living and income for professional groups; spreading the award over a number of years; refusing to extend awards on the Danckwerts scale to consultants and dentists; terminating compulsory arbitration for those earning £1,500 and above.[77] Butler told Churchill that he would be able to limit repercussions of Danckwerts. His officials were less confident.[78]

'Great botheration' was Crookshank's reflection on his experience of announcing the Danckwerts award and confronting the Lobby and the Opposition.[79] This award was additionally discomfiting because it precipitated the announcement of a Supplementary Estimate, so resurrecting all the unpleasant memories of past NHS Supplementary Estimates with their embarrassing consequences for the previous Government.

A final decision over the Danckwerts award was delayed until June 1952, when Crookshank's successor was in office. None of the radical proposals for holding up the award was adopted. Instead it was decided to try and break the chain at its first link by preventing application of the Danckwerts principle to consultant grades.[80] One final token of Crookshank's discomfort with his office as Minister of Health is provided by his response to the 'Use the NHS Sensibly' campaign. This exercise was the major publicity initiative of the Ministry of Health following the establishment of the NHS. Its aim was training the public in discriminating use of the new service. This campaign was also a response to mounting BMA accusations that patients were abusing family doctors by frivolous calls on their time. Both the BMA and the Central Office of Information issued leaflets and posters, and other arms of the media co-operated in teaching the public to 'Help your Doctor to Help You'. The campaign was regarded by the Cabinet NHS Committee as a useful contribution to the economy drive. In this context Marquand gave his support for the campaign during his brief term of office. Officials expected Crookshank also to co-operate by warning the public to avoid excessive use of the service during the winter of 1951/52. It was thought that this action by the Minister would defuse BMA calls for action against ill-disciplined patients. However this request met with Crookshank's blank rejection. Such public appeals were in his view inappropriate to the status of his office. The publicity campaign was then abandoned.[81]

The appointment of Crookshank to supervise transfer of the National Health Service into Conservative hands was not a success. His few months in office coincided with three varied catastrophes, concerning health charges, the Dentists Bill, and the Danckwerts award. Such problems underlined the need to place the National Health Service under a Minister having an undiluted commitment to this office.

(ii) NEW STABILITY: MACLEOD AND HIS SUCCESSORS: 1952–1957

By the end of April 1952 it was apparent that Crookshank's divided responsibilities were adding to shortcomings in his capacities both as Leader of the House and Minister of Health. The possibility of his removal from the Ministry of Health was rumoured in February 1952, but he remained in this office until Churchill's first Cabinet reshuffle in May 1952.[82] Crookshank was thoroughly relieved by the change. He felt adequately compensated by being made Lord Privy Seal. In this capacity he remained involved in health affairs because of his membership of the Home Affairs Committee. Indeed he frequently chaired this Committee as substitute for the Marquess of Salisbury. Crookshank stayed as Lord Privy Seal until his retirement in December 1955.[83] The delay from February to May 1952 in rotating Ministers operated to the advantage of his successor because Crookshank was left to struggle with some unenviable problems connected with the transition to Conservative government. It also gave an opportunity for Iain Macleod to emerge as a contender for ministerial office.

I N Macleod was the son of a Skipton general practitioner of Isle of Lewis origin, a background which is often cited as the source of his interest in health affairs. Of more immediate relevance were responsibilities relating to social services as an officer at the Conservative Party Research Department. He entered Parliament as MP for Enfield West at the 1950 General Election.[84]

As noted above Macleod established an immediate reputation in the field of health with a maiden speech delivered within a few days of assembly of the new Parliament. Thereafter the majority of Macleod's interventions in the House of Commons related to the health service. He was particularly active on the question of inflated dentists' fees and the collapse of the priority dental services, accusing the Government of creating a 'paradise for the spiv dentists'.[85] His grasp of technicalities was particularly evident in contributions made during the 1951 and 1952 NHS legislation. It is therefore possible that his co-authorship with Enoch Powell of a Conservative Political Centre pamphlet, *The Social Services: Needs and Means* (January 1952), together with his appointment as Chairman of the Conservative Party Health and Social Services Committee in February 1952, contributed to rumours that Crookshank was about to stand down as Minister of Health. The matter seems to have been finally decided by his pungent and effective onslaught on Bevan during the Second Reading debate on the 1952 NHS Bill. Officials recognised that, as a debater in the Bevan style, Macleod was seemingly 'the coming man' among Conservatives.[86]

On 7 May 1952 when Macleod became Minister of Health, he had only been in Parliament for two years, and he was the first incumbent, apart from Bevan, to hold this office without having previous ministerial experience. Notwithstanding absence of Cabinet rank, Macleod had, by any standards, made a spectacular leap forward in his political career.

Macleod was fortunate in presiding over his department at a time of relative tranquillity. Charges and economies had been pushed as far as was feasible in the short term. Following the 1952 NHS Act the process of amending the 1946 legislation was completed. In fact Macleod's only piece of legislation was the Dentists Bill, which was revived in 1955. Health service expenditure was stabilised. Following Government humiliation over the Danckwerts award, general practitioners and the BMA were temporarily in a quiescent mood. Crookshank had ruled out any radical interference with the structure of the health service. Most of the pressure for further reforms and economies was relieved by the setting up of the Guillebaud Committee, the prolonged deliberations of which effectively froze action on many fronts. Similarly, establishment in February 1954 of a Royal Commission to report on mental health temporarily defused problems in this difficult area. The period from May 1952 to the end of 1955 thus turned out to be a propitious time for an inexperienced Minister to establish a firm political foothold.

By contrast with his predecessor Macleod supported the main principles upon which the National Health Service was founded. As an initiator of the 'One Nation' group of Conservative MPs, a leading author of the *One Nation* (October 1950) pamphlet, Macleod championed the Disraelian philosophy. His group set out to revive positive Conservative commitment to the social services, and to restore public confidence in conservatism as the guardian of social welfare. Among previous Ministers of Health his model was Neville Chamberlain. Macleod even took the trouble to write a monograph on the discredited Chamberlain, in order to draw attention to the success of his early career as a constructive thinker in the field of health and housing.[87] As Minister of Health, Macleod believed that he was pursuing 'the ideals of a true Disraelian policy', by using the National Health Service as an instrument to 'elevate the condition of the people'.[88]

To officials Macleod seemed like the polar opposite to Crookshank. They felt more comfortable with him because he was a family man from a less elevated social rank. But they were less happy about his strong ideas concerning policy, which furthermore were thought not to be widely shared within the Conservative Party.[89] There was a risk that Macleod might prove troublesome and say unwise things. Seldon finds that officials reacted variably to Macleod. Some found him a good companion, others thought him cold and unfriendly.[90] One important source contrasted his strong public image with a tendency to timidity in facing up to Cabinet colleagues. If this conclusion is correct, it is a reminder of the weakening of the political position of the National Health Service consequent on loss of Cabinet rank of the Minister of Health, a disadvantage that was not overcome until the mid-sixties.[91] Notwithstanding difficulties caused by his relatively junior position among Ministers, officials counted his period of office as a success in establishing the National Health Service on a new plane of stability, lasting for a sufficient time for it to become protected by strengthening bonds of consensus.[92]

Macleod remained Minister of Health during the changeover from Churchill to Eden as Prime Minister in April 1955, and after the General Election of May 1955 which increased the Conservative majority, but in the major reshuffle of December 1955 he was transferred to the Ministry of Labour – echoing the change made by Bevan four years previously. At this point Macmillan succeeded Butler as Chancellor of the Exchequer. Officials were disappointed to lose the experienced Macleod, whom they had come to regard as an effective Minister and shrewd politician. Nevertheless it was appreciated that their department was only a first stepping stone to a career for an ambitious politician like Macleod. The Permanent Secretary predicted that Macleod's replacement would be 'very affable and very ineffectual and that . . . we should lose every fight with the Treasury from now on'.[93] Macleod's successor, Robert H Turton (1903-, subsequently Baron Tranmire) was at the end of his short career in government. He had entered Parliament in 1929, but had not held office until 1951. After junior appointments in Pensions and National Insurance he was promoted by Eden to become Parliamentary Under-Secretary at the Foreign Office in October 1954, from which position Eden transferred him to the Ministry of Health in December 1955.[94] Turton gained familiarity with the problems of the hospital service through his participation in a long Select Committee on Estimates investigation in 1951.

Following the resignation of Eden in January 1957 Harold Macmillan became Prime Minister and Thorneycroft Chancellor of the Exchequer. Turton was replaced as Minister of Health by the younger and more promising Dennis F Vosper (1916–1968). The latter was more in the cast of Macleod, having entered Parliament in 1950 and serving as Parliamentary Secretary to Eccles in the Ministry of Education from October 1954. After a promising start at the Ministry of Health Vosper was taken seriously ill in June 1957 and he resigned in September, when he was replaced by Derek C Walker-Smith, who continued until the appointment in 1960 of Enoch Powell, Macleod's old associate and competitor.[95]

Through working as Parliamentary Secretary to the Ministry of Health from 1951 to 1957, Patricia Hornsby-Smith was one of the longest-serving holders of this post. She was succeeded briefly by John K Vaughan-Morgan, MP for Reigate since 1950. He carried major responsibilities during the illness of Vosper. Upon Vaughan-Morgan's transfer to the Board of Trade in 1957, he was succeeded by Richard H M Thompson, who remained Parliamentary Secretary until 1959.

Stuart's team at the Scottish Office was the most stable one within the Government. The first change occurred in April 1955 when Galbraith was promoted to become Minister of State in the department. He was replaced by J Nixon Browne, a Glasgow MP and businessman, formerly Parliamentary Private Secretary to Stuart. Nixon Browne served as Parliamentary Under-Secretary responsible for housing, health and local government from 1955 until 1959.[96] Stuart, although not an adventurous politician, was popular in his department and respected in the Government. He was replaced by John Maclay (later Viscount Muirshiel) who was a much lesser political force. Maclay had served briefly as Minister of Transport (1951/52) before resigning because of ill-health. He returned to the Government in October 1956, where he served briefly at the Colonial Office before being appointed Secretary of State for Scotland in January 1957, a post which he occupied until 1962.[97]

The remaining sections of this chapter consider the major political problems affecting the health services in the period between the appointment of Macleod and the beginning of 1957. This period is framed by the Guillebaud Report, which is the first full-scale inquiry into the working of the National Health Service.

(iii) THE GUILLEBAUD REPORT

Like its Labour predecessor the Conservative Government was haunted by the spectre of rising costs on the National Health Service. Expenditure of £400m pa took on some kind of totemic significance. All public expenditure in excess of this level was taken as indefensible concession to wanton extravagance.

Painful experience of the 1951 and 1952 legislation taught that recourse to minor charges was frustrating and unproductive. Learning from Labour's lack of success in controlling the NHS by committee, this course was not pursued by the Conservative Government.

Although estimates for 1953/54 were only slightly in excess of £400m, the Treasury was so alarmed by the prospect for increase in future years that decisive action was called for to bring NHS spending under control. Seemingly without much prior discussion, in November 1952 the Treasury decided to refer this problem to a small independent inquiry. Macleod wanted this investigation to be extended to the social services as a whole, but he was overruled by Butler.[98] A more serious objection emanated from the Department of Health, where it was urged that an inquiry would reveal the extent of unmet need in the areas of tuberculosis, mental health, mental handicap, elderly, and chronic care. Consequently the 'Treasury are here playing with fire and are liable to get very badly burned'.[99] At this stage the Treasury was confident that the committee of inquiry would 'come down on the right side' providing its membership and terms of reference were correctly determined. In practice it proved impracticable and impolitic to predetermine the outcome of this inquiry. In discussion of the terms of reference Lord Cherwell and Peter Thorneycroft, President of the Board of Trade, urged that the committee should be primarily directed towards reducing the cost of the NHS to the Exchequer. With difficulty Thorneycroft was persuaded by Butler that less restrictive terms of reference were necessary in order to avoid the accusation that the Government was embarking on a destructive onslaught on the welfare state.[100]

After much redrafting of its terms of reference, it was agreed that the committee should merely consider how 'rising charge' upon the Exchequer might be avoided. Of the Treasury suggestions for chairman, Ernest Brown the ex-Minister of Health was ruled out by Macleod. Brown's reputation as an agent of retrenchment in the pre-war National Governments would have made him objectionable to Labour. Although publicly not well known, the

Cambridge economist Claude W Guillebaud, nephew of the famous economist Alfred Marshall, was accepted because of his unexceptionable middle-of-the-road record. His reputation as a 'professional just man' was arguably more valuable for disarming Labour critics than for determining that the committee should be economy-minded.[101]

Other members of the Committee were J W Cook FRS a Glasgow chemist, Miss B A Godwin nominated by the TUC, Sir John Maude the former Permanent Secretary to the Ministry of Health, and the industrialist Sir Geoffrey Vickers. The Guillebaud Committee was announced by Macleod in the House of Commons on 1 April 1953. In response to Labour critics he gave assurances that this exercise was an 'independent and objective inquiry' and not an 'economy cuts committee'.[102]

From the standpoint of the Treasury the Guillebaud Committee as eventually constituted was an imperfect instrument for guaranteeing the primary objective of economy. A second disadvantage was lack of urgency in the work of the committee. Guillebaud took on the chairmanship only on the understanding that the committee could be fitted in with his existing engagements. At the outset it was agreed that the Report would take a year or even longer. In the end the deliberations of the committee took two and a half years and its Report was not published until January 1956.[103] Even more important, the very existence of the Guillebaud Committee acted as a brake in the Treasury's relentless quest for economy in the National Health Service. Indeed, the committee was increasingly invoked in favour of arguments for additional expenditure. The Cabinet meetings at which the Guillebaud Committee was launched were also considering the imposition of additional health charges. The committee was given as one of the factors causing this latter proposal to be deferred. Butler admitted that 'the [increased prescription] charge is dead until after the committee has reported'.[104] Macleod argued that it would be improper to embark on policy changes while the Guillebaud Committee was sitting. By virtue of the slow pace of the committee's deliberations and because they intended to make no interim report, the opportunity to introduce fresh economies was considerably delayed.[105] The Health Ministers were also reticent about bringing to a head their disputes with the pharmaceutical companies over either profits from proprietary drugs or introducing a limited list of drugs, until it was clear what attitude to these problems was taken by the Guillebaud Committee.[106] As noted below, Macleod increasingly relied on assertions of support from the Guillebaud Committee to buttress his argument with the Treasury for increased capital allowance, especially for hospitals. On the basis of this issue it was concluded that Guillebaud, 'like all other committees which set out to secure economy, is likely to recommend big increases in expenditure'.[107]

At the first meeting Guillebaud advised, on the question of rising costs of the NHS, that 'it might well be that, at least in times of inflation, there could be no satisfactory answer'.[108] Although the committee was concerned with the economical administration of the service, it took little account of radical proposals that would be required to effect substantial economies. It was basically concerned with the improvement in the performance of the service as it was currently operating. In most respects such improvement involved additional expenditure rather than economy.

The reasons for the tendency of the Guillebaud Committee to support the status quo are easy to detect. First, the members were genuinely open-minded and undoctrinaire. Also, with the exception of Maude they were inexperienced in health affairs. Even Maude admitted that he had lost touch with the health service since his retirement. The Committee was thus dependent on the guidance and advice it was offered. The whole work of the committee was organised by a secretary drawn from the Ministry of Health. Members' experience of the National Health Service was dominated by sources associated with reinforcing the views of the health departments. In these quarters there was strong preference for a period of stability in order to give an opportunity for maximising the performance of existing arrangements. Secondly, because the committee adopted a liberal interpretation of its remit, it operated as an economically biased committee of inquiry into all aspects of the service rather than conducting a narrow investigation into costs and potential economies. Much of the time of the committee was spent in wide-ranging interviews with representatives from all parts of the NHS, and from professional organisations representing many classes of health worker. Twenty such meetings were held at monthly intervals until the end of 1954, after which the whole ground of the health service was again covered in a series of two-day meetings held in 1955. The great majority of the above witnesses were resistant to upsetting the delicate balance of interests inherent in the existing organisation of the health service. Their preference for improvement lay with additional expenditure within the current range of options, even where this did not entail the most rational disposition of resources. Thirdly, the committee was more free to dissipate its energies because Guillebaud transferred the more technical work in the field of social accounting to a separate investigation conducted under the aegis of the National Institute of Economic and Social Research. This investigation was undertaken by Brian Abel-Smith, a young Cambridge economist, using

Professor R M Titmuss as a consultant. Their contact with the Guillebaud Committee was minimal, but their memorandum, first read by Guillebaud in January 1955, was fundamental to setting the tone of the Guillebaud Report, and in its separately published form the elegant work of Abel-Smith and Titmuss overshadowed the pedestrian Report, and achieved stature as a minor classic of modern social analysis.[109] Abel-Smith and Titmuss were less concerned with cheese-paring economies than with detecting current and prospective shortcomings in social service provision. From this standpoint of commitment to welfare they furnished Guillebaud with convincing economic arguments refuting the widely held assumption that the National Health Service was extravagantly conceived and escalating in cost. Indeed, according to certain standard social accounting criteria it was demonstrated that the NHS was seriously under-financed. The social scientists were not concerned with diluting their argument about the relative economy of the existing mechanism by raising wider questions of the appropriateness of the philosophy under which the NHS was established.

Compilation of the Report, which was largely delegated to the committee's secretary, was accomplished smoothly. The final stage of preparation involved assimilation of essential material from the Abel-Smith and Titmuss memorandum, which was undertaken in June 1955. Until this time the committee remained in harmony. However at the last stage Miss Godwin entered a reservation arguing for the assimilation of teaching hospitals into the regional structure and also making the case against direct charges for services. This minor concession to Labour opinion was not regarded as a significant embarrassment to the committee. Much more anxiety was provoked by a lengthy reservation entered by Sir John Maude, which vigorously argued the case against the current organisation of the NHS, and advocated return at an appropriate time to the form of unitary local government organisation of the kind favoured within official circles at the outset of planning for a National Health Service.[110] Such a view, emanating from an eminent source, was felt to be deeply subversive to the Report. Strenuous efforts were made to persuade Maude to withdraw his reservation, but to no avail.[111]

The main virtue of the Guillebaud Report was subsidiary to its ostensible purpose. It provided for the first time an ordered digest of information about the working of the National Health Service during its first seven years. In all essential respects the Report saw that it was good.

On the sensitive question of efficiency the Report decisively concluded that, 'Any charge that there is widespread extravagance in the National Health Service, whether in respect of the spending of money or the use of manpower, is not borne out by our evidence'.[112] The committee was accordingly unable to suggest any source for major economies and it was not favourable to additional charges. Although not going quite as far as Miss Godwin, the committee concluded that, having considered each proposal for charges strictly on its merits with regard to the efficiency and economy of the service, 'no convincing case has been made out for the imposition of new charges'.[113] While not explicitly advocating abolition of all existing charges the committee recommended that 'high priority should be given to modifying them, so soon as other conditions permit' in order to remove the deterrent effect in cases of genuine need.[114]

Having ruled out major economies and further charges the committee warned that a further increment in expenditure was required to make up for deficiencies in existing services. Identification of significant shortcomings according to current estimates reminded the committee that changing standards of adequacy were likely to increase pressure for higher expenditure on health care. Finally the committee warned that higher costs should be accepted as an inevitable consequence of the inflationary spiral. The committee thus concluded:

> We have sought to ascertain where, if anywhere, there is opportunity for effecting substantial savings in expenditure, or for attracting new sources of income, within the existing structure of the Service; but . . . we have found no opportunity for making recommendations which would either produce new sources of income or reduce in a substantial degree the annual cost of the Service. In some instances—and particularly with regard to the level of hospital capital expenditure—we have found it necessary, in the interests of the future efficiency of the Service, to make recommendations which will tend to increase the future cost.[115]

The most notable conclusions of the Guillebaud Report were derived from Abel-Smith and Titmuss. The Guillebaud case rested on the social scientists' calculation that the current net cost of the NHS to public funds, expressed as a percentage of the Gross National Product, had fallen from 3.75 in 1949/50 to 3.24 in 1953/54. The Abel-Smith-Titmuss calculation was for England and Wales only, and it reallocated expenditure to the appropriate year, a procedure designed to iron out perturbations caused by phenomena such as the Danckwerts award, where a large retrospective element was involved. They pointed out that 'had the proportion of resources devoted to the Service in 1953/54 been the same as in 1949/50 the net cost would have been £67 million higher'.[116] Discussion of the cost of the NHS with reference to changing prices showed a decline from a peak in 1950/51.[117] Reference to demographical factors, such as population growth, or ageing, also showed NHS expenditure in a favourable light.[118] The only major weapon in this armoury not used by their investigation was comparison of NHS expenditure with other sectors of public expenditure. The authors also failed to take up the invitation to conduct international comparisons. The latter would in fact have been extremely difficult to pursue and inconclusive in outcome.

A further telling finding of Abel-Smith and Titmuss related to the low level of NHS capital expenditure. It was demonstrated both that capital expenditure was extremely low, and that the cost of new fixed assets as a proportion of gross fixed capital formation had fallen as a percentage from 0.83 in 1949/50 to 0.53 in 1953/54.[119] Virtually all of the capital allocation was absorbed by the hospital sector. Various comparisons, all suggestive of current underprovision, were conducted by the social scientists. First, they confirmed the Ministry of Health's view that capital expenditure pre-war was at least three times higher than the 1952/53 level if changes in prices were taken into account. Secondly, the balance of capital to current expenditure was shown to have declined from 19.6% in 1938/39 to 4.1% in 1952/53. Thirdly, making one of their rare international comparisons, it was pointed out that the comparable capital/current balance for the United States for 1951 was 23.4%. The investigators reached the moderate conclusion that an annual expenditure of between £20m and £30m would raise hospital capital to a reasonably adequate level.[120] This brave speculation was taken up by the Guillebaud Committee and it became the central recommendation of their Report that hospital capital expenditure should be returned for a seven-year period 1957/58 to 1965/66 to its asserted pre-war level of £30m.[121] The committee to only a limited degree, and the experts not at all, gave consideration to the possibility of reversal of the past tradition and current trend towards increasing hospitalisation.

Subsidiary recommendations of the Guillebaud Committee with significant financial implications comprised: (a) substantial modification or reduction of charges for dental and ophthalmic services, and (b) introduction of a 50% exchequer grant for residential accommodation, mainly for the elderly as provided under section 21(1) of the National Assistance Act.[122] The latter recommendation was particularly advocated on the committee by Vickers, who developed a special interest in welfare and preventive services.

Publication of the Guillebaud Report was delayed from 18 to 25 January 1956 because of the ministerial change at the Ministry of Health. The official press release headed 'No fundamental changes recommended. Service needs time to settle down' set the tone for the reception of this Report. The response was generally low-key and mildly supportive. There was no overt disappointment over the failure of the Report to advocate major economies in the National Health Service. The left-wing press regarded the Report as a shock for the Government and a vote of confidence for Labour's declared view of the NHS. The *Daily Worker* called the report a 'damp squib'. The more serious newspapers, the weeklies and the medical press devoted most attention to the Abel-Smith and Titmuss findings, and they generally sympathised with Maude's concern over the organisation of the service. *The Lancet* regarded the Report primarily as a 'starting point for all further discussion'. *The Times* declared that 'a new enquiry is urgently necessary'. There was a feeling that the Guillebaud Report had carried the debate over problems of health care very little further forward.[123]

Within the Government the Report evoked contrasting responses from the various departments involved. The health departments outwardly expressed dissatisfaction, but enjoyed inner contentment. The Treasury was infuriated by the perceived waywardness of its brainchild.

The draft Report was announced by the committee's secretary to his colleagues as a 'puffball'. The Ministers reported that the text 'runs to over 500 pages of typescript and the Conclusions alone to more than fifty pages. But it says very little'. Macleod confessed to the Prime Minister that 'I'm afraid it has very few useful proposals'.[124]

During the Treasury post-mortem the Guillebaud Report was described as 'pretty awful' and 'highly disappointing and indeed unsatisfactory'. Because the committee was judged to have evaded major aspects of its terms of reference the Treasury objected, albeit unsuccessfully, to the Minister's intention to pay warm tribute to its work.[125] The Treasury was particularly annoyed by the Report's sanction for additional expenditure, its failure to give clearance for additional charges, its evasiveness about preventing rising costs, and its lame comments about such technical problems as hospital cost accounting and the cost of proprietary medicines. Having failed to achieve control of NHS expenditure through the medium of an independent inquiry, the Treasury urged establishment of a Ministerial Committee to consider ways of controlling social service expenditure in general. This step is reminiscent of the Labour Government's ill-fated experiment with its NHS Committee. Butler argued for holding back Government comment on the Guillebaud Committee until the Social Services Committee was under way.[126]

In defending the National Health Service at the Home Affairs Committee Macleod admitted that he found the Guillebaud Report 'almost embarrassingly favourable'. Nevertheless he felt that it supported his contention that the service had become increasingly efficient. It was reported that:

The Minister came away from the meeting with the impression that there was general sympathy with what I think is his own view, that any idea of major economies, whether in the form of so-called administrative economies, or in the form of cuts in the Service through new charges or other methods, can no longer hold the field.[127]

This impression of the meeting was not shared in Treasury circles, where it was felt that Cabinet agreement to delegate preparation of a statement on Guillebaud to a committee of Ministers and to establish a Cabinet Committee to examine social services expenditure would effectively reopen the question of further economies in the health service.

Final preparations for the statement on the Guillebaud Report were interrupted by the ministerial changes of December 1955. Upon the insistence of Macmillan, the new Chancellor of the Exchequer, promises of action to implement the few positive recommendations of Guillebaud involving additional expenditure were deleted from statement.[128] In its final form the statement lamented that 'in view of the economic situation the Government cannot undertake any additional financial commitments in respect of the Health Services at the present time'.[129] Not only were Turton and Stuart unable in the short term to gain any tangible benefits from the Guillebaud Report, but they were also thrown back to defend existing commitments to increased hospital capital expenditure, and they were even faced with demands for further economies and additional charges from the direction of the new Social Services Committee.

(iv) CONTAINING COSTS AND IMPLEMENTING CHARGES

Faced with pressure from the Treasury to contain rising costs of the National Health Service, Macleod followed the course of his two predecessors by proposing to levy further charges. His first choice was the simple option of increasing the prescription charge from 1s per form to 1s per item. However Stuart was unwilling to go along with this proposal, arguing that: (a) abuses had been contained, (b) such a change would be deeply unpopular, (c) he was averse to reopening arguments about exemption, and (d) it was unwise to modify a decision made only a few months earlier.[130] In view of these arguments, the decision to use the Guillebaud Committee to work out economies, and the additional unpopularity of the introduction of such a measure at the seasonal peak illness period and at a time of general grief because of the east coast floods, the Cabinet decided that it was an inopportune moment to increase the prescription charge.[131]

Although the Guillebaud Committee constituted an effective block on short-term action the Treasury continued to ruminate about the whole range of options for increased health service charges. An arbitrary 5% cut in the hospital maintenance budget, hotel charges for hospital patients, the increased prescription charge, introduction of full prescription charge for drugs not contained on a limited list, or increasing the National Insurance contribution were all considered, but ruled out in the short term. At this stage interfering with the National Insurance arrangement was particularly stoutly resisted in Treasury thinking, and it was noted that the Conservative Policy Committee favoured completely abandoning the National Insurance appropriation in aid towards the National Health Service.[132]

Fresh economies in the health service were next broached in the context of the recommendations of the Cabinet Committee on Civil Expenditure, chaired by Viscount Swinton, Secretary of State for Commonwealth Relations. This committee aimed to peg civil expenditure for 1955/56 to the 1954/55 level by introducing reductions of £125m. The target of £446m adopted for the NHS involved the minor reduction of £14m, to be achieved by a 40% cut in hospital capital expenditure, increasing the prescription charge to 1s per item, and virtual elimination of the small allowance on hospital maintenance expenditure.[133] The Swinton Committee also considered imposition of a hotel charge for hospital patients, but this was abandoned in view of its small yield and likely unpopularity. Macleod and Stuart accepted the reduction in capital expenditure, but argued that the elimination of the small allowance on hospital maintenance expenditure would be difficult to observe and they opposed the increased prescription charge, citing many of the objections raised when this issue was last discussed. The Prime Minister sensed a mood of buoyant confidence in the country which he attributed to the success of Government policies. Accordingly the Swinton axe was allowed to strike more lightly, with the result that the proposal to increase the prescription charge was once again shelved.[134]

Notwithstanding relaxation of the Swinton economies Butler was unwilling to let social service expenditure run its natural course over the next few years. It was pointed out that the social services were costing 35% more in 1955/56 than in 1951/52, whereas GNP had increased by only 25%. In fact the increases were very uneven across the social service field. Butler's figures showed an 18% increase in the National Health Service compared with a 35%

increase in education. Without showing particular alarm the Cabinet agreed to Butler's suggestion that a survey should be undertaken to estimate the likely extent of expansion of the social service budget.[135]

Butler's survey, completed without cognisance of the financial implications of the Guillebaud Report, suggested that between 1955/56 and 1960/61 social service expenditure would continue to rise at a steady pace. The projected overall increase in net expenditure was 16.6%, the rates for education and the NHS being 27.5% and 15.4% respectively. The NHS was expected to increase in net cost by £72m giving a prospective total of £544m for 1960/61. Although the target of £400m was now completely discarded this prospective increase was not viewed with equanimity by the Treasury, where the suspicion that NHS expenditure might easily get out of control seemed justified in the light of recommendations of the Guillebaud Committee and the Phillips Committee on the elderly.[136]

Establishment of a committee of Ministers to review expenditure on the social services was delayed until after the Cabinet reshuffle of December 1955. This committee came under the experienced and informed chairmanship of the Lord Privy Seal (Butler). Its members comprised the Secretary of State for Scotland (Stuart), Minister of Housing (Sandys), Minister of Agriculture (Amory), Minister of Education (Eccles), Minister of Pensions and National Insurance (Boyd-Carpenter), Minister of Health (Turton), and Financial Secretary to the Treasury (Brooke).[137] The committee held four meetings spread over five months and it considered twenty-nine memoranda. Although beginning with the ambitious goal of £200m reduction in social services expenditure in 1956/57, and considering a variety of radical proposals for cuts in services, the committee ended up with a lower target of £100m and commitment to only minor economies. Thus in briefer space the Conservative Social Services Committee re-enacted the experience of the Labour NHS Committee. Major economies considered for the NHS included charging in full for all drugs prescribed except in hospital treatment; introduction of a hospital boarding charge, perhaps covered by insurance contribution; and either abolition or transfer to an insurance basis for the dental and ophthalmic services. Although not expected to yield significant revenue it was also recommended that aliens should be charged for NHS treatment on the grounds that this measure would have a beneficial psychological effect. These proposals were soon whittled down on grounds of political objection, complaints from Boyd-Carpenter about increasing dependence of the NHS on his hard-pressed National Insurance fund, inconsistency with Guillebaud recommendations, or in response to rear-guard counter-proposals from Turton. The only major item of NHS economy given serious attention was the increased prescription charge. The Treasury demanded an increase to 2s per item. Turton countered with the long-standing proposal for 1s per item. The committee agreed that the latter was all the chronically sick could be expected to shoulder.[138]

There was some hesitation before proceeding with the increased prescription charge. At one stage the Policy Review Group of senior Ministers headed by Macmillan decided to 'quietly drop' the increased charge because it was likely to spur on wage claims.[139] However this increase was included in Macmillan's package of £100m economies announced on 25 October 1956. This was an unhappy occasion, first because the Opposition could claim that the social services were being raided to pay for the Suez expedition, and secondly because Macmillan's replies to supplementaries introduced serious ambiguities over the scope of exemptions.[140]

The Government announcement on prescription charges met with unanticipated hostility, directed from most sections of the press, the *BMJ* and *The Lancet*, the BMA and the MPU, Government supporters and the Opposition. The Conservative Health and Social Services Committee complained to Macmillan. The influential London Executive Council passed a resolution condemning the charges. Such an intervention by an official body caused consternation at the Treasury.[141]

Notwithstanding his official announcement Macmillan once again hesitated before pushing ahead with the increased prescription charge. A Cabinet Committee was asked to consider whether they could evolve an alternative 'more acceptable to public opinion'.[142] Privately it was conceded that this increase seemed 'brutal'.[143] At the meeting of Ministers, Macleod proposed a 2s flat rate charge per prescription, but this was rejected because the immediate yield would be lower. On this ground and because change in policy would be taken as a sign of indecision and weakness Butler recommended that the official announcement should be honoured. It was however agreed that the increase should be applied as humanely as possible.[144] There was also a feeling that an appropriate countervailing concession was called for and it was proposed that local authorities should be allowed to develop a chiropody service, as recommended by the Guillebaud Committee. Despite Treasury objection that this innovation would set a precedent for relaxation on other Guillebaud proposals, the chiropody service was accepted in order to 'sweeten the pill' for the elderly.[145] The way was now clear for Turton to clarify the Government's position on charges, and defend the decision in a debate in which the Government obtained a majority of 303 against

231.[146] It was calculated that the charge would reinstate to the 1952 level of 15% the patient's contribution towards the cost of prescriptions. The anticipated yield of this new charge introduced on 1 December 1956 was £12.7m per annum.[147]

The loss of confidence in sterling brought about by the Suez crisis resulted in fresh pressure for reduction in estimates for 1957/58. Of the £300m reduction sought, £100m was the allotted contribution of the social services, and the Cabinet looked to the NHS for the largest part of this massive economy.[148]

Intensive discussions concerning ways of meeting this formidable demand took place during the opening months of Macmillan's administration, and they involved new appointees as Chancellor of the Exchequer (Thorneycroft), Secretary of State for Scotland (Maclay), and Minister of Health (Vosper). Vosper repeated his predecessor's claim that the NHS deserved favourable treatment in view of its steadily receding demands on the national economy. Using the Abel-Smith-Titmuss approach it was pointed out that the share of GNP absorbed by the NHS had fallen from 3.26% in 1949/50 to 2.80% in 1955/56. Health, it was argued, had fared badly compared with education.[149] In response Thorneycroft called for 'courageous steps', involving such measures as substantial reduction in the dental service and introduction of hospital boarding charges.[150] The Cabinet was firmly of the opinion that the National Health Service was costing more than the Exchequer could bear, but it was unable to agree on further cuts in services or on new direct charges to the user. By a process of elimination Ministers fell back on reconsideration of the hitherto little favoured option of increasing the contribution of the National Insurance fund towards the National Health Service. There was 'general agreement that the National Health Service should now be established on a compulsory contributory basis'. Initial objections from Boyd-Carpenter were overcome by the suggestion that the NHS and NI contributions should be firmly separated, with the distinction between the two schemes being indicated on the insurance stamps themselves.[151] Intensive discussions took place about realising such a policy, with the intention of raising £20m in 1957/58. From the perspective of Vosper the insurance plan was the least painful of his alternatives. But the Ministry of Pensions and National Insurance remained unenthusiastic, with the result that Boyd-Carpenter was kept provided with fresh objections. The scheme eventually foundered because no way could be discovered of introducing an increased insurance contribution without sparking off accumulating latent demands for improvements in pensions and other benefits. Thorneycroft was left wringing his hands over the growing and seemingly insoluble problem of expanding NHS expenditure.[152]

(v) CAPITAL FOR HOSPITALS

One of the major problems facing the early National Health Service was modernisation of its largely obsolete hospital stock. Of the hospitals housing its 500,000 in-patients about half dated from before 1900. In the case of mental and mental deficiency hospitals about 70% dated from before 1900. A variety of factors added to this problem, (a) much of the hospital stock was inappropriate for modern use; (b) most voluntary hospitals were severely under-financed pre-1939; (c) hospital building had virtually ceased after 1939; (d) much war-time damage remained unrepaired; (e) mental and mental deficiency hospitals were severely over-crowded and long waiting lists had built up; and (f) the slender resources available under the NHS were dissipated on uneconomical emergency schemes.

The hospital surveys conducted during World War II estimated that £500m of capital work was required. Evolving priorities for capital expenditure was delayed until after the complex operation of setting up the new hospital organisation was completed. Once the new hospital authorities were firmly established their opportunity for undertaking capital projects was limited by the economy drives which dominated the early history of the NHS. Holding back on capital development was the most easily effected short-term economy in the hospital sector, but neglect of capital work had increasingly deleterious longer-term consequences.

From 1948/49 to 1953/54 capital investment averaged at about £7m per annum, which compared with the equivalent of £35m in 1938/39.[153] The seriousness of this problem was apparent to Crookshank, who made representations to the Economic Affairs Committee in April 1952. Macleod issued a memorandum summarising the case in June 1952, but no positive outcome is reported.[154] In 1954 Macleod put in a plea for an increase in hospital capital investment from £10m in 1954/55 to £16m for 1955/56. He warned that his department had made representations to the Guillebaud Committee on this point. His case was regarded sympathetically within the Treasury and consideration was given to granting £14m or perhaps £13m. But there was also a view that no substantial increase should be conceded unless economies were offered elsewhere in the hospital budget. There was also a disinclination to act in advance of the Guillebaud Report. Butler warned: 'we must hold Hospitals to £11½m'.[155] Finally only £10m was allowed for hospital capital expenditure for 1955/56 as a result of the economies imposed by the Swinton Committee. Macleod was particularly disappointed that abandonment of investment control regulations and relaxation of building controls was not bringing proportionate benefits to the hospital sector. It was 'quite tragic that the result of the introduction of a National Health Service should be to cripple the capital development of our hospitals and to put us in effect right back where we were before the much needed expansion that started in the thirties when local authorities were given general hospital responsibilities'.[156]

In the more favourable climate of the autumn of 1954 Macleod entered a fresh plea for higher hospital capital expenditure. The strength of his case was again recognised in the Treasury, and he was warmly supported at the Economic Affairs Committee. He pointed out that during a period when capital investment in education and housing had increased by 100% and 43% respectively, investment in hospitals had been reduced by 2.3%.[157] When referred to the Cabinet Macleod's memorandum evoked no controversy. Churchill was now 'impressed by the extent to which this country was falling behind others in the provision of up-to-date hospitals, and by the urgent need to improve the hospital services . . . He considered that a great campaign should be undertaken to improve this part of our social services as soon as the Government's programme for pensions was completed'.[158]

This was an agreement in principle. No figures were produced or discussed. Informal soundings suggested that the Ministry of Health was reconciled to low spending in the short term providing that £19m per annum was adopted for 1957/58. This target, which the Treasury found 'formidable', represented only 50% of the estimated pre-war level of hospital capital expenditure.[159]

There followed a lively exchange between Macleod and Brooke concerning realisation of the 'great campaign'. The details of their rival proposals and the eventually agreed levels of expenditure are given in Table I below.[160]

Although the House of Commons announcements by Macleod and Galbraith made in February 1955 were presented as a major step forward in the hospital building programme they entailed for 1956/57 expenditure of only £2m more than the austerity package approved in July 1954. The £18m agreed for 1957/58 fell far short of the £30m first mentioned by Macleod in December 1954 as the desirable target for hospital expenditure. This aspiration was conveniently backed up by the Guillebaud Report a year later, but although constantly reiterated as an ideal it proved extremely hard to attain.

The health departments even found it difficult to hang on to their slender gains. The decision of the Cabinet in September 1955 to introduce stringent capital investment controls in the public

TABLE I

Rival Proposals for Hospital Capital Expenditure
1954/55–1957/58

(in £ millions)

	1954/55	1955/56	1956/57	1957/58	
Swinton, July 1954	10	10	12	17	(England & Wales)
Macleod, Dec 1954	10	10	13	18	
Brooke, Jan 1955	10	10	13	16.5	
Macleod, HC Feb 1955	10	10	13	18	
Galbraith, HC Feb 1955	1.9	1.9	2.2	2.5	(Scotland)

sector was primarily directed at local authorities, but it had inevitable repercussions on other public agencies. Both Stuart and Macleod stoutly resisted applying the new restrictions to the hospital building programme, to which they argued the Government was irrevocably pledged. A promise was extracted from Butler that already announced programmes would not be affected. Macleod publicly thanked the Chancellor for having 'been able to keep the green light fixed on' the hospital programme.[161]

The above argument was repeated in January 1956 between the new team of Ministers. Macmillan warned Stuart and Turton that hospitals could not be exempted from cuts in the capital programme. The Health Ministers reminded Macmillan of the substantial Government commitment to the hospital building programme and they agreed to work closely together to protect this facet of their spending.[162] Macmillan still called for a 'modest reduction' in the 1956/57 programme, but the Cabinet sided with the Health Ministers on this point.[163] However Macmillan prevented inclusion in the official statement on the Guillebaud Report of any promise concerning commitment to the recommended £30m target for hospital capital expenditure.[164]

Having at last secured the £18m capital allocation for 1957/58 the debate moved on to the level for 1958/59. Turton asked for £21m, which was refused by Macmillan, as was the compromise bid of £20m. Macmillan insisted on his original offer of £19m.[165] At this point the Financial Secretary felt that the Ministry of Health was being treated somewhat harshly, 'This is sound, strict Treasury doctrine. But I feel bound to express my view that since the war the Exchequer treatment of Education has been lavish and of hospitals niggardly, and as to capital investment, the gaps here in dispute for hospitals . . . are almost insignificant compared with the £600m a year now going into house building'.[166] Brooke was reminded that the hard line over capital expenditure stemmed from Treasury conviction that the Minister of Health was making insufficient effort to economise in other areas of his £580m budget.[167] This disagreement over the paltry sum of £1m thus assumed symbolic importance. Because neither side would give way the issue was taken to the Cabinet, where Turton was supported by Eden and the sum of £20m was agreed.[168]

The arguments used by Turton, although not well articulated, aptly illustrate the growing crisis of hospitals, especially those concerned with problems of chronic illness:

(a) The conditions at many of our hospitals are very unsatisfactory, some of them being an inheritance from the old poor law days.

(b) In certain places we are still making use of wartime hutted hospitals that cannot be kept weatherproof.

(c) A large number of our mental and mental deficiency hospitals are over a century old and lack modern conveniences.

(d) Overcrowding in mental hospitals is serious. A figure of 40 per cent on the female side is not uncommon.

(e) Shortage of beds for the chronic sick is filling the mental hospitals with old people who could be housed elsewhere.

(f) Our policy of restricting the number of hostels that local welfare authorities can build under Part III of the National Assistance Act, 1948, is aggravating the problem.

(g) The number of old people who have to be cared for will increase considerably in the next few years.

With these problems in mind Turton warned that they were 'in danger of a breakdown in the hospital service'.[169] It seemed that the seriousness of the hospital problem was at last effectively communicated to the Cabinet. But Turton had scored only a Pyrrhic victory. In the wake of the Suez crisis fresh restrictions on capital investment were called for, and the hospital capital programme was expected to take a substantial cut. Thorneycroft asked for a reduction of the hospital investment programme to £14m for 1956/57, and to £15m for 1957/58.[170] These reductions were successfully resisted by Vosper, who pointed out that NHS capital spending in 1955/56 was only 0.56% of gross fixed capital formation compared with 0.83% in 1949/50. He claimed that hospitals had become the Cinderella of the social services. Even maintenance of the hospital capital programme at £20m was insufficient to raise capital development out of the trough into which it had fallen since the establishment of the NHS.[171] Vosper went on to obtain £20m for 1958/59, and his successor Walker-Smith, after resisting a further round of cuts, secured £22m for 1959/60. It was calculated that increases in the hospital capital development budget were just about sufficient to offset rising prices, although a persistent problem of underspending tended to undermine this stability. However, even if a minor upturn was attained from 1957/58 onwards, the level fell drastically short of the £30m wanted by the Ministry of Health and advocated by the Guillebaud Report. The first twelve years of the National Health Service thus made virtually no contribution to the hospital modernisation problem. This delay greatly added to the scale of the difficulties facing Enoch Powell in 1960, when he initiated the first attempt at comprehensive hospital planning since the establishment of the NHS.

(vi) CAPITAL FOR WELFARE

As noted above the build-up of pressure on the hospital chronic sector was in part a reflection of the failure to develop alternative community-based services. For this purpose local authorities were the relevant agency. Under either the National Health Service Act (1946) or the National Assistance Act (1948) local authorities were empowered to build and equip health centres, maternity and child welfare centres, school clinics, day nurseries, occupation centres for the mentally handicapped, and old people's homes. The capital outlay of local authorities also went towards ambulance stations and housing for their nursing staff. There was particularly urgent pressure for maternity and child welfare centres and school clinics for new housing developments, occupation centres to maintain the mentally handicapped outside residential institutions, and old people's homes to prevent the growing population of the elderly drifting into mental institutions or geriatric hospitals. For reasons discussed in chapter IX below a variety of factors inhibited the development of health centres. But there was growing public support for improved services for mothers and infants, the mentally handicapped and the elderly. Local authorities were keen to meet the demand, but the usual restrictions on capital expenditure severely limited development.

During the early years of the NHS the local health and welfare capital budgets were each kept fairly constant at about £2m per annum. Maternity and child welfare centres were the largest commitment of the local health authority budget, absorbing about 40% of the total. The local welfare authorities provided about 3,200 places (England and Wales) and 400 (Scotland) each year in old people's homes.[172] Under section 21 of the National Assistance Act the cost of these homes was borne by the rates, a subsidy being provided in the form of an exchequer payment of £7 10s per annum for each place. This expenditure was regarded favourably by the Treasury. The substantial local authority investment constituted an economy for the exchequer. Furthermore it was appreciated that many of the local authority services reduced pressure on hospitals and were of a preventive character. It was remarked that these services were as much a contribution towards economy as the replacement of inefficient boilers in hospitals.[173]

The first bid to expand the local authority capital programme was made in 1955. It was proposed to increase local health authority spending to £2.6m for both 1956/57 and 1957/58, and the local welfare authority programme for the same years to £2.8m and £2.9m.[174] In defence of welfare spending the Ministry of Health invoked the recently published Phillips Report, growing demand from local authorities for loan sanctions, and the need to relieve pressure on hospitals.[175] Inadequacy of services for the elderly showed signs of attracting political attention.[176] Unluckily for the health departments, what constituted reasonable demands according to Treasury reckoning, were introduced at precisely the moment chosen by Butler for restriction on local authority capital expenditure. In the light of Butler's request for 'local authorities to hold back their schemes for capital expenditure as far as they can', the local health authority programme for 1956/57 was reduced to £1.3m. However in compensation a modest increase in welfare spending was conceded for 1956/57, loan sanctions of £3.1m being permitted.[177]

Following the above announcement, and a further Cabinet discussion, in September 1955 Butler wrote to Ministers specifically asking for restraint in capital spending.[178] Butler's colleagues were generally supportive, the noticeable exceptions being Eccles and his adjutant Vosper at the Ministry of Education, where every loophole was exploited to evade this economy measure. As noted above Stuart and Macleod objected to cutting back their hospital programme. Since plans for expansion of their local health and welfare authority programmes had already been rejected, these were for the moment immune from further cuts. However, soon after Macmillan succeeded Butler as Chancellor of the Exchequer, he asked for immediate suspension of local authority loan sanctions except in urgent cases. Turton argued that local authority welfare provision should be exempted from this embargo, but Macmillan refused, leaving Turton with the option, which the Minister declined, of taking the matter to the Cabinet. It was agreed that no further loans would be sanctioned in 1955/56, but loans to a limit of £1m would be allowed to local welfare authorities in the first half of 1956/57.[179] The effect of this economy was reduction of local authority health expenditure for 1955/56 to £0.6m and a reduction of local welfare authority expenditure to £2.25m. The economies introduced in February 1956 therefore reduced the total 1955/56 programme from £4.4m to about £3m, a reduction of 25% below previous years. Turton now entered into debate with Macmillan to avoid a further reduction in local health and welfare spending in 1956/57. For the whole year £0.5m and £2.5m were demanded for the local health and welfare services respectively, which would preserve the reduced level of spending permitted in the previous year. However Macmillan insisted on reduction of the welfare programme to £2m. For the remaining years of the decade local health authority spending reverted to £2m per annum and the local welfare programme was maintained at £2.5m. Thus, despite formidable backing from major independent inquiries such as the Guillebaud Committee, the Phillips Committee on the elderly, the Piercy Committee on the disabled, and the Royal Commission on Mental Illness, as well as mounting public indignation over the plight of the elderly, the disabled, the mentally ill and the mentally handicapped, it proved impossible to achieve a real increase in capital outlay on facilities for these groups, even in the latter part of the decade.[180]

Neglect of community care did not signify ignorance of the problem or unawareness of longer-term implications. Turton warned Macmillan that in failing to provide accommodation for the elderly they were neglecting 'one of the most urgent of our social problems'. He pointed to the 'economic absurdity' of Treasury decisions which spurned the cheap and desirable local authority care for the elderly only to incur the expensive and undesirable hospital alternative. Turton also found it 'difficult to provide any reasonable answer' why normal children were supplied with places for education and training from the age of five while the mentally handicapped were left unprovided. The Treasury sympathised with these arguments, but underprovision in the field of community care was regarded as a regrettable consequence of the failure of the health departments to economise elsewhere in their spending.[181]

(vii) CONTROLLING DRUGS

Macleod admitted that expenditure on pharmaceutical products caused him 'more concern than any other item, even including the hospitals'.[182] As Table II indicates both the overall drug bill and the cost per prescription climbed unremittingly. The Health Ministers described this trend as 'frightening'. The phenomenon was less frightening to Abel-Smith and Titmuss, but their scientific analysis tentatively concluded that the pharmaceutical service was one of the few components of NHS expenditure in which 'net cost continued to rise after 1950/51 in real terms'.[183] None of the methods

TABLE II

Cost of the Pharmaceutical Service 1947–1956

England, Wales, Scotland

Year	Total Cost to the Exchequer (in £ millions)	Charges paid by Patients (in £ millions)	Cost per Prescription (in pence)
1947 (calendar year, NHI)	6.8		24
1948/49 (original estimate)	11.5		24
1948/49 (from 5.7.48)	17.5		33.5
1949/50	35.5		38
1950/51	39		40.5
1951/52	51		47
1952/53	47.7	5.5	50.5
1953/54	50.3	7.1	52
1954/55	52.0	6.8	53
1955/56	55.6	7.6	58

Sources: HA(53)25, CAB 134/913; Annual Reports, Ministry of Health and Department of Health, Scotland. Select Committee on Estimates 7th Report 1948/49, p 54.

adopted during the early years of the NHS for containing these costs was more than trivially successful. The greatest energies went into the prescription charge, which was attractive in principle both because of its deterrent effect and on account of its direct revenue contribution. However, the deterrent effect was only temporary and it was indiscriminate in its application. Also, as suggested by the preceding narrative, because of the political unpopularity and contentiousness of this charge, the difficulty in raising and maintaining it at an economic level was disproportionate to its contribution towards costs. Attempts to cut back costs by 'educating' patients to use the service sensibly were abandoned after some slight and amateurish experiments. Consequently, controlling the drug bill through the medium of the user was unsuccessful.

As indicated in chapter IX below it also proved impossible to reduce the drug bill by educating or disciplining the doctors who wrote the prescriptions. Macleod blamed the 'wholly improper pressure put upon doctors by patients on the one hand and more seriously by manufacturers on the other'.[184] Increasing the flow of more balanced information to doctors and introducing refinements to the disciplinary machinery made no difference to the relentless march forward of the cost of the pharmaceutical services.

Gradually attention turned to dealing with the problem at source through closer scrutiny of the prices charged to the NHS by the pharmaceutical companies. This approach was induced by irrefutable evidence that the basic reasons for increase in the drugs bill were (a) the emergence of new and expensive drugs such as antibiotics and hormones, and (b) the increased reliance on proprietary rather than standard preparations. In the last year of National Health Insurance proprietary drugs accounted for only 5% of prescriptions. By 1953 proprietary preparations were accounting for 25% in number but about 50% in cost of drugs dispensed by chemists. By the end of 1954 proprietary preparations accounted for 60% and by 1959 75% of this bill.

The health departments were stung into action by the adverse comments of the Public Accounts Committee (Third Report 1951/ 52, paras 46–51) concerning negligence over determining fair levels of profits made by suppliers. This committee could not 'view with equanimity the continued payment of prices which . . . include a profit margin substantially in excess of that hitherto accepted as appropriate for government contracts'. The first instinct of the Health Ministers was to investigate whether Defence Regulations could be used to force information from the drug companies, and if necessary to impose prices. In view of the need to meet the objections of the Public Accounts Committee there was support in the Home Affairs Committee for invoking Defence Regulations, but it was agreed that this should only be used as a threat and in the last resort because of the fear of creating a precedent for more draconian use of Defence Regulations by a future Labour Government.[185]

From the Treasury perspective the Ministry of Health 'unwillingly and under Treasury pressure' entered into discussion with the Association of the British Pharmaceutical Industry (ABPI) concerning voluntary cost investigation. Following contacts beginning late in 1952 working parties were established to look into the cost of basic drugs and the earnings of secondary compounders and wholesalers. The main investigation conducted related to fourteen firms producing standard drugs. This turned out to be inconclusive and it was decided to take no action. The only positive benefit emerged from an investigation into the production of bulk drugs where minor reduction in prices was negotiated.[186]

The Health Ministers reported to colleagues on action taken in 1953 to assuage the Public Accounts Committee.[187] It was proposed to build on the work of the joint committee of the Central and

Scottish Health Services Councils presided over by Sir Henry Cohen, which had evolved a classification of drugs in current use. This committee suggested that two classes of preparation should not be prescribed under the NHS: first, those advertised direct to the public; and secondly, 900 items in categories (5) and (6) of their six-part classification, comprising drugs of no proven therapeutic value. It was hoped that doctors would voluntarily comply with the recommendation to avoid the above preparations. There still remained 4,000 proprietary preparations in classes (2)–(4), which the committee accepted for NHS use, 'subject to satisfactory arrangements for price being made between the Health Departments and the manufacturers'.[188]

The Ministers considered alternative ways of pricing acceptable proprietary preparations. Either the Government could insist on a price no higher than that paid for a comparable standard preparation, or the Government could work out a fair price based on the actual cost of manufacture. It was admitted that the industry was vigorously opposed to the first alternative on the grounds that it would undermine the whole financial structure of its operations. The industry argued that profits from proprietary preparations subsidised standard drugs, that buoyant profits were essential for marketing proprietary drugs abroad, and that research and development would be undermined by restricted profits. The alternative method of assessing a fair price for each preparation was also problematical. It was likely that a substantial margin of profits would need to be admitted. But the main difficulty was the complexity of the operation required to fix fair prices on an individual basis for large numbers of preparations. There was a risk that this method was administratively impracticable.

Lack of confidence about evolving an efficient pricing mechanism led the Ministers to consider other alternatives. In particular they felt that at some stage 'a limit will have to be placed on the unrestricted supply' of drugs under the health service. Doctors would be free to prescribe any drug, but patients would pay the full cost of drugs not contained on an approved list. It was realised that this proposal would require legislation and that it would be controversial. It was hoped that the Guillebaud Committee would give a firm lead towards this solution. A further long-term alternative mentioned was the possibility of introducing some form of statutory registration for new proprietary preparations.[189]

The Home Affairs Committee favoured evolving a scheme for pricing at the level of standard equivalents as their short-term option, while agreeing that the 'approved list' idea was the desirable long-term objective.[190] Further discussion of this latter policy was suspended pending further insight into the views of the newly formed Guillebaud Committee. On the advice of a specialist sub-committee the Home Affairs Committee's short-term option was also quickly abandoned. It was thought unwise to embark on a major confrontation with the industry and thus become exposed to the criticism of undermining exports, before knowing whether the Guillebaud Committee would be supportive. The Home Affairs Committee therefore fell back on its only other option, investigation of the pricing of individual drugs. With the aid of Board of Trade accountants it was estimated that 20 firms, responsible for 30–40 preparations, would be covered in the course of a year. It was proposed to concentrate effort on smaller firms, because (a) these were thought to be the worst offenders, (b) it was difficult to isolate the costs of individual drugs in larger firms, and (c) most smaller firms were not committed to research and development. Where firms refused to reduce their profit to what was judged a reasonable level the health departments intended to 'blacklist' their products, relying on voluntary co-operation from doctors.[191]

The Ministry of Health embarked on investigations into 91 proprietary preparations, representing £4.7m in value, with the aim of limiting profits to 15% on capital employed. By the end of 1954 negotiations were in progress with the six companies involved to reduce profits on some of these products. In the course of these inquiries two asthma inhalants were blacklisted.[192]

Disapproving of the fixed profit criterion, in July 1954 the ABPI submitted its own scheme for arriving at acceptable prices. The ABPI formulae were first discussed with officials on 9 August 1954. Ministry of Health officials were disinclined to follow up this option, believing it to be unacceptable to the Public Accounts Committee because ABPI formulae would not reveal information about profits. However, at the insistence of Macleod and the Treasury negotiations with the ABPI were resumed and revised formulae were submitted by ABPI in June 1955.[193] Once again the negotiations were undertaken reluctantly by the Ministry of Health. The Treasury was by no means confident of success but it was argued that full consideration of the ABPI scheme would strengthen the position of the Government in the event of negotiations break-ing down.[194] Not that the Treasury found the ABPI scheme instinctively attractive. Indeed, at the eleventh hour a strong move was mounted to abandon all previous approaches and impose a fixed percentage (perhaps 10%) rebate on all pharmaceutical prod-ucts. Although backed by the Public Accounts Committee (Third Report 1955/56, para 28) this experiment was dropped in the light of warning of an antagonistic response from the industry.[195]

In the final stages of the negotiations the Treasury and Ministry of Health switched preferences, the former coming down in favour of firm by firm review and statutory price control, while the latter was persuaded of the advantages of a limited trial of the price formulae advocated by the industry. The Ministry of Health had gradually become disillusioned with product by product investigation, which after initial euphoria over certain easy cases was turning out to be onerous and of uncertain outcome. Furthermore the industry was increasingly restive about co-operating in these investigations. The ABPI approach promised smaller economies, but it applied to all products, was straightforward to operate and promised certain returns. The Health Ministers favoured a scheme in which the departments worked in harmony with industry, provided the formulae were adjusted to give better guarantees of economies. In the face of opposition from Macmillan, Turton completed his negotiations with the ABPI, the two sides reaching agreement in December 1956.[196]

At this point Treasury objections to the ABPI scheme were dropped and with very little formality the Voluntary Price Regulation Scheme was accepted for a trial period of three years.[197] This decision was publicly announced on 8 April 1957.[198] All parties were relieved by the termination of 'a very long wrestle with this problem'. The limited savings of £750,000 per annum seemed preferable to the 'horrors of war, and uncertain outcome of individual negotiations after cost investigation'.[199]

It was unfortunate that, after this great concentration of effort on reducing the cost of proprietary preparations, the yield was almost negligible, amounting to £250,000 in the first year, and £400,000 in the second.[200] With the drug bill approaching £70m per annum Thorneycroft demanded that the Ministry of Health should get 'this business under control'. The idea of the limited list was again broached. History once more repeated itself. Just as this proposal was deferred in 1953 pending expectation of support from the Guillebaud Committee, so in 1957 the Chancellor was asked to wait for the views of the newly formed Hinchcliffe Committee.[201] However, Hinchcliffe, like his forebear, gave neither support for the limited list, nor offered any decisive clue to the elusive quest for control of the drug bill.

(viii) PAYING DOCTORS AND DENTISTS

The Danckwerts award settled the long-running dispute over the remuneration of general practitioners, only to create problems of equal difficulty concerning extension of the award to consultants and related hospital medical staff, as well as raising the prospect of repercussions throughout the NHS and indeed elsewhere in the economy. As noted above the National Health Service began before there had been an opportunity to apply the Spens recommendations to hospital medical staffs. Terms and conditions consistent with Spens were not fixed until July 1949. Thereafter the Labour Government was much concerned with the alleged over-generosity towards part-time consultants. Gaitskell complained that the latter enjoyed the best of both worlds, 'well-paid apprenticeship followed by secure and superannuable employment and at the same time salaries comparable to the earnings of the risk-bearing private practitioners of former days'.[202] Labour Ministers were particularly antagonistic to the merit award system. Improving the status of full-time consultants and cutting back the advantages of the rest was a major obsession with the NHS Committee of the Labour Government. However no action was taken, partly for fear of provoking consultants to join their general practitioner brethren in demanding a major cost of living increase.[203]

The Danckwerts award was taken as a bitter blow by the Government. This award constituted 'total rejection' of the Government's case; it risked establishing the precedent that doctors, alone among the professions, would be guaranteed index-linked salaries, and it more than wiped out the effect of hard-won economies and charges imposed on patients.[204]

Macleod's first attendance at a Cabinet meeting was occasioned by the problem of preventing repercussions from Danckwerts. The staff side of the Medical Whitley Council had just given notification that they expected the Danckwerts principle to be extended to hospital medical staff. Taking account of merit awards, direct application entailed increasing the existing scale (£1,700–£5,250) to £2,750–£7,130. Ministers were adamant that the chain should be broken at its first link.[205] Butler accordingly made a statement explaining that the Government could not accept that the Danckwerts award necessarily involved adjustment in remuneration elsewhere. There was no justification for the view that 'the appropriate standard of remuneration for the professional classes is a rate of 100 per cent above that in force in 1939'.[206]

Once the management side rejected the claim made on behalf of hospital medical staffs the discussion moved on to the possibilities of arbitration. Although hospital medical staff were not covered by the Industrial Disputes Order it was difficult to refuse access to arbitration because, (a) this had been conceded in the recent parallel case of general practitioners, (b) consultants could claim that the Government's promise to implement the Spens Report had not been fulfilled, and (c) the Minister had in 1949 given an undertaking that disputes about remuneration would be settled by arbitration 'save in exceptional circumstances'. However the Health Ministers proposed to reject arbitration on the grounds that the Danckwerts award constituted 'exceptional circumstances', and because the Spens Report was obsolete. Realising that this response courted accusations of breach of faith and likely countervailing action from the BMA, the Ministers proposed that a modest offer should be made to hospital medical staffs, costing a total of £5m per annum.[207]

Moran lobbied both Salisbury (chairman of the Home Affairs Committee) and Churchill on behalf of the consultants, pointing out that their acceptance of NHS contracts was conditional on the understanding that the Spens Report would be fully implemented. According to Moran, specialists would be reasonable, expect no retrospection, and perhaps not the full betterment, but he argued that some increase was needed for the sake of recruitment.[208] Salisbury was converted, calling on Macleod to be 'as generous as possible' to this elite profession.[209]

In addition to the proposal for an all-round increase from the Health Ministers, the Home Affairs Committee was faced with rival suggestions, from Boyd-Carpenter (Financial Secretary) wanting the award to be limited to junior hospital staff, while Monckton (Minister of Labour) favoured an independent inquiry. Monckton argued that refusal to arbitrate would add to pressure for consultants to be included among the various professional groups who were about to be included under the amended Industrial Disputes Order.[210]

The Home Affairs Committee was divided over this issue. Galbraith kept to the line of the memorandum of the Health Ministers. Macleod also argued the case for an all-round increase for hospital medical staffs, but he conceded the strength of his friend Monckton's argument in favour of an independent committee of inquiry. Boyd-Carpenter also agreed that the latter was an acceptable secondary option. Fyfe (Home Secretary), Simonds (Lord Chancellor), and Salisbury favoured making a realistic offer capable of winning over moderate elements in the profession. The meeting narrowly decided in favour of a committee of inquiry on the grounds that this would give the best chance to prevent the increase spreading to part-time consultants.[211]

Before embarking on the formal inquiry Macleod and Galbraith held two meetings with Sir Russell Brain, chairman of the staff side of the Medical Whitley Council. Brain echoed Moran's moderate view, confirming that consultants had no wish to embarrass the Government by insisting on full implementation of the Spens-Danckwerts principle. From his hints about possible lines of a settlement it seemed that something below £4m might be acceptable to consultants. Despite these positive signs Macleod was doubtful whether Brain could convince the rest of the staff side on proposals acceptable to the Government, especially since all eighteen members were part-time consultants. He therefore favoured pressing on with an inquiry, a conclusion still unacceptable to Galbraith, but accepted by the Home Affairs Committee.[212] However, when the terms of reference of the proposed committee of inquiry were considered, Galbraith, supported by the chairman, Crookshank, once again made the case for a negotiated settlement and it was agreed that Ministers should invite a costed proposal from the staff side.[213] The staff side claim was indeed moderate, the main element being a flat rate increase of £400 for consultants. The total cost amounted to £3.25m. They also agreed to defer implementation until April 1954. Macleod now joined Galbraith in favouring acceptance of a modified form of the above proposals. Other Ministers still preferred an inquiry, largely because they were concerned that announcement of an increase for consultants would adversely affect the current wage round. It was agreed to work out terms of a settlement, on the understanding that announcement would be delayed until an opportune moment.[214]

In the final negotiations some minor changes were introduced by the health departments, the only significant one being adoption of a scale tapering from £400 to £350 for the consultants' increase. The staff side was asked to accept abolition of the 'weighting' allowance given to part-time consultants. This was refused, but a minor adjustment of the weighting system was adopted to reduce marginally the advantage of part-time consultants. This was the only concession to improving the relative standing of full-time consultants. Macleod admitted that the settlement was more favourable to part-time consultants than the Government had originally wished, but he warned against penalising them because this might be taken as a precedent by Labour for abolition of the part-time arrangement. Bearing in mind that a full settlement along lines obtained by general practitioners would have cost £17m, the Home Affairs Committee was satisfied that it could not improve on its £3.25m deal.[215]

Between April 1954 and June 1956 there was no major controversy between the profession and the Government over medical salaries. This was the only significant spell of peace on this matter between the start of the service and 1960.

Pressure for improved remuneration built up within the BMA during 1955. For purposes of their renewed campaign consultants and general practitioners joined together.[216] The formal case for an increase of 24%, costing £20m, was presented in June 1956.[217]

The profession argued for the increase on the basis of an existing contractual right confirmed by the Spens Report and Danckwerts award. The Treasury and health departments were satisfied that the 1954 specialists' award had effectively ended any credibility possessed by the Spens-Danckwerts argument. It was agreed to refuse to consider an increase, although at the outset Macmillan realised that a totally negative stance was unrealistic. Privately he considered a Royal Commission or a standing advisory committee to be an appropriate basis for placing remuneration of the profession on a sounder footing.[218] Many obstacles had to be overcome before this constructive approach was adopted.

Although appreciating the strength of argument in favour of a general inquiry into remuneration the Cabinet initially favoured flat rejection of the profession's claim. On Macleod's advice it was agreed that the adverse economic situation should not be cited as grounds for rejection because this would create expectation of an increase when economic conditions improved.[219] The BMA was accordingly informed that the Minister did 'not feel justified in giving consideration to any claim for a general increase in medical remuneration'.[220] The BMA leadership was incensed that its 6,500-word reasoned case was answered by a perfunctory 94-word rejection. The *BMJ* affected an air of outrage. The Ministry of Health was accused of a breach of faith and the Permanent Secretary was singled out for particular blame.[221] The situation was not improved by a meeting between Turton, Nixon Browne and representatives of the profession on 1 August 1956, when the profession was asked to justify the legal basis for its claim. Consideration of the legal argument deferred further action until after the end of the year.[222] The Permanent Secretary's letter to the BMA disposing of their legal argument further exacerbated relations with them.[223]

Another unproductive meeting with the Minister was held. The *BMJ* spoke of a 'crisis of confidence between medicine and the state' and called, in terms reminiscent of 1943, for an investigation from the ground upwards, no doubt with a Spens-type resolution in mind.[224]

The last two months of 1956 were marked by agitated discussion concerning avoidance of a major confrontation with the profession. As in 1954 the respective merits of negotiation and a commission of inquiry were considered. In the light of the Danckwerts experience arbitration was the most feared outcome. Discussion of alternatives revolved around the conundrum of evading arbitration.[225] With difficulty the Treasury persuaded Hawton to commit his department to a full-scale inquiry, arguing that the 'exceptional importance' of the doctors' claim merited a 'lengthy inquiry'. Because the BDA was joining the BMA in its complaints, it seemed inescapable to deal with the two professions simultaneously. It was proposed to deflect any accusations of procrastination by offering an interim increase for junior hospital doctors. Once a commission of inquiry was accepted the main difficulty was deciding the boundaries of its operation. It was agreed to include local authority doctors at the Ministry of Health's insistence, and in the face of the Treasury objection that this would invite comparability claims in the local authority sector. However the Treasury was successful in excluding university research personnel, in order to block comparability increases in the higher education field.[226] This exclusion was known to disappoint Salisbury in particular, because he was persuaded by Himsworth that one of the major functions of a full-scale inquiry would be reappraising the relativities between clinicians and medical researchers. Himsworth had pointed out that only 6 out of 68 FRSs, and none of the four current Nobel Prize winners, were eligible for merit awards.[227]

The first memorandum to the Cabinet outlining proposals for a Royal Commission to investigate remuneration of doctors and dentists was issued by Stuart and Turton, and the second by Maclay and Turton. A third paper was circulated by Salisbury outlining the grievances of biomedical researchers. In his view the ineligibility for a merit award of one of the discoverers of penicillin was a crucial instance indicting the whole merit award system.[228] The Cabinet agreed to establish a Royal Commission, with the aim of establishing some form of permanent advisory machinery at its conclusion. The problems of medical researchers were left for the Commission to recognise. Vosper was pessimistic concerning the prospects of limiting an interim pay increase to junior hospital doctors.[229]

Relations with the profession had deteriorated to the point where a Royal Commission presented to them as a fait accompli, and with membership excluding medical and dental representatives, was regarded with deep distrust. During the opening months of 1957 meetings of doctors and dentists expressed overwhelming antagonism to the Government's proposals. Even after Macmillan's personal intervention and the offer of an interim all-round increase of 5%, with 10% for junior hospital doctors, the profession agreed to co-operate with the Commission only by a narrow majority, and after experiencing a painful crisis of confidence between the rank and file and the leadership. Under the chairmanship of the industrialist Sir Harry Pilkington, the Royal Commission conducted the most elaborate investigation into the incomes of the British medical profession ever undertaken, and it satisfied the Government's wishes by basing its recommendations on comparisons with the earnings of other professions. The outcome was a 22% award, the cost of which was £12m, compared with the £35m estimated cost of the BMA claim. The Commission also paved the way for establishing a more permanent mechanism to conduct periodic reviews of doctors' incomes. Thus after twelve years in existence the NHS entered into a more stable arrangement for determining professional remuneration.

The 1956/57 dispute was relevant to certain other longer-term developments. Evolution of alternative arrangements for providing treatment during their 'snowball strike' set doctors thinking more seriously about alternatives to the NHS, including insurance arrangements for health care. Reflecting the air of general disenchantment with the NHS the BMA Council was asked by the Representative Meeting to institute an inquiry into the whole field of the publicly administered medical services. A committee under the chairmanship of Sir Arthur Porritt was set up in 1958 and it reported in 1962. The Porritt Report constituted the first collective deliberation of the profession on the future of health care since the ill-fated Medical Planning Commission of 1942. Although less widely noticed than the Medical Planning Commission report, the Porritt Report is of permanent interest because it constituted the first sign of a significant drift of opinion in favour of National Health Service reorganisation.

(ix) DETECTING NEW GIANTS

The birth of the National Health Service coincided with the dawning of the knowledge that lung cancer was emerging as one of the major causes of death and disease in modern Britain. The steady increase in incidence of lung cancer caused concern immediately after World War II. In the year 1951 recorded lung cancer deaths in England and Wales reached 13,000, and for the first time exceeded deaths from tuberculosis. At precisely this moment the famous paper by Doll and Hill indicted cigarette smoking as the predominant cause of lung cancer. During the 1950s cigarette smoking grew in popularity, deaths from lung cancer steadily increased, and scientific evidence concerning their interrelationship mounted until it became incontrovertible. Combating the smoking habit consequently emerged as one of the most significant steps that could be taken towards realisation of the preventive ideal of the National Health Service. For a variety of reasons this problem was not treated with an urgency commensurate with its importance. Dealing with the issue was complicated because of the wider interests involved. Health Ministers were obliged to consult their colleagues before declaring their policy.

Within the NHS this question first came to the attention of the Cancer and Radiotherapy Standing Advisory Committee at the instigation of one of its members. The Cancer SAC recommended that the MRC should sponsor further research on this problem. It was felt that convincing evidence concerning the relationship between smoking and lung cancer might not materialise for some 20 years.[230] The MRC rebuffed the scepticism of the Cancer SAC. Himsworth informed the Chief Medical Officer that MRC was 'satisfied that the case against smoking as such is proven, and that no further statistical enquiry on the general aspect of the problem is necessary'.[231]

Two parliamentary questions on smoking and lung cancer tabled for 28 June 1951 resulted in the Cancer SAC reconsidering its position. Notwithstanding the committed line taken by the MRC, the Cancer SAC confirmed its former view and it was supported by the CHSC. The Minister was advised that the available evidence of a direct relationship between smoking and carcinoma of the lung was insufficient to justify publicity on this subject.[232]

Macleod was closely questioned on the connection between smoking and lung cancer again on 19 June 1952. Subsequently further pressure in Parliament, press coverage, reference to this subject on television, and prompting from the CHSC forced the Cancer SAC to consult a panel of independent adjudicators, which decided firmly in favour of Doll and Hill. The Cancer SAC now revised its advice to conclude that there was a 'real' connection between smoking and lung cancer, and it agreed that the young should be warned of the dangers of excessive smoking.[233] On this occasion Macleod decided to consult colleagues before making a further public statement, partly because the connection between smoking and lung cancer was now irrefutable, partly because the Imperial Tobacco Company wished to donate £250,000 to MRC for research on this subject and to make an announcement in its annual report, scheduled for 25 February 1954. Macleod appreciated that he was faced with a problem requiring 'delicate public relations handling'. The Permanent Secretary was keen that the Ministry should not open itself to the charge of suppression.[234] In view of the wider public issues involved, including the tobacco tax, it was agreed that a sub-committee should consider the text of an announcement, and that the latter should be cleared with the full Cabinet. Despite some ministerial reservations the Cabinet authorised acceptance of funds donated by the tobacco industry for research into the causes of cancer.[235]

The advice transmitted from the Cancer SAC proved sufficiently unalarmist to be acceptable as the basis for the parliamentary statement. Despite Macleod's cautious approach, Monckton, Salisbury and Boyd-Carpenter favoured toning down the announcement, and also its postponement.

Macleod warned that the statement would create less of a sensation if made early. He appreciated that quiet handling of this subject was essential, because 'we all know that the Welfare State and much else is based on tobacco smoking'. It was in his view impossible to delay because the 'prime mover in all this is a man of extremely advanced left wing opinions and would not hesitate to embarrass the Government if nothing appears soon'.[236] This view was accepted and Macleod's statement made on 12 February 1954 was successful in temporarily defusing criticism. Macleod was unenthusiastic about going beyond his initial statement. His officials warned that 'the Minister is not at the moment in favour of an official propaganda campaign . . . being launched by the Ministry or by local health authorities at the Ministry's request'. However, pressure on this subject was uncontainable and discussion within the Standing Advisory Committees erupted again in 1955. On this occasion the Medical SAC advocated a publicity campaign on the connection between smoking and lung cancer. After some procrastination this suggestion was not supported by the CHSC.[237] However the Medical SAC immediately revived its advice, which on this occasion was supported by the CHSC.[238] The advice given was sufficiently decisive and grave for the matter to be referred to the full Cabinet. Turton informed his colleagues that deaths from lung cancer had mounted to 17,000 in 1955. He cited the view of the MRC Secretary that evidence on this subject was now 'so massive as to be incontrovertible', and also that identification of the precise causal agent was of secondary importance. The Cabinet decided that a 'restrained rather than alarmist' statement should be drawn up by a committee of Ministers. In the absence of direct proof of causal connection it was agreed that a propaganda campaign was not justified.[239] The Ministers advised that 'from the point of view of social hygiene, cancer of the lung is not a disease like tuberculosis; nor should the Government assume too lightly the odium of advising the general public on their personal tastes and habits where the evidence of the harm which may arise is not conclusive'. It was also urged that substantial Treasury interest should be taken into account. Macmillan reminded his colleagues that tobacco duty yielded £670m pa and he persuaded them to delay the statement until after the Budget announcement. Finally it was agreed that the statement should be made in advance of the publication of further findings by Doll and Hill expected in the near future.[240] A brief statement made by Turton in the House of Commons on 7 May 1956 accordingly reported on recent research and promised that the public would be kept informed of further developments. Within the Medical SAC it was felt that the ministerial statement had failed to reflect the spirit of urgency of the advice given, but it was decided not to press the issue.[241]

Renewed action awaited the publication of a full MRC report in June 1957, in connection with which a committee of Ministers recommended a more positive public statement and also minor publicity in the field of health education.[242] The first uninhibited official support for the conclusions reached by Doll and Hill in 1950, was consequently expressed by Vaughan-Morgan in the House of Commons on 27 June 1957. Thereafter the health and education departments asked local health and education authorities and the Central Council for Health Education to give prominence to the relationship between smoking and lung cancer in their health education activities. However very little momentum was achieved until after the publication of the Royal College of Physicians Report, *Smoking and Health* (1962). Following the latter report a temporary check occurred in the consumption of cigarettes. The more permanent check was a phenomenon of the late seventies. By that stage it had become evident that cigarette smoking was implicated in a wide range of diseases, including various cancers, coronary heart disease, bronchitis and emphysema. The 1984 *Annual Report* of the DHSS publicised the fact that in 1981 'some 100,000 deaths in the UK (15–20 per cent of the total) were attributable to smoking'. In retrospect it is clear that the critics of smoking during the early years of the NHS were by no means underestimating the scale of the health problem attributed to the tobacco smoking habit. As the revised Royal College of Physicians Report noted, cigarette smoking was as important 'a cause of death as were the great epidemic diseases such as typhoid, cholera and TB that affected previous generations in this country'.[243] In fact tobacco smoking was destroying life on a scale greater than the infectious diseases that had inspired the sanitarian movement of Victorian times. The National Health Service was noticeably less resilient in identifying and combating the new and more formidable giants of disease characterising the modern age. Problems such as tobacco smoking, like similar hazards connected with other addictions, diet, and environment, indicate the formidable nature of the obstacles standing in the way of the realisation of the preventive ideal of the modern health service. Shortcomings in adapting to this new situation were recognised at an early stage. In reviewing his ten years as Chief Medical Officer to the Scottish Department of Health, Sir Kenneth Cowan frankly admitted that his pleasure concerning successes in the preventive field such as the 1957 mass radiography campaign or introduction of the Salk vaccine against polio was tempered by the realisation that the modern health service had failed to inhibit the increase in lung cancer. Accordingly he advocated a much more vigorous commitment to campaigning against smoking, a view that was totally shared by his counterpart, Sir George Godber, at the Ministry of Health.[244]

CHAPTER VII

The Advisory Services

Responsibility for the National Health Service was divided between the Ministry of Health and the Department of Health for Scotland. During our period the latter was a stable entity, the interests of which were represented in the Cabinet by the Secretary of State for Scotland. As noted in chapter V, following the departure of Bevan the Ministry of Health lost its Cabinet status. Besides affecting the general prestige of the department, this demotion weakened the position of the Ministry with respect to its two great negotiating partners, the Treasury and the medical profession. Eckstein has commented on the ambivalence within the profession concerning the decline in status of the Ministry.[1] The chairman of the powerful Joint Consultants Committee blamed lack of seniority of the Ministry for the failure to correct underspending on hospital development.[2] The Acton review concluded that 'most observers would agree that fears as to the Ministry's loss of prestige and status have been confirmed'.[3] In terms of size the reorganisation of 1951 resulted in the staff of the department shrinking from 5,300 to 2,724. In its senior ranks the Ministry retained 21 officials of assistant secretary rank and above,[4] which was a small force to command fourteen Regional Hospital Boards, 377 Hospital Management Committees, 138 Executive Councils, 145 Local Health and Welfare Authorities, as well as the complex central consultative machinery, or the powerful and articulate leadership of the medical profession.

Internally the changes of 1951 were less disruptive because the NHS was already run as a 'practically self-contained compartment' of the Ministry of Health.[5] Further changes in the administration of the reduced health department were introduced after 1951. An establishment division was formed, later a small organisation and methods branch, and in 1955 an embryonic statistical department.[6] The Guillebaud Report, the Acton survey and other experts pressed for a more fully developed research and intelligence department, and for the effective exploitation of the skills of accountants, economists and statisticians in health service research.[7] The Treasury was sympathetic to this aim and it also wanted reorganisation of the divisional structure to facilitate liaison with the hospital regional organisation.[8] In the Treasury view, deficiencies of the

Ministry were regarded as a reflection of problems of an 'old fashioned regulatory Department who have suddenly got landed with a senior managerial job'.[9]

In addition to difficulties created by its diminished size, the Ministry of Health also faced special problems of internal co-ordination. Traditionally the most striking difficulty of the department was the division between its administrative and medical branches. During the tenure of Sir George Newman as Chief Medical Officer there had been a particularly disharmonious relationship between the two sides. In later years there remained the difficulty of defining a precise role for the medical branch. On the basis of his historical review Mackenzie suggests that 'on questions of health policy the initiative lies with the medical side, on matters of resource allocation and administrative structure it lies with the generalist class of the Civil Service'.[10] Unfortunately, problems rarely fell into these discrete categories. From the perspective of the under secretary in charge of Division 4 'the lay administrative staff, while not in any way interfering with or overruling the activities of their medical and other professional colleagues, have the ultimate responsibility for reconciling differences and securing the prompt and orderly conduct of business. Of course, there are informal exchanges in correspondence or discussion between the professional staff in the Ministry and their opposite numbers outside, but it is the lay administrative staff which has to bring all the threads together'.[11] There was a tendency for the Chief Medical Officer and his staff to drift into the position of technical advisers or intermediaries in negotiation with their professional colleagues in the NHS. Thus under the NHS the medical branch assumed a less robust status than their predecessors during the early days of the Ministry of Health. This to some extent reversed Morant's philosophy concerning the centrality of expert guidance in the formation of policy. As noted below in chapter VIII the balance of influence between senior officers at the regional level more closely accorded with Morant's conception.

Problems of integration within the Ministry of Health were not eased by the continuing semi-autonomous status of the Board of Control and the Welsh Board of Health. As will be seen in chapter VIII, on the basis of its special legal functions the Board of Control coveted its independence. Under its long-serving chairman, Sir Laurence Brock, the Board of Control assumed a superior air. When the National Health Service was formed the Board of Control took on a dual function, retaining its separate statutory existence and also doubling as the mental health division of the Ministry of Health. Under the new arrangement, 'while the Board will act in its corporate and semi-independent capacity in dealing with the liberty of the subject, the personnel of the Board will become the Mental Health Division of the Ministry of Health and will deal with the administrative and medical questions as officers of the Minister and an integral part of his Department'.[12] Further erosion of the independent status of the Board of Control took place with the retirement of Brock's successor, Sir Percy Barter, in 1953, and finally the Board of Control was abolished following the Mental Health Act of 1959.

A further administrative complication was created by the existence of the Welsh Board of Health. The latter was established in 1919, under section 5 of the Ministry of Health Act, taking over the functions, staff and Cardiff offices of the Welsh Insurance Commissioners.[13] The Board of Health introduced an element of regional co-ordination in Wales, but it was less authoritative than the agency advocated by the Welsh Consultative Council on Medical and Allied Services. In response to the 'traditional sentiment of nationality deeply imbedded' in the Welsh consciousness, the Consultative Council called for a Welsh National Council for Health, modelled on the Welsh National Memorial Association co-ordinating the tuberculosis service. It was further proposed that the principality should be divided into five areas for health planning purposes.[14] The Welsh Board of Health never took on the representative character proposed for the National Council, and its powers were more limited. During the inter-war period the Board of Health exercised in Wales the National Health Insurance and public health functions of the Ministry of Health; civil defence, housing and other functions were acquired in the years leading up to and following the outbreak of World War II. The Board of Health moved into new headquarters in Cathays Park, Cardiff in 1938 and continued to grow until, by early 1945, it employed more than 500 staff. From this peak the Board of Health gradually declined, losing about 300 of its staff with the formation of the Ministry of National Insurance in 1945, while its housing functions were lost in 1951. The Board of Health continued to exercise most of the functions of the Ministry of Health relating to the administration of the National Health Service in Wales.[15] With its staff of about 150, in the 1950s the Board played a minor technical and co-ordinating role. Its usefulness was severely eroded by the existence of the Welsh Regional Hospital Board, which commanded most of the resources of the NHS in Wales. The Welsh Board of Health was generally regarded as a minor anachronism. The Acton survey doubted whether its retention could be justified on administrative grounds. However, the Association of Executive Associations was relatively isolated in calling for its abolition.[16] Reassertion of Welsh political identity temporarily preserved this

Welsh institution, until eventually it was transmuted into the Health Division of the Welsh Office in 1969.

(i) THE CENTRAL ADVISORY MACHINERY

When the Ministry of Health was first established in 1919 the Minister was advised by an influential Consultative Council on Medical and Allied Services, which in 1920 was responsible for the famous Dawson Report, widely taken as the blueprint for a modern comprehensive health service. At the time the Report was ignored, the Consultative Council was allowed to lapse, and no other central advisory machinery was constructed in its place. Although Ministers subsequently made some use of a Medical Advisory Committee, as well as specialist technical committees, no formal machinery existed for conveying expert advice on the development of the health services.[17]

In this respect the Ministry of Health differed from the Board of Education, which made active use of consultative committees. The Ministry was also departing from the conception of expert advisory committees proclaimed in the Haldane Report on the machinery of government (1918).

Failure of the Ministry of Health to exploit its opportunities to develop an advisory mechanism accounts for the almost disproportionate importance assumed by this subject in negotiations between the profession and the Government in the run-up to the National Health Service. Other organisations such as the voluntary hospitals and local authorities also attached importance to the central advisory mechanism as a vehicle for compensating for their loss of status in the new local health service administration. The Labour Government set the minds of its critics at rest by promising them a role in a strong statutory central advisory apparatus. At the TUC congress the influential secretary of the Medical Practitioners' Union, Dr Bruce Cardew, called for the CHSC to become a 'Parliament for the Health Services to receive ideas from the nurses, the cleaners, and the rank and file'.[18] Naturally, the expectations aroused were difficult to reconcile in practice. In particular the medical profession was alarmed by the prospect of its influence being diluted by a substantial lay presence, while lay organisations were antagonistic to the proprietorial attitude of the medical profession.

The symbolic importance of the central advisory machinery was signified by the prominent place of the clauses relating to the Central Health Services Council (or Scottish Health Services Council) and Standing Advisory Committees in the 1946 and 1947 NHS legislation. These bodies were given the duty of advising on

questions referred to them by Ministers, but they were also empowered to initiate advice and also to publish reports.

Establishment of the CHSC and SHSC was an early task for
the administrators, and until this exercise was completed the more
elaborate process of setting up the advisory committees could not
be undertaken. Originally it was hoped that the CHSC would
begin operations in February 1947, but in the event its first meeting
was not held until 27 July 1948. Consequently the SACs were not
set up until after the new service had begun.

The CHSC comprised 41 and the SHSC 35 members. In both a
bare majority (21 and 18 respectively) were medically qualified.
Ministers selected the members from lists of names submitted by
relevant organisations. With the CHSC the largest identifiable
group of 15 medical practitioners was largely drawn from the BMA
list. The three Presidents of the Royal Colleges and three others
were included as ex officio members. Two medical members
(reinforcing two representatives of lay organisations) were chosen
to represent the interests of mental health. The remaining members
of the CHSC represented other professional groups (including
three dentists but no opticians), voluntary hospitals and local
government. A similar balance was observed in the SHSC. The
average age of members was about 60, and this remained the case
during the first decade of the service.[19]

Tension over medical and lay influence on the CHSC surfaced
at the first meeting when, as the first item of business, the question
of the chairmanship was raised. The medical interest temporarily
acquiesced to the lay chairman, Frederick Messer, the Labour MP
and chairman of the NW Metropolitan RHB. This solution was a
tactful concession to the sensitivities of the Labour administration.
In 1957 Messer was replaced by the physician, Sir Henry Cohen,
chairman of the Medical SAC, and increasingly the dominant
voice in the advisory machinery. The first chairman of the SHSC
was also a layman, Sir Humphrey Broun Lindsay, who was
replaced by another layman, J P Younger in 1953, and then by
the pathologist, G L Montgomery in 1955. Broun Lindsay and
Younger both vacated the chairmanship of the SHSC to become
chairmen of RHBs, of Edinburgh and Glasgow respectively. The
first major responsibility of the CHSC and SHSC was determining
the structure of the advisory committees. At the outset it had been
intended to specify the SACs in the health service legislation, but
in view of absence of agreement on any obvious logical arrangement
this problem was deferred until after establishment of the central
councils. In pre-legislation negotiations the BMA had pressed for
an advisory committee to deal with the general medical service,
while the voluntary hospitals had wanted an advisory committee

for the hospital service. It was thought that such committees would determine the main lines of policy in their respective areas. In initial planning for England and Wales it was proposed to establish a hospital and specialist services SAC, with sub-committees representing cancer, tuberculosis and mental health. Eventually the three latter were elevated to the rank of separate SACs, while the remaining hospital and specialist interest was subsumed into a general Medical SAC. The other SACs established for England and Wales were Dental; Pharmaceutical; Ophthalmic; Nursing; and Maternity and Midwifery, making nine in all. These committees absorbed some or all of the functions of pre-existing bodies such as the Medical Advisory Committee (1930-), Standing Advisory Committee on Tuberculosis (1939-), Eye Services Committee (1946-), and the Radium Commission (1929-).[20] Proposals for SACs to deal with child health, health centres, or health education were not proceeded with.[21]

In Scotland the SACs were constructed on a slightly different pattern, relating more to the structure of the service and to geography than was the case in England. The nine SACs were Medical; Dental; Nursing and Midwifery; Pharmaceutical; Hospital and Specialist Services; Local Authority Services; GP Services; Health Centres; and Highlands and Islands. In keeping with their traditional independence the Scottish advisory mechanism for the most part operated without reference to its English counterpart. The two sets of advisory committees thus ran in parallel, addressing themselves to similar problems, and reaching similar conclusions. In a few unavoidable cases, especially in the early days, there was some joint action between the Scottish and English arms of the advisory mechanism.[22]

Although formally the SAC structure was proposed by the CHSC and SHSC, the basic schemes were evolved by officials. Contrary to official advice the CHSC insisted on a substantial share of the places on standing advisory committees, consequently considerably diluting both the latter's independence and expert character. The English Medical SAC membership was drawn overwhelmingly from the CHSC. A major disagreement erupted within the CHSC over the constitution of the Medical SAC, which BMA representatives wanted to reserve entirely for the profession, and it was pointed out that Bevan had promised such a constitution. After much controversy Bevan confirmed this promise, with the result that the Dental, Pharmaceutical, and Ophthalmic Committees were also reserved for 'professional' representatives. It was then necessary to increase the 'professional' element on the Nursing SAC. It was agreed that defining 'profession' in the context of these committees admitted no logically consistent solution. In effect this arrangement was implemented by removing lay members, which caused resentment, and led to difficulties over the position of the CHSC chairman, who was appointed ex officio to all committees.[23] In Scotland the issue of professional representation was pushed to its logical conclusion. It was reported that 'no medical interlopers' would be allowed on the Nursing and Midwifery SAC, which would thus be reserved for the 'uninhibited expression of views by nurses and midwives'.

The problem of lay participation also erupted with respect to CHSC committees. The TUC complained about its exclusion from the Committee on General Practice. On the other hand the BMA complained about lay participation. It also regretted that the medical members were drawn directly from the CHSC rather than from the BMA itself. It was admitted that the BMA had 'purposely nominated people whom they no longer regarded as particularly effective for the CHSC on the grounds that they had thought it would be merely a façade'.[24]

The two advisory structures persisted with very little modification being made during the first decade of the service. Their work was recorded in the annual reports of the CHSC and SHSC, the former being published separately, and the latter as a brief appendix to the annual report of the Department of Health. During this period the CHSC and its SACs issued more than 200 pieces of advice to the Minister, and they published 18 reports. The SHSC was less active in offering advice to the Secretary of State, but it issued 14 reports and also participated in preparation of seven of the CHSC reports.

While the central advisory structure made some useful contributions, the impression of assiduous and consistent industry is to some extent illusory. After an initial phase of euphoria, many of the advisory bodies showed signs of loss of momentum. A variety of factors rendered the advisory apparatus unsuited to give dynamic leadership. First, the infrequency of meetings, combined with elaborate arrangements for consultation between committees, precluded advice being given promptly on all but the most trivial issues. Secondly, the members selected were already committed to other professional or NHS bodies. Many members recorded poor attendance, and some were also too unadaptable or elderly to be helpful. The willing members stretched their talents by serving on too many SACs and ad hoc sub-committees. The real work of the advisory bodies fell on too few shoulders. Thirdly, the advisory committees lacked cohesion; they were for the most part miscellaneous collections of delegates representing diverse and discordant interest groups. Accordingly, the committees were insufficiently vigorous or effective for the most part of the membership to transfer their loyalties to this new advisory machinery. Finally, the morale of advisory committees was undermined by failure to gain the confidence of the departments concerned. It was felt that significant business was deflected elsewhere, while on occasions the department seemed flagrantly to disregard the advice given by the CHSC.[25] In the absence of positive encouragement from officials the advisory mechanism drifted away from the main ground of policy problems. There was sufficient work to sustain the quarterly meetings of the CHSC until 1954, but in the following three years only three meetings were held each year. Annual reports reflected tailing off in the contribution of the CHSC and its associated SACs. Regular quarterly meetings were sustained only by the Medical, Nursing, and Mental Health committees. These were the only committees that performed the function originally envisaged for the SACs. Reflecting a similar trend in Scotland, in 1952 the SHSC proposed a merger of the Hospital and GP Services SACs, and dissolution of the Health Centre SAC.[26]

Ministers, in their ritual addresses to the CHSC, emphasised the importance of the consultative process, but little that mattered was entrusted to the advisory committees.[27] Indeed, the central advisory committees were deflected away from more important problems, (a) because other avenues of inquiry were more appropriate, (b) because of the risk of raising major policy questions prematurely, or (c) because of dangers of straying into the forbidden territory of pay and conditions of employment. Officials realised that they risked 'appearing to restrict their field to merely trifling by banning burning topics'.[28] Reacting to reported jealousy of the CHSC over establishment of the Cranbrook Committee, Turton explained that no disrespect was intended, but he needed advice from a carefully balanced expert group, in view of the divergent opinions expressed on the maternity services within the medical profession.[29] Only the more determined committees sustained a sense of useful purpose. Most perished on the trivial business put their way from official sources. By the end of the decade a sense of crisis was reached. A meeting was held to consider how to infuse new life into the advisory machinery.[30] Members were complaining that there was 'little before these bodies' and that all important inquiries were being directed elsewhere. Officials frankly admitted that ad hoc inquiries, hand-picked specialist committees, or direct consultation with bodies representing the profession were more suitable vehicles for obtaining advice. It was concluded that 'All this activity inevitably reduces the field in which use can be made of the CHSCs and SACs'.[31] By a process of elimination it was decided that the CHSC and SHSC might profitably look into the neglected area of preventive medicine, the practical outcome being formation in 1960 of the Joint CHSC and SHSC Committee under Cohen to report on health education.

The major success of the advisory set-up was the joint CHSC-SHSC committees on prescribing and the definition of drugs, which evolved guidelines on prescribing and produced lists of substances that were not eligible for consideration as drugs, and also devised a system for the classification of proprietary preparations.[32] These committees provided politically useful evidence that the health departments were making a beginning in the control of excessive prescribing.[33] Also politically useful was the Committee on Health Centres, which was the first CHSC committee to be established. This inquiry was promised in the light of the decision in January 1948 to place an effective freeze on the development of health centres. The two years of deliberation by the Health Centre Committee, from December 1948 to December 1950, and the further delay of four months before publication of an extract from the report, provided valuable respite on this delicate issue. Neither the CHSC nor the SHSC was successful in breathing life into the health centre experiment, but they prompted a minor change in the 1949 Act making it permissible for doctors to see private patients in health centres, and they kept up pressure on officials to leave open the possibility of building health centres in new housing developments. As noted below in chapter IX their efforts were poorly rewarded.

The Committee on Health Centres illustrates the value of the advisory machinery as a shelving device, justifying inaction pending a lengthy independent inquiry. A remit to the slow-paced advisory engine was particularly useful when it was unlikely that it would come up with embarrassing conclusions. In Scotland, the report of the Committee on Ageing, set up in 1949, was not published until 1953, while the report of the Committee set up in 1953 on Mental Deficiency was not published until 1957. As pointed out above, even with respect to such a serious health hazard as lung cancer occasioned by cigarette smoking, the advisory machinery proved to be inadequate for backing up the findings of MRC-conducted research. Notwithstanding the fanatical dedication of one member of the CHSC, it took six years of slow and inconsequential deliberation before firm advice recognising the dangers of cigarette smoking was offered to the Minister. Even after 1957 sustained pressure on this issue was not forthcoming from the advisory machinery, the low priority attached to this question being evident as late as 1964 in the Cohen report on health education.[34] It is a plausible hypothesis that the influence of advocates on the smoking and lung cancer issue was more than matched by imperatives on the other side emanating from the Treasury.

The advisory committees were particularly ineffective in dealing with major administrative problems within the health service. In the absence of a Hospital and Specialist Service SAC in the English advisory service it was agreed to establish a hospital sub-committee of the Medical SAC. Because of internal dissent over the scope and composition of the committee, action was delayed for a year. In June 1949 a committee was established to examine the general structure of the hospital service. This committee reported in June 1950 and recommendations of the CHSC based on its findings appeared in the annual report published in April 1951. The report itself was not published, and the relatively anodyne recommendations of the CHSC were issued only after much disagreement.[35]

Having failed to make a mark with a report on external administration, in January 1950 the CHSC set up a Committee on Internal Hospital Administration, the report of which was eventually published in 1954. Once again this report occasioned disagreement and was subjected to much amendment before issue, with the result that it was silent on questions upon which policy guidance was required.[36] Ironically similar disarray attended the preparation of the report on the improvement of co-operation between the three parts of the health service.[37]

It is perhaps an unsurprising outcome that large and heterogeneous advisory committees tended to fragment into their component parts when addressing the more intractable problems of the NHS. The BMA representatives were particularly prone to defend their party line. Thus, when the prospect of establishing a committee on health centres emerged, BMA representatives, backed up by the BMA itself, protested when this topic was remitted to the CHSC rather than the Medical SAC.[38] Similarly the BMA complained about the CHSC's intervention on general practice. It was alleged that the CHSC had excluded 'sound general practitioners'.[39] In both cases, although the eventual outcome was uncontroversial, the BMA group objected to an issue relating to their members being referred to a body containing non-professional representatives, no doubt appreciating that the BMA influence was stronger on the Medical SAC than elsewhere in the advisory machinery.[40] Because of their differing composition there was a tendency for SACs to react differently to the problems with which they were confronted. When, at the instigation of the Ministry, the Nursing SAC set about preparing a series of technical memoranda for guidance of trained nurses on approved techniques on such points as the sterilisation of syringes, this initiative was opposed both in principle and in detail by the Medical SAC, and disagreement spilled over to the CHSC.[41] Similarly the Mental SAC entered into a protracted dispute with the Nursing SAC over the latter's proposal to introduce a scheme for enrolment of assistant nurses in mental hospitals. In both of these disputes committees dominated by the medical profession reacted adversely to independent initiatives exercised by the body upon which nurses were dominant. The Nursing SAC, although consistently active, attained little influence. It was noticed that this committee remained weak and was treated by professional bodies 'with contempt'.[42]

Notwithstanding the shortcomings of the advisory mechanism, the Scottish advisory committees produced useful reports on neglected subjects such as the welfare of hospital patients, preventive medicine, child health, and the ageing population. In England the Medical and Mental SACs operated with full agenda. They addressed themselves to some important questions, and gave useful advice to the departments on numerous technical questions. They considered cross-infection in hospital, safety in operating theatres, privacy of patients, visits to children in hospital, control of infectious diseases, and the services to such neglected groups as the aged or epileptic. On occasions they pressed ahead with their investigations and advice against the wishes of the departments. In 1956 the Medical SAC complained that the Minister's statement on smoking and lung cancer 'did not meet the advice given by the Committee'.[43] Such confrontation with the Minister was rare. In general the committees were directed towards problems upon which their approach was likely to reinforce the instincts of the departments.

The low profile of the central advisory mechanism was not offensive to the departments. While the advisory bodies operated with greater regularity than their pre-NHS equivalents, the departments showed little enthusiasm for drawing out their potential. As noted above the structure itself was ill-designed for its intended purposes. There was accordingly a tendency for officials to depend on other avenues for advice. Much of the responsibility for the indifferent performance of the advisory committees must lie with the members themselves. Their right to initiate was not restricted, yet it was used to only a limited degree. The example of Horace Joules illustrates the capacity of a single member to make a decisive impact. With rare exceptions the committees failed to undertake sustained initiatives. Nevertheless their shortcomings attracted relatively little public comment. However, a scattering of criticism emanated from such sources as the Royal College of Physicians and the Acton Society Trust. *The Lancet* regarded the advisory mechanism as a failure. Gradually, what Mackenzie called the

'present extraordinary system of consultation' developed a reputation for being 'too passive or inconclusive', or acting as a 'rubber
stamp' on routine clinical matters, which was scarcely the role
envisaged when the NHS was established.[44]

(ii) OTHER CHANNELS OF CONSULTATION

Given inherent limitations in the central advisory machinery the
health departments relied on more specialised avenues of advice
outside the statutory framework. Some of this consultation was a
prior condition for the entry of the medical profession into the
NHS.

Potentially more compact and effective vehicles for guidance of
Ministers than the rambling central advisory machinery, were the
regular gatherings of chairmen and senior officers of the Regional
Hospital Boards. Owing to the numbers involved the English and
Welsh chairmen met separately from their officers. Such meetings
had no statutory basis, but they were vital to maintaining smooth
co-ordination of the major branch of the service. Not only were
these meetings appropriate for considering problems of the hospital
and specialist service, but their deliberations necessarily extended
to the service as a whole. Compared with the central advisory
mechanisms, the RHB senior officers and chairmen possessed the
advantage of front-line experience at the hub of the new service.
The success of this mechanism depended on the calibre of the
officers and chairmen, as well as on the spirit in which these
meetings were approached by the Minister and officials.

The meetings of RHB chairmen in London began auspiciously
enough. The Ministry of Health announced that it would 'consult
and discuss with chairmen any question of major policy in the
hospital service before any action is taken'. The meetings began
on a monthly basis, but at the request of the department they
were reduced to two-monthly from June 1950. With rare exceptions,
Ministers' contacts with chairmen were limited to perfunctory
attendances, for the purpose of introduction, at the beginning of
their ministerial appointment. When Hawton became Permanent
Secretary, the chairmanship of the meetings was frequently delegated to his deputy. Increasingly the agenda was taken up by local
grievances. The chairmen were consulted about procedures for
supply of dustbins, or travelling expenses for hospital chaplains.
Such triviality generated a sense of frustration. It was felt that the
higher purpose of the chairmen's meetings was not being
observed.[45] Led by Schuster, in late 1953 the chairmen tried to
enhance the status of their meetings. They asked for reference to
more important policy issues, and more regular access to the
Minister. Minor improvements in procedure were wrung out of

the department, where it was suspected that the chairmen were usurping the role of the central advisory machinery.[46] The chairmen remained dissatisfied. Their meetings continued to be dominated by routine and trivial business. It was not until 1960 when Enoch Powell assumed office that the chairmen were taken more genuinely into the Minister's confidence on significant points of policy.[47]

One of the reforms suggested by the English chairmen was holding regular joint meetings of all senior RHB officers for discussions of policy. This was ruled out by the department for various reasons, including the unwieldy size of the meeting. However, in Scotland regular joint meetings of RHB chairmen, senior administrative medical officers, and secretaries were held. These meetings were generally more successful and harmonious than their counterparts in England. This outcome was facilitated by the more positive standing of the Scottish RHBs, whereas the English and Welsh chairmen were very much more on the defensive. The meetings of chairmen and senior officers perhaps reinforced the status of RHBs, but they remained essentially reactive in character and were not mobilised to tackle major problems of policy facing the early NHS.

Because of the large numbers involved no regular meetings were held for purposes of consultation with representatives of Hospital Management Committees, Executive Councils, or Local Health Authorities. The HMCs and Executive Councils established associations to represent their interests, while the Local Health Authorities relied on the traditional machinery of the County Councils Association and the Association of Municipal Corporations. These bodies made frequent representations to the health departments concerning the administration of their respective services. In the case of Executive Councils and Local Health Authorities arrangements for consultation roughly continued what had existed previously. However difficulties existed with the Association of HMCs, the very creation of which was offensive to some Regional Hospital Boards. Thus, although the Ministry of Health was in contact with individual hospital groups, it was slow to enter into regular dealings with the Association of HMCs, for fear of further alienating the regional boards, and also because of the risk of setting up two rival channels for advice within the hospital sector. Relations with the Executive Councils Association and the local authority associations were sporadic and limited to technical questions of administration. These channels were not exploited for purposes of planning the development of Part III and Part IV services. Since neither the Scottish nor the English SAC arrangement served this end, there was no channel for the communication of expert advice on these branches of the service to compare with the arrangements existing for the hospital service. As noted below, this defect was to some extent compensated for by the establishment of ad hoc working parties to deal with specific problems.

Commentators are impressed by the permeation of the influence of doctors and their professional associations in the administration of the National Health Service.[48] The new service created a multiplicity of avenues for the influence of the BMA and its satellite committees. Such factors as numerical strength, an effective organisational framework, and hard-won experience in exerting pressure on the health departments, enabled the BMA to exceed more formally constituted advisory bodies in building itself into the policy-making and administrative framework. Consequently a great deal of the business of the NHS was transacted directly between the health departments and representatives of the medical profession. Eckstein argues that the health departments and BMA were drawn into a sort of symbiotic relationship, resulting in intimate and amicable relations between the two sides. This form of transaction is characterised as a 'backstairs network' conducted on the basis of mutual interest rather than because of ties of social affinity between the parties involved. The great number of low-level transactions between the two sides must have generated some sense of identity among the lower-order principals involved. However the unending stream of issues upon which disagreement existed prevented the more senior officials and the negotiators of the profession entering into much mutual accord. With respect to higher-level negotiations the two sides displayed little sense of mutual confidence. Thus disagreements easily escalated, periodically threatening a total breakdown of relations, especially when remuneration was in dispute.

The precedent for direct professional participation was set at the negotiation stage. The profession demanded full consultation on account of its fear of control by bureaucrats. The health departments relied on professional expertise in the framing of regulations and in settling routine problems of administration. Negotiation and consultation became inextricably intertwined. Paradoxically the Negotiating Committee of the profession and its six sub-committees set up early in 1947, were settling detailed points of administration long before it was evident that the profession's involvement in the new service would be recommended. As already noted, the Negotiating Committee, although representing the profession as a whole, was in most respects dominated by the BMA. The existence of a separate negotiating body was extremely useful to the BMA for public relations purposes.

Professional participation was not limited to the preparatory stages of the National Health Service. After the Appointed Day the existing negotiating sub-committees silently evolved into a settled mechanism for regular consultation. The position of the profession was also strengthened by virtue of its substantial representation on the major administrative authorities and advisory committees, as well as by its domination of the statutory Medical Practices Committees, formed to regulate the distribution of general medical practitioners. Although formally appointed by the Ministers, the Medical Practices Committees were in reality composed of nominees of the profession, the English Committee being chaired by the Sheffield BMA veteran, W E Dornan. The Medical Practices Committees liaised with the General Medical Services Committee and built up cordial relations with the professionally dominated Executive Councils.[49] It is therefore not surprising that the fears of the profession concerning compulsory deployment of labour were quickly dispelled.

The profession scored a further notable success through obtaining exclusive control over the distribution of distinction awards to consultants. The Standing Advisory Committee on Distinction Awards, formed in 1949, was one of the few professional committees associated with the NHS to be devoid of BMA influence.[50] The Awards Committee was firmly under the control of the Royal Colleges, and it was headed and dominated by Lord Moran, the strongest counterweight to BMA influence within the profession. The sole lay member was Sir Horace Hamilton, formerly Permanent Under-Secretary of State at the Scottish Office, who served as vice-chairman until 1961, when he was replaced by Lord Brain. From 1949 to 1961 the other fifteen members were male and medical.

For the purpose of regular consultation on problems relating to general medical practitioners the general practice sub-committee of the Negotiating Committee handed over in late 1948 to the GMSC. Although constitutionally accountable to the Local Medical Committees, the GMSC was in reality more akin to the standing committees of the BMA.[51] Illustrating the closeness of this relationship, in 1952, Dr Solomon Wand, the GMSC chairman, was elected chairman of the BMA Council. Routine meetings between officials and GMSC representatives were at first held monthly, then quarterly from 1950, and only twice-yearly from 1953 onwards.[52] This decline in frequency indicates the gradual elimination of many points of longstanding disagreement concerning the administration of Part IV services. A steady stream of minor problems emerged, the meetings being frequently concerned with some thirty items of separate business. Usually the GMSC was represented by a small group headed by the chairman and the deputy secretary of the

BMA. Many of the minor problems were disposed of by correspondence.

Fuller GMSC delegations came into action when disputes related to levels of remuneration. On these occasions discussions with officials tended to end in impasse.[53] In exceptional circumstances the GMSC saw the Minister and Secretary of State. They met Bevan in April 1950, and Marquand in February and September 1951 in the run-up to the Danckwerts adjudication. In 1957 they held meetings with both the Ministers and Prime Minister before their compliance with a Royal Commission on remuneration was obtained.

The GMSC was a reincarnation of the Insurance Acts Committee which had represented panel doctors under National Health Insurance legislation.[54] No analogous machinery existed for representing the interests of hospital staffs. The two obvious contenders were the BMA-influenced Regional and Central Consultants and Specialists Committees, and the Royal Colleges. In the event a Joint Consultants and Specialists Committee was established in November 1948, to represent both of these interests, the Royal Colleges and Scottish Corporations being preponderant by 11 members to 6. The first chairman of this committee was Sir Lionel Whitby, who was replaced in 1951 by Sir Russell Brain. By 1953 only six of the original committee remained in post. The Joint Consultants Committee possessed certain advantages over the GMSC in its sphere owing to its compactness and direct representation on Whitley Council B. But the Joint Committee was not so successful as the GMSC in protecting the financial position of its constituent groups, or as sensitive to the interests of the lower echelons. The Joint Committee repeatedly neglected its responsibilities towards whole-time consultants. In 1950 it complied with a draft circular which would have resulted in redundancy for 1,000 registrars and senior registrars. Direct intervention by the BMA was needed to restore the position. The poor showing of the Joint Committee in negotiations concerning application of the Danckwerts principle to specialists has already been described.[55] However, in 1949 when negotiating terms for consultants' contracts, it was successful in wringing out of the Minister a concession concerning the right to arbitration.

Relations between officials and the Joint Committee were noticeably more cordial than with the GMSC. Numerous minor problems were dispatched without too much difficulty. But the Joint Committee was not effective in obtaining concessions on more significant issues. Progress in discussions was slow. The same business tended to appear on successive agenda. The pace of meeting slowed down. At first meetings were held bimonthly, whereas in 1954 only one meeting was convened.[56] Negotiations over consultant trainee establishments illustrate the declining pace of the consultative process. In late 1952 an official reported that the Joint Committee complained that the Ministry was 'consulting them less than we did in the early days of the NHS, and less than we do now on the general practitioner service'.[57] Relations between the Ministry and the Joint Committee deteriorated over the problem of hospital staffing. Having suffered embarrassment over junior hospital posts the Joint Committee was more vigilant when manpower controls were applied to consultant establishments. The Joint Committee were dismayed when in December 1952 the manpower control circular RHB(52)133 was issued without prior consultation. The Joint Committee insisted that 'representatives of the profession should be consulted on all important matters at all levels of the Health Service, including the Ministry itself'.[58] Notwithstanding these strictures the joint consultative machinery soon faced another crisis when, in November 1952, detailed consultant establishments were proposed for teaching hospitals without prior consultation. Joint Committee anxieties concerning tightening central control of consultant appointments were reduced with the formation in 1953 of the Advisory Committee on Consultant Establishments, which met under the Deputy CMO bimonthly, and contained representatives of the Joint Committee and the Ministry of Health.[59] However this committee was essentially reactive rather than constructive. The Joint Committee pressed for a total review of the consultant establishments, which was resisted by the Ministry in the light of predicted inflationary consequences. Further progress in resolving this conflict was not made until 1958 when a working party was set up under Sir Robert Platt to examine the medical staffing structure in the hospital service.

Direct consultation with committees representing the profession was the favoured mechanism for dealing with routine problems. Indeed even on broader issues such as the state of general practice, the medical career structure in hospitals, or medical advisory committees, the Ministry placed its primary emphasis on direct discussions with the profession and in each of these cases the GMSC or Joint Consultants Committee tried to ward off separate consideration by the statutory advisory committees. On wider issues of policy the health departments preferred informal consultation with its panel of consultant advisers, together with separate inquiries, undertaken by individuals or working parties. The Platt working party, just noted, is one of a long sequence of such exercises. Working parties were favoured because they enabled expert opinion to be concentrated on the point at issue. Such expert investigation was not always a means to prompt intervention.

An example of successful application of the working party is provided by the group set up to consider the distribution of the Central Pool, following the Danckwerts award made on 24 March 1952. Agreement to the findings of this working party was reported on 5 June 1952. This rapid exercise, conducted by representatives of the health departments and the GMSC, smoothed out some major points of contention between the Government and the medical profession, which had been the subject of inconsequential discussions, in some cases extending back to 1946. The distribution arrangements for general medical practice laid down by this working party persisted until 1966. Among the innovations introduced was greater incentive for practitioners to engage in group practice, an important outcome in the light of the failure of the Government's health centre plans.[60] Although less influential in their conclusions, three working parties set up under William Penman represented a necessary reaction to problems relating to remuneration among chemists, dentists and opticians. A further example of positive outcome was the report produced by Sir Noel Hall in 1957, which resulted in the simplification of the grading structure on the administrative side of the hospital service.[61]

Working parties were often set up to examine problems of shortage of personnel, or the training and regulation of emergent occupational groups. Nursing recruitment was one of the longest standing areas of concern. Here the Ministry of Labour's National Advisory Council on the Recruitment of Nurses and Midwives was the main forum for discussion. This inter-departmental arrangement proved to be inefficient and inappropriate. Liaison between Ministry of Labour officers and hospital authorities was never effectively developed. During the early years of the National Health Service the National Advisory Council recorded some particularly notable failures in the field of mental nurse recruitment. Working parties or small committees examined a variety of more specific problems in the nursing and social work area: the recruitment and training of midwives (chairman, M D Stocks, 1947-49); social workers in the mental health services (chairman, Prof J M Mackintosh, 1948-51); training of district nurses (chairman, Sir F Armer, 1953-55); recruitment and training of health visitors (chairman, Sir W Jameson, 1953-56); social workers (chairman, E Younghusband, 1955-59).

There were great variations in the speed of implementation of the findings of working parties. The committee chaired by Zachary Cope was set up to unify professional structures relating to eight groups of medical auxiliaries. This complex issue was investigated expeditiously. The committee began its work in 1949 and it reported in 1951. But there followed nearly a decade of controversy before the Professions Supplementary to Medicine Act (1960) came to fruition.[62] In the case of hospital costing, where there was urgent need to establish a modern and uniform system, a series of working parties established by RHB treasurers, the King's Fund, the Nuffield Trust, and the Ministry of Health deliberated between 1948 and 1955. Only in 1957 was a limited trial of a new system begun. The Costing Committee formed to facilitate the new system was judged to be inactive, and it was found that the Advisory Council for Management Efficiency, which was also relevant to this task, was lacking in decisive leadership over the application of schemes which it was agreed were essential for the efficiency of the service.[63] On the issue of hospital costing the procession of working parties and specialist committees was complemented by deliberations of statutory advisory bodies. Although often useful documents, their reports exercised remarkably little short-term influence. They illustrate the tendency of reports and circulars to become ends in themselves, and substitutes for action.

In some cases strategically important reports turned out to have disproportionately slight effect. The National Health Service Committee of the Cabinet had high expectations of the report commissioned from Sir Cyril Jones. This report was circulated at a crucial point in the debate on economies in the National Health Service.[64] However none of the recommendations was implemented and the report was almost immediately forgotten. It has already been pointed out that the impact of the Guillebaud Report was slight considering the length of time taken to conduct its inquiries. The Committee on Medical Manpower (chairman, H U Willink, 1954–57) turned up with conclusions which, while satisfying in the short term to the advocates of retrenchment, proved impossible to implement, and were embarrassing in the longer term because they failed to take realistic account of the demands of modern health services for trained medical personnel.[65]

CHAPTER VIII

The Hospital Service

The major innovation of the National Health Service was its state-owned and exchequer-funded hospital service. For the first time comprehensive hospital and consultant care was made available to all, and without imposition of direct charges. Inadequacy of specialist services was the most glaring defect of the inter-war system of medical care. Alleviation of this defect was a primary incentive for the first tentative moves towards a national hospital plan. With unpremeditated haste in the preparation for war, the Emergency Hospital Service plunged the nation into an experiment in integrated hospital planning. Once this step was taken it was impossible to revert to the pre-war situation. Some kind of national hospital service was inevitable. Wartime planning for a National Health Service largely turned on the problem of reorganising hospital services. Especially when the decision to integrate the mental sector into the new service was taken, the scale of the hospital side of the NHS operation completely dwarfed everything else. Klein's remark is especially pertinent 'The 1948 NHS was, essentially, a national hospital service'.[1]

(i) COST OF THE SERVICE

On account of its massive size the hospital service naturally absorbed a substantial proportion of the funds of the NHS. It has already been pointed out that the scale of exchequer commitment to hospital and specialist care was largely responsible for the crisis of the NHS under the Labour Government. Although economies and charges were mainly directed elsewhere, the cost of the hospital service was the predominant worry, and this is reflected in the affairs of the Cabinet NHS Committee and the Public Accounts Committee. The only interventions on health care of the Select Committee on Estimates related to the hospital sector, which was the subject of three of its major reports between 1949 and 1957.

There was no objective estimate of a reasonable level of expenditure on the new hospital service. As noted in chapter V the impression of overspending derived primarily from artificially low expectations of the cost of the service aroused prior to the Appointed Day. Early calculations and the estimates for the first year of the service set spending limits at an unrealistically and unattainably low level. As a secondary factor, it is possible that the cost of the service was augmented owing to adoption of an entirely novel form of hospital administration creating maximum discontinuity with the previous system, and involving a major shift from rate to exchequer funding.

In December 1945 the Cabinet was quoted £97m as the annual cost for the hospital service (England and Wales £87m, Scotland £10m).[2] The first formal estimates submitted in 1948 increased this figure to £121m (annual rate £164m) for the first nine months of the service, while the outcome was £145m, which constituted an annual rate of £196m. Consequently the January 1948 estimates were 61% above those of December 1945, while the outcome for the first year of the service exceeded the estimates by 20%. Such figures suggested that expenditure on the new and untried system of hospital administration was out of control. Expenditure on hospitals continued to mount, reaching £345m in 1955/56, which was 54% above the level in the first full year of the service. As a percentage of expenditure on the NHS as a whole the hospital service rose from 53% at the beginning to 57% in 1955, at which level it remained until 1962.

Table I shows the trend in expenditure on the hospital service for England and Wales in slightly more detail. As already noted it was originally speculated that hospital expenditure would run at £87m, whereas in the first full year of the service it reached £214m. Thereafter the pace of increase slowed down, although hospital expenditure still reached £316m in 1955/56.

As Table I indicates, capital expenditure on hospitals was insignificant. The difficulties in securing funds for capital spending on anything like a realistic scale have been considered in chapter VI. Expansion of hospital spending was almost entirely on the revenue side. In their evidence to the Select Committee on Estimates, officials explained that £69.2m of the increase of £103.8m on hospital expenditure between 1949/50 and 1955/56 was due to increases in pay, prices and other unavoidable costs. They attributed the remaining £34.6m to the 'net effect of developments and improvements'.[3] The scale of increase in the cost of maintaining hospitals looks even less formidable when seen in the context of the rise in real prices. Table II shows total revenue spending in actual and constant prices. Between 1949/50 and 1955/56 revenue expenditure on the hospital service rose by 48.3%. The retail price index rose by 38.6% during the same period. Expressing hospital costs in constant price terms reduces the increase between 1949/50 and 1955/56 from £99.4m to £20m, a rise of 9.7%. Furthermore, most of this increase had taken place at the very beginning of the period. After taking account of inflation the sharp increases in expenditure

TABLE I

Maintenance and Capital Expenditure in the Hospital Service
(England and Wales 1949-1956)

£m actual prices

	1949/50	%	1950/51	%	1951/52	%	1952/53	%	1953/54	%	1954/55	%	1955/56	%
Capital & Maintenance														
Capital Expenditure	8.6	4.2	8.8	3.9	9.6	3.9	9.1	3.5	8.8	3.3	11.3	4.0	11.5	3.8
Maintenance Expenditure	205.6	95.8	227.2	96.1	246.3	96.1	256.9	96.5	269.7	96.7	281.1	96.0	305.0	96.2
Breakdown of Maintenance														
Salaries and Wages														
(i) Medical	22.0	(18.4)	25.6	(19.3)	25.0	(17.6)	26.0	(16.8)	27.2	(16.8)	30.8	(17.8)	31.7	(17.0)
(ii) Nursing	45.2	(37.9)	49.1	(37.0)	51.1	(36.0)	56.2	(36.4)	59.2	(36.5)	62.6	(36.2)	68.7	(36.9)
(iii) Other	52.1	(43.7)	58.1	(43.7)	65.7	(46.4)	72.2	(46.8)	75.8	(46.7)	79.3	(46.0)	85.7	(46.1)
Total Wages and Salaries	119.3	58.0	132.8	58.5	141.8	60.2	154.5	60.2	162.1	60.1	172.7	61.4	186.2	61.0
Provisions	21.9	10.7	23.6	10.4	27.1	11.5	30.9	12.0	32.9	12.2	34.3	12.2	36.4	11.9
Fuel, light, power etc	12.7	6.2	14.3	6.3	16.1	6.8	17.7	6.9	18.9	7.0	20.4	7.3	22.7	7.4
Other	51.7	25.1	56.5	24.8	61.3	21.5	53.8	20.9	55.8	20.7	53.7	19.1	59.7	19.7

Source: *Summarised Accounts of RHBs*.
Note: Percentages for Wages are given as a percentage of total wages.

TABLE II

Maintenance Expenditure on the Hospital Service in Actual,
and 1949/50 Prices
(England and Wales 1949/50–1955/56)

£m

	1949/50	1950/51	1951/52	1952/53	1953/54	1954/55	1955/56
Total Expenditure of the Hospital Service in Actual Prices	205.6	227.2	246.3	256.9	269.7	281.1	305.0
Total Expenditure of the Hospital Service in 1949/50 Prices	205.6	214.7	208.5	208.2	219.1	221.7	225.6
Index	100	104.4	101.4	101.3	106.6	107.8	109.7

fell away after the first two years of the service. Consequently the index of hospital expenditure corrects the impression of substantial and unremitting increase in hospital costs. Once the initial difficulties were over, the picture was basically one of stability. The King's Fund concluded that 1953 and 1954 were a major historical turning point. It was now clear that the hospital service was responding to economies and that 'it is no longer felt that the cost of hospitals is getting out of hand'.[4] The Guillebaud Committee failed to detect evidence of excessive expenditure in the hospital service, and the Select Committee on Estimates likewise concluded that 'there is no evidence of declining efficiency on the part of hospital authorities'.[5] The 9.7% increase, while a significant increment, was a relatively small price to pay for the expanding responsibilities of a new social service.

In their pioneering study of this problem Abel-Smith and Titmuss concluded that the increase was primarily occasioned by a rise in staff numbers, which in their view was merited by the substantial increase in both the quantity and quality of service. As they expressed it 'the hospitals did more work for a larger national population; more confinements took place in hospital; more services were rendered to general practitioners; more road accidents were treated; more provision was made for industrial accidents; more people were trained as doctors, nurses etc; more research was undertaken and completed. All these are quantitative indices of activity; what cannot be assessed is the changing work of the hospital as an agent of humanity'.[6]

The main justification for the substantially higher than envisaged cost of the hospital service rests not only on the expansion of services but also on unavoidable commitments consequent upon taking over a system verging on a state of dereliction. Neither the public nor the voluntary sector had adapted with sufficient alacrity to the needs of modern medicine. Both systems were weighted down with anachronisms. Their buildings were decaying, their services were out of date, and their staffing arrangements were untenable. Adaptation of this ramshackle and largely bankrupt edifice into a rational, modern and humane hospital structure to serve the whole population was inconceivable without revolutionary reorganisation and a secular increase in capital and revenue expenditure.

There was no excuse for innocence over the scale of this commitment. Reviews undertaken before World War II demonstrated the incapacity of current services to meet wartime demands. On the basis of temporary expediency the Emergency Hospital Service introduced many communities to modern specialist care facilities for the very first time. The hospital surveys sponsored during the war confirmed that despite EHS activities, services were still desperately inadequate. Their combined findings suggested that a substantial proportion of the 225,000 beds surveyed in England and Wales were substandard, while in addition there was a calculated deficit of 98,000 beds. These calculations took no account of the mental sector, which was of approximately similar total size, and where the problems of shortage and defective facilities were equally prevalent. The independent findings of the survey teams were 'monotonously unanimous' in their verdict.[7] Every regional survey revealed a similar pattern of deficiencies, outmoded physical facilities, maldistribution and uneven quality of services, shortage of nursing and medical staff, inadequate training, idiosyncrasy and lack of co-ordination, and inadequate funding, owing to either poverty or neglect.

Typically the surveyors concluded that 'the bulk of the hospitals in the region are out of date, their arrangements do not conform to modern needs and they are often too small with no possibility for expansion. Out-patient departments at general hospitals are especially poor, inconvenient and cramped'.[8] The old voluntary hospitals were often in noisy central locations. Public Assistance institutions occupied more spacious peripheral sites, but 'almost without exception these are bad. The buildings are dark, old, devoid of modern sanitary conveniences, death-traps in the case of fire; and in short unfit for the Nursing of Chronic Sick or any other form of Sick Person'.[9] Each region produced its list of deficiencies in the consultant service. Characteristically the 'dearth of consultants is particularly noticeable in gynaecology and obstetrics, paediatrics, dermatology, nervous diseases and psychiatry'.[10] Even when consultants of sufficient quality were present in a region, their effective service was limited to the largest medical centres. Away from the narrow perimeter of the teaching hospital vast tracts of the country were dependent on whatever consultant skills local general practitioners could muster.

There was nothing in the diagnosis of the hospital surveys to suggest that improvements envisaged in the National Health Service could be accomplished without almost complete replacement of the hospital stock, extensive modernisation of facilities, and a completely different basis for the remuneration of staff. Because the NHS was committed from the outset to providing an unrestricted service, it picked up the bill for decades of resource starvation. During the early stages of the service basic steps were taken towards modernisation. Wages and salaries were adjusted, extra staff recruited, and services provided on a more adequate scale. In retrospect these changes are judged as only a modest step towards realising the goals agreed by the surveyors. Further reforms were ruled out and hospital expenditure was fixed at a ceiling that effectively limited capacity to introduce improvements in services on anything like the scale required. The modest expansion permitted took place at the sacrifice of renovation and replacement of the antiquated hospital stock.

(ii) REGIONAL HOSPITAL SERVICE

Unification of hospital services under Regional Hospital Boards was the most striking innovation of the National Health Service. Although during wartime planning the regional theme was not emphasised owing to the assumption that hospital services would be administered by local authorities, either singly or in small combinations, the regional principle was deep-rooted, and it eventually reasserted itself.

The Dawson and Cave Committees just after World War I recommended integrated hospital planning. The idea of adopting the regional principle in local government administration also took root at this time. Application of the regional idea for planning hospital services was adopted most quickly in Scotland. The Mackenzie *Report on the Hospital Services of Scotland* (1926) proposed five regions, four based on the teaching hospitals of Aberdeen, Dundee, Edinburgh and Glasgow, and the other on Inverness. This view was also taken in the 1929 Scottish Local Government Act, after which the voluntary hospitals constituted regional committees to co-ordinate their effort. The same regional principle was asserted in the Cathcart *Report on Scottish Health Services* (1936), which recommended setting up statutory regional committees 'charged with the duty of facilitating the co-ordination of hospital services within the region' (para 677). The Scottish Branch of the BHA then put new life into the regional committees. Establishment in 1940 of the Nuffield Advisory Committee on Regionalisation of Hospital Services in Scotland facilitated discussions between voluntary and local authority representatives. Finally the regional plan was given backing by the Hetherington Committee (1943). It is therefore not surprising that wartime negotiations on the hospital service in Scotland paid implicit regard to regionalisation, and since the teaching hospitals had always been regarded as the linchpin of regional organisation, their exclusion from the RHB structure was not considered. Consequently the regional hospital structure adopted in Scotland in 1947 (see Map 1) was largely foreshadowed by the plan of 1926. The minor differences between the proposals of the Mackenzie Report (1926), the mature BHA proposals (1942), and the structure adopted in 1947 are summarised in Table III. By contrast with England and Wales none of the Scottish RHBs cut across local government boundaries. In this extremely settled arrangement the main problem was the concentration of population and resources in the Western region. The latter contained a population of 3m, and it controlled more than half the hospital resources in Scotland. In population size it compared with the larger English regions, while the South Eastern region was slightly smaller than the two smallest English regions. The other three Scottish regions in total possessed a smaller population than the smallest English region. Their separate existence was justified on geographical considerations.

Regionalisation was slower to evolve in England and Wales. However the areas into which the BHA was organised were recognised as a loose framework for regional co-operation. Also the larger local authorities represented regions in embryo. Two positive steps towards regionalisation occurred in 1937, with the Report of the Commission set up by the BHA under Lord Sankey, and the Report of the Royal Commission on Local Government in the Tyneside Area. The latter recommended that a single authority should be constructed to administer all the services in a region comprising the Newcastle conurbation and Northumberland. The Sankey Commission proposed division of the country into hospital regions and the formation of hospital regional councils to co-ordinate voluntary hospital services in their areas. Following the Sankey Report the BHA set up a Provisional Central Council which drew up proposals for regional organisation, based on advice received from its area committees. The mature proposals of the Provisional

TABLE III

The Scottish Hospital Regions, compared with Ancestral Plans

Mackenzie Regions (1926)	BHA Regions (1942)	RHB Regions (1946)
1. NORTHERN Inverness, Skye, Outer Hebrides, Ross and Cromarty, Moray and Nairn, Sutherland and Caithness.	1. NORTHERN Inverness, Skye, Outer Hebrides, Ross and Cromarty, Moray and Nairn, Sutherland and Caithness.	1. NORTHERN Inverness, Skye, Outer Hebrides, Ross and Cromarty, Nairn, Sutherland and Caithness.
2. NORTH EASTERN Aberdeen, Orkney and Shetland, Kincardine, Banff.	2. NORTH EASTERN Aberdeen, Orkney and Shetland, Kincardine, Banff.	2. NORTH EASTERN Moray, Aberdeen, Orkney and Shetland, Kincardine, Banff.
3. EASTERN Angus, Perth, Fife, Kinross.	3. EASTERN Angus, E. Perth, N&E Fife, Kinross.	3. EASTERN Angus, Perth, Kinross.
4. SOUTH EASTERN Clackmannan, EW & Midlothian, Peebles, Berwick, Roxburgh, Selkirk.	4. SOUTH EASTERN EW & Midlothian, S & W Fife, Peebles, Berwick, Roxburgh, Selkirk.	4. SOUTH EASTERN EW & Midlothian, Fife, Peebles, Berwick, Roxburgh, Selkirk.
5. WESTERN Argyll, Stirling, Dunbarton, Renfrew, Lanark, Ayr & Bute, Dumfries, Kirkcudbright, Wigtown.	5. WESTERN Argyll, W Perth, Stirling, Clackmannan, Dunbarton, Renfrew, Lanark, Ayr & Bute, Dumfries, Kirkcudbright, Wigtown.	5. WESTERN Argyll, Stirling, Clackmannan, Dunbarton, Renfrew, Lanark, Ayr & Bute, Dumfries, Kirkcudbright, Wigtown.

Council envisaged formation of 14 regional councils and some 60–70 divisional councils. As in Scotland the Nuffield Provincial Hospitals Trust acted as a catalyst to the establishment of regional and divisional councils, involving participation of both voluntary hospitals and local authorities.[11] By the time of the Nuffield intervention the Government had set up the Emergency Hospital Service, which imposed on hospital services the eleven divisions of the Civil Defence regions. Differences between the BHA and EMS regions are summarised in Table IV. In 1940 there were accordingly two rival regional schemes in existence. Based on common principles, they were reasonably compatible with one another. The Nuffield Provincial Hospitals Trust was sufficiently at ease to hint that it would accept units coinciding with the Civil Defence regions.[12] As in Scotland it was anticipated that the 'key hospital' of each region

ЛЭnal Health Service

SCOTLAND

Showing Regional Hospital Board Areas
Counties and County Boroughs

эn

IDINE

REGIONAL HOSPITAL AREAS

1. **Northern**
2. **North-Eastern**
3. **Eastern**
4. **South-Eastern**
5. **Western**

Note: Shetland and the Orkney Islands
(not shown) are included in No. 2
area

would be a teaching hospital.[13] In summary the philosophy of regionalisation involved 'improvement in staffing and equipment, extensive adaptation of existing facilities, the provision of new services and accommodation, and substitution of a unified plan on a regional basis developed from considerations of geography, population, transport, communications, existing hospital accommodation and, where possible, a teaching centre'.[14]

Notwithstanding impetus for regionalisation from the voluntary sector the ministerial statement on 9 October 1941 spoke only of planning on the basis of 'areas substantially larger than those of individual local authorities'. Thereafter planning was undertaken largely on the basis of integrating county councils and associated county boroughs. Addition of regional councils was a somewhat reluctant concession offered in the course of discussions following the 1944 White Paper. The Labour Government reverted to the regional concept in very much the form advocated by the voluntary hospital lobby, except on the vital question of ownership. Breaking with the limitations of local government boundaries satisfied voluntary hospitals that they were not being handed over to the local authorities. The latter were to some extent consoled by the prospect of substantial representation on the new RHBs.

The final Willink scheme proposed about 30 Regional Councils. First plans by the Labour Government envisaged between 16 and 20 regional authorities, but the number was reduced in deference to the principle of linking regions with teaching hospitals (see Map 2). As indicated by Table IV the regional divisions adopted bore striking resemblance to the Civil Defence regions. Outside London the main modifications of the Civil Defence boundaries were brought about by the requirement to form regions around the teaching hospitals. Other Government departments, such as the newly established Ministry of Town and Country Planning, kept more closely to the Civil Defence regions. The NHS scheme split Civil Defence region 10 between Manchester and Liverpool. The southern boundary of region 2 was adjusted to align Sheffield with the E. Midland region 3, which otherwise would have lacked a teaching hospital. Even in the London area the structure built on the EMS sectors, which radiated from the centre. The main changes were reduction of these segments from ten to four, and increasing the radial span of the regions to include most of the territory occupied by regions 6, 7, and 8 of the BHA plan. Thus the regional plan of the NHS bore the strong imprint of the two ancestral types. It was much less radical than the BHA scheme in departing from local authority boundaries, but county boundaries were not observed in a number of cases. The LCC was divided into four segments, while Wiltshire was split between three RHBs.

TABLE IV

The English and Welsh Hospital Regions, compared with Ancestral Plans

BHA Regions (1939)	Civil Defence Regions (1939–1945)	RHB Regions (1946)
1. NORTH EAST Northumberland, Durham.	1. NORTHERN Northumberland, Durham, N Riding Yorkshire.	1. NEWCASTLE Cumberland, Northumberland, Durham, N Westmorland.
2. YORKSHIRE Yorkshire, with N Derby, N Notts, Lincs.	2. NORTH EASTERN W & E Riding Yorkshire.	2. LEEDS Yorkshire, except South W Riding.
3. EAST MIDLAND S Derby, S Notts, S Lincs, Leicester, Rutland, Northants, Warwick, Staffs.	3. NORTH MIDLAND Derby, Notts, Lincs, Leicester, Rutland, Northants.	3. SHEFFIELD South West Riding, Lincolnshire (except S Kesteven), Nottinghamshire, Rutland, Leicestershire, S Derbyshire.
4. EAST ANGLIA Norfolk, Suffolk, NE Essex, Cambridge, Huntingdon.	4. EASTERN Norfolk, Suffolk, Cambridge, Huntingdon, Essex, Bedford, Hertford.	4. E ANGLIA Norfolk, Suffolk, Cambridgeshire, Huntingdonshire, S Kesteven of Lincs.
6. LONDON Hertford, SW Essex, Middlesex, LCC, W Berks, Surrey, Kent.	5. LONDON LCC, Greater London.	5. NW METROPOLITAN NW London, Middlesex, Hertfordshire, Bedfordshire.
		6. NE METROPOLITAN NE London, Essex.
7. SUSSEX Sussex.	12. SOUTH EASTERN Sussex, Kent.	7. SE METROPOLITAN SE London, Kent, E Sussex.
8. SOUTHERN Hampshire, Isle of Wight, Dorset, S Wilts.		8. SW METROPOLITAN SW London, Surrey, W Sussex, Hampshire, S Wiltshire, Dorset, Isle of Wight.

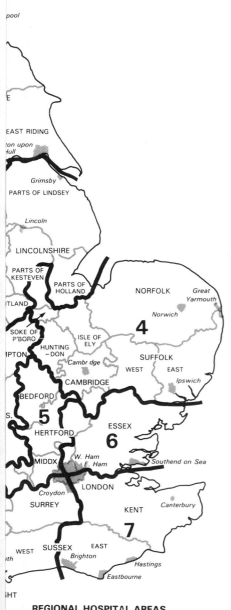

:ional Health Service

GLAND AND WALES

howing Regional Hospital Board Areas
Counties and County Boroughs

pool

E

EAST RIDING

ton upon
Hull

Grimsby

PARTS OF LINDSEY

Lincoln

LINCOLNSHIRE

PARTS OF
KESTEVEN

PARTS OF
HOLLAND

NORFOLK

Great
Yarmouth

Norwich

TLAND

SOKE OF
P'BORO

ISLE OF
ELY

HUNTING
–DON

IPTON

Cambr dge

SUFFOLK

WEST   EAST

Ipswich

CAMBRIDGE

BEDFORD

4

S.

5

HERTFORD

ESSEX

6

MIDDX

W. Ham
E. Ham

Southend on Sea

Croydon

LONDON

SURREY

KENT

Canterbury

7

WEST   SUSSEX   EAST

th

Brighton

Hastings

Eastbourne

s

HT

REGIONAL HOSPITAL AREAS

Newcastle
Leeds
Sheffield
East Anglia
N.W. Metropolitan
N.E. Metropolitan
S.E. Metropolitan

8. S.W. Metropolitan
9. Oxford
10. South Western
11. Welsh
12. Birmingham
13. Manchester
14. Liverpool

BHA Regions (1939)	Civil Defence Regions (1939–1945)	RHB Regions (1946)
5. OXFORD Oxford, Bucks, Berks, NE Wilts, Bedford	6. SOUTHERN Oxford, Bucks, Berks, Hampshire.	9. OXFORD Oxfordshire, Northamptonshire, Buckinghamshire, Berkshire, E Gloucestershire, E Wiltshire.
10. BRISTOL Gloucester, Hereford, NW Wilts, Somerset. 9. SOUTH WESTERN Devon, Cornwall	7. SOUTH WESTERN Gloucester, Wiltshire, Somerset, Dorset, Devon, Cornwall.	10. SOUTH WESTERN W Gloucestershire, W Wiltshire, Somerset, Devon, Cornwall.
11. SOUTH WALES Pembroke, Cardigan, Radnor, Brecknock, Carmarthen, Glamorgan, Monmouth.	8. WALES	11. WALES
12. MIDLAND & CENTRAL WALES Warwick, Worcester, Shropshire, Staffs, Montgomery, Merioneth.	9. MIDLAND Warwick, Worcester, Hereford, Shropshire, Staffs.	12. BIRMINGHAM Staffordshire, Warwickshire, Worcestershire, Herefordshire, Shropshire.
13. LANCASHIRE & CHESHIRE Cheshire, NW Derby, Lancashire, Flintshire, Denbigh, Caernarvon, Anglesey.	10. NORTH WESTERN Cheshire, NW Derby, Lancashire, Westmorland, Cumberland.	13. MANCHESTER E Lancashire, E Cheshire, NW Derbyshire, S Westmorland.
14. NORTH WEST Westmorland, Cumberland.		14. LIVERPOOL W Lancashire, W Cheshire

Notes: 1. In the first two columns counties are denoted by standard abbreviations, or by county towns, as in Map 2.
2. Scotland constitutes Civil Defence Region 11.

Counties divided into equal or unequal halves included Gloucestershire, Hertfordshire, Lancashire, Sussex, Westmorland and the West Riding of Yorkshire. Many other administrative counties and metropolitan boroughs were dissected into uneven segments for purposes of hospital organisation. In many cases geographical arguments justified the division, but lack of coterminosity between counties and hospital authorities inevitably added to the difficulties of co-ordinating services. Counties such as Westmorland, Hertfordshire and Bedfordshire objected to being split between hospital regions.[15] Others appreciated that the divisions were necessary to preserve traditional lines of communication.

Because of the substantial preliminary work on regionalisation the plans circulated by the Ministry of Health in November 1946 met with relatively little resistance, and they were only slightly modified in the form adopted in December 1946. However, the establishment of RHB areas was not accomplished without dispute.[16] Drawing the boundaries between the Liverpool and Manchester RHBs proved to be particularly difficult. In the analysis of the sagacious Secretary of the Lancashire Asylums Board, 'the main factors to be borne in mind were the jealousy felt by Liverpool for Manchester, and the reluctance of Preston to consider any scheme centred on Liverpool or Manchester'.[17] When Liverpool turned out to be the smaller of the two regions, Liverpool University complained about threats to the prestige of its medical school. Liverpool made an unsuccessful bid to annex N Wales, as well as N Lancashire and S Westmorland. Liverpool not only failed to extend its territory but it also lost a substantial slice of central Cheshire to the Manchester RHB. Only with difficulty was the loss of Warrington to Manchester prevented. Despite professional support for linking N Wales with Liverpool, and suspicion between N and S Wales, it was decided to establish a hospital region following the national boundary, and therefore fitting in with the administrative pattern of the Welsh Board of Health and the Welsh National Memorial Association.[18] Liverpool became reconciled to the loss of N Wales, but it continued to covet Preston, Wigan, and parts of Cheshire, as well as part of Shropshire.[19]

The proposals for four Metropolitan regions were enthusiastically accepted by the King's Fund, the teaching hospitals and other voluntary hospitals. Certain technical changes were suggested. Particularly favoured was increasing the number of regions in north London from two to three, in order to reduce the accumulation of teaching hospitals in the proposed NW Metropolitan region. It will be recalled that the EMS scheme had established seven sectors to the north, and only three to the south of the Thames. A sustained rearguard action against the whole scheme was mounted by the LCC. The LCC dwelt on the anomalies created by the sectoral division, and especially the arbitrary distribution of many of the hospital resources that would ensue. The LCC also argued against the break-up of its hospital system and proposed a rival plan involving linkage of teaching hospitals with designated areas in the home counties.

Local anxieties were aroused by the regional proposals. For instance N Wales feared the dominance of Cardiff, Bradford feared Leeds, while the E Midland towns feared domination from Sheffield. At the microcosmic level small towns disliked association with larger neighbours. Hence Whitby fought bitterly to transfer from the Leeds to the Newcastle region in order to escape the imperialism of Scarborough. This was described as a turn in an historic 'savage feud' between the Yorkshire seaside towns.[20]

The majority of the regions in England and Wales contained populations between 3 and 4m. The two smallest (E Anglia, Oxford), with populations of 1.5m were completely viable. There was most doubt over the largest region, the SW Metropolitan, which stretched from London to the west country. Sub-regional status was suggested for natural divisions of heterogeneous regions. Such subdivision was a strong feature of the BHA regional plan. The obvious candidates meriting sub-regional committees were Devon and Cornwall (South Western), Western (SW Metropolitan), N Lancashire and S Westmorland (Manchester), Cumberland and N Westmorland (Newcastle), and N Wales (Wales). The first four were recommended both in correspondence and in the important circular RHB(47)1. Strong local campaigns were mounted on behalf of the prospective sub-regions. The Government's intentions were carried out in two cases, Western, and Cumberland and N Westmorland. In the case of N Wales, and also N Lancashire and S Westmorland, opposition on their respective RHBs blocked action, while the committee for Devon and Cornwall, although formed, was later dissolved because of inaction.[21] In 1951 the Welsh RHB partly compensated N Wales by setting up a special advisory committee to liaise with Liverpool.[22] Although initially regarded by the SW Metropolitan RHB as no more important than its other area committees, the Western committee grew in authority, obtained an area office in Winchester, and developed separatist inclinations. In 1950 proposals were made for upgrading the area into a Western region, which were decisively rejected by the Ministry at the time, although they were supported by the Select Committee on Estimates.[23] However, the Western area was comparable with the Oxford RHB in its population, geographical size, and bed resources. Its major defect was lack of a teaching hospital, which was used as a technical reason for excluding regional status in 1950.[24] The Western committee was unpopular with the Ministry of Health. It was described as a 'constant source of friction' within an RHB which, although large, was regarded as efficient. It is therefore not surprising that the Guillebaud Committee was persuaded to recommend against regional status for the Western committee.[25] Nevertheless, pressure continued to build up for separation and the strength of the case was recognised in 1959 with the establishment of the Wessex RHB.[26]

The Cumberland and N Westmorland Special Area committee of the Newcastle RHB reflected the difficulties of a region straddling the Pennines. The area committee operated from offices in Carlisle. The population covered was only 300,000 and the hospital services were assimilated into four HMC groups. Consequently separatism was out of the question. This committee was an asset to the area and relations with the Newcastle RHB were cordial, which was a contrast with the Wessex case.[27] The success of this devolution is indicated by the fact that the first new general hospital facility in the region, and indeed the first outside the south of England, was located in W Cumberland, at Hensingham, near Whitehaven.[28]

(iii) TEACHING HOSPITALS

Paradoxically, although the whole philosophy of regionalisation was based on the idea of the undergraduate teaching hospital as the key hospital of the region, the teaching hospitals in England and Wales side-stepped integration in the regional framework, thinking of themselves as *dei ex machina*. This contrasted with the situation in Scotland, where all hospitals were integrated under the regional boards. Selection of hospitals for designation as teaching hospitals in England and Wales was not an entirely simple exercise. Indeed designation called for special discretion and tact. It was not accomplished without much controversy and pain. The orders detailing the designation of teaching hospitals were not issued until March 1948 (provincial) and May 1948 (London). The ten provincial teaching hospitals comprised about 70 hospital units and 12,000 beds. The twelve London undergraduate teaching hospitals included about 50 hospitals and 10,000 beds. In addition, in London 14 postgraduate teaching groups were formed, comprising some 30 hospitals and 5,000 beds. Thus the elite corps of ex-voluntary hospitals were granted privileged status under the NHS, and they annexed a substantial slice of the first-class hospital accommodation in their regions. Teaching hospitals maintained their separate identities and were administered by Boards of Governors acting as agents of the Minister. There was therefore no third party intervening between them and the Minister as was the case with hospital groups outside the teaching fraternity.

The chairmen and Boards of Governors comprising on average 28 members were appointed by the Minister, on the basis of one-fifth from each of the universities, the teaching staff of the medical school, and the RHB. The remaining two-fifths were appointed after consultation with local authorities and other relevant groups.[29] In the view of the Teaching Hospitals Association the burden of the work of Boards of Governors fell on the ministerial category. It was asserted that the energies of the other members were absorbed in rival commitments. The Association accordingly stressed that special care should be given to selection of ministerial appointees.[30]

The problem of designating teaching hospitals involved more than identifying existing undergraduate teaching hospitals and their existing assets. Major difficulties were presented over selection of hospitals eligible for postgraduate teaching status, and in evolving viable arrangements for grouping. As noted above the bed requirements declared by undergraduate teaching hospitals necessitated incursion into the territory of the regional boards. In the cases of East Anglia and Oxford in particular, there was no way of satisfying the demands of both teaching hospitals and regional authorities.

Policy with respect to undergraduate teaching hospitals was guided by the view of the Goodenough Committee on Medical Education (1944) that 1,000-bed teaching units were desirable for balanced medical training. Teaching hospitals naturally aspired to reach this target as much as possible from resources under their direct control. Consistent with this principle, both Oxford and Cambridge universities laid claim to all the local general hospital facilities. Such appropriation of their key hospital resources was clearly unacceptable to the regional boards. On the other hand the universities were unable to fulfil their teaching obligations without access to considerably more beds than were available in the groups based on the Radcliffe Infirmary and Addenbrooke's. Sharing of facilities was ruled out. It was reluctantly agreed to grant the teaching hospitals control of most hospital facilities in their area, with the understanding that they would provide facilities for the regional boards on an agency basis. Officials suspected that either teaching and research, or the interests of patients requiring routine treatment, would be neglected. This formula was therefore initially adopted on a strictly temporary basis.[31]

London undergraduate teaching hospitals also displayed a propensity to swallow up prize hospitals of the regions and exchange them for unattractive alternatives.[32] In cases such as the Hampstead

General Hospital, detachment from the region was resisted on the grounds that its status would suffer under the proposed amalgamation with the Royal Free teaching group. The regions, especially the NW Metropolitan, were concerned that their capacity to provide district hospital services would be prejudiced by loss of resources. In the tug of war over hospital designation the regions were forced to make concessions. In the case of the NW Metropolitan RHB, 4,133 beds were lost to five undergraduate teaching hospitals, and 2,164 beds to nine postgraduate teaching hospitals.[33]

The greatest difficulty lay in defining postgraduate teaching groups. St Mark's hospital was rescued from the NE Metropolitan RHB, and was initially intended for amalgamation with the St. Bartholomew's undergraduate teaching hospital, but it was diverted into a miscellaneous postgraduate amalgamation involving the distant Hammersmith (LCC) and W London (initially scheduled as an undergraduate teaching hospital). Officials were disappointed that the Board of Governors seemed unable to unify this heterogeneous assembly of hospitals.[34] Rationalisation of postgraduate groups was difficult to achieve in view of the independence and status consciousness of the specialist hospitals involved. The proposal to amalgamate the Maida Vale hospital with the National Hospital, Queen's Square, to form a single institute of neurology was vehemently resisted by Queen's Square.[35] The proposal to unite the Queen Elizabeth and Great Ormond Street hospitals for children was unattractive to both parties. Demands by the former for separate designation were resisted and it was omitted from the list of postgraduate teaching hospitals, which produced a renewed outcry in which the feelings of the Royal Family were cited on Queen Elizabeth's behalf.[36]

Separate administration was not regarded by the teaching hospitals themselves as conferring special advantages. Direct proximity to the Ministry of Health was thought to lead to undue official interference. Accustomed to their old freedoms and idiosyncrasies, teaching hospitals found irksome the uniformity of the new system. However, when viewed from neglected recesses of the regions, teaching hospitals seemed like a select club of mandarins, imbued with privilege without responsibility.[37] Even a review that was persuaded by the justice of the case for maintaining the independence of the London teaching hospitals at least, concluded that it was 'wrong to write off simply as jealousy the deeply felt sentiments of resentment which we encountered among matrons and secretaries of short-staffed Regional board hospitals, at what they felt to be the unjustifiable extravagance of the London teaching hospitals in particular'.[38]

Although not an argument in itself for ending the separate status of teaching hospitals, a main objection against them was unnecessary extravagance. Sustaining this argument was virtually impossible in view of the primitive state of hospital cost accounting, and because of the acceptance that a differential between teaching hospitals and others was justified. The Abel-Smith and Titmuss study helped the case of teaching hospitals by pointing out that on the basis of current trends in costs, regional hospitals were catching up the teaching hospitals.[39] Nevertheless, even if it was a myth, the idea of extravagance of London teaching hospitals remained proverbial wisdom in the HMC world.[40] Guillebaud admitted that he was 'staggered by the differences' between costs at the Edinburgh Royal Infirmary and the London teaching hospitals.[41] For the Ministry of Health it was admitted that 'there remained some doubt whether the differences were entirely justified'.[42]

A more serious problem was lack of co-ordination between teaching hospitals and the regional service. Experience of this problem varied greatly. The Liverpool RHB, building on a tradition of co-operation, expressed itself completely satisfied. On the other hand the E Anglia and Sheffield RHBs were critical of their teaching hospitals. Sheffield was particularly concerned about failure to co-ordinate staffing development and hospital planning. Examples were given to illustrate needless duplication and inefficiencies forced on the region by lack of co-operation. The complaints of E Anglia are particularly pertinent, because of its reliance on the teaching hospital in Cambridge for general hospital services. E Anglia confirmed the fears expressed when this anomalous relationship was sanctioned. The Cambridge Board of Governors was accused of being over-concerned with the prestigious specialisms and neglectful of the chronic sick. This view was backed up by the Association of HMCs, which concluded that separation of the teaching hospitals had been detrimental to planning of regional services. The Association was 'unanimous that teaching hospitals should be absorbed by the RHBs'. Similarly, the E Anglia RHB concluded that 'creation of independent Boards of Governors had been fundamentally a mistake'.[43] The Royal Medico-Psychological Association also recommended amalgamation on the grounds that the status of the mental health sector was prejudiced by separation.[44] Despite their support for teaching hospitals, the Acton Society Trust doubted whether these institutions were acting as a centre for the radiation of higher standards of scientific medicine to the regions as a whole.[45] Notwithstanding such criticisms, and the overwhelming support for amalgamation from Scottish

witnesses, the Guillebaud Committee argued the case for maintenance of the Boards of Governors, especially on the grounds of the
'dangers of overstandardisation and uniformity'. It was concluded
that it would be 'short-sighted' to 'subordinate' to RHBs 'these
institutions upon which so much depends for the future development of the service'.[46] This verdict indicates that there was no
diminution of faith in those arguments in favour of special status
for teaching hospitals that had won the day in 1946.

(iv) REGIONAL HOSPITAL BOARDS AND HOSPITAL MANAGEMENT BODIES

Each of the thirty-six teaching hospitals in England and Wales was
managed by a separate Board of Governors directly responsible to
the Minister. This left the great majority of hospitals in England
and Wales under the administration of the fourteen Regional
Hospital Boards. In Scotland all hospitals were administered by
the five Regional Hospital Boards. In each region a chairman was
selected by the Minister. Then, after relevant consultations, the
boards were appointed. Among the first duties of the boards
was evolving a system for grouping hospitals under Hospital
Management Committees in England and Wales, and Boards of
Management in Scotland. Once these groupings were accepted by
the Ministers the RHBs appointed chairmen and other members
of the management committees, of which there were at the outset
377 in England and Wales and 85 in Scotland.

Scrupulous care was taken over the selection of chairmen of
regional boards and indeed with the whole selection procedure for
the boards. Whatever their shortcomings the chairmen represented
the elite of the available voluntary effort.[47]

Bevan went to extreme lengths to avoid any suspicion that the
new Regional Hospital Boards were being handed over to the
Labour local government interest. Among the initial fourteen
appointed chairmen, only three had Labour Party or trade union
connections. This representation would have been smaller had
Bevan not intervened to secure appointment of two Labour nominees in the Metropolitan regions.[48] The remaining eleven were
businessmen (seven) and members of the professions (four), mostly
with conservative and voluntary hospital associations. During the
first decade of the service the Labour presence gradually declined,
the last Labour chairman being replaced in 1957. During this
decade, of the twenty-six persons serving as chairmen, fourteen
were drawn from business and commerce, eight from the professions (four academics, two accountants, one town clerk, and one
solicitor), compared with four from the labour movement.

Only two of the academics—Stopford (Manchester), and Collingwood (Newcastle)—remained in office for any length of time. For most of this period Stopford was the sole medical presence, and he was not among the most active chairmen. Of the fourteen initial appointees, nine were aged 65 or more. By far the youngest was the Earl of Cranbrook of the E Anglia board, who was 47. Four of the 65-plus age group of initial appointees were retained for about ten years. Among the new appointments made during the first ten years the veteran was Sir George Schuster, who became chairman of the Oxford board in 1951 at the age of seventy, and who retired in 1963 at 82. The only woman to hold a chairmanship during the early years was the distinguished pathologist Janet Vaughan, who stepped in for a brief interim period in 1950. The first woman to hold a chairmanship for any length of time was Dame Isabel Graham Bryce, who was appointed in 1963, also in Oxford.

Although one of the oldest, Schuster was one of the most dominant voices among the chairmen. About eight of the other appointees during the first decade are identifiable as conscientious and active members of the meetings of chairmen. Two (Cranbrook and Elliot) were also chairmen of county councils. Also conspicuous at the meetings of chairmen were Gibson (Sheffield) and Alban (Wales), both of whom were experienced in health administration in the poorer regions.

The initial chairmen in Scotland were more overtly Labour in complexion than their colleagues in England. Labour local government provided three of the five chairmen, one of whom (May Baird) was the wife of Professor Dugald Baird, the leading obstetrician. In addition the chairman of the large Western Region was the retired MOH for Glasgow, who was accordingly experienced in working with Labour-controlled local government. Only the chairman of the Scottish SE region represented the voluntary interest. Scotland also differed from England in the fact that two of the first five chairmen were medically qualified. The Labour and medical bias among the chairmen of the Scottish RHBs gradually dwindled in the late 50s. By the end of the decade these offices were dominated by representatives of business and commerce.[49]

The third schedule of the English NHS Act was relatively unspecific about the constitution of boards, merely stating that the Minister should consult the local universities involved in medical teaching, the medical profession, local authorities, and other organisations at his discretion. A letter circulated in January 1947 to relevant organisations indicated that boards were likely to comprise members with the following backgrounds, $\frac{1}{4}$ voluntary hospital; $\frac{1}{4}$

local authority; less than $\frac{1}{4}$, medical profession and university with teaching involvement; the remainder representing varied interests, including two with mental health service experience.[50] The recommended size for boards was between 20 and 30.

The above guidelines were generally observed. The original boards ranged in size from 22 to 33 and there was little subsequent change. The proportion of medical appointees was higher than originally anticipated and it tended to increase. Medical representation stood at 29% in 1947 and 31% in 1956. In 1947 the highest was Leeds with 38% and the lowest E Anglia with 12%. In 1956 the highest were NW Metropolitan with 47% and Liverpool with 43%, and the lowest Leeds with 21%. The risk of medical dominance of regional boards alerted the Guillebaud Committee to recommend that medical representation should not normally exceed 25%, which was duly accepted as a desirable goal by the Ministry of Health.[51] The Guillebaud Committee discounted advice suggesting that medical representation should be restricted to advisory committees as was the case with other classes of employees.[52]

Some other features of the boards caused little comment at the time. For instance, women comprised only 14% of the boards in 1947 and 15% in 1956. Also the members were relatively old, about 60% being aged over 60. Finally the boards were relatively inbred, 32% of the original appointees being still in office in 1956.

In view of the diversity in size of the Scottish regions it was agreed that the boards were likely to range in size from 20 to 35, in order to accommodate all the interests involved. In the event the Scottish boards initially ranged from 18 to 33 in membership. The Permanent Secretary was in favour of retaining boards of this size, suspecting that smaller boards would place undue responsibility in the hands of officers. However Galbraith favoured substantial reduction. By way of compromise modest reductions were gradually introduced, the boards ending up with between 15 and 24 members.[53]

The Scottish NHS Act specified that more than 50% of the membership of RHBs and BMs should be non-medical. Medical representation on regional boards was from the outset above 25%, and it increased as the boards were reduced in size, reaching 50% by 1956.

It is difficult to generalise about the influence or effectiveness of boards administering the regions. It was a common complaint that the real work of the boards was forced on too few individuals. Some of the most active members formed bad relationships with colleagues. Mediocre members having a poor attendance record were too readily reappointed. Such shortcomings resulted in a dearth of first-class internal candidates for succession to the chairmanship. Also, contrary to the Government's intentions, authority fell away from the boards, towards officers and committees. Notwithstanding such limitations there was little pressure for changing the character of regional boards. Dr Stephen Taylor's advocacy of small boards with paid members attracted little support, and this proposal was not considered seriously in the Guillebaud Report.[54] The Ministry of Health had considered introducing salaries for chairmen of RHBs and HMCs, but this idea was not taken up because voluntary status was a 'fundamental principle of the service'.[55] An equally negative response was evoked by the suggestion of Macleod that ministerial patronage was an unsound basis for making board appointments. His proposal to compose boards from nominees of relevant local health authorities was criticised by Lord Cranbrook on the grounds that it would 'bring politics in with a vengeance'.[56] It was generally felt that political divisions between members had not intruded into the work of the boards. One reason for this must have been the insignificant representation of the labour movement on regional and local administrative bodies.

Labour had built up a large stake in health administration owing to its strength on some of the largest local authorities. Wartime planning commitment to municipalisation of health services had heightened Labour expectations of greater control in the future. It was naturally hoped that substitution of nationalisation for municipalisation would not diminish the degree of Labour involvement, particularly in view of the large share of hospital resources emanating from the public sector.

Procedures for determining the composition of regional boards left little room for Labour representation. Even when discretion could be exercised by the Minister, as the case of selection of chairmen demonstrates, Bevan's repeated promises that he would rely exclusively on the criterion of personal merit and 'avoid any suggestion of political bias' worked in favour of over-compensation with regard to appeasing critics of the new service.[57] Labour's chance for representation was in effect limited to its share of the 25% of places reserved for local authority members, and to the small residue intended for mental health and miscellaneous interests. In practice in a regional board with 30 places, in which medical representation stood at 33%, Labour was limited to a share of seven local authority seats and four others. Not all local authorities in a region could be represented, and fair geographical distribution was required. Consequently, even in Labour strongholds such as London or the W Riding, the local Labour authorities in the area were likely to be restricted to three places on their local regional boards. Labour's only realistic hope for representation in the 'others' category rested on consultation with the TUC. At his first meeting with the TUC Bevan assured them that 'Trades Unions would be represented on the RHBs'. Most regional boards in England and Scotland initially contained one or two TUC nominees. Consequently the Labour interest in the regional boards was only rarely above five members.

Revelation of the constitution of RHBs resulted in cries of anguish from the labour movement, and this issue was a continuing cause of complaint. Even Attlee expressed his displeasure that the boards were dominated by the old regime who had been 'active in resisting the progressive march of public activity'.[58] It was pointed out that known critics of the NHS had been appointed as chairmen of regional boards, while Labour chairmen of public health committees had not found a place on RHBs.[59]

The Labour presence waned still further after 1951, due to factors such as erosion of its political position, ineptitude of many of its nominees, reduction of trade union representation, and in Scotland as an effect of the reduction in the size of the boards. In England and Wales trade union presence for all boards stood at about 16 members until 1953. Thereafter it gradually fell to a low ebb of 10 in 1956. In 1955 and 1956 there were eight boards without a trade union representative, including such working-class areas as Sheffield, Liverpool and Newcastle. Sheffield was one of the few boards never to include a TUC representative. This decline in trade union membership was peculiar to England and Wales. Every Scottish regional board included one or two trade unionists at the outset, and this level was preserved.[60]

One reason for the decline in trade union membership of RHBs and HMCs was refusal to accept those TUC nominees who were employed in the hospital service. In the light of Bevan's promises concerning industrial democracy in the NHS, health service unions anticipated that their members employed in the hospital service would be eligible to serve on hospital management bodies. In the event industrial democracy was reserved almost exclusively for the medical profession. Others were excluded on the grounds that advisory committees were the appropriate level for employee participation. However this rule was not applied with consistency. A handful of nurses were initially appointed to RHBs, and to a substantial number of HMCs. COHSE complained about unjustifiable prejudice against subordinate grades of health worker. The union was supported by the General Secretary of the Labour Party, but the Ministry of Health kept to its line that the TUC was consulted, not as the body representing NHS employees, but to reflect the interests of the 'consumer'.[61] When the political tide turned, it was in order for TUC representation to be reduced on the grounds that it was merely one of a number of organisations representing the consumer and industry.[62] The TUC headed a list of organisations representing health workers aggrieved by their omission from regular consultations regarding appointments to RHBs. The Royal College of Midwives, the Royal College of Nursing, and the Society of Medical Officers of Health were in turn informed that their rightful place was on the advisory committees of the hospital authorities, rather than on the boards or management committees.[63] The RCN attached importance to Bevan's hint given in February 1946 that nurses were likely to find a place on RHBs, albeit in a personal capacity. The original boards contained thirteen nurses, but this number dwindled to seven in 1956, and to one in 1974. This weeding out of nurses may well reflect increasing difficulties in keeping at bay other groups of health workers.

Notwithstanding the substantial medical presence on RHBs the BMA was dissatisfied by the haphazard way in which general practitioners were represented. Feeling was aroused when the first changes in board membership reduced the original 20 general practitioners to 13 in 1950. By 1952 in some RHBs there was no general practitioner and on others the appointee was not the nominee of the BMA. The latter insisted that its own nominees had sole right to represent general practitioner opinion in the area, whereas in official circles such nominees were often regarded as medical politicians holding a brief for the BMA, and accordingly were excluded. The matter was complicated by emergence of the College of General Practitioners as a rival forum for general practitioner opinion.[64]

When hospital groups were defined in 1948 the RHBs were encouraged to form natural groups drawn from major district hospitals and functional satellites.[65] Nevertheless it was realised that local circumstances, or the need for associations of specialist hospitals, would result in adoption of a 'wide diversity of arrangements'. Consequently no attempt was made to impose a uniform pattern. Nevertheless the health departments played an active role in framing schemes, and many RHBs were persuaded to make significant changes, usually in the direction of increasing the number of groups.[66] Pressure by the Board of Control for separate grouping of mental hospitals added to this trend. Consequently the Sheffield regional plan was revised upward from 22 to 30 groups, and that of the NW Metropolitan from 15 to 22.

For England and Wales, 377 hospital groups were formed and 85 for Scotland. The number of groups ranged from 52 in the largest English region to 14 in the smallest. In the Scottish Eastern region there were only 8 groups, but in the Western 37. E Anglia felt that 20 was the maximum number of HMCs for a RHB to control, whereas larger RHBs tended to place this figure higher. The SW Metropolitan was not dissatisfied with its 52.

The above arrangement became generally accepted as a natural order, but there was discontent over the results in some regions. Small groups were prominent in Newcastle and the South Western regions whereas Birmingham opted for large groups. Thus Newcastle adopted 33 groups for 191 hospitals (one for every 815 beds), whereas Birmingham adopted 27 for 224 (one for every 1,582 beds). Birmingham boasted that in the face of opposition it had maintained groups that were large and mixed, even containing psychiatric hospitals.[67] Between 1948 and 1956 only minor modifications to groupings were introduced, a small increase to 388 in England and Wales being explained mainly by take-over of miners' rehabilitation centres from the National Coal Board, and splitting off of some large mental hospitals into single hospital groups.

The Guillebaud Committee recommended breaking up large groups and amalgamating small ones. Guillebaud advocacy of greater uniformity, closer proximation to the 'ideal hospital arrangement' of the satellite type, constituted the sort of rationalisation opposed by the same committee with respect to teaching hospitals.[68] The Ministry of Health was sympathetic to regrouping along these lines, while the Treasury was hostile on account of cost implications. When examined in detail it was found that little change was likely, but a target of increasing the groups to 427 was adopted.[69] Regions varied in their reaction. The NW Metropolitan RHB considered that there was only one possible candidate for change, but after examination this was not pursued. No alterations were made in the controversial Birmingham groupings.[70] In practice, running down of infectious diseases hospitals resulted in assimilation of these units into a smaller number of groups. The total for hospital groups in England and Wales was 381 in 1961 when further consideration was given to eliminating the small number of non-psychiatric groups with under 600 beds, or above 2,000.[71]

In Scotland the chairmen of management committees were appointed by the members, but in England they were appointed by the regional board. The Third Schedule of the 1946 Act required that management committees should be appointed after regional board consultation with Local Health Authorities, Executive Councils, hospital staffs, initially voluntary hospital governors, a list of named organisations, and other organisations at the discretion of the board. The process of consultation was laborious. Regions varied in their choice of organisations consulted on a discretionary basis. The only common denominator was trades councils. A few consulted health service unions, rotary clubs, and even Toc H. Regions over-zealous in consultation were accused of stirring up public unrest owing to inevitable disappointment over selection.[72]

The Ministry of Health advised the following model constitution for management committees: 4–5 Local Health Authority; 2–3 Executive Council; 3–4 medical and dental; 4–5 voluntary hospital; 3 others. A suitable size recommended for management committees was 15–20.[73] Regions varied in their policy for HMCs. Sheffield established committees with a uniform membership of 15. Birmingham adopted a range from 15 to 25.

Membership problems of the management committees followed the pattern described above for regional boards. Medical membership was higher than expected. In Scotland the 1947 Act specified ⅕th medical membership, but this was inflated because of choice of medical representatives by universities or the Minister.[74] Bevan expressed his concern to board chairmen over a PEP finding that in some cases medical representation was reaching almost 50%.[75] He warned of the dangers of syndicalism, domination by 'one section of the community', and of the tendency of the medical profession to act in unison. He called on regional boards to appoint younger people and manual workers.[76] RHB(49)143 warned against over-representation of the medical profession, but little change in the situation was evident when the problem was again raised in the context of recommendations of the Guillebaud Committee.[77]

Bevan was more embarrassed because he had fended off criticisms over regional board appointments by promising Labour local government members that they would achieve opportunities for representation on the management committees. However, complaints received by Bevan from the labour movement related as much to HMCs as RHBs. For instance, in a particular detailed analysis an observer from Leeds described how in the Leeds region only 102 out of 514 members were known to support Labour. Labour was in a small minority on the HMCs both in Leeds and Bradford. This position was contrasted with Labour's predominance in local government in the area. It was argued that the new system was controlled both at the RHB and HMC level by members fundamentally disaffected with the NHS.[78]

The primary obsession during the first few years of the NHS was satisfying the rival claimants for places on RHBs and HMCs. The major criticism at first was the absence of new blood. In following years the main problem was the low quality and poor participation rate of many members, a factor which led the Department of Health in Scotland to reduce the size of its RHBs. The Governors of St Bartholomew's Hospital pressed for reduction in the size of Boards of Governors on the grounds that large governing bodies reduced efficiency.[79] The Select Committee on Estimates urged that closer attention be given to the qualifications appropriate for HMC appointments. It was recommended that ability to contribute to efficient administration should become the primary qualification for selection, with representation of local interests being regarded as a secondary factor, a conclusion which was passed on to RHBs in 1958.[80]

(v) TRIPARTITE RELATIONS: HEALTH DEPARTMENTS, RHBs, HMCs

Once it was decided to depart from the local authority model for health service administration and to interpose regions between local hospital committees and the central departments, awkward questions arose over the relationship between the two tiers of local administration. The voluntary hospitals, which before 1946 were apostles of Regional Councils because of their value in obstructing the influence of local authorities, now favoured maximum devolution to the group level. Throughout its planning exercises the Ministry of Health had emphasised that planning and administration should be inseparably linked. Both the English and Scottish legislation located these powers at the regional board level. Regional boards were viewed as the agent of the Ministers, while management bodies exercised their functions as the agent of regional boards. Superiority of regional boards was implicit in the powers they were given to appoint chairmen and members of management committees in England and Wales. During the passage of the English Bill amendments diluting the powers of regional boards were resisted. Nevertheless substantial autonomy was promised to hospital groups, and indeed this was regarded as essential to attract the voluntary service of management committee members. This degree of independence was seen as a fundamental concession calculated to purchase willing compliance of the voluntary hospitals.

Consequently the 1946 White Paper promised both regions and groups 'a high degree of independence and autonomy within their own fields'. There was therefore some idea of division of labour between the two bodies. The regional board would 'plan and execute the plan', while the management committee would 'carry out day-to-day management'.[81] The management committees were promised 'a real measure of responsibility within their own sphere'.[82] It was insisted that it was never contemplated that the HMCs would be merely subordinate.[83] However the agency principle was on occasions given more prominence. For instance the Select Committee was advised that regional boards 'plan and administer a co-ordinated and specialist service', while the management committees were concerned with 'day-to-day management of the hospitals on behalf of the Regional Boards'.[84] Bevan expressed the relationship slightly differently when addressing RHB chairmen. He stressed the independence of RHBs, but warned them that they must delegate to HMCs, 'while reserving major policy to themselves'.[85]

Imprecision over the boundaries of responsibility between regional boards and management committees was regarded by the Select Committee as the source of 'a great deal of doubt and difficulty'. Sir Cyril Jones called the administrative structure 'far from clearly defined'.[86] In Scotland there was much less uncertainty about the respective functions of regional boards and Boards of Management. Initially the agency principle was applied in its most literal form. The Department of Health avoided direct dealings with Boards of Management, its directives being transmitted to the groups through the region. A firm chain of command was thus established, which was regarded as fundamental to the character of the Scottish system.[87] The Boards of Management were taken in hand over preparation of their first budgets. They were 'supposed to have their particular autonomy, but we recognised that they were just "groping"'. Consequently Scottish regional boards insisted that Boards of Management should submit for approval all projects for capital expenditure, all requests for major supplies of equipment, and all additions to establishments.[88] This detailed supervision of Boards of Management was exercised through the agency of regional boards. When the system was operating smoothly the regions discontinued detailed approval of staff complements; the number of sub-heads under which budgets were approved were reduced to a minimum and transfer of expenditure from one sub-head to another was permitted without reference to the regional boards. The latter felt in firmer control of Boards of Management because they were responsible for audits of hospital groups which was not the case in England.[89]

The less defined relationship between the region and the group in England and Wales promoted diversity of practice. For instance, uncertainties over integration between the region and the group raised questions over cross-membership. Initially both health departments discouraged cross-membership, viewing management committees as an apprenticeship for the regional board.[90] Regions varied in their response to this advice. Boards such as Birmingham and Wales were dominated by members who were also management committee chairmen, whereas the Liverpool and NW Metropolitan boards contained no management committee chairmen. The fact that 231 out of 374 regional board members in 1956 were also members of management committees demonstrates how little the official advice was heeded. In Scotland separation between management committees and regional boards was more strictly heeded, except in the two northern regions, where cross-membership was accepted in order to facilitate liaison in their scattered areas.[91]

Prospects for evolving a stable equilibrium between regional boards and management committees were undermined by the deepening political controversy surrounding the NHS, which resulted in pressures on the health departments to bring hospital administration under tighter rein. The immediate instinct of the Ministry of Health was to clamp down directly on the management committees, which resulted in complaints from the regions that they were being bypassed.

Originally, regional boards were gratified that RHB (47)1 para 2 promised them 'the largest possible measure of discretion' in the administration of their areas. In practice the boards found that the deluge of circulars from the Ministry of Health (102 in 1948, 159 in 1949) severely limited their scope for action. Thus, even before the NHS began, RHB chairmen discovered that the Ministry insisted on approving the annual estimates of management committees. The chairmen also complained that the groups were too independent. Boards consequently objected that they lacked effective control over financial matters and establishments. However the Ministry resisted trends towards reducing management committee officers to subordinates of their regional counterparts, or which would erode the degree of control exercised by management committees.[92] The regions also complained that they were insufficiently informed about group finances because auditing of groups was conducted by the internal audit organisation of the Ministry.[93]

Complaints from the regions led to a change of arrangements for approving the 1950/51 estimates, which resulted in the regional boards determining allocations to the groups. This provided the boards with their first opportunity to exercise the powers alluded to in RHB (47)1. Regions recorded minor extensions in their hold over groups, but their major demands for closer supervision were almost invariably rebuffed. Advances were wiped out by direct actions taken by the Ministry to bring expenditure under tighter control following Cripps' parliamentary statement of March 1950.

RHB(50)41 of April 1950 initiated monthly HMC expenditure returns to be made directly to the Ministry as well as to the boards. The Ministry then intervened directly to influence management committees, although the regional boards were sceptical about the central departments' capacity to monitor 400 different operations. Then, diverging from recently agreed procedures, under RHB(50)80 the Ministry took away the power of *virement* from the regions. It also introduced central reviews of hospital staffs. Finally, the regional boards were also offended by new authority given to the Ministry's principal regional officers, who now received papers and attended meetings at both regional and group level. It looked as if preparations were being made to transfer the administration of regions to the Ministry's regional offices. Indeed the regional chairmen were warned that there was a suggestion that a civil servant should have the right of veto at board meetings.[94]

Erosion of the influence of regional boards was noticed on all sides. The board chairmen felt that hospital groups were being run directly from Whitehall.[95] The Chairman of the Portsmouth HMC claimed that regional boards 'could be washed out entirely'. He advocated direct relations between the Ministry and management committees, as in the case of local authorities. Regional boards were described as an unnecessary cog in the wheel.[96] The Select Committee on Estimates urged the Ministry of Health to clarify its position. It should either 'give greater scope to the Regional Hospital Boards or they must move towards reorganising the service on the basis that the functions of the Regional Hospital Boards are primarily of a planning and advisory nature'.[97]

By 1951 a confused situation had developed. The most serious problems related to the handling and timetabling of estimates. Each of the three parties in the tripartite relationship was inclined to blame the others for failings that had led to substantial Supplementary Estimates in the first two years of the service. The succession of changes in procedures for handling estimates were unpalatable to one or other of the agents of local administration.

In the light of the above factors it is not surprising that the Jones Report recommended abolition of regional boards, or that the Labour Government accepted this recommendation. The regional boards consequently spent the greater part of two years uncertain whether they would survive, even as planning bodies. On the other hand management committees were temporarily on the ascendant. To the irritation of the regional boards the management committees formed an association which constituted an effective counterbalance to the collective influence of the regional board chairmen.[98] In the view of the Guillebaud Committee 'this period of doubt as to the future role of the Regional Hospital Board did real harm to the service'. One of the members of the Committee was more forthright, advocating unreservedly application of the Scottish system. He could not understand why 'both the Ministry and the HMCs appear to be obsessed by the fear that RHBs, if given power, will use it dictatorially'.[99]

It was not until 1952 that the RHBs restored their credibility. They were granted some of their old rights, and were assured of continuation. England and Wales followed Scotland in granting control of HMC establishments to regional boards. Once this function was assumed the Treasury was satisfied that regional boards should be retained.[100] Although this work proved onerous and frustrating for the boards, it at least gave them a more active supervisory role. However, as the Guillebaud Committee noticed, earlier events cast a long shadow. In the absence of unambiguous support from the Ministry of Health, the authority of regional boards remained in doubt and it was apt to be challenged.[101] Nevertheless, from 1952 onwards the authority of RHBs gradually expanded, and they were increasingly used as agents by the Ministry. By 1954 the Association of HMCs was complaining of undue control by the regions.[102]

In their evidence to the Guillebaud Committee most regional boards pressed for further supervisory influence over management committees. They wanted control over establishments and greater powers to ensure that items on budgets such as maintenance were used for the intended purpose.[103] Many regions favoured adoption of the Scottish relationship between regional boards and management committees. The Guillebaud Committee accepted that there was substance in the complaints of the regional boards. It was concluded: 'Regional Hospital Boards should be told, and Hospital Management Committees should accept, that the Regional Boards are responsible for exercising a general oversight and supervision over the administration of the hospital service in their Regions'.[104] However the Guillebaud Committee's specific recommendations made little contribution towards strengthening the powers of regional boards. The Select Committee on Estimates reiterated the Guillebaud Committee's views, and offered a few further hints on strengthening the authority of regional boards.[105] The advice given was sufficiently unspecific to excuse inaction from the Ministry of Health. Indeed the Permanent Secretary thought that the wishes of the Committee had already been accomplished: 'progress since the scheme began has been definitely in favour of increasing the powers of regional boards, particularly their financial control over management committees, and giving them more control of the service than was envisaged at the beginning'.[106]

As noted above, concessions towards management committees appeased local interests connected with the former voluntary hospitals. Development of house committees at the unit level served the same function. The 1946 White Paper accordingly promised that management committees would be empowered to set up house committees 'as required'.[107] However provision for house committees was not made in the NHS legislation and amendments to this effect were resisted. None the less, both Bevan and Rucker alluded to house committees as a necessary link in the chain of delegation.[108] Bevan continued to favour formation of house committees.[109] In the absence of firm instructions, management committees evolved a variety of arrangements for delegation within the group. In Scotland house committees were not called for because of the prevalence of medical administration at the unit level.[110] Detecting a tendency towards 'fragmentation of the hospital service by breaking down the two tier system of administration', circular RHB(47)11 deprecated giving house committees executive powers. In the same vein RHB(49)107 asked boards to ensure that house committees were uniform in character and not subversive to the executive functions of management committees.[111] This official line was supported by the Bradbeer Committee.[112] However some hospital boards and management committees seem to have ignored this advice. The Newcastle board from the outset encouraged management committees to establish strong house committees with authority to make all appointments except senior staff. Thus within the sub-regional committee structure, the W Cumberland HMC divided up its area into four district house committees. In this case the 'disintegrative tendency' worrying the Ministry was carried to an extreme. The two-tier system had escalated to four: RHB-Sub-regional Committee-HMC-House Committee.[113] The Oxford regional board was also a keen advocate of devolution to house committees.[114] The Association of HMCs was divided on the issue. An official warned that house committees would prove to be 'millstones round the Hospital Secretaries' necks'.[115]

(vi) OFFICERS AND COMMITTEES

The major responsibility within a regional board resided with the chairman and the two senior officers, the Senior Administrative Medical Officer and the secretary. In Scotland, England and Wales most of the original appointees to the administrative posts were still in office in 1957. The secretaries changed in one region in England and two in Scotland. SAMOs were replaced in two regions in England and one in Scotland. The largest group of recruits to SAMO posts came from local authority service, while the second largest had worked as medical officers in government service. The secretaries were diverse in their backgrounds. Only a minority were recruited from the voluntary hospital sector, whereas three were retired Indian civil servants. The majority came from various local government backgrounds. Appointment of civil servants to the senior posts was discouraged on the grounds that it would be open to serious misrepresentation by suggesting that the hospital service was a branch of the civil service.[116]

The SAMO was described primarily as 'adviser of the Board on the planning, organisation and staffing of the hospital and specialist service', whereas the secretary would primarily 'arrange for the conduct of the proceedings of the Board and its committees', and also 'conduct its business management generally, including general supervision of the finance, supply and establishment organisation of the Board'.[117] This remit intentionally avoided the question of relative status of the two chief officers. However, because of professional demands for the SAMO to be given consultant status, this post carried a considerably higher salary. Thus, although it was hoped that the SAMOs and secretaries would work out an amicable partnership, the former began at an advantage. Furthermore, the Industrial Court witnessed telling concessions from the management side, in which the SAMO was acknowledged to be the 'senior administrative officer', 'keyman', 'senior officer of the team', etc.[118] Official guidance continued to emphasise teamwork, but where the chairman's authority was weak, and the incumbents inclined to be factious, conflict tended to break out among the senior officers, not only between SAMOs and secretaries, but also between all the senior officers, including treasurers and architects. Avoidance of hierarchy was thus a recipe for anarchy in certain boards.[119]

RHB chairmen frequently complained that their senior officers were underpaid compared with equivalent administrators outside. It was felt that recruitment of medical staff was adversely affected by the superior position of consultants, while secretaries, treasurers, legal advisers and engineers were also thought to be at a disadvantage to their counterparts outside the NHS.[120] Lack of incentives at the highest level was a reflection of the general shortcomings of the career structure in the hospital service. Complaints made about the position of regional officers were repeated with respect to administrative and clerical staff at group and unit level.

Management committees in England and Wales were left with wide discretion concerning the appointment of officers.[121] Practice varied greatly, but especially in general hospital groups there was a tendency to appoint separate secretaries, finance officers and supplies officers.[122] It was noted that 'there is some eagerness to build up as heavy a barrage of officers as can be squeezed into a liberal interpretation of the Ministry's intention'.[123] As in the case of regional boards there was no designated chief administrative officer, with the result that the authority of the group secretary was open to question. Finance officers in particular regarded themselves as part of the regional financial network rather than as junior to group secretaries. Appointment of finance officers to serve a number of groups encouraged this thinking. Scotland was spared this ambiguity because the chief officer acted both as secretary and treasurer, while supplies were handled regionally. Scotland also appointed group medical superintendents, which pointed to the absence of a medical administrator at group level in the English system.[124] This was regarded as a defeat by SAMOs, who lacked a counterpart with whom to liaise in the hospital group.

Links were formed between regional officers and their group counterparts, but the regions chafed over their lack of participation in appointment of the chief group officers. Notwithstanding the accusation that unsatisfactory appointments were being made, demands by the regions for involvement in selection were decisively rejected by the Ministry of Health on grounds of infringement of the independent status of management committees.[125] Complaints continued and were regarded seriously enough by the Select Committee on Estimates for changes in appointments procedures to be requested.[126] The Select Committee was more impressed by the complaints of the regional boards than by the negative responses of the Ministry of Health, which it judged disquietingly complacent.[127]

Concern about defects in the appointment mechanism prompted attention to the wider problem of recruitment and training. The Oxford and Newcastle boards pressed for a programme of recruitment and training of administrative and clerical staff of the kind prevalent in the nationalised industries. Newcastle described the current position as one of 'few vacancies, poor prospects, few applicants'.[128] Oxford was also annoyed that this problem had been referred to the Whitley Council rather than the regional boards. Improvement of recruitment and training became a major obsession with Schuster the Oxford chairman.[129] While the regional boards accepted that improved staff training was needed they were not entirely agreed on the mechanism. Sheffield, for instance, was not in favour of a graduate training programme, preferring to take its entrants direct from school.[130]

Proposals for a unified recruitment and training scheme were slow to evolve. The staff side of the relevant Whitley Council submitted proposals in February 1952. The management side was opposed to the staff suggestion that a diploma in administration should be a condition of appointment to higher administrative posts, and it also opposed granting special allowances for such qualifications. After more than two years the management side produced rival proposals for a National Training Scheme, which involved arrangements for graduate entry.[131]

Lack of progress was lamented by both the Guillebaud Committee and the Select Committee on Estimates. The latter noted that minor initiatives had recently been forthcoming, but it pointed out that 'dangers inherent in the absence of a satisfactory career structure, or of national recruitment, training, and promotion schemes, must have long been apparent'.[132]

The two-tier organisation of the NHS deflected attention away from the hospital unit. Although it was hoped that hospital groups would take on corporate identity, the weight of tradition favoured continuing importance of the hospital unit. As noted above, formation of house committees strengthened the sentiment for the hospital unit. It was widely felt that the services of secretaries of hospital units were severely undervalued under the NHS, with the result that the quality of entrants to these key posts was suffering.[133] The absence of a medical administrator at the group or hospital level in most hospitals also raised the question of extending the use of medical superintendents. Such officers occupied a firm place in the Scottish system and in the English mental sector. However, in England and Wales the role of medical superintendent was not without its ambiguities. Medical superintendents and group secretaries in mental hospital groups experienced the same difficulties in working out their relationships as did SAMOs and secretaries at the regional level.[134] Medical administration at the unit level exposed disagreement among regional boards. Certain boards were pleased to jettison medical superintendents as an unpalatable hangover from the local authority hospital system. Other boards regretted that medical superintendents were being superseded by lay administrators. It was argued that medical administrators were the only ones equipped to bring order among consultants. It was also suggested that absence of medical administrators was likely to result in neglect of functions such as prevention of infection and kitchen hygiene.[135]

The Oxford board advocated the new system in which the lay administrator at the unit level was guided by a Medical Advisory Committee. However both the Bradbeer and Guillebaud Committees recognised the strength of the argument for extension of medical administration. They proposed an intermediate solution under which a consultant would act as 'consultant-medical administrator' of the hospital unit. It was argued that this officer would 'help to restore that loyalty which, before the inception of the National Health Service was centred on the hospital but has since tended to shift towards individual specialties'.[136]

Given the increasing predominance of lay administration, medical advisory committees at the unit level exercised an important influence. The profession was insistent that parallel medical advisory committees should also be established at the regional level. Such an arrangement was consistent with the view taken throughout negotiations that medical advisory committees should be established at every level in administration. This demand was conceded by the health departments, but provision for these committees was not embodied in the legislation.[137] General encouragement was given for medical advisory committees at regional and group level. However, the Ministry of Health was opposed to dictating to regional boards a precise mechanism for obtaining medical advice. Indeed it resisted stipulating any particular committee structure for regional boards, even with respect to mental health. Notwithstanding obduracy of the Ministry, the Joint Consultants Committee pressed for statutory recognition of the regional Medical Advisory Committee.[138] Failing legislation, the Joint Committee pressed for a departmental memorandum requesting formation of 'democratically elected' advisory committees at regional, group and unit levels. The Ministry agreed that these committees were desirable, but doubted whether a memorandum was really needed.[139] Lying behind the reticence of the Ministry was fear that the medical advisory machinery would fall into the hands of the Regional Committees of Consultants and Specialists, which were closely identified with the BMA, and therefore in the eyes of the department 'medico-political' in character.[140]

The Joint Committee was not appeased by subsequent events. It was regaled with information concerning the elaborate advisory mechanisms established by the regional boards, but these were criticised by representatives of the profession on account of their lack of uniformity, inappropriateness, and failure to reflect the voice of local specialists.[141] The Joint Committee insisted on the principle of 'representative staff committees elected by the staff'. The department agreed to put this proposal to chairmen of regional boards, and also to recommend more regular establishment of such committees at group level, with sub-committees acting at unit level. The agreed draft constitution of regional medical advisory committees received a 'chilling reception' from regional chairmen, who were disinclined to depart from their existing advisory arrangements.[142] Other aspects of the agreed proposals ran into difficulties with the Bradbeer Committee, which objected to unit medical advisory committees being sub-committees of the group committees. The Bradbeer Committee wanted the unit committee to represent only the staff of that hospital, whereas it recommended that the group committee should contain general practitioner and MOH representatives. This view was backed by the Medical SAC and the CHSC.[143] The Bradbeer Committee produced a detailed exposition of the case for unit medical staff committees and for group medical advisory committees, conclusions which were supported by the Guillebaud Committee.[144] The latter also agreed with the profession concerning regional arrangements, recommending against the advice of the Ministry of Health that there should be set up 'a single consultative committee for each Region to strengthen the link between the senior medical staff and the Regional Hospital Board'.[145]

This advice created no problem in Scotland, where there was already in existence an advisory machinery approved of by the Regional Consultants and Specialists Committees. However, the regional boards in England remained overwhelmingly opposed to modifying their consultative procedures. Only Liverpool and Wales had established advisory committees of the type recommended by the Guillebaud Committee, and they advocated their extension.[146] But the other regions were cool to antagonistic. Subsequent reconsideration caused some boards to draw nearer the model wanted by the profession, but most made the minimum adjustment of their existing committees. The degree of consultation with professional bodies remained inadequate to satisfy the BMA, the Joint Committee and the Regional Consultants and Specialists Committees.[147]

(vii) RESOURCE ALLOCATION

During the first years of the NHS relatively little attention was given to the question of resource allocation. Official reports dating from that period contain a vast amount of statistical data, often on trivial aspects of the service, but they are conspicuously silent with respect to distribution of resources, whether financial, human, or material, between the regions, or between teaching and non-teaching hospitals.

There was an undercurrent of concern. Those regions that were better provided at the outset of the service retained their advantages over the rest. Although deficiencies in the service were endemic to all areas, some regions were recognised as particularly backward. E Anglia, Sheffield and Wales were described as the most backward regions in 1947.[148] On the whole deprivation tended to be located in the north and the west. Impoverishment of services was an inherited pattern, closely reflecting the long-term problems of the economy in the areas worst affected by the depression. The Ministry was officially committed to levelling up the depressed regions. At the time of economies the poorer regions were treated more leniently than others, while they were also given slightly more advantage from funds available for development.[149]

Data presented in Table V give a rough impression of the problem of uneven resource distribution. The value of such information is limited because it gives no insight into differences within regions, or disparities between types of institution or service. However this tabulation suggests that contemporary impressions

TABLE V

Regional Distribution of Hospital Resources and Staff

	1	2	3	4	5	6	7	8
Regional Board	% Population	% Revenue Allocation		% Capital Allocation	% Beds (RHB + BG)	% Consultants (RHB + BG)		% Nursing & Midwifery Staff
	Mid-1953	1950/51	1955/56	1948/49–1956/57	31.12.53	31.12.49	31.12.55	31.12.49
Newcastle	6.6	5.26	5.89	8.68	5.4	5.91	6.61	6.42
Leeds	6.9	6.67	6.71	6.29	7.1	6.02	5.67	7.31
Sheffield	9.5	7.08	7.44	8.96	7.4	6.70	6.66	8.24
E Anglia	3.3	2.76	2.70	3.22	3.0	3.49	3.20	2.84
NW Met.	8.8	9.79	9.02	7.89	8.6	12.19	11.27	8.74
NE Met.	6.9	8.52	8.33	6.13	7.1	8.44	8.96	8.19
SE Met.	7.2	9.15	8.48	7.38	8.5	8.33	9.35	8.88
SW Met.	10.5	14.26	13.06	11.71	14.0	12.27	12.04	14.90
Oxford	3.3	2.95	3.21	3.93	3.0	3.63	3.61	3.09
S Western	6.3	6.80	6.94	6.89	7.2	6.21	5.85	8.02
Wales	5.9	5.39	5.82	7.03	5.4	5.18	5.37	6.27
Birmingham	10.1	8.32	8.72	8.69	9.1	8.78	9.04	9.49
Manchester	9.9	8.37	8.83	8.31	9.2	6.72	7.25	10.02
Liverpool	4.8	4.69	4.86	4.90	5.0	6.14	5.12	5.49

Sources: T.SS 267/02A, col 1 (from Reg Gen), col 5.
 Acton Soc Trust, *Hospitals and the State*, no 6 (1959), cols 2,3,4.
 DHSS 94II2/4/102/1, cols 6 & 7.
 Select Committee on Estimates, 11th Report, 1950/51, col 8.

Notes: 1. Nursing staffs total numbers are used in column 8 rather than whole-time equivalent.
 2. For consultants in columns 6 and 7 total numbers are used. Percentages for the metropolitan RHBs, especially NW Met. RHB, are understated because they exclude consultants working exclusively for teaching hospitals.
 3. The figures relate to regional boards, except where stated.

293

concerning the superiority of the metropolitan regions, and under-provision in the north and west were basically correct. Adding in the teaching hospitals would increase the advantage of the better provided regions. Generally resources were in surplus over population in the metropolitan areas, while they were in deficit in the north and the west.

Scotland also betrayed substantial differences between the regions, but it is more difficult to identify general disadvantage. Thus, the North Eastern region was at the bottom of the league of beds for its population, but it was at the top for its level of nursing staff. The Northern region was poorly provided with nurses, but well-supplied with specialists.[150]

The disadvantages of the poorer regions are confirmed by reference to less coarse estimates. For instance, the ratios of total staff to 100 staffed beds showed the metropolitan boards, Oxford and South Western at the top of the league table for the various sizes and types of hospital, with Newcastle, Sheffield and E Anglia consistently at the bottom.[151] Not only was a region such as Sheffield relatively under-provided with consultants, but also the quality of these consultants, as measured by the awards system, was inferior. Thus the 1949 league table of awards showed that 26.9% of consultants in the Manchester region received awards, whereas the level for the NW Metropolitan region was 37.9%.[152] Even within the provinces there were substantial differences, as illustrated by some representative figures from Oxford and Sheffield. The latter's population was three times the size of the former's, but in 1951 Sheffield employed 5% of the national total of consultants in general medicine (with 5.9% of the awards), 7.0% of consultants in mental health (3.5% of awards), and 5.9% of consultants in anaesthetics (3.7% of awards); whereas Oxford employed 3.1% of consultants in general medicine (3.5% of awards), 2.9% of consultants in mental health (6.5% of awards), and 3.8% of consultants in anaesthetics (5% of awards).[153] Oxford was consequently in advance of its population norm with respect to the supply of consultants in the various specialties, and considerably in advance in the proportion receiving awards, whereas Sheffield was in marked deficit in both respects. Such discrepancies seem to have been taken philosophically within the Sheffield region, where it was concluded that their low consultant/population rating was a sign of the virtue that 'it is often wise to hasten slowly and also to insist upon quality'.[154]

To some extent regional boards could influence resource distribution. Some regions were notably more successful than others in improving their position. For instance Newcastle significantly improved its standing with respect to consultants. Newcastle in

1949 started with 280 consultants (74 awards, including 6 As), whereas in 1959 it employed 463 consultants (140 awards, including 16 As). On the other hand Sheffield began in 1949 with 332 consultants (96 awards, including 4 As), while it ended up in 1959 with 465 consultants (140 awards, including 14 As).[155] Newcastle thus recorded a 65% increase, whereas the increase in Sheffield was only 40%. The smaller northern region caught up the larger one. The relatively good performance of Newcastle, or the relatively poor showing of most of its northern neighbours is probably explained by local factors, including the efficiency of the regional board, and perhaps especially the quality of leadership exercised by the SAMO and expert committees. It is relevant that the Newcastle SAMO was regarded as the best in England and Wales, whereas the others in the north were relatively unimpressive. Notwithstanding the crudity of comparisons included in it, Table V suggests a problem of redistribution very similar to that revealed by the infinitely more sophisticated methods of the Resource Allocation Working Party in 1976, even to the extent of containing a similar league table of deprivation.

There were some calls for a bold solution to this problem. Indeed one observer in 1950 suggested principles for reallocation of the type adopted nearly thirty years later, 'Some regions inherited a much better developed hospital service than others, but present financing methods are likely to have the effect of perpetuating this situation, owing to the very uneven distribution of funds over the various parts of the country. An allocation of whatever sum is to be made available for the hospital service over the regions, on a formula basis calculated according to population, hospital needs, and so on, would probably yield better results over the country as a whole even if it meant transfer of some of the funds from the well-provided to the ill-provided areas'.[156] At the time adoption of a strict formula for resource allocation met with little support. However there was a steady stream of criticism concerning uneven distribution. As early as 1950 the Welsh regional board complained that it was receiving an inadequate share of resources.[157] However this problem was not actively taken up by the RHB chairmen. A careful analysis of the pattern of resource distribution, undertaken by *The Hospital*, noted trends towards compensating the poorer regions on the capital side, but it also noted persistent disparities in the revenue allocation.[158] The Treasury increasingly believed that since regions were comparable, they should receive 'fair shares' of allocations, based on the size of their populations.[159] The Guillebaud Committee was actively interested in comparison of spending between hospital types, but it devoted almost no attention to regional distribution. A late request for data on expenditure per head of population was denounced as a 'futile exercise' by the official involved. The pattern revealed is consistent with Table V. In 1953 the average for England and Wales was £5 per head, the highest region being SW Metropolitan, with £6.3, and the lowest Sheffield with £3.9. The ratio of population to staffed beds averaged 100, the highest region being Sheffield with 124 and the lowest SW Metropolitan with 72. Comparisons excluding London also placed Sheffield at the bottom of the league table, with S Western at the top. Similar differences were evident in Scotland, with the Eastern region being best endowed, and the NE region worst.[160] This differential had persisted since the beginning of the service.

The slow drift towards ironing out the more gross factors in distribution of resources had produced measurable improvement by the late 50s. Between 1950/51 and 1958/59 the share in resources of the six poorest regions had increased from 39.1% to 42.2%, whereas the metropolitan share had declined from 41.7% to 38.3%. This effect was reinforced by a slight decline in the share of the teaching hospitals.[161] But notable differences still remained. Unequal distribution first became a public issue in 1957, when the Select Committee on Estimates questioned closely Treasury and Ministry of Health witnesses on this point. It was admitted that resource allocation had been largely dictated by the 'inherited pattern'.[162] Notwithstanding the Minister's policy to reduce variations, it was admitted that inequalities in resource distribution were tending to become entrenched.[163] The only evidence before the Committee related to the cost per week of hospital maintenance, which showed that Oxford was the most expensive and Newcastle the least.[164] The published version of this evidence showed that throughout the period 1951–1956 the NW Metropolitan board was the most expensive and Manchester the cheapest.[165] Ministry of Health witnesses produced no convincing defence of the perpetuation of differences inherited from pre-NHS days.[166] The Select Committee was unhappy about persistence of inequalities in resource allocation, yet no specific guidance was given on solutions to this difficulty.

It has already been noted that regional data are aggregates derived from extremely diverse data relating to individual hospital units. It was a major problem to evolve accounting methods which would permit meaningful comparisons between hospital functions. When the NHS was established it took over the subjective method of accounting, itemising salaries, wages, fuel, provisions etc, which had limited value for comparative investigations. From 1946 onwards *The Accountant* and other expert authorities bombarded the health departments with advice on cost accounting, suggesting that a system of 'objective' or 'unit' accounting should be adopted for the NHS which, it was argued, would provide more realistic insight into the cost of natural hospital functions. Objective accounting was offered as a more effective instrument of administrative control. It would allow identification and elimination of waste, provide a scientific basis for building up annual estimates, and allow allocations to be made on an equitable basis. When the health departments failed to adopt objective accounting methods they were reviled by *The Accountant*. The subsequent problems of overspending on the hospital service were blamed to some extent on defective accountancy procedures. *The Accountant* was joined by the King's Fund, the Nuffield Provincial Hospitals Trust, the Public Accounts Committee, the Select Committee on Estimates, a committee of CHSC and eventually the Guillebaud Committee in demands for objective cost accounting.

The health departments took guidance from their regional treasurers, on whose advice separate English and Scottish systems were established for reducing the subjective accounts to a form amenable to comparative uses. However the unit of comparison adopted, the average in-patient cost per week for each hospital, was regarded by *The Accountant* and other critics as a totally futile basis for comparison. It was argued that the health departments were introducing methods that had been abandoned pre-war on account of their inefficiency.[167]

The further thoughts of the regional treasurers presented in 1952 showed more sympathy for objective accounting, but the proposals were still unacceptable to the purists because cost accounts were proposed as a supplement rather than replacement for subjective accounts. The treasurers were primarily concerned with arriving at a more scientific basis for separating in-patient from out-patient expenditure to replace the arbitrary formula then in use. Their methods were designed specifically for large general hospitals.[168]

Reports on hospital costing were also solicited by the Ministry from the Nuffield Provincial Hospitals Trust and the King's Fund, both of whom recommended that objective accounts should replace the existing system. The Nuffield and King's Fund reports differed significantly on points of detail.[169] In an attempt to preserve the best of both worlds the Ministry in 1953 established a working party to devise a departmental costing system, to operate within the existing subjective framework. A similar committee was established in Scotland.[170]

The Guillebaud Committee was struck by accounts of the application of functional costing at the Glasgow Royal Infirmary.[171] The Oxford regional board was impressed by this system and it complained about the Ministry's lethargy in taking up cost accounting.[172] However the NW Metropolitan and the E Anglia regions were sceptical. They suspected that unit costing would be expensive to operate, and that it might not yield comparisons capable of leading to savings.[173]

The English report, completed in July 1955, proposed that all larger hospitals should produce a 'main scheme' cost statement for in-patients and out-patients separately, in which all expenditure would be shown per patient week and per case, and allocated either to wards and out-patient departments or to medical service departments.[174]

The Scottish report completed in March 1955 showed a more cautious approach. It was proposed to limit their experiment to 30 hospitals, and the system adopted would be simplified, involving reference only to prime costs (salaries, wages, direct supplies and services).

Support for the new costing scheme was not unanimous in England. A minority of the expert working party put in a reservation doubting the value of uniform costing and therefore suggesting reduction to an experiment involving 50 hospitals rather than the 200 scheduled for participation in the main scheme. The long drawn-out deliberations of the Ministry of Health on cost accounting were accompanied by increasing scepticism on the part of the Treasury. It was suspected that cost accounting would become an expensive investment which was unlikely to bear fruit in either economies or more efficient reallocation of resources. The Treasury consequently favoured adoption of the cheaper Scottish system. However, commitment had gone so far that it was impossible to reverse the trend in events. It was therefore reluctantly decided to proceed, and the new schemes were introduced in April 1957.[175]

(viii) CONTROL OF ESTABLISHMENTS

With the build-up of concern over the cost of the NHS, critical attention became fixed on the hospital service as the largest element within the NHS, and consequently upon salaries and wages as the largest component of hospital costs. Since it was impossible to hold down remuneration without jeopardising the existence of the recently formed Whitley Councils, control of establishments offered the only realistic means to assail the problem of staff costs. Suspicion that hospitals were overstaffed was provoked by the large numbers involved, and by increases during the early years of the service. In England and Wales, between December 1949 and September 1952, the total number of full-time staff went up from 303,600 to 325,000, and part-time staff from 75,000 to 90,000, which amounted to an increase of 15%.[176] In Scotland staff numbers rose from 47,000 in 1948 to 53,000 in September 1952, an increase of 12%.[177] A fuller statement of the staffing position with respect to the major groups of staff is shown in Table VI. This indicates a diverse pattern between 1949 and 1952, with the large categories of full-time nursing, midwifery and domestic staff showing only modest annual increments. The more substantial percentage increases took place among the three less numerous groups; in all these cases after the first full year the rate of change quickly declined. Indeed, it was generally felt that the greatest increases of all had taken place before March 1949, the transitional period for which few reliable statistics are available. These increases are attributable to a variety of factors, including partial correction of the pre-NHS staff shortage, building up of a new administration, and to real expansion. Inevitably suspicions were aroused that not all increases were justified. Even within the health authorities themselves there were frequent accusations of waste, albeit usually elsewhere. As noted in the previous section the regional personnel accused the teaching hospitals of lavish staffing, while the regional boards were convinced that the management committees were overdeveloping their administrative and clerical empires. For instance the Sheffield region felt that the 63% increase of HMC administrative and clerical staff between July 1948 and December 1949 was unjustified.[178]

Lack of confidence in the capacity of management committees to determine establishments correctly lay at the heart of demands by regional boards for closer control over establishment matters. Such demands were firmly rebuffed because they were contrary to the conception of local management responsibility, which was held fundamental to the hospital service. The official countersuggestion that sufficient influence over establishments could be exerted through scrutiny of estimates was dismissed as insufficient by the regional boards.[179]

The first intervention of the Treasury occurred in March 1949 when Cripps called on Bevan to control hospital staff numbers and also to introduce firm guidelines for determining establishments. Bevan assured him that they were collecting relevant data, but prescription of staffing levels was ruled out because it was inconsistent with their policy of local autonomy.[180] The discovery that in Scotland regional boards exercised detailed control over staffing levels of Boards of Management encouraged the Treasury in September 1949 to return to the suggestion that a similar method should be applied in England. The Ministry of Health was thrown into turmoil by requests from the Treasury for statistics and reviews of staffing levels. Adverse comments from the Public Accounts Committee and the Select Committee on Estimates added to the

TABLE VI

Staff of the Hospital Service 1949–1956 (England and Wales)

thousands

	31.12.49	31.12.50	%	31.12.51	%	31.12.52	%	31.12.53	%	31.12.54	%	31.12.55	%	31.12.56	%	1956/ 1949 % increase
1. Medical and Dental	11.9	12.9	8.4	13.7	6.2	14.3	4.4	14.4	0.7	15.0	4.2	15.3	2.0	15.8	3.3	32.8
2. Professional and Technical	12.5	13.7	9.6	15.1	10.2	15.8	4.6	16.0	1.3	16.5	3.1	17.4	5.5	18.0	3.4	44.0
3. Administrative and Clerical	23.8	27.3	14.7	27.3	—	27.3	—	26.7	-2.2	27.0	1.1	27.5	1.9	28.5	3.6	19.7
4. Nursing and Midwifery																
w.t.	125.8	132.4	5.2	136.2	2.9	141.0	3.6	144.6	2.6	144.7	0.1	143.4	-0.9	145.8	1.7	15.9
p.t.	23.1	25.0	8.2	25.8	3.2	26.6	3.1	28.8	8.3	30.5	5.9	32.9	7.9	35.6	8.2	54.1
5. Domestic Staff																
w.t.	101.2	103.3	2.1	105.4	2.0	108.1	2.6	109.1	0.9	109.3	0.2	111.3	1.8	112.9	1.4	11.6
p.t.	27.1	29.9	3.3	33.6	12.4	35.7	6.2	36.7	2.8	41.5	13.1	44.4	7.0	46.6	5.0	72.0

Source: Ministry of Health, *Summary 1949–1966* (1967).
Note: The totals are given as whole-time equivalents in 1–3 and as whole-time and part-time in 4 and 5.

incentive for action. Instead of conceding the Treasury request for a joint working party to control staffing levels, the Ministry set up two-person teams to inquire into establishments throughout the hospital service.[181] Hospital authorities were informed about this development in August 1950 and the teams began work in September. Upon the basis of the fieldwork of these teams it was proposed to fix establishments for all categories of staff. The Minister would then stipulate detailed establishment ceilings, which were only to be exceeded with the agreement of the next highest authority.[182] Central teams of four types were appointed to investigate the following staff categories: medical and dental (9 teams for RHBs, 1 team for BGs), nursing (5 teams), administrative and clerical (6 teams), and domestic (1 team). Even given the number of teams involved, the magnitude of this operation was formidable. The slowness of the operation resulted in the findings of the teams becoming obsolete before they were put into effect. Among the multiplicity of problems facing this exercise were, difficulty in evolving objective staffing norms, findings which revealed understaffing and therefore implied recruitment rather than economy, lack of consistency between review teams, the capacity of entrenched Boards of Governors and management committees to reverse the Minister's recommendations, and finally, difficulty in deciding an honourable course of action in the case of staff made redundant or regraded as a result of review. Such difficulties severely reduced the effectiveness of the review teams. All expectations of decisive conclusions from this exercise were rapidly dispelled. The review teams worked in an atmosphere of increasing scepticism. Early in 1953 most of them were unobtrusively wound up. Of the large-scale reviews, only that concerning administrative and clerical staffs was completed. The much more manageable review of consultant staff was finished, but only the review relating to teaching hospitals was used to determine establishments.[183] As early as August 1951 the Treasury believed that the reviews were a farce, conducted as a face-saving exercise to appease the Public Accounts Committee, but without any real prospects of the recommendations becoming effective.[184]

Regardless of their utility in certain fields, the review teams were clearly not an appropriate instrument to bring about rapid control of hospital establishments. In November 1951, the newly appointed Crookshank demanded a more aggressive approach to the control of establishments.[185] In the summer of 1952 the health departments were urged by the Treasury to take more decisive action. First, they were asked to extend to other staffs the effective freeze placed on administrative and clerical staff numbers in December 1951. Secondly, the Treasury requested a 5% reduction in staffs other than medical or nursing, to be attained within a year. The Scottish Department of Health acceded to these requests more readily than the Ministry of Health. Within the Ministry there was strong opposition to increasing use of central direction, and objection to the 5% cut as an arbitrary device, potentially damaging to standards of care because medical and nursing staff were dependent on the services of the staff selected for cuts.[186]

Treasury thinking was reluctantly accepted by the Ministry of Health. Establishments were fixed at the level of 5 December 1952. Thereafter permission for increases in staff required approval of the next highest authority, which meant that the majority of establishments were controlled by the regional boards, but increases in RHB staff and senior medical and dental staff required ministerial approval.

The above proposals were embodied in the 'Economy in Manpower' circular RHB(52)133 of 5 December 1952, which Macleod identified as 'political dynamite', and which received the predicted stormy response. Despite careful preparation by the department to prevent the circular causing much stir at its date of public release, negative reactions were sparked off by a leak of the circular to the *Daily Herald* on 30 October 1952. The *Daily Herald* headline 'Hospitals Slash: Staff Cuts on the Way' caused panic among health workers and their representatives.[187] Urgent representations were made by the ancillary staffs' unions, especially by C F Comer, General Secretary of COHSE, and W D Goss, secretary of the staff side of the Ancillary Staffs Whitley Council. The circular also elicited adverse response from Conservative MPs, as well as from labour organisations. These groups were assured that essential staff were not threatened, and that recruitment would not be inhibited in shortage areas.[188]

The more severe critics of RHB(52)133 came from within the health service. With few exceptions it was denounced by regional boards and management committees. In Scotland 'unanimous and violent opposition' was voiced by the regional chairmen, who demanded a Government declaration concerning limitation in standards of treatment as a precondition for such a circular. The Secretary of State met the chairmen and sent out a cautious letter before issuing his Economy in Manpower circular.[189] In England only one regional chairman even hinted at support. It was argued that the policy would generate numerous undesirable side-effects without achieving its proclaimed end. Chairmen offered to co-operate but they held out no hope of reaching a 5% cut in one year. They reiterated their long-standing claim that the realistic solution to this problem was regional control over group establishments and control through budgets rather than numbers.[190] The

Teaching Hospitals Association protested on behalf of Boards of Governors, who were particularly concerned that promises of prior consultation before imposition of controls had not been honoured.[191]

Although unpopular and seemingly draconian, the manpower economy circular was regarded by officials as a temporary and negative expedient. The Treasury wanted a more scientific basis for determining establishments. The primary emphasis was on improving the quality of statistical returns, with a view to achieving comparability between institutions of similar type. The Treasury was influenced by exercises of this kind undertaken by the SW Metropolitan RHB. League table comparisons were advocated for use within and between regions. The Ministry of Health was unreceptive to such proposals.[192] A second approach, which was the subject of considerable but inconclusive discussion, involved selection of a single region for specific investigation. Such a region would constitute a guinea pig, or the 'eyes and ears' of the department. It would serve as a centre for experimentation before ideas were tried out in other regions.[193]

As Table VI indicates, 1953 saw a sharp fall in the rate of increase in all major categories of staff, and indeed an actual decrease in administrative and clerical staff to below the level appertaining in December 1950. The situation might almost be described as a freeze. In the first year of operation of the new controls total hospital staff increased by only 1%.[194] But there was nothing like an aggregate fall of 5% in categories 1, 3 and 5 in Table VI, which comprise category 'D' of RHB(52)133, where this reduction was required. The Ministry of Health was relieved that seven secretaries of regional boards reacted positively to RHB(52)133. However, the majority of their letters were by no means supportive. Most secretaries felt that stabilisation of staff was primarily a reflection of the increasingly uncompetitive nature of hospital wage rates. Indeed it was pointed out that the current rules would permit substitution of cheap ancillary staff by expensive professionals. A particularly destructive review of RHB(52)133 from the secretary of the E Anglia RHB pointed out that the 'casual vacancies' loophole enabled management committees to inflate their nominal rolls, with the result that it was easy to accomplish a paper saving. Also the widespread use of part-time staff provided a device for evading the freeze.[195] Table VI shows that the rate of increase in part-time employees in nursing was not inhibited by the freeze.

Regional boards were uncomplimentary about both RHB(52)133 and the review teams in their testimonies to the Guillebaud Committee. It was claimed that review teams sanctioned unrealistically high establishments, with the result that their finding obstructed attempts by the boards to reduce staffing levels. The regional boards petitioned to take over the work of the review teams.[196] Such views disposed the Guillebaud Committee to make its firm recommendation concerning relaxation of the controls introduced in RHB(52)133.[197] The Guillebaud Committee was also influenced by the evidence that staffing levels were under control. During 1953 and 1954 the overall increase in staff in the hospital sector was only 1% per annum. Subsequently, as Table VI indicates, rates of increase began to climb, but this caused no particular alarm.

In April 1952 the Treasury suggested radical means for long-term regulation of staff numbers. Despite various reminders no reply from the Ministry was forthcoming.[198] When the problem became less urgent Treasury interest in its solution noticeably waned. The initiative for reviews of staff and elaboration of new arrangements for control was now left to the health departments and the regional boards. In Scotland an expert team conducted a general review of six hospitals and came to the conclusion that there should be a 7% reduction in staff compared with the 0.7% estimated by Boards of Management. A further investigation into 42 hospitals also suggested room for savings. This problem was then referred to the Scottish Health Services Council in 1955, but no contribution to resolving this problem emanated from this source.[199]

In Scotland central controls on staff numbers were relaxed without adverse effects, except in the case of consultants, where in 1956 the Department of Health took over control of all additional consultant appointments.[200] This followed the practice of England and Wales, where a permanent mechanism for central control over additional consultant appointments had been introduced in 1953. With other classes of personnel England followed the Scottish example, delegating responsibility for review and control of hospital establishments to regional boards.[201] Some boards, such as SW Metropolitan, undertook detailed reviews and attempted to fix group establishments on a scientific basis. Others, such as NW Metropolitan, took the view that only management committees could fix establishments efficiently. Accordingly these latter boards merely continued the existing arrangement whereby determination of establishments depended on totals submitted by management committees, which were known to be inflated.[202]

Given the relative stability of the situation, and the strong positive recommendation of the Guillebaud Committee, as well as its own decreasing conviction in the efficacy of the measures introduced in RHB(52)133, the Treasury found it difficult to reject the appeal from the Ministry of Health for abolition of direct controls on establishment numbers. It was felt that the capacity of regional boards to manage establishments would not be tested until direct controls on numbers were removed.[203] However, relatively simple administrative change was delayed repeatedly on the plea of unripeness of time. The circular on manpower control was eventually superseded in June 1959 by HM(59)61.[204]

(ix) CONSULTANTS AND TRAINEES

Consultant services were the pivot upon which the National Health Service turned. Consultants were the elite corps, whose willing participation was regarded by Bevan as fundamental to the image of the NHS as a first class service. Consultants were therefore ushered into the state hospital system on privileged terms. The voluntary teaching hospitals were adopted as the model for the new regime, while the dispiriting ethos of the old municipal hospitals was shunned. Consultants were offered many fresh inducements, without being expected to sacrifice too many of their traditional privileges.

The most attractive feature of the new system to the profession was the high degree of financial security provided, even for those opting for part-time contracts. Thus the financial deterrent which had hitherto prevented consultants from leaving major medical centres was removed. Consultants were free to colonise the tracts of Britain formerly deprived of their services.

A fundamental problem facing the hospital service was determination of both its immediate and optimum requirement for specialists. These questions were closely related to the calculation of norms for bed complements, since consultant establishments were determined on the basis of ratios of staff to beds. The wartime surveys adopted no uniform standard for their estimation of regional bed requirements. The experience of the surveys was distilled into RHB(48)1, 'The Development of Consultant Services', which was reissued with minor amendments in January 1950 as an official publication. This document constituted one of the rare excursions of the Ministry of Health into the arena of idealistic planning. The norms adopted were presented as long-term goals. They were markedly in excess of current levels of provision and except for limited categories such as chronic illness, they were markedly in excess of targets included in the ambitious Hospital Plan of 1962. Consistency with RHB(48)1 would have required the Sheffield region to add 26,000 beds to its existing complement of 16,000. Reference to the more modest estimates of the wartime survey would have required addition of 11,500 beds. In its own review, based on immediate priorities, the Sheffield region adopted 6,000 as its target for additional beds. Even on the most modest estimates the more deprived parts of the region such as Doncaster required a doubling of their hospital resources.[205]

Other hospital authorities performed a similar exercise to that undertaken in the Sheffield region. Their findings were broadly similar. An urgent need existed to expand the hospital service. It was realised that shortage of materials and funds would limit capital development, but there was no such obvious impediment to extension of consultant and specialist services, in anticipation of their further expansion when the hospital building programme was inaugurated.

The NHS therefore began in confident anticipation that consultant services would be rapidly expanded. Regional boards and management committees exploited their powers to initiate ambitious programmes for recruitment of consultants, trainees and full supporting staff. Immediate progress on the consultant front was limited because of the delay in settling terms and conditions of employment for hospital medical staffs. Temporary contracts were extended until December 1949. In the preceding months 'professional committees' in each region graded existing staffs, while other committees worked out the establishments required by the regional hospital service.

The medical career structure laid down in early circulars was complex and during its early history a number of minor alterations and changes in nomenclature were introduced. The new arrangements were broadly based on the existing pattern in the London undergraduate teaching hospitals. The classic career structure for intending specialists involved a pre-registration year as a house officer, followed by a further year as a senior house officer, and then two years as a registrar, prior to a final three-year trainee phase as a senior registrar before promotion to tenured consultant rank.[206] In order to maintain high and uniform status for consultant appointments substantial numbers of existing hospital appointees were excluded from this rank and appointed as Senior Hospital Medical Officers (SHMO), who were essentially inferior consultants. The initial grading in NW Metropolitan region created 788 consultant posts compared with 194 SHMOs. A further grade of Junior Hospital Medical Officer (JHMO) was created as an afterthought for lower-ranking hospital medical staff needed for routine or menial duties. Both the SHMO and JHMO grades proved to be troublesome. Their existence carried the risk that in some specialties a back-door route to becoming a consultant would be created. Also, because of shortages in these same specialties JHMOs were granted extended tenure, so creating a second inferior rank of sub-consultant.[207]

The initial grading exercise caused considerable dissatisfaction among SHMOs, who were granted a once and for all review in 1951 as a result of which a small minority were upgraded. Professional bodies were concerned that this category, originally created to deal with a residuum, would become consolidated into a permanent secondary consultant class, the exploitation of which would result in dilution. Consequently, the Joint Committee extracted agreement that the SHMO grade be limited to the minor specialties. In such reservations the SHMO quickly became established as a basic career grade. SHMOs constituted about 20% of the consultant and specialist workforce in England and Wales, and 30% in Scotland. On the official side the predominant concern related to the early age of appointment of SHMOs. However nothing was done to prevent JHMOs leap-frogging to relatively high salary positions through securing SHMO appointments in their mid-twenties.[208]

The above anomalies, together with dissatisfaction over distinction awards paid to consultants, provoked doubts about the staffing structure initially adopted. The Scottish Department of Health made a strong bid to sweep away the SHMO anomaly by establishing a subsidiary grade of consultant to be known as a 'specialist'. The Department of Health expected that two-thirds of the consultant and specialist workforce would be transferred to this new grade, whereas the Ministry of Health preferred one-quarter. The Scottish proposal also involved organising specialist care on a more hierarchical basis, whereas the English insisted on equality among consultants. In the absence of agreement on basic structural points the Scottish plan was withdrawn.[209] It was not, however, forgotten. As noted below cognate proposals were later introduced in the context of the senior registrar problem.

Initially it was assumed that the consultant career structure would operate like an escalator with trainees being carried smoothly upwards until the minority reaching the end of the complete training programme would graduate to consultant vacancies made available either through retirement or expansion. Substantial recruitment of junior medical staff was undertaken in expectation of unimpeded expansion of the consultant corps. The numbers graduating from medical schools were swollen by demobilised doctors, whose training had been interrupted by the war. Many of them had taken up temporary supernumerary positions created under a special scheme by the Government after the war.

It was soon realised that high recruitment to lower ranks created expectations of huge expansion in consultant numbers. Bevan, as his major concession to mounting pressure for economies in hospital costs, offered a drastic cut-back in the numbers of trainees.[210] The first tightening-up, signified by RHB(50)78, transferred appointment of registrars and senior registrars from management committees to regional boards. The next step was enforced reduction in the number of registrars and senior registrars as a means of limiting expansion of consultant numbers to not more than 150 per annum. The Ministry of Health proposed 950 registrars and 175 third-year senior registrars. The Joint Committee agreed to 1,100 and 225 respectively, making 600 senior registrars in all. These allocations were included in RHB(50)106 (November 1950). In addition to the overall total, each region and each specialty was awarded an allocation of senior registrars. Notwithstanding minor modifications in the numbers involved, this 'training plan' remained intact for the whole of our period with respect to senior registrars.

The above limitations were subversive to regional development plans. For instance the Liverpool region calculated that it required 128 registrars and 71 senior registrars. Under RHB(50)106 it was granted 52 registrars and 28 senior registrars. In response to protests from the teaching hospital and the regional board the allocation of senior registrars was increased to 44.[211] RHB(50)106 became a focus for extreme hostility from both the profession and the hospital authorities. The campaign mounted by the profession to circumvent redundancies of trainees is selected by Eckstein as an example of successful negotiation by the BMA.[212] Significant concessions were introduced. First, in September 1951 the limit on registrars was removed. Registrars were henceforth employed according to the routine staffing needs of the regions. Notwithstanding this reclassification the Ministry of Health refused to return responsibility for appointment of registrars to the management committees. Secondly, in May 1952 for certain minority specialties all senior registrars in post in September 1952 were allowed to complete their full training. Thirdly, in order to create more vacancies existing consultants were retired at 65. Fourthly, a small number of additional consultant posts was created. Fifthly, the training period for senior registrars was extended from three to four years. Finally, in May 1953, senior registrars who had completed four years' training and were unable to obtain consultant appointments, were allowed to occupy special 'transitional posts'.[213] These adjustments relieved the position of 'time-expired senior registrars', although their position remained far from attractive. Officials blamed the profession for having refused to accept more stringent limitations in the training programme, and they blamed the trainees for unwillingness to transfer to less prestigious specialties, less attractive parts of the country or out of hospitals into general practice. An awkward situation emerged in which senior registrars trained predominantly in general medicine and general surgery were faced with openings almost exclusively in fields such as psychiatry, anaesthetics, pathology or radiology. Consequently the few posts in general medicine and general surgery attracted an inundation of applicants, whereas in the shortage areas vacancies went unfilled, or when appointments were made, severe doubts were harboured concerning the quality of the appointees.[214] The mismatch between the products of the training system and the demands of the service was lamented as a reflection of the 'imperfectness of the medico-advisory machinery'.[215]

The training system thus produced excess in some directions and deficiencies in others. Distortions apparent at the top of the pyramid were exaggerated at the bottom, where posts in the less prestigious specialties and the less favoured regions became extremely difficult to fill. These problems forced the already less well-endowed regions to inflate salaries in order to attract routine staff. The erosion of junior hospital staff was also increased by loss to general practice following the advances consequent on the Danckwerts Award, which were only partly compensated for by the hospital award of 1954.

Staffing shortages were evident even in the outlying parts of the metropolitan regions, but they were worse in the north. The Sheffield region found, for instance, that casualty departments in the mining areas were dependent on the services of local general practitioners. In 1953 Sheffield reported overall vacancies in junior establishments of 20% (with 50% in some areas), Leeds 30%, and Newcastle 32%. This problem made such regions dependent on immigrant doctors, mainly from India and Pakistan, most of whom were spending short periods of training in Britain. By 1958 it was estimated that up to 2,500 overseas doctors were working in hospitals in England and Wales.[216]

Details concerning the expansion in consultant numbers are given in Table VII. The base from which this increase took place cannot be ascertained because of uncertainties about the figures for 1948, and because of the difficulty of translating the numbers into whole-time equivalents. One informed estimate suggested that there were about 3,500 whole-time equivalents in 1948, and it was speculated that 7,000 were required to staff the service. This target was not reached until 1958, by which time demands and expectations were considerably higher. As Table VII indicates numbers increased rapidly during the early years of the service. Paradoxically, one of the effects of the economies in junior staff made during 1951 was substitution by more expensive consultant staff in 1952. It was only after the introduction of rigid manpower controls in December 1952 that expansion was pegged to the 150 per annum regarded as the 'right' figure by officials. Although

TABLE VII

Consultant Numbers 1949-1955

1. *England and Wales*	31.12.49	31.12.51	%	31.12.53	%	31.12.55	%	1955/1949 % increase
General Medicine	642	734	14.3	773	5.3	801	3.6	24.8
Diseases of Chest	199	245	23.1	305	24.5	310	0.2	55.8
Mental Health	405	481	18.1	535	11.2	568	0.6	40.2
Neurology	49	55	12.2	60	9.1	63	5.0	28.6
Paediatrics	150	182	21.3	195	7.1	196	0.5	30.7
Radiology	295	358	21.4	389	8.6	414	6.4	40.3
Pathology	453	498	11.0	575	15.5	610	6.9	34.7
General Surgery	792	818	9.9	851	4.0	859	0.9	8.5
Anaesthetics	459	605	10.0	695	14.9	742	6.8	61.7
Neurosurgery	31	36	16.1	40	11.1	44	10.0	41.9
Plastic Surgery	27	30	11.1	39	30.0	46	17.9	70.4
Thoracic Surgery	44	60	36.4	81	35.0	85	4.9	93.2
Orthopaedic Surgery	227	262	5.4	294	12.2	307	4.4	35.2
Obstetrics & Gynaecology	370	389	5.1	411	5.7	426	6.1	15.1
Total Consultants	5,184	5,882	13.5	6,412	9.0	6,650	3.7	28.3
2. (a) England and Wales	4,959	5,649	13.9	6,165	9.1	6,400	3.8	29.1
(b) Scotland	633	707	11.8	780	10.3	844	8.2	33.3
Total Consultants (Britain)	5,592	6,356	13.7	6,945	9.3	7,244	4.3	29.5
3. England and Wales:	4,711	5,582	18.5	6,323	13.3	6,720	6.3	42.6
Consultants and Specialists (whole-time equivalent)	(3037)	(3665)	20.7	(4303)	17.4	(4634)	7.7	52.6

Sources:

DHSS 94112/4/102/1–5, VII, section 1.

Willink Report, p 14, VII, section 2.

Ministry of Health, *Summary 1949–1966* (1967), VII, section 3.

Notes:

1. The numbers of consultants are given for selected specialties. Consultants specialising in more than one area are counted in both. The totals indicate the number of individuals with no double counting.

2. Total numbers of individuals are given for 1 and 2, and whole-time equivalents for 3. This category includes Senior Hospital Medical Officers, who numbered 1,860 in 1949, 2,130 in 1951, 2,245 in 1953, and 2,318 in 1955. They were predominantly full-time. The figure in brackets gives the approximate full-time equivalent level for consultants on the assumption that SHMOs were 90% part-time.

this was regarded as a realistic long-term target, it proved difficult to achieve. In evidence to the Willink Committee the Ministry of Health admitted to 390 new appointments in 1950, 196 in 1951, 300 in 1952, 99 in 1953, 141 in 1954, and 167 in 1955.[217]

The transition to central control in December 1952 resulted in a dramatic, but strictly temporary, reduction in new appointments. By 1957 new consultant appointments had again reached their pre-1953 level. Even a poorly staffed region like Sheffield built up its consultant strength from about 362 in 1948 to 483 in 1952. Before 1953 the pattern of new consultant appointments was determined regionally. The change to central control in 1953 made relatively little difference. The list of 76 new appointments in the Liverpool region between 1948 and 1955 was headed by 14 in psychiatry, 13 in anaesthetics, 8 in general surgery, 8 in obstetrics and gynaecology, 6 in chest diseases, 5 in general medicine, and 4 in orthopaedics.[218] Pathology was the noticeable shortage area not represented, but in Liverpool pathologists were relegated to the SHMO level, 7 appointments being made between 1948 and 1955. Anaesthetics and psychiatry were also prominent in the SHMO lists. Such a pattern supports the trends noted in Table VII, and it also confirms anxieties about the failure of the training system to reflect the changing demands of the service.

Reduction in the level of new consultant appointments was associated with transfer of control, first to the Ministry of Health and then to the newly formed Central Advisory Committee on Consultant Appointments.[219] This severe centralisation was undertaken in response to pressure from the Treasury for rigid control of consultant numbers. In the short term the Advisory Committee exercised little control over the general pattern of the consultant service because it was exclusively concerned with new appointments, which constituted only a small fraction of the total consultant and specialist workforce. As noted in chapter VII this mechanism involved an incursion of the profession into territory formerly controlled by regional boards. The Advisory Committee was therefore more attractive to the Joint Consultants Committee than to the regional boards. At first the regional boards, led by Newcastle, subjected the Advisory Committee to a barrage of destructive criticism. Minor modifications in procedure were introduced, but the urgent requests of the regional boards for direct contact with the Committee were refused. Because of the sharp cut-back in the total number of consultant appointments, the ration for each regional board was at first extremely small, with the consequence that they felt meanly treated.[220] Thus the Liverpool region, which made about 12 additional consultant appointments each year before 1953, was reduced to about two each year there-after. Additional indignation was caused by the tendency of the Advisory Committee to consign to SHMOs services which the regions wanted placing under consultants. Privately officials recognised that the system was not operating fairly and there was sympathy for the idea of introducing regional allocations, but instead a compromise was arranged whereby the applications from each region were considered *en bloc*.[221]

At the outset of the hospital economy drive in 1950 the Ministry of Health initiated its comprehensive review of hospital establishments. Unlike the other reviews, investigation of consultant establishments was realistic, practicable, and also desirable because of the need to standardise development of this key service. The operation was set up with a view to achieving prompt results. Nine teams, each comprising two senior consultants, reviewed regional board consultant establishments, while three consultants examined the teaching hospitals.[222] The regional boards were warned that their establishments would be fixed on the basis of these reviews. Both sides of the review exercise ran into serious difficulties. The regional surveys were so idiosyncratic that they were virtually useless and had to be suppressed. An embarrassed official reported: 'one not in, one lost, two or three fragmentary, one or two not intelligible, one making no recommendations'.[223] In the case of the teaching hospital reviews, the conclusions were submitted to the Boards of Governors for comment, only to be met with an outraged response from individual boards, the Teaching Hospitals Association and the Joint Consultants Committee.[224]

The question of an objective inquiry into consultant services passed temporarily into abeyance, but it soon resurfaced, this time in a confused attempt by the BMA and Joint Consultants Committee to provide a lasting solution to the senior registrar problem. In 1954 and 1955 the Joint Consultants Committee and the Central Consultants and Specialists Committee of the BMA plied the Ministry with documents containing outlines for a new grading structure. For a short time the Joint Committee favoured creation of an inferior rank of consultant, but this option was quickly abandoned in favour of increase in consultant numbers. The Joint Committee argued the case for a new survey persistently and in the face of intransigent official opposition. Both sides anticipated that objective reviews would expose understaffing. This end was desired by the Joint Committee as the solution to the senior registrar problem, while it was feared by officials on account of inevitable cost consequences. It was concluded that, 'Any review of ideal needs on an expansionist basis would be both useless and dangerous'.[225] It was only in 1958, and after direct representations of the Joint Committee to the Minister, that the deadlock was broken and a compromise was reached, which resulted in the formation of a working party under Sir Robert Platt to examine the hospital medical staffing problem. This move deflected energies into the realm of general principles and it temporarily released pressure for direct planning exercises.

Originally the Labour Government wanted whole-time service by consultants to be predominant in the NHS, but part-time contracts were allowed for the small number of consultants retaining an interest in private practice. In response to pressure from the profession the possibility of taking up part-time contracts was left open to all consultants. In the event the terms for part-time consultants were so advantageous that there was little inducement for them to remain in full-time service. The latter became reserved for a small minority of technicians and practitioners of minor specialties. The great majority took up part-time contracts, conferring not only the right to engage in private practice, but also generous relief for travelling time, access to lucrative domiciliary consultations, advantageous income tax treatment, and virtual monopoly of distinction awards. The last constituted such an important social and economic custom among consultants that it deserves further consideration. As a method of remuneration, distinction awards were an anomaly within the public service.[226] This system was particularly exceptional because distribution of the awards was vested in the beneficiaries themselves.

The awards system came into being as part of the Spens agreement concluded with consultants. The rationale for distinction awards was relatively ill-defined. They were regarded variously as compensation for loss of private practice, an inducement to recruitment, a means of attracting consultants away from major teaching centres, or a substitute for honours, equivalent to the FRS awarded to scientists. The awards system was acceptable to Bevan because it gratified the leadership of the profession. It was not uncongenial to the Ministry of Health because it offered a device for evading a generally applied salary scale with a high ceiling. Payment of 'C' awards worth £500 to 20%, 'B' awards worth £1,500 to 10%, and 'A' awards worth £2,500 to 4% of consultants, was an economical way of rewarding seniority. The awards system suited consultants because it was consistent with the long tradition of the scramble for 'glittering prizes' by which esteem was measured in their profession. The part-time consultants, who expected to monopolise the highest awards, were accordingly guaranteed high earnings from public service without prejudicing their chances of exploiting whatever remained of private practice. During their long and arduous training, junior medical staff were consoled by the distant lure of distinction awards.

The architect of the awards system was Lord Moran, who then presided over the awards committee. The place of this committee in the advisory machinery of the health departments has already been discussed. The committee and its Scottish sub-committee conducted a regular routine of consultations with professional and regional bodies. Despite the complexity of the consultative process and the authority of his committee, Moran seems to have dominated events. He reduced the meetings of the committee to a minimum, and cut back on the circulated papers, preferring for instance to furnish the committee with summary short-lists rather than complete lists and fuller particulars.[227] Moran's own prejudices intervened at both the general and the particular level. For instance Moran's limited regard for such fields as psychiatry or anaesthetics contributed to their under-representation in the awards.[228] Moran also resisted departure from the absolute confidentiality under which the system was established. Moran believed that publication even of statistical information would provide 'ammunition for mischief makers'.[229] It was particularly emphasised that publicity concerning individual awards would undermine public confidence in equality of standards of treatment. The first limited statistical information about distribution of awards between specialties was not made available until 1958, in response to a parliamentary question from Kenneth Robinson.[230] Notwithstanding objections from Moran to the publication of regional, specialty, or RHB-teaching hospital breakdown, slightly fuller statistical information was included in the Report of the Royal Commission on Doctors' and Dentists' Remuneration.[231] Consequently the only thing known about the operation of the system before 1958 was the total number of awards made annually in the three price categories.

The Spens Committee recommended roughly equal specialty and geographical distribution to provide the proper incentives to equalisation. Scotland was granted 34% of the awards, but the committee opposed regional quotas on the grounds that the criterion of merit should be strictly applied. The committee finally agreed to restrict the use of rough quotas to 'C' awards.[232]

Consultants employed by London teaching hospitals received the largest share of awards; those working for provincial regional boards the least.[233] Initially there were substantial differences between provincial teaching hospitals, and between provincial regions. The best rewarded provincial region was Oxford, where 39.1% received awards. The lowest was Newcastle with 26.4%; E Anglia was only slightly higher with 27.4%. A large London teaching hospital held as many awards as a medium provincial region. Guy's possessed as many 'A' awards as the Newcastle, Leeds and Sheffield regions together. Differences between the provincial regions had narrowed down by 1956, but the essential disparities were still present. The patterns tended to persist, with Oxford and the metropolitan boards faring well, and with E Anglia and the northern regions doing badly.

The most obvious differences related to distribution between the specialties. In 1949 the best rewarded was neurology with 71.4% of incumbents receiving awards. Large specialties such as general medicine received 46.6% and general surgery 44.9%. At the other end of the scale pathology received 28.0%, psychiatry 19.5% and anaesthetics 15.9%. In 1955 the order was similar, with neurology receiving 73.0%, general medicine 55.6%, general surgery 51.1%, pathology 27.7%, psychiatry 15.8% and anaesthetics 13.5%. Ten years later the position was very little different. If anything the percentage share of the less prestigious specialties marginally declined.

Notwithstanding the prevalent view in the Ministry of Health that there was no escape from distinction awards because of their association with the Spens agreement, the awards system was subjected to a barrage of criticism on account of its secrecy, because of alleged discrimination against certain specialties, because of geographical inequalities, and because of the implied hierarchy of hospital types. Others argued that distinction awards were unsound in principle, because they discriminated against full-time consultants, medical research and university teaching personnel. The Scottish Department of Health only agreed to participate in the scheme on the understanding that it would soon be superseded by a new career structure for specialists and consultants. Distinction awards came under attack from Gaitskell and the Labour NHS Cabinet Committee, from Willink the Conservative former Minister of Health, and persistently from Sir Harold Himsworth, the Secretary of the MRC.[234] It was anticipated that the Royal Commission on Doctors' and Dentists' Remuneration would suggest sweeping changes in the awards system. In the Treasury view distinction awards should be abolished as a 'blot on the landscape' of public finance.[235] The Scottish Department of Health suggested abolition of 'C' and 'B' awards, with substitution of payments attached to particular posts. The MRC pressed for extension of awards to medical research workers. The Ministry of Health wanted the status quo. Reluctantly the Treasury withdrew its opposition on the grounds that the awards system offered the cheapest means of granting a pay increase, and because of support for this system among the 'big battalions' of the profession. It was accepted that 'arguments of expediency outweigh those of principle'.[236] Accordingly, notwithstanding criticism of the awards system and a poor defence from Moran, the Commission ratified and strengthened the existing system. Uneven distribution of awards between specialties was not regarded as an inexcusable anomaly.

The only concession to the critics was a request for regular publication of basic statistical data.[237] Discussions of distinction awards conducted in the context of the Royal Commission show that some of the original purposes of the awards system had been lost from sight. By 1957 the awards were primarily viewed as a means of rewarding the elite of the profession. The Spens Committee idea that they might be used as an inducement for consultants to serve in unpopular areas, or in less prestigious specialties, was not emphasised. Indeed, it could be argued that the workings of the system had induced precisely opposite effects. Although secrecy disguised the true picture, popular mythology within the profession recognised that the chances of earning distinction awards fell away sharply for those vacating the major teaching centres, or opting for the less prestigious specialties.

(x) SPECIAL SERVICES

Public Health Laboratory Service

Formation of a national bacteriological service was a response to the threat of bacteriological warfare. The Emergency Public Health Laboratory Service, formed at the outset of World War II, constituted a network of bacteriological laboratories which were administered by MRC on behalf of the Ministry of Health. In 1944 it was agreed that this service, designed to 'assist in the diagnosis, control and prevention of infectious diseases', should be continued as a national service after the war. Provision for the Public Health Laboratory Service was contained in section 17 of the 1946 NHS Act. The MRC agreed to continue to administer the PHLS on behalf of the Ministry of Health, detailed administration being handled by a PHLS Board under the chairmanship of the Second Secretary of the MRC.[228]

The PHLS initially consisted of a central laboratory at Colindale in London, five regional laboratories, about 40 'constituent laboratories', and various other laboratories conducting work on an agency basis. Under the NHS this network was extended and new functions such as virology were taken on. By 1955 the PHLS was employing about 1,000 staff, 125 of whom were medically qualified, while 250 were laboratory technicians. The PHLS was reasonably well treated financially. Between 1949/50 and 1956/57 its allocation increased by 59%, which was higher than for the hospital service as a whole.[239] The ideal arrangement envisaged involved siting regional public health laboratories, as well as regional blood transfusion laboratories, in close proximity to teaching hospital pathology services. Active collaboration between these laboratories was anticipated.

Notwithstanding eagerness for co-operation importance was attached to the independence of the PHLS. Basic to the philosophy of the PHLS was the view that public health bacteriology was fundamentally different from parallel clinical pathology services developed by regional hospital authorities. 'Public health bacteriology differs in several respects from hospital pathology, both in its origin and in its functions. Public health bacteriology arose as a direct outcome of the work of the great sanitary reformers of the last century on the control of diseases engendered by filth, poverty and overcrowding. From the beginning it was closely linked with epidemiology, and then, as now, its purpose was mainly preventive. Clinical pathology, on the other hand, arose as a hand-maid to the clinician in the hospital for the diagnosis and treatment of the individual patient'.[240] The PHLS accordingly looked outward to the community and provided services for the MOH and others faced with problems of environmental origin.

Regardless of this principle, the problems of staff and accommodation shortage caused hospital and public health laboratory facilities to be telescoped together in some areas. Also, in Scotland, under section 3 of the 1947 NHS Act, hospital pathology and public health laboratory services were integrated and administered by the Regional Hospital Boards, with a joint committee on laboratory services advising on policy. In the most populated regions the laboratory services were largely delegated to the Boards of Management.[241] It was accepted that the laboratory service in Scotland had 'lagged considerably behind that of England', owing to neglect by hospital authorities.[242] Nevertheless, the committee set up in 1956 to review this problem recommended continuation of the integrated arrangement. Responding to pressures from the Treasury for economies, the Ministry of Health reviewed the PHLS. Following the recommendations of MRC, it was concluded that the service should remain nationally organised and independent of the hospital laboratory service.[243] Continuation of the existing administrative arrangement was accepted by both the Ministry and MRC. The latter was pessimistic about prospects for the PHLS if it were transferred to the Ministry and its hospital boards.[244]

Although MRC agency continued until 1960, the permanent viability of this arrangement was undermined in 1954.[245] The essential cause of disruption was the 1954 pay award to hospital staffs. As noted in chapter VI, the increase involved was modest compared with the Danckwerts award to general practitioners, but it increased the differential between clinicians and research workers, and it perpetuated distinction awards, which were only available to clinicians. In 1949 it was agreed to remunerate public health bacteriologists on the same basis as hospital pathologists. Clinicians on the PHLS staff were therefore paid at clinicians' rates and they were eligible for distinction awards, with the result that a major differential was created between PHLS clinicians and comparable MRC grades. Indignation caused by this discrimination echoed through the ranks of the MRC and it precipitated a demand for a change in the agency arrangement. The MRC worked up some additional arguments justifying change, suggesting that the PHLS was more a routine than a research function, and pointing to the underfunding of the service consequent on Ministry control. However the intensity of the demand for change was largely due to the salary issue. With a view to securing maximum continuity, Sir Landsborough Thomson suggested that the PHLS Board should be incorporated under the Companies' Act. The new board would then become the employer, but the MRC could continue to administer the service and to give scientific direction.

This simple adjustment proved difficult to accomplish. Between September 1954 and the summer of 1958 elaborate tripartite discussions between the Ministry, MRC and the Treasury considered ways of resolving the MRC dilemma over the Public Health Laboratory Service. Maintenance of the status quo was the most favoured alternative, but this was ruled out when the Royal Commission on Doctors' and Dentists' Remuneration failed to reform the distinction awards system. A second means to preserve the MRC arrangement involved regrading PHLS staff to remove their rights to clinical salaries, but changing the terms agreed in 1949 was held to be unrealistic. Adoption of the Scottish form of administration was ruled out for reasons stated in the 1951 review. Various hybrid solutions were also abandoned on account of their complexity. Direct transfer of the PHLS Board to the Ministry of Health was at first ruled out because it involved a nominal increase in the size of the civil service at a time when the Government was committed to a reduction. There was an additional fear that the superior earnings of senior PHLS staff would lead to pay demands among other civil servants. Thus after going round in circles, the negotiators were left with Thomson's original suggestion, which was itself liable to objection on account of the undesirability of proliferating independent government-financed bodies, and because it was liable to be more expensive than the other solutions. However, one particular advantage of the incorporated Board was avoidance of legislation. By the time the departments were agreed on action, Government sensitivities over increases in the civil service were reduced, with the result that it was agreed to proceed on the lines of the more straightforward solution involving reconstitution of the PHLS Board under the Ministry of Health. Legislation to this effect was introduced in December 1959.

Blood Transfusion Service

Pre-war blood transfusion services were very small-scale enterprises, confined to major centres. They were almost exclusively concerned with maintaining lists of volunteer blood donors. The wartime Emergency Blood Transfusion Service transformed the scale of this operation and it established a modern framework for the collection and storage of blood, and for the preparation of blood products. The need to continue the service after the war was universally accepted. At a meeting of the senior regional advisers involved in the service, held in March 1945, the Chief Medical Officer recommended that the Blood Transfusion Service should be retained in its current form. He stressed the need for regional organisation of blood collection, and co-operation with university laboratories and with the national processing centres. For logistical reasons and because of the need to maintain advanced and uniform technical standards, Jameson conceded that national organisation should be retained. The blood transfusion service established under the NHS was organised on the same regional basis as the hospital system. The transfusion service was well-adjusted for the transition because its organisation followed the Civil Defence regional pattern. The English and Welsh Civil Defence regions were readily adapted to the Regional Hospital Board arrangement, especially because Civil Defence region 10 was already divided into Liverpool and Manchester sectors for blood transfusion purposes. The only departure from the hospital regions occurred in London, where one centre served the two hospital regions to the north of the Thames, while another served the two regions to the south. In Scotland the blood transfusion service organisation fitted in with the five regional hospital divisions.[246]

The sister Public Health Laboratory Service was regionally distributed, but it was not organised into regional units. Consequently its links with the regional boards were more distant. On the other hand the regional boards were responsible for the routine administration of the Blood Transfusion Service, a proximity which resulted in occasional difficulties over the relative responsibilities of regional secretaries and the medical directors of the regional blood transfusion centres.[247] The centres themselves were responsible for a variety of functions, including obtaining a supply of blood from donors, mobile teams, supply and maintenance of transfusion apparatus, hospital blood stores, typing, special preparation such as concentration and washing of red cells, investigation of specimens, research and education.[248] The regional centres were linked to the Blood Plasma Drying Plant and the Blood Group Reference Laboratory, both associated with the Lister Institute in London.

The most obvious characteristic of the blood transfusion service was its growth. For instance, in Scotland the quantity of blood supplied increased from 36,000 bottles per annum in 1949 to 111,000 bottles in 1956.[249] In England and Wales the number of donations of blood rose from 457,000 in 1949 to 803,500 in 1956.[250] The costs of the early service are difficult to ascertain, but in England and Wales costs increased from £1m in 1954/55 to £1.4m in 1957/58.[251] These developments reflect a general increase in demand for blood and blood products occasioned by new trends in surgery. This increase in volume of work was associated with modernisation and extension of facilities, as well as new building. Some of the expansion in the service was permitted for civil defence purposes.[252]

As noted above, one of the reasons for organising the blood transfusion service on a national basis was to ensure that the most advanced technical standards were observed. Indeed, the regional directors met regularly to discuss administrative and technical problems. At an early stage they produced a model scheme for a regional blood transfusion centre which was quietly suppressed on account of its 'idealistic' character.[253] Not all of their initiatives demonstrated efficiency and common purpose. For instance, the attempt to introduce improved blood transfusion apparatus represented a notable false start. Discussions began in 1950 with maximum standardisation being a major objective. Progress towards a solution was slow, and regions varied in their enthusiasm for the improved apparatus. The exercise was also undermined by serious defects in the new 'sets' introduced in 1952. Before the teething troubles were over, it had become clear that the glass and rubber equipment introduced was rapidly becoming obsolete because of the superior qualities of disposable plastic sets. Although discussions started in 1954, trials with plastic sets were not begun until 1956. Largely because of Treasury anxieties concerning the additional cost of plastic equipment, its introduction was delayed until 1958.[254]

A further difficulty experienced within the Blood Transfusion Service, which reflected a problem of the hospital service as a whole, was shortage of student and junior technical staff. By 1955 this problem was affecting many regions, especially in the midlands and the north, and it was threatening maintenance of standards.

Because work in blood transfusion placed students at a disadvantage in the intermediate examination of the Institute of Medical Laboratory Technicians, they tended to be deflected into general pathology laboratories, where their prospects of success were greater. Dramatic solutions were considered, such as creating a new professional organisation and separate examinations specifically for blood transfusion technicians. But in the event, long and tortuous discussions with the Institute of Medical Laboratory Technicians resulted in minor modifications to the existing examinations. This amelioration, together with improved pay resulting from a Whitley award, produced sufficient improvement for the crisis to be overcome.[255]

Tuberculosis Service
As noted in chapter I, between 1911 and World War II local authorities established the foundations of a comprehensive tuberculosis service. Tuberculosis was a major cause of death, a source of deep public concern, and a high priority area in the field of public health. The 30,000 beds in tuberculosis hospitals signify the importance attached to the tuberculosis service. World War II constituted a serious set-back to the institutional system. Many beds were lost owing to appropriation for military use, or shortage of nurses.

In 1947 deaths from respiratory tuberculosis amounted to 55 per 100,000 in England and Wales, and 80 per 100,000 in Scotland. Although the already established trend towards remission of the disease continued, the number of notifications increased, with the consequence that hospital waiting lists reached embarrassing proportions.

The importance of tuberculosis was therefore still sufficient for it to claim major attention from the planners.[256] Earlier plans for the NHS would have permitted continuation of an integrated tuberculosis service under local authorities. Under the NHS tripartite structure existing services were split between Regional Hospital Boards and Local Health Authorities. Nevertheless it was urged that chest physicians, the 'medical specialists responsible for the treatment of tuberculosis may be closely and directly concerned alike with diagnostic and curative work under the Board and with prevention and care work under the Local Health Authority'.[257] Experts in the field were by no means satisfied that the new service would give sufficient emphasis to preventive and after-care work. It was urged that the arrangement whereby chest physicians were remunerated 8/11ths by the regional board, and only 3/11ths at a lower administrative rate by Local Health Authorities, would result in neglect of preventive work. Thereby recruitment would be impeded.[258] Inferior remuneration identified the chest physician as a second-class citizen, even compared with officers engaged in blood transfusion or public health bacteriology. Critics such as the Welsh National Memorial Association, the Joint Tuberculosis Council and the Society of Medical Officers of Health, attached high importance to retaining an integrated service.[259] However in 1948 the main parts of the service, hospitals, sanatoria, village settlements, dispensaries and mobile X-radiography units, were transferred to the regional boards, while residual functions were left with Medical Officers of Health.

Continuing development of an integrated tuberculosis service was to some extent dependent on the Tuberculosis Standing Advisory Committee at the centre, and liaison arrangements between regional boards and local authorities at the periphery. Neither worked particularly well. After an initial burst of activity the Standing Advisory Committee became a dead letter. Most regional boards pressed ahead with their own services with very little reference to the local authorities. A review conducted for the Standing Advisory Committee in 1949 asserted that chest physicians were neglecting the local authority side of their work, that liaison was poor, that there was vagueness over the distribution of functions, and that the service was suffering from lack of positive direction.[260] Experts in the field noted continuing reliance on surgical treatment and they detected a general inertia within the service.[261]

Superficial examination suggests that the NHS marked a fundamental turning-point in the treatment of tuberculosis. During the early days of the NHS, quality controls were imposed on milk, miniature mass radiography was introduced on an extensive scale, BCG vaccination was made available, streptomycin and other forms of chemotherapy were applied, and research initiatives such as the MRC tuberculin test survey were undertaken. Furthermore the tuberculous benefited from general improvements in the hospital and consultant service such as the general expansion and modernisation of radiology and pathology departments. Typically, in the Liverpool region examinations in X-ray departments increased from 382,000 in 1950 to 937,000 in 1955, while specimens examined in pathology laboratories increased from 0.55m in 1950 to 2.1m in 1955.[262]

However there is some reason to doubt the appropriateness of medical intervention. As Bryder demonstrates Britain fell behind western neighbours in exploitation of BCG vaccination and chemotherapy. Consequently over-reliance on thoracic surgery and traditional sanatorium treatment largely wasted the advantages gained through extension of mass radiography. Committees appointed by the profession to examine the state of the tuberculosis service pressed for major improvement. One of these committees described the problem as a 'national scandal'.[263] In Scotland BCG vaccination was introduced in 1950. By the end of 1956 about 200,000 persons had been vaccinated.[264] In England and Wales BCG vaccine was first made available for contacts of those suffering from tuberculosis, such as nurses and medical students (circular 72/49). In 1953 vaccination was conceded for secondary pupils (circular 22/53), but the general guidance given on prevention stressed co-ordination more than vaccination (circular 8/54). By the end of 1954 only 250,000 persons had been vaccinated, while only 88 LHAs had taken up the option of vaccinating school children. By the end of 1956 600,000 persons had been vaccinated (about half of them being school children) and 120 LHAs were involved. In 1956 the first notification (circular 14/56) of the successful outcome of an MRC trial on vaccination of school children breathed new life into the lethargic vaccination campaign.[265]

Prevailing fashions in treatment created maximum pressure on beds, at a time when the service had not recovered completely from the wartime emergency. Thus in 1948 3,500 beds in England and Wales and 500 in Scotland were closed for want of nurses. The waiting list in England and Wales was 9,000. By December 1949 4,400 beds were closed and English and Welsh waiting lists had increased to 10,000. Although, as noted above, tuberculosis deaths were declining, the number of notifications continued to rise owing to more effective early diagnosis.[266]

It was pointed out that means to ease the bed shortage included reversing the tendency for more lengthy sanatorium treatment, making more accurate early diagnoses, more effective exploitation of domiciliary care, and reduction in surgical treatment.[267] The solutions adopted concentrated on bed provision, by gaining access to additional beds in teaching or general hospitals,[268] or by seconding student nurses from teaching hospitals to tuberculosis sanatoria. The latter suggestion, emanating from the Nursing SAC, was accepted by the CHSC only after active opposition from teaching hospital members.[269] The NW Metropolitan board was one of the few to organise an effective secondment scheme.[270]

Prior to the NHS, local authorities were allowed to send tuberculosis patients for treatment in Swiss sanatoria. This idea seemed relevant to the difficulties of the NHS tuberculosis service because the Swiss sanatoria had considerable spare capacity. Bevan was closely questioned by Arthur Greenwood on the possibility of use of Swiss sanatoria by NHS patients. Bevan responded that the NHS legislation gave no equivalent powers to hospital authorities, and he was distinctly unhelpful. [271] The plight of tuberculosis sufferers touched the conscience of the public. The Swiss sanatorium idea caught the popular imagination as an appropriate solution to this tragic problem.[272] The theme was taken up in the popular and professional press.[273]

Experiencing an even more serious shortage of tuberculosis beds in the industrial regions of Scotland than in England, McNeil appealed to Cripps for additional funds to support Swiss sanatorium treatment, but Cripps was unwilling to release extra resources for this purpose, or even to allow a scheme within the present budgetary ceiling. However, as noted in chapter V, Gaitskell's mind was changed when it emerged that the Swiss sanatorium scheme could soften the blow of the 1951 health charges.[274] The £400,000 per annum made available was divided equally between the two health services north and south of the border.

Swiss sanatorium treatment was at first heralded as a great humanitarian gesture, but it was administratively inconvenient, while the medical results were unimpressive and even suspect.[275] Furthermore, from a public relations point of view it was disastrous. At first the health departments were inundated with letters from the families of sufferers who were not selected for the Swiss sanatoria.[276] Later the press took up reports of the miserable condition of the sanatorium patients.[277] By this stage the home waiting lists had been considerably reduced. Consequently the Swiss sanatorium experiment was quietly closed down.[278] In total 1,043 Scottish patients and 1,025 English patients were treated in Switzerland.[279] The size of the scheme and consequently its cost were considerably less than was originally envisaged.

By 1955 there was a surplus of tuberculosis beds in Scotland, and in the following year the waiting list had been virtually eliminated in England and Wales. The UK mortality rate had declined by 73% between 1948 and 1956, from 440 per million to 109 per million. However there was no ground for complacency because of the continuing high incidence of notifications, which were still above 30,000 in 1956. Mass radiography consequently remained an important service. The use of miniature mass radiography for civilian purposes was slow to develop in Britain. It was introduced in England and Wales in 1943, and in 1944 in Scotland. When the NHS was established mass radiography units were taken over from 21 local authorities in England and Wales.[280] By 1954 70 units were operating in England and Wales, and 10 in Scotland. In the Sheffield region the number of miniature film examinations increased from 190,000 in 1950 to 357,000 in 1957.[281] Increasingly the service concentrated on campaigns in particularly exposed areas such as Liverpool or Glasgow, where especially notable and intensive efforts involving collaboration between hospital and Local Health Authorities were undertaken.[282] The success of this work promoted continuing attention to improvement in technique. By the mid-50s a clear trend had developed towards the use of static units and 100m film.[283]

Mass-radiography was increasingly involved with screening for conditions other than tuberculosis, in particular industrial lung diseases and lung cancer. Chest physicians gradually became diverted towards these latter conditions. Local investigations revealed unexpectedly high levels in the incidence of pneumoconiosis among men and tuberculosis among women. An investigation into the community of Rhondda Fach revealed levels of lung disease which officials found 'very disturbing', and it also showed how few, even among the miners had previously been X-rayed.[284] Screening for tuberculosis also became materially relevant to checking the state of health of the increasing immigrant population. Unsuccessful attempts were made to follow the procedure in other countries whereby immigrants were screened for tuberculosis on entry.

Mass radiography was merely one aspect of the expansion of radiological facilities. It has already been noted that expansion of X-ray departments was one of the most conspicuous manifestations of modernisation in the early NHS. As in the case of the laboratory and blood transfusion services the expansion of radiological facilities was soon threatened by a shortage of technicians.[285] At one stage frustration over the shortage caused the Sheffield RHB to break ranks with other regions, and infringe Whitley agreements, by paying preferential rates for overtime to its radiographers.[286] The number of radiographers required by the NHS was 3,600, but only 3,000 were in service in the late 50s. The worst hit authorities experienced a 25% staff shortage. Although the number of students increased slightly, it was not enough to meet the deficit. Students spent two years studying at professionally-approved schools maintained by the hospital authorities. In 1957 it was reported that schools in the midlands and north were operating at 50% capacity.[287]

This problem was converted into a crisis by the decision in 1954 of the Ministry of Education to cease payment of grants to radiographers and other medical auxiliaries, on the grounds that they were receiving 'training' rather than 'education'. It was difficult for the Ministry of Health to resist the argument that radiographers were receiving a training similar to that of nurses. The most obvious solution was to pay student radiographers a training allowance similar to that given to student nurses. However this proposal ran into two difficulties. First, the Treasury opposed it on account of its adding to the number of civil servants, and secondly it flew in the face of the Cope Committee recommendations concerning the training of medical auxiliaries. Accordingly the Ministry of Health reluctantly took over the burden of bursaries from the LEAs and in 1957, at first on an emergency basis, bursaries were paid to student radiographers. While not sufficient to solve the problem of staffing this prevented further erosion in the ranks of the radiographers.[288]

(xi) MENTAL DISORDER AND MENTAL HANDICAP

Although, following the recommendations of the 1926 Report of the Royal Commission on Lunacy, it was generally accepted that the 'treatment of mental illness should approximate as nearly to the treatment of physical ailments' as possible, remarkably little was done to achieve integration between the mental and non-mental hospital services. When plans for a National Health Service were first formulated it was assumed that the general and mental health services would not be integrated organisationally, but that they would develop in tandem. Continued separation was justified on grounds of the vast scale and characteristic identity of mental and mental deficiency institutions, the positive advantages of separate development, and the difficulties of achieving integration before full reform of the law relating to mental and mental deficiency patients. In the light of these apparently compelling arguments emanating from the authoritative Board of Control the mental sector was left out of the wartime surveys of hospital resources and the first drafts of plans for hospital reorganisation.[289]

The attitude of the Board of Control was by no means complacent or negative. Defects of the existing system were recognised, but it was firmly held that reorganisation of the mental health services could not be undertaken without extensive revision of the law relating to lunacy and mental deficiency. The chairman of the Board advised that no Government could undertake such revision without the sanction of a Royal Commission.[290] The Ministry of Health therefore agreed that the mental sector should be left out of their deliberations concerning national hospital co-ordination, and the same line was taken when the first plans for a comprehensive health service were devised.[291] There was in fact only a minor measure of disagreement on the future of the service among specialist bodies concerned with mental health. All ostensibly favoured moves towards integration, with the mental sector retaining some kind of separate identity. The Board of Control and the Mental Hospitals Association wanted approximation, ie maintenance of the existing separate system of administration, while the BMA Mental Health Committee and the Department of Health for Scotland (on the authority of the Cathcart Committee) argued that improvement of the service would not come about without administrative integration with the National Health Service.[292]

It was not until the summer of 1943 that the Board of Control relinquished its argument concerning the prerequisite for a Royal Commission and wholesale revision of the law. It was conceded that the Board of Control would preserve its identity, while entering into closer association with the Ministry of Health and that the interests of the mental health services locally would be protected by the creation of strong Mental Health Committees at the local authority level.[293] Consequently, at the eleventh hour the draft White Paper was modified to include the mental health services.

After the 1944 White Paper the Board of Control answered critics of integration by recounting the arguments in favour of ending 'isolation' of the mental sector and achieving full functional 'integration' with other parts of the health service. It was hoped for instance that there would be full interchangeability of medical and nursing staffs in the general and mental sectors, redistribution of hospital resources to cater for the special needs of disadvantaged groups, and integration between hospital and community services. Amalgamating all services under local authority joint boards, as proposed by the 1944 White Paper, was regarded as an important step towards unification of mental and mental deficiency services, which were currently scattered between Visiting Committees, Mental Deficiency Committees, Public Assistance Committees and Local Education Authorities.

Under this new arrangement the Board of Control anticipated that the consolidated mental health services would retain their identity, with supervision being exercised by a separate Mental Health Services Committee and a Medical Director of Mental Health Services. As in the case of the Board of Control at the centre it was argued that continuing judicial functions rendered it necessary to preserve the identity of mental health organisation at the periphery.[294]

Administrative separation of the hospital and local authority health services under the 1946 and 1947 NHS legislation precluded unified local administration of mental health services. Responsibilities were divided between new hospital authorities and Local Health Authorities. The Regional Hospital Boards superseded a medley of pre-existing arrangements for mental and mental deficiency hospital administration. In Scotland the RHBs took over the voluntary Royal Mental Asylums, each of which had been managed independently. But the majority of mental hospitals were derived from the public sector. The traditional model for mental hospital administration involved local authorities delegating control to semi-autonomous Visiting Committees responsible for single institutions, but the Lancashire and West Riding Asylums Boards, which were joint boards, administered all the mental hospitals in their areas. The most modern arrangement existed in the LCC, Middlesex and Surrey, where mental health services were delegated to a committee of each county council.

Mental deficiency services were more recent and more uniform in character. The RHBs took over institutions administered by local authority Mental Deficiency Committees, while Local Health Authorities became responsible for ascertainment and after-care. The scale of the problem taken on by the new hospital authorities was formidable. In 1946 there were 147,000 mental patients, and 53,000 mental deficiency patients under institutional care, as well as 47,000 ascertained in the community, about 5,000 of whom awaited admission to an institution. It was thought that a further 100,000 mental defectives in the community required some kind of care. These numbers were swollen by the inmates of Poor Law institutions, 'when the Workhouses are abolished, questions will arise as to the disposal of patients detained in them under Sections 24 and 25, as well as to the disposal of the nondescript medley of uncertified but mentally enfeebled persons now usually to be found in them'. It was calculated that workhouses contained 10,000 persons of unsound mind, 10,000 mental defectives, and a much greater number of enfeebled elderly.[295]

Hospitals housing mental patients were unsuited to modern hospital purposes. They were old, geographically isolated, and often too large. The 'desirable maximum' number of beds in a mental hospital was given as 1,000, yet the Leeds and Manchester RHBs between them had seven mental hospitals with more than two thousand patients, while the SW Metropolitan RHB had seven institutions of this size.[296] Sixty-seven of the 140 mental hospitals housed more than 1,000 patients. In Scotland the institutions were smaller. Six of the seven institutions with over 1,000 patients were concentrated in the Western RHB area.

The problems of the mental and mental deficiency sector had been made worse by World War II, when 35,000 beds had been requisitioned for EMS purposes.[297] As noted below, the ejected patients risked becoming displaced persons. In the London area many mental hospitals suffered bomb damage. There were long delays before accommodation was restored to its former use, thus adding to an already serious problem of overcrowding. Even when requisitioned property was returned, the hospital authorities often lacked the finance or nursing staff to be able to restore services.[298]

The first tallies of institutional services confirmed initial impressions that facilities were overstrained. It was recommended that beds should be provided at the level of 3.5 – 4.0 per 1000 population (mental), and 2.0 per 1000 (mental deficiency).[299] At the end of 1948 nine RHBs fell below 4 per 1000 for the two sectors combined, the lowest being Newcastle and Sheffield.[300] The first detailed review, giving the position at the beginning of 1952, showed that the provision had improved only slightly. Virtually all regions experienced a substantial overcrowding problem. In mental hospitals only 1,000 beds had been added since the start of the service; seven regions contributed no new beds. The Manchester and Liverpool regions, despite overcrowding (eg Liverpool, 41% on the male, and 42% on the female side in mental deficiency institutions), had provided no additional mental or mental deficiency beds since 1948. It was confirmed that endemic staff shortages were exacerbating the problem of overcrowding and long waiting lists.[301] Data provided for the Guillebaud Committee suggested that a marginal improvement had taken place. The average bed provision for the English regions had increased from 4.5 per 1000 in December 1948 to 4.7 per 1000 in December 1953, the Scottish average in December 1953 being 5.5.[302] Newcastle and Sheffield remained the worst provided regions, with levels below 4.0. These two regions were also among the three worst in 1964, by which stage bed provision had declined to near its 1949 level.[303]

During the early years of the Service shortage of accommodation for mental and mental deficiency patients was one of the major recurrent problems faced by hospital authorities. Relaxation of pressure owing to reduction in the average length of stay of younger mental patients was offset by rapid increase in voluntary admissions and by the growth of the psychogeriatric population. Regions argued that their beds were blocked by large numbers of patients evacuated during the war, who had not been accepted back by their places of origin. This problem generated much friction and mutual recrimination. At one stage about half the RHBs were demanding ministerial intervention to relieve them of this burden.[304]

As early as 1949 officials predicted that the boards would be confronted by breakdown of their services. Alarm among RHB chairmen prompted a national review of the service in 1952. As predicted the findings were depressing. Officials expressed relief that there was a major 'discrepancy between the size of the problem and the public awareness of it'. On behalf of the RHB chairmen Schuster demanded a radical solution. Officials responded that they were impotent to initiate a decisive improvement without a change in Government policy. It was explained that 'what we need is more money, more buildings, more steel and more staff — none of which seems likely to be available'.[305] Very little improvement had occurred by 1956. A Treasury official admitted that conditions in some institutions were 'little short of a public scandal' and that Macleod had regarded under-development of the mental sector as his 'most difficult problem'.[306] By this stage greater attention was being paid to this question in view of signs of disquiet from among MPs, especially Kenneth Robinson, a future Minister of Health, at that time chairman of the Mental Health Committee of the NW Metropolitan RHB.

At the initial meeting of RHB chairmen Bevan urged 'blending' or 'integrating' the mental and general hospital services.[307] It was still unclear whether the mental sector would benefit by reorganisation. There was certainly a danger of drifting into a worst of both worlds situation, with the mental services remaining isolated, and not deriving benefits from integration, while possibly suffering penalties through being deprived of their proper share of resources. This latter possibility quickly became apparent when regional schemes for reorganising hospital accommodation involved detachment of better mental hospital accommodation and its appropriation to other uses. The boards were reminded that accommodation designated under the Lunacy and Mental Treatment Acts could not be diverted without express consent of the Minister.[308] Such ministerial intervention could only be evoked under exceptional circumstances. Given the administrative structure of the service it was difficult to ensure that the vast mental sector would be able to derive benefits proportionate to its needs.

Administrative devices at the regional and local level designed to protect the interests of the mental sector included appointment of Regional Mental Health Committees, Regional Psychiatrists, and the separate grouping of mental and mental deficiency hospitals.

No statutory provision was made for the establishment of Regional Mental Health Committees or for the appointment of Regional Psychiatrists. However this course was strongly advocated in circulars RHB(47)1 and 13. The Ministry of Health was unwilling to impose a rigid structural framework on RHBs. Division 8 was reassured that RHBs were unlikely to depart from model schemes for administration proposed in major circulars.[309] In the event, the RHBs, with their characteristic show of independence, proposed a variety of methods for organising their committees.[310] At an initial discussion only two chairmen supported the arrangement for Mental Health Committees proposed in the circulars. Only a minority of regions were persuaded to follow the approved pattern. Division 8 urged the appointment of mental health services committees having high status and containing co-opted experts in the field.[311] In practice these committees lacked the standing demanded by Division 8. The mental services committees were lost among the welter of sub-committees of standing committees of the RHBs, ranking with sub-committees dealing with problems such as hospital pharmacy or laundry services.

Division 8 was also frustrated in its attempts to establish a full-time Regional Psychiatrist of approximately equal rank to the SAMO. The Negotiating Committee of the profession and the Board of Control were agreed that a full-time 'Medical Director of Mental Health' was required for purposes of planning, and for co-ordination of services. It was agreed to adopt the title Regional Psychiatrist to emphasise the clinical rather than administrative bias of this post.[312] RHB chairmen objected to adding the Regional Psychiatrist to their small group of senior officers. It was felt that such an appointment would stand in the way of integration. It was also difficult to attract a consultant of sufficient standing in view of the relatively unattractive salary. Accordingly, at the regional level there was a preference for part-time Regional Psychiatrist appointees, who were also involved in clinical work. Despite the urgent entreaties of officials, the Regions tended to backslide over making Regional Psychiatrist appointments.[313] Circular RHB(50)20 accepted that a variety of arrangements were permissible. A survey undertaken in 1955 showed that in six cases the work was done by a medical officer of the Regional Board, while in the others the appointees held part-time clinical appointments.[314] The Ministry of Health was prepared to allow the Regional Psychiatrist appointments to lapse, but questions in the House of Commons from Kenneth Robinson led the chairmen of RHBs to agree to retain them.[315]

Reflecting the views of the Board of Control, circulars RHB(47)11 and 13 recommended that large institutions should be designated as single hospital groups, while smaller mental and mental deficiency institutions should be linked into groups appropriate for nurse training. Mental hospitals and mental deficiency institutions were generally grouped separately. This practice was followed in the majority of cases, but integration required creation of mixed groups containing general and mental hospitals. The NW Metropolitan RHB was a particularly strong advocate of this arrangement, but its plans were turned down by the Minister. After direct discussions with Bevan the NW Metropolitan RHB reluctantly abandoned its mixed groups. The only boards to persist with mixed groups on any scale were Leeds and Birmingham.[316] In the case of Birmingham, mixed groups were unsuccessfully resisted and then constantly criticised by Division 8. They were a source of resentment from medical superintendents of mental institutions. But this arrangement was reluctantly accepted and it persisted.[317] However, it was not the beginning of a general trend, despite the aspirations of RHBs such as Newcastle and Sheffield to establish mixed groups. Separate administration in the mental sector was ratified by the Guillebaud Report, after which there was little incentive to embark on further experiments in regrouping.[318]

The mental sector was affected by a chronic personnel shortage, reflected in both the quantity and quality of its staff. This problem was evident at the highest level. It was increasingly evident that recruits of the requisite standard were not coming forward to become medical superintendents of the key institutions. Mental hospitals cherished a long tradition of medical administration. In the past medical superintendents had presided over their isolated domains like benevolent grandees. The NHS reduced the prestige, power and financial advantages of their office. They were burdened with judicial and administrative responsibilities, but were at a financial disadvantage to part-time consultants. The balance of advantage was thus reversed between medical superintendents and their senior medical colleagues. In the modern age many of the incidental characteristics of medical superintendents' life style seemed less advantageous, and the breed itself was dwindling. Although the Bradbeer and Guillebaud reports recommended continuation of medical administration in mental hospitals, in all other classes of hospital in England and Wales this tradition was dying out, hastened into its grave by the fading importance of tuberculosis and infectious diseases hospitals, where medical administration had also been dominant.

The remuneration of medical superintendents was known to be too low for the responsibilities involved, but improvements were blocked for fear of creating a precedent with respect to other classes of medical administrators, especially Medical Officers of Health and their staff. Consequently market forces dictated trends and RHBs complained there were insufficient well-qualified and active medical superintendents to give leadership towards modernisation.[319]

In 1950 the problem of quality and quantity in the consultant field was raised at the Mental Health SAC.[320] It was thought that 670 represented the full specialist complement for England and Wales, but in the RHBs only 360 consultants and 180 SHMOs were employed. Official sources usually gave 405 as the total for consultant appointments in December 1949. This shortage was invoked against application of the notorious circular RHB(50)106 to cut back the training grades in psychiatry. In the event no reductions in psychiatric training positions were needed because the modest norms allowed for in the training plans were not reached. Between 1951 and 1956 the norms for senior registrars were raised from 118 to 142, but the number of senior registrars in training fell over the period from 117 to 96. Each year only a handful of senior registrars reached their fourth year of training. Consequently there was considerable wastage, and the medical experts deliberated at length on the manifold causes for the paucity of fully-trained recruits for consultant positions. On the academic side 'dearth of training facilities and lack of contact with active medical schools' were blamed for failure to attract good candidates.[321] Further investigation revealed that senior registrars were dropping out at an early stage to become SHMOs.

Since the majority of consultant appointments were being made by upgrading SHMOs there was no incentive to complete training. Consequently, even the most recently appointed consultants were inadequately qualified. Thus specialist work was being conducted by an indifferent set of consultants, supported by a large medley of poorly qualified SHMOs.[322] As a result data indicating a rise in specialist numbers are not indicative of an improvement in quality. The precise numerical position is far from clear in the official statistics. The Ministry of Health *Annual Reports* show an increase of consultants from 405 to 592 between 1949 and 1956, a percentage increase higher than for any specialism other than anaesthetics. Taken together with an increase of SHMOs from 180 to 381, the senior specialist grades might seem to have been fully staffed. But many of these personnel were part-time appointees, their whole-time equivalent in 1956 being 480 (consultants) and 330 (SHMOs).[323]

These figures suggest that by 1956 the official staffing norms were being met. There had been only a minor overall increase in the number of beds in the mental sector between 1949 and 1956. Indeed, after reaching a peak in 1954 of 140,500, the number of patients resident in mental hospitals declined slightly in 1955, and this trend continued, so marginally reducing the overcrowding rate. Allowing for changes in the service, such as great increase in admissions and in out-patient work, and the development of more elaborate therapy, it was still arguable that the mental hospitals were understaffed on the medical side, regardless of questions of the quality of that staff. Indeed, on the basis of a survey of vacancies made in 1954 the Mental Health SAC concluded that there existed an overall 20% shortage in staff, and that the position was very much worse in the less-favoured regions. The mounting burdens on the service led to a sense of despondency. Concerned members of the profession called for urgent government action to correct a situation which they felt was 'steadily growing more grave'.[324]

Perhaps the great problem of the mental sector under the early NHS was the shortage of nursing staff. An urgent investigation conducted at the behest of RHB chairmen indicated that 2,819 mental beds and 2,145 mental deficiency beds were closed for want of nursing staff.[325] Because of the staff shortage, voluntary admissions to mental hospitals were curtailed, the mentally handicapped could not be transferred back from their temporary wartime accommodation to their home institutions, and the mental handicap waiting list had grown from 5,000 to 8,000. Staff shortage was blamed for the unwillingness of boards to invest a great proportion of their limited capital allocation in provision of new accommodation.[326] In order to achieve accepted norms (1 nurse to 4.5 - 4.7 patients in mental; 1 nurse to 6 patients in mental deficiency) mental hospitals required to increase nursing staff from 25,000 to 37,000. However, the first review of the figures showed that in both mental and mental deficiency institutions recruitment had slumped since the beginning of the NHS.[327] There were shortages in every grade. The problem was especially serious on the female side in both mental and mental deficiency institutions, where the great majority of recruits were lost before completion of their training. In the absence of trained staff there was increasing reliance on untrained nursing assistants and part-time staff. Properly qualified staff were a diminishing asset, and this erosion was reflected in the difficulty of obtaining senior nursing staff with the requisite double qualification.[328] In sombre reflection on the data, the Mental Health SAC judged this problem 'desperately serious', 'catastrophic and likely to become worse'. The situation was described as a downward spiral, only to be arrested if 'something almost revolutionary' was done.[329]

Stagnation in recruitment, and the trend towards dilution in quality of the staff continued, with the result that both experts and administrators viewed the situation with increasing alarm. In 1954 it was estimated that the mental hospitals were understaffed by 20% on the male side and 35% on the female side.[330] Mental deficiency institutions were fully staffed on the male side, but 17% below strength on the female side. Dilution was particularly apparent on the female side, where registered nurses had fallen to 36% of the nursing staff, compared with the desirable 75–80%.[331]

The mental sector nursing staff situation in 1949 and 1956 is indicated in Table VIII. It shows a significant decline in student numbers, stagnation in the numbers of trained nurses in mental hospitals, but slight improvement in mental deficiency institutions. The most notable change was the growth in untrained nursing staff, and especially whole-time nursing assistants in mental hospitals, where the numbers doubled between 1949 and 1956. These figures graphically demonstrate the way in which mental and mental deficiency nursing fell behind the general and teaching

TABLE VIII

Comparison of Nursing Staff Levels in the Mental Sector 1949–1956 (England and Wales)

	1949 (30 Dec)				1956 (30 Sept)			
	male		female		male		female	
	wt	pt	wt	pt	wt	pt	wt	pt
Mental Trained	7,232	13	3,824	1,134	7,319	138	3,721	1,512
Student Nurses	2,537	—	2,664	—	1,625	—	2,491	—
Other Nursing Staff	1,273	4	1,629	4,419	1,427	154	3,280	5,129
Total	11,042	17	8,117	5,553	10,371	322	9,492	6,641
Mental Deficiency Trained	1,538	—	1,075	250	2,001	51	1,249	422
Student Nurses	617	—	518	—	470	—	431	—
Other Nursing Staff	860	2	940	1,520	982	109	1,491	1,958
Total	3,015	2	2,533	1,770	3,453	160	3,171	2,380
M + MD Total	14,057	19	10,605	7,323	13,824	482	12,663	9,021

Sources: Mental Health SAC, 'Supply of Nurses', 18 February 1954, DHSS 94198/2/1B; Ministry of Health, *Report 1956*.

sectors in the expansion of staffing levels which occurred under the early NHS.

The first try at solving the mental nursing problem involved taking steps to boost recruitment. Circular RHB(53)54 explained that two departmental nursing officers were being appointed to visit hospitals and advise on recruitment. A call was made for mental hospitals to be 'jolted out of the rut' of their 'atmosphere of defeatism'. The Ministry of Labour planned to convene conferences and frame a strategy for local campaigns.[332] RHB chairmen were sceptical about the prospect for recruitment campaigns unless wages and conditions of work were drastically improved. Their pessimism was justified. Recruitment campaigns recorded negligible successes.[333] Not to be deterred, officials issued a circular on the improvement of working conditions in the institutions, making numerous recommendations concerning changes which were largely cosmetic. A travelling mental health exhibition was then devised, with the hope of boosting recruitment by showing institutional services in a good light.[334] This joint Ministry of Labour—Ministry of Health exhibition was launched on 7 November 1955. The RHB chairmen were once again sceptical. The ill-starred Mental Health Exhibition took to the road, but whatever good was done was counteracted by adverse publicity for the service, because the exhibition became a focus for protest demonstrations from COHSE, the union representing mental nurses.[335]

The second line of advance on the mental nursing front favoured by officials was the much wider use of Enrolled Assistant Nurses. Introduction of a special roll of assistant mental nurses would require legislation, but the lower professional grade was favoured as a spur to recruitment, and because lower qualifications were thought appropriate to mental nursing duties. This approach was supported by the National Advisory Council, the Nursing SAC and by some RHB chairmen.[336] The change was bitterly resisted by the Royal Medico-Psychological Association, COHSE and most effectively by the Mental Health SAC. Critics of the enrolled nurse scheme pointed out that (a) it had not materially helped to solve the staffing problem in general hospitals, (b) it was likely that recruitment to this grade would undermine recruitment to full training, (c) it would not be attractive to those currently engaged as nursing assistants, whose circumstances often precluded taking up training, (d) adoption of three routes into mental nursing would cause undesirable administrative complications, (e) statutory registration would create inflexibility over employment, and (f) it was an expression of 'dangerous fallacies, quite out of keeping with modern medical thought' to conclude that mental nursing involved less medical skill than other types of nursing. It was therefore held that 'it would be inimical to the future of mental nursing and the welfare of patients to recognise an inferior qualification'. The Mental Health SAC concluded that 'the tendency towards further dilution should be strongly resisted and that everything possible shall be done to encourage the recruitment of larger numbers of students'. In their view, at the crux of this problem lay levels of pay, conditions of work, and methods of teaching and training. Given the likelihood of continuing staff shortage the Mental Health SAC acknowledged the 'unfortunate necessity' of employment of nursing assistants, for whom it would be necessary to arrange some elementary training. It was urged that such assistants should not constitute more than 20% of the nursing workforce.[337] In the face of sustained opposition to the extension of the use of enrolled nurses in the mental sector this scheme was temporarily abandoned. In December 1954 the CHSC announced agreement between the rival parties. It was accepted that enrolment was not relevant in the short term. As an alternative it was agreed to introduce more training opportunities for nursing assistants.[338]

Front-line witnesses generally advised that improvement in wages and conditions of work offered the only realistic means to ease the problem of shortage of mental nurses. The combination of inferior pay and unattractive conditions of work placed mental nursing in an extremely weak position in a market where employment opportunities were expanding. Furthermore, within mental nursing, qualified nurses were at a financial disadvantage to unqualified staff. Action to benefit trained mental nurses depended on the Whitley Nurses and Midwives Council. The staff side, dominated by the general nursing interest, was reluctant to open up differentials between mental nurses and other nursing groups. The settlement of 1949 had given trained mental nurses a 'lead' of £20 per annum over general nurses. A claim for a further £50 increase made in November 1952 dragged on until April 1954, when the Industrial Court granted £25. Slight improvements were given to mental student nurses in November 1955. These were the only increases awarded specifically to mental nurses before April 1956.[339] Inevitably frustration built up among nurses in mental institutions. Resentment was expressed over such varied issues as the death of a nurse at Whittingham Hospital, Lancashire, and the superior economic position of imported nursing assistants, or indeed of mentally handicapped patients working on licence. In support of demands for improved pay and conditions COHSE branches organised protests at the mental health touring exhibition, and unofficial bans on overtime spread through the mental sector in the early months of 1956, until some forty institutions and 10,000 workers were involved.[340] This was the first nationwide industrial action under the NHS. A national work-to-rule, planned to begin on 1 May 1956, was narrowly averted. Further small concessions to student mental nurses and nursing assistants were granted in the 1 April 1956 general pay award, but the COHSE leadership made little other headway in securing differentials for trained nurses, either in its direct negotiations with the health departments, or on the Whitley Council. When the Industrial Court refused the claim of mental nurses for enhanced overtime payments in July 1956, a national overtime ban was once again narrowly averted, although a new wave of unofficial protest swept through the mental hospitals in October, and thereafter there were sporadic outbreaks of industrial action, including sit-in strikes.[341]

The major development priority in the mental sector during the early years of the NHS was modernisation and extension of existing institutions. In 1954 Macleod declared that he regarded the capital needs of the mental hospital services 'as unquestionably taking priority over anything else'.[342] His aim was to create 2,800 extra beds. As noted above, publicity concerning the plight of mental institutions lay behind the Cabinet decision to sanction a capital development plan for hospitals.

In 1938/39 local authority capital expenditure on mental and mental deficiency institutions stood at £2.3m, which represented 50% of local authority spending on hospitals.[343] Between 1948 and 1954 the NHS devoted about £1m pa to this purpose. Between 1954 and 1957 the average was just less than £2m pa. Thus, even the expanded level of capital commitment left spending in real terms at less than one-third the pre-war level. As a percentage of NHS capital spending on hospitals, the mental sector received 16% between 1948 and 1954, rising to 25.2% in 1954/55, and 28.1% in 1955/56. The Ministry of Health Report conceded that the mental sector received a 'smaller proportion than was reasonable' during the early years. Concern over low spending caused the Ministry of Health in 1950 to advise RHBs to devote at least 20% of their capital allocation to the mental area. The subsequent increase was not sufficient to compensate for earlier neglect. As in all things, wide discrepancies existed between the RHBs. For instance, between 1948 and 1955 the Newcastle and Sheffield RHBs devoted 30% of their capital allocation to the mental sector, whereas Manchester and Liverpool allowed only 16% and 17%.[344]

Given the paucity of support for capital projects the Oxford RHB evolved plans for constructing new institutions on a cheap, prefabricated basis, which was undertaken on a small scale, although not without controversy with other RHBs and the Ministry of Health, where objections to the Oxford scheme both in principle and in detail were raised.[345]

Most of the capital spending went on minor schemes for modernisation and additional beds. Thirty institutions were identified as needing major improvement, the largest group comprising eight in the S Western region.[346] In order to meet this need, in May 1953 the Ministry announced that it was setting aside £1m for schemes costing less than £200,000 designed to increase accommodation. This 'mental million' was expended between 1954 and 1959 on schemes selected by the Ministry from bids placed by the RHBs. Adaptation of a hutted military camp to make the Bradwell Grove mental deficiency institution (Oxford RHB) constituted one of the more unusual projects supported by the 'mental million'. The mental sector fared relatively well in the first phase of 'major schemes' chosen by the health departments. The Greaves Hall mental deficiency institution, Southport (Liverpool RHB), started in 1953, was the first new in-patient facility to be built in England and Wales since World War II. Its foundation stone was laid on

8 May by Macleod. Intended for 1,000 patients, the scheme began with a small first phase completed in 1958. Balderton Hall mental deficiency institution (Sheffield RHB) was the only other mental sector major scheme in the eight undertaken during the early years of the NHS. Greaves Hall exemplifies the painfully slow pace of hospital development. A further example is provided by the Lea Castle mental deficiency institution, Kidderminster (Birmingham RHB), where contracts were placed just before the Appointed Day by the local authorities, but this modest project was not completed until 1966.[347] Beginning in 1955/56, planning was undertaken on a much larger scale. Six RHBs hoped to build new mental hospitals. None of these schemes materialised. The first phase of significant building took place between 1956 and 1958, when priorities switched from mental to mental deficiency institutions. Starts were made on extensions to six mental deficiency institutions and one mental hospital (Digby, near Exeter, S Western RHB).[348]

The major Scottish schemes in the mental sector involved extensions at three mental deficiency institutions (at Banff, Dundee and Larbert) and two mental hospitals, Westgreen (Dundee) and Royal (Edinburgh). Of these developments, the first to be started was Westgreen in 1955/56, the extensions to the three mental deficiency institutions beginning in the following year, and the Royal Edinburgh Mental Hospital, not until 1957/58. Hardly any of these projects were completed before the unveiling of the 1962 Hospital Plan.[349]

The switch in capital development away from mental hospitals towards mental deficiency institutions reflects a shift in policy in the field of mental health. Provision of extra beds in the mental deficiency field was regarded as a less avoidable necessity, the only means to satisfy the long list of urgent cases awaiting admission. On the other hand it was realised that continuing pressure for expansion of mental hospitals could be relieved if the growing population of elderly patients in mental hospitals, who were often marginal cases, could be accommodated in some other manner. This class of patient was at risk of placing intolerable pressures on resources of mental hospitals. The percentage of patients over 65 in mental hospitals had risen from 16.4% to 20.1% between 1944 and 1954. The continuation of this trend, together with the emergence for the first time of a significant population of over-75s, was a cause for growing concern. A Mental Health SAC sub-committee concluded that 'the burden on the state, in terms of money and absorption of manpower, of provision to this extent, would be serious indeed in relation to any view of the future economy'.[350] Accordingly, arresting this influx of elderly patients assumed high priority.

Faced with their crisis of accommodation mental health planners became enthusiastic about forms of therapy permitting more rapid turn-over of patients, and they were alerted to the advantages of treatment less dependent on in-patient facilities. Out of necessity and then choice preferences turned towards out-patient clinics and community care. It was also realised that this alternative could also be exploited for the benefit of the mentally handicapped. The mounting advocacy on behalf of these alternatives unleashed a torrent of literature in the 1960s, but it was already strong enough in the 1950s to influence the Royal Commission on Mental Illness and Mental Deficiency (1954–1957). The Mental Health SAC held its first discussions on community care, day hospitals, special arrangements for the care of the elderly, and preventive psychiatry in 1949 and 1950. These initiatives were reflected in official circulars, while a BMA report on the care of the elderly also received wide publicity. There was broad support for the creation of short-stay units for observation and for long-stay annexes. It was calculated that some 26,000 patients could be transferred from mental hospitals to such annexes.[351] There was, however, some disagreement whether such developments should be associated with geriatric departments of general hospitals, or with mental hospitals. Emphasis gradually shifted to more radical alternatives, involving establishment of day hospitals and associated local authority support services. Such co-ordinated services were given the support of the Mental Health SAC in 1955.[352] The model schemes established in York, Worthing, Salford, Oldham and Nottingham attracted wide publicity.[353] The Mental Health SAC also backed proposals to remove as many as 50% of the population of mental deficiency institutions to hostels, sited where their residents could take up employment and lead independent lives. This proposal could not be implemented without local authority participation.[354] Such initiatives were indicative of a shift in attitudes among planners, but in the first decade of the service their influence was relatively limited. By 1956, despite their major capacity to effect savings, only twenty day hospitals had been established in Britain.[355] There were in England and Wales about twenty psychiatric social workers and just one psychologist employed by a Local Health Authority. Only a handful of authorities were providing hostel accommodation for mental or mental deficiency patients. The many constraints facing schemes relying on co-ordinated action by hospital and local authorities reduced the scope for more radical ventures in community care. The more common successes of the system tended to be limited to improvements mounted by single authorities. The rapid transformation of such institutions as the Glengall Mental

Hospital, Ayr, illustrated how much could be achieved by reorganisation of a hospital unit, at only minimum cost. Such projects maximised opportunities for rehabilitation, and they made real concessions to the dignity of the patients suffering from mental disorder.[356] Whether application of such principles was helped or hindered by the more widespread application of the forms of chemotherapy and surgery that also gained ground in the 1950s, is a question requiring further evaluation.

(xii) HOSPITAL DEVELOPMENT

It has already been pointed out that the constant pressure for economy exerted during the early years of the NHS was resolved in the hospital sector by cutting back expenditure on maintenance and capital development to a minimum. For one reason after another capital spending on hospitals had been extremely limited ever since World War I. The NHS thus inherited building stock in a severe stage of dilapidation, and still bearing the scars of World War II. Repairing the manifold defects of the system exposed by the war-time surveys necessarily involved massive capital commitment. Estimates of the cost of modernising the hospital stock were upwards of £300m.[357] Yet it was not until after 1960 that capital expenditure rose in real terms above the pre-war level. Failure of the NHS authorities to mount a capital programme on anything like the appropriate scale was at first little noticed. Spartan conditions in hospitals were traditional, and they were tolerated with stoicism by staff and patients alike. However, the relative destitution of the hospital service became strikingly obvious when the building boom was under way. It was for instance noted that 'The 14 new towns now rising in Britain have houses, churches, factories, schools, shops, cinemas, inns, but not a hospital between them'.[358] RHB chairmen were alarmed that the rising cost of maintenance was stifling their attempts to undertake much-needed rationalisation and modernisation.[359] It has been noted in chapter VI that Churchill and his Cabinet wanted a campaign to correct this shortcoming. Spirits were to some extent raised by the ministerial statements made on 9 February 1955 outlining a modest package of hospital building schemes. There was alas little to show in the short term. Soon weighty authorities voiced their alarm in the press, now dwelling on the adverse position in Britain compared with European neighbours, particularly those countries where hospitals had been destroyed during the war. It seemed a particular indignity for Britain to tolerate hospitals which were inefficient, uncomfortable, obsolete, squalid, and unhealthy. The hospital authorities were accused of squandering their resources on emergency maintenance when complete reconstruction represented sounder long-term investment.[360] Such strictures were a common-place of representations by the health departments to the Treasury. Officials were possessed by pessimism concerning the pace and scope of hospital development. One of them caricatured projects undertaken during the years of restriction, '*stage one:* site works, followed by *stage two:* out patient and casualty department. Nothing for a year or two until local politics dictate, say, *stage three:* twin operating suite and a new acute surgical block, perhaps a new laboratory and mortuary'. Even small schemes were only accomplished after much delay and frustration.[361] The mechanism for planning was by no means efficient, but the basic problems boiled down to lack of resources. Even the Treasury witness conceded that hospital capital expenditure had been 'manifestly inadequate'.[362]

The overall division of the meagre capital allocation between regions is summarised in Table V. Given the slender resources, distribution could scarcely reflect objective need. Necessarily, major improvements were very localised. Most of the capital allocation was swallowed up in maintenance work, much of the distribution of which was determined by emergencies. The capital allocation of regions fluctuated from year to year according to the apportion-ment of major schemes, but as Table V shows, by 1956 expenditure roughly followed the pattern of distribution of population between the regions. Among the less well-provided regions Newcastle and Wales derived some benefit from redistribution. When spending on the teaching hospitals is taken into account the balance of advantage remains with the metropolitan area.

Administration of the capital allocation was not without its problems. Many hospital authorities favoured carrying over of unspent balances as a means of ensuring more balanced and efficient use of resources.[363] Others wanted to raise loans for capital works in the same manner as local authorities, emphasising that the loss in interest payments would be more than compensated for by savings through introduction of more efficient heating systems, laundries etc.[364] Requirements for health department and Treasury approval of plans were criticised as unnecessary and time-consum-ing. Slight relaxation of the ceilings in July 1953 failed to assuage critics. Particular objection was aimed at Treasury involvement with building works costing more than £30,000. This view was supported by the Guillebaud Committee, which suggested raising this limit to £100,000.[365] By way of compromise the level adopted in 1957 was £60,000, with a rise from £10,000 to £30,000 for schemes requiring health department approval. In defence of centralised supervision officials argued that reference to the health departments was desirable for planning purposes.[366] RHBs tended to blame delays on the complex machinery for consultations with the health departments and the Treasury, while Government officials complained that the boards were indecisive and inefficient in their handling of large schemes.[367]

Notwithstanding a more liberal regime for vetting capital schemes, in reality the health departments obtained greater control of development because an increasing share of the capital budget was absorbed by 'major schemes' chosen centrally from a list of bids placed by the regions. Consequently, firm central control was maintained over the distribution of projects costing upwards of £250,000. Armed with strong central control, the departments in 1955 evolved arrangements whereby the regions were given formal forecasts of their capital allocations for three years in advance. Once the momentum of hospital building had increased, the Ministry of Health established a small Hospital Design Unit, to promote efficient and economical design of hospital building. It was generally felt that the Unit was not in a position to make the same impact as the successful Building Unit at the Ministry of Education.[368]

The regional capital allocation was largely absorbed in execution of unglamorous but essential works such as replacing boilers, rewiring, and upgrading kitchens and laundry services. Infectious diseases and Poor Law hospitals required adaptation for use by other classes of patient, or in the latter case they needed raising to a more humane standard. The more ambitious routine developments involved building operating theatres, X-ray departments, or pathology laboratories. Many of the proposals for modernisation, and especially those for new out-patient departments, fell under the 'major schemes' allocation decided centrally. The major schemes project began in 1950, but it was not until 1954/55 that it reached a significant scale. Of the eight major schemes costing £200,000 or more started before 31 March 1956, there were two extensions of mental deficiency accommodation (discussed above in section xi), one heating and boiler replacement, one pathology institute and regional blood transfusion centre, one casualty unit and war damage reinstatement, one out-patient department, one first stage of a new hospital in West Wales, and one beginning of a major teaching hospital extension. Only just over £1m had been spent on major schemes by March 1956.[369] By the same date, under the major schemes arrangement in Scotland, starts had been made on neurosurgical radiotherapy facilities at the Western General Hospital, Edinburgh, a surgical block at the Kirkcaldy Victoria Hospital, and the Bellshill Maternity Hospital, Lanarkshire.[370]

Given the low level of capital allocations there was little opportunity for co-ordinated planning of hospital development, either locally or nationally. At first the energies of regional boards were largely absorbed in honouring commitments taken on by predecessor hospital authorities. Gradually a picture was built up of the state of services within the regions. The regional boards were faced with unenviable decisions concerning priorities for major schemes urged on them by the hospital groups. Judgement was not always sound. For instance the Leeds region wanted to establish a new 300-bed tuberculosis sanatorium at a time when demand for tuberculosis beds was entering into terminal decline.[371]

It was not until November 1953 that the Treasury received a detailed account of the forward plans of the Ministry of Health.[372] Of the numerous schemes listed between 1953 and 1956, few reached fruition before 1960. High priority was attached to reconstruction or resiting the major teaching hospitals, St Thomas's, Guy's, St George's, Charing Cross, Cambridge and Cardiff were in the first list. Manchester, Oxford, Sheffield, Royal Free, and St Mary's were added, in that order. In 1953 it was firmly intended to move Charing Cross to Northwick Park, but by 1958 this plan was dropped and Fulham was substituted as an alternative site. This switch of preferences illustrates the confusion existing over resiting London teaching hospitals. The only one of the above London projects to be started before 1960 was the surgical block at Guy's. The most active provincial teaching hospital redevelopment took place at the Radcliffe Infirmary in Oxford. The wisdom of this course was thrown in doubt by the decision to resite the teaching hospital in Headington. From the outset Cambridge was committed to evacuating its central site. The first stage of work at Hills Rd Cambridge began in 1958. Two other schemes begun before 1960 were reconstruction of the Manchester Royal Infirmary made necessary through severe structural problems in the existing buildings, and the building of an out-patient department as the first stage of the new teaching hospital in Sheffield.

Of the numerous proposals for improved hospital facilities in areas of particular need, special priority was attached to general hospitals for the new towns to the north of London at Welwyn and Harlow, and for W Cumberland, Swindon, W Cornwall and W Wales. Replacement of temporary war-time hutted accommodation was often invoked as one of the grounds for action. Of this list, only W Cornwall had not started by 1960. Additional schemes introduced for reason of special priority included an accident block at the Middlesbrough General Hospital because no burns or head injuries facilities existed for this industrial area nearer than Newcastle, the redevelopment of the Doncaster Royal Infirmary because of extreme pressure on facilities and reliance on temporary hutted accommodation, and extensions at Swansea, Bangor,

Northampton, Kettering, Leeds, S Ockenden, and Bristol. Some progress on all of these developments had been made by 1960. Proposals favoured before 1955, but subsequently dropped down the priority list included most of the London teaching hospital schemes, the Cardiff teaching hospital redevelopment and new hospitals for Slough, W Cornwall, Coventry, S Lincolnshire, Huddersfield, Lowestoft, Gillingham and Wythenshawe.[373]

Dearth of capital resources severely limited opportunities for major redevelopment. Consequently hospital authorities were driven to incur expenditure on obsolete hospitals that often merited relocation on an entirely different site. However, framing a settled policy was affected by factors other than finance. The arguments in Oxford over the merits of a central or peripheral site for the teaching hospital were repeated in many instances. This problem existed in its most acute form in London, where population was shifting to the periphery yet hospital resources remained concentrated in the central area. The problem was eased by the commitment to new hospitals or major extensions at such places as Welwyn, Harlow, Hillingdon, Slough, Isleworth, Crawley and Kingston. But this left unsolved the maldistribution of the vitally important teaching hospitals.

This difficulty was apparent to the Goodenough Committee and to the wartime surveyors. Both made timid recommendations concerning relocation. Neither suggested amalgamations. Charing Cross, St George's and the Royal Free were favourite candidates for removal to the periphery, and the designation of teaching hospitals made in 1948 granted hospital facilities to Charing Cross in Wembley and Harrow, and to the Royal Free in Hampstead, on the understanding that relocation would take place. It was assumed that the Royal Free would be redeveloped on the site of its satellite, the NW London Fever Hospital, Lawn Rd, Hampstead. The Northwick Park site, Harrow, was purchased for Charing Cross. It was originally intended to commence building in 1952/53, but the economy drive resulted in delay. Charing Cross was, however, included as a high priority in a list given to the House of Commons by Macleod in July 1955. By this time the Grove infectious diseases hospital at Tooting had been designated as a teaching hospital to prepare for the removal of St George's. The Ministry of Health was reconciled to rebuilding and modernisation of the other undergraduate teaching hospitals on their crowded central sites.

The modest intentions of the Ministry were taken account of in the Greater London development plan. Progress was undermined by a complete change of attitude on the part of the UGC and London University Senate. Their 'new thinking' of 1954 resisted removal of teaching hospitals from their central sites on the grounds that teaching needed to be conducted in proximity to research and general university life. Accordingly the three hospitals resumed their preference for redeveloping on central sites. The only concession offered was a 'twin-star' arrangement whereby, in addition to the central teaching hospital, a satellite facility would be developed in the suburbs. This alternative was vigorously resisted by the Ministry of Health, which in 1957 campaigned for its earlier plan. Reluctant agreement was obtained from the Charing Cross and Royal Free teaching hospitals to move to peripheral sites, on the understanding that high priority would be accorded to their redevelopment. A significant change introduced at this stage diverted Charing Cross to Fulham, abandoning the Harrow site favoured since the wartime hospital survey.[374]

CHAPTER IX

Primary and Preventive Services

The Dawson Report proposed that neighbourhood preventive and curative services should be assembled into a single organisation, the physical basis for which was the 'primary health centre'. This report was the first official publication to introduce the primary-secondary distinction into the field of health care. The Dawson Report also advocated linking the domiciliary services provided by the doctor, dentist, pharmacist, nurse, midwife and health visitor in a single domiciliary or primary framework in which teamwork was a fundamental point of emphasis.

In the event the National Health Service failed to heed the advice of the Dawson Report that 'preventive and curative medicine cannot be separated on any sound principle, and in any scheme of medical services must be brought together in close co-ordination'.[1] As explained in chapter IV, Dawson's primary services were split between Local Health Authorities and Executive Councils under part III and part IV of the 1946 Act. A similar cleavage was introduced in Scotland. Functional efficiency depended on a high degree of co-operation between part III and part IV services, commitment to which was symbolised by the intention to make the development of health centres a central feature of the National Health Service.

Except for transfer of functions from metropolitan boroughs to the LCC and from district councils to county boroughs and county councils, the structure of Local Health Authority administration continued much as before the NHS. The primary change affecting Local Health Authorities was the drastic reduction in their responsibilities following transfer of their institutional services to hospital authorities. Local Health Authorities were left with a miscellaneous collection of services. However, when taken together with the school health service and local welfare service, local public health departments retained control over community care services of considerable potential importance. Early plans for the NHS assumed that it would be possible to implement the recommendations of the 1926 Royal Commission on National Health Insurance by placing general medical services under Local Health Authorities. The profession favoured retention of the National Health Insurance form of administration. In the event the NHI arrangements were cosmetically adjusted to the needs of the NHS. The biggest adjustment related to the addition of statutory dental and optician services. Additional minor modifications were required for purposes of accommodation to the Medical Practices Committee with respect to filling of vacancies, and for dealing with disciplinary matters. Many changes of detail were introduced in connection with the larger scale of the NHS operation, but the new Executive Councils and their subsidiary committees retained the essential ethos of the old Insurance Committees. Consistent with the name they were given, their role was essentially neutral and routine. They avoided policy issues and thereby played little part in developing the services they administered. Their silent operations were largely unnoticed by the public, to the irritation of improvers who complained that Executive Councils were not established 'merely to administer the system of medical care but to promote steady improvement'.[2] Administrators wanting to give the ECs a more positive image suggested a change of name, to something like 'Family Health Services Council'.[3] Many alternatives were considered before the title Family Practitioner Committee was adopted in 1974.

Originally it was hoped that under the NHS the number of administrative areas for the general medical services would be reduced. However, the proposed amalgamations 'ran counter to local patriotism, and unfortunately raised feelings of a semi-political nature'. Accordingly planners retreated. In England and Wales 146 Insurance Committees were replaced by 138 Executive Councils. In Scotland where local authority units were much smaller, 54 Insurance Committees were reduced to 25 Executive Councils.

While changes in the short term were ruled out, officials wanted the framework to be maintained in a form compatible with local health authority organisation, 'If and when the time came to link the EC to some other administrative body, that body should clearly be the local health authority; and it would be folly meantime to set up yet another area pattern differing from that of the local health authorities'.[4]

As noted in chapter IV the chairmen of ECs were originally ministerial appointees. As a concession to the profession the Councils were allowed to appoint their own chairmen under the 1949 amending legislation. Unlike the hospital authorities, and consistent with NHI practice, only five members of ECs were ministerial appointees, while others were direct nominees of Local Health Authorities (8), the local medical committee (7), local dental committee (3), and the local pharmaceutical committee (2). There was consequently a fine balance between lay and professional representation.[5] The strongest elements within the first group of

EC chairmen were solicitors and former Insurance Committee chairmen. Typically, the first chairman of the giant London EC was Henry Lesser, former chairman of the London Insurance Committee. The composition of ECs caused little controversy, although in conservative areas labour organisations complained that they were virtually unrepresented, and that the ECs were controlled by interests unsympathetic to the NHS.[6] In the 'Minister's group', Trades Council nominees were accepted as the representatives of the working-class consumer. In addition 'a family woman, preferably young, married with children' was wanted by Bevan. Difficulty was experienced in keeping up this representation.[7] The major criticism of ECs was the persistent poor attendance record of some members, especially LHA nominees, and the tendency of duties to fall on too few shoulders.[8] In this respect the ECs experienced similar problems to the hospital authorities.

(i) GENERAL PRACTITIONER SERVICE

The twenty thousand general practitioners were the largest, best-organised and most forceful professional group involved in the NHS. Periodically they came together to exercise dramatic influence, especially when questions of remuneration were involved. But for the most part they were individualists, fiercely protective of their independence, and concerned with nothing other than their immediate practice. The Executive Council machinery was designed to interfere to the minimum degree with the exercise of general practitioners' skills. The ECs accordingly presided less over a single coherent general practitioner service, than over 20,000 separate and competing services.

Notwithstanding the intentions of the NHS legislation to cultivate a greater corporate sense among general practitioners, in the event there was a trend towards greater fragmentation. As a BMA leader noted, retention of the old NHI method of remuneration and abolition of sale of practices was destructive to the build-up of group practice. 'Present-day methods of remuneration make for large and competitive practices. New partnerships are not being readily formed. In fact, the abolition of the sale of practices so loosened partnership financial ties, that many partnerships have been dissolved. We pay the busy doctor in such a way to make it advantageous for him to employ an assistant, but not to take that assistant into partnership; while on his National Health remuneration the doctor with a small list can afford neither assistant nor partner'.[9] The virtual collapse of health centre development left general practitioners without incentive to engage in teamwork. Furthermore the system of remuneration also discriminated against conscientious doctors who kept their lists within reasonable limits and who improved and equipped their surgeries. It was accepted that the system was unfair 'since the doctor with a large list gets a bigger cut of practice expenses than the doctor with a small list, though his practice expenses per patient on his list may be lower if he lives in a poor area, as is commonly the case'. However the allowance for practice expenses on the basis of an average agreed in negotiation between the profession and the Government departments was convenient for both sides. It suited the dominant element within the profession because it over-compensated established doctors. It was especially agreeable to the Treasury because of its simplicity in operation, whereas the alternative would have involved examining individual returns. In addition payment of actual expenses was feared because it would 'stimulate increased expenses' and so create an incentive to 'lavish expenditure which cannot be controlled'.[10] In spite of widespread criticism that adoption of an arbitrary average for practice expenses constituted one of the major impediments to the improvement of general practice, this formula was not modified until the reforms introduced in the wake of the 1966 'Doctors' Charter'.

The above comments and earlier sections on NHS negotiations show how the whole tenor of general practice was determined by the mode of remuneration adopted. Consequently attempts to improve general practice tended to rest on controls exercised through remuneration. The only opportunity for effective action emerged with the Danckwerts award in 1952 which raised the Spens recommendation of £1,111 for average annual net remuneration to £2,222. Acceptance of this award was made conditional on acceptance of revised arrangements for distribution of the central pool. Among the various aims were 'discouraging unduly large lists, a relative improvement in the position of those practitioners least favourably placed under the present plan of distribution', rendering 'it easier for new doctors to enter practice', and stimulating group practice.[11] As already noted in chapter VII the Working Party on Distribution achieved a rapid settlement on some contentious and divisive issues, in some respects flying in the face of fetishes of the profession, and thereby exposing the GMSC to criticism from its own ranks. In retrospect the reforms seem very anodyne. In order to smooth the transition to the new rules, the working party proposals came into force on 1 April 1953.

The most obvious targets for correction were the large list doctors. Under the NHI panel, the limit for single doctors was 2,500, which was met only in industrial areas. The NHS generously permitted a maximum for a single-handed doctor of 4,000. This was generally regarded as too high for efficient service. The working party reduced the limit to 3,500, with similar reductions for members of partnerships and in respect of the employment of permanent assistants.[12] It was calculated that about 2m patients would be redistributed. Most of the benefit was likely to go to partners or neighbouring practitioners rather than to new doctors.[13]

Because calculation of the central pool was determined by the number of doctors rather than population there was no particular incentive on the part of the profession to resist recruitment of extra doctors, or reduction of maximum lists. Both the Medical Practices Committees and the BMA accepted this as a generally desirable object. The Hadfield survey of opinion among general practitioners discovered general support for a 2,500 maximum in towns and 2,000 in rural areas. Despite its receipt of much evidence favouring further reduction in list size, the CHSC Committee on General Practice accepted that the Working Party on Distribution formulae 'fairly reflect present needs and conditions'.[14]

Other groups campaigned for further reduction of the maximum list. The MPU adopted first 3,500, then 3,000, and later 2,500 as desirable limits for principals.[15] There was some support for a 2,500 maximum from the Association of English ECs.[16] At an extreme the General Practice Reform Association wanted a maximum of 2,000.[17] Although not prescribing maxima, the Willink Committee calculated future demands for personnel on the assumption that the average list size would be 2,500 in industrial areas and 2,000 in rural areas.[18]

Because of its retrospective effect the Danckwerts award rewarded the large list most conspicuously and consequently drew further attention to the adverse economic position of young entrants. Furthermore, although in order to give better compensation for the medium list doctor a 'loading' of an additional 10s on the capitation was introduced for every patient on the list between 500 and 1,500, the Medical Practitioners Union argued that the new entrant with a list below 1,000 was worse off than if the fixed annual payment had been retained and a flat rate increase of the capitation had been made.[19] The Government conceded that young practitioners would face difficulties if they settled in adequately doctored areas, but it was claimed that their chances were much improved if they migrated to regions where shortage existed.

The £300 fixed annual payment introduced to assist young doctors inherited all of the opprobrium attached to the Labour Government's Basic Salary proposal that it superseded.[20] Besides smacking of the repugnant notion of payment by salary, the major practical difficulty of the fixed annual payment was its priority claim on the local pool. Recipients of the fixed annual payment reduced the capitation payments of their established neighbours. It is therefore unsurprising that Executive Councils in consultation with their Local Medical Committees, when assessing the 'reasonable justification' for the fixed annual payment, adopted rigorous criteria for qualification. Instinctively, the local bodies turned down applications for the fixed annual payments, while equally instinctively, and with the moral backing of Bevan, the Ministry allowed appeals from appellants.[21] The BMA unsuccessfully tried to intrude the Medical Practices Committee and later the GMSC into the central appeals procedure to ensure an outcome more favourable to established practitioners.[22] Between July 1948 and July 1951, out of 545 appeals against Executive Council decisions concerning fixed annual payments, 202 were allowed by the Minister.[23] Fears that the fixed annual payment was the thin end of the wedge to the introduction of salaried service gradually subsided. By the termination of the scheme only about 1,000 general practitioners had succeeded in scrambling over the hurdles to obtain these payments.

From 1 April 1953, under the Working Party report, the fixed annual payment was replaced by the initial practice allowance.[24] The new scheme limited aid to three years, and it was available only in areas 'designated' by the Medical Practices Committee. The payment tapered down from £600 in the first year to £200 in the third. This inducement was no more successful than its predecessor. By 1965 only about 225 doctors were in receipt of the initial practice allowance.[25] It was generally accepted that the positive inducements offered by the initial practice allowance were insufficient to offset other difficulties facing young practitioners trying to establish themselves in the deprived areas.[26]

The most successful aspect of the Working Party report related to encouragement of group practice. First, the new regulations relating to list size were more advantageous to partners than to single-handed practitioners and assistants. Secondly, £100,000 was set aside annually to give financial assistance to partnerships.[27] This fund was directed into improvement of group practice premises. Although not designed for this purpose the group practice loan scheme effectively replaced the health centre programme. This alternative was preferable to the Treasury because it was a deduction from the pool rather than a separate call on the exchequer. Thus fine adjustment in the remuneration mechanism facilitated an important piece of social engineering among general practitioners. In 1952 in England and Wales there were 7,459 single-handed principals and 9,745 doctors in partnership. The respective totals for 1956 were 6,691 and 12,272. The percentage of doctors in partnership in England and Wales therefore increased from 56% to 64.7%. In 1952 in Scotland there were 1,111 single-handed principals and 1,269 doctors in partnership. The respective totals for 1956 were 952 and 1,599. The percentage of doctors in partnership in Scotland therefore increased from 53.3% to 62.7%.[28]

Following implementation of the recommendations of the Working Party on Distribution, incentives for group practice were combined with minor disincentives against engagement of permanent assistants. The number of such assistants fell from 1,689 in 1952 to 1,504 in 1954, but a continuing high rate of recruitment then prevented further decline in assistantships.[29] There was widespread feeling that permanent assistants, who were often immigrants, were an exploited group. Gaitskell took up their cause, complaining to Marquand about their low pay and lack of tenure.[30] Marquand had been separately alerted to this problem by the Medical Practitioners Union. Assistants formed their own pressure group, the Unestablished Practitioners Group, to press their case for improved opportunities for promotion to independent practice.[31] Assistants received little encouragement from one of the Medical Practices Committees, which regarded them as mediocre candidates, whose attitudes had been soured by frequent failure in competition for appointments in more prestigious areas.[32] The only significant help received by assistants stemmed from the Medical Practitioners Union, which instigated a GMSC inquiry, the results of which led the Ministry of Health to issue guidelines to Executive Councils calling for the tighter regulation of consents for assistantships.[33]

It was open for the Working Party on Distribution to recommend a compulsory retirement age, or at least to discourage working into extreme old age. Phasing out of elderly practitioners was the most obvious means to ease the lot of younger practitioners and its relevance to the improvement of efficiency was self-evident. However this problem was evaded by the working party, and by the CHSC and BMA committees on general practice, and it received little public attention. Granted standard safeguards for the client, unrestricted liberty to continue in practice was regarded as an inalienable right of the higher professions. Before 1948 long service was an economic necessity. After 1948 eligibility for superannuation was conditional on ten years' NHS service, with the result that elderly practitioners were inclined to delay retirement until 1958 so that they could collect both superannuation and compensation for loss of their right of sale of practice. Introduction of further financial inducements to earlier retirement was unacceptable to the Government. The public was judged to have sufficient protection against any lapse in efficiency of old doctors or indeed against other incompetent practitioners.[34] Dignified restraint on the retirement issue was occasionally broken by an unguarded comment, such as, 'The NHS is after all a publicly organised service and it is a little worrying to have them going on well into their 90s and costing the Exchequer about £3,000 pa'.[35] Old practitioners were an endemic feature of the system and they were sometimes local celebrities. In Reid Ross's Factory Town the oldest practitioner with 41 years' experience was the most highly esteemed.[36] In England and Wales in 1954, 1,188 out of its 18,513 principals were aged 66 or over. In 1954 in Scotland 37 out of its 2,514 principals were aged above 75. In the Kent and Canterbury EC area, 5% of all principals were aged above 70.[37] This information indicates the prevalence of medical practice beyond the normal age of retirement. It should be considered in association with comments offered below about the state of general practice.

One of the major aims of the NHS was correction of the maldistribution of general practitioners. Sale of practice was abolished in the interests of this policy, and two national Medical Practices Committees were formed to influence distribution. As noted in chapter IV the powers of the Medical Practices Committee were reduced during negotiations. Eventually the emasculated committee was placed in the hands of nominees of the profession. Under the sixth schedule of the 1946 NHS Act the Medical Practices Committee comprised eight members and a chairman, all but two being appointed by the Minister after consultation with the profession.[38]

The role of the Medical Practices Committee was much less interventionist than originally envisaged. In the majority of cases partnerships and practices determined successors with very little intervention from Executive Councils, while the Medical Practices Committee for the most part acted as a referee. It was the arbiter of legality. The Committee also collected and classified data. In the small percentage of cases where advertisements were involved, and with respect to certain partnership arrangements, it played a more active part. The best-known function of the Medical Practices Committee was closure or restriction of entry into practice in certain areas where the number of doctors was considered to be adequate.[39] The Medical Practices Committee for England and Wales operated on the basis of a four-part classification until 1953. Thereafter, on the advice of the Working Party on Distribution, it adopted a three-part classification. During negotiations, closure or restriction was resisted by the profession on account of its limitation of the traditional freedom to practise anywhere. Closure turned out to be an attractive proposition to incumbent doctors because it reduced competition for patients in their area. The Medical Practices Committee applied its powers to close an area with great reserve. In its original classification closures were confined to areas where average list sizes were below 1,600. Under the revised classification averages in 'restricted' areas were below 1,500.

'Intermediate' areas included average lists from 1,500 to 2,500, while higher averages were classified as 'designated'.[40] Quite contrary to original expectations the Medical Practices Committee came under pressure from Executive Councils to extend closures, in some cases to embrace areas with average list sizes of 4,000, which would have closed virtually the whole country to new entrants.[41]

On account of geographical factors low list averages were common in Scotland. Consequently the Scottish Medical Practices Committee only intermittently closed an area.[42]

In England and Wales designated areas in 1952 contained 21.7m or 51.5% of the population, whereas in 1955 this figure had declined to 10.0m, or 23.4% of the population. In Scotland 'listed' areas contained 13.4% of the population in 1952, and 10.5% in 1955. In England and Wales the average list size in the designated areas fell from 2,851 to 2,736 between 1952 and 1955, while in Scotland the list size in listed areas was reduced from 2,875 to 2,740.[43] Improvements in industrial areas were offset by the tendency for these areas to include an increasing percentage of elderly single-handed practice doctors.[44] Improvement in the supply of doctors in designated areas was primarily a reflection of a general influx into the profession, occasioned by expansion of the medical schools and restriction of opportunities for promotion in hospitals. Between July 1948 and July 1955 the number of principals in general practice in England and Wales rose by about 10%, from 19,450 to 21,350.[45] Between 1952 and 1956 the average list size fell from 2,436 to 2,286 in England and Wales, and from 2,078 to 1,971 in Scotland.[46]

When considered in the light of long-term trends the NHS marked a phase of rapid recruitment to general practice. The rank and file of the profession became uneasy about increased competition, while the Government departments were concerned about paying a growing number of doctors to provide a fairly constant service. Assessment of the 'saturation point' for general medical practice was a primary motivation for establishing the Willink Committee.[47] Consensus on this issue was virtually impossible owing to the wide divergence of opinion on optimum list size, and because of the difficulty in assessing the future work-load of general practitioners. The Ministry of Health believed that ageing of the population could be accommodated without increasing numbers of general practitioners, whereas the Willink Report allowed an increase of 75 general practitioners per annum for this factor.[48] On the basis of reducing the average list to 2,000 the English Medical Practices Committee calculated a need for 3,135 additional principals.[49] The Ministry of Health favoured an increase nearer to the 424 required to reduce the average to 2,500 in the designated areas.[50] The Willink Committee came down nearer to the Ministry's position, accepting that 600 additional principals would be needed in England and Wales, and 25 in Scotland, to reach the desirable target of average list sizes of 2,000 in rural areas and 2,500 in urban areas.[51] The Willink limit was quickly passed and the number of principals in service gradually increased to reach 23,254 in 1983, when the average list size was 2,116.[52]

As the NHS became more settled, doubts emerged concerning the success of the new service in overcoming the notorious weaknesses of general practice under the previous regime. The moderate increases in numbers or partnerships mentioned above were not themselves instrumental in working the required transformation of standards and attitudes. During the early years of the service general practitioners were immersed in their financial grievances, while the health departments were preoccupied with keeping down costs. Earlier promises of a great initiative to improve the general medical service remained unaccomplished. Inertia characterised the system.

Stagnation was, however, not absolute. Between 1950 and 1953 reports on general practice emanated from the BMA and the CHSC, as well as from a variety of independent observers. Furthermore the College of General Practitioners and more modest groups such as the General Practice Reform Association were formed to improve standards in general practice. These developments were less a manifestation of leadership from above than a reaction to a mounting tide of criticism from below. The single most effective factor in mobilising opinion in favour of constructive change was the paper produced in *The Lancet* by an Australian visitor, J S Collings.[53] Many subsequent developments spring from this source.

Collings was not universally applauded for his work and his intervention is susceptible to criticism. But most of his shots hit their mark with explosive impact. In bald terms Collings concluded that the 'overall state of general practice is bad and still deteriorating'.[54] His survey of practices in England and Scotland, whether of the industrial, mixed or rural type, found little to inspire confidence. His bleakest experience related to the industrial areas, where little seemed to have changed since the last century.[55] Other inquiries generally confirmed the findings of Collings. The National Health Service had largely severed links between general practitioners and the hospital service, with the result that practitioners' prestige had suffered.[56] Even where general practitioners retained posts as clinical assistants in hospital their status declined, and they complained generally about being treated as inferiors by their hospital colleagues. Echoing a common complaint, the Executive

Councils Association claimed that general practitioners had degenerated into 'glorified clerks' referring their patients to hospitals, even for the most minor treatment.[57]

There was little agreement on the ideal relationship between general practitioners and the hospital service. Some hospital authorities regarded phasing out of general practitioners as a sign of a natural evolutionary change, whereas others regarded them as useful for maintenance of certain essential hospital services.[58] General practitioners were themselves divided over hospital work. Some wanted general practice to develop its independent identity,[59] others regarded hospital experience as essential for maintenance of specialist skills among general practitioners.[60] In the interests of economy and efficiency the Ministry of Health tried to reverse the decline in general practitioner hospital appointments.[61]

A conscientious single-handed practitioner working from a converted workman's cottage in an industrial town conducted between 40 and 55 consultations each day. On a busy day he saw 42 patients in three hours. In addition he made 25 domiciliary visits each day, and gave out 50 certificates each week. His holidays comprised one half-day each week, plus an annual summer break. Apart from abandonment of direct billing of non-insured patients, and some change in prescribing habits, this routine was little different from experience recorded in similar places during the depression.[62] In Factory Town, where findings echoed those of Collings, it was noted that the average length for consultations was 4 minutes.[63]

In the survey undertaken for the BMA, practitioners frankly admitted their shortcomings. Their problems were summarised as:

Lack of time in the heavy demands for treatment for trivial ailments. The haste necessitated by crowded surgeries was said to induce mental fatigue and strain, diminish alertness of mind, and cloud clinical judgement. This led to a tendency to 'spot diagnosis' and to the reference to hospital of any cases requiring much thought.[64]

Consequently, notwithstanding improvements in recruitment, general practice remained greatly in arrears of the standards anticipated when the NHS was devised. The incremental changes taking place were insufficient to bring about the desirable standard of primary care. The more concerted attempts to modernise general practice will be further considered in section (v) below.

(ii) DENTAL SERVICE

The Dawson Report's outline of the future medical service gave a high place to the dental service. In Dawson's primary health centres dental treatment was projected 'for all classes of the community' and for all age groups.[65] The reality in inter-war

Britain was very different. Compared with other western nations Britain possessed fewer dentists, a smaller proportion of qualified dentists, a poorer service and lower expectations among the public. In a BDA review undertaken in 1941, National Health Insurance dental benefit was dismissed as a 'breakdown service'.[66] Other public dental services were seriously underdeveloped. Acceptable standards were limited to a few special schemes. Further erosion of services available to the civilian population took place during World War II.

Although the Beveridge Report assumed that dental benefit would be universalised under the comprehensive social security plan, the Ministry of Health was unconvinced that it was realistic to promise such a service. Realising that a complete dental service would require far more dentists than the 12,000 available at that time, the Ministry opted for a gradualist policy based on extension of the existing dental service for priority classes.[67] The BDA and Incorporated Dentists Society were also opposed to a comprehensive service on account of the risk of dilution by ancillaries. The lead for a comprehensive dental service was given by the interim report of the Teviot Committee in August 1944. Doubters within the Ministry and the dental profession were quickly persuaded to accept the Teviot conclusion.[68]

As already seen in chapter IV negotiations with the dental profession ran into severe difficulties. Confrontation over the concentration of the dental service into health centres, where dentists would be salaried, was avoided when it became clear that health centres on any scale were a distant proposition. More serious difficulties resulted from disagreements over the mode of remuneration for the general dental service. Refusal by the health departments to countenance the grant-in-aid system advocated by the consultative committee of the profession led to imposition of a revised version of the existing NHI scale of fees. The resultant BDA-led boycott of the new service failed for a variety of reasons. First, the generality of dentists were accustomed to the scale-of-fees system. They were not unhappy to sacrifice the grant-in-aid which in any case had only been narrowly approved by their negotiators. Acceptance of the scale of fees by a Government known to favour salaried service was recognised as a conciliatory gesture. Secondly, the revised scale of fees was considerably more generous than the NHI scale. Thirdly, joining the NHS entailed a guarantee of remuneration at the level suggested by the Spens Committee, and also some back-dated payments. As noted above, within a few months of the introduction of the new service 95% of effective dentists had joined the general dental service.

TABLE I

Cost of the General Dental Service 1948–1956

£m at actual prices

	(6 months) 1948	1949	1950	1951	1952	1953	1954	1955	1956
Fees to dentists	10.0	41.9	40.5	33.0	22.0	20.0	22.2	26.1	29.5
Payments by patients				0.9	5.0	6.4	6.8	7.1	7.6
Total cost	10.0	41.9	40.5	33.9	27.0	26.4	29.0	33.2	37.1

Sources: Ministry of Health, Annual Reports; Estimates, 7th Report, pp 23–5.

The high initial level of expenditure on the general dental service is common knowledge. Dental benefit under NHI cost about £1m pa. An early estimate for the NHS assumed that the full service would cost £10m pa.[69] The figure adopted for a full year during preparation of the first estimates was £12m, which was reduced to £7m for the first nine months of the service, and also in light of expected delays in payments to dentists. The basis for these calculations was the experience that only 7% of the NHI beneficiaries took advantage of the service in any one year. In addition, following the Teviot Committee, it was thought that the public would need persuading to avail themselves of a dental service.[70] Payments to dentists in England and Wales amounted to £19.5m in 1948/49 (nine months), £46.5m in 1949/50, and £39.5m in 1950/51. Stringent measures then introduced quickly reduced the cost of the dental service by half. Trends in the cost of the dental service are shown in Table I.

The high cost of the dental service was explained by two factors, first the unexpectedly high level of demand, and secondly high earnings of dentists. Officials candidly admitted that they were taken by surprise by the initial rush at the service. In Scotland because 13.6% of the population used the service in the first six months Sir George Henderson could not 'see how it can fail to come down, and come down pretty rapidly'. Bevan also predicted a rapid fall-off in demand. On that account he confidently reduced the estimate for 1949/50 from £40m to £29m. Expectations of slackening demand constituted a further miscalculation.[71] Demand for dental treatment remained high until it was artificially suppressed, although the character of that demand was gradually changing.

In the first months of the service claims handled by the Dental Estimates Board ran at the rate of 6.8m pa, compared with the

2.4m expected.[72] During the first nine months 4.2m teeth were filled, 4.5m extracted and 33.4m artificial teeth were provided. The amount of conservation work greatly increased under the NHS, but the most spectacular change was the massive increase in artificial teeth provided. In 1950/51 65.6m artificial teeth were handed out. The early NHS dental service can thus be characterised as a 'denture boom', the most prominent element in which was the supply of replacement dentures. Such replacements must often have been given for old, ill-fitting vulcanite dentures. Others were replacements for recently provided dentures that had been fitted before the gums had stabilised. The ratio of artificial teeth supplied to teeth extracted under NHI dental benefit was 2:1, indicating a low rate of replacement.[73] In 1948/49 this ratio increased to 7:1. In 1950/51 the ratio declined slightly to 5:1, suggesting that the replacement element in the denture boom was declining. In 1950/51 8.7m teeth were filled, indicating a steady rise in conservation work.[74] Consequently, although the NHS dental service was still predominantly a denture supply agency, the germ of the trend towards conservation was apparent, even before external incentives were applied to hasten this trend.

Estimates for fees paid to dentists were based on the Spens recommendation that dentists should receive an average of £1,778 pa. Immediately the service began it was clear that earnings would exceed this figure. Much publicity was attracted by evidence of gross earnings in the region of £20,000 by dentists who were effectively proprietors of 'denture factories'. There was also alarm at the inversion of the recommendations of Spens with respect to the relative earnings of dentists and doctors. It was pointed out that the net earnings of general practitioners were £1,530 pa, while dentists were receiving £2,300 pa.[75] Precise characterisation of the salary situation was difficult in the fluid situation of the early NHS, when recruitment was still taking place and the Dental Estimates Board was fresh to its work and operating in a state of seige.

Early Dental Estimates Board investigations suggested excess earnings. The first indicated that 7% were earning twice the Spens recommended salary. The second, more adequate survey, covering the period October 1948 to March 1949, showed that 59% were earning more than £1,778, while 22% were receiving twice this figure.[76] Average net earnings appeared to be about 20% in excess of £1,778. A truer picture of earnings was not known until after 1952, when it emerged that average net earnings during the early NHS were 45% higher than the recommended Spens figure.[77] This later analysis also demonstrated the advantageous position of younger, more active dentists, and 'organised practices' employing assistants. Later reassessments showed that dentists' financial advantage was even greater than earlier realised because their allowed expenses of 52% were overestimated by 10%.

Dentists were quite easily able to inflate their earnings by working more than the chairside 33 hours regarded as a full working week by Spens. They could also exploit the more lucrative denture work, and they benefited by errors in the timings for dental operations adopted in calculating the scale of fees.

The health departments were slow to bring dentists' earnings under control. The first token effort was made in February 1949 when fees above £400 a month were reduced by 50%. At this stage the excessive earnings problem was attributed to a small number of irresponsible practitioners. Such action temporarily appeased critics, and it was not offensive to the profession. However this 'ceiling cut' was quite ineffective. Fees were reduced by only 7%, and the effect was temporary. Organised practices easily compensated for this minor obstacle.[78]

In order to establish a firm basis of fact for future action, in January 1949 a working party under William Penman was formed to review timings for dental operations. The Penman inquiry also examined the general problem of earnings. It was found that dentists were working an average of 37½ hours each week, which the Ministry wished to adopt as a revised working week for dentists, but this idea was unanimously rejected by the profession. The Penman working party suggested that average earnings were only 14% in excess of £1,778, or 19% including private practice earnings. Of this excess 11% was attributed to extra hours, and 8% to faster working. The Penman Report advised that the only justifiable reduction in fees related to the timing factor. It sided with the profession's view that fees should be paid on a sliding scale, so that only high income earners would be penalised. Under the Penman recommendations much of the saving extracted from high income earners would have been transferred to lower-paid dentists.[79]

The Penman Report was published in August 1949. It was silent on the expenses issue, and it offered nothing to aid the Government's quest for economy in the general dental service. Consequently it was quietly bypassed. The health departments acted unilaterally before the appearance of the Penman Report to impose a cut in fees of 20%. This reduction was announced in May and it was applied from 1 June 1949. The Ministry contemplated a 25% cut, but Dental Estimates Board findings cited above suggested that 20% would be sufficient. Application of this cut involved construction of a new scale of fees, which applied a mild incentive towards conservative treatment. Underestimation of the proportion of denture work being undertaken (assumed to be 40% of total, but actually 60%) resulted in reduction of the anticipated savings to 15%.[80]

The 20% reduction in fees applied in June 1949 was as ineffective as the earlier cut introduced in February. Its impact was reduced because the ceiling cut on high earnings was removed, with the result that private work was deflected back into the NHS. Also demand was sufficient for dentists to be able to take on more work to offset cuts, while continuing influx of dentists into the service added to costs. The reduction in fees accomplished by this second cut was consequently no more than 6%.[81] The exercise was counterproductive in other respects because it alienated the dentists, who regarded the Government's action as a breach of faith. Dentists undertaking a greater amount of denture work were most annoyed, which accounts for sporadic strike action of dentists in the north of England. This was the first step in reducing the economic advantage of dentists specialising in denture work. From this point onward economic advantage turned against the more traditional dentists of the north and Wales.

Confirming the low yield from the 20% cut, the Dental Estimates Board found early in 1950 that dentists' earnings were still on average 8% above the Spens level. Because the average was depressed by numerous elderly dentists who were not fully active, it was decided to impose a further 15% cut. The BDA reported that the cuts were striking unfairly at the middle-income earners. Consequently it refused to negotiate and withdrew its co-operation from an investigation into practice expenses. The Government imposed a 10% cut with effect from 1 May 1950.[82]

On this occasion, as Table I indicates, the tide of fees began to ebb. Between May 1950 and the introduction of charges a year later a 15% reduction in fees paid to dentists took place. Average earnings were reduced from 45% above the Spens level to 20% in excess.[83]

This adverse change resulted from gradual drying up of lucrative replacement denture work, and transfer to less remunerative conservative dentistry. The impact of the 10% cut was reinforced by the charges imposed on dentures in May 1951. The acute political controversies surrounding this measure have been fully discussed in chapter V. Denture charges exercised a more pronounced deterrent effect than had been expected. Gross dental earnings fell by a further 20% in the year 1951/52. The additional dental charges introduced in 1952 resulted in a further reduction of 15% in gross earnings.[84] Thus, by early 1953 dentists were earning on average 22% below the Spens level. The burden of cuts was spread unevenly. Organised practices and younger dentists in the south survived the cuts, but single-handed dentists, especially in the north and Scotland, fared badly.

The combined effect of changes in the scale of fees, charges, and natural reduction of demand destroyed the denture boom. Between 1950/51 and 1953 there was a 66% fall in the number of artificial teeth supplied. The ratio of artificial teeth to extractions was only 2.5:1, almost back to the pre-war level. On the other hand over the same period the number of teeth filled increased by 40%, showing that the public was willing to avail itself of conservative treatment regardless of charges. By 1953 the ratio of fillings to artificial teeth was 1:1.9. Notwithstanding its use as a political weapon the general dental service was slowly undergoing a transformation and casting off its image as a breakdown service.[85]

Despite a positive shift in the character of the dental service, it was left with problems. There were for instance doubts about the quality of conservative dentistry, and indeed about the probity of its practitioners. The Comptroller and Auditor General spoke darkly of 'scamped work and even of fraud', and the Public Accounts Committee kept up its pungent criticism of the administration of the dental service.[86] The chairman and members of the Dental Estimates Board accepted that its system gave 'every opportunity for practising petty deception and even fraud'. They believed that 30% of the fees paid were giving no value. In the light of the experience of the Board, a Treasury witness concluded that there was 'more waste of public money here than in any other part of the NHS'.[87] There was general feeling that the machinery of inspection and discipline was operating in only a perfunctory manner.

Decisions concerning the general dental service exercised profound influence on the priority dental services. These services to mothers and infants and to school children were provided in clinics maintained by Local Health and Education Authorities, and they were staffed by salaried dental officers. Places like Cambridge had developed extensive priority services, but mostly these clinics were underdeveloped. It was anticipated that the above classes would be treated with genuine priority under the NHS. But the system adopted effectively placed the clinics in competition with the general dental service for the same staff. The contest was uneven and predictably dentists abandoned the priority services for more lucrative general dental practice.

Owing to an influx from the armed services recruitment to the priority services reached a peak in 1948 when there were in England and Wales 921 dental officers. By 1950 the number had fallen to 738 and by 1951 it was 717. This decline caused public alarm.[88] Paradoxically the dental charges of 1952 did much to revive services to the priority classes. Recruitment again improved because the general dental service was no longer so attractive, while exclusion of adolescents from the charges greatly increased the amount of treatment received by this group.[89] The 1953 Education Act strengthened the responsibility of Local Education Authorities to provide dental treatment for those at school. According to official interpretation, public disenchantment with private dentists and the cheapness of the clinic alternative resulted in the priority services obtaining a new lease of life. However the profession was no admirer of dental clinics, which were dismissed as the 'cinderella' of the local authority services. It was alleged by the BDA that the record of clinics was poor both on examination and treatment. It was thought that the dull, routine work of school clinics would never attract competent dentists. Given their increasing tendency to spare capacity private dentists made a bid to take over the work of the school dental service on an agency basis.[90]

The NHS was confronted by the anticipated problem of shortage of dentists. The aura of instability surrounding the early service reduced its attractiveness to potential recruits. The Teviot Committee urged an increase of the effective dentist workforce from 12,000 to 20,000. In 1953 it was noted that 24,000 dentists would produce a staffing standard equivalent to American dentistry.[91]

The Teviot Committee advised that the entry into dental schools should be increased from the pre-war level of 400 to 900. Dental schools were gradually expanded to allow for an increased intake. The intake stood at about 650 between 1946 and 1948, largely owing to the influx of ex-servicemen, but afterwards, with increasing dependence on younger entrants, recruitment fell away to about 470 in the mid-50s. Entry into the Scottish dental schools fell by 50% between 1950 and 1952. There was alarm in Scotland because many of the trainees, such as the 60 Norwegians recorded in 1954, were unlikely to practise in Britain.[92] The profession blamed the drop in recruitment on the threat of introduction of ancillaries, the inferior status of dentistry compared with medicine, controls exercised by the Dental Estimates Board, the heavy cost of entry into the service, current insecurity and uncertainty about future prospects, and bad publicity for the profession under the NHS.[93]

Whatever the justification of the pessimistic prognosis by the profession the number of dentists failed to increase. In the decade following World War II there were about 15,500 registered dentists, but an active workforce of only about 9,500. A particular reason for concern was the imminent decline in numbers consequent on retirement of the '1921 dentists'. This group, whose registration had been permitted in 1921 on account of experience rather than qualifications, still accounted for 25% of the profession in 1955. It was expected that a substantial number of them would retire in 1958 when they had fulfilled minimum conditions of eligibility for NHS superannuation.

The combination of declining recruitment and escalating retirement faced NHS dentistry with a renewed crisis. Furthermore it revived the argument over the respective roles of qualified dentists and dental ancillaries. The profession pressed for an inquiry into the recruitment problem. Officials were resistant to creating a platform for rehearsal of professional grievances, especially concerning pay, an issue upon which the Government was becoming increasingly vulnerable.[94] But an inquiry under Lord McNair was established in 1955, after the profession agreed that it was committed to disinterested analysis rather than short-term advantage. The McNair Committee reported in October 1956.[95] The report covered much of the ground of the Teviot Report and its general tenor was similar, but less optimistic. Diffuseness of the problem of the professional standing of dentistry was matched by diffuseness of the proposed solutions. It was hoped that by projecting a more positive image, recruitment from schools and among women would be increased.

Inevitably the McNair Committee drifted into consideration of income levels of the dentists. It was accepted that the current system had failed to establish a secure career pattern for dentists. Blame was directed against the current scale of fees, but no particular solution was proposed.[96] Because the McNair Report presented something of a depressing account of the state of dentistry, without making convincing suggestions for improvement, it contributed little towards restoring morale or confidence in the future of NHS dentistry.

Current economic factors rather than the McNair Report were instrumental in bringing about the improvement in recruitment which took place in the late 50s. From 1952 onwards the health departments urged that restoration of the 10% cut in remuneration made in 1950 was justified and that this was the single measure most likely to raise entry into dentistry. An unresponsive Treasury was eventually persuaded to accept restoration, but only after conclusion of a lengthy Inland Revenue inquiry into practice expenses.[97] The 10% cut was restored in April 1955. By this stage dentists' earnings were regaining their buoyancy owing to recovery of the market from the effect of the 1951 and 1952 charges. Also in the more relaxed atmosphere prevailing in the late 50s the health departments took tentative steps towards encouragement of dental health.[98] Even with such improvements standards still fell drastically short of the kind of comprehensive dental service envisaged in the 1920 Dawson Report.

(iii) PHARMACEUTICAL AND OPHTHALMIC SERVICES

Pharmacists. The major problems of the pharmaceutical service, occasioned by high demand and increasing cost of the drugs prescribed, have already been discussed in chapter VI. The cost of the pharmaceutical service was essentially determined by these factors. Compared with their other part IV colleagues, the general practitioners, dentists, or sight-testing opticians, pharmacists occupied a relatively uncontroversial niche in the NHS. Their major initial concern was the extent to which health centres would employ salaried pharmacists, and thereby enter into competition with private contractor chemists. In early planning documents it was left open to individuals to decide whether they obtained 'their supplies on the prescription of their doctor either from the shops or other premises of a pharmacist or from any health centre where dispensing services are provided'.[99]

On account of the plentiful supply of chemists' shops pharmacy services were played down in early health centre planning. The Joint Committee on a National Pharmaceutical Service was assured that health centres would be limited to a few carefully controlled experiments and that the question of including pharmaceutical services would only arise on new estates. In the light of these assurances, it seemed to the Joint Committee that as far as pharmacists were concerned the NHS was retaining continuity with NHI. Most of the minor adverse changes anticipated by the Joint Committee failed to materialise.[100]

As with the other groups the major problem of the pharmacists was establishing a sound basis for remuneration. In March 1946 the Secretary of State promised the Scottish chemists an inquiry of the Spens type. This was designed to allay their fears concerning possible loss of the differential which they were paid under NHI. The result was a working party headed by William Penman which undertook a comparative study of pharmacists' earnings. The report demonstrated peculiarities in the Scottish system, which became the basis of a minor difference in the remuneration arrangements. The report was completed in April 1948, giving very little time for pay negotiations before the Appointed Day.[101] In June 1948 an agreement was concluded, which essentially involved updating the NHI scale. Under the NHS the chemist received (a) the wholesale cost of ingredients as contained in the Drug Tariff, (b) an on-cost allowance of $33\frac{1}{3}\%$ to allow for overheads, (c) an average dispensing fee of 1s, with separate rates for certain special services, and (d) a container allowance of $2\frac{1}{2}$d per prescription. Of these payments (a) and (b) repeated the NHI pattern, (c) increased the NHI rate of 6d to 1s, and (d) was a new payment compensating the chemist for supplying a container for medicine. Under NHI, patients either brought their own bottles, or paid a deposit. The new arrangement ended an old tradition, but it was more civilised. Given a constant cost of ingredients and the on-cost, the NHS rate to chemists would have been 30.5d compared with 22d per prescription previously. This factor, reinforced by increase from 70m to 241m in the annual total of prescriptions, and a 66% increase in the average price of prescriptions, contributed to the greatly inflated cost of the pharmaceutical service in the first year of the NHS.[102] In Scotland chemists preserved their higher dispensing fee, being granted 1s 3d instead of 1s.[103]

About 14,000 chemists joined the service in England and Wales. Their first and most persistent grievance related to the change introduced in pricing the prescriptions submitted to the pricing offices. Because of the unanticipated level of work, the profession agreed to accept payment on the basis of a 25% sample for all prescriptions under 2s 6d, but with full costing being made for more expensive items. An element of inaccuracy was inevitably introduced by this method, compared with the full pricing policy pursued under NHI. Even with the sample method the work of the pricing bureaux rapidly fell ten months into arrears. The pricing bureaux were reorganised, more staff were recruited, and slowly the arrears were cleared, but it took until the end of 1954 to reach an acceptable timetable. In Scotland the arrears were ended in 1952. However, despite introduction of various modifications, both pricing systems remained based on averages, which was unacceptable to the profession, and it was also the source of division of opinion within the Ministry and among experts. The Treasury resisted pressure to readopt full pricing on the ground that additional financial outlay was not merited by an exercise that brought no proven return to the taxpayer. This problem was somewhat eased by adoption in England of the Scottish level of 55% for the pricing sample, while full pricing was applied to about 60% of prescriptions.[104] The departmental advocates of full pricing believed that the 'chaotic state' of the pricing system over a period of five years had contributed to laxity over excessive prescribing.[105]

Inevitably, in the course of the Government's economy drive, fees received by chemists came under scrutiny. In their case no target incomes had been established, and there was little objective justification for the fees adopted. In 1949 consideration was given to abolishing the container allowance, reducing the on-cost fee from 33% to 16%, and also reducing the dispensing fee. In the event, after protracted departmental discussions and negotiations with the profession the container allowance was reduced from $2\frac{1}{2}$d to $1\frac{1}{4}$d, and on-costs from 33% to 25%, but these savings were quickly wiped out by backdated claims made through the Whitley machinery, which resulted in the Scottish dispensing fee being increased from 1s 3d to 1s 6d, backdated to 5 July 1948, while the English dispensing fee was increased from 1s to 1s 1d with effect from 1 May 1950. The profession then entered into prolonged negotiations to secure further increases in all their fees.[106] As in the case of the eye service the Government discovered that imposing charges on patients was a more straightforward and effective means of introducing economies than the alternative of striking at the remuneration of the professionals involved with these services.

Opticians. Ophthalmic benefit was the most highly developed additional benefit available to participants in the National Health Insurance scheme. By 1942 12m persons, mostly men, comprising 60% of the insured population, were receiving ophthalmic benefit. Under this arrangement members paid half of the cost. Children with eye defects were treated under the school medical service. Most of the remaining 75% of the population made their own arrangements. The working classes customarily used the 'sixpenny' service at Woolworth's, or else they obtained glasses from itinerant vendors, or second-hand from market stalls.

The Beveridge Report recommended extension of an ophthalmic service to the whole population. Although this proposal introduced no particular technical difficulty, it inevitably precipitated renewed hostilities in the thirty-years war between the medical profession and sight-testing opticians. Under the NHI scheme the argument had gone in favour of the opticians. Their cheap service suited the Approved Societies; they seemed to be competent enough to handle the majority of the work involved, and there were too few medically qualified ophthalmologists to deal with anything other than the more serious eye defects. The medical profession was reconciled to a minority role, but it wanted opticians to work as auxiliaries under medical supervision. Sight-testing opticians consolidated their position during the inter-war period, but without gaining the full formal independence they desired owing to failure of their attempt to introduce statutory registration. Through the medium of the National Ophthalmic Treatment Board general practitioners invaded the field, using authorised 'dispensing opticians' as their auxiliaries. This alternative was not particularly successful, in 1942 dealing with less than one-quarter of the NHI business.[107]

At the time of the Beveridge Report the eye service was dispersed between specialist ophthalmic departments in hospitals, general practitioners involved with the National Ophthalmic Treatment Board and their sight-testing assistants, dispensing opticians, and eye clinics of local authorities. The health departments had always regarded reconciliation between the conflicting parties as a 'vexed problem'. Their general line was to encourage the development of a medical eye service, but without ostentatiously undermining sight-testing opticians. Discussions concerning the future comprehensive service concluded that a full medical service was desirable, but impracticable, owing to the shortage of specialists. Accordingly in 1944 it was agreed to persist with the current compromise arrangement, allowing the bulk of the work to be undertaken by dispensing opticians, but looking forward to the eventual phasing out of their service.[108]

The first active negotiations were held in the spring of 1945. Ophthalmologists and opticians were told that the current distribution of work would continue until a committee was set up to determine the form of a permanent service. Providing their independence was protected, opticians accepted health centres as a basis for the new service. Ophthalmologists on the other hand wanted clinics transferred from health centres to hospitals, where they hoped to build up an 'ideal service for future development'.[109]

After the 1945 election the Government was pressed by the ophthalmologists to accept their 'ideal form of eye service' as an immediate objective. Although the health departments were sceptical about this possibility, the memorandum outlining the future service was strongly influenced by this point of view. It accepted 'provision as soon as possible of special clinics, as part of the hospital service', staffed by ophthalmologists and refractionists working under them. Although such services would become 'the sole arrangements for eye-testing' recognised under the NHS, it was conceded that in the short term 'temporary supplementary arrangements' would be available under Executive Councils, where authorised sight-testing opticians would provide glasses to patients possessing a certificate from their general practitioner. It was emphasised that this supplementary service would in due course be abolished. In order to prevent sight-testing opticians from gaining security, their profession was denied places on the CHSC or Executive Councils.[110] They were also left out of the superannuation and disciplinary arrangements, and unlike general practitioners, dentists, or pharmacists, no local professional committees were formed. However, somewhat unavoidably, opticians were included in the Ophthalmic SAC. Opticians were unhappy with these restrictions, but they participated in the Eye Services Committee set up to organise conditions of entry of their group into the supplementary eye service. The medical profession warned that once in place a supplementary service would be difficult to dismember. The opticians worked hard to convert this suspicion into reality.[111]

The Eye Services Committee recommended that the Ministers should introduce a formal machinery for regulating the supplementary eye service, but the Government favoured a more informal mechanism. Consequently, on the recommendation of the Eye Services Committee a Central Professional Committee was formed to draw up lists of accredited practitioners. The main list, including 4,000 sight-testing opticians (now also called 'ophthalmic opticians'), was submitted in May 1948. The committee retained responsibility for this aspect of regulation in the profession until its lists were superseded by the statutory register in 1961.[112] In March 1949, about 5,000 individual sight-testing opticians, and opticians working for some 2,000 firms, represented the backbone of the supplementary service. In addition there were about 1,000 ophthalmic medical practitioners, and 530 dispensing opticians. The balance of personnel thus remained about the same as under National Health Insurance.[113]

The service offered also remained similar to that given under NHI. Ten types of spectacles were available free of charge, and seven others could be obtained for extra cost. After some hesitation, two types and limited colours of plastic frames were available on the free list. A sufficient range of free frames was introduced to avoid a 'utility' image, but care was exercised not to boost demand artificially.[114] There was little idea of likely demand. The industry feared that the public would not be attracted by the new service. Official estimates were based on the assumption that the NHI level of demand would continue. This placed the cost of the service at £3.5m for a full year, and £2m for the first nine months. An official pleaded that 'nobody knew what sort of demand there would be or whether people had not already got the spectacles they wanted. The actual rush shows that for some reason or other people wanted new spectacles'.[115] It was expected that about 5% of the population would use the service each year. In Scotland the initial rate ran at 20%. In England and Wales in the first nine months 5m persons were tested, while the total cost in this period was £11m, which represented an annual rate of £15m. A member of the Select Committee on Estimates called this episode an 'egregious miscalculation'.[116] The cost of the supplementary eye service in England and Wales reached a peak of £21.7m in 1949/50, and it fell only slightly in the following year. At its peak, in England and Wales there were about 5m sight-tests each year, and 7.5m pairs of spectacles were supplied.[117]

Control of the cost of the supplementary eye service became an increasingly serious political issue. In order to avoid a reduction in their fees the profession pressed for the introduction of charges. The first modest proposal for removing plastic frames from the free list was at first rejected by Bevan, but soon afterwards accepted. From 1 May 1950 patients paid all but 5s of the cost of plastic frames. This charge made virtually no difference to demand.[118]

During 1950 officials considered a range of further options, from introduction of a 1s flat rate charge on lenses, to charging for the whole cost of the service, except for sight-testing.[119] Desultory official deliberations were eventually overtaken by the political exchanges described in chapter V, which resulted in imposition on 21 May 1951 of charges of 10s per lens, and the full cost of frames. These charges precipitated a dramatic reduction in demand. Comparing the second and third quarters of 1951, sight-tests fell by 35%, and the number of pairs of glasses supplied by 45%. Comparing the fourth quarters of 1950 and 1951, fees paid for sight-testing fell by 35%, while payments to opticians for supply and repair fell by 63%.[120] The cost of the supplementary service fell from £19.6m in 1950/51 to £8.5m in 1951/52.

Introduction of charges was backed up by a less forceful attempt to reduce fees. In negotiations concerning the original scale of fees the profession asked for an increase of the sight-testing fee from the NHI level of 7s 6d to 21s. In negotiations 15s 6d was agreed. The Ministry evolved a fee for dispensing based on investigation of current practice, 25s being proposed and eventually accepted. The combined testing and dispensing fee was therefore 40s 6d.[121] As a result of Whitley Council negotiations conducted between January and April 1949 this combined fee was reduced to 38s, and minor adjustments were introduced in other fees. Receipts of opticians were little affected by these changes. Further reductions were ruled out when a Penman Working Party, after a brief investigation made in 1950, concluded that the scale of fees was essentially correct. The primary financial benefit to opticians had accrued from high demand and resultant reduction in overheads.[122] With the collapse of demand the profession pressed for increased fees to compensate them for loss of income; 51s was demanded as the combined sight-testing and dispensing fee. Under the scrutiny of the Public Accounts Committee and the Treasury, the health departments resisted an increase on the grounds that a thorough inquiry was needed to reveal the economic circumstances of opticians. This inquiry was delegated to the profession, and it was undertaken between 1953 and 1955, but owing to lack of co-operation by members the data were unusable.[123] The financial position of sight-testing opticians improved because of gradual recovery in NHS demand and increasing private fees. Their morale was also restored owing to virtual abandonment of plans for a hospital eye service.

The position of sight-testing opticians was also assisted by the report of the committee under Lord Crook which in 1952 recommended registration. The Crook Report also made practical proposals for ironing out differences between opticians and their medical critics.[124] The latter were at last reconciled to accepting ophthalmic opticians as an independent profession. The positive view of the supplementary eye service emerging from the Guillebaud Report provided the final spur to registration, which was introduced following the Opticians Act of 1958.

Apart from health centres the hospital eye service provides the other major example of departure from the intentions of the NHS legislation. A hospital eye service was favoured because it was medically superior, potentially cheaper, and more acceptable to the consultant lobby. Detailed proposals for a hospital eye service were drawn up by the Eye Services Committee and the Faculty of Ophthalmologists. But there were major obstacles to development of a hospital eye service. This exercise involved high initial capital cost and it was impeded by a shortage of both consultant and auxiliary staff. Consequently circulars to hospital authorities in July and October 1948 warned that the supplementary service would be the main provider 'for some time', while the hospital service was expected to increase only gradually. Nevertheless in 1950 it was still mentioned that hospital authorities should 'develop the refraction service at hospitals and eye clinics as rapidly as may be to replace the interim service'.[125]

In practice ophthalmic services in hospitals developed little differently from other specialties. Some expansion was occasioned by absorption of the school eye service, but reference to hospital eye clinics for regular eye defects was virtually a dead letter.[126] In 1950, when consideration was given to abolishing the supplementary eye service as an economy, it seemed possible that a hospital eye service would become a minor reality.[127] But the imposition of substantial charges for the supplementary service proved to be such an effective way of reducing costs and suppressing demand that the hospital eye service lost one of its major attractions.

Gradually expectations of a hospital eye service faded, and the supplementary service became accepted as a regular part of the NHS. Taking what seems to have been a personal initiative with respect to the section of the 1946 Act giving the Minister powers to close down the supplementary service, Macleod promised that 'he had no intention of using Section 41(4) and while he could not bind other Ministers of Health, he could not conceive anyone attempting to end the Supplementary Scheme in any time which need be a matter of concern at present'.[128]

This commitment made to the Joint Emergency Committee of the Optical Profession was reported in Macleod's address to the Association of Executive Councils in December 1955. It seems to have been accepted reluctantly by his officials. In their testimonies to the Guillebaud Committee it was urged that the hospital service would be cheaper but the Minister had decided not to accelerate development in this direction.[129] RHB chairmen were also reminded of the Minister's statement in response to their demand for firm commitment to development of a hospital eye service.[130] The Guillebaud Committee was swayed by evidence concerning the efficiency, cheapness and popularity of the supplementary eye service. Accordingly it recommended against its replacement by a comprehensive hospital eye service. Thereby the long struggle waged by opticians since the birth of National Health Insurance was finally concluded to their satisfaction under the National Health Service.[131]

(iv) LOCAL HEALTH AUTHORITIES

As already indicated the National Health Service profoundly reduced the part played by local authorities in health care. This change was traumatic for local authorities because it represented a sudden and unexpected reversal of policies followed since the beginning of the century.

The largest losses to local authorities were the general, poor law, tuberculosis, infectious diseases, mental and mental deficiency hospitals and institutions, which were transferred to the hospital authorities. Local authorities were left with a variety of residual functions not easily disposed of elsewhere in the service. Otherwise they were subsidiary partners in services, the main body of which was provided by part II or part IV authorities. In cases such as maternity and child welfare, tuberculosis, mental health and mental deficiency, or care of the elderly, where previous to 1948 local authorities had provided a comprehensive service, under the NHS these services were distributed between the three branches of the system, with local authorities becoming in each case the junior partner. Local authorities in England and Wales administered the ambulance service used predominantly by hospital authorities. Under either the NHS or National Assistance legislation, local authorities provided a variety of care and after-care services for the elderly, the mentally handicapped, or for those suffering from mental disorder or tuberculosis. The main body of services for these groups was provided by hospital authorities. In the case of health centres the controlling influence rested with part IV contractors. Maternity and child welfare services were divided uncomfortably between parts II, III and IV authorities. Even within local authorities themselves there was often not complete unification between health services provided by local health, welfare and education authorities. Services developed unevenly. Situated within an expanding education system, the School Health Service entered a phase of buoyant growth. Services for mothers and pre-school children lagged behind. Services for the elderly and handicapped were even more depressed.[132] Transfer of maternity and child welfare functions from districts to counties reduced the status of many medical officers and created friction between the two levels of authority.[133] Local Health Authorities depended for their rehabilitation on co-operation from other branches of the NHS, but this was difficult to achieve and it was not helped by survival of deep-rooted animosity between Medical Officers of Health and other members of the profession. In view of the disruption experienced, and obvious demotion, local health departments were reduced to a dispirited rump. Their sense of purpose was not regained before they were finally abolished in 1974.

From the outset of the NHS a sense of impending doom hung over Local Health Authorities. In its evidence to the Guillebaud Committee the Society of Medical Officers of Health admitted that 'the Local Health Authority service had suffered so much in status and prestige under the NHS that their medical staff had greatly degenerated both in quantity and quality'. Loss of administration of hospitals had 'sapped' their energies. They felt that there was 'no real future in the local authority field'.[134] Medical Officers of Health were criticised for not grasping the opportunities of the new service, either because of lack of commitment to community care, or because of unwillingness to incur expenditure on the rates.[135] Local Health Authority expenditure was consequently restricted from two directions. The weak political position of health departments meant that they were vulnerable locally. Since many of their services relied on capital development they were convenient targets during Government economy drives. The rigid control of local authority health and welfare expenditure has already been described in chapter VI, while the restriction of health centre development is discussed below.

The early years of the NHS witnessed the slow incremental growth of the miscellaneous services administered by Local Health and Welfare Authorities without very much reference to integrated planning or rational goals. Even in the case of the health visitors, where a review was undertaken in 1953, the report was not completed until 1956 and a circular making recommendations was not issued until 1959.[136] In the meantime local authorities varied in their attitude to this service. In 1955 it was reported that health visitor staffs ranged from 0.16 per 1,000 to 0.05 per 1,000, the norm recommended by the Jameson Report being 0.23 per 1,000. By 1960 there were on average 0.12 health visitors per thousand population. In 1960 the average for the home nursing service was 0.17 per 1,000, variation in provision ranging from 0.16 per 1,000 to 0.25 per 1,000.[137] Diversity was even greater in the home help service, which was recommended, but was not obligatory under the 1946 NHS Act. Employment of whole-time home helps diminished, but the number of part-time workers increased from 8,230 to 42,000 between 1948 and 1958. By 1960 this service contained the equivalent of 23,000 whole-time staff. The better areas provided as many as 2 home helps per 1,000 population, the worst as few as 0.07 per 1,000.[138] Whereas home helps and home nurses were concerned mainly with the elderly, health visitors worked primarily with infants, but to an increasing extent with the elderly. Provision of other services to the elderly was on a sporadic and miniscule scale. As noted above additional funds for the chiropody service were made available in compensation for the 1955 increase in the prescription charge. At this time only the LCC provided anything approximating to a chiropody service.[139]

The above examples illustrate a pattern in local health and welfare services. Provision was considerably in arrears of reasonable expectations, while expansion was slow and uneven. Local authority services themselves were lacking in plan and they were poorly co-ordinated with the work of other branches of the health service. In its notes for the CHSC Committee on General Practice the Ministry of Health candidly accepted that one of the most striking deficiencies of the NHS was 'lack of liaison between the services provided by Executive Councils and those provided by the Local Health Authorities . . . unhappily anything in the nature of a comprehensive team is still difficult to seek'.[140] In 1955 it was admitted that the recently formulated 'doctrine of domiciliary teams' had made little headway.[141] Although the Minister and Ministry 'have been doing all they can to build up the idea of the domiciliary team under the clinical leadership of the general practitioner, and I am sure that there is still a great deal of preventive work, particularly in the socio-medical field, for the teams to do . . . The difficulty is of course to attract the interest of general practitioners, who are at present reluctant to make use of the Health Visitors and other domiciliary services provided by Local Health Authorities'.[142]

The work of home nurses, home helps, health visitors, social workers, and chiropodists, as well as other functions such as the meals-on-wheels undertaken by voluntary agencies, were important for maintaining the elderly in their homes. It was the frequently reiterated policy of the Government that the elderly should be cared for in this way, but the services were inadequate in scale and their extension was insufficient to meet the needs of the expanding population of the elderly.[143] The home care services were thus an area of relative neglect. The importance of sheltered accommodation, an appropriate second line of defence, was even less appreciated.[144] Energies were diverted into the more traditional and less appropriate alternative of building residential homes for the elderly. This policy developed incrementally, starting with adaptation of grossly unsuitable accommodation inherited from Poor Law authorities, and extending to building of new units. Between 1948 and 1958 welfare authorities under section 21 of the 1948 National Assistance Act converted about 1,000 buildings into homes, and they also built 133 specially designed homes for the elderly. As noted in chapter VI capital expenditure controls severely limited this development during the 1950s. Satisfaction of the demand from local authorities for loan sanctions would have resulted in building of new homes at the rate of about fifty each year, but only about twenty-five schemes each year were permitted. Financial restrictions also resulted in adoption by the Ministry of Health of lower specifications for new accommodation. By 1960 part III residential accommodation housed a total of 84,000 persons, including 39,000 in homes opened since 1948. Residential homes were provided mostly for the elderly, but a small number of homes were given over to the handicapped, or other groups.[145] Although residential homes of the model type containing places for about 60 residents received much publicity, they were arguably a worst-of-both-worlds solution. The whole philosophy of this development was questioned in Townsend's penetrating critique.[146] The residential homes policy came into favour primarily because it offered an economical alternative to expensive hospital provision for the elderly. With mounting concern over the escalation of the cost to the exchequer of hospital care, residential homes paid for by the rates with a minor exchequer subsidy, and involving direct payments by residents, were an attractive alternative.

Following the precedent set for the elderly, residential homes were increasingly canvassed for other groups for whom hospital accommodation was only doubtfully appropriate. Residential homes, or half-way houses, were adopted as a means to reverse the demand for additional accommodation in mental hospitals and mental deficiency institutions. In 1955 a sub-committee of the Mental Health SAC examined the potentialities for developing this form of community care. Its report, produced in 1956, was enthusiastic for a combined policy of homes and training centres, but action was delayed pending the report of the Royal Commission on Mental Illness.[147]

Under the NHS local authorities retained their responsibility for services known as 'community care of defectives'. The concept of community care evolved in this context.[148] Development of junior and adult training centres for the mentally handicapped outside institutions proceeded at an embarrassingly slow pace. Curbs on capital spending held up development of this economical alternative, with the result that pressure on expensive institutional accommodation was increased. Although the arguments in favour of training centres were conceded, their establishment on any scale was delayed until the late fifties. In 1960 there were places for only about 20,000 mentally handicapped in training centres. A rate of provision of at least 1 per 1,000 of the population was recommended. Only Salford and Nottingham approached this level. The average rate in 1960 was 0.66 per 1,000.[149]

The first hostels for the mentally handicapped were established in Leeds and London in 1955. Notwithstanding warm support for such hostels from the Royal Commission on Mental Illness, by 1962 there were only 30 hostels, providing about 600 places, to cover the needs of the entire mental disorder and mental handicap service.[150]

As noted above it was hoped that domiciliary teams involving general practitioners and Local Health Authorities would expand health promotion and prevention. Local authorities were pioneers in the field of health 'propaganda'. During the inter-war period they established and funded the Central Council for Health Education to co-ordinate work in this field. Local authorities mounted some notable campaigns concerning diphtheria immunisation, or mass-X-radiography for tuberculosis, but their effort noticeably dwindled under the NHS and the Central Council for Health Education became moribund. Major preventive issues such as class, occupational, or regional differentials in health, family planning, nutritional habits, fluoridation of water, cigarette smoking, alcohol abuse, mental health or cancer education, or rubella immunisation were either neglected, or else provoked such fears of public controversy that concerted action was precluded. Because of instinctive avoidance of the more critical issues the content of health education was trivialised and cynics were liable to claim that it was 'appalling nonsense' to claim that social medicine or preventive medicine could make a significant contribution to the health service.[151] Writing four years after the paper by Doll and Bradford Hill on smoking and lung cancer, in his memorandum prepared for the Guillebaud Committee, the Chief Medical Officer concluded that 'there is no likelihood that research in the field of preventive medicine would offer any promise of early marked alteration in the country's morbidity'. There were therefore 'no new fields for preventive action'.[152] Advances in the areas of preventive medicine, epidemiology, or social medicine, failed to generate more robust leadership on prevention and health promotion. Early promises that the National Health Service would give priority to a positive conception of health were largely lost from sight. Official guidance on health promotion tended to be lacking in real content.[153] Nevertheless, within the advisory committees, or the specialist committees looking into the cost of the health service, mental health, maternity, child health, or problems of the elderly, there was a persistent and increasing undercurrent of concern about preventive medicine. Writers such as McKeown aroused the suspicion that preventive medicine had greater potential than was allowed in the health service at that time. Formation in 1959 of the Cohen Committee to consider whether 'there are any fresh fields where health education might be expected to benefit the public' represented an administrative response to these pressures.

The primary educational effort of local health authorities was aimed at mothers and infants. The main vehicle for this action was the system of maternity and child welfare centres, the total number of which had already reached 4,700 by the start of the National Health Service. Besides monitoring health and giving out supplementary food these centres had traditionally regarded education as their most fundamental activity. In the years before the NHS maternity and child welfare clinics took on additional significance as one component in an increasingly comprehensive local authority maternity service. The NHS disrupted this tendency and divided responsibility for maternity between the three branches of the service. Local authorities were relegated to a minor role in this uneasy partnership. Maternity and Child Welfare Centres were the only major institutional expression left with Local Health Authorities. Accordingly they took on special symbolic importance. Every attempt was made to sustain a programme for new M&CW centres and also to keep up the associated medical and midwifery staff. It was a particular point of principle to furnish new housing estates with M&CW centres at the same rate as schools. There was also the problem of replacing old M&CW centres located in improvised buildings such as church halls. The average annual expenditure on M&CW centres between 1950 and 1955 was about £250,000. In 1957 it was estimated that half the 5,000 M&CW centres were located in unsatisfactory buildings.[154]

The clamp-down on capital investment adversely affected the M&CW programme and attracted bad publicity. The Labour Party made political capital out of refusal of loan sanctions for M&CW centres in areas of high infant mortality.[155]

Superficial expressions of confidence about Local Health Authority maternity and child welfare services disguise increasing doubts about their viability. The crisis overtaking Local Health Authority services originates with the rise in institutional confinements. In 1937 39.7% of births took place in hospital. In 1957 this level had increased to 64.6%. Because of this trend hospital authorities emerged as the dominant influence in the maternity field. Under the NHS the Royal College of Obstetricians and Gynaecologists pressed consistently for an integrated maternity service controlled by hospital authorities. In 1944 the College advocated a 70% hospital confinement norm. In 1954 it concluded that all births should take place in maternity units.[156] The principal aim of the RCOG was to restore continuity of care, the basis for which was disturbed under the National Health Service. The RCOG struck out equally at general practitioners and local authority medical officers. It wanted obstetric care limited to general practitioners with approved qualifications and included on properly constituted Executive Council obstetric lists.[157] It was envisaged that these authorised obstetrician-general practitioners would staff antenatal clinics and supervise deliveries in local obstetric units. Accordingly local authority maternity facilities would become redundant and local authority employed domiciliary midwives, of whom there were some 5,000 in 1955, would be transferred to the hospital service. The steady decline in attendance at local authority antenatal clinics was regarded as a sign of their obsolescence.[158]

Reforms proposed by the RCOG were not greeted with enthusiasm in official circles. Official policy ordained that 'confinement which is expected to be normal is as safe at home as in hospital'.[159] At the outset of the NHS 50% was adopted as the figure for cases which on social or medical grounds would merit institutional confinement. It was realised that the 1954 RCOG report would give fresh impetus to the already strong public pressure for extension of maternity hospital provision. It was also feared that current research would lend weight to the RCOG contention that hospital confinement was safer. Failure of the health departments to bring general practitioner obstetricians under control, or to persuade them to work in partnership with local authority domiciliary midwives provided further justification for the RCOG case. The RCOG line was unacceptable to either the BMA or Local Health Authorities. Both defended their record in the field of obstetrics. General practitioners resented the imperialism of their consultant colleagues, while Local Health Authority medical officers and midwives claimed that they were supplying a wide range of educational and social services, as well as providing complete and effective care in the majority of domiciliary confinements. An investigation conducted in Birmingham showed that general practitioners were called in for only 10% of domiciliary cases handled by local authority midwives.[160] It was argued that the status of midwives was higher when acting under the part III service than when assisting general practitioners under part IV, when they were relegated to the status of maternity nurses.

The health departments were inclined to reject the RCOG proposals, first because the case for 100% hospital confinement was not medically proven, secondly because such a policy would result in controversy within the profession, thirdly because of the cost involved, and finally on account of the positive merits of diversity. The professional parties in the controversy were so entrenched that the Ministry was pressed to work out a definitive policy. The Guillebaud Committee called for 'an appropriate body to review the whole of this field'.[161] This subject was regarded as too delicate for the CHSC and officials feared that an expert committee would side with the RCOG.[162] The official preference was for maximum delay before instituting an inquiry with the hope that the controversy would die down and in order to allow further objective evidence to accumulate. But growing political controversy surrounding this problem ruled out inaction. Consequently a committee under the Earl of Cranbrook was established in April 1956 to review the organisation of the maternity services. This committee opted for 70% hospital maternity provision and for gradual replacement of local authority medical officers by general practitioner obstetricians in local authority antenatal clinics.[163] The M&CW clinics therefore persisted and domiciliary midwives were not transferred to the hospital authority. The last star in the Local Health Authority firmament thus narrowly survived into the final decade of the unreorganised NHS.

(v) HEALTH CENTRES AND GROUP PRACTICE

The Dawson Report of 1920 introduced the term 'health centre' into the currency of medical planning. Thereafter more ambitious schemes for development of the health service exploited the health centre concept. Generally accepted characteristics of the health centre were collaboration and division of labour among a range of personnel working under one roof, exploitation of modern diagnostic and therapeutic techniques, and finally the diffuse implication that health centres would pay more positive regard to maintenance of health, rather than merely react by treating disease. The health centre particularly confronted the old-fashioned individualistic ethos of general practice.

It was not until the mid-thirties that health centre development occurred on any scale. By 1939 the term health centre was widely used to designate new buildings housing Local Health Authority services. The health centre became increasingly important in planning documents.[164] From 1933 onwards the health centre was a major feature in the policy statements of the Socialist Medical Association, Medical Practitioners Union and the Labour Party. The *Interim Report* of the Medical Planning Commission (1942) signified approval of the health centre by an influential group within the profession. As noted in chapter III early plans for the NHS accepted the health centre as the principal basis for the organisation of general medical practice. The profession exhibited growing antipathy to the health centre idea owing to fear of salaried employment by local authorities. Accordingly later wartime plans limited the health centre to the status of an experiment.

Consistent with Labour Party policy, the health centre returned to a more central place in section 21 of the 1946 NHS Act and section 15 of the 1947 NHS (Scotland) Act. The medico-political controversies of 1946–1948 did nothing to win the hearts of the profession for health centre practice. However there was no need for concern on their part because it was not practicable for local authorities to establish health centres without the full compliance of general practitioners for whom the facility was projected.

Preparations for the NHS went ahead on the assumption that health centres would be a 'key feature' of the service and the major focus for Local Health Authority development plans. Documents from the Socialist Medical Association, Medical Practitioners Union and the Society of Medical Officers of Health provided detail to assist the planners. A report from the BMA accepted the health centre as a suitable candidate for experiment in the short term, with the likelihood that it would become the regular basis for the organisation of general practice in the longer term.[165] Despite antipathy to health centres having been whipped up among the rank and file of the profession only 47% of them recorded opposition in a survey conducted in 1951. Accordingly, under the NHS professional opposition to the health centre was not as great as might have been expected. A contemporary expert commentator felt 'the promise of health centres represented the chief hope of the general practitioners for a "new deal"'.[166]

As indicated in chapter VI there was no ambiguity over the Labour Government's commitment to health centres, nor in the legislation itself. The 1946 White Paper declared that 'A main feature of the personal practitioner services is to be the development of Health Centres. The object is that the Health Centre system should afford facilities for the general medical and dental services and also for many of the special clinic services of the local health authorities, and sometimes also for out-post clinics of the hospitals and specialist services. The Centres will also serve as bases for various activities in health education'.[167] Health centres thus assumed a high degree of importance. The first authoritative survey of the health centre problem correctly concluded that there was general expectation that the new service would facilitate 'the creation of health centres which would become the focus of preventive, curative and socio-medical practice in the neighbourhood'.[168] Friends and critics alike regarded health centres as an inevitable development which it was unrealistic to resist. In the media, advocacy of health centres was led by *The Times*. However the health centre policy first faltered and then failed. This episode attracts the attention of commentators because it represents the most obvious case of non-compliance with a central provision of the NHS legislation.[169] Indeed Eckstein identifies this as 'perhaps the greatest failure of the Service'.[170] A contemporary witness for the reforming side of the profession believed that 'many practitioners now regard the promise of health centres as a political trick, designed to gain their support at the time of negotiations, or at least as an unfulfilled promise whose fulfilment is now unlikely'.[171] Analysts disagree with one another about the main cause for the failure of the health centre policy.

A variety of factors contributed to the collapse of confidence on this important issue. The first difficulty related to the irregular army of existing institutions aspiring to health centre status under the NHS. The largest groups of contenders were the clinics belonging to the Friendly Societies Medical Alliance in England, the Medical Aid Societies in Welsh mining communities, or miscellaneous clinics run by local authorities, all of them in the London area. Both general practitioners and dentists were known to have an aversion to all of these institutions, and reviews of their facilities suggested that they were an unsuitable basis for the health centre programme. Even the well-known miners' Medical Aid Societies or GWR Medical Fund Society in Swindon were regarded as hopelessly antiquated, whereas such fine facilities as the Finsbury Health Centre were unacceptable to providers of the general medical service. The instinct of the planners was to start with a virtually clean slate. Local authorities were discouraged from trying to translate old dispensaries into modern health centres.[172] It was felt that such inferior hybrids would bring 'the whole conception of health centres into disrepute'.[173] In practice a consistent line was impossible to maintain because of the strong bond of sentiment connecting Bevan with his native Medical Aid Societies. Although these institutions were not wanted by the relevant county councils, nor by local doctors and dentists, they were given a last-minute reprieve and became known as health centres.[174] In all some 25 institutions were recognised as health centres when the NHS came into existence.[175] Of these nine provided general practitioner services. Most were soon closed down because they were not viable. Others offered a decreasing range of services. After the failure of numerous rescue missions, the prestigious Peckham Health Centre was converted into an LCC recreation centre.[17]

The success of the Government's health centre policy clearly rested on erasing the derelict image of the appropriated health centres. In line with other services administered by them, Local Health Authorities, in circular 22/47 (19 February 1947), were asked to submit proposals for health centres. Although resources were regarded as a limiting factor, no restraints on long-term planning were introduced. The first backward steps were marked by circulars 176/47 (17 December 1947) and 3/48 (14 January 1948). The former cancelled the requirement to submit plans for health centre development. The latter restricted applications to 'urgent new projects', giving shortage of building materials as the reason for planning restriction. It was also discovered that insufficient research had been undertaken on health centre planning. Accordingly further action was deferred pending the results of a review by the Central Health Services Council.

The timing of this retraction is probably significant. First, the above circulars were issued at the lowest ebb of Bevan's relations with the BMA, when it looked as if the profession would refuse to enter the service, and when health centres were being portrayed by medical politicians in the most odious light. Secondly, the extravagant schemes for health centres which the larger Local Health Authorities were promulgating unilaterally, were calculated to alienate the profession and surprise the Treasury, which was totally unprepared for capital development on this scale. During the first half of 1948 officials became reconciled to the fundamental inertia of general medical practice. Since the BMA would tolerate nothing more than updating the panel system, health centres became a virtual irrelevance.

In order to avoid headlong clashes between Local Medical Committees and Local Health Authorities it seemed better to restrict health centres to green field sites. Consequently the few positive moves towards health centre development were conducted in the context of new towns and housing estates with more than 2,500 houses. Even this narrow conception left room for considerable initiative, since 9 new towns and 50 large housing estates were scheduled for development.[177] Soon this new policy was overtaken by events. First, the NHS came under pressure because of escalation of costs, with the result that virtually all capital development was eliminated. Secondly, the first few health centre proposals considered by the Ministry illustrated the extreme difficulty of reconciling the various interests involved. Official thinking was influenced by two particular failures, in Birmingham and Sheffield. In Birmingham a much publicised row developed because general practitioners were forbidden to see their private patients in the new health centres. This caused them to refuse to participate in the Stechford health centre, after which the Birmingham county borough dropped its health centre plans. The CHSC health centre committee took the side of the doctors, and it was supported by the CHSC.[178] As noted in chapter V the Government reluctantly gave way to the doctors' demands and a relevant amendment was introduced at a late stage into the 1949 NHS Act. Bevan regarded this concession as a humiliation. It must have further soured his attitude towards general practitioners and health centres. Despite the concession to doctors, the Birmingham schemes were not revived. In the second example, in Sheffield, where trivial expenditure was involved in converting public assistance facilities into a health centre at Firth Park, changes of personnel among local practitioners during the prolonged negotiations introduced doubters, and given an atmosphere of suspicion among other practitioners in the neighbourhood, the health centre team withdrew from the project. The Sheffield county borough then dropped its health centre scheme. The Ministry was dismayed by this 'blackmail' on the part of local doctors. It was realised that no health centre scheme would be immune from sabotage by neighbours jealous of the alleged superior prospects, hence unfair competition, of health centre doctors.[179] With the bitter experience of Birmingham and Sheffield in mind the Ministry of Health in circular 117/50 (12 December 1950) advised Local Health Authorities to give priority to conventional doctors' housing and surgeries in new housing developments.[180]

The above advice resulted in a further clash with the CHSC and its health centre committee, because the latter had come down firmly in favour of health centres as the standard form of organisation for general practice on large housing developments. It was pointed out that no more materials or costs were involved in health centres than in doctors' houses and surgeries. Echoing declared Government policy the health centre committee expressed its concern to end 'the evils of competitive practice'.[181] In order to improve chances for health centre doctors the CHSC and its health centre committee unsuccessfully pressed the Government to introduce protection against competition from other doctors in the area, if necessary by legislation.[182]

By this stage the cankerworm had eaten too deep for the decay of support for health centres to be arrested. Bevan refused to endorse the advice of the CHSC, and furthermore he insisted that his reticence should not be blamed on financial restrictions.[183] It was agreed to proceed with extreme caution, acceding to health centres only when they entailed modest expenditure, and when the arguments in favour of this alternative were overwhelming.[184] Gradually policy hardened still further. In July 1952 a new official line was adopted that 'owing to lack of community of interest between general practitioners and local health authorities the present procedure for the provision of health centres was largely unworkable'. Instead efforts were directed towards encouraging group practice using the £100,000 per annum set aside for this purpose from the enlarged central pool created by the Danckwerts award.[185] The Danckwerts award also hardened the Treasury against health centres. Given the improved economic circumstances of general practitioners the Treasury opposed giving them further advantages in the form of subsidies involved in health centre practice. Health centres were dismissed as a redundant experiment.[186]

Official policy stopped short of an embargo on health centres, but they were tolerated with minimum enthusiasm. At the opening of the Aveley Health Centre at Thurrock, Essex, a project which had been subject to much delay, Macleod urged that 'the health centre can never afford and probably will never be able to afford to pull down what is already good in order to put up something that is perhaps only a little better'.[187] Fresh restrictions on local authority capital development introduced in 1956 further reinforced this judgement. The seemingly marginal advantages offered by health centres deterred the Guillebaud Committee from advocacy, and this set the tone for official reports until there was a sharp change in 1966.[188]

The Aveley Health Centre was only the seventh to be opened since the beginning of the NHS. One further health centre was completed in 1956, and two more before 1960. To bring a regular section 21 health centre proposal to successful fruition demanded a rare concatenation of local circumstances and perseverance in overcoming obstacles set up by the central authority. Six of the seven early health centres were located on housing estates. Two of the seven were cheap conversions, one of a cottage hospital (Faringdon, 1951), the other of council houses (Clifton, Nottingham, 1952). One was a modest prefabricated building (Knowle West, Bristol, 1952).

With one exception, the other purpose-built health centres were reasonably economical buildings combining general medical, local health, welfare and education authority services (Harold Hill, 1954, and Aveley, 1955, Essex; Hester's Way, Cheltenham, 1955; and Springwell, Sunderland, 1956). The one extravagant health centre was Woodberry Down, Stoke Newington (LCC), expenditure on which was £180,000, virtually the cost of all the remaining new health centres put together. The expense of Woodberry Down was used as an excuse by critics for not embarking on a general health centre programme.[189]

In addition to the above health centres, a few others were established on the basis of special arrangements of Local Health Authorities and Executive Councils with other organisations. These included Darbishire House, Manchester 1954 (university, Rockefeller, Nuffield Provincial Hospitals Trust), Corby new town, 1954 (RHB, NPHT), and four at Harlow 1952–1955 (new town corporation, NPHT).[190] Harlow was consequently the only new town to feature health centres and it was the only community in Britain served by doctors working exclusively from health centres.[191]

In Scotland health centre development was undertaken by the Department of Health. Although the central department remained more committed to health centres than its English counterpart, few of its provisional schemes materialised. The major example was Sighthill, Edinburgh (1953), which was the approximate equivalent of Woodberry Down and cost almost as much. The only other health centre completed before 1960 was Stranraer (1954), which was a realistic and successful small scheme.[192]

Few health centres were completed, but many more were projected. For instance, in 1948 the LCC produced a comprehensive programme for 166 health centres. Woodberry Down was the sole survivor. This is indicative of a general pattern, elaborate provisional plans, scaling down of plans to modest short lists, even more selective applications for loan sanctions, long consultations; with few successful outcomes. In 1949 seventy applications were under consideration, in June 1952 fifty-four, whereas in 1956 only four new applications were made.[193] Consequently, although the majority of local authorities showed interest in health centres, most were quickly deterred from further action, although a significant number became enmeshed in long and fruitless negotiations with the Ministry of Health.[194]

Some of the contenders conducted vigorous and much publicised campaigns. At a new housing development at Eston in the Cleveland area there was unanimous local support for a health centre, but the proposal made in 1949 was turned down. In January 1950 the Executive Council complained that thirty or more patients, some with influenza, were obliged to queue, standing in slush outside overfull surgeries. It was asserted that 'only the establishment of a health centre could improve the existing scandalous conditions'. The local MP made representations in favour of this project but the Ministry adhered to the view that local support and need for improvement of surgeries constituted insufficient grounds for acceptance. The campaign for this health centre continued into the next decade.[195]

The first thorough review of health centre applications concluded that some of the failures were attributable to obstruction by doctors and their representatives. A further contributory factor was the limitation on capital spending, but 'finally the Ministry must shoulder the main blame that the network of health centres over the whole country envisaged in the early days of the NHS failed to materialise'.[196]

The few health centres established tended to become showpieces. The Sighthill and Woodberry Down Health Centres in particular were used as propaganda bearing witness to advances in primary care brought about by the NHS. Scattered circumstantial evidence, or the few critical evaluations made of health centres, demonstrated a substantial gulf between expectations and realities. It was virtually impossible to establish non-competitive health centre practice in a system which placed a premium on open competition. Consequently the six incumbents of Woodberry Down were surrounded by sixty-two other competitors practising within a half-mile radius of the health centre.[197] Except in rare cases such as Harlow, health centres were treated by their occupants as branch surgeries. The facilities were severely under-exploited. General practitioners admitted that they took up sessions in the health centre not because of any positive enthusiasm, but in order to keep out their competitors. Health centre doctors collaborated neither with one another, nor with other users. Relations between general practitioners and local authority staff were particularly distant, even to the extent of partition walls being erected between the two groups. Patients consequently derived no particular benefit from attending health centres. They received the customary treatment. If anything patients found health centres inconvenient and inhospitable. The few positive enthusiasts for health centre practice among the health centre doctors were as a result totally unrepresentative of their fellows.[198] As a vehicle for promoting co-operation, or for revitalising general practice, health centres were thus a catastrophic failure.

Although less spectacular manifestations of modernisation than health centres, improved group practices were looked to as a means for achieving many of the same ends, but on a more economical basis. The group practice loans scheme was an additional inducement for establishment of modern group practices. Between 1953 when it began, and December 1956, 239 applications were made, of which 100 were approved. Of the £452,000 allocated, £306,500 had been spent. Thus this extra incentive for group practices involved expenditure of the same order as spending on health centres, but it was spread over a very much larger number of schemes, and interest-free loans were of course reclaimed.[199]

In 1951 Marquand felt that he could allay fears of Labour critics by giving a positive lead on group practice centres.[200] In 1952 the Minister was advised that in the absence of 'community of interest' between general practitioners and local health authorities, encouragement of group practices should be adopted as the alternative policy.[201] The Ministry encouraged applicants for health centres to transfer to schemes for Local Health Authority clinics and group practices in the same vicinity.[202] The first representative of the 'new type of health care' was at Oxhey in Hertfordshire, where a group practice centre was built adjacent to a county council clinic.[203] Treasury approval for an integrated health centre at Oxhey was granted in 1949. In its revised form, the health centre was opened in 1959.

The Ministry admitted to the Cohen Committee that it was 'unhappily true three years after the start of the NHS, anything in the nature of a comprehensive team is still difficult to seek'.[204] The more advanced group practices built up by the most competent general practitioners were increasingly looked upon as the model for future progress. Although in most cases these initiatives owed virtually nothing to the NHS, they were adopted and encouraged under the new service. The leading example was the Skipton group practice, which was built up under J G Ollerenshaw from 1938 onwards.[205] Other lively groups such as those at Corbridge in Northumberland, or Tenterden in Kent, originated in the 1930s. A review of such group practices was impressed by their general competence. However, reservations were expressed about the unimaginative nature of much of the practice. Relations with consultants were variable, while with Local Health Authorities they were generally hostile. This resulted in poor relations with most local authority health workers. Midwives were sometimes appreciated, while health visitors were usually ignored. In rare cases the survey discovered good relations with both consultants and with Local Health Authorities. In such places the midwife, district nurse and health visitor were regarded as helpful associates. Such exceptional cases were much appreciated as examples of the primary care teamwork the National Health Service was designed to promote. It was hoped that these models would eventually become imitated throughout the service.[206]

CONCLUSIONS

Any assessment of the National Health Service on the basis of its early history cannot have more than interim value. Nevertheless by 1957 the NHS had taken on the settled appearance that it was to preserve until the mid-seventies. Parliamentary debates on the Guillebaud Report, those marking the tenth anniversary of the service, or utterances of leading medical politicians made at that time, confirm that the initial fierce objection to the service had almost completely died away. Critics who formerly had lamented the creation of the NHS now congratulated themselves on being its originators.

Public opinion had long been favourable towards a state-provided comprehensive health service. Regardless of the limitations in the performance of the new service, it was such an improvement over its antecedents that public satisfaction was guaranteed.[1] Because the National Health Service was tied up in the minds of the rank and file of the medical profession with the long-term trend towards extension of public medical services, almost everything about the new service had initially unleashed anxieties concerning loss of traditional medical freedoms. In the event these fears were rapidly dispelled. Feeling against the NHS was somewhat artificially worked up at times of crisis over doctors' remuneration, but such perturbations were insufficient to deflate the growing mood of inner contentment within the medical profession. Most other groups of workers in the health service experienced their difficulties, but they behaved in less raucous fashion than the medical profession. In no case were grievances sufficient to undermine confidence in the essential soundness of the NHS. After the bouts of acrimonious controversy between 1943 and 1948, and instability between 1948 and 1952, the implements of combat were discreetly stowed away.

There emerged a tacit agreement to work within the framework of compromises in existence at that time. All parties accepted the imperfections of the system rather than jeopardise its survival. Polls conducted in 1956 showed that virtually all doctors accepted that the NHS was a permanent institution. In a Gallup poll 67% of them said that they would vote in favour if there was a question of starting this kind of service afresh.[2]

Thus by the mid-fifties the NHS was protected by a broad consensus, embracing all social classes, both political parties, all but an eccentric fringe of the medical profession, and all others employed in the service. An eminent Harvard clinician commented that the NHS was 'in harmony with the total pattern of the British state'. His colleague, a Harvard political scientist, concluded that the NHS had become 'accepted as an altogether natural feature of the British landscape, almost a part of the Constitution'.[3]

Notwithstanding different points of emphasis, testimony from major political and medical witnesses confirmed the above impressions. Turton described the Guillebaud Report as a 'welcome vindication of the National Health Service'. Given the service's 'record of achievement', Turton urged that 'the greatest need is for stability for a period of years'.[4] Walker-Smith, Turton's indirect successor as Minister of Health, emphasised the record of efficiency of the NHS. In his view 'the country was getting a good bargain for the very large amount of money which the Health Service was costing'.[5]

The general calls among back-bench politicians of all parties for extension and improvement in services reflect the shared assumption among the rank and file that the NHS was inviolable and that its comprehensiveness was a desirable objective. As one prominent Conservative noted, it was feasible to cut defence spending, raise taxes, or even allow a 'dose of unemployment. But meddle with National Health? That's political suicide'.[6] The great difficulty experienced by both Labour and Conservative Governments in mobilising support for health charges, and the extremely modest scale of the charges eventually levied, also illustrate the extent of political support for the original conception of a service essentially free from direct charges. Representing expert opinion, the King's Fund in 1954 noted that the 'grave anxieties that hung over the early years of the Service had ceased to look as menacing as they did'. Summarising the mood of the nation at the tenth anniversary, The Times concluded that 'the nation has good reason to be proud of the Health Service'.[7]

Once the NHS was established as a national institution there was a tendency to read back consensus into earlier history. The new service has increasingly been viewed as the inevitable outcome of reflections concerning the limitations of the inter-war health services. The intellectual origins of the National Health Service are traced back to a consensus built up during the 1930s, uniting a broad spectrum of lay and professional opinion. From this perspective, wartime commitment to social reconstruction and the welfare state provided the final catalyst to practical realisation of a comprehensive health service.[8]

The first three chapters of the present study give only moderate support for the above interpretation. There was certainly a generally shared belief that all members of the community should have access to medical attention and it was realised that existing services fell short of this objective. There was of course nothing new in advocating that the state should facilitate the health of its people. In this respect twentieth-century social reformers were largely modernising the vocabulary of their Victorian sanitarian forebears.

Concerning the mechanism for extending provision and bringing greater order into the chaotic assemblage of health services there was remarkably little unity of outlook. At the outset of the inter-war planning process Morant and Dawson disagreed fundamentally on the administrative framework for a comprehensive service. Morant wanted expansion on the basis of existing county councils and county boroughs. Dawson favoured ad hoc health authorities containing a mixture of elected representatives and co-opted professional members. Inter-war schemes for extending the coverage of health services variously took voluntary hospitals, National Health Insurance, or the local authority services as their basis. From the time of Morant the Ministry of Health assumed that a National Health Service would be built up by accretion of local authority provided health services. This process was appreciably advanced by 1939. The Labour Party generally favoured this option. On the other hand the BMA increasingly canvassed state superintended contributory insurance as the model for an extended health service. No positive steps were taken during the inter-war period to realise this latter objective, although the Cathcart Report opted for the contributory principle. Even on the Cathcart Committee a substantial minority argued for the rate and tax supported alternative. This committee was also divided over the merits of municipal administration of health services. Such patent lack of unanimity within the Cathcart Committee reflects growing polarisation of outlook on important aspects of health policy.

Opinion was also divided over the future role of the voluntary hospitals. While certain large municipalities in England after 1929 made rapid steps towards providing comprehensive municipal hospital services, envisaging that voluntary hospitals would play a diminishing part in their schemes, in Scotland it was expected that local authorities would play only a subsidiary role.

By the outbreak of war there were sharp divergences of opinion concerning the future development of the health services and little sign that duplication, competition and lack of co-ordination would be ended. It was unclear to what degree the future services would be funded by taxes, rates, or contributory insurance, and it was uncertain whether voluntary hospitals would survive as dominant partners or would enter into slow decline. By this stage there was a distinct polarisation of opinion between the Ministry of Health, LCC and Labour Party on the one hand, and the BMA, voluntary hospital pressure groups and the political right on the other. The famous ministerial statement concerning a comprehensive hospital service made in October 1941 was less a reflection of deliberate planning than an attempt to deter an outbreak of fratricide between the municipal and voluntary hospital lobbies.

The subsequent process of wartime preparation for the National Health Service shows remarkably few concessions to the spirit of solidarity and altruism which is supposed to have taken precedence over self-interest. Notwithstanding verbal posturing in favour of the principle of reconstruction, the vested interests used the wartime planning initiative as a means to reinforce their position in any post-war settlement. Officials over-estimated the tolerance of the medical profession for real change in the organisation and administration of the health services. The result was lasting disillusionment among the planners, and a prolonged legacy of distrust on the part of the profession.

Although a skilful cosmetic exercise, the 1944 White Paper signified little progress in resolving acute disagreements over the future direction of policy. The planners notably failed to bring the profession and the voluntary hospitals round to their way of thinking. Having for one of the first occasions in more than thirty years of dispute with the health departments obtained a position of advantage, the BMA inclined to an uncompromising line, and it scented indecisiveness within the Government. The Minister responsible for the health service in Scotland struck off in a different direction from his colleague responsible for England and Wales, while the fragile agreement between the coalition partners over the 1944 White Paper broke down. Thus in the last year of the coalition the two partners kept their separate counsels. The line followed by Willink between February 1944 and June 1945 represented capitulation rather than the emergence of consensus.

Labour emerged from the 1945 election as the defender of the 1944 White Paper, but reserving the right to depart from it on the basis of the precedent set by Willink. The Labour Government was faced with unenviable decisions concerning the degree to which it should compromise on its long-standing policy commitments in order to purchase conciliation from the medical profession. Paradoxically nationalisation of the voluntary hospitals represented one such conciliatory gesture, because it was less offensive to consultants than the municipal alternative. But concession to one party inevitably caused offence elsewhere, in this case predictably to the British Hospitals Association, but also to the local authority associations, and the repercussions were felt within the Labour Cabinet. Accordingly the Government went forward not only with its health service legislation beset by external critics, but also with considerable self-doubt concerning some major aspects of policy. Yet further dilution of Labour expectations took place during the negotiations leading up to the Appointed Day. The major departure of the Government from its original intentions lay in the abandonment of unitary organisation and adoption of three separate forms of administration for the hospital, Executive Council, and Local Health Authority sectors of the service. Thus the original intention of resolving the lack of cohesion of services by placing all services under about 60 local health authorities was abandoned. Instead services were distributed between some 700 local and regional bodies in England and Wales, and 170 in Scotland. The only significant steps towards rationalisation involved bringing all hospitals into a single administration, and in Scotland reducing the number of Executive Council areas.

Labour was disappointed by other aspects of the health service as it turned out in practice. Opportunities for labour or trade union participation in hospital administration turned out to be unexpectedly limited. Local authorities were precluded from developing health centres along the lines originally envisaged. Instead of working as full-time salaried officers in health centres, general practitioners and dentists evaded salaried service almost completely and preserved the competitive systems to which they were accustomed under National Health Insurance. Labour opinion was also to some extent offended by the autonomy granted to teaching hospitals, by pay beds, by merit awards, and by the rights given to NHS consultants to engage in private practice.

The post-war Labour Government accordingly paid relatively dearly for the settlements that eventually drew the profession into the health service. To apply such terms as 'consensus' or 'convergence' to the planning process outlined above implies a greater degree of cohesion among the parties involved than is merited by the evidence. The service established in 1948 was regarded by both the Government and the profession as the best compromise that could be secured in the circumstances. Rather than risk destabilising the system the opposing sides came to accept the lines of truce as permanent boundaries. Gradually a spurious consensus grew up around the system as a whole, thereby granting permanence to many features that had been regarded as temporary expedients.

The period between the Danckwerts award and the Royal Commission on Remuneration provided welcome respite for all sides. The Ministry of Health in particular bore the scars of war-weariness. Macleod advocated 'a time of tranquillity in which the different parts of the service were properly integrated and all the resources available, however limited, were being used to the best advantage'.[9] The Guillebaud Committee was urged to accept stabilisation, and its recommendations to this effect were warmly accepted in official circles. Turton declared that 'the greatest need is for stability for a period of years'.[10]

Agreement to work within the original framework of the NHS added to the difficulty in meeting some of the major objectives of the service. Fragmentation into three entirely separate and distinctive structures, with hundreds of local administrative components, placed almost impossible demands on the health departments with respect to co-ordination. It is ironic that a service created to unify effort and overcome serious defects in co-operation should itself become subject to this same criticism.[11] The quite different characteristics of the three branches of the service guaranteed incompatibility rather than cohesion. Executive Councils and Local Health Authorities were roughly coterminous, but the former were purely regulatory and they developed no taste for co-ordination. In general they reflected the instinct of the local medical committees to keep Local Health Authorities at arm's length. Ancestral experiences warned that co-operation was a likely prelude to assimilation. It was self-evident that fusion of part III and part IV services was the most straightforward means to simplify NHS administration, but the strength of feeling within the medical profession against such a move was sufficient to cause deletion of this suggestion from the agenda.

Both Executive Council and local authority branches of the service suffered a sense of inferiority with respect to the hospital service. The BMA complained to the Guillebaud Committee that 'there was a real danger of the country developing a National Hospital Service instead of a National Health Service'.[12] The massive hospital authorities were tempted to develop their services without regard to their lesser part III and part IV neighbours, with whom no common boundaries existed. Both general practitioners and public health medical officers complained that they were being arbitrarily pushed out of the hospitals. The CHSC committee on co-ordination made elaborate suggestions for creating greater harmony between the three parts of the service, but integrated planning and joint use of personnel was limited to isolated and unrepresentative cases.[13]

Absence of symmetry and lack of co-ordination between the three arms of the service obstructed continuity of treatment in important fields like maternity, and it stood in the way of community care policies to which the Government was increasingly committed as their response to the seemingly inexorable advance of the hospital sector. The Government's ideal of domiciliary teams was held up as a means 'to make it possible to keep out of hospitals, including mental hospitals, all patients who can be equally well treated at home'.[14] However realisation of this objective was held up by the underdevelopment and backward looking character of part III and part IV services, which tended to leave the whole planning initiative to the hospital authorities. The latter were naturally slow to respond to inducements towards community care. Consequently, a precious opportunity was lost to transfer loyalties and resources into the field of community care. With respect to such important priority groups as the elderly, the mentally and physically handicapped, or the mentally disordered, appropriate forms of care were evolved too slowly, and multidisciplinary teams remained a feature of reports of expert committees rather than the service itself. In 1961 Titmuss acidly pointed out that expenditure on community mental health and mental handicap services was less in real terms than a decade earlier, and less than the current level of compensation given for fowl pest.[15]

Co-ordinated planning was also poorly developed within the separate branches of the NHS. Attempts by the health departments to remedy the desperately backward state of general medical practice were limited to minor financial inducements towards group practice. Formation of group practices, or improvements in the standards of work, were left to the vagaries of local inclinations, until the new College of General Practitioners developed into a forum for more positive initiative. Hadfield's review of general practice ended with a complaint about the lack of unity in the profession and in the health services as a whole. He concluded that the service 'is crying out for a unified administration'.[16]

Local health authorities were not co-ordinated with one another, and internally their health functions were scattered between various departments. Medical officers worked as specialists in isolation from one another and they failed to come to terms with the newly developing social service side of their departments.[17]

Within the hospital service regionalisation was adopted to bring order to the archaic legacy of unco-ordinated institutional facilities. However no effective arrangement for attaining the right balance of resource distribution between regions developed, while ambiguity during the early years of the service over the relationship between regional boards and management committees in England and Wales resulted in a delay in co-ordinating the work of hospital groups. The separate administration of teaching hospitals provided an additional complication in the planning of regional services.

The Select Committee on Estimates complained that the distribution of resources had become set in the 'inherited pattern' created before the NHS was established. But, it was less concerned with reallocation of resources to the advantage of the poorer regions than with arriving at means of rewarding the most efficient authorities.[18] The Select Committee identified areas of waste that had been causing concern for some time, but where effective remedial steps had not been adopted. It was for instance noted that beds for private patients and amenity beds were seriously under-occupied. Insufficient attention had been devoted to economising on hospital supplies. The high level of domiciliary consultations in some regions suggested lack of proper controls on this service. Because of the slowness in developing hospital costing the Committee complained that it was difficult to identify areas of waste. As in the case of resource distribution the Select Committee was not particularly alert to endemic deficiencies affecting major services in the less well-favoured regions.

The main concern of the Select Committee related to the quality of administration as a whole. It was doubted whether training and selection procedures for hospital administrative staff were adequate to meet the level of responsibility involved in the new system.[19] The Select Committee was also disturbed about the neglect of long-term planning in the hospital service. It was 'depressed by the apparent lack of vigour with which some fundamental problems are being faced by the Ministry'. The findings of the Select Committee, including the censure of the Ministry of Health for its lack of leadership, were echoed by the Acton hospital survey.[20] If this assertion was justified the responsibility lay with the Ministers. Between 1951 and 1957 there were six Ministers of Health, only Macleod remaining in office for any length of time. This rapid rotation, together with the demotion of the Minister of Health from Cabinet rank, reduced confidence in the capacity of Ministers to give leadership, or to 'stand up against the importunities of the Treasury'.[21]

The extensive investigation into the hospital service by the Select Committee on Estimates is illustrative of the current of constructive criticism faced by the National Health Service. Many of the shortcomings revealed by such inquiries could be corrected within the existing administrative framework. Other difficulties led to suggestions that the framework itself would require reconstruction. Various witnesses before the Guillebaud Committee recommended administrative unification of the health services, and evidence in favour of this solution was gathered in a long reservation entered by Sir John Maude. The latter argued that the line of policy pursued in the Ministry of Health from 1920 to 1945 was justified by subsequent events. He therefore proposed that health services should be unified under local authority control at some time in the future. Although Maude's intervention was not welcomed by officials, they were not unsympathetic with his point of view.[22] On the assumption that local government would be reformed Bevan also favoured this outcome. He regarded transfer of the hospital services to elected local authorities, and termination of the separate status of teaching hospitals, as tasks for the next phase in the development of the health service.[23]

The remuneration dispute of 1956 quickened anxieties within the profession about the service as a whole. A *BMJ* editorial asserted that a plebiscite taken among the profession would 'show a majority highly critical of the Service and in favour of a reform'.[24] The BMA leadership consequently instituted a thorough review of the service along the lines of the wartime Medical Planning Commission. The new committee chaired by Sir Arthur Porritt began its work shortly after the tenth anniversary, and its report issued in 1962 marked the first tangible step towards National Health Service reorganisation. It is significant that this move came from a body designed to make up for the failings of the CHSC machinery and the deficiency of the health departments in the 'corporate capacity for constructive thinking'.[25]

From the time of Morant and the Dawson Report onwards, preparations were made for redesigning the British health services according to a consistent rational plan. The aim of this exercise was the most efficient mobilisation of scientific knowledge and material resources for optimising the health of the whole community. During the depression frustrations mounted concerning the gulf between potential and prevalent standards of health care. By 1946 positive health was regarded as a fundamental civil right, and this ideal was confirmed by the constitution of the World Health Organisation, which was adopted during the passage of the 1946 National Health Service legislation.

Despite the many compromises involved in the course of converting the plan devised in 1943 into the service inaugurated in 1948, the National Health Service was at that time and has remained the most ambitious publicly provided health service to be established by a major western democracy. Although socialisation was not carried to the extent wanted by the Labour Party the service involved a high degree of direct ownership and employment by public bodies. Also, as Bevan emphasised, besides the more obvious aim of providing a 'comprehensive, free, health service' the NHS fulfilled a secondary redistributive function. This latter aspect of the service was reinforced by the transference to the exchequer of the major burden of funding.[26]

Although the National Health Service achieved only limited equalisation of services, it provided the less well-off with a variety of forms of care to which previously they had only limited access. All members of the family were now treated equally with respect to the services of a general practitioner. The most important innovation related to freedom of access to specialist and consultant services, which were gradually built up from the modest framework available in 1948. Provision of dentures, spectacles and hearing aids on a massive scale under the early National Health Service, although subsequently caricatured as an eccentricity, represented a vital contribution to elevating the standards of life of a vast section of the community, and such services were of particular benefit to the elderly. In this context Bevan recognised the importance of the 580,000 hearing aids supplied between 1948 and 1957 in rescuing poor people from a 'kind of twilight life'.[27] The special benefit of these services to the poorest sections of the community lay at the root of the objections to health charges.

The above example reminds us that one of the greatest problems of the early National Health Service was dealing with the backlog of demand, and with the deficiencies in the health care facilities that had been accumulating since before World War I. The new service was only moderately successful in dealing with these difficulties. Because of competing claims on a limited budget hospital rebuilding was largely postponed until the 1960s. It was not possible to delay demands for higher remuneration. For the first time in the history of health care in Britain all classes of health worker were paid on a more realistic basis, and in the case of general practitioners the settlements involved redressing grievances going back to 1911. Inclusion of Whitley Councils in the National Health Service prevented health workers from sinking back to the artificially low standards prevalent in voluntary hospitals before 1948. As a monopoly employer of labour the NHS unavoidably became entangled in problems of professionalisation. In cases such as nurses, midwives, dentists, opticians and medical auxiliaries legislation was involved. With respect to other groups such as health visitors or social workers expert committees provided guidelines on training and responsibilities. Once the National Health Service was established, the health departments found it necessary to take up problems which their predecessors either evaded or circumvented owing to the absence of unitary responsibility.

The financing of the health service made little allowance for correction of inherited problems, such as maldistribution and general deficiency in standards. Furthermore, after the brief initial phase of expansion, spending on the service was kept at a level which placed Britain at a growing disadvantage compared with other western nations. Nevertheless services were gradually modernised and an increasing volume of care was provided without a great expansion in physical facilities. Hospitals greatly expanded their out-patient departments and increased their turn-over of in-patients. Day hospitals and community care services were developed, although not on a scale commensurate with need.[28] Despite its reservations about administration of the hospital service the Select Committee on Estimates accepted that 'increase in standards of service must have mainly been financed by economies resulting from increased efficiency, skill and individual effort'.[29]

Although the National Health Service was not responsible for all medical advance made during this period, it constituted a vehicle transmitting the advantages of modern medicine to an ever increasing section of the population. Discrepancies in standards and expectations of health care inherited from the past were so ingrained that their correction was beyond the capacities of the early National Health Service. Limitations of finance, administration and attitude precluded a concerted assault on inequalities in health. However the National Health Service had conceded the principle of unrestricted entitlement of access to health care. By establishing a system permitting care to rise to the level of demand, Britain had indeed set on foot an ambitious experiment, which its architect described as 'the most civilised achievement of modern Government'.[30] Bevan's audacious campaign to permit natural expansion of the health service led to one of the great confrontations of modern politics. Bevan's Cabinet colleagues, despite their long-standing commitment to a free, comprehensive health service, were completely taken aback by the cost entailed in this exercise. Like the officials who prepared those notorious early estimates for the new service, the expectations of the Labour Cabinet were conditioned by standards prevalent during the depression. The Labour Government rapidly retraced its steps and imposed severe limits on further development of services. Under the regime prevalent until 1960 expansion was conditional on the product of economy measures, or upon the imposition of charges. In the atmosphere of retrenchment dominant in the 1950s the idea of a comprehensive health service was consigned to the realm of utopian dreams. In this new mood of realism the Guillebaud Committee accepted that its 'Report should point out that the country would not be in a position to provide a fully comprehensive health service in the foreseeable future, whether it was provided free or otherwise'.[31]

NOTES

Chapter I
INCESSANT CONSTRUCTION

1. John Simon, memorandum to Lord President, PC8/164, 27 July 1869, quoted from R Lambert, *Sir John Simon 1816-1904 and English Social Administration* (McGibbon & Kee, 1963), p 606.

2. Sir Farquhar Buzzard, *The Hospital*, January 1945, p 10. Buzzard was recently retired as Regius Professor of Medicine at Oxford, and he was a leading adviser to the Nuffield Provincial Hospitals Trust.

3. Willink, HC Debates, vol 398, col 428, 16 March 1944, introducing the debate on the 1944 National Health Service White Paper.

4. Bevan, CP(48)302, 13 December 1948, CAB129/3; Bevan, address to Whitley Management Side Chairmen, 1949, DHSS 94601/1/17.

5. Woodburn, CP(48)308, 29 December 1948, CAB129/3. See also A K Bowman, SAMO for Western Regional Hospital Board, Scotland to Sir George Henderson [1949], T.SS 226/5/01A, and p viii above.

6. Bevan, Government Expenditure, 14 September 1949, T. 227/185.

7. For the pre-war health services, see PEP, *The British Health Services* (PEP, 1937) and *A National Health Service*, Cmd. 6502, 1944, pp 53-74. See also R Stevens, *Medical Practice in Modern England* (Yale UP, 1966), pp 11-64.

8. B Abel-Smith, *The Hospitals 1800-1948* (Heinemann, 1964); R Pinker, *English Hospital Statistics 1861-1938* (Heinemann, 1966); I Levitt, 'Welfare and the Scottish Poor Law, 1890-1948', Univ Edinburgh PhD, 1983.

9. Pinker, pp 50, 52, 57; *WP*, pp 55, 68-9, England and Wales 78,000 beds and Scotland 14,000 beds in 1939.

10. Pinker, p 161. £15m according to SC Alford, MH77/22 and MH77/24.

11. Pinker, p 59.

12. Pinker, pp 73, 81.

13. Pinker, pp 152-3. Voluntary gifts and investments 36%, and payments from patients 53%, according to Sources of Income of Voluntary Hospitals, PR(43)90, 29 October 1943, CAB87/13.

14. 27% according to PR(43)90, CAB87/13.

15. Abel-Smith, pp 323-51.

16. *Social Insurance and Allied Services*, Cmd. 6404, 1942, para 432, 10 million wage earners paying an average of 3d per household. Also, Voluntary Hospital Contributory Schemes, 19 December 1941 MH77/22; Alford, February 1942, MH77/22.

17. It was estimated that voluntary services in these categories were in 1938 costing about £3m pa (*The Lancet*, 1942, ii, 609).

18. The Scottish provision came under the Poor Law (Scotland) Act, 1845. M A Crowther, *The Workhouse System 1834-1929* (Batsford, 1981), pp 156-90; *idem*, 'Paupers or Patients? Obstacles to Professionalisation in the Poor Law

Medical Service before 1914', *Journal of the History of Medicine*, 1948, *39*: 33–54; A Digby, *Pauper Palaces* (Routledge, 1978), pp 166–79; M W Flinn, 'Medical Services under the New Poor Law', in D Fraser, ed, *The New Poor Law in the Nineteenth Century* (Macmillan, 1976), pp 45–66; R Hodgkinson, *The Origins of the National Health Service. The Medical Services of the New Poor Law 1834–1871* (Wellcome, 1967); P Townsend, *The Last Refuge, A Survey of Residential Institutions and Homes for the Aged in England and Wales* (Routledge, 1962), pp 17–39.

19. G W Oxley, *Poor Relief in England and Wales 1601–1834* (David & Charles, 1974); E G Thomas, 'The Old Poor Law and Medicine', *Medical History*, 1980, *24:* 1–19.

20. Crowther, 'Paupers or Patients?', p 35; W A Robson, *The Development of Local Government* (Allen & Unwin, 1931), pp 293–304.

21. *WP*, p 56; Abel-Smith, pp 252–83.

22. Levitt, pp 276–88; Memorandum for Committee on Post-War Policy Problems, 21 February 1942, MH77/22, for details of Scottish schemes, the largest being for Glasgow, which was approved in 1941. By 1939 Scottish local authorities were providing 1,600 beds under the 1929 Local Government Act.

23. Alford, 19 December 1941, MH77/22; Townsend, pp 28–9.

24. Sir A S MacNalty, Local Authority Specialist Services, 15 March 1937, MH80/24.

25. Robson, p 311.

26. Alford, 19 December 1941, MH77/22; Levitt, p 368. Abel-Smith (p 383) gives 53,000 for England and Wales.

27. Alford, February 1942, MH77/22.

28. Education Act (1921), sections 80–1. *PEP Report*, pp 119–26.

29. C Webster, 'The Health of the School Child During the Depression', in N Parry and D McNair, eds, *The Fitness of the Nation* (History of Education Society, 1983), pp 70–85.

30. J Lewis, *The Politics of Motherhood: Child and Maternal Welfare in England 1900–1939* (Croom Helm, 1980); *PEP Report*, pp 90–119; Royal College of Obstetricians and Gynaecologists, and Population Investigation Committee, *Maternity in Great Britain* (OUP, 1948).

31. *PEP Report*, pp 98–9, 105.

32. *PEP Report*, p 96.

33. *PEP Report*, pp 100–2; Domiciliary Midwifery Services, 29 September 1944, MH80/33.

34. R M Titmuss, *Problems of Social Policy* (HMSO, 1950), p 221.

35. Pinker, p 77; *PEP Report*, pp 99–100; Alford, February 1942 (MH77/22) gives 1,966 for England and Wales. This figure relates to beds outside maternity wards of Poor Law hospitals. Local authorities also booked about 2,000 beds in voluntary hospitals for maternity cases.

36. L Bryder, 'The Problem of Tuberculosis in England and Wales, 1900–1950', Univ Oxford DPhil, 1985; *PEP Report*, pp 282–9; *WP*, pp 56–60, 70.

37. Sir A S MacNalty, *The Reform of the Public Health Services* (OUP, 1943), p 68.

38. In Scotland beds were provided under the 1897 Public Health (Scotland) Act. Alford, February 1942, gives 15,000; *PEP Report* (pp 286–7) 23,000; Robson (p 292) 17,000. Such variations are accounted for by choice over inclusion with respect to England of, (a) 8,000 beds for tuberculosis patients in

voluntary hospitals, or (b) 7,000 beds for tuberculosis patients in isolation and general hospitals (Bryder, p 112).

39. WP, p 60; MacNalty, *Reform of Health Services*, pp 70-1.

40. C Webster, 'Health, Welfare and Unemployment during the Depression', *Past and Present*, 1985, No 109: 204-30.

41. Fred Messer, HC Debates, vol 398, col 562, 17 March 1944.

42. Robson, pp 292-3.

43. K Jones, *Mental Health and Social Policy 1845-1959* (Routledge, 1960).

44. Rather different Scottish legislation comprises the Lunacy (Scotland) Acts, 1857 and 1919.

45. WP, pp 61-2, 70-1; *PEP Report*, pp 271-6.

46. J Ryan with F Thomas, *The Politics of Mental Handicap* (Penguin, 1980), pp 102-16; *WP*, p 61; *PEP Report*, pp 276-81.

47. C P Blacker, *Neurosis and the Mental Health Services* (OUP, 1946), pp 82-5; Jones, pp 80-90.

48. N R Eder, *National Health Insurance and the Medical Profession* (Garland Publishing Inc, 1982); B B Gilbert, *The Origins of National Insurance* (Joseph, 1968); *idem*, *British Social Policy 1914-1939* (Batsford, 1970).

49. *National Insurance Act* (1911), section 15 (2).

50. Sir A S NacNalty, Local Authority Specialist Services, 15 March 1937 (MH80/24) notes that specialist services were considered in 1911, and again in 1920-22, when they were delayed as an economy measure.

51. Sidney Webb *et al*, 'Interim Report of the Committee of Enquiry . . . on the Working of the Insurance Act', *The New Statesman*, Special Supplement, 14 March 1914, p 9.

52. For another view, see Frank Honigsbaum, *The Division in British Medicine* (Kogan Page, 1979).

53. A Peacock and D Wiseman, *The Growth of Public Expenditure in the UK*, 2nd edn (Allen & Unwin, 1966) demonstrates that social service expenditure increased from 4.2% GNP in 1910 to 10.9% in 1937.

54. From estimates made by J E Bray in T W Hill, *The Health of England* (Cape, 1933), pp 43-6; and *WP*, pp 80-4.

55. Pinker, p 162.

56. Expenditure on public health services (£65m) is taken from Table I, column (C), p 13 above.

57. I Gough, *The Political Economy of the Welfare State* (Macmillan, 1979), p 77.

58. MacNalty, *Reform of Health Services*, p 5.

59. M W Flinn, ed, *Scottish Population History from the Seventeenth Century to the 1930s* (CUP, 1977); R Mitchison, *British Population Change since 1860* (Macmillan, 1977); T. McKeown, *The Modern Rise of Population* (Arnold, 1976).

60. McKeown, *Rise of Population*.

61. R M Titmuss, *Poverty and Population. A Factual Study of Contemporary Social Waste* (Macmillan, 1937).

62. *PEP Report*, p 394. Titmuss, *Problems of Social Policy*, chapter xxv, gives a résumé of health problems facing wartime planners.

Chapter II
VISIONS OF UTOPIA

1. Churchill, Memorandum, 12 January 1943, *The Second World War* (Cassell, 1952), iv, pp 861–2. Based on memorandum by Sir William Jowitt, Reconstruction is not the Framing of Utopias, WP(42)507, 14 November 1942, CAB66/30. See also Sir Kingsley Wood to Churchill, 17 November 1942 attacking 'Golden Age' idealists, PREM 4/89/2. This critique was taken up by Lord Cherwell, warning against oversimplified schemes for 'our post-war Utopia', Memorandum, 20 October 1943, WP(43)465, CAB66/42.

2. S Webb and B Webb, *The Break Up of the Poor Law* (Longman, 1909), pp xi, 291.

3. *Second Report of the Royal Sanitary Commission*, PP 1871, XXXV, p 174.

4. *Royal Commission on the Poor Laws and Relief of Distress*, Cd. 4499, 1909, Minority Report, reissued separately as *The Break Up of the Poor Law, op cit.*

5. S and B Webb, *Break Up of the Poor Law*, pp 292–3; *idem, The State and the Doctor* (Longman, 1910), p 231.

6. S and B Webb, *Break Up*, pp 293, 524–7; *State and Doctor*, pp 248–50.

7. S and B Webb, *State and Doctor*, p 230.

8. Sketch by Morant, Bodleian Library, Addison Papers, Box E3; note on Morant's plans for the Ministry of Health, MH79/377; Sir Bertrand Dawson, *The Nation's Welfare: The Future of the Medical Profession* (Cassell, 1918).

9. S Stacey, 'The Ministry of Health 1919–1929: Ideas and practice in a Government Department', Univ Oxford DPhil, 1985.

10. Historical note for Minister, 24 December 1943, MH80/26.

11. *Interim Report on the Future Provision of Medical and Allied Services*, Cmd. 693, 1920.

12. Dawson, 'Medicine and the State', *The Medical Officer*, 1920, 23:223–4.

13. Robson, *Development of Local Government*, pp 287–354.

14. Note on Morant's plans, MH79/377, pp 2–3.

15. MH77/50; MH77/54.

16. MacNalty, Memorandum on Provision of Specialist Services, 15 March 1937, MH80/24. A similar conclusion was expressed in *Report on Scottish Health Services*, Cmd. 5204, 1936 (chaired by E P Cathcart): 'We do not doubt that the abandonment of the contributory system so far as concerns the medical side of insurance will be found to be an ineluctable stage in the development of our health services. Some of us think that the time has now come to take this step'. (Reservation by seven members on Part IV, paras 764–81).

17. Office Meetings, 7 February and 6 March 1938, MH80/24.

18. Office Meetings, 7 February 1938, 6 April 1938, 31 May 1938, and 27 June 1938, MH80/24.

19. Proposals for Subvention to London Voluntary Hospitals, March 1938, MH80/24. Meeting of officials with experts, 19 May 1938, MH80/24.

20. Meeting of officials, LCC and voluntary hospitals, 27 January 1939, MH80/24, MH79/513.

21. MacNalty to Sir George Chrystal, 21 September 1939, Sir E R Forber to Chrystal, 17 September 1939, A W Neville to Chrystal, 22 September 1939, MH80/24.

22. MacNalty to Forber, 8 January 1940, MH80/24.

23. *The Lancet*, 1939, ii, 947, 28 October 1939.

24. C L Dunn, ed, *The Emergency Medical Services*, 2 vols (HMSO, 1952); Titmuss, *Problems of Social Policy*, pp 442-505; Description of the Emergency Hospital Service, 21 February 1942, MH77/22; J B Hunter, 'The Emergency Medical Service and the Future', *BMJ*, 1941, i, 326-9.

25. For instance, Sir Edward Forber argued that the regional hospital scheme was not permanently useful, A Regional Organisation for Hospital Service, 23 November 1939, MH80/24; and *WP*, p 57, which admits the impermanence of regionalisation despite achievements of EMS.

26. Dunn, *Emergency Medical Services*, i, pp 42-3.

27. The London Hospital covered two sectors.

28. Sir E Rock Carling to Sir John Maude, 4 March 1943, MH80/25.

29. H A Clegg and T E Chester, *Wage Policy and the Health Service* (Blackwell, 1957), pp 5-12; S Ferguson and H Fitzgerald, *Studies in the Social Services* (HMSO, 1954), pp 284-331.

30. D Hamilton, *The Healers, A History of Medicine in Scotland* (Canongate, 1981), pp 255-8.

31. Department of Health Scotland, *Health and Industrial Efficiency: Scottish Experiments in Social Medicine* (HMSO, Edinburgh, 1943); Sir Andrew Davidson, *Scottish Experiments in Social Medicine* (Johns Hopkins, 1947); Titmuss, *Problems of Social Policy*, pp 472-3; Thomas Johnston, *Memories* (Collins, 1952), pp 152-3, concluded that the Clyde basin experiment 'blazed the trail for the NHS'.

32. Johnston, *Memories*, pp 152-3.

33. G S Wilson, 'Public Health Laboratory Service', *British Medical Bulletin*, 1951, 7: 146-53; A L Thomson, 'The Organisation of a National Public Health Laboratory Service', *British Medical Bulletin*, 1943, 1:, 38-9; Dunn, i, pp 334-55, ii, pp 68-71.

34. Department of Health Scotland, circular 3/1942. For England and Wales, see Dunn, i, pp 166-8; Titmuss, *Problems of Social Policy*, pp 466-8.

35. MacNalty, *Reform of Health Services*, p 38. MacNalty had been chairman of the sub-committee of the Imperial Defence Committee that had in 1938 designed the Emergency Hospital scheme: Dunn, i, pp 12-14.

36. *The Times*, Leader, 19 November 1943.

37. Maude, Suggestions for a Post-War Hospital Policy, August 1941, MH77/22.

38. See also, Liberal Party, *Health for the People* (1942); Communist Party, *Britain's Health Services* (1942).

39. For example, A Bourne, *Health of the Future* (Penguin, 1942); D Stark Murray, *The Future of Medicine* (Penguin, 1942).

40. E D MacGregor to Maude, 20 January 1941, MH77/22.

41. TUC Report, included in Memorandum, 14 January 1942, SIC(42)2, CAB87/77.

42. BMA, *A General Medical Service*, para 27; meeting between Ministry of Health officials and Beveridge, 17 February 1942, MH80/81.

43. BMA, *A General Medical Service*, para 5; *Draft Interim Report of the Medical Planning Commission* (1942), para III; *Beveridge Report*, para 427.

44. First meeting, 7 May 1941, *BMJ*, 1941, i, 759-61, 17 May 1941.

45. *BMJ*, 1942, i, 743–53, 20 June 1942.

46. *Draft Interim Report of MPC*, para III.

47. British Hospitals Association, *Voluntary Hospitals Commission Report* (1937).

48. Nuffield Provincial Hospitals Trust, *A National Hospital Service* (October, 1941).

49. Elliot to Nuffield, December 1939, in LP(41)167, 14 October 1941, CAB71/2; *A National Hospital Service*, p 9.

50. Forber, Post-War Hospital Policy, 8 May 1940, MH80/24.

51. N M Goodman, *Wilson Jameson Architect of National Health* (Allen & Unwin, 1970), pp III–12; H M C Macaulay, 'Reflections on the Origins of the National Hospital Service', *Public Health*, 1974, 89:1–3.

52. *The Lancet*, 1939, ii, 945–50, 28 October 1939; *The Lancet*, 1942, ii, 599–622, 21 November 1942.

53. PEP, Memorandum, May 1942, SIC(42)65, CAB87/77, Introduction, para 5, Text, para 22.

54. *Picture Post*, vol 10, No 1, 4 January 1941.

55. T Hopkinson, ed, *Picture Post 1938–50* (Penguin, 1970), p 90.

56. *New Statesman*, 23 August 1941, p 184.

57. Memorandum by Nuffield College Social Reconstruction Survey, SIC(42)65, CAB87/77.

58. Minute, 10 July 1942, SIC(42)100, MH80/24.

59. Ministry of Information, Public Feeling on Post-War Reconstruction, November 1942, CAB118/73.

60. Maude, Suggestions upon which a policy must be framed, August 1941, MH77/22.

61. *The Times*, Leader, 10 November 1941.

62. Maude, Suggestions for a Post-War Hospital Policy, August 1941, MH77/22.

63. Goodman, pp 81–2.

64. Meetings, 9, 14 and 23 January 1941, HH65/93.

65. Meetings between MacDonald and officials, 7 December 1940, 24 January 1941, MH80/24.

66. MacDonald to W M Goodenough, *The Times*, 15 January 1941, and LP(41)167, 14 October 1941, CAB71/2.

67. *The Times*, Leader, 15 January 1941.

68. Maude, Suggestions for a Post-War Hospital Policy, August 1941, MH77/22.

69. Memoranda, December 1940 to September 1941, MH80/24; J E Pater, *The Making of the National Health Service* (King's Fund, 1981), pp 26–9.

70. Nuffield, *A National Hospital Service*, pp 12–13.

71. *Star*, 12 August 1941. Brown reported to colleagues that Latham's remarks had provoked much comment, LP(41) 48th mtg, 15 October 1941, CAB71/2. Johnston argued that it was preferable to establish a committee of inquiry rather than make premature commitments, HH65/93.

72. HC Debates, vol 374, cols 1116–20, 9 October 1941. For background papers, 1–6 October 1941, HH65/93 and 97.

73. Press release, 9 October 1941, MH77/22; Pater, pp 31–3.

74. RP(41)ist mtg, 6 March 1941, CAB87/1. Health was not specifically mentioned in Greenwood's grandiose memorandum on reconstruction, RP(41)3. P Addison, *The Road to 1945* (Quartet, 1977), pp 167-8.

75. LP(41)47th mtg, 9 October 1941, CAB71/2.

76. LP(41)167, 14 October 1941, CAB71/2.

77. LP(41)48th mtg, 15 October 1941, CAB71/2.

78. HC Debates, vol 374, cols 1653-703, 21 October 1941; vol 379, cols 507-62, 21 April 1942.

79. Scottish Branch of the BHA, *Memorandum of a Scheme for the Regionalisation and Co-ordination of the Hospital Services of Scotland* (September, 1942).

80. Meetings, 28 November 1941, 27 December 1941, HH65/71-72.

81. Johnston set up his Office Committee in April 1941, HH65/93. For its initial policy deliberations, HH65/70.

82. Meetings summarised in *Memorandum of a Scheme*, pp 27-9. On 4 September 1941 Johnston told his officials that the Department's hospitals 'should be retained as a directly run State contribution to the hospital service', HH65/93.

83. SC(41)4, 2 December 1941, MH77/25.

84. A Bullock, *The Life and Times of Ernest Bevin* (Heinemann, 1967), ii, pp 225-6; J Harris, *William Beveridge. A Biography* (Clarendon, 1977), pp 382-3.

85. RP(41)6, 23 June 1941, CAB87/1; SIC(41)ist mtg, 8 July 1941, CAB87/76. The terms of reference of this committee were not publicly revealed.

86. HC Debates, vol 372, col 45, 10 June 1941.

87. J Harris, *Beveridge*, pp 378-418.

88. Beveridge, Basic Problems of Social Security with Heads of a Scheme, 11 December 1941, SIC(41)20, CAB87/76; Harris, p 390.

89. SIC(42)100, 10 July 1942, PIN 8/87. This draft contained an extended definition of the scope of the new health service (Part VI, para 19), which was embodied unchanged into the published report (para 427): the 'comprehensive national health service will ensure that for every citizen there is available whatever medical treatment he requires, in whatever form he requires it, domiciliary or institutional, general, specialist or consultant, and will ensure also the provision of dental, ophthalmic and surgical appliances, nursing and midwifery and rehabilitation after accidents'. The final Report also contained a briefer and obscurely placed reference, 'a national health service organised under the health departments and post-medical rehabilitation treatment will be provided for all persons capable of profiting by it' (para 19, xii).

90. Memorandum to Advisory Panel on Home Affairs, 25 June 1942, APH(42)5, revised as Address to Engineering Industries Association, 30 July 1942, and included in Beveridge, *The Pillars of Security* (Allen & Unwin, 1943), pp 41-58.

91. Beveridge to Maude, 22 February 1942, MH80/31.

92. *Beveridge Report*, paras 432-6.

93. Beveridge to Maude, 2 February 1942, Maude to H A de Montmorency, 20 January 1942, Montmorency to Maude, 6 February 1942, MH80/31.

94. Maude to Montmorency, 17 February 1942, MH80/31.

95. Meeting of Health Departments with Beveridge, 17 February 1942, MH80/31.

96. Jameson, Diary, cited in Goodman, *Jameson*, p 117.

97. Maude to Montmorency, 9 February 1942, Maude, Post-War Medical Policy: General Practitioner Service, February 1942, MH80/31.

98. J E Pater, Salaried Medical Service, nd, MH77/26.

99. Buzzard, 'Reconstruction in the Practice of Medicine', Harveian Oration 1941, *The Lancet*, 1942, i, 343-7, 21 March 1942; J A Ryle, 'Social Medicine', *BMJ*, 1942, i, 801, 27 June 1942; *idem*, 'Social Medicine: Its Meaning and its Scope', *BMJ*, 1943, ii, 633-6.

100. Sir W Dalrymple-Champneys, Minute on MPC report, 1 July 1942, MH80/31.

101. Comparison of MPC Report and Ministry of Health Scheme, September 1942, MH77/26.

102. General Practitioner Service, March 1942, MH80/24.

103. Draft of a Paper by Sir John Maude for Ministers on a proposed General Practitioner Service, November 1942, MH77/26; revised from J M K Hawton, Medical Practitioner Service, September 1942, MH80/24.

104. Maude to Sir Alan Barlow, 17 November 1942, Barlow to Maude, 8 November 1942, MH80/24.

105. W R Fraser, Post-War General Practitioner Service, 5 December 1942, MH80/24.

106. *BMJ*, 1942, ii, Supplement, 30-2, 19 September 1942; 33-6, 26 September 1942.

107. Sir Beckwith Whitehouse, 'The British Tradition and the New Outlook', *BMJ*, 1942, ii, 357-9, 26 September 1942.

108. Official Committee Report, RP(43)6, 14 January 1943, CAB143/45; Draft Report of Reconstruction Priorities Committee, PR(43)9, 7 February 1943, CAB87/13; Interim Report of the Reconstruction Priorities Committee, WP(43)58, 11 February 1943, paras 12-15, 55(iii), CAB66/34.

109. WM(43)28th mtg, 12 February 1943, CAB66/34.

110. HC Debates, vol 386, cols 1655-78 (especially cols 1660-3), 16 February 1943.

111. HC Debates, vol 386, cols 1825-38, 2030-50.

112. *The Times*, 22 March 1943; Churchill, *War Speeches*, ed C Eade (Cassell, 1944), pp 32-45.

113. Addison, *Road to 1945*, pp 222-8.

114. WP(43)255, 308, 324, July 1943, CAB66/39; WM(43)40th mtg, CAB65/36.

115. Notes on a Comprehensive Health Service, February 1943, MH80/25.

116. First Draft of a Scheme, 4 January 1943, 4th Draft, 29 January 1943, MH80/25.

117. First Draft, 4 January 1943, MH80/25.

118. PR(43)3, 2 February 1943, CAB87/13.

119. PR(43)3, para 4.

120. Maude to Sir Alexander Maxwell, 19 April 1943, MH80/25.

121. PR(43)3, paras 7-8.

122. PR(43)3, paras 9-10.

123. PR(43)3, 2 February 1943, CAB 87/13; PR(43) 3rd mtg, 4 February 1943, CAB 87/12.

Chapter III
INFINITE REGRESS

1. HC Debates, vol 386, col 1661, 16 February 1943 'in consultation with them, the shape of a reorganised service will be worked out'.

2. Education Green Book, June 1941; White Paper, July 1943; Bill, October, 1943. R. Barker, *Education and Politics* (Clarendon, 1972), pp 75-80; P H J H Gosden, *Education in the Second World War* (Methuen, 1976).

3. Brown to George C Anderson, 10 March 1943, MH80/25.

4. Brown, Speech at Watford, 26 March 1943, *The Times*, 27 March 1943, *The Hospital*, April 1943, pp 115-16, 123.

5. RP(43)6, 14 January 1943, para 61, CAB123/45.

6. NHS(18), 16 April 1943, Maude to Maxwell, 19 April 1943, meeting with the profession, 17 May 1943, MH80/25.

7. *The Times*, Leader, 12 April 1943.

8. *The Times*, Leader, 17 May 1943.

9. G C Anderson, letter, *The Times*, 9 June 1943.

10. *BMJ*, 1943, i, Supplement, 61-2, 22 May 1943, summarised in Pater, pp. 61-3. For a more statesmanlike review, R M F Picken, 'The Comprehensive Health Service', *Public Administration*, 1943, 21: 59-67.

11. NHS(3), 26 February 1943 (draft), NHS(4), March 1943, MH80/25.

12. NHS(4), para 8.

13. NHS(4), para 11.

14. London, 11 March, 30 March, 3 and 26 May 1943, Edinburgh, 12 March and 25 May 1943, MH80/25.

15. *Report of the Committee on Post-War Hospital Problems in Scotland*, Cmd. 6472, 1943. For background papers, see HH65/62 and 69.

16. *Hospital Problems in Scotland*, paras 31-63.

17. *Hospital Problems in Scotland*, paras 118-30.

18. *Hospital Problems in Scotland*, paras 65-84. For Johnston's discussion of this point with voluntary hospital representatives, 13 January 1944, HH65/57.

19. London, 10 March, 23 March, 16 April and 23 June 1943, Edinburgh, 8 March, 12 July and 30 August 1943, MH80/25, HH101/4.

20. London, 27 July 1943, Edinburgh, 12 July 1943, MH80/25, HH101/4.

21. Maude to Brown, 23 June 1943, MH80/25.

22. Medical Advisory Committee, 4 March 1943, MH80/25. No indication is given of the reaction of the Scottish Medical Advisory Committee on 2 March 1943, HH101/1.

23. London, (Representative Committee), 9 March, 25 March, 15 April, 17 May and 14 July 1943, Edinburgh, (Liaison Committee), 8 March, 27 March, 12 May, 25 May, 15 June and 26 July 1943, MH80/25, HH101/1.

24. Negotiating Committee, 24 May, 3 June and 28 June 1943, MH80/25. This committee comprised G F Buchan, of Soc MOH, H S Souttar and Sir Alfred Webb-Johnson of R Coll Surgeons, H Boldero of R Coll Physicians,

H G Dain, E A Gregg and A Talbot Rogers of BMA, and Anderson or Hill as officials of the BMA.

25. Anderson to Maude, 12 May 1943, H G Dain, 15 April 1943, MH80/25.

26. J I Cameron, 26 July 1943, MH80/25.

27. Maude to Brown, 3 May 1943, MH80/25.

28. Sir E Rock Carling to Maude, 4 March 1943, MH80/25.

29. Anderson to Maude, 12 May 1943, Webb-Johnson, 17 May 1943, MH80/25.

30. Negotiating Committee, 24 May 1943, MH80/25.

31. Maude, 23 June 1943, MH80/25.

32. Especially, Negotiating Committee, 28 June 1943, MH80/25.

33. Sir A Robinson to Maude, April 1943, MH80/25.

34. Anderson to Brown, 13 May 1943, MH80/25.

35. Anderson to Maude, 12 May 1943, MH80/25.

36. Souttar, Representative Committee, 14 July 1943, MH80/25.

37. NHS(S) Med 7, 26 July 1943, MH80/25.

38. Maude to Brown, 3 May 1943, MH80/25.

39. Maude to Brown, 23 June 1943, MH80/25.

40. Pater, pp 69-73, overlooks earlier discussion at the Reconstruction Priorities Committee on 4 February 1943.

41. PR(43)45, 29 July 1943 (Johnston), PR(43)46, 28 July 1943 (Brown), CAB87/13.

42. PR(43)46, paras 4-7; PR(43)45, para 2.

43. PR(43)46, para 16.

44. PR(43)45, para 4.

45. PR(43)46, paras 40-1, 44.

46. PR(43)46, para 36.

47. PR(43)46, para 24.

48. PR(43)45, para 5.

49. *Economist,* 2 October 1943.

50. Addison, *Road to 1945*, pp 235-7; K Harris, *Attlee* (Weidenfeld & Nicolson, 1982), pp 225-6; Woolton, *Memoirs* (Cassell, 1959), p 259.

51. *Manchester Guardian,* 12 November 1943.

52. Churchill, *War Speeches,* pp 263-8.

53. PR(43)15th mtg, 30 July 1943, CAB87/12.

54. PR(43)16th mtg, 18 August 1943, PR(43)18th mtg, 8 September 1943, CAB87/12.

55. PR(43)49, 17 August 1943, PR(43)48, 13 August 1943, CAB87/13.

56. PR(43)51, 3 September 1943, CAB87/13.

57. PR(43)17th mtg, 18 August 1943, CAB87/12.

58. PR(43)19th mtg, 16 September 1943, CAB87/12; R(44)2nd mtg, 10 January 1944, CAB87/5.

59. PR(43)60, 4 September 1943, CAB87/13.

60. NHS(S)LA7, 12 July 1943, CAB80/26.

61. PR(43)24th mtg, 15 October 1943, CAB87/12.

62. R(44)4th mtg, 10 January 1944, CAB87/5.

63. PR(43)24th mtg, 15 October 1943, PR(43)29th mtg, 1 November 1943, CAB87/12.

64. PR(43)76, 12 October 1943, PR(43)88, 29 October 1943, CAB87/13. Johnston's view was supported by the Scottish Branch of the BHA, NHS(S)BHA3, 5 November 1943, MH80/26. See also, *The Hospital*, November 1943, p 336.

65. R(44)3rd mtg, 10 January 1944, CAB87/5.

66. R(44)13th mtg, 4 February 1944, CAB87/5.

67. Apology for the White Paper in response to Attlee, January 1944, CAB124/244.

68. Representation to Woolton by BHA, 18 January 1944, CAB124/442.

69. Attlee to Woolton, 1 February 1944, Attlee to Churchill, Woolton to Eden, Woolton to Churchill, 10 February 1944, CAB124/244.

70. WM(44) 17th mtg, 9 February 1944, WM(44) 18th mtg, 11 February 1944, WM(44) 21st mtg, 15 February 1944, CAB65/41.

71. MH77/28.

72. T C W Mitchell to Hawton, 21 December 1943, Hawton on Scottish draft, December 1943, MH77/28.

73. White Paper, First Draft, p 12, MH77/28. *WP*, p 5, cited by Pater, p 78. Similar modifications at the end of section I removed the reference to 'the fullest opportunity of positive good health' as the aim of the service.

74. Summary in H Eckstein, *The English Health Service: its origins, structure and achievements* (OUP, 1959), pp 136-9; Pater, pp 78-81.

75. Proof, 3 February 1944, WM(44)17th mtg, 9 February 1944, CAB65/41.

76. Historical material was transferred from the introduction of the early draft to appendices in the White Paper.

77. *WP*, p 12; *Brief WP*, p 5.

78. *WP*, p 12.

79. The first draft also proposed a Central Hospitals Council.

80. *WP*, pp 14-19, 77-9; *Brief WP*, pp 21-3.

81. *WP*, pp 20-6.

82. *WP*, pp 26-38; *Brief WP*, pp 5-12.

83. *WP*, p 28.

84. *WP*, p 35.

85. *WP*, pp 42-6; *Brief WP*, pp 23-6.

86. *WP*, pp 42-6; *Brief WP*, pp 23-6.

87. *WP*, pp 80-5; *Beveridge Report*, paras 268, 270.

88. Pater, p 78.

89. *The Times*, Leader, 18 February 1944.

90. Report on BMA Conference, MH80/27; BMA Press Statement, 17 February 1944, MH80/76.

91. Maude to Willink, 1 and 4 September 1943, MH80/26.

92. Maude to Willink, 7 June 1943, MH80/26.

93. K McGregor, 16 July 1943, MH80/26.

94. T Fife Clark to S F Wilkinson, [January] 1944, MH80/26.

95. Rock-Carling to Jameson, February 1944, MH77/28.

96. Buzzard, 'The Voluntary Hospital System is Dead: Long Live the Voluntary Hospitals', *The Hospital*, January 1944, pp 9-12. Communicated to Ministry of Health in draft and discussed November 1943, MH77/28.

97. *The Lancet*, 1944, i, 279-80, 313-14, 26 February and 4 March 1944.

98. *News Chronicle*, 9 August 1944.

99. HC Debates, vol 398, cols 427-518, 535-633, 16 and 17 March 1944. Pater, pp 81-2; Eckstein, p 139, exaggerates the positive tone of this debate.

100. A Greenwood (col 557), L Silkin (col 574), E Summerskill (col 581).

101. HL Debates, vol 131, cols 70-116, 118-19, 16 and 21 March 1943.

102. Willink, Birmingham, 14 April, and Croydon, 17 May 1944, *The Hospital*, May 1944, pp 138, 158, June 1944, pp 177-8. Brief, May 1944, MH77/31.

103. See above, p 45.

104. *BMJ*, 1943, ii, Supplement, 75, 30 October 1943.

105. *BMJ*, 1944, i, 293-5, 26 February 1944. Eckstein, pp 143-7.

106. *BMJ*, 1944, i, Supplement, 41-3, 11 March 1944.

107. NHS(44)1-3, April 1944, MH80/27. Apart from this, the only other direct contacts with the profession were, (a) a meeting with the Negotiating Committee, 4 August 1944, NHS(44)10, MH80/31, and (b) a meeting with the Representative Committee, 10 October 1944, at which the Minister announced his revised ideas, NHS(44)14, MH80/34.

108. Report, *BMJ*, 1944, i, 643-8, and Editorial, 663-4, 13 May 1944. Pater, pp 83-5.

109. *BMJ*, 1944, ii, Supplement, 147-65, 16 December 1944.

110. *BMJ*, 1944, ii, Supplement, 25-9, 5 August 1944, 40-1, 19 August 1944.

111. King's Fund, *Statement of Principles,* and *Memorandum on the National Health Service* (July 1944), BHA, *A National Health Service* (July, 1944).

112. NHS(44) 6 and 7, 14 and 20 June 1944, CAB80/27. Pater, pp 85-7. Resolutions of Executive Council of County Councils Association, *The Hospital,* June 1944, p 179.

113. Local authorities and the hospital services, [August] 1944, MH80/33.

114. NHS(44)5, April 1944, MH80/27; NHS(44)8, [June 1944], MH80/27; Regional Councils, 3 August 1944, MH80/33; Local Authorities and the Hospital Service, [August, 1944], MH80/33; Notes on Regionalism, [August 1944], MH80/33; T S McIntosh to Charles, 10 August 1944, MH80/33.

115. NHS(44)5, April 1944, MH80/27.

116. Local Authorities and the Hospital Service, [August 1944], MH80/33.

117. Sir Arthur Rucker to Sir Miles Mitchell, 6 September 1944, followed by meeting with AMC, 19 October 1944, and with CCA, 26 October 1944, MH80/33.

118. NHS(44)15 and 16, 17 and 18 October 1944, MH80/33. Payments from local authorities occasioned an acrimonious correspondence between Rucker and Wettenhall of BHA in November 1944, MH80/34.

119. Rucker to Moran, 27 October, 9 November, and 23 November 1944, MH80/32.

120. Rucker to Mitchell, 22 December 1944, MH80/33.

121. Meeting between Johnston and Willink, 20 December 1944, MH80/27; R(44)168, 27 September 1944, CAB87/6.

122. Executive Committee of BHA, 'Considerations affecting the Service in Scotland', in BHA, *A National Health Service*, pp 12–15; Scottish BMA Report and Conference on White Paper, *BMJ*, 1944, ii, Supplement, 73–6, 97–101, 7 October and 4 November 1944. For regular meetings with local authorities and voluntary hospital representatives beginning August 1944, HH101/4, 5.

123. *The Times*, 22 November 1944. Cobb to Willink, 19 December 1944, Willink to Cobb, n.d., MH77/88.

124. Webb-Johnson to Willink, 8 December 1944, MH77/88.

125. R(44)65th mtg, 2 October 1944, CAB87/5.

126. Hill to Maude, 8 January 1945, MH80/27; list of members, MH80/28.

127. Moran to Rucker, 18 and 20 December 1944, complaints about the 'arbitrary and provocative' behaviour of BMA, MH77/119.

128. NHS(45)45, 24 May 1945, MH80/32.

129. NHS(45)8, 3 February 1945, MH77/119.

130. NHS(45)45, 24 May 1945, MH80/32.

131. NHS(45)18, March 1945, MH77/30B.

132. NHS(45)11 and 13, 6 and 13 February 1945, MH80/32; NHS(45)18, March 1945, MH77/30B.

133. NHS(45)45, 24 May 1945, Resolutions 2–4, MH80/32.

134. NHS(45)4 and 6, 16 and 23 January 1945, MH80/32.

135. NHS(45)11 and 13, 6 and 13 February 1945, MH80/32; NHS(45)45, 24 May 1945, MH80/32.

136. NHS(45)11 and 13, 6 and 13 February 1945, MH80/32; Moran to Willink, 29 January 1945, MH77/119.

137. NHS(45)20 and 30, February and 13 March, 1945, MH80/32.

138. NHS(45)45, 24 May 1945, Resolutions 7–17 and 18–21, MH80/32.

139. NHS(45)8, 3 February 1945, MH77/119; NHS(45)11, 13, and 30, 6 and 13 February, 13 March 1945, MH80/32.

140. A point also made by Willink to BHA, NHS(45)17, 22 February 1945, MH80/28.

141. NHS(45)8, 3 February 1945, MH77/119; NHS(45)18, March 1945, MH77/30B.

142. NHS(45)45, 24 May 1945, Resolutions 18–21, MH80/32.

143. NHS(45)30, 13 March 1945, MH80/32.

144. NHS(45)45, 24 May 1945, MH80/32.

145. NHS(45)8, 3 February 1945, MH77/119; NHS(45)18, March 1945, MH77/30B.

146. NHS(45)9, 30 January 1945, MH80/32.

147. NHS(45)8, 3 February 1945, MH77/119; NHS(45)18, March 1945, MH77/30B.

148. NHS(45)26, 14 March 1945, MH80/28.

149. NHS(45)8, 3 February 1945, MH77/119;. NHS(45)18, March 1945, MH77/30B.

150. NHS(45)9 and 13, 30 January and 13 February 1945, MH80/32.

151. NHS(45)18, March 1945, MH77/30B.

152. NHS(45)39, 24 April 1945, MH80/32.

153. NHS(S)BHA9A, 10 January 1945, HH101/5; NHS(S)LA 34, 20 April 1945, HH101/4.

154. NHS(45)13 and 20, 13 February and February 1945, MH80/32.

155. Woolton to Churchill, 26 March 1945, CAB124/245.

156. R(45)12th mtg, 12 March 1945, R(45)32 and 33, 6 March 1945, CAB87/10.

157. R(45)13th mtg, 20 March 1945, R(45)35, 17 March 1945, CAB87/10.

158. Woolton to Churchill, 26 March 1945, CAB124/245.

159. For example, *Daily Mirror,* 28 and 29 March 1945, 'Doctors Win'; *Daily Worker,* 27 March 1945, 'Government Abandon Health Plan'; *Municipal Journal,* 1 June 1945, pp 1075, 'Death of a White Paper'; resolutions from labour and union organisations complaining about 'whittling down' of the White Paper, April 1944, MH77/44.

160. *The Times,* Leader, 6 and 14 April 1945.

161. HC Debates, vol 409, cols 1954–8, 1987–8, 12 April 1945; vol 410, cols 1095–1107, 26 April 1945.

162. *The Times,* 18 April 1945, speech by Summerskill.

163. *The Times*, 25 May 1945; *Labour Party Conference Report* (1945).

164. Willink to Bevin, 26 April 1945, MH77/119; draft, MH80/32.

165. K O Morgan, *Labour in Power 1945–1951* (Clarendon, 1984), pp 35–6; Addison, pp 256–8; Harris, pp 249–51.

166. MH80/28.

167. NHS(45)38, 8 May 1945, MH80/28.

168. Woolton to Willink, and Willink to Woolton, 18 May 1945, CAB21/2032.

169. NHS(45)45, 24 May 1945, MH80/32.

170. *The Times,* Leader, 12 June 1945.

171. CP(45)13, 4 June 1945, and draft 'National Health Service', CAB66/66. Pater, pp 100–4.

172. Progress with the Proposals, June 1946, CAB66/66.

173. Home Affairs Committee, 6 June 1945, CAB21/2019. See also Willink to Woolton, 7 June 1945, renewing his plea for publication, CAB21/2032.

174. CM(45)9th mtg, 15 June 1945, CAB65/53; CP(45)32, 11 June 1945, CAB66/66.

175. MH77/30A.

Chapter IV
LABOUR ASCENDANT

1. Morgan, *Labour in Power*, pp 45–93; Socialist Medical Association, *The New Chapter* (August, 1945).

2. *Manchester Guardian*, 4 August 1945.

3. Russell-Smith Letters, 27 July 1945.

4. Bodleian Library, Attlee Papers, vol 18.

5. Attlee, *As It Happened* (Heinemann, 1954), p 178. See also Harris, *Attlee,* p 405; A Bullock, *Ernest Bevin Foreign Secretary* (Heinemann, 1983), p 77; M Foot, *Aneurin Bevan*, 2 vols (Paladin, 1975), i, pp 507-9; Morgan, pp 57-9.

6. Russell-Smith Letters, 3 August 1945.

7. Russell-Smith Letters, 21 and 22 August 1945.

8. G Pottinger, *The Secretaries of State for Scotland, 1926-76* (Scottish Academic Press, 1979), pp 101-5. J M Bellamy and J Saville, eds, *Dictionary of Labour Biography* (Macmillan, 1972), ii, 402-3. Morrison to Attlee, 29 November 1947, suggested that Dalton should replace Bevan as Minister of Health, Morrison Papers, f 27. B Pimlott, *The Political Diary of Hugh Dalton 1918-40, 1945-60* (Cape, 1986) sheds no light on this possibility.

9. Pottinger, pp 106-16; H Tracey, ed, *The British Labour Party,* 3 vols (Caxton, 1948), iii, pp 141-2.

10. A Turner, *Scottish Home Rule* (Clarendon, 1952), p 35; Morgan, pp 307-8.

11. Among the standard works, Eckstein plays down Labour involvement; others tend to by-pass the question. The few authors more specially concerned with socialist issues, such as Stark Murray and Honigsbaum, lack perspective on major developments. Nevertheless, Honigsbaum, *Division in British Medicine* is an invaluable source on left-wing associations and general practice.

12. Sir F Menzies, *BMJ*, 1941, ii, 60-1, 12 July 1941.

13. An SMA memorandum of January 1944 was praised as a 'sound and well-reasoned document' by one official, while another ordered that the SMA should be thanked for its help at a particularly opportune moment; minutes, 14 and 18 January 1944, MH77/63.

14. Morgan, pp 36-44; R B McCallum and A Readman, *The British General Election of 1945* (OUP, 1947).

15. HC Debates, vol 374, col 1119, 9 October 1941. Bevan repeated this remark in his speech on the Second Reading of the 1946 NHS Bill.

16. HC Debates, vol 386, col 1657, 16 February 1943, one of about half a dozen disruptions of Anderson's speech.

17. E Bunbury to Bevan, 9 August 1945, MH77/63.

18. *The Times*, 6 September and 22 October 1945; *The Lancet*, 1945, ii, 340, 15 September 1945. The argument for urgency was made in a draft Cabinet paper initially, it seems, prepared for Willink and revised for Bevan in August 1945, MH80/28.

19. HC Debates, vol 413, cols 258, 568, 17 and 21 August 1945 (Greenwood, Morrison). HL Debates, vol 137, col 78, 16 August 1945 (Addison).

20. Memorandam on National Health Service, October 1945, National Health Service, November 1945, Comparison of Schemes [November 1945], MH80/30. D Stark Murray, 'New Views on the Health Service', September 1945, Brynmor Jones Library, Hull University, Socialist Medical Association Archive, DSM1/29.

21. Industrial Health Services, November 1945, MH80/28.

22. Hospital and Consultant Services, October 1945, MH80/28.

23. Stark Murray, 'New Views'.

24. Medical Practitioners Union, *Transition to a State Medical Service* (August 1942).

25. Menzies, *BMJ*, 1941, ii, 60-1, 12 July 1941.

26. *The Lancet*, 1945, ii, 347, 15 September 1945; Murray, 'New Views' notes Bevan's stated desire for 'industrial democracy' in the health service, involving control by all workers.

27. Buchanan's 'cordial agreement' reported by T D Haddow to Rucker, 4 October 1945, Hospital Services: Preliminary Views: Scotland, 30 October 1945, MH80/34.

28. Hospital Services: Preliminary Views, 30 October 1945, MH80/34. Documents from September 1945 describing the hospital service in Scotland had repeated the 1944 White Paper proposals, MH80/28, MH80/34.

29. Pater, National Hospital Service, c 10 August 1945, MH80/34.

30. Memoranda on voluntary hospitals and the national hospital scheme, 7 August to 22 September 1945, MH80/28, MH80/34. The draft Cabinet paper prepared for Bevan's consideration, Outline of Proposals for a National Health Service, 9 September 1945, closely followed the Willink compromises, HH101/7.

31. Sir W S Douglas to Bevan, 22 September 1945, MH80/28, repeating comment by Rucker.

32. Bevan, CP(45)205, 5 October 1945, Buchanan, CP(45)207, 5 October 1945, CAB129/3. Buchanan noted that this view was framed without consultation with Westwood (CM(45)43rd mtg, CAB128/1).

33. CM(45)40th mtg, 11 October 1945, CAB128/1.

34. Morrison, CP(45)227, 12 October 1945, Bevan, CP(45)231, 16 October 1945, CAB129/3.

35. CM(45)43rd mtg, 18 October 1945, CAB128/1. Pater, pp 109–11. Acceptance 'in principle' replaced an earlier minute of this meeting which concluded that 'before the Cabinet came to a final decision, however, they should have an opportunity of seeing the scheme worked out in detail'.

36. Bevan, CP(45)339, 13 December 1945, brief supplementary memorandum by Westwood, CP(45)345, 13 December 1945, CAB129/5. Pater, pp 114–15. Morgan, p 155.

37. CM(45)65th mtg, 20 December 1945, CAB128/2. Pater, pp 115–16.

38. CP(46)3, 3 January 1946, CAB129/6. CM(46)3rd mtg, 8 January 1946, CAB128/5.

39. Briefs on SS(45)33 and 34, and CP(46)3, T.161/1243. Foot, ii, pp 136–7, gives high praise for Dalton as next to Bevan 'chief architect' of the NHS. There is little evidence to support this view. Pimlott's biography of Dalton sheds no further light on this claim, B Pimlott, *Hugh Dalton* (Cape, 1985), p 495.

40. Bevan, CP(46)86, 1 March 1946, Westwood, CP(46)89, 1 March 1946, CAB129/7. SS(46)4th mtg, 4 March 1946, CAB134/698. CM(46)22nd mtg, 8 March 1946, CAB128/5. Pater, pp 118–19.

41. Morrison and Greenwood, CP(46)94, 6 March 1946, CAB129/7.

42. Foot, ii, pp 122–4; Pater, p 107.

43. *Sunday Pictorial*, 4 November 1945; *Daily Herald*, 5 November 1945; *Daily Worker*, 6 November 1945.

44. HC Debates, vol 415, cols 1455–7, 8 November 1945. CM(45)51st mtg, 8 November 1945, CAB128/2.

45. Proposals for a National Health Service, December 1945, MH80/28, MH77/119. Derived from CP(45)339, Appendix, 13 December 1945, CAB129/5.

46. NHS(46)2, 8 January 1946, MH80/30. See also meeting in December 1945, MH80/28. Westwood met the Scottish TUC on 31 January 1947, HH101/8.

47. NHS(46), 5, 10, 22 and 29, 15 January 1946 to 26 February 1946, MH80/30. NHS(S) LA(46) 1 and 2, 17 January and 8 February 1946, for Westwood's first meetings with the local authority associations, HH101/4.

48. Meeting of Bevan with SMA, 17 January 1946, MH77/63. See also correspondence of Hastings and Murray with Bevan, 1946, MH77/85-86.

49. NHS(46)6 and 23, 21 January and 11 February 1946, MH80/30. Wettenhall to Bevan, 14 February 1946, MH80/30. BHA, *A Plan for a National Hospital Service* (March, 1946). NHS B6, 18 November 1946 for Westwood's discussion with voluntary hospital representatives, HH101/6.

50. Bevan to Wettenhall, 23 February 1946, MH77/100.

51. For Buzzard, see above, p 58. Cohen, 'A Comprehensive Health Service', *Agenda,* February 1943, pp 1-20; *idem,* 'Our Hospital System—A Retrospect and Prospect', (November 1945), MH77/54. Bevan to Cohen, 25 January 1946, points out that he had already adopted most of Cohen's proposals in advance of seeing them, MH77/54.

52. NHS(46)19, 5 February 1946, meeting with King's Fund, MH80/30. Sir George Aylwen to Bevan, 18 January, 11 and 27 March 1946, MH77/100.

53. CP(45)298, 23 November 1945, CAB129/4. For background exchanges between Ministry of Health and the Treasury, MH80/32.

54. Hawton to Douglas, 22 November 1945, MH80/32.

55. CM(45)58th mtg, 3 December 1945, CAB128/2. HC Debates, vol 416, cols 2511-12, 6 December 1945.

56. NHS(45)47 and 48, 4 and 13 December 1945, MH80/32; NHS(46)1 and 11, 2 and 29 January 1946, MH80/30. Correspondence between Government Actuary and Ministry of Health, 15 February to 11 March 1946, MH80/30, MH80/32.

57. Maude to Hill, 17 May and 10 July 1944, MH77/172.

58. BMA evidence, October 1945, MH77/172.

59. Hill, oral evidence, 16 October 1945, MH77/173.

60. *Report of the Inter-Departmental Committee on the Remuneration of General Practitioners,* Cmd. 6810, 1946.

61. *Spens GP Report,* para 13.

62. *Spens GP Report,* Appendix II.

63. Meeting, 26 February 1946, MH77/173.

64. *Spens GP Report,* para 14.

65. *Spens GP Report,* para 19. Rucker to H H George, 12 June 1946, MH77/172.

66. Rucker to George, 28 March 1946, MH77/176.

67. Hill to Bevan, 8 November 1945, MH77/119.

68. Bevan to Hill, 13 November 1945, NHS(45)47, 4 December 1945, MH77/119.

69. Seven Principles, 13 December 1945, MH77/119; *BMJ,* 1945, ii, 833, 15 December 1945; Pater, pp 112-13.

70. NHS(46)3, 10 January 1946, MH80/30.

71. NHS(46)17, 6 February 1946, MH80/30.

72. *The Times,* 16 March 1946.

73. *Health Service: Draft of a Bill,* 6 April, 1945, *National Health Services Bill,* 2 August 1945, *National Health Service Bill (94),* 19 March 1946, MH80/36.

74. The draft of 18 January 1946 contained no provision for amenity or pay beds, only a clause 5 declaring a free hospital service. The amenity and pay bed provision was added in the draft of 11 February 1946.

75. *The Times,* 1 May 1946. Pater, pp 126–9.

76. HC Debates, vol 422, cols 63–81, 30 April 1946.

77. Cols 397–407, 2 May 1946.

78. Cols 247–54, 1 May 1946.

79. Cols 43–63, 30 April 1946.

80. Cols 222–42, 1 May 1946.

81. Cols 231–2, 1 May 1946.

82. Cols 136–45, 30 April 1946.

83. Cols 260–6 (S Marshall), 270–4 (Sir Harold Webbe).

84. Cols 407–12, 2 May 1946. The amendment declared that the Bill 'prejudices the patient's right to an independent family doctor; which retards the development of the hospital services by destroying local ownership, and gravely menaces all charitable foundations . . . and which weakens the responsibility of local authorities without planning the health services as a whole'.

85. HC Debates, vol 425, cols 766–91, 26 June 1946; cols 1980–2005, 23 July 1946.

86. HC Debates, vol 426, cols 392–475, 26 July 1946.

87. HL Debates, vol 140, cols 822–32, 16 April 1946.

88. HL Debates, vol 140, cols 832–66, 16 April 1946.

89. HL Debates, vol 143, cols 1–138, 17 October 1946. Pater, pp 133–6.

90. HL Debates, vol 143, cols 381, 388–9, 391–2, 17 October 1946; cols 750–2, 28 October 1946.

91. HL Debates, vol 143, cols 408–23, 21 October 1946; cols 757–60, 28 October 1946.

92. HL Debates, vol 143, cols 431–6, 21 October 1946.

93. HL Debates, vol 143, cols 423–9, 21 October 1946. A further small amendment introduced by the Opposition and agreed at the Report stage allowed honorary consultant staff to join their colleagues in undertaking private work, HL Debates, vol 143, cols 747–50, 28 October 1946.

94. HL Debates, vol 143, cols 461–2, 21 October 1946; cols 764–9, 28 October 1946. A similar amendment had been rejected at the Commons Committee stage, HC Debates, vol 425, cols 1734–74, 22 July 1946.

95. HC Debates, vol 425, cols 456–90, 5 June 1946; cols 1822–42, 22 July 1946. HL Debates, vol 143, cols 463–84, 21 October 1946. The Earl of Munster's amendment enabling local authorities to make use of external midwifery services organised by hospital authorities was accepted, HL Debates, vol 143, cols 502–7, 22 October 1946, col 770, 28 October 1946.

96. HL Debates, vol 143, cols 507–10, 22 October 1946; cols 771–3, 28 October 1946.

97. HC Debates, vol 425, cols 590–617, 18 June 1946. HL Debates, vol 143, cols 501–22, 22 October 1946; col 935, 31 October 1946.

98. Addison to Bevan, and Bevan to Addison, 29 October 1946, MH80/40. This issue was sensitive enough for Bevan to seek Cabinet support, CM(46)93rd mtg, 31 October 1946, CAB123/6.

99. HC Standing Committee C 1946–47, vol I, cols 1244–5, 23 May 1946; HL Debates, vol 143, cols 802–5, 28 October 1946. Jowitt to Bevan, 29 October 1946, Bevan to Jowitt, n.d., MH80/40.

100. HC Debates, vol 428, cols. 1082–1158, 4 November 1946.

101. National Health Service Act, 1946, 9 & 10 Geo 6, ch 81. During the parliamentary process the Bill had expanded from 51 to 80 clauses.

102. HC Debates, vol 422, col 392, 2 May 1946.

103. SS(46)7th mtg, 18 July 1946, CAB134/689. Background papers to NHS (Scotland)Bill, HH101/974.

104. CAB21/2020. Bill (II), 26 November 1946, HPC(46)26th mtg, 22 October 1946, prints of Bill, May–November 1946, HH101/150.

105. HC Debates, vol 431, cols 995–1106, 10 December 1946. For notes on clauses, HH101/975–980.

106. HC Standing Committee C, 1946–47, vol I, cols 801–1650.

107. HC Debates, vol 436, cols 619–778, 21 April 1947.

108. HC Standing Committee C, 1946–47, vol I, cols 1170–89, 25 February 1947; HC Debates, vol 436, cols 621–35, 21 April 1947.

109. HC Debates, vol 436, cols 725–78, 21 April 1947.

110. HL Debates, vol 147, cols 300–35, 12 May 1947.

111. HL Debates, vol 147, cols 595–607, 755–62, 12 and 15 May 1947; HC Debates, vol 437, cols 2287–90, 20 May 1947.

112. HL Debates, vol 147, cols 607–9, 747, 12 and 15 May 1947; HC Debates, vol 437, col 2290, 20 May 1947.

113. HL Debates, vol 147, cols 612–19, 748–51, 12 and 15 May 1947; HC Debates, vol 437, cols 2290–1, 20 May 1947.

114. HL Debates, vol 147, cols 619–22, 12 May 1947; HC Debates, vol 437, col 2292, 20 May 1947.

115. HL Debates, vol 147, cols 570–86, 751–2, 12 and 15 May 1947; HC Debates, vol 437, col 2292, 20 May 1947.

116. HL Debates, vol 147, cols 627–33, 752–3, 12 and 15 May 1947; HC Debates, vol 437, cols 2292–3, 20 May 1947.

117. HL Debates, vol 147, cols 638–40, 754, 12 and 15 May 1947; HC Debates, vol 437, col 2293, 20 May 1947.

118. HL Debates, vol 147, cols 755–62, 15 May 1947; HC Debates, vol 437, col 2379, 21 May 1947. National Health Service (Scotland) Act, 1947, 10 & 11 Geo 6, ch 27.

119. BMJ, 1946, ii, 163, 3 August 1946. For other perspectives, Pater, pp 139–64; Stevens, pp 80–94; A Lindsey, *Socialised Medicine in England and Wales: The National Health Service, 1948–1961* (N Carolina UP, 1962); P Jenkins, 'Bevan's Fight with the BMA', in M Sissons and P French, eds, *Age of Austerity 1945–51* (Penguin, 1964), pp 240–65.

120. Rucker to Souttar, 6 June 1946, meeting of Hill and Douglas, 10 May 1946, MH80/32.

121. NHS(46)30, 31 and 32, 13, 20 and 27 May 1946, MH 80/32.

122. Meeting of Bevan, officials and Insurance Acts Committee of BMA, 17 June 1946, exchange of letters between Douglas and Hill, 22 July 1946 to 8 August 1946, MH77/177.

123. *BMJ*, 1946, ii, 163-4, 3 August 1946.

124. Dain, *BMJ*, 1946, ii, 747-50, 16 November 1946; Hill, *Evening Standard*, 20 November 1946.

125. *The Lancet*, 1946, ii, 909-10, 21 December 1946.

126. *BMJ*, 1946, ii, 956, 21 December 1946.

127. *The Times*, 6 January 1947.

128. Royal College Presidents to Bevan, 2 January 1947, Bevan to Presidents, 6 January 1947, MH77/177, *BMJ*, 1947, i, 66-7, 11 January 1947; Pater, pp 139-41.

129. *BMJ*, 1947, i, Supplement, 18, 1 February 1947.

130. Exchange of letters between Hill and Douglas, 16 January 1947 to 10 February 1947, MH77/119, DHSS94256/5/2A. For parallel negotiations in Scotland beginning June 1947, HH102/502-503.

131. DHSS94256/5/2A.

132. Meeting of Ministers, officials, and Negotiating Committee, 2 and 3 December 1947, DHSS94256/5/2B.

133. *BMJ*, 1947, ii, Supplement, 141-62, 20 December 1947. Woodburn was dissuaded by Bevan from addressing a personal letter to members of the profession in Scotland, DHSS94256/5/2B.

134. *BMJ*, 1947, ii, 1046-7, 27 December 1947; *BMJ*, 1948, i, 56, 10 January 1948.

135. See for instance, *The Times*, Leader, 14 January 1948; *The Lancet*, 1948, i, 144-5, 24 January 1948.

136. *The Lancet*, 1948, i, 149-50, 24 January 1948.

137. *The Times*, 19 January 1948. Speech at opening of E Glamorgan County Hospital, 17 January 1948.

138. CM(48)6th mtg, 22 January 1948, CM(48)8th mtg, 29 January 1948, CAB128/12.

139. CM(48)9th mtg, 2 February 1948, CAB128/12.

140. HC Debates, vol 446, col 1203-5, 29 January 1948.

141. HC Debates, vol 447, cols 35-160, 9 February 1948. Notes for Bevan's speech, making different, but equally pungent remarks about the BMA leaders, DHSS94256/5/2B. The *Manchester Guardian* reported that the Labour benches were 'wild with delight' at Bevan's 'brilliant performance' or 'gladiatoral triumph' (10 February 1948). For the special status of this speech, Foot, ii, pp 176-88.

142. *BMJ*, 1948, i, 454-5, 6 March 1948.

143. *BMJ*, 1948, i, Supplement, 49-56, 27 March 1948.

144. Douglas to Hill, 18 October 1946, 20 December 1946, MH77/177.

145. Discussions on remuneration, October 1946 to December 1947, MH77/177, DHSS94256/5/2A, T.SS 5/150/01A.

146. Hawton to Spens, January 1948, Spens to Hawton, 1 March 1948, MH77/179.

147. BMA, *The Doctors Case* (April 1948), paras 6, 7.

148. NHS(47)30, 25 November 1947, MH77/125.

149. Russell-Smith to Hawton, 6 January 1948, MH77/125.

150. Pater, p 158.

151. Moran to Bevan, 24 March 1948, MH77/119; Moran to Bevan, 4 April 1948, DHSS94256/1/16. *The Lancet,* 1948, i, 561, 10 April 1948; *BMJ,* 1948 i, 694-5, 10 April 1948.

152. HC Debates, vol 449, cols 164-6, 7 April 1948; HL Debates, vol 154, cols 1194-7, 7 April 1948.

153. Announcement by Bevan of the names of the Legal Committee appointed to consider the implications of the NHS Acts in relation to partnerships, HC Debates, vol 449, cols *23-4*, 8 April 1948.

154. Moran to Bevan, 8 April 1948, DHSS94256/1/16.

155. Bevan to Moran, 10 April 1948, DHSS94256/1/16.

156. Meeting, 12 April 1948, DHSS94256/5/2B.

157. *BMJ,* 1948, i, 742-4, 17 April 1948. NHS(48)7, 8 and 11, 7, 13 and 25 May 1948, MH80/57, DHSS94256/5/2B.

158. Exchanges between Treasury and Ministry of Health, February to May 1948, MH77/177.

159. Hill, 25 May 1948, DHSS94256/5/2B.

160. *Report of the Inter-Departmental Committee on the Remuneration of Consultants and Specialists,* Cmd. 7420, 1948. Stevens, *Medical Practice,* pp 90-1. *The Times,* Leader, 16 June 1948.

161. *BMJ,* 1948, i, 893-4, 8 May 1948.

162. *BMJ,* 1948, i, 936-7, 15 May 1948.

163. Douglas to Hill, 26 May 1948, DHSS94256/5/2B. *BMJ,* i, 1948, Supplement, 147-55, 5 June 1948.

164. DHSS94256/2/20. Lindsey, *Socialised Medicine,* pp 66-7.

165. *Report of the Inter-Departmental Committee on the Remuneration of General Dental Practitioners,* Cmd. 7402, 1948.

166. Cripps, 24 May 1948, T.SS 5/154/02A.

167. Bevan, Woodburn and Consultative Committee, 7 June 1948, DHSS94257/1/21.

168. Bevan to 3 dental organisations, 16 June 1948, DHSS94257/2/50A. *The Times,* Leader, 15 May 1948.

169. GEN181/1st mtg, 15 May 1947, CAB130/11; HC Debates, vol 438, col 701, 9 June 1947.

170. For an early compilation of NHS statistics, c March 1946, MH80/34.

171. Summary of Action Required, DHSS94256/5/2A.

172. The following chronology summarises events which are described in more detail in chapters VII to IX below, where sources are cited. The Scottish preparations began slightly later, but by mid-1948 the two sets of arrangements were running in tandem. See also, 'The National Health Service Act in Great Britain. A Review of the First Year's Working', *The Practitioner,* Extra Number, Autumn 1949.

173. MH90/52.

174. Fife Clark to Rucker, 10 October 1946 and subsequent memoranda, MH55/962. Central Office of Information, Social Services Publicity, 24 December 1947, CAB124/1015.

175. Meeting of Ministers to discuss publicity for the Appointed Day, 12 February 1948, CAB124/1015.

176. Ministry of National Insurance, *Family Guide to the National Insurance Scheme*, 1948; title changed from 'Short Guide . . .'

177. D Stephens to H B Riddle, 6 January 1947, and following papers, MH55/962.

178. Fife Clark, 16 December 1947, MH55/962.

179. F Byers MP to Bevan, 16 February 1948, Bevan to Byers, nd, DHSS94256/2/20.

180. Fife Clark to Hawton, 24 April 1948, MH55/962.

181. Ministry of Health, circular 36/48, 15 March 1948, and related papers, DHSS94202/1/14.

182. The National Health Service, 20 February 1948. Cited in T Wildy, 'Propaganda and Social Policy in Britain 1945-1951', Leeds University PhD, 1985, pp 190-2.

183. Wildy, pp. 194-200; for reaction of officials, Russell-Smith Letters, 13 February 1948, 16 March 1948.

184. *Report of the Ministry of Health for 1949* (HMSO, 1950), pp 337-8.

185. BMA, *The Private Patient and the New Health Service* (1948). For criticisms DHSS94256/2/20.

186. *The Times*, 18 June 1948.

187. *The Lancet*, 1948, ii, 24, 3 July 1948.

188. Morrison to Attlee 25 June 1948, Attlee Papers, vol 71, fol 161; Bevan to Attlee, 2 July 1948, Attlee Papers, vol 72, fols 13-14.

189. Drafts and text of broadcast, Attlee Papers, vols 71 and 72, CAB124/1016. For background discussions, Wildy, pp 172-83.

190. Harris, pp 424-5; Foot, ii, pp 234-8.

191. Russell-Smith Letters, 5 July 1948.

192. Russell-Smith Letters, 6 July-8 July 1948.

193. 'The Ministry and the Service', *The Practitioner* Review (n 172 above), p 72.

194. Russell-Smith Letters, 28 July 1948.

195. Ministry of Health, *Report 1949*, p 117.

196. Hill to Douglas, 8 December 1948, 3 January 1949, D Stevenson to Douglas 22 April 1949, meeting of officials with BMA, 1 June 1949, MH80/57.

197. Russell-Smith to Hawton, 18 December 1948, MH80/57.

198. See also Sir L Whitby, *The Times*, 20 June 1949.

199. Hill to Douglas, 11, 12 and 19 May 1949, Douglas to Hill, 13 May 1949 (twice), MH80/57.

200. Sir T D Harrison to I E Ellis, 2 June 1949, MH80/57. HC Debates vol 464, col 1853, 11 May 1949.

201. Bevan to Morrison, 7 April 1949, Morrison to Bevan, 14 April 1949, MH80/57.

202. HC Debates, vol 468, cols 599-600, 19 October 1949.

203. HC Debates, vol 468, cols 589-94, 19 October 1949.

204. HC Debates, vol 468, cols 629–45, 19 October 1949.

205. HC Debates, vol 463, cols 2439–40, 8 April 1949. Morrison to Bevan, nd, Bevan to Morrison, 13 May 1949, CAB21/2035.

206. CM(49)43rd mtg, 30 June 1949, CAB128/15.

207. CP(49)190, 14 September 1949, CP(49)196, 29 September 1949, CP(49)206, 17 October 1949, CAB129/37.

208. CM(49)59th mtg, 18 October 1949, CAB128/16.

209. HL Debates, vol 165, cols 799–801, 17 November 1949. The National Health Service (Amendment) Act received Royal Assent on 16 December 1949, (12, 13, & 14 Geo 6, ch 93).

Chapter V
CRISIS OF EXPENDITURE

1. These totals exclude appropriations in aid from National Health Insurance. The NHS [Money] debate was almost exclusively preoccupied with the £66m compensation for general practitioners. Just one speaker, Major Guy Lloyd, complained that the estimate for the cost of the service was 'grossly inadequate', HC Debates, vol 422, cols 432–4, 2 May 1946.

2. *PEP Report*, Hilliard and McNae, and Medical Planning Research, sources cited above, p 13. A H T Robb-Smith, 'The Conjectures of Appendix E. With A Backward Glance to 1912', *The Lancet*, 1944, i, 545–6, 22 April 1944; office discussions, April 1944, MH77/84. Robb-Smith's information was also shown to Bevan, Russell-Smith, 29 November 1945, MH77/85.

3. E Hale to Sir Herbert Brittain, December 1948, H B Liddle to H G Smyth, 10 May 1949, T.SS 226/5/01A. For details of estimates for Scotland, England and Wales 1948–1957, see Tables I and II.

4. A Johnston to A R W Bavin, 27 January 1949, CAB21/2035.

5. Cripps, 16 December 1948, T.SS 226/5/01A.

6. Bevan, CP(48)302, 13 December 1948, Woodburn, CP(48)308, 29 December 1948, CAB129/3.

7. CM(49) 12th mtg, 17 February 1949, CAB128/15.

8. Hale to Brittain, November 1948, B F St-J Trend to L N Helsby, 17 December 1948, Johnston to Bavin, 27 January 1949, Sir Norman Brook to Johnston, 31 January 1949, T.SS 226/5/01A.

9. Attlee to Cripps, cited by E G Cass, 12 April 1949, Cripps to Bevan and Woodburn, 20 December 1948, T.SS 226/5/01A.

10. Bevan to Cripps, 4 January 1949, T. 227/185.

11. Woodburn offered a reduction of £3.4m compared with the £12.5m requested, Sir B Gilbert to Sir Edward Bridges, 12 January 1949, T. 227/185.

12. Cripps to Bevan, 5 January 1949, T. 227/185.

13. Hale, 11 January 1949, T. 227/185.

14. Gilbert to Bridges, 12 January 1949, T. 227/185.

15. Cripps to Attlee, 24 January 1949, T.SS 226/5/01A.

16. Notes for meeting between Cripps and Bevan, 25 January 1949, Hale to Cripps, November 1949, T.SS 5/333/01A.

17. *Statement on Personal Incomes, Costs and Prices*, Cmd. 7321, February 1948.

18. Bevan, 18 January 1949, DHSS94601/1/17. Morgan, pp 371-3, 378-9; C R Dow, *The Management of the British Economy 1945-60* (CUP, 1970), p 35; A Cairncross, *Years of Recovery British Economic Policy, 1945-51* (Metheun, 1985), 404-8.

19. HC Debates, vol 466, col 2153, 6 July 1949, vol 468, cols 26-7, 27 September 1949.

20. Bevan, CP(49)220, 1 November 1949, CAB129/37; CM(49) 64th mtg, 7 November 1949, CAB128/16.

21. Cripps to Bevan and Woodburn, 9 March 1949, T.SS 226/5/01A.

22. Bevan to Cripps, 21 March 1949, Woodburn to Cripps, 23 March 1949, T.SS 226/5/01A.

23. Briefs on 1949 Budget, drafts of Budget speech, broadcast text, T. 171/399; HC Debates, vol 463, cols 2082-4, 6 April 1949.

24. Sources cited in n22 above.

25. T J Bligh, 12 May 1949, Gilbert to Bridges, 17 May 1949, T.SS 226/5/01A.

26. J A R Pimlott to Morrison, 5 January 1949, CAB21/2035.

27. *Seventh Report from the Committee on Estimates 1948-49* (HMSO, 1949), p xxiv.

28. Bevan, CP(49)105, 6 May 1949, Woodburn, CP(49)106, 10 May 1949, CAB129/34; CM(49) 37th mtg, 23 May 1949, CAB128/15.

29. Pimlott to Morrison, 17 May 1949, CAB21/2035.

30. D J Mitchell to Hale, 17 August 1949, T.SS 226/5/01A.

31. EPC(49)76, 7 July 1949, CAB134/220. Also confirms £57m for 1949/50 Supplementary Estimates.

32. Cripps, EPC(49)111, 13 October 1949, CAB134/220; EPC(49)34th mtg and 35th mtg, 14 October 1949, CAB134/220. Background papers submitted by health departments, September 1949, T. 227/185. For Bevan's criticism of polypharmacy, HC Standing Committee C, 1946-47, vol I, cols 1604-5, 19 June 1946.

33. Attlee, CP(49)205, 20 October 1949, CAB129/37; CM(49) 61st mtg, 21 October 1949, CAB128/16.

34. Bevan to Attlee, 21 October 1949, Attlee to Bevan, nd, Attlee Papers, vol 89, fols 282-7. Foot, ii, pp 273-4.

35. Attlee Papers, vol 89, fols 288 ff; vol 90, fols 1-92; vol 91, fols 19 ff. HC Debates, vol 468, col 1019, 24 October 1949.

36. Morrison to Attlee, 20 October 1949, Attlee Papers, vol 91, fol 19.

37. *The Times*, 25 and 26 October 1949. See also *Manchester Guardian*, 25 October 1949.

38. Bevan, addresses to Parliamentary Labour Party and at University College London, *The Times*, 26 October 1949, 16 November 1949.

39. Hawton to Pater, 28 October 1949, MH80/57.

40. Morrison to Attlee, 24 October 1949, and subsequent exchanges ending 31 October 1949, Attlee Papers, vol 90, fols 106-12, vol 92, fol 4.

41. Harris, p 439.

42. Bevan, LP(49)77, 1 November 1949, CAB132/13; LP(49) 19th mtg, 4 November 1949, CAB132/11.

43. Hale to Gilbert, 6 January 1950, T.SS 5/333/01A 'The fact is that the Minister has come down in favour of the charge per script because its yield is lower'.

44. Haddow to Hale, 18 November 1949, T.SS 5/333/01A.

45. E J S Clarke to Harrison, 21 October 1949, MH80/57.

46. NC15/15/2, MH80/57.

47. HL Debates, vol 165, cols 796-9, 17 November 1949; HC Debates, vol 470, cols 2233-86, 9 December 1949.

48. Woodburn to Cripps, 24 December 1949, T. 227/185.

49. Cripps, LP(50) 3, 10 January 1950, CAB132/15; LP(50) 1st mtg, 20 January 1950, CAB132/14.

50. Bevan, CP(50)14, 26 January 1950, CAB129/38.

51. Bevan to Attlee, 2 February 1950, CAB124/1187; Attlee to Morrison, 3 February 1950, Attlee to Cripps, 3 February 1950, T.SS 5/333/01A.

52. HC Debates, vol 487, col 43, 23 April 1951.

53. Hale, 11 November 1949, T. 227/185.

54. Cripps to Bevan and Woodburn, 28 November 1949, T. 227/185.

55. Bevan to Cripps, 12 December 1949, Woodburn to Cripps, 24 December 1949, T. 227/185.

56. Bridges, comment on Hale to Gilbert, 16 December 1949, T. 227/185.

57. F W S Craig, *British General Election Manifestos 1900-1974* (Macmillan, 1975), pp 148-58; N Fisher, *Iain Macleod* (Deutsch, 1973), p 63.

58. H G Nicholas, *The British General Election of 1950* (Macmillan, 1951); Morgan, pp 402-6.

59. P M Williams, *The Diary of Hugh Gaitskell 1945-1956* (Cape, 1983), pp 61-2, 236, 238; Morgan, p 465; *DNB* (Kenneth Younger); Pottinger, pp 117-29; Bullock, pp 757-8. Foot, ii, p 317, describes McNeil as a 'Daltonian', but nothing is said of this in Pimlott's biography of Dalton.

60. Foot, ii, p 288; Gaitskell, *Diary*, pp 163-4, 174.

61. Russell-Smith Letters, 28 February and 1 March 1950.

62. Dalton, *High Tide and After: Memoirs 1945-60* (Muller, 1962), p 350; Williams, *Hugh Gaitskell* (Cape, 1979), p 211.

63. Harris, p 449; Pimlott, pp 576-7.

64. LP(50) 1st mtg, 20 January 1950, CAB132/14.

65. Bevan, CP(50) 31, 10 March 1950, CAB 129/38.

66. CP(50)31, paras 13-14, 45.

67. CP(50)31, para 26.

68. CP(50)31, paras 32, 40.

69. CM(50) 10th mtg, 13 March 1950, CAB 128/17.

70. CM(50) 11th mtg, 16 March 1950, CAB 128/17.

71. Harris, p. 451.

72. HC Debates, vol 472, cols 916-1038, 14 March 1950. For Crookshank's liking for this image, see his Second Reading speech on the 1952 Act, 27 March 1952.

73. Cols 933-9, especially col 939.

74. Cols 950-5.

75. Cols 960-4.

76. Cols 1022-34.

77. E M Nicholson to Morrison, 11 and 17 March 1950, CAB124/1188.

78. Johnston to Brook, 20 March 1950, CAB21/1733.

79. Brook to Bridges, 21 March 1950, CAB21/1733.

80. Williams, p 210.

81. Gaitskell, *Diary*, pp 174-5, 21 March 1950. Williams, p 212, credits Wilson with arrangement of this 'compromise'. If Wilson intervened, his action would seem to belong to a date later than 21 March.

82. Nicholson to Morrison, 31 March 1950, CAB21/1733.

83. Brook to Attlee, 1 April 1950, CAB21/1733.

84. BC(50)15, 22 February 1950, paras 22-31, T. 171/400.

85. Foot, ii, p 291; Williams, p 212; L Smith, *Harold Wilson* (Hodder & Stoughton, 1964), p 150.

86. Cripps to Attlee, 2 April 1950, Attlee Papers, vol 100, fols 2-4, and T. 171/402. Harris, p 451.

87. Attlee to Cripps, 3 April 1950, T. 171/402.

88. Cripps, CP(50)53, 29 March 1950, CAB129/39. CM(50) 17th mtg, 3 April 1950, CAB128/17. See also Nicholson to Morrison, 5 April 1950, CAB21/1733.

89. Bevan, CP(50)56, 30 March 1950, CAB129/39.

90. McNeil, CP(50)57, 31 March 1950, CAB129/39.

91. CM(50) 18th mtg, 4 April 1950, CAB128/17.

92. Drafts of Budget statement, T. 171/402.

93. CM(50) 19th mtg, 6 April 1950, CAB128/17. Brook to Attlee, 4 April 1950 (CAB21/1733) notes Morrison's failure to tie the Cabinet to its earlier 'decision' concerning public expenditure cuts.

94. Draft Budget statement, 7 April 1950, CAB21/1733 and T. 171/402.

95. HC Debates, vol 474, cols 59-60, 18 April 1950.

96. Douglas to Gilbert, 12 April 1950, Gilbert to W Armstrong, 13 April 1950, T.SS 226/5/01A.

97. L L H Thompson, 12 April 1950, T.SS 226/5/01A.

98. Douglas to Gilbert, 26 April 1950, T.SS 226/5/01B.

99. Draft terms, Brook to Attlee, 11 April 1950, CAB21/1733. See also CP(50)79, 21 April 1950, CAB129/39, and NH(50)1, 22 April, 1950, CAB134/518.

100. Morrison to Brook, 17 April 1950, CAB21/1733.

101. CP(50)79, 21 April 1950, CAB129/39.

102. Gilbert on NH(50)2, 3, and 4, T.SS 226/5/01B. Johnston to Attlee, 25 April 1950, CAB21/2027.

103. NH(50)2, 3 and 4, 6 May 1950, CAB134/518.

104. Johnston to Attlee, 8 May 1950, CAB21/2027.

105. NH(50) 1st mtg, 10 May 1950, CAB134/518.

106. Foot, ii, pp 291-2.

107. Gaitskell, *Diary*, p 143, 11 August 1950; Williams, p 214.

108. McNeil to Morrison, 19 May 1950, Morrison to McNeil, 26 May 1950, CAB124/1187.

109. Johnston to Attlee, 12 May 1950, Hawton to Johnston, 17 May 1950, CAB21/2027.

110. NH(50) 2nd mtg, 23 May 1950, CAB134/518.

111. Johnston to Brook, 26 June 1950, CAB21/2027.

112. Gaitskell, NH(50)6, 23 June 1950, CAB134/518, drafted by Johnston and toned down by Gaitskell, T.SS 226/5/01B.

113. Bevan, NH(50)7-11, 24 June 1950, CAB 134/518. For criticism of the schemes for loans, J H Lidderdale to Morrison, 20 July, 1950, CAB21/2027.

114. McNeil, NH(50)12-13, 24 June 1950, CAB134/518.

115. NH(50) 3rd mtg, 28 June 1950, CAB134/518.

116. Johnston to Brook, 26 June 1950, CAB21/2027.

117. Gaitskell, *Diary*, pp 192-3, 11 August 1950; Williams p 214.

118. Foot, ii, p 293.

119. Foot, ii, pp 293-4, citing Bevan to Cripps, June 1950.

120. Bevan, NH(50) 14-16, 15 July 1950, Woodburn, NH(50)18, 17 July 1950, CAB134/518. The Treasury was still unhappy because of Bevan's failure to give assurances concerning keeping within his estimate: brief on NH(50) 16, CAB 21/2027.

121. Bevan, NH(50) 17, 15 July 1950, CAB 134/518.

122. Brief on Jones Report, July 1950, CAB21/2027.

123. Lidderdale to Morrison, 20 July 1950, CAB24/1188.

124. NH(50) 4th mtg, 21 July 1950, CAB134/518.

125. Bevan to Gaitskell, 25 July 1950, T.SS 226/5/01B.

126. Bevan, NH(50)21, 21 September 1950 (originally dated July 1950, suggesting procrastination over submission), CAB134/518.

127. McNeil, NH(50)20, 20 September 1950, CAB134/518.

128. Bevan, NH(50)22-25, 21 September to 13 October 1950, CAB134/518.

129. Gilbert to Attlee, 23 September 1950, T.SS 226/5/01B.

130. NH(50) 5th mtg, 16 October 1950, CAB 134/518. At this stage Dalton was backing Bevan against Gaitskell, Pimlott, p 573.

131. E W Playfair to Johnston, 29 November 1950, J G Owen to Mitchell, 29 November 1950, T.SS 226/5/01B.

132. Hale to Gilbert, 1 August 1950, T.SS 226/5/01B.

133. HL Debates, vol 168, cols 1215-23, 18 October 1950.

134. Gaitskell, NH(50)26, 6 November 1950, CAB134/518.

135. Bevan, NH(50)31, 17 November 1950, McNeil, NH(50)32, 17 November 1950, CAB134/518.

136. Johnston to Attlee, 20 November 1950, CAB21/2027.

137. NH(50) 6th mtg, 21 November 1950, CAB134/518. Bevan had written to Attlee expressing 'consternation and astonishment' about Gaitskell's appointment, Harris, pp 459-60; see also Foot, ii, pp 296-8; Williams, 236-8.

138. Bevan NH(50)29, 16 November 1950, McNeil NH(50)30, 17 November, 1950, CAB134/518.

139. Johnston to Attlee, 23 November 1950, CAB21/2027.

140. Johnston to Brook, 24 November 1950, CAB21/2027.

141. Johnston to Brook, 25 November 1950, CAB21/2027.

142. Johnston to Playfair, 27 November 1950, Playfair to Johnston, 29 November 1950, CAB21/2027.

143. Gaitskell, *Diary*, pp 215-16, 3 November 1950; Dalton, *Diary*, p 490, 30 October 1950. Harris, pp 469-70; Foot, ii, pp 308-9; Morgan, p 438.

144. Foot, ii, p 309.

145. M Jenkins, *Bevanism, Labour's High Tide* (Spokesman, 1979), pp 81-4, an episode little noticed by Foot.

146. Russell-Smith Letters, 19 January 1951. For Dalton's perspective, Pimlott, p 594.

147. Gaitskell, *Diary*, pp 228-9.

148. Marquand, LP(49)76, 25 October 1949, CAB132/14. Three letters from Ministry of Pensions to Treasury, October 1949, T.SS 5/333/01A.

149. Marquand to Bevan, c 16 March 1950, CAB124/1188.

150. Marquand, NH(50)5, 19 May 1950, CAB134/518.

151. NH(50) 6mtg, 21 November 1950, CAB134/518.

152. Marquand to Brook, 16 March 1951 and related memoranda, CAB21/3370.

153. Russell-Smith Letters, 22 January and 15 February 1951. *The Times*, 8 November 1972.

154. Owen to Playfair, 24 January 1951, Mitchell to Owen, 29 January 1951, T.SS 226/5/01C.

155. Budget Committee, July 1950-March 1951, T. 171/403.

156. Owen to Playfair, 2 February 1951, T.SS 226/5/01C.

157. Gaitskell, c 4 February 1951, T.SS 226/5/01C.

158. Gaitskell to Marquand and McNeil, 6 February 1951, T.SS 226/5/01C.

159. Marquand to Gaitskell, 12 February 1951, T.SS 226/5/01C.

160. McNeil to Gaitskell, 13 February 1951, T.SS 226/5/01C.

161. NH(51) 1st mtg, 15 February 1951, CAB134/519. Gaitskell, *Diary*, pp 239-40.

162. Marquand, NH(51)2, 20 February 1951, CAB134/519.

163. McNeil, NH(51) 3, 20 February, 1951, CAB134/519.

164. Owen to Playfair, 21 February 1951, T. 171/404.

165. Gaitskell to Marquand and McNeil, 21 February 1951, T. 171/404.

166. Armstrong to Gilbert, 1 March 1951, T. 171/404.

167. Brief, 5 March 1951, meeting, 6 March 1951, T. 171/403. Gaitskell, *Diary*, pp 240-1.

168. Owen to Playfair, 8 March 1951, T.SS 226/5/01C.

169. Gaitskell, NH(51)6, 13 March 1951, CAB134/519. See also Armstrong to Gilbert, 7 March 1951, T.SS 226/5/01C.

170. NH(51) 3rd mtg, 14 March 1951, CAB134/519. Gaitskell, *Diary*, p 241.

171. Armstrong to Gilbert, 7 March 1951, Johnston to Attlee, 8 March 1951, T. 171/404.

172. Consideration of Bevan for Bevin's post is discussed by Harris, p 472, Williams, pp 238, 249, Bullock, p 758. Pimlott, pp 595-6, gives Dalton's list,

in which Bevan is not included. Likewise Gaitskell, *Diary*, p 238. Foot does not consider the issue.

173. Minute of meeting of 15 March 1951, GEN357/1 and 2, and T. 171/404. Gaitskell, *Diary*, p 241; Williams, pp 250, 837.

174. Gaitskell to Attlee, 20 March 1951, Attlee Papers, vol 119, fols 30-1, T. 171/404, draft T.SS 226/5/01C. Gaitskell, *Diary*, p 242.

175. Attlee to Gaitskell, 20 March 1951, Attlee Papers, vol 119, fol 32, T. 171/404.

176. CM(51) 22nd mtg, 22 March 1951, CAB128/19. Gaitskell, *Diary*, p 242.

177. Foot, ii, p 317, for an account of this meeting from Bevan's perspective. Dalton reports Bevan making 'very heavy weather' of the problem, *Diary*, p 514, 22 March 1951. Gaitskell, *Diary*, pp 242-3.

178. Gaitskell, *Diary*, pp 242-3; Williams, p 250; Dalton, *Diary*, p. 515, 22 March 1951.

179. Williams, p 250; Foot, ii, p 317.

180. Foot, ii, p 292.

181. Gaitskell, *Diary*, p 252, 4 May 1951, and testimony of Lord Armstrong, Williams, p 250.

182. Foot, ii, pp 317-18.

183. Dalton, *Diary*, pp 518-20, 5-6 April 1951; Gaitskell, *Diary*, p 243; Williams, pp 250-1; Pimlott, pp 598-9; Foot, ii, pp 318-20.

184. CM(51) 25th mtg, 9 April 1951, CAB128/19. Gaitskell, *Diary*, pp 245-7, 30 April 1951; Williams, p 250.

185. B Donoughue and G W Jones, *Herbert Morrison: Portrait of a Politician* (Weidenfeld & Nicholson, 1973), p 487, Morrison's notes on his interview. Williams, p 251; Pimlott, pp 598-9; Dalton, *Diary*, pp 521-2, 9 April 1951.

186. Gaitskell, *Diary*, pp 243-5.

187. Foot, ii, p 321, and Harris, p 475, locate this meeting on evening of 9 April.

188. Gaitskell, *Diary*, pp 245-6.

189. Gaitskell, *Diary*, pp 246-7; Williams, p 252; Foot, ii, p 321; Harris, p 475.

190. Gaitskell, *Diary*, p 246; Williams, p 253.

191. Gaitskell, *Diary*, p 247. Brook to Morrison, 26 April 1951, ascribing this change to a 'message' possibly stemming from Attlee, CAB21/2367.

192. Draft Budget speech (T. 171/407, p 23) erases 'to prevent forestalling, the new charges will apply to dentures and spectacles ordered after April 12th'. HC Debates, vol 486, col 852, 10 April 1951.

193. Gaitskell, *Diary*, p 252; Foot, ii, pp 324-5; Pimlott, p 599.

194. CM(51) 27th mtg, 12 April 1951, CAB128/19. Gaitskell, *Diary*, p 252; Dalton, *Diary*, p 529, 12 April 1951.

195. Russell-Smith Letters, 17 April 1951.

196. Foot, ii, pp 323-7; Williams, pp 256-7; Morgan, pp 451-2.

197. Attlee to Bevan, 18 April 1951, Foot, ii, p 327; Harris, p 476.

198. CM(51) 29th mtg, 19 April 1951, CAB128/19. Gaitskell, *Diary*, pp 253-4; Dalton, *Diary*, p 532, 19 April 1951.

199. Gaitskell, *Diary*, p 254; Williams, p 256.

200. Gaitskell, *Diary*, pp 254–5; Foot, ii, p 327; Williams, p 257; Pimlott, p 600 for Dalton's interventions.

201. Attlee to Bevan, 20 April 1951, Harris, p 477.

202. Bevan to Attlee, 21 April 1951, Attlee to Bevan, 21 April 1951, Harris, p 477, Foot, ii, pp 328–9, Williams, p 258. Some sources date these letters 21 April, and others 22 April. Some ascribe them to Saturday, others to Sunday. Correspondence included in *The Times*, 23 April 1951.

203. Harris, pp 478–80; Pimlott, p 601; Morgan, p 453.

204. HC Debates, vol 487, cols 34–43, 23 April 1951, extensively quoted in Foot, ii, pp 331–5.

205. Foot, ii, pp 336–7; Williams, pp 260–1.

206. HC Debates, vol 487, cols 228–31, 24 April 1951.

207. Williams, pp 259–61; Jenkins, pp 152–3; Morgan, p 454.

208. Russell-Smith, 13 March 1951, MH80/58, T. 227/92. Marquand to Gaitskell, 15 March 1951, Gaitskell to Marquand, 17 March 1951, T.SS 226/5/01C.

209. Owen, minute of meeting of Ministers, 12 April 1951, T. 227/92.

210. M I Michaels to S I Smith, 16 April 1951, MH80/58; Marquand to Ede, April 1951, CAB21/2027.

211. CM(51) 29th mtg, 19 April 1951, CM(51) 30th mtg, 23 April 1951, CAB128/19.

212. CM(51) 31st mtg, 26 April 1951, CAB128/19.

213. CM(51) 32nd mtg, 30 April 1951, CAB128/19; Hawton to Marquand, 1 May 1951, MH80/58.

214. Russell-Smith Letters, 10, 11, 12 and 13 April 1951.

215. Hawton to Marquand, 11 April 1951, MH80/58.

216. Brook to Morrison, 26 April 1951, CAB21/2367.

217. HC Debates, vol 487, cols 232–347, 24 April 1951. This Bill received Royal Assent on 10 May 1951, 14 & 15 Geo 6, ch 31.

218. Hawton to Michaels, 18 April 1951, MH80/58.

219. J E Pollard to Haddow, 3 May 1951, Marquand to Foot, April 1951, MH80/58.

220. Haddow to H K Ainsworth, 29 March 1951, MH80/58. HC Debates, vol 487, cols 234, 333–4, 24 April 1951.

221. HC Debates, vol 487, cols 331–8, 24 April 1951.

222. HC Debates, vol 487, cols 1275–306, 2 May 1951.

223. HC Debates, vol 487, cols 1306–14, 2 May 1951.

224. HC Debates, vol 487, cols. 1293–306, 2 May 1951. Discussions among officials, 3 May 1951, Haddow to Russell-Smith, 27 March 1951, MH80/58.

225. HC Debates, vol 487, cols 1206–37, 2 May 1951.

226. HC Debates, vol 487, cols 1375–7, 2 May 1951.

227. HC Debates, vol 487, cols 1250–6, 1374–5, 2 May 1951. Russell-Smith Letters, 3 May 1951.

228. HC Debates, vol 487, cols 1601–716, 7 May 1951; col 2185, 10 May 1951. HL Debates, vol 171, cols 812–28, 9 May 1951.

229. Playfair to Hale, 13 March 1951, T.SS 226/5/01C.

230. Russell-Smith to Michaels, 18 January 1951, MH80/59.

231. Playfair to Owen, 25 May 1951, T.SS 226/5/01C.

232. Mitchell to Owen, 14 April 1951, T.SS 226/5/01C.

233. NH(51)9, 25 May 1951, CAB134/519.

234. NH(51) 3rd mtg, 25 May 1951, NH(51) 4th mtg, 31 May 1951, CAB134/519.

235. The last paper circulated to the Committee, NH(51)14, 18 September 1951, CAB134/519.

Chapter VI
CONSERVATIVES AND CONSENSUS

1. F W S Craig, *British General Election Manifestos 1900–1974*, 1951 Conservative Manifesto, pp 169–73, 1951 Labour Manifesto, pp 173–6.

2. A Seldon, *Churchill's Indian Summer. The Conservative Government 1951–55* (Hodder & Stoughton, 1981), pp 76–8. Bodleian Library, Crookshank Diary, fol 48, 28 October 1951. D E Butler, *The British General Election of 1951* (Macmillan, 1952).

3. Seldon, pp 91, 540.

4. Seldon, pp 82, 91–2; Obituary, *The Times*, 18 October 1961. Crookshank was handicapped by his association with Chamberlain's appeasement policy.

5. Russell-Smith Letters, 7 November 1951, 17 January 1952.

6. Russell-Smith Letters, 8 November 1951, 1 February 1952, 18 March 1952, 8 May 1952. Crookshank's Diary supports this reputation for aversion to his health duties.

7. Russell-Smith Letters, 26 March 1952.

8. Seldon, p 133.

9. Seldon, p 92; Fisher, *Macleod*, p 84; Pottinger, pp 130–45.

10. Seldon, pp 133–5, 550; Russell-Smith Letters, 27 March 1952, 2 April 1952.

11. Seldon, p 267; Russell-Smith Letters, 1, 6, 13 and 29 November 1951.

12. Crookshank Papers, Diary, fol 54, 19 December 1954.

13. Goodman, *Wilson Jameson*, pp 144–5.

14. Hill to Douglas, 19 May 1949, MH80/57.

15. Crookshank Papers, Diary, fol 49, 9 November 1951.

16. Crookshank, note, nd, MH80/59. Conservative Party, *Britain Strong and Free* (1951), p 29.

17. Butler to Crookshank, 12 November 1951, MH80/59.

18. Butler to Churchill, 19 December 1951, T.SS 226/5/01D.

19. Meeting of officials, 19 November 1951, MH80/59.

20. Owen, nd, MH80/59; Mitchell, 26 November 1951, T. 227/185.

21. Office meeting with Crookshank, 14 November 1951, MH80/59.

22. Meeting of Treasury and health department officials, 19 November 1951, Pater to Russell-Smith, 20 December 1951, MH80/59.

23. Haddow, nd, MH80/59.

24. Economy in the National Health Service, [December 1951], Board of Control minute, 12 December 1951, MH80/59.

25. NHS Estimates, 3 December 1951, T.SS 226/5/01D. This increase included £13.5m additional commitment to civil defence.

26. Owen, 4 December 1951, T.SS 226/5/01D.

27. EA(E)(51)10, 6 December 1951, CAB134/856.

28. Crookshank Papers, Diary, fol 53, 6 and 7 December 1951.

29. EA(E)(51) 4th mtg, 7 December 1951, 6th mtg, 12 December 1951, CAB134/856.

30. Crookshank to Cherwell, 14 December 1951, Cherwell to Crookshank, 18 December 1951, T.SS 226/5/01D. With respect to this exchange Butler noted 'the writer is perpetually with the PM and will be for some time ahead'.

31. Playfair to Gilbert, 18 December 1951, T.SS 226/5/10D; Crookshank Papers, Diary, fol 54, 17 December 1951.

32. CC(51) 19th mtg, 20 December 1951, CAB128/23. Russell-Smith minute, 20 December 1951, MH80/59. See Table I, p 135 above, for the outcome.

33. Playfair to Sir Geoffrey King, Ministry of National Insurance, 5 January 1952, Playfair to Armstrong, 21 January 1952, T.SS 226/5/01D.

34. EA(E)(52) 1st mtg, 10 January 1952, CAB134/856. J P Dodds to I F Armer, 21 January 1952, MH80/59.

35. HC Debates, vol 495, cols 54-5, 29 January 1952; cols 210-321, 30 January 1952; cols 371-496, 31 January 1952.

36. CC(52) 17th mtg, 14 February 1952, CAB128/24.

37. Owen, minute, 13 February 1952, T. 227/106.

38. CC(52) 4th mtg, 17 January 1952, CAB128/24; Playfair to Owen, 18 January 1952, T 227/106.

39. CC(52) 17th mtg, 14 February 1952, CC(52) 30th mtg, 13 March 1952, CAB128/24.

40. Owen to Playfair, 19 February and 5 March 1952, T. 227/106. Russell-Smith to E Bullard, National Assistance Board, 11 February 1952, MH80/59.

41. *The Backbench Diaries of Richard Crossman*, ed J Morgan (Hamilton/Cape, 1981), p 77.

42. Russell-Smith to Bullard, 11 February 1952, MH80/59; Owen to Playfair, 19 February 1952 and 3 March 1952, T. 227/106.

43. Butler to Crookshank and Stuart, 12 March 1952, Stuart to Butler, 19 March 1952, Crookshank to Butler, 19 March 1952, T. 227/106. The Department of Health argued against relinquishing the charge on hearing aids on the ground that these were equivalent to glasses, upon which there was already a charge, Haddow to Pater, 14 March 1952, MH80/59.

44. Butler to Crookshank, 21 March 1952, T. 227/106.

45. CC(52) 32nd mtg, 20 March 1952, CAB128/24.

46. Crookshank Papers, Diary, fols 61-2, 19 and 20 February 1952.

47. Stuart to Crookshank, 29 January 1952, MH80/59; Butler to Crookshank, 31 March 1952, and related papers, T. 227/106.

48. NHS(52)4, 18 February 1952, MH80/59. Russell-Smith Letters, 6 May 1952, described this measure as a 'rotten Bill'.

49. Russell-Smith Letters, 6 and 9 May 1952.

50. Second Reading Debate, HC Debates, vol 498, cols 841-56, 27 March 1952.

51. HC Debates, vol 498, cols 886-95, 961-7, 27 March 1952.

52. Fisher, *Macleod*, pp 81-4; Foot, ii, pp 357-8; Russell-Smith Letters, 27 March 1952.

53. Crookshank Papers, Diary, fol 64, 27 March 1952.

54. CC(52) 41st mtg, 10 April 1952, CAB128/24. HC Debates, vol 498, cols 419–686, 23 April 1952.

55. Macleod to Crookshank, 31 March 1952, MH80/60.

56. Russell-Smith Letters, 10 April 1952.

57. HC Debates, vol 498, cols 1941–1990, 3 April 1952.

58. HC Debates, vol 498, cols 1997–2042, 3 April 1952.

59 HC Debates, vol 498, cols 1740–56, 3 April 1952.

60. *Backbench Diaries of Crossman*, pp 101-2, 29 April 1952; Russell-Smith Letters, 3 April 1952.

61. Foot, ii, p. 372.

62. *The Times*, 20 May 1952.

63. Macleod to Woolton, 20 May 1952, MH80/60. See also Marquand, letter, *The Times*, 14 August 1952.

64. HL Debates, vol 176, cols 799–952, 13 May 1952. The Bill received its Royal Assent on 22 May 1952, National Health Service Act, 1952, (15 & 16 Geo. 6 & 1 Eliz. 2, ch 25). *National Health Service (Charges for Drugs and Appliances) Regulations, 1952* (SI 1952, No. 1021).

65. Macleod to Salisbury, 22 May 1952, Salisbury to Macleod, nd, MH80/60. Russell-Smith Letters, 6, 13 and 15 May 1952.

66. DHSS 95005/1/85A-D. For publicity on dental nurses, *The Times*, 25 October 1950.

67. Russell-Smith Letters, 22 January, 4, 5 and 28 February, 4 March 1952.

68. HL Debates, vol 174, cols 1019-60, 5 February 1952; vol 175, cols 422–74, 4 March 1952; cols 766–77, 18 March 1952; cols 912-14, 25 March 1952.

69. Russell-Smith Letters, 21 February 1952, 25 March 1952.

70. Russell-Smith Letters, 19 February 1952, 2 April 1952.

71. Given in full in J S Ross, *The National Health Service in Great Britain* (OUP, 1952), p 387.

72. CC(52) 33rd mtg, 25 March 1952, CAB128/24.

73. Russell-Smith Letters, 25, 26 and 27 March 1952.

74. Churchill to Butler, nd, Playfair to Dodds, 19 April 1952, T. 227/107.

75. Crookshank to Churchill, 22 April 1952, T. 227/107.

76. HL Debates, vol 175, cols 982-92; Russell-Smith Letters, 26 March 1952.

77. Draft memorandum, 18 April 1952, T. 227/107; C(52)190, 11 June 1952, CAB129/32.

78. Butler to Churchill, 24 April 1952, and annotations, T. 227/107.

79. HC Debates, vol 498, cols 209-13, 25 March 1952; Crookshank Papers, Diary, fol 64, 25 March 1952.

80. CC(52) 63rd mtg, 26 June 1952, CAB128/25.

81. Use the NHS Sensibly Campaign, 1949-51, MH55/965.

82. Crookshank Papers, Diary, fol 51, 20 and 21 February 1951. It was rumoured that his successor would be Walter Monckton. Seldon, pp 81, 91, 264-5.

83. Crookshank Papers, Diary, fols 68-9, 1-8 May 1952.

84. Seldon, p 265; Fisher, *Macleod*, pp 72–86.

85. HC Debates, vol 487, cols 299–306, 24 April 1950.

86. HC Debates, vol 498, cols 886–95, 27 March 1952. Fisher, pp 80–4; Foot, ii, pp 357–8. Russell-Smith Letters, 27 March 1952.

87. Macleod (with P Goldman), *The Life of Neville Chamberlain* (Macmillan, 1961).

88. Lecture at Conservative Political Centre, 1954, 'Sanitas Sanitatum', reproduced by Fisher, pp 327–36.

89 Russell-Smith Letters, 8 and 9 May 1952.

90. Seldon, p 265.

91. Russell-Smith Letters, 26 June 1952, 27 January 1953, 4 September, 1953. Fisher p 104.

92. Fisher, pp 102–6; Seldon, pp 265–70.

93 Russell-Smith Letters, 14 and 16 December 1955.

94. Seldon, pp 288, 385; *Who's Who*, 1985. In the General Election on 26 May 1955 the Conservative Party was returned with an increased majority, Seldon, pp 72–5, 462; D E Butler, *The British General Election of 1955* (Macmillan, 1955).

95. Seldon, p 279; Fisher, Obituary, *The Times*, 22 January 1968.

96. Seldon, pp 133–5, 543.

97. Seldon, pp 226–8 and *passim*, Pottinger, pp 146–55.

98. Macleod to Butler, 14 January 1953 and attached notes, T.SS 5/13/02A.

99. Haddow to Gilbert, 29 November 1952, T.SS 5/13/02A, 8 December 1952, DHSS 94501/9/1.

100. C(53)30 and 58, 28 January and 11 February 1953, CAB129/59; CC(53) 6th mtg, 3 February 1953, CC(53) 11th mtg, 12 February 1953, CAB128/26; Butler to Thorneycroft, 17 February, 1953, Thorneycroft to Butler, 18 February 1953 and notes, T.SS 5/13/02A.

101. Playfair to Gilbert, 11 March 1953, T.SS 5/13/02A.

102. HC Debates, vol 513, cols 1228–35, 1 April 1953.

103. Playfair to Gilbert, 23 March 1953, T.SS 5/13/02A. *Report of the Committee of Enquiry into the Cost of the National Health Service*, Cmd. 9663, 1956. Although E Halliday, secretary to the committee, is not mentioned in the Report, his role was vital, both in guiding the committee and in drafting the Report.

104. Playfair to Owen, 12 February 1953, T.SS 5/332/01B.

105. K G H Binning to Mitchell, 3 October 1953, Mitchell to Clarke (citing letter of Macleod to Butler, 28 October 1953), 14 November 1953, T. 227/185.

106. HA(53) 7th mtg, 20 March 1953, HA(CP)(53) 1st mtg, 29 April 1953, CAB134/912; R M J Harris to Crookshank, 13 May 1953, CAB21/3370.

107. Clarke to K E Couzens, 28 January 1955, T.SS 267/02B.

108. GC(53) 1st mtg, 13 May 1953, DHSS 94501/9/2A.

109. B Abel-Smith and R M Titmuss, *The Cost of the National Health Service in England and Wales* (CUP, 1956). For initial adverse reaction of Guillebaud to certain aspects of this investigation, Guillebaud to E Halliday, 20 January 1955, DHSS 94501/9/7/2.

110. *Guillebaud Report*, pp 270–3 (Godwin); pp 274–86 (Maude).

111. Correspondence and comment, August to December 1955, DHSS 94501/9/7/2, 94501/9/9A.

112. *Guillebaud Report*, para 725.

113. *Guillebaud Report*, para 573.

114. *Guillebaud Report*, para 774.

115. *Guillebaud Report*, paras 720-1.

116. *Cost of the NHS*, p 60. Estimation of trends on the basis of the unadjusted appropriation accounts reveals a broadly similar conclusion.

117. *Cost of the NHS*, p 62.

118. *Cost of the NHS*, pp 68-73.

119. *Cost of the NHS*, p 49. Treasury estimates suggested a fall from 1.0% to 0.7%, T.SS 5/13/02B.

120. *Cost of the NHS*, pp 51-7.

121. Capital expenditure was not discussed by the Guillebaud Committee until 4 and 5 July 1955 (GC(55) 7th mtg, DHSS 94501/9/2D), where the pre-war level was introduced as a reasonable basis for comparison. *Guillebaud Report*, paras 67-8, 319, and p 249.

122. *Guillebaud Report*, paras 580, 586, 612.

123. *Daily Worker*, 28 January 1956; *Daily Herald*, 19 December 1955; *The Economist*, 31 January 1956; *The Lancet*, 4 February 1956; *The Times*, 31 January 1956. *The Times* and *Manchester Guardian*, 7 May 1956 suggest growing disenchantment with the *Guillebaud Report*.

124. Halliday, 27 July 1955, draft memorandum by Macleod and Stuart, 22 November 1955, Macleod to Eden, 22 November 1955, DHSS 94501/9/9A.

125. Treasury discussion of draft statement on Guillebaud, November 1955, T.SS 5/13/02B. HC Debates, vol 546, col 147, 24 November 1955.

126. Butler on HP(55)89, 23 November 1955, T.SS 5/13/02B.

127. AS Marre to Haddow, 2 December 1955, DHSS 94501/9/9A; HP(55)89, 24 November 1955, CAB134/1252; HP(55) 16th mtg, 25 November 1955, CAB134/1250.

128. Macmillan to Turton and Stuart, 18 January 1956, T.SS 267/02C; HP(56)6, 19 January 1956, CAB134/1254.

129 HC Debates, vol 548, cols 207-9, 25 January 1956.

130. Stuart to Macleod, 22 January 1953, Macleod to Stuart, c 30 January 1953, T.SS 5/332/01B.

131. CC(53) 6th mtg, and 8th mtg, 3 and 10 February 1953, CAB128/26.

132. Binning to Mitchell, 3 October 1953 and 14 November 1953, T. 227/185; Binning to Mitchell, 20 October 1953, T.SS 226/5/01D.

133. C(54)232, 15 July 1954, CAB129/69.

134. C(54)240, 17 July 1954, CAB129/69; CC(54) 51st mtg, 20 July 1954, CAB128/27. See Table I, p 135 above, for the outcome.

135. CP(55)57, 1 July 1955, CAB129/76; CP(55) 20th mtg, 5 July 1955, CAB128/29.

136. CP(55)188, 3 December 1955, CAB129/78; CM(55) 45th mtg, 6 December 1955, CAB128/29. *Report of the Committee on the Economic and Financial Problems of the Provision for Old Age*, Cmd.9333, 1954.

137. CM(56) 3rd mtg, 11 January 1956, CAB128/30.

138. SS (56) 5, 14, 19, CAB16/8/10/1 (briefs for Butler); T.SS 5/333/01C (Treasury briefs, January to May 1956).

139. Treasury minute, 14 June 1956, T.SS 5/333/01C.

140. HC Debates, vol 558, cols 831–40, 25 October 1956. Exchanges between Health officials and Treasury over exemptions, T.SS 5/333/01C.

141. *The Times*, Leader, 12 November 1956. For a summary of reactions, T.SS 5/333/01D.

142. CM(56) 83rd mtg, 13 November 1956, CAB128/30.

143. Treasury minute, 8 November 1956, T.SS 5/333/01D.

144. GEN559/1st mtg, 15 November 1956, CAB21/3370.

145. Butler to Eden, 16 November 1956, and Treasury minutes, CAB21/3370, T.SS 5/333/01D.

146. HC Debates, vol 560, cols 1353–8, 19 November 1956; vol 561 cols 661–726, 29 November 1956.

147. *National Health Service (General, Medical & Pharmaceutical Services) Amendment (No. 2) Regulations, 1956* (SI 1956, No. 1745).

148. CM(57) 2nd mtg, 8 January 1957, CAB128/30.

149. C(57)17, 30 January 1957, CAB129/85.

150. C(57)16, 30 January 1957, CAB129/85.

151. CM(57) 2nd mtg, 8 January 1957, CAB128/30; CC(57) 5th and 7th mtg, 31 January and 2 February 1957, CAB128/31.

152. Thorneycroft, 21 March 1957, T.SS 5/333/01D.

153. Macleod to Butler, 26 April 1954, T.SS 267/02A. The data given by Abel-Smith and Titmuss, *Cost of the NHS*, p 50, suggest that £9.2m is the average for this period.

154. EA(52)86, 16 June 1952, EA(52) 19th mtg, 18 June 1952, CAB134/843.

155. Treasury minutes, March 1954 to April 1954, T.SS 267/02A.

156. Macleod to Butler, 26 April 1954, T.SS 267/02A.

157. EA(54) 25th mtg, 25 November 1954, T.SS 267/02A. Treasury minutes, November 1954, T.HOP 223/443/01.

158. C(54)348, 16 November 1954, CAB129/69; CC(54) 80th mtg, 29 November 1954, CAB128/27.

159. R L Workman to Clarke, 2 December 1954, T.HOP 223/443/01.

160. Correspondence between Macleod and Brooke, 8 December 1954 to 4 February 1955, T.SS 267/02A–B.

161. Stuart to Butler, 17 September 1955, Macleod to Butler, 19 September 1955, T.SS 66/226/02A. HC Debates, vol 545, cols 217–18, 26 October 1955; cols 542–3, 28 October 1955 (Butler); cols 642–4, 31 October 1955 (Macleod).

162. Macmillan to Stuart and Turton, 18 January 1956, Stuart to Macmillan, 19 January 1956, Turton to Macmillan, 19 January 1956, T.SS 267/02C; Stuart to Turton, 19 January 1956, DHSS 94501/9/9B.

163. Macmillan to Turton, 23 January 1956, T.SS 267/02C, CM(56) 6th mtg, 24 January 1956, CAB128/30.

164. HC Debates, vol 548, cols 207–9, 25 January 1956; col. 1346, 6 February 1956, where Turton is challenged on the £30m Guillebaud recommendation and replies that he will bear this figure in mind.

165. Correspondence between Turton and Macmillan, 25 June 1956 to c 20 July 1956, T.SS 267/02C.

166. Brooke, 15 July 1956, T.SS 267/02C.

167. Brief on CP(56)188, July 1956, T.SS 267/02C.

168. N F Cairncross to P Benner, 25 June 1956, T.SS 267/02C; CM(56) 55th mtg, 31 July 1956, CAB128/30.

169. CP(56)188, 20 July 1956, CAB129/82.

170. Brief on CM(56)16, 24 January 1956, T.HOP 223/443/01.

171. C(57)17, 30 January 1957, CAB129/85.

172. Investment Review 1954, 30 October 1954, T.HOP 223/443/01.

173. J Kelly to Workman, 2 December 1954, meeting of Treasury and Ministry of Health officials, 3 December 1954, T.HOP 223/443/01.

174. Workman to Clarke, 3 June 1955, T.SS 267/02A.

175. *Report of the Committee on the Economic and Financial Problems of the Provision for Old Age*, Cmd. 9333, 1954.

176. HL Debates, vol 192, cols 79-142, 23 March 1955.

177. HC Debates, vol 544, cols 826-35, 25 July 1955. Treasury comment on Investment Review 1955, November 1955, T.SS 267/02A.

178. See above, pp217-8.

179. F F Turnbull to Brittain, 8 February 1956, T.SS 66/226/02A. Correspondence between Turnbull and Marre, 7 to 13 February 1956, T.SS 267/02C.

180. Treasury minute, 26 June 1957, Walker-Smith to Amory, 13 January 1958, T.HOP 223/443/01; HA(57)138 and 146, 14 and 26 November 1957, CAB134/1971. HA(57) 27th mtg, 6 December 1957, CAB134/1968.

181. Correspondence between Turton and Macmillan, 20 July 1956 to 2 August 1956. Investment Review 1956, and Treasury minutes, August 1956, T.SS 267/549/01A.

182. Macleod to Stuart, January 1953, T.SS 5/333/01B. Macleod had discussed this problem with Crookshank as early as February 1952, ie before he became Minister of Health (noted in HA(52) 28th mtg, 24 October 1952, CAB134/908).

183. HA(53)25, 10 March 1953, CAB134/913. *Cost of the NHS*, p 38 and Appendix E.

184. Macleod to Stuart, January 1953, T.SS 5/333/01B.

185. HA(52)136, 18 October 1952, CAB134/911; HA(52) 28th mtg, 24 October 1952, CAB134/908.

186. Progress on Drugs Control, February 1955; T B Williamson to Workman, 30 July 1954, T.SS 5/333/02A.

187. HA(53)25, 10 March 1953, CAB134/913.

188. *Report of the Joint Committee on Prescribing on Form EC10* (HMSO, 1954).

189. This possibility was briefly and unfavourably considered in the *Guillebaud Report* (paras 479-81). For the Ministry of Health's unsuccessful attempt to promote action of registration of drugs, 1951-1952, HH101/230.

190. HA(53) 7th mtg, 20 March 1953, CAB134/912.

191. (HA)(CD)(53)2 and 3, 21 April and 11 May 1953, CAB134/912. HA(CD)(53) 1st mtg, 29 April 1953, HA(CD)(53) 2nd mtg, 15 May 1953, HA(53)11 mtg, 15 May 1953, CAB134/912.

192. Workman to Clarke, 22 November 1954, T.SS 5/333/02A.

193. Meeting of Macleod, Hornsby-Smith, Treasury and Ministry of Health officials, 17 March 1955, Clarke to F E Figgures, 30 March 1955, T.SS 5/333/02A.

194. Workman, 1 December 1955, T.SS 5/333/02A.

195. Playfair to Turnbull, 17 and 20 February 1956, T.SS 5/333/02C.

196. Treasury minutes, 17 May 1956 to 19 December 1956, T.SS 5/333/02C.

197. Turton to Macmillan, 19 December 1956, T.SS 5/333/02C; HA(57)25, 8 March 1957, CAB134/1969; HA(57) 7th mtg, 22 March 1957, CAB134/1968.

198. HC Debates, vol 568, col 91, 8 April 1957.

199. Treasury minutes, 17 May 1956, 12 June 1956, 22 March 1957, T.SS 5/333/02C-D.

200. Treasury minutes, 13 December 1957, 14 October 1958, T.SS 5/333/02D-E.

201. *Final Report of the Committee on Cost of Prescribing* (HMSO, 1959).

202. NH(50)26, 6 November 1950, CAB134/518.

203. The conclusion of the last paper submitted to the Committee, NHS(51)14, 18 September 1951, CAB134/519.

204. CC(52) 33rd mtg, 25 March 1952, CAB128/24.

205. C(52)190, 11 June 1952, CAB129/32; CC(52) 63rd mtg, 26 June 1952, CAB128/25. Haddow to A H Clough, 9 May 1952, Dodds to Owen, 28 June 1952, T. 227/107.

206. HC Debates, vol 503, cols *47-48*, 2 July 1952.

207. HA(53)41, 4 May 1953, CAB134/913. For background discussions, T.ED 365/023A.

208. Moran to Salisbury, 7 May and 10 June 1953, CAB124/1189.

209. Salisbury to Macleod, 8 June 1953, CAB124/1189.

210. HA(53)43, 6 May 1953 (Boyd-Carpenter), HA(53)49, 13 May 1953 (Monckton), CAB134/913.

211. HA(53) 11th mtg, 15 May 1953, CAB134/912. Macleod wrote to Churchill, 1 June 1953 about the discussions within the Committee, CAB124/1189.

212. HA(53)55, 9 June 1953, CAB134/913; HA(53) 13th mtg, 12 June 1953, CAB134/912.

213. HA(53)50, 20 May 1953, CAB134/913; HA(53) 12th mtg, 21 May 1953, CAB134/912.

214. HA(53)72, 21 July 1953, CAB134/914; HA(53) 18th mtg, 24 July 1953, CAB134/912.

215. HA(54)27, 9 March 1954, CAB134/916; (HA(54) 6th mtg, 12 March 1954), CAB134/915. The major reservation at this point came from Sir Harold Himsworth of MRC who complained that the generous offer to part-time consultants would have repercussions in universities and among scientists. Butler agreed that 'widespread and extensive' repercussions were likely (CAB124/1189).

216. Letter of Russell Brain (chairman, staff side, Medical Whitley Council) and Talbot Rogers (chairman, GMSC), *BMJ*, 1956, i, Supplement, 44, 11 February 1956.

217. A Macrae to Hawton, 17 June 1956, T.SS 5/150/01F.

218. Treasury brief on CP(56)160, 4 July 1956, T.SS 150/01F.

219. CP(56)160, 3 July 1956, CAB129/82; CM(56) 47th mtg, CM(56) 49th mtg, 3 and 12 July 1956, CAB128/20.

220. Hawton to Macrae, 13 July 1956, T.SS 5/150/01F.

221. *BMJ*, 1956, ii. 144-5, 216-17, 21 and 28 July 1956.

222. Minute of meeting 1 August 1956, T.SS 5/150/01F; *BMJ*, 1956, ii, 350, 406-7, 11 and 18 August 1956. Turton to Macmillan, 22 October, 1956, Treasury minute, 20 November 1956, T.SS 5/150/01F. HP(56)128, 8 November 1956, CAB134/1256; HP(56)15th mtg, 12 November 1956, CAB134/1253.

223. Correspondence between Hawton and Macrae, 21 November to 5 December 1956, T.SS 5/150/01F-G.

224. *BMJ*, 1956, ii, 1290-1, 1 December 1956. The *Manchester Guardian*, 6 December 1956, declared that the doctors had a 'strong moral case'.

225. Treasury and health department minutes, 13 November 1956 to 22 January 1957, T.SS 5/150/01F-G.

226. Treasury minute, 22 January 1957, T.SS 5/150/01G.

227. Salisbury to Macmillan, 8 July 1956, minute of visit of Himsworth to Treasury, 26 September 1956, T.SS 5/150/01F.

228. CP(57)11, 10 January 1957 (Stuart and Turton), CAB129/82; C(57)33, 13 February 1957 (Maclay and Vosper), C(57)34, 13 February 1957 (Salisbury), CAB129/85.

229. CC(57) 3rd mtg, 24 January 1957, CC(57) 11th mtg, 15 February 1957, CAB128/31.

230. Cancer SAC, 18 January 1951, DHSS 94200/2/1A.

231. Himsworth to Charles, 22 February 1951, MH55/1011.

232. Cancer SAC, 26 July 1951, DHSS 94200/2/1A; CHSC, *Report for 1951*, p 17.

233. Cancer SAC, 23 November and 22 December 1953, DHSS 94200/2/1A; CHSC, *Report for 1953*, p 28.

234. Macleod, 22 January 1954, Ministry of Health minutes, 9 January 1954 to 12 February 1954, MH55/1011.

235. HA(54)9, 26 January 1954, CAB134/916; HA(54) 3rd mtg, 5 February 1954, CAB134/915; CC(54) 8th mtg, 10 February 1954, CAB128/27.

236. Macleod to Boyd-Carpenter, 29 January 1954, MH55/1011. The prime mover referred to was Dr Horace Joules, medical superintendent of the Central Middlesex Hospital, and member of the Cancer and Medical SACs.

237. Medical SAC, notes for chairman, 8 March 1953, SAC(M)55 1st mtg, 18 March 1955, DHSS 94192/2/7. CHSC(55) 2nd mtg, 11 October 1955, DHSS 94151/2/2H.

238. SAC(M)56 1st mtg, 13 March 1956, DHSS 94192/2/8; CHSC(56) 1st mtg, 13 March 1956, DHSS 94151/2/2K.

239. CP(56)99, 19 April 1956, CAB129/80; CM(56) 30th mtg, 19 April 1956, CAB128/30.

240. CP(56)111, 1 May 1956, CAB129/81; CM(65) 32nd mtg, 3 May 1956, CAB128/30.

241. SAC(M) 2nd mtg, 16 June 1956, DHSS 94192/2/8. HC Debates, vol 552, cols 803-5, 7 May, 1956.

242. C(57)135, 4 June 1957, CAB129/87.

243. Royal College of Physicians, *Smoking and Health Now* (Pitman, 1971), p 9.

244. Sir Kenneth Cowan, 'Retrospect', *Health Bulletin*, January 1964, No 1; Sir George Godber, 'Health versus Greed', *New York State Journal of Medicine*, December 1963, pp 1248–9.

Chapter VII
THE ADVISORY SERVICES

1. H Eckstein, *Pressure Group Politics, the case of the British Medical Association* (Allen & Unwin, 1960), pp 53–8.

2. Sir Russell Brock, *The Times*, 26 May 1956.

3. Acton, 5, p 9.

4. Acton, 5, p 73.

5. Enquiry into the Financial Working of the NHS, NH(50)17, 15 July 1950, paras 85–7, CAB134/518.

6. T.SS 5/376/01B; Guillebaud Committee, 5 July 1955, DHSS94501/9/2D.

7. *Guillebaud Report*, paras 70–3; Acton, 6, pp 25–6; *Local Government Finance*, September 1950, p 221.

8. Treasury minutes, 27 July to November 1953, T.SS 44/59/02A–B.

9. Treasury minute, December 1952, T.SS 44/59/02D.

10. W J M Mackenzie, *Power and responsibility in health care. The National Health Service as a political institution* (NPHT, 1979), p 154.

11. Pater to Grosvenor, 28 December 1956, DHSS 94101/2/80.

12. Note on provisions relating to the Mental Health Service, April 1946, MH80/36.

13. Acton, 5, pp 20–1; E K Jones, *The Story of the Welsh Board of Health* (Welsh Office, unpublished typescript).

14. Welsh Consultative Council on Medical and Allied Services, *First Report*, Cmd. 703, 1920; *Second Report*, Cmd. 1448, 1921.

15. Jones, pp 55–66.

16. Acton, 5, p 21; Guillebaud Committee, 26 January 1954, DHSS 94501/9/2B.

17. Background notes on CHSC, 24 December 1943, MH80/26.

18. TUC, Annual Congress 1950 and related correspondence, DHSS 94157/1/1.

19. DHSS 94151/1/1A, 94151/2/1A.

20. The Medical Advisory Committee, 'functioned spasmodically', notes on CHSC, 24 December 1943, MH80/26.

21. DHSS 94151/2/1A.

22. HH91/91, 96, 100.

23. DHSS 94151/2/1A, 2A, especially meeting of chairman's committee, 27 October 1948. Haddow to Dodds, 8 July 1948, DHSS 94151/3/1.

24. Ministry of Health minute, 8 May 1951, quoting BMA deputy secretary, D Stevenson, DHSS 94157/1/1.

25. Rock Carling, January 1951, on circular 117/50, DHSS 94157/1/1.

26. Acton, 5, p 31.

27. Brief for Marquand, 13 March 1951, DHSS 94151/2/1C.

28. Ministry of Health minute, 29 September 1950, DHSS 94192/2/2.

29. CHSC, 13 March 1956, DHSS 94151/2/17.

30. Russell-Smith to Dodds, 10 June 1959, DHSS 94151/21/1.

31. Ministry of Health minute, 20 August 1959, DHSS 94151/21/1.

32. Committee established June 1949, DHSS 94151/2/2B.

33. Joint Committee on Prescribing, *Interim Report*, 1950; *Report*, 1954. Definitions of Drugs Joint Sub-committee, 3 reports, 1950–1951.

34. Ministry of Health minute, June 1959, DHSS 94151/21/1. CHSC-SHSC, *Health Education* (HMSO, 1964), paras 41, 79–86.

35. DHSS 94151/2/2B.

36. *Report on Internal Administration of Hospitals* (HMSO, 1954).

37. *Co-operation between Hospitals, Local Authority and General Practitioner Services* (HMSO, 1952).

38. DHSS 94192/2/2.

39. DHSS 94192/2/3.

40. It was complained that the BMA put names forward for the Medical SAC 'for BMA purposes rather than in the interests of the SAC', Ministry of Health minute, June 1952, DHSS 94151/1/1D.

41. DHSS 94192/2/1, 2D.

42. DHSS 94151/1/1F.

43. Medical SAC, 16 June 1956, DHSS 94192/2/8.

44. Mackenzie, *Power and responsibility*, p 157; Acton, 6, pp 44–5; *The Lancet*, 1958, ii, 27–30, 5 July 1958; Royal College of Physicians, 7 February 1954, Guillebaud Committee, DHSS 94501/9/2B.

45. MH90/56.

46. Schuster to Hawton, 23 February 1954, MH90/57.

47. MH90/83.

48. Eckstein, *Pressure Group Politics*; Stevens, *Medical Practice*, pp 259–69.

49. DHSS 94256/6/117/1A.

50. DHSS 94112/4/3.

51. Eckstein, *Pressure Group Politics*, pp 63–4.

52. DHSS 94256/5/22.

53. DHSS 94256/5/22B.

54. Eckstein, *Pressure Group Politics*, p 64; Stevens, *Medical Practice*, pp 93, 277–80.

55. DHSS 94II/3/6B; Eckstein, *Pressure Group Politics*, pp 113–25.

56. DHSS 94III/3/6.

57. Dodds to Haddow, 16 December 1952, DHSS 94III/3/61A.

58. Brain to Dodds, 19 December 1952, DHSS 94III/3/61A.

59. Stevens, *Medical Practice*, pp 228–30. See below chapter VIII.

60. Stevens, *Medical Practice*, pp 131–3. See below chapter IX.

61. *Report on the Grading and Structure of Administrative and Clerical Staff* (HMSO, 1957).

62. G Larkin, *Occupational Monopoly and Modern Medicine* (Tavistock, 1983), pp 157–79.

63. C Montacute, *Costing and Efficiency in Hospitals* (NPHT, 1962), pp 35-42.

64. Enquiry into the Financial Working of the NHS, NH(50)17, 15 July 1950, CAB134/518.

65. *Report of Committee to Consider the Future Numbers of Medical Practitioners* (HMSO, 1957).

Chapter VIII
THE HOSPITAL SERVICE

1. R Klein, *The Politics of the National Health Service* (Longman, 1983), p 7.

2. CP(45)339, 345, CAB129/5.

3. Estimates, 6th Report, para 7, evidence, p 1. Figures for hospital expenditure cited here are slightly different from those in Table 1.

4. King's Fund, *Annual Report 1954*, p. 1.

5. Estimates, 6th Report, para 6.

6. *Cost of the NHS*, p 34.

7. Nuffield Provincial Hospitals Trust, *The Hospital Surveys* (NPHT, 1946), p 1.

8. Summary of NE Survey, MH80/36.

9. Summary of Oxford Survey, MH80/36.

10. Summary of NE Survey, MH80/36.

11. *British Hospitals Yearbook 1939*, Introduction; *The Hospital*, July 1938, pp 239-43, August 1939, pp 279-83, January 1940, pp 15-16.

12. *The Times*, 15 January 1941.

13. Nuffield Provincial Hospitals Trust, *A National Hospital Service* (October, 1941), pp 17-18.

14. H Cohen, 'A Comprehensive Health Service', *Agenda*, February 1943, p 12.

15. MH90/2.

16. The following section is based on MH90/2-6.

17. Sir George Etherton, reported by Pater, 1 April 1942, MH77/5.

18. MH77/104.

19. Liverpool RHB, 20 April 1954, DHSS 94501/9/2B.

20. MH90/6-7.

21. Pater, 4 July 1955, DHSS 94501/9/2D; MH90/6.

22. Welsh RHB, 20 April 1954, DHSS 94501/9/2D.

23. Estimates, 11th Report, paras 36-7.

24. DHSS, RHB 1/3.

25. *Guillebaud Report*, para 233.

26. MH90/20.

27. MH88/11; *Report of the Special Area Committee for Cumberland and N Westmorland 1947-1949*; W J Ball, 'The Hospital services of Cumberland and N Westmorland', *The Hospital*, August 1950, pp 585-91.

28. MH88/17, 18, 21.

29. RHB(48)2.

30. 20 April 1954, DHSS 94501/9/2B.

31. MH93/12, 19.

32. The following section is based on MH93/1, 13–18.

33. NW Metropolitan RHB, *Survey 1947-1950*, pp 13–15.

34. L Granshaw, *St Mark's Hospital London* (King's Fund, 1985), p 281. Pater to Hawton, 6 January 1954, MH90/11.

35. MH93/13.

36. MH93/14.

37. E Anglia RHB, 29 September 1953, 'superior species', DHSS 94501/9/2A; Association of HMCs, 26 January 1954, 'exaggerated sense of their own importance', DHSS 94501/9/2B.

38. Acton, 4, p 44.

39. *Cost of the NHS*, pp 28–9.

40. Association of HMCs, 26 January 1954, DHSS 94501/9/2B.

41. W O Chatterton to Marre, 11 July 1953, DHSS 94501/9/2A.

42. Pater, 30 June 1953, DHSS 94501/9/2A.

43. E Anglia RHB, 29 September 1953, Sheffield RHB, 30 December 1953, Assoc HMCs, 26 January 1954, DHSS 94501/9/2B.

44. RMPA, 20 April 1954, DHSS 94501/9/2B.

45. Acton, 4, p 44.

46. *Guillebaud Report*, para 183.

47. The following section is based on MH90/8, 9, 20.

48. MH90/8.

49. HH101/160-161.

50. Ministry of Health to RHB chairmen, 11 January 1947, MH90/8.

51. DHSS 94101/2K; *Guillebaud Report*, para 262.

52. *Guillebaud Report*, paras 257-61.

53. HH101/158-159.

54. S Taylor, 'SOS-RHBs', *The Lancet*, 1951, ii, 725–30, 20 October 1951; *Guillebaud Report*, para 264.

55. Pater, 30 June 1953, DHSS 94501/9/2A.

56. Minute following visit to Oxford and E Anglia, 28 September 1954, MH90/11.

57. Bevan to Attlee, 7 August 1947, MH90/9.

58. NHS(46)2, MH80/30; Attlee to Bevan, 1 August 1947, MH90/9.

59. MH90/9; MH88/1-2; DHSS, RHB 8/1/1; Labour Party Archives, Morgan Phillips Papers, 1947.

60. Macleod to Tewson, 30 November 1955, DHSS 94101/1/2J. For continuing complaints, DHSS 94101/1/2M, 2P; DHSS 9/H 165/6.

61. COHSE to Ministry of Heath, October 1947, MH90/9; Pater to Benner, 29 November 1955, DHSS 94101/1/2J.

62. TUC delegation, 7 February 1952, DHSS 94101/1/2M.

63. NHS(46)20, 12 February 1946, MH80/30; MH90/8, 9, 25.

64. MH90/10; DHSS 94256/5/23.

65. RHB(47)1.

66. RHB chairmen, 17 February 1948, MH90/54.

67. *Birmingham RHB 1947–1966*, p 6.

68. *Guillebaud Report*, para 238.

69. DHSS 94501/9/21.

70. NW Metropolitan RHB, *Survey 1954–1958*, pp 7–8; *Birmingham RHB 1947–1966*, p 6.

71. DHSS, RHB secretaries 6/62.

72. RHB chairmen, 21 September 1954, MH90/57.

73. RHB chairmen, 20 January 1948, MH90/54.

74. DHSS 94501/9/2D.

75. Newcastle RHB reported 30% medical, Liverpool 37% reduced later to 25%, Nov-Dec 1953, DHSS 94501/9/2B.

76. Bevan to RHB chairmen, 23 July 1947, MH90/54.

77. DHSS 94101/1/2K.

78. J T Anson to Bevan, 1 June 1948, Labour Party Archives, Morgan Phillips Papers, 1948.

79. Estimates, 6th Report, Appendix II, pp 398–400.

80. Estimates, 6th Report, q 1628–1635, para 10, MH90/61.

81. *WP 1946*, paras 19–23. For similar statements made in Parliament 1946, *Guillebaud Report*, p 78.

82. HMC(48)1.

83. Pater, 4 July 1955, DHSS 94501/9/2D.

84. Estimates, 11th Report, Appendix I.

85. Bevan to RHB chairmen, 23 July 1947, MH90/52.

86. Estimates, 11th Report, para 5; Jones Report, para 8; NH(50)17, 15 July 1950, CAB134/519.

87. RHB(S) (52)17.

88. H W Scarth, secretary, W Region RHB, Estimates, 7th Report, p 99.

89. Haddow, 14 August 1953, DHSS 94501/9/2A; *Guillebaud Report*, paras 204–6.

90. RHB(49)143.

91. RHB chairmen, 18 March 1952, MH90/55; Haddow, 14 August 1953, DHSS 94501/9/2A; Acton, 4, pp 6–8.

92. Estimates, 7th Report, pp 86-90; RHB chairmen, 17 February and 16 March 1948, MH90/54.

93. Estimates, 7th Report, pp 100-1, 11th Report, para 9 and p 114.

94. RHB chairmen, 21 December 1948, MH90/54 (closer supervision); 17 October 1950, MH90/55 (virement); 21 March and 16 May 1950 (civil servants), MH90/55.

95. RHB chairmen, 16 March 1948, MH90/54.

96. Estimates, 11th Report, pp 163–4.

97. Estimates, 11th Report, para 53.

98. RHB chairmen, 16 June 1949, MH90/54; 21 February 1950, MH90/55; 20 March 1956, MH90/60.

99. *Guillebaud Report*, para 197; Vickers, August 1955, DHSS 94501/9/2D.

100. RHB deputation, 25 February 1952, supported by Report of Committee on Hospital Administration, 1950, DHSS 94151/2/2C. Playfair to Crombie, 18 September 1952, T.SS 434/02B.

101. *Guillebaud Report*, para 197.

102. 26 January 1954, DHSS 94501/9/2B.

103. DHSS 94501/9/2B.

104. *Guillebaud Report*, para 212.

105. Estimates, 6th Report, para 7.

106. Estimates, 6th Report, q 2698.

107. *WP 1946*, para 23.

108. Bevan, Standing Committee C, 4 June 1946, col 422.

109. Bevan to RHB chairmen, 23 July 1947, MH90/52; Rucker, *The Hospital*, June 1947, p 284; see also RHB secretaries, 5 April 1949, MH90/67.

110. 19 June 1950, DHSS 94501/9/10.

111. RHB chairmen, 19 July 1949, MH90/54; Ministry of Health, September 1953, DHSS 94501/9/2B.

112. CHSC, *Report of Committee on the Internal Administration of Hospitals* (HMSO, 1953), paras 220-5.

113. *The Hospital*, November 1948, pp 496-8; Newcastle RHB, 23 November 1953, DHSS 94501/9/2B.

114. 29 September 1953, DHSS 94501/9/2B.

115. 26 January 1954, DHSS 94501/9/2B. See also Ministry of Health minute, 17 August 1955, DHSS 94501/9/9A.

116. Bevan to RHB chairmen, 23 July 1947, MH90/52.

117. Minister of Health to RHB chairmen, 27 June 1947, MH90/45.

118. *Industrial Court (No 2322) NHS*, April-May 1951; MH90/51.

119. DHSS 94101/2/80, C J Ham, *Policy Making in the National Health Service* (Macmillan, 1981), pp 36-9.

120. RHB chairmen, 20 January and 19 May 1953, MH90/56,; Newcastle RHB, 23 November 1953, DHSS 94501/9/2B. For RHB engineers versus architects, MH90/46.

121. HMC(48)2.

122. Acton, 3, p 9.

123. *The Hospital*, November 1948, p 499.

124. Haddow, 19 August 1953, DHSS 94501/9/2A.

125. RHB chairmen, 18 January 1955, MH90/58.

126. Estimates, 6th Report, paras 12-15.

127. Estimates, 6th Report, q 2706-2756.

128. Oxford and Newcastle RHBs, 23 November 1953, DHSS 94501/9/2B.

129. RHB chairmen, 19 January 1954, MH90/56.

130. Sheffield RHB, 30 December 1953, DHSS 94501/9/2B.

131. Institute of Hospital Administrators, 20 April 1952, DHSS 94501/9/2B; Dodds, August 1954, and Guillebaud Committee 14 March 1955, DHSS 94501/9/7/2; Pater to Halliday, 17 August 1955, DHSS 94501/9/9A.

132. *Guillebaud Report*, para 395; Estimates, 6th Report, para II; Acton, 6, p 22.

133. Oxford and Newcastle RHBs, 23 November 1953, DHSS 9450I/9/2B.

134. RHB chairmen, 2 and 16 November 1948, MH90/50; *The Hospital*, November 1948, pp 493-4.

135. Newcastle, E Anglia, Liverpool, and Sheffield RHBs, September to December 1953, DHSS 9450I/9/2B.

136. *Report of the Committee on the Internal Administration of Hospitals* (HMSO, 1953), paras 62-84; *Guillebaud Report*, paras 407-15.

137. RHB(47)I, para 9; HMC (48)I, para 13.

138. NHS(49)II, 10 March 1949, DHSS 94III/3/6A.

139. NHS(50)4, 15 March 1950, DHSS 94III/3/6B.

140. NHS(50)15, II October 1950, DHSS 94III/3/6B.

141. Summary of regional advisory committees in 1952, DHSS 94III/3/45.

142. RHB chairmen, 21 October 1952, MH90/55; notes for Joint Consultants Committee, 15 July 1954, DHSS 94III/3/6E.

143. CHSC(53)12, DHSS 9415I/2/2F; CHSC, 17 March and 16 June 1953, DHSS 9495I/2/2D.

144. For summary of group advisory committees in March 1950, DHSS 94III/3/45; *Report on Internal Hospital Administration*, paras 62-3, 77-84; *Guillebaud Report*, para 407.

145. *Guillebaud Report*, paras 224-8; Pater, 4 July 1955, DHSS 9450I/9/2D.

146. T Lloyd Hughes, *The Lancet*, 1954, ii, 647-8, 25 September 1954; RHB chairmen, 20 March 1956, MH90/60.

147. Joint Consultants Committee, 4 October 1956, DHSS 94III/3/6G; RHB chairmen, 19 March 1957, MH90/60; DHSS 9450I/9/2D.

148. Godber to M Reed, 28 August 1947, MH90/45.

149. Estimates, IIth Report, q 3227-3235 (F L Edwards).

150. RHB(S) (51)I, 25 January 1951.

151. T.SS 434/02D (1951).

152. DHSS 94II2/4/102/I.

153. DHSS 94II2/4/102/2.

154. Sheffield RHB, *Quinquennial Report 1952-1957*, p 27.

155. DHSS 94II2/4/65.

156. W L Abernethy, *Local Government Finance*, September 1950, p 221.

157. RHB chairmen, 21 February 1950, MH90/55.

158. *The Hospital*, October 1952, pp 674-7.

159. R B Moberly to Mitchell, 2 April 1953, T.SS5/376/01B.

160. Ministry of Health, February 1955, DHSS 9450I/9/9A; Department of Health, 2 February 1955, DHSS 9450I/9/7/2.

161. Acton, 6, pp 5-7.

162. Estimates, 6th Report, q 529.

163. Estimates, 6th Report, q 449, 530, 2686.

164. Estimates, 6th Report, q 428.

165. Estimates, 6th Report, Appendix 3, pp 377-8.

166. Estimates, 6th Report, q 428–43.

167. *The Accountant*, 11 March 1950, 16 August 1952.

168. *Hospital Cost Accounting* (HMSO, 1952).

169. NPHT, *Report of an experiment in Hospital Costing* (1952); King's Fund, *Report on Costing Investigation* (1952).

170. T.SS 5/376/01B.

171. Glasgow RI, 29 September 1953, DHSS 94501/9/2B.

172. Oxford RHB, 23 November 1953, DHSS 94501/9/2B.

173. NW Metropolitan and E Anglia RHBs, 29 September 1953, DHSS 94501/9/2B.

174. *Report of the Working Party Set up to Devise a System of Costing* (HMSO, 1955); DHSS 94501/9/2D.

175. T. SS 5/376/01B. For subsequent developments, see C Montacute, *Costing and Efficiency in Hospitals* (NPHT, 1962).

176. RHB(52)133.

177. Haddow to Owen, 8 October 1952, T. SS434/02B.

178. Estimates, 11th Report, paras 24–8.

179. RHB chairmen, 21 December 1948 and 21 March 1949, MH90/55.

180. T.SS 434/02A; DHSS 94III/1/23A.

181. Cripps to Bevan, 9 March 1949, Bevan to Cripps, 21 March 1949, T.SS 434/02A.

182. Marquand, statement in CHSC, *Report 1950*, p ii.

183. T.SS 434/02B–C; DHSS 94III/1/23A, 29A. For administrative survey, see G A Paines, *Municipal Journal*, 30 April 1954, p 943.

184. Treasury minutes, 15 August 1951, DHSS 94III/1/23A, 4 August 1952, T.SS 434/02B.

185. Ministry of Health, office meeting, 29 November 1951, DHSS 94III/1/26.

186. DHSS 94III/1/29A.

187. DHSS 94III/1/29A.

188. DHSS 94III/2/48.

189. Department of Health, 16 September 1952, DHSS 94III/1/29A, HH 101/115.

190. RHB chairmen, 11 November 1952, DHSS 94III/1/29A; S G Hill, secretary Northampton HMC, 2 January 1953, DHSS 94III/2/48.

191. Howard to Hawton, 10 and 13 December 1952, DHSS 94III/3/61A.

192. Treasury minute, 24 February 1953, T.SS 434/02D.

193. Treasury minute, 4 August 1952, T.SS 434/02B.

194. Ministry of Health minute, 18 March 1954, T.SS 434/29A.

195. Reports from RHB secretaries, October to November 1953, T.SS 434/29A.

196. Liverpool, Newcastle, Oxford and Sheffield RHBs, DHSS 94501/9/2B.

197. *Guillebaud Report*, para 222.

198. T.SS 434/02D.

199. DHSS 94III/1/29A; HH 10/115.

200. DHSS 94III/1/29B.

201. Office meeting, 18 March 1954, DHSS 94III/1/29A.

202. NW Metropolitan RHB, *Survey 1954-1958,* pp 76-7.

203. Treasury minute, 22 May 1956, DHSS 94III/1/02D; DHSS 94III/1/29B.

204. T.SS 434/02E.

205. Sheffield RHB, *Quinquennial Report 1947-1952*, pp 23-36.

206. Stevens, *Medical Practice*, pp 139-52.

207. DHSS 94III/3/6A, 50, 58.

208. DHSS 94III/3/6A-B.

209. CAB131/518; DHSS 94II2/4/15.

210. NH(50) 6th mtg, 21 November 1950, CAB134/518.

211. Liverpool RHB, *Report 1954-1955*, pp 48-52.

212. Eckstein, *Pressure Group Politics*, pp 113-25.

213. DHSS 94III/3/6C-D.

214. Joint Consultants Committee, 16 July 1952, DHSS 94III/3/6C.

215. Joint Consultants Committee, 15 July 1954, DHSS 94III/3/6E.

216. Guillebaud Committee, 23 November and 30 December 1953, DHSS 94501/9/2B, 94256/6/117/1A, 94III/3/58, 70, 85.

217. DHSS 94256/6/118 (numbers slightly different from those implied by Table VII).

218. Liverpool RHB, *Report 1954-1955*, p 49.

219. DHSS 94III/1/23A, 94III/3/77A, MH90/56, 57.

220. RHB chairmen, 19 January and 13 April 1954, MH90/56, 57; Guillebaud Committee, 23 November 1953, DHSS 94501/9/2B, 94III/3/77A.

221. DHSS 94III/3/77A.

222. T.SS 434/02A; DHSS 94III/1/23A, 94III/3/61A.

223. Ministry of Health minute, 2 December 1952, DHSS 94III/3/61A.

224. DHSS 94III/3/61A-B; Sir Russell Brain, *The Lancet*, 1952, ii, 1033, 22 November 1952.

225. Joint Consultants Committee, 27 April 1955, DHSS 94III/3/6F.

226. Stevens, *Medical Practice*, pp 212-22.

227. DHSS 94II2/4/3A.

228. DHSS 94II2/4/2A, 8A.

229. DHSS 94III/4/65.

230. HC Debates, vol 585, cols *85-86*, 31 March 1958.

231. *Report of the Royal Commission on Doctors' and Dentists' Remuneration*, pp 76-9; DHSS 94II2/4/15.

232. DHSS 94II2/4/3A.

233. DHSS 94II2/4/102/1, 5.

234. CAB134/518 (Labour NHS Committee); DHSS 94II2/4/2A (Willink); T.SS 5/150/01L (Himsworth).

235. Treasury minute, 25 February 1958, T.SS 5/150/01L.

236. Treasury minute, 27 February 1958, T.SS 5/150/01L.

237. *Report on Doctors' and Dentists' Remuneration*, paras 214-30.

238. G S Wilson, 'Public Health Laboratory Service', *British Medical Bulletin*, 1951, 7: 146–53, closely follows MRC 51/117, DHSS 94141/1/15; Report on the PHLS, 1951, DHSS 94142/2/2B.

239. Treasury minute, 15 March 1955, T.SS 5/363/04A–B.

240. MRC 51/117, DHSS 94141/1/15.

241. Scottish Health Services Council, *The Organisation of Laboratory Services* (HMSO, 1958).

242. *The Organisation of Laboratory Services*, para 37; Haddow to Dodds, 20 January 1955, DHSS 94141/1/26A.

243. Organisation of the PHLS, 19 February 1951, DHSS 94141/1/15.

244. Treasury minute, November, T.SS 5/363/04A.

245. The following paragraphs are based on MRC A91/1–2, T.SS 5/363/04A–B, DHSS 94141/1/24A.

246. DHSS 93285/19/1.

247. DHSS 94115/1/9.

248. Blood transfusion service, February 1946, DHSS 93285/19/1.

249. Department of Health, *Report 1956*, pp 68–70.

250. Ministry of Health, *Report 1956*, pp 24–5.

251. DHSS 94115/8/1.

252. DHSS 94115/1/54.

253. DHSS 94115/1/9.

254. DHSS 94115/3/21, 509, 511.

255. DHSS 94115/2/9A; DHSS 94115/5/8; RHB chairmen, 20 September 1955, MH90/58.

256. L Bryder, 'The Problem of Tuberculosis in England and Wales', pp 283–335; O L Peterson, *A Study of the NHS* (Rockefeller Foundation, 1951), pp 29–31.

257. RHB(49)9, para 3.

258. RHB chairmen, 18 October 1949, MH90/50, 18 March 1952, MH90/55.

259. Welsh National Memorial Association, April 1946, Joint Tuberculosis Council, 16 August 1946, MH77/83; Bryder, pp 322–3.

260. SAC(T)(49)9, DHSS 94192/2/1.

261. *BMJ*, 1950, ii, 61–8, 1382–5, 8 July and 16 December 1950; Bryder, p 327.

262. Liverpool RHB, *Annual Reports 1951, 1957*, Appendices.

263. *BMJ*, 1950, ii, 1384, 16 December 1950; *The Times*, 15 December 1950.

264. Department of Health, *Report 1956*, p 30.

265. Ministry of Health, *Report 1954*, pp 98–9; *1956*, pp 98–9.

266. DHSS 94192/2/1A.

267. Heaf, Tuberculosis SAC, 11 March 1949, DHSS 94192/2/1A; DHSS 94192/2/1A; RHB chairmen, 20 September 1949, MH90/50; Peterson, p 30.

268. Tuberculosis SAC, 5 October 1949, DHSS 94192/2/1A.

269. CHSC, 18 October 1950, DHSS 94151/2/2C.

270. NW Metropolitan RHB, *Survey 1951–1954*, p 37.

271. HC Debates, vol 459, col 547, 9 December 1948.

272. RHB chairmen, 19 October 1948, MH90/50.

273. *The Scotsman*, 11 August 1950; *The Practitioner*, August 1950, pp 106–7, 176–81.

274. Correspondence of McNeil with Cripps and Gaitskell, 1 August 1950 to 29 March 1951, HH102/316.

275. HH102/137.

276. DHSS, RHB I 29/101.

277. *Daily Herald*, 13 November 1954; HC Debates, vol 533, cols *107–8*, 23 November 1954.

278. HC Debates, vol 546, cols 2307–9, 30 November 1955.

279. Department of Health, *Report 1956*, p 30; Ministry of Health, *Report 1955*, pp 20–1.

280. MH90/31.

281. Sheffield RHB, *Quinquennial Report 1947–1952*, p 51; *1952–1957*, p 33.

282. HH102/488 (Glasgow); HH102/518.

283. DHSS 94192/2/1A.

284. *BMJ*, 1952, ii, 843–53, 18 October 1952; DHSS 94192/2/5.

285. Medical SAC, 1949, DHSS 94192/2/1.

286. RHB chairmen, 18 July 1950, MH90/55.

287. RHB chairmen, 15 November 1955, MH90/59; September 1957, MH90/61.

288. RHB chairmen, 15 November 1955, MH90/59; DHSS 94111/12/10A; Ed50/338.

289. Maude, Suggestions for Post-War Policy, August 1941, MH80/24.

290. Sir Laurence Brock to Maude, 4 September 1941, MH77/25.

291. Maude to G Anderson, 4 May 1943, MH80/31.

292. Post-War Hospital Policy, 23 September 1941, HH65/93; Department of Health Scotland minute, 20 September 1941, MH77/25; R Howat to Pater, 13 April 1943, MH77/26.

293. P Barter to Maude, 22 June 1943, MH80/31.

294. Board of Control, minutes, 1944, MH77/71.

295. Board of Control, Mental Health Services, March 1947, DHSS 94101/4/1.

296. Ministry of Health, *The Development of Consultant Services* (HMSO, 1950), p 17.

297. Neville, Emergency Medical Service, 2 September 1941, MH77/25.

298. For difficulties in regaining use of EMS accommodation, Barter to Douglas, 19 November 1948, and RHB chairmen, 21 December 1948, MH90/54.

299. RHB(47)13, paras 12, 23.

300. RHB chairmen, 1950, MH90/54. Adopting lower norms of 3.5 per 1,000 (mental), and 1.5 per 1,000 (mental deficiency), it was estimated in 1955 that 30,000 additional mental beds and 12,000 MD beds were required. The cost of modernisation of the mental sector was placed at £105m, Bavin to Pater, 26 February 1955, DHSS 94501/9/9A.

301. Review of Services, May 1952, MH90/55.

302. Bed Provision, 31 December 1953, DHSS 94501/9/6.

303. Stevens, *Medical Practice*, p 239.

304. Gedling to Pater, 16 June 1949, MH90/54; Barter, minute, December 1951, MH90/55.

305. RHB chairmen, 15 July 1952, MH90/55.

306. Treasury minute, 2 March 1956, T.SS 365/294/08E. For expression of concern from Newcastle RHB, 1956–1958, MH88/29.

307. RHB(47)3, 23 July 1947, MH90/52.

308. Barter to Hawton, 19 November 1948, RHB chairmen, 21 December 1948, MH90/54.

309. Division 8, Mental Health Services, March 1947, DHSS 94101/4/1. For Board of Control unease concerning Ministry of Health compliance with 'undertakings' concerning Mental Health Committees and Mental Health Medical Officers, MH90/8.

310. Mental Health SAC, 22 June 1949, DHSS 94198/2/1A.

311. RHB chairmen, 25 November 1947, MH90/54.

312. Mental Health Services, March 1947, DHSS 94101/4/1, 94256/5/4.

313. MH90/50.

314. RHB chairmen, 17 January 1956, MH90/59.

315. RHB chairmen, 17 January 1956, 20 March 1956, MH90/59; summary in MH90/50.

316. NW Metropolitan RHB, *Survey 1947–1950*, pp 13–15; RHB chairmen, 25 November 1947, MH90/54.

317. Mental Health SAC, 28 February and 2 May 1951, DHSS 94198/2/1B; representations from Central Hospital Warwick, 28 January 1957, MH90/36; Grouping of Psychiatric Hospitals, 1962, MH90/29, DHSS 94101/4/1, 94198/4/18.

318. MH90/29.

319. DHSS 94111/3/89.

320. Mental Health SAC, 22 November 1950, DHSS 94198/2/1A.

321. Mental Health SAC, 28 April and 28 July 1954, DHSS 94198/2/1B.

322. RHB chairmen, 19 July 1955, MH90/58.

323. Medical Staffing in Mental Hospitals, June 1957, DHSS 94198/4/17.

324. Mental Health SAC, 28 July 1954, DHSS 94198/2/1B; E B Strauss and five others, 'Medical Staffs of Mental Hospitals', *The Lancet*, 1957, i, 930, 4 May 1957 (see also 1041–2, 1143).

325. Mental Health Service, May 1952, MH90/55.

326. RHB psychiatrists, 10 September 1952, DHSS 94198/4/1.

327. Mental Health SAC, 23 July 1952, DHSS 94198/2/1B.

328. Professor Aubrey Lewis, Supply of Nurses, August 1949, DHSS 94198/4/2A.

329. Mental Health SAC, 28 September 1949, DHSS 94198/2/1A.

330. Note on Statistics, 30 September 1952, DHSS 94198/4/2B; Mental Health SAC, 18 February 1954, DHSS 94198/2/1B.

331. For Sheffield RHB situation, September 1953, MH90/56.

332. Russell-Smith to RHB secretaries, 7 July 1953, MH90/56. A sub-committee of the SHSC reporting in 1953 mainly blamed substandard teaching for low recruitment, SHSC, *Report 1953*, pp 137–9.

333. RHB chairmen, 21 July and 17 November 1953, MH90/56, 21 September 1954, MH90/57.

334. RHB chairmen, 15 August 1955, MH90/58.

335. Itinerary for Mental Health Exhibition, Ministry of Health, *Report 1955*, p 12; *Report 1956*, pp 18–19.

336. RHB chairmen, 21 July and 15 September 1953, MH90/56.

337. Mental Health SAC, 23 July 1952, Mental Health SAC, Supply of Nurses, 18 February 1954, DHSS 94198/2/1B.

338. CHSC, 15 June and 14 December 1954, DHSS 94151/2/1E.

339. T.ED 365/294/08A–E.

340. *The Times*, 17 February and 8 March 1956. Russell-Smith, March 1956, expresses concern over cancelled bookings for Mental Health Exhibition, MH90/59.

341. MH90/60–61; DHSS 94607/5/23A–B.

342. Macleod to Butler, 26 April 1954, T.SS 267/02A.

343. C C Lucas to R W B Clarke, 23 November 1953, T.HOP 223/443/01.

344. Ministry of Health, *Report 1954*, p 11; *Report 1955*, p 13; *Report 1956*, pp 14–16.

345. RHB chairmen, 1952–1953, MH90/56.

346. RHB chairmen, 21 September 1954, MH90/58.

347. Liverpool RHB, *Annual Report 1957/58*, pp 46–7, 61; *Birmingham RHB 1947–1956*, pp 40, 228.

348. Circular MH(55)64, 1 July 1955, DHSS 94202/1/36; T.HOP 223/443/01; Ministry of Health, *Report 1955*, p 177; MH 88/29 for extensions at Prudhoe, Newcastle.

349. T.HOP 223/443/01; Department of Health, *Report 1956*, pp 58–9; Department of Health, Capital Investment Review 1958/59–1959/60, CAB139/237.

350. Mental Health SAC, 25 April 1956, DHSS 94198/2/1B. RHB chairmen, 15 March 1955, gives 29% as the figure for over 65s in 1954, MH90/57.

351. DHSS 94198/4/1.

352. Mental Health SAC, 20 June and 26 October 1955, DHSS 94198/2/1B.

353. H Freeman, 'Mental Health Services in an English County Borough before 1974', *Medical History*, 1984, *28*: 111–28 (Salford). D Macmillan, 'Community Health Services and the Mental Hospital', in H Freeman and J Farndale, eds, *Trends in the Mental Health Services* (Pergamon, 1963), pp 226–237 (Nottingham). H L Freeman, 'Oldham and District Psychiatric Service', *The Lancet*, 1960, i, 218–21, 23 January 1960. J Carse, N E Panton and A Watt, 'A District Mental Health Service. The Worthing Experiment', *The Lancet*, 1958, i, 39–41, 4 January 1958.

354. Mental Health SAC, 23 July and 24 September 1952, DHSS 94198/2/1B.

355. Mental Health SAC, 25 July 1956, DHSS 94198/2/1B; J Farndale, *The Hospital Day Movement in Great Britain* (Pergamon, 1961).

356. D Sherret, *BMJ*, 1958, i, 994–6, 26 April 1958; A A Baker, 'Breaking up the Mental Hospital', *The Lancet*, 1958, ii, 253–4, 2 August 1958 (Banstead, Surrey).

357. Bavin to Pater, 26 February 1955, DHSS 94501/9/9A (£360m); Macleod to Brooke, 30 January 1955, T.SS 267/02B (£600m).

358. J Pringle, 'Crisis in the hospitals', *Daily Telegraph*, 9 February 1955. For similar complaints, NW Metropolitan RHB, *Survey 1951–1954*, pp 26–7; NW

Metropolitan RHB to Guillebaud Committee, 29 September 1953, DHSS 94501/9/2B.

359. RHB chairmen, 16 November 1954, MH90/57.

360. J B Oldham, *The Times*, 21 May 1956; Russell Brock, *The Times*, 26 May 1956.

361. Treasury minute, 29/30 September 1959, T.SS 267/491/01E.

362. Estimates, 6th Report, para 29.

363. E Anglia RHB, 29 September 1953, Newcastle RHB, 23 November 1953, Sheffield RHB, 30 December 1953, Guillebaud Committee, DHSS 94501/9/2B.

364. Oxford RHB, 29 September 1953, Guillebaud Committee, DHSS 94501/9/2B; RHB chairmen, 21 February 1950, MH90/55.

365. *Guillebaud Report*, paras 213-18, 311. See also Acton, 6, pp 12-14.

366. Guillebaud Committee, 4 and 28 July 1955, DHSS 94501/9/2D.

367. RHB chairmen, 21 February 1950, MH90/55, 16 February 1954, MH90/56.

368. Acton, 6, pp 19-20; T.SS 267/02B.

369. Summary of schemes started before 31 March 1956, July 1957, T.SS 267/491/01A.

370. Health Services Investment Scotland, 1950-1957, T.HOP 223/443/01; Capital Investment Review 1958/59-1959/60, CAB 139/237.

371. Ham, *Policy Making in the NHS*, p 57 (Leeds RHB).

372. Treasury minute, 23 November 1953, T.SS 267/02A.

373. The above summary is derived from T.SS 267/491/01A-B, T.HOP 223/443/01, DHSS 94202/1/36, MH90/58.

374. MH93/5.

Chapter IX
PRIMARY AND PREVENTIVE SERVICES

1. *Dawson Report*, para 6.

2. *The Times*, 2 June 1950.

3. Chairman, Birmingham EC, 1954, DHSS 94251/3/19.

4. Ministry of Health, Guillebaud Committee, 21 July 1953, DHSS 94501/9/2A.

5. MH77/156; DHSS 94251/1/5.

6. DHSS 94251/1/15, 94256/5/2A.

7. DHSS 94251/1/18A.

8. DHSS 94251/1/18C-D.

9. A Talbot Rogers, in H Lesser, ed, *The Health Services* (Allen & Unwin, 1951), p 33.

10. Treasury minute, 15 April 1958, T.SS 5/150/01M.

11. *Distribution of Remuneration among General Practitioners* (HMSO, 1952); Ministry of Health, *Report 1953*, pp 61-4.

12. *Distribution*, para 5.

13. DHSS 94256/18/16.

14. CHSC, *Report of the Committee on General Practice within the NHS* (HMSO, 1954), para 42. For relevant discussions of the CHSC General Practice Committee, 2 July 1953, DHSS 94157/2/1C.

15. For MPU views, CHSC General Practice Committee, 25 March 1952, DHSS 94151/2/1B, 30 October 1952, 94256/18/16; Willink Committee, 3 July 1956, DHSS 94256/6/108.

16. Willink Committee, 23 May 1955, 94256/6/117/1B.

17. Willink Committee, 1955, DHSS 94256/6/117/1B.

18. *Willink Report*, para 34.

19. *Distribution*, para 22; Cardew to Macleod, 18 June 1952, DHSS 94256/18/16.

20. ECL44, 2 July 1948. See also ECL112/48.

21. DHSS 94256/6/20.

22. Ministry of Health minutes, October 1948, April–October 1951, DHSS 94256/6/20.

23. DHSS 94256/6/40.

24. *Distribution,* paras 10–21.

25. Ministry of Health, *Report 1956,* p 57.

26. Scottish Medical Practices Committee, 11 July 1955, DHSS 94256/6/117/1A.

27. *Distribution*, paras 28, 29.

28. DHSS 24256/6/118.

29. Ministry of Health, *Report 1956,* p 56.

30. Gaitskell to Marquand, 8 June 1951, DHSS 94157/2/1M.

31. DHSS 94256/6/84, 94157/2/1A.

32. Ministry of Health memorandum, 2 May 1951, CHSC General Practice Committee, DHSS 94157/2/1A.

33. DHSS 94256/2/29 (1955-56); ECL59/56, 27 August 1956.

34. Office discussion, July 1953, DHSS 94157/2/1C.

35. Ministry of Health minute, 23 May 1955, DHSS 94256/6/108.

36. D Reid Ross, 1953, CHSC General Practice Committee, DHSS 94157/2/1C.

37. DHSS 94256/6/117/30.

38. Medical Practices Committee, CHSC General Practice Committee, 12 June and 12 December 1951, DHSS 94157/2/1A; Reports of the Medical Practices Committee, DHSS 94256/6/117/1A. See also W E Dornan, in Lesser, *The Health Services*, pp 36–42.

39. *Distribution*, paras 8–9.

40. Medical Practices Committee, 4th Report, January 1953, DHSS 94256/6/117/1A.

41. Dornan, p 41.

42. DHSS 94256/6/117/1A; HH102/520.

43. *Willink Report*, paras 30, 32.

44. HH102/520.

45. *Willink Report*, para 28.

46. DHSS 24256/6/118.

47. For events leading to establishment of Willink Committee, January 1954 onwards, DHSS 94256/6/108. Original concern about saturation, Ministry of Health minutes, July 1951, DHSS 94157/2/1B, 94157/4/7. See also T.SS 434/02B (Ministry of Health and Treasury meeting, 8 May 1952).

48. Ministry of Health, memorandum NDMS 47, DHSS 94256/6/117/1B. *Willink Report*, para 35.

49. Medical Practices Committee, Willink Committee, DHSS 94256/10/117/1A.

50. Ministry of Health minute, 13 December 1955, DHSS 94256/10/117/31.

51. *Willink Report*, para 34.

52. DHSS, *The Health Service in England 1984* (HMSO, 1985), p 18.

53. J. S. Collings, 'General Practice in England Today: A Reconaissance', *The Lancet*, 1950, i, 555–85, 25 March 1950.

54. Collings, p 568.

55. Collings, p 558.

56. For decline in status, Medical Practitioners Union, CHSC General Practice Committee, 25 March 1952, DHSS 94157/2/1B.

57. Association of Executive Councils, Guillebaud Committee, 26 January 1954, DHSS 94501/9/2B.

58. For Regional Hospital Boards' views, Guillebaud Committee, DHSS 94501/9/2B.

59. S Taylor, memorandum, 3 December 1952, DHSS 94157/2/5.

60. For example, Barnet General Hospital, DHSS 94157/2/1A.

61. Ministry of Health memorandum, February 1952, DHSS 94111/3/58.

62. B Spencer of Burnley, 30 April 1952, CHSC General Practice Committee, DHSS 94157/2/1B. For pre-war practice, see MH77/173.

63. D Reid Ross, 1953, CHSC General Practice Committee, DHSS 94157/2/1C.

64. S J Hadfield, *BMJ*, 1953, ii, 683–706, 26 September 1953.

65. *Dawson Report*, paras, 116–27.

66. 'Interim report of Sub-committee of BDA Council on Dental Benefit to the Insured Population', July 1941, BDA War Council 1939–43 Minute Book.

67. Report of a Committee on Post-war Dental Policy, February 1943, MH80/35. One estimate made for this committee suggested that 62,000 dentists would be required for a full service (PWDP2), MH77/183.

68. MH77/124.

69. George to Hale, 22 November 1944, T.SS 5/154/02A.

70. Estimates, 7th Report, pp 23–33. Bevan to Cripps, 4 January 1949, T. 227/185.

71. Cripps to Bevan, 4 January 1949, T. 227/185; Estimates, 7th Report, pp 30–2.

72. Bevan to Cripps, 4 January 1949, T. 227/185; DHSS 94262/1/3A.

73. DHSS 94262/1/3A–B, 94262/1/4A.

74. DHSS 94262/1/6.

75. *The Times,* 14 March 1950.

76. DHSS 94257/2/50A–B; T.SS 5/154/02B; *The Times*, 20 May 1949.

77. DHSS 94262/1/11.

78. DHSS 94257/6/9A, 16, 94257/3/6, 94262/1/3A, 4A.

79. DHSS 94257/11/1. Penman to Russell-Smith, 16 April 1949, 94257/2/5B.

80. DHSS 94257/2/50B, 94257/6/15, 94262/1/3B, 4A.

81. DHSS 94257/2/50B, 94262/1/3B, 4A.

82. DHSS 94257/2/50C; agreed by Cripps, 20 April 1950, T.SS 5/154/02B.

83. DHSS 94257/2/50C, 94262/1/3B, 6.

84. DHSS 94257/1/69, 94408/7/26, 94262/1/3D, 4C, 94257/6/44B.

85. DHSS 94262/1/4C, 30.

86. Public Accounts Commitee, 4th Report 1950/51, paras 54–73.

87. Mitchell to Owen, 21 March 1953, T.SS 5/154/02C. For Dental Estimates Board, see DHSS 94262/2/34–35.

88. HC Debates, vol 458, cols 1592–604, 26 November 1948.

89. B L Pearson to P M Rossiter, 22 March 1952, T.SS 5/154/02B.

90. BDA, Guillebaud Committee, 12 October 1954, DHSS 94501/9/2C.

91. Russell-Smith, Guillebaud Committee, 21 July 1953, DHSS 94501/9/2A.

92. DHSS 95005/1/III.

93. Haddow to Owen, 2 April 1953, T.SS 5/154/02C; BDA, Guillebaud Committee, 12 October 1954, DHSS 94501/9/2C; *Guillebaud Report,* paras 527–30.

94. DHSS 94257/2/150A.

95. *Report of the Committee on Recruitment to the Dental Profession,* Cmd. 9861, 1956.

96. DHSS 94257/2/156A–B.

97. T.SS 5/154/02C; DHSS 94257/6/34A–C, 94257/6/31.

98. DHSS 95005/1/134; circular 11/55 expressed the aim of the service as 'elimination of oral disease'.

99. *WP 1946,* para 59.

100. Meeting of officials with Joint Committee on a National Pharmaceutical Service, 17 June 1947, DHSS 94258/1/3.

101. DHSS 94258/4/1A; *Report of the Working Party on Differences in Dispensing Practice between England, Wales and Scotland* (HMSO, 1948).

102. DHSS 94501/9/4A; Estimates, 7th Report, pp 54–61.

103. Estimates, 7th Report, p 58.

104. DHSS 94258/1/63–70, 94258/7/9, 94501/9/2C.

105. Ministry of Health, memorandum on Pharmaceutical Service, 1954, DHSS 94501/9/4A.

106. DHSS 94258/1/65B–C.

107. Larkin, *Occupational Monopoly,* pp 24–51; MH58/234; MH80/35.

108. MH80/35.

109. MH77/74; MH80/35.

110. NHS(46)8, February 1946, MH80/35; *WP 1946,* paras 65–8.

111. MH 77/75; MH80/35.

112. DHSS 94259/2/4A.

113. Ministry of Health, *Report 1949,* p 270.

114. DHSS 94346/1/3, 94259/1/9.

115. Estimates, 7th Report, p 47 (H H George).

116. Estimates, 7th Report, pp 43–54.

117. Ministry of Health, *Report 1952,* p 69.

118. DHSS 94259/3/8; MH77/123.

119. MH77/123; DHSS 94259/1/69.

120. Ministry of Health, *Report 1952*, p 3, Appendix XIV.

121. DHSS 94259/1/9.

122. DHSS 94259/3/9.

123. DHSS 94259/3/25.

124. DHSS 94259/5/1-14; *Report of the Inter-departmental Committee on the Statutory Registration of Opticians,* Cmd. 8531, 1952. Larkin, pp 54-9.

125. DHSS 94114/1/2A-B. Ministry of Health, *Development of Consultant Services* (HMSO, 1950), p 28.

126. Ed. 50/388; DHSS 94259/1/5B.

127. DHSS 94259/2/88, 94114/1/2A-B.

128. DHSS 94259/2/84A. For a similar statement by Marquand, 13 March 1951, DHSS 94259/2/86A.

129. Guillebaud Committee, 21 July 1953, DHSS 94501/9/2A, 17 August 1955, DHSS 94501/9/9A.

130. RHB chairmen, September 1956, MH90/60.

131. *Guillebaud Report*, para 562.

132. LCC, Guillebaud Committee, 12 October 1954, DHSS 94501/9/2C. P Henderson, *The School Health Service 1908-1974* (HMSO, 1975).

133. MH77/83.

134. Guillebaud Committee, 29 June 1954, DHSS 94501/9/2C; see also Peterson, *A Study of the NHS*, pp 77-8, for further examples.

135. Guillebaud Committee, 19 August 1953 (Department of Health, Scotland), DHSS 94501/9/2A; 13 July 1954 (BMA), DHSS 94501/9/2C.

136. Circular 26/59.

137. Ministry of Health, Guillebaud Committee, 2 July 1955, DHSS 94501/9/2D, 94202/5/1.

138. Guillebaud Committee, 4 July 1955, DHSS 94501/9/2D, 94501/9/10, 94202/5/1.

139. Guillebaud Committee, 4 July 1955, DHSS 94501/9/2D.

140. Ministry of Health minute, October 1951, DHSS 94157/2/1A.

141. Ministry of Health minute, 10 January 1955, DHSS 94501/9/9A.

142. Halliday to Vickers, 21 January 1955, DHSS 94501/9/7/2.

143. Townsend, *The Last Refuge*, p 394.

144. Townsend, pp 399-404.

145. Circular 3/55; Ministry of Health, *Reports 1948-1958*; DHSS 94202/5/1; T.SS 267/549/01A.

146. P Townsend, *The Last Refuge. A survey of Residential Institutions and Homes for the Aged* (Routledge, 1962).

147. DHSS 94198/3/1.

148. Circular 100/47; Mental Health Services, 1947, DHSS 94101/4/1, 94202/1/5.

149. DHSS 94202/5/1, 4A, 94202/1/63.

150. DHSS 94202/1/63, 94202/3/1.

151. Guillebaud Committee, 22 January 1955, DHSS 94501/9/9A; 19 April 1955, DHSS 94501/9/7/2. For class and occupation, see J N Morris and J A Heady,

The Lancet, 1955, i, 554-9; W P D Logan, *British Journal of Preventive Medicine*, 1954, *8*: 128-38.

152. Preventive Medicine, 1955, DHSS 94501/9/9A.

153. SHSC, *What Local Authorities can do to promote Health and Prevent Disease* (HMSO, 1951).

154. T.SS 267/549/01A.

155. DHSS 94501/9/16/2; HC Debates, vol 556, cols 721-32, 12 July 1956.

156. RCOG, *Report on National Maternity Service* (May 1944); The Maternity Service, 10 April 1956, MH77/91; CHSC Committee on General Practice, DHSS 94157/2/1B; RCOG. *Report on the Obstetric Service under the NHS* (July 1954).

157. For problems of local obstetric lists, DHSS 94254/1/3, 94151/2/1C.

158. Ministry of Health, *Report 1954*, p 14; DHSS 94501/9/2C (decline of antenatal clinic attendances).

159. Ministry of Health minute, 4 September 1954, DHSS 94254/2/19.

160. Ministry of Health, *Report 1954*, p 23.

161. *Guillebaud Report*, para 637.

162. Ministry of Health minute, 14 February 1955, DHSS 94254/2/19.

163. *Report of the Maternity Services Committee* (HMSO, 1959).

164. For a brief review, see P Hall, in P Hall *et al*, eds, *Change, Choice and Conflict in Social Policy* (Heinemann, 1975), pp 278-84; See also Honigsbaum, *Division in British Medicine*; Ministry of Health, memorandum on health centres, January 1949, CHSC Health Centre Committee, DHSS 94152/1/1A.

165. BMA Committee, appointed April 1947, Interim Report June 1948, revised Interim Report July 1948.

166. S J Hadfield, 'A field survey of general practice 1951-1952', *BMJ*, 1953, ii, p 702, 27 September 1953; J S Collings, 'General Practice in England Today: A Reconaissance', *The Lancet*, 1950, i, 555-85, 25 March 1950 (p 575).

167. *WP 1946*, para 42.

168. Ministry of Health minute, 8 July 1959, DHSS 94203/4/3A.

169. P Hall, pp 277-310; M Ryan, 'Health Centre Policy in England and Wales', *British Journal of Sociology*, 1968, *19*:34-46; Eckstein, *National Health Service*, pp 247-52.

170. Eckstein, *English Health Service*, p 252.

171. Collings, p 575.

172. MH77/93, 94, 95.

173. Russell-Smith to Douglas, 10 June 1949, MH77/95.

174. MH77/94, DHSS 94203/1/4C.

175. CHSC(HC) 49, 4 January 1949, DHSS 94152/1/1A; Ministry of Health, *Report 1949*, p 253.

176. DHSS 93285/2/23C, 94142/1/11.

177. DHSS 94203/1/9.

178. CHSC Health Centre Committee, 12 May 1949, DHSS 94152/1/1A; CHSC, 21 June 1949, DHSS 94151/2/2B.

179. DHSS 94203/2/14.

180. DHSS 94203/1/4C.

181. CHSC Health Centre Committee, 8 June 1950, DHSS 94152/1/1A; CHSC, 21 June 1950, DHSS 94151/2/2B.

182. CHSC, 13 December 1949, DHSS 94151/2/1B.

183. Bevan, 27 July 1950, DHSS 94203/1/4C.

184. Office discussion, September 1950, DHSS 94203/1/18.

185. Office meeting, 1 July 1952, DHSS 94203/1/18.

186. Mitchell to J Hogarth, 25 January 1954, HH101/1887.

187. DHSS 94203/2/13.

188. *Guillebaud Report*, paras 627-9. Guillebaud Committee, criticism of health centres, Ministry of Health, 21 July 1953, DHSS 94501/9/2A; County Councils Association, 16 September 1954, MOH of LCC, 12 October 1954, DHSS 94501/9/2C.

189. *Guillebaud Report*, para 627.

190. DHSS 94501/9/7/2, 94203/4/3A.

191. Lord Taylor of Harlow, *Update*, 15 June 1979, pp 1537-47; Taylor *et al*, *The Lancet*, 1955, ii, 863-70, 22 October 1955.

192. DHSS 94203/4/1; HH101/1887, 1888-1891.

193. Ministry of Health, *Report 1949*, p 254; DHSS 94203/1/4C.

194. DHSS 94203/2/14.

195. N Riding EC, DHSS 94203/2/14. For similar complaints about patients waiting in the street, *The Lancet*, 1949, i, 359, 26 February 1949; *The Lancet*, 1950, i, 557, 25 March 1950.

196. Ministry of Health minute, 14 October 1960, DHSS 94203/2/14.

197. BMA, CHSC General Practice Committee, 14 May 1953, DHSS 94157/2/1C.

198. DHSS 94203/4/3A-B, 94501/9/7/2.

199. Ministry of Health, *Report 1956*, p 53. For Scottish group practice loans, HH101/668, 669.

200. Marquand to Hawton, 1 June 1951, DHSS 94203/1/4C.

201. Office meeting, 1 July 1952, DHSS 94203/1/4C.

202. Correspondence with LCC, 1954-1955, DHSS 94203/1/4C; Turton, 22 February 1956, DHSS 94203/1/20.

203. Opened 9 January 1959, DHSS 94203/2/12/1.

204. Ministry of Health minute, October 1951, DHSS 94157/2/1A.

205. DHSS 94203/4/3; Ollerenshaw, memorandum, 25 June 1952, DHSS 94157/2/1B; G A Fisher, *Practitioner*, 1953, *170*: 619-26.

206. DHSS 94203/4/3A-B.

CONCLUSIONS

1. The Gallup poll in 1956 reported an 89% favourable view of the NHS, P F Gemmill, *Britain's Search for Health* (Univ Pennsylvania Press, 1960), p 152.

2. Gemmill, pp 151-2; *idem, BMJ*, 1958, ii, Supplement, 17-21, 5 July 1958.

3. James Howard Means, *Practitioner*, 1953, *170*: 57; Harry Eckstein, *English Health Service*, p 2. See also the foreword to Eckstein, written by Means.

4. HC Debates, vol 552, cols 846-7, 7 May 1956.

5. HC Debates, vol 592, col 1401, 30 July 1958.

6. *US News and World Report*, 12 April 1957, p 66.

7. At the opening meeting of his Committee, Guillebaud declared that 'Nobody would wish to return to the system prevailing before the act came into force' (13 May 1953, DHSS 94501/9/2A). King's Fund, *Annual Report 1954*, p 1; *The Times*, 'NHS Supplement', July 1958, p ii. For a summary of contemporary estimates, Gemmill, pp 134-54.

8. Eckstein, *English Health Service*; R M Titmuss, 'War and Social Policy', in *Essays on the Welfare State* (Allen & Unwin, 1958), pp 75-87; R Klein, *The Politics of the National Health Service*; P Addison *The Road to 1945*, pp 277-8.

9. Macleod, Address to CHSC, 17 June 1952, DHSS 94151/2/1C.

10. HC Debates, vol 552, col 847, 7 May 1956.

11. *The Times*, 19 April 1958; Sir H Platt, *BMJ*, 1958, ii, Supplement, 5-7, 5 July 1958. Eckstein, *English Health Service*, pp 240-7. See also note 13 below.

12. BMA, Guillebaud Committee, 13 July 1954, DHSS 94501/9/2C.

13. CHSC, *Report on Co-operation between Hospital, Local Authority and General Practitioner Services* (HMSO, 1952). For admission of the failure of co-operation, Turton, HC Debates, vol 552, cols 851-3, and Messer, col 897, 7 May 1956.

14. Turton, HC Debates, vol 552, col 854, 7 May 1956. G E Godber, 'Health Services Past, Present and Future', *The Lancet*, 1958, ii, 1-6, 5 July 1958: 'hospitals must be organised primarily for the support of home care' (p 6). Walker-Smith, HC Debates, vol 592, cols 1404-6, 30 July 1958.

15. R M Titmuss, 'Community Care—Fact or Fiction?', in H Freeman and J Farndale, eds, *Trends in the Mental Health Services* (Pergamon, 1963), p 222 (originally published without title in, *Everybody's Business, the 1959 Mental Health Act and the community* (NAMH, 1960), pp 66-70).

16. S J Hadfield, *BMJ*, 1953, ii, p 706, 26 September 1953.

17. Turton, HC Debates, vol 552, col 854, 7 May 1956.

18. Estimates, 6th Report, para 19.

19. Estimates, 6th Report, paras 10-17.

20. Estimates, 6th Report, para 37; Sir C Nicholson, HC Debates, vol 592, cols 1437-46, 30 July 1958; Acton, 6, pp 15-25.

21. Bevan, HC Debates, vol 592, cols 1395-6, 30 July 1958; *The Lancet*, 1958, ii, 27, 5 July 1958.

22. *Guillebaud Report*, pp 274-86; DHSS 94501/9/2D. Unexpected support for Maude's view emanated from Lord Cranbrook, the influential chairman of the E Anglia RHB, 29 Sept. 1953, DHSS 94501/9/2B.

23. Bevan, *Municipal Journal*, 12 March 1954, p 544, *In Place of Fear* (Heinemann, 1952) p 91; Eckstein, *English Health Service*, pp 246-7. A detailed case for the change advocated by Bevan was made by the Society of Medical Officers of Health, Guillebaud Committee, 20 April 1954, DHSS 94501/9/2B.

24. *BMJ*, 1958, ii, 33-4, 5 July 1958.

25. *The Lancet*, 1958, ii, 28-9, 5 July 1958; *A Review of the Medical Services in Great Britain* (Social Assay, 1962).

26. Bevan, HC Debates, vol 592, cols 1387-90, 30 July 1958.

27. Bevan, HC Debates, vol 592, col 1397, 30 July 1958.

28. Godber, Health Service, GC45, DHSS 94501/9/2B; Treasury memorandum, 28 July 1955, DHSS 94501/9/2D; Walker-Smith, HC Debates, vol 592, cols 1401-6, 30 July 1958; Estimates, 6th Report, Appendices; Acton, 6, pp 72-80.

29. Estimates, 6th Report, para 5.

30. Bevan, HC Debates, vol 592, col 1398, 30 July 1958.

31. Guillebaud Committee, 19 April 1955, DHSS 94501/9/2D.

Abbreviations

A *General Abbreviations*

ABPI	Association of the British Pharmaceutical Industry
Acton	Acton Society Trust, *Hospitals and The State,* 6 Parts (1955–1959)
AMC	Association of Municipal Corporations
Beveridge Report	*Social Insurance and Allied Services* (Cmd. 6404, 1942)
BDA	British Dental Association
BHA	British Hospitals Association
BG	Board of Governors
BM	Board of Management
BMA	British Medical Association
BMJ	*British Medical Journal*
CCA	County Councils Association
CHSC	Central Health Services Council
COHSE	Confederation of Health Service Employees
Cost of the NHS	B Abel-Smith and R M Titmuss, *The Cost of the National Health Service in England and Wales* (CUP, 1956)
Dawson Report	Consultative Council on Medical and Allied Services, *Interim Report on the Future Provision of Medical and Allied Services* (Cmd. 693, 1920)
Estimates, 6th Report	Select Committee on Estimates, Session 1956/57, Sixth Report (HC 222)
Estimates, 7th Report	Select Committee on Estimates, Session 1948/49, Seventh Report (HC 176, 178)
Estimates, 11th Report	Select Committee on Estimates, Session 1950/51, Eleventh Report (HC 261)
EC	Executive Council
GMSC	General Medical Services Committee
GNC	General Nursing Council
Guillebaud Report	*Report of the Committee of Enquiry into the Cost of the National Health Service* (Cmd. 9663, 1956)
HMC	Hospital Management Committee
JHMO	Junior Hospital Medical Officer
LCC	London County Council
LHA	Local Health Authority

M & CW	Maternity and Child Welfare
MOH	Medical Officer of Health
MRC	Medical Research Council
NHI	National Health Insurance
NHS	National Health Service
PEP	Political and Economic Planning
PEP Report	*The British Health Services* (PEP, 1937)
PHLS	Public Health Laboratory Service
RCN	Royal College of Nursing
RCOG	Royal College of Obstetricians and Gynaecologists
RHB	Regional Hospital Board
SAC	Standing Advisory Committee
SAMO	Senior Administrative Medical Officer
SHMO	Senior Hospital Medical Officer
SHSC	Scottish Health Services Council
TUC	Trades Union Congress
UGC	University Grants Committee
Willink Report	*Report of the Committee to Consider the Future Numbers of Medical Practitioners and the Appropriate Intake of Medical Students* (HMSO, 1957)
WP	*A National Health Service* (Cmd. 6502, 1944)
WP 1946	*National Health Service Bill. Summary of the Proposed New Service* (Cmd. 6761, 1946)

B *Abbreviations Relating to Official Records*

(a) Departmental Records in the Public Record Office

CAB	Cabinet Office
Ed	Ministry of Education
MH	Ministry of Health
T. (followed by numbers only)	Treasury

(b) Departmental Records in the Scottish Record Office

| HH | Department of Health, Scotland |

(c) Records in Government Departments

DHSS	Department of Health and Social Security
MRC	Medical Research Council
T. (followed by capital letters and numbers)	Treasury

INDEX

Individual institutions are located by town or county, except in the case of London, where no location is given. First references are given to authors of books or civil servants cited in the notes. At this point full names and relevant bibliographical details are stated.